A Long Walk to Church

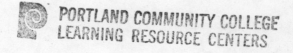

A LONG WALK TO CHURCH

A Contemporary History of Russian Orthodoxy

NATHANIEL DAVIS

WESTVIEW PRESS
Boulder • San Francisco • Oxford

Copyright © 1995 by Westview Press, Inc.

Published in 1995 in the United States of America by Westview Press, Inc., 5500 Central Avenue, Boulder, Colorado 80301-2877, and in the United Kingdom by Westview Press, 36 Lonsdale Road, Summertown, Oxford OX2 7EW

Library of Congress Cataloging-in-Publication Data
Davis, Nathaniel.
    A long walk to church : a contemporary history of Russian orthodoxy / Nathaniel Davis.
        p.   cm.
    Includes bibliographical references and index.
    ISBN 0-8133-2276-6. — ISBN 0-8133-2277-4
    1. Russkaia pravoslavnaia tserkov—Soviet Union—History.
2. Orthodox Eastern Church—Soviet Union—History.   3. Church and
state—Soviet Union—History.   4. Soviet Union—Church history.
I. Title.
BX492.D38   1995
281.9′47′0904—dc20
                                                                                                94-22735
                                                                                                CIP

Printed and bound in the United States of America

(∞)   The paper used in this publication meets the requirements
       of the American National Standard for Permanence of Paper
       for Printed Library Materials Z39.48-1984.

10   9   8   7   6   5   4   3

*To my wife, Elizabeth, who has sustained me always,
and my son, Tom, who has labored mightily on this book*

Contents

Tables and Figures

Prologue

ON A WINTER DAY forty years ago, I remember standing in a country village far from Moscow looking for a church—as was my wont. I approached a bent, much bundled, aged woman. I asked her if there was a church close by and, if so, where I might go to find it. Her eyes were the pale, watery blue sometimes characteristic of the old. A deeply melancholy expression came over her face, and she answered: "It's a long, long walk to church."

In point of fact, for the quarter century between Khrushchev's campaign against religion and Gorbachev's revision of policy in 1988, one could travel east from Chita for 1,000 kilometers on the Trans-Siberian Railroad without passing a single church. One could also travel 600 kilometers west from there without passing a church. Sakha-Yakutia, with an area more than the size of the United States east of the Mississippi, has had only one church from the time of the Khrushchev drive until 1993. Most of the million Russians living east of the Urals and north of the sixty-second parallel have had to travel almost 2,000 kilometers to reach the nearest functioning church. Truly, it has been a long walk to church.

Nathaniel Davis

Preface

THIS STUDY IS A SECULAR examination of the history of the Russian Orthodox Church in recent times. It is difficult to be objective about religion. I am reminded of a cartoon published long ago of a matron in a bookshop asking for "an impartial history of the [U.S.] Civil War, written from the Southern point of view." For those who might be curious, I am a member of the United Church of Christ.

For those unfamiliar with Orthodox ecclesiastical usage, a monastic priest takes a saint's name when he becomes a monk and drops his surname. Sometimes, in written works, the surname is added in parentheses after the saint's name in order to avoid confusion. For example, one might write "Metropolitan Kirill (Gundyaev)." The metropolitan's name as a boy was Vladimir Mikhailovich Gundyaev.

I am indebted to Zbigniew K. Brzezinski, to the late Philip E. Mosely, and to the late Frank Nowak, who reviewed early work that ultimately led to this manuscript. Haym Jaffe of Drexel University assisted me in statistical projections. William C. Fletcher of the University of Kansas read this manuscript and prepared a perceptive, enlightening, and immensely helpful commentary on the book and all its parts. Donald W. Treadgold of the University of Washington encouraged me to go to Westview Press and introduced me to senior editor Peter W. Kracht, who has proved extremely helpful and unfailingly supportive of my efforts—as has his associate, Mick Gusinde-Duffy. The project editor, Mary Jo Lawrence, and the copy editor, Ida May B. Norton, have been extremely helpful and untiring in their care, patience, and support. I am also indebted to my wife, Elizabeth, my son, Thomas Rohde Davis, and my daughter, Margaret Davis Mainardi, for criticism, editing, and work on the draft. The manuscript was typed by my son, and some early materials were typed by my daughter. James F. Winstead of Harvey Mudd College prepared the graphs in the volume.

Research for this study was supported in part by a grant from the International Research and Exchange Board (IREX), with funds provided by the National Endowment for the Humanities and the United States Information Agency. Research was also supported by a fellowship from the John Randolph Haynes and Dora Haynes Foundation. None of these organizations is responsible for the views expressed.

N.D.

Introduction: Communism and Religion

WHEN THE COMMUNISTS took control in Russia, they were determined to subdue all opposition forces, including the Russian Orthodox Church. More fundamentally, as Marxists, they wanted to build a society without God, and the church blocked the way. Not only in the lands that became the Soviet Union but in every country where the communists seized power after World War II, a struggle between the state and the churches ensued.

Twice in the history of communist rule in the Soviet Union, the Bolsheviks and the Soviet state drove the church to the threshold of institutional death, or at least to its antechamber. The first time was at the end of the 1930s, when Stalin's men had wiped out virtually all of the resources of the church. The second time, although less dramatic, was in Brezhnev's "period of stagnation." Following Khrushchev's headlong assault in the early 1960s, the subsequent slow erosion of Orthodox institutional strength exposed the possibility of the church's ultimate extinction.

Both times, fortuitous events saved the institutional body of the church. In 1939, the turnaround followed the Molotov-Ribbentrop Pact, Soviet annexations, Hitler's invasion of the USSR, German permissiveness toward Orthodox Church renewal in the occupied zones, and Stalin's later policies toward liberated areas. In the late 1980s, the millennium of the baptism of Rus in 988 (the Millennium), glasnost and democratization, Gorbachev's felt need for new sources of support, his desire for international acceptance, and his pragmatism led to a new Soviet religious policy. Now, after the collapse of the communist institution, aggressive Marxist ideological materialism in Russia is a whispered memory. For a second time the church is rising like a phoenix from the ashes of misfortune.

Why has the church twice been renewed in vigor and strength? Was it luck, which could change? Was it something intrinsic in the natural order that prevents the triumph of antireligion? Was it the constancy of God, which ultimately rules human history, politics, and society?[1] There are at least two problems in any attempt to answer these questions. First one must consider whether the things observed in the external realm of life—church buildings, priests, church attendance, and other religious activities—truly reflect the inner reality. Second, one must consider whether the world's historical and social experience makes it possible to say that the communists, in trying to build an atheist society, assumed an inherently impossible task.

Religion has been defined as "the outward act or form by which men indicate their recognition of the existence of a god ... the outer form and embodiment [of] the inner spirit."[2] Outward manifestations are all that can really be examined, as a secular analysis of the inner spirit is uncongenial to the instincts of social scientists and historians. It was also beyond the communists' natural reach.

Nevertheless, churches are earthly institutions, rooted in the terrain of observable reality. They are not made of disembodied ectoplasm, conjured up out of nothingness. In June 1991, Patriarch Aleksi II (Ridiger) responded to those who claimed that the head of the Russian Orthodox Church in the late 1920s, Metropolitan Sergi (Stragorodski), could have defied the communists and refused to make a declaration of loyalty to a godless state:

> Metropolitan Sergi wanted to save the Church. I know that many people, hearing these words, protest that it is Christ who saves the Church and not people. This is true. But it is also true that, without human efforts, God's help does not save. The Ecumenical Church is indestructible. But where is the celebrated Church of Carthage? Are there Orthodox believers today in Kaledoniya, in Asia Minor, where Gregory the Illuminator and Basil the Great earned their renown? Before our eyes the Church in Albania was destroyed. . . . And in Russia there were powers wishing to do the same thing.[3]

Think of a "City of God" in the Soviet Union, which the communists assaulted in their days of militant atheism. The city's "temples" might represent the various religious bodies, each one rooted in the earth, where the city could be attacked and where its dimensions on the ground could be measured. Each of the temples also had—and has—a vertical dimension in the realm of the spirit, and no one who stood on the earth could clearly see to the tops of the columns, domes, and towers, as they were shrouded in mist. That is the realm of philosophers and theologians, who are not earthbound. This study will describe the situation on the ground; it is at this level that the communists made their assault, because they too were earthbound.[4]

When they were young and filled with optimism and arrogance, the communists honestly believed that they could destroy the temples by knocking out the bottoms of the columns and by blocking all efforts to shore them up. Faith might have died within a generation or two in a nation where no house of worship stood, where no priest celebrated the liturgy, where no one taught a child about God, and where an empty silence of the spirit ruled the land. Even a catacomb church was within reach of the communists' bulldozers. Dedicated Christians worshiping secretly in the deep forest might have been hard to find and apprehend, but their activity was still of flesh and blood and not beyond the grasp of state authority if the believers were pursued with sufficient means and determination.

The image of an earthbound "temple" is intended only to distinguish the inquiries of the historian and the philosopher, not to describe the churches as inert or the historian's task as a simple measurement of dimensions and unchanging forms. At its heart a church consists of people; it might better be described as "an army on the march."[5] Moreover, religious institutions do not always grow or shrink incrementally, which would enable the scholar to count churches, priests, and other resources and project trends in some linear fashion. Hegel wrote that "history is in fact a spiral process; great creative periods are followed by periods of reaction in which the spirit, apparently dying, is restoring itself to emerge in new creativity at a higher level."[6] The Chinese philosopher Lin Yutang said much the same thing: "Thoughts and ideas are somewhat like seeds. They have a way of lying dormant underground until a more favorable climate brings them again to life."[7]

The appearance on the world stage of great individuals also results in imponderables and discontinuities. Perhaps this is the curse of historians, particularly those who write their histories too soon. Augustus, who left a memoir of the most notable events of his reign, made no mention of the birth of Christ. The year before the Millennium of the baptism of Rus, 1987, may have been like 1533—the year before Luther completed his translation of the Bible, Calvin began to write the *Institutes,* and the Society of Jesus was conceived. By the time 1991 had drawn to a close, the collapse of communist government and of the USSR had provided a discontinuity no less portentous than the events that followed the year 1533. History's great periods of tumult are inherently uncontrollable, unpredictable, ruled by personality and chance, and also by those furious, primordial forces that characterize social revolutions in every epoch.

Some anthropologists and historians have argued that the communists' objective of eradicating religious practice was intrinsically unattainable. They point out that secular power has never succeeded in eradicating religious practice in any society and that this suggests some fundamental human need to worship. Were the communists necessarily doomed to failure?

As a step toward providing the answer, we may all agree that secular political power has been able to change religious patterns, even if not to eliminate them. In 1555 the Treaty of Augsburg, between the Catholics and Protestants in

Germany, decreed that the religion of a territory would be determined by its prince. With few exceptions, it was. Similarly, in Kievan Rus, Prince Vladimir accepted Orthodox Christianity in 988, thereby determining the prevailing religion in his land. It is also clear from history that redirecting religious allegiances has always been a bloody and a difficult business. A realistic communist would have concluded that the destruction of a competing religion required a great and sustained effort. Nevertheless, religions—indigestible though they may be—have been devoured by the adherents of other faiths.

Religions can undeniably be changed, but can religion be destroyed? To prove that communist power could not have eradicated religion, one must show both that (1) religion is an intrinsic and universal social need, and (2) communism is not a substitute faith.

The renowned anthropologist Ruth Benedict wrote in the 1930s that religious phenomena are universal, and her findings are still accepted by her colleagues:

> The striking fact about . . . [the] plain distinction between the religious and the non-religious in actual ethnographic recording is that it.needs so little recasting in its transfer from one society to another. No matter into how exotic a society the traveler has wandered, he still finds the distinction made and in comparatively familiar terms. And it is universal. There is no monograph in existence that does not group a certain class of facts as religion, and there are no records of travelers, provided they are full enough to warrant such a judgment, that do not indicate this category.[8]

A note of caution must be added here. Although it is broadly true that religion can be found in every society, not all individuals feel the need to worship. Therefore, it would seem that religion is not essential in individual terms, even though it appears to be so in social and societal terms.

Alternatively, an inquiry into past realities might indicate whether religion is an intrinsic social need. A record of constancy in the intensity of religious observance throughout history—regardless of state policy or other secular influences—would strengthen the argument that religion is an elemental force that cannot be suppressed. There have been vast changes over time, however, in the level of apparent religious loyalty. In the history of the West, the age that followed Christ's life and teaching has been characterized as intensely religious, as has the thirteenth century—the age of the cathedral builders, St. Thomas Aquinas, and St. Francis of Assisi. For an age of reduced religious intensity in Western civilization, one might choose Greece at the time of Alexander's conquests, when even the mystery religions appeared to have become stagnant. Before Mohammed, the religious ideas of the pagan Arabs were said to have been vague and scanty. Then came the Prophet, followed by the triumphant march of Islam.

If we think of the religious impulse as something that can be stimulated, we must also concede that it can be reduced or can atrophy. In fact, some historical support might be found for the communists' contention that social progress brings secularization.

As a matter of historical record, atheism has seldom been espoused, and the lack of historical adherence to atheism means that there are few examples from which to argue that the communists' atheistic experiment had to fail. The precedent that most readily comes to mind is the campaign against religion during the French Revolution, but this attack was not sufficiently coherent or prolonged to demonstrate the intrinsic strengths or weaknesses of a godless social order. The very fact that the communists' road has been so nearly unexplored makes it difficult to assert with confidence that natural forces would block it.

Moreover, totalitarianism is a modern concept, and communism probably went further than its competitors in imposing control over people's lives and minds. The communists developed techniques of mass psychological manipulation that might have enabled them to accomplish more ambitious social mutations than authoritarian states had been able to achieve previously.

For a communist theoretician, the universality of religion did not present a serious problem—religion was consistently regarded by the Marxists as a symptom of exploitation, suffering, fear, and ignorance. Exploitation was considered universal prior to the establishment of socialism in Russia; thus it was not surprising that religion was also universal. Because the world the communists sought to create was avowedly unique, a society without religion likewise would have been unique. Nevertheless, when all is said and done, the apparent universality of religious observance remains an arresting historical and social fact.

Was communism a substitute faith? If it was, one can make the argument that religion is a universal societal phenomenon by pointing out that the communists were simply trying to replace the traditional religions in the Soviet Union with their own creed. Here we must not confuse Christianity and the other highly developed doctrines with religious manifestations that appear to be universal. According to Ruth Benedict, religion is not the "pursuit of ideal ends" or "the desire to live more virtuously and to interpret the transitory in terms of the eternal." She explained that primitive cosmologies are often elaborated in direct contradiction of the theme of good and evil and observed that "religion is not historically a citizenship in an ideal world, but had to do with success in this world."[9]

Communism actually had most of these elements, including the "pursuit of ideal ends," citizenship in an ideal world, and success in this one. One of the most important attributes scholars ascribe to the world religions is an integrated belief system that gives meaning and regularity to the human experience and unites doctrine with action. In the glory days of the Bolshevik movement, the communists' godless creed accomplished this. Reinhold Niebuhr argued that the real faith of modern society is faith in history, which has the promise and meaning of existence and takes the place of God. In this sense, Marx founded a "historical" religion.

Paul Tillich observed that both Old Testament prophetic revelation and Marxism "regard the fight between good and evil forces as the main content of history."[10] John C. Bennett commented:

> If religion is defined as man's relationship to whatever he regards as ultimate or to whatever he trusts most for deliverance from the evils and hazards of life, then Communism is undoubtedly religious. . . . Communism occupies the place in life for the convinced Communist that religions occupy in the lives of their adherents. Communism offers a goal for life. It offers a faith in redemption from all recognized evils.[11]

Communism shared with many religions and several secular callings the physical accompaniments of worship, including ceremonies, shrines, and rites. Lenin's mausoleum and the Red Square parades, complete with icons of Lenin and other communist saints, were examples. It takes an act of faith to be an atheist for the same reasons it takes an act of faith to be a believer.

Of course, there are some characteristics associated with religion that communism never shared. One of these is the immortality of the soul, which some—but not all—religions espouse. Communism's denial of the afterlife may not have been troublesome to a young person building Soviet socialism in the mid-1920s. However, in times of war, bereavement, or approaching death, the individual who was otherwise satisfied with communism might have been inclined to seek the comfort of religion. The communists acknowledged that this was the case during World War II. They explained such backsliding by saying that insufficient time had elapsed after the 1917 revolution to erase the earlier religious culture.

Perhaps the key element in religion that communism lacked is the recognition of the supernatural. Ruth Benedict defined the supernatural in primitive religions as a "wonderful power," or a "voltage, with which the universe is said to be charged."[12] In other religions it is God. This assertion of the supernatural is universal in religion and constitutes for many scholars its definitive quality. In actuality, however, the emphasis on the supernatural has varied widely from one religion to another. Moreover, if the only element lacking in communism that can be surely identified in all the world's religions is supernaturalism, this would mean that the essential difference between communism and religious faith is an element shared by religion, magic and superstition. This was the view of the communists, who asserted that tribal peoples feared the natural forces that destroyed crops or threatened the community's welfare. Failing to understand these natural forces, tribal peoples made gods of them. The cure was knowledge.

Albert Boiter commented:

> Others see Soviet communism as a new religion in everything but name, lacking only belief in a transcendental being. But even this void is seen by some as being

filled by the deification of science and progress. Franz Cardinal Koenig (1975) of Vienna has accused the Soviet government of maintaining a confessional state of the traditional type, with the state acting as protector of one established faith.[13]

Although it is true that the supernatural element in primitive religion is not exalting, each society lives according to its own sophistication of thought and complexity of experience. Both the primitive and the advanced society, each in its own terms, may find some fulfillment in acknowledging a higher or different power beyond human grasp or understanding. The communists, who believe there is no heaven, saw no need to build toward it in the vertical dimension of the spirit. To those who believe that altars should point toward the sky, the communists appear to have constructed their temples by marbling over the barren ground, which stretches out in one vast, glittering, empty temple floor.

Earlier in this discussion I argued that secular influences have a genuine impact on a church's inner condition or, to phrase it another way, that a church's foundations are embedded in the real world. I also asked whether the communists tried to create a religious void or merely to clear a place for their own faith. Even if one could find a religious essence in terms which disqualify the communist "creed," this would still leave a number of alternative possibilities. I posed several of them thirty-five years ago when I was completing a dissertation on the church under communism. I suggested that the pressure of natural forces to fill the religious vacuum in the communists' realm might have crumpled the materialists' social order; alternatively, it might have pushed the communists back from any effort to destroy the churches. For their part, the churches conceivably might have been pushed into the narrow corner of human experience occupied by superstition and magic. Another possibility was that the sharpness of the communists' determination to annihilate religion might have dulled and that fraternization and compromise might have grown from a tactic to a condition.[14]

What is interesting today is how close to having been answered and resolved these questions and alternatives seem to be. Fraternization and compromise did grow from a tactic to a condition in the Soviet Union, but the onrush of events did not stop there. The communist faith disintegrated. Totalitarian communist power, after a spasm in August 1991, crumbled. The communist motherland fragmented. Relatively few people, at least in the developed "first world," still think of communism as a compelling substitute faith. Arthur Koestler was correct when he called communism "the God that failed." Corruption, careerism, and cronyism in Brezhnev's "era of stagnation" washed away the materialists' commitment. Successor governments in the former Soviet Union abandoned the effort to destroy the churches. Most of them are, almost poignantly, now seeking the support of Russian Orthodoxy, Islam, and other religious communities. The dogmatists of atheism are stumbling in the wilderness.

Whether the present situation will be permanent is another question. Not much in the former Soviet Union today can be regarded as stable, lasting, or reliable. An attempt to resolve this question here, however, would be to jump to the end of this story, and we are just beginning.

This introduction should not end without a glimpse of the passion, beauty, and faith that characterize the Russian Orthodox Church world. Anyone who has been present during Orthodox services over the years has a head filled with pictures. They are of bundled old women in scarves and felt boots creaking to their knees and bowing down over the cold stones of the sanctuary floor. They are of the deeply lined countenances of aged priests, a distant light shining from tired eyes. They are of the faces of the women carrying collection plates through crowds of worshipers, cheeks illuminated by sturdy candles planted among the ruble notes. They are of the exhilaration, crush, and, yes, odor of immense crowds as midnight turns to Easter morn. They are of the catch in one's breath when the news is passed that Christ is risen. They are of the woman behind the candle counter who presses a single egg painted blood red into one's hand at Eastertime.[15]

The pictures are of alert, intelligent young men and women presenting themselves for baptism, diffidently, uncomfortably, but resolutely. They are of the dark shadows of faithful, ancient nuns. They are of thousands of flickering candles, white beards, glittering miters, and golden robes and of the resonance of choral singing by unaccompanied voices. They are of the eyes of Jesus and the Mother of God looking out from icons into one's own eyes, no matter where one stands. They are of the smell of incense. They are of little, wooden country churches with shingled onion domes approached by walking across wet fields. They are of a dark-suited, bearded man walking down a street, looking to neither the right nor the left, who turns into a churchyard and unlocks the door of an empty church before scheduled services.

The pictures are of the robust woman in the bell tower of the St. Florus nunnery in Kiev pulling on dozens of big and little ropes in an almost frenzied but joyous dance as her bells peal out to the world in a triumphal cacophony. They are of the priest in the village of Ib telling U.S. visitors matter-of-factly that there were 120 priests in Komi until the late 1930s when 100 of them were taken to the airport and were shot dead as "enemies of the people." They are of the old widower made bishop of Brest in 1990, shown with his arms around a sturdy peasant who has knelt and buried his head in the folds of the bishop's cassock. They are of the round old woman in the Kharkov cathedral, just before services, telling a U.S. student to take his hands out of his pockets and stand erect, after her rotund form had perfectly imitated his long and languid slouch. They are of the old mother in the Kiev railroad station in Moscow blessing her grown and visibly embarrassed son before he takes his train. They are of the published snapshot of another old bishop and a young priest taken from across a meadow as they sit on a bench near a church, two distant black figures, talking of eternal things.[16]

The pictures reflect the affirmation of Orthodox writers that the church is a living body where today's believers are surrounded by all the saints who have ever lived. As one Russian Orthodox priest put it, "Today *living* saints walk the face of the earth in Russia."[17]

1

From the Bolshevik
Revolution to World War II

THE YEAR 1939 WAS the worst in history for the Russian Orthodox Church. Never before had the institutional and human situation of the church been quite so desperate. Never again, after the Soviet territorial acquisitions of 1939–1940 brought new priests, bishops, and resources to the church, would it become quite so bad.

In 1939 the acting head of the church, Metropolitan Sergi (Stragorodski), lived in Moscow, virtually cut off from the few score churches still functioning in the vast Soviet land. According to a well-informed observer, Wassilij Alexeev, "Sergi awaited arrest each minute. . . . His attendant went away during the night, fearing that he would be arrested with the Metropolitan [if he stayed]. . . . The aging hierarch remained completely alone . . . and if something like a heart attack had occurred, he would have died without aid of any kind."[1]

All the monasteries, nunneries, and seminaries were closed. Dioceses did not exist as administrative units. A few of the separated churches sent irregular letters to the metropolitan, but even this meager correspondence consisted mostly of greetings.[2] The Russian Orthodox Church was in agony.

How did the church reach this pass? Although this book focuses on post–World War II events and more particularly on the contemporary situation, a brief review of the church-state struggle between 1917 and 1939 may be in order.

When the Bolsheviks seized power in 1917, the Russian Orthodox Church was electing its first patriarch since the time of Peter the Great (1682–1725). After the fall of the czar, even the modernists in the church had become convinced that a strong, unifying leader was needed, and the provisional government had given permission for a church council with the authority to act. Eleven days after the storming of the Winter Palace, Metropolitan Tikhon (Belavin) of Moscow was chosen by lot from among three elected candidates.[3]

The new Soviet government already had nationalized all church lands, and it would soon decree the separation of church and state, cancel the church's status as a juridical entity, ban state subsidies to clergy and religious bodies, seize church bank accounts, deny legal standing to church marriages, divorces, and baptisms, and ban organized religious education of the young.

Still, most of the church leaders believed that the communist government was an affliction that would pass. After electing Patriarch Tikhon, the council affirmed that the Russian Orthodox Church was the national church of Russia, that the state needed church approval to legislate on matters relating to the church, that blasphemy should remain illegal, that church schools should be recognized, and that the head of the Russian state and the top appointees in education and religious affairs should be Orthodox.[4]

In January of 1918, the patriarch excommunicated the faith's "open and secret enemies."[5] Other pronouncements from the patriarch and the church council followed, excommunicating priests or laymen who connived against duly appointed ecclesiastics, facilitated antichurch legislation, laid hands on Orthodox churchmen, or committed acts against the church.[6] The stage was set for confrontation, and it came, despite the patriarch's refusal to support the Bolsheviks' enemies in the civil war that soon engulfed the nation. In fact, the church-state struggle was but a part of the cataclysm through which Russia was passing. All of society had been riven asunder, and the misfortunes of the church seemed to be, in a sense, by-products of revolution and chaos.

On the all-European scene, Russia was losing World War I, having suffered over 9 million casualties—more than any other belligerent. Appalling conditions had characterized the situation at the front. Sometimes Russian soldiers had been obliged to wait in backup trenches, lacking even rifles, until the deaths of comrades allowed them to scavenge arms. As the British military attaché described it, the soldiers had been "churned into gruel" by German artillery.[7] In the peace treaty with Germany signed in March 1918, the Soviet Union lost a third of its population and a third of its arable lands.

The defeat abroad hardly matched the upheavals at home. Soldiers streamed home to their villages to grab pieces of land. Russia's erstwhile allies invaded— Britain and the United States in the far north, Britain and France in the south, and Japan and the United States in the far east. Anti-Bolshevik forces advanced toward Petrograd and Moscow from the north, south, east, and west. In the meantime, former Czech and Slovak prisoners of war seized the Trans-Siberian Railroad. Cruelty, brutality, and torture were appalling. Just as the anti-Bolsheviks faltered and the Western powers began losing stomach for their interventions, the Poles attacked. Kiev changed hands seventeen times between 1918 and 1921 before a peace favorable to Poland was signed in Riga.

In the countryside, the Bolsheviks organized Committees of the Village Poor and sent out workers and soldiers from the cities to seize grain. Peasant revolts swept the countryside, and the civil war became a peasant war. Industrial output plummeted to one-seventh of its prewar level. Citizens fled Moscow and Petrograd seeking food and safety in the countryside; more than half the people in those cities abandoned them. The ruble stood at one two-hundred-thousandth of its prewar value.

Over 7 million people died from hunger and epidemics; cannibalism spread. The editor of *Pomoshch* [Relief], the organ of the All-Russia Famine Relief Committee described it: "People mainly ate members of their own families as they died, feeding on the older children, but not sparing newborn infants either . . . despite the fact that there wasn't much to them."[8]

In this context of desperation, the Bolshevik regime demanded the church's valuables for famine relief. On February 19, 1922, the patriarch duly asked parishes to surrender all precious articles except those used in sacraments and worship. A few days later the government launched a propaganda campaign against a "heartless" church and ordered virtually every treasure confiscated, including consecrated vessels.[9] Loyal Orthodox believers rallied to defend their sacramental treasures, and the Russian press reported some 1,400 bloody fights as priests and parishioners tried to guard their churches.[10] The bloodiest incidents occurred in Shuya, east of Moscow, where church supporters and Bolsheviks battled for days. Throughout the country churches were closed by force, and priests and hierarchs were arrested. Although there had been bloody incidents before, this was the first great crisis in the church-state struggle.[11]

Almost a half century later it was revealed that Lenin had sent a secret memorandum to his Politburo colleagues on March 19, 1922, in which he wrote with brutal candor that the campaign to seize church treasures was intended to break the power of the clergy, not simply to obtain resources with which to buy food. Lenin called the opportunity "exceptionally beneficial," the only moment "when we are given ninety-nine out of 100 chances to gain a full and crushing victory" over the clerical enemy and

> assure ourselves the necessary positions for decades ahead. It is precisely now and only now, when there is cannibalism . . . and corpses are lying along the roads that we can (and therefore must) carry out the confiscation of valuables with fanatical and merciless energy. . . . No other opportunity but the current terrible famine will give us a mood of the wide masses such as would provide us with their sympathies or at least neutrality. . . . Now our victory over the reactionary clergy is guaranteed. . . . The trial of the Shuya rioters for resisting aid to the hungry [should] be conducted in as short a time as possible, concluding in the maximum possible number of executions. . . . If possible, similar executions should be carried out in Moscow and other spiritual centers of the country.[12]

The fight over church treasures had ongoing consequences. On May 6, 1922,

Patriarch Tikhon was placed under house arrest—accused of resisting the confis-
cations. Leaders of reformist and leftist currents that had developed within the
church, particularly after the 1905 Edict of Toleration, took advantage of Tikhon's
confinement to seize control of the patriarchal chancery and church administration.[13] Calling themselves Renovationists, these clerics had coalesced into three
factions. The largest of them, the Living Church, was led by Archpriest Vladimir
Krasnitski, a radical-rightist cleric before World War I, who emerged as a leader
of the married priests who wanted to change the Orthodox rule that permitted
only monastic clergy to aspire to episcopal office. The second Renovationist grouping was led by Father Aleksandr Ivanovich Vvedenski, a charismatic preacher who
was alleged to be a libertine and police collaborator. Clerics in Vvedenski's Union
of Communities of Ancient Apostolic Churches also wanted to open the door to
married priests becoming bishops. The smallest but most respected grouping
was led by Bishop, then Metropolitan, Antonin (Granovski), an opponent of autocracy even in the prerevolutionary time. The Renovationists had Bolshevik
support, clearly motivated by the authorities' desire to split and thereby rule the
church. The government turned over the majority of the functioning Orthodox
churches in the country to the collaborating Renovationists.[14]

For moral, traditional, and political reasons, most of the Orthodox laity dis-
dained the Renovationists. The church schism was a blow to the institutional integrity of the patriarchal church, however, and it influenced Tikhon in his decision to "confess" anti-Soviet acts, renounce them, and declare that he was "no
longer an enemy of the Soviet Government." The authorities freed him on June
26, 1923, and he was able to reassert his authority and turn the tide against the
Renovationists.[15]

By late 1924 the Renovationists had lost their control over a third to a half of
the churches the authorities had given them. In the meantime, Lenin had died
and Stalin was slowly consolidating his power. The New Economic Policy was
bringing economic recovery and a modicum of normality. During this time, the
strength of the patriarchal church grew.[16]

On April 7, 1925, Patriarch Tikhon died, and his death plunged the church into
a rolling crisis of leadership. By 1927, ten out of eleven prelates successively
named to act as head of the church were in prison or exile, and most of the bishops were in similar straits.[17] The man who emerged as acting head of the church
was Metropolitan Sergi (Stragorodski) of Nizhni-Novgorod. Arrested more than
once, Sergi was released from prison in March of 1927 and issued a loyalty declaration to the Soviet government on July 24 of that year. Its key passage, which outraged many Orthodox in the Soviet Union and in the Russian emigration, recognized "the Soviet Union as our civil motherland, whose [the motherland's] joys and
successes are our joys and successes, and whose misfortunes are our misfortunes."[18]

Under the leadership of Metropolitan Antoni (Khrapovitski), formerly of Kiev, émigré Russian churchmen had met in the Serbian town of Sremski Karlovci in 1921 and established the Karlovci Synod, which ultimately became the Russian Orthodox Church Abroad. Promonarchist and prointerventionist resolutions of the synod had complicated Tikhon's position at the time of the first great anti-church campaign in 1922. Although Sergi did not collaborate with the Karlovcians, he had confidential correspondence with them, and the synod published a letter from Sergi in 1926 that the Bolsheviks used as a pretext for Sergi's arrest. After Sergi's loyalty declaration of 1927, the Karlovcians fiercely opposed Sergi and his perceived capitulation and came to regard the underground True Orthodox Church and True Orthodox Christians as the legitimate voices of Orthodoxy in the USSR. Metropolitan Iosif (Petrovykh), Metropolitan Agafangel (Preobrazhenski), Metropolitan Kirill (Smirnov), Bishop Aleksi (Bui), and the majority of the bishops imprisoned in the camps on the Solovetski Islands distanced themselves from Sergi and his loyalty declaration, although not all of them repudiated his authority.[19]

The quieter times of the New Economic Policy were shattered by the forced industrialization and collectivization drives that started in 1928. At the end of 1929 and at the beginning of 1930, as had been the case in 1921 and 1922, troops and party workers fanned out into the countryside, this time to force the peasants to join collective farms. Peasant resistance produced violence once again, and farmers slaughtered their livestock and ate or destroyed stores of food and seed. Hunger returned. Although Stalin temporarily reined in the collectivization drive in March of 1930, pressures on the peasants soon resumed and a man-made famine spread. It reached appalling proportions in Ukraine and the northern Caucasus in 1932. At least 5 million people died from hunger and attendant diseases. A Soviet demographer noted a population loss of 7.5 million. In his memoirs, Nikita Khrushchev described how trains pulled into Kiev loaded with corpses of people who had starved to death; railroad workers had picked them up all along the route from Poltava. The rivers of the northern Caucasus carried thousands of bodies to the sea.[20]

As in the famine of 1922, the church was among the victims. Farmers posted guards and defended their churches and priests with scythes and pitchforks, but many priests and peasants were swept away in the general violence. The campaign changed the face of the countryside, which has been dotted ever since with the shells of churches serving as granaries, overcrowded dwellings, storehouses, and workshops, their rusting and disintegrating cupolas standing hollow against the sky. In 1932 city churches also became targets, and the 1929–1933 period became the second great wave of church closings.[21]

In a dissertation completed some years ago, I made an effort to analyze the communist authorities' strategies and the churches' counterstrategies in their struggle in both the Soviet Union and in Eastern Europe.[22] I shall not repeat the argument here. It was notable, however, that the evolution of communist strategy in the USSR came rather close to repeating itself in the "people's democracies" of Eastern Europe three decades after the battles between the Bolsheviks and Russian Orthodox believers. In both areas there was an initial political struggle characterized by violence, arrests, and church closings. The pattern continued with communist efforts to divide the various religious communities and split the ranks of clerical adversaries—the Orthodox in Russia, Bulgaria, Romania, and Serbia; the Roman Catholics in Poland, Czechoslovakia, Hungary, and Croatia; and the Lutherans in East Germany. Church leaders in the Soviet Union and Eastern Europe were subsequently forced to make declarations of political submission, with varying degrees of exception in Poland, East Germany, and one or two other places.

Both in the Soviet Union and in Eastern Europe, the frontal assault on religious communities receded over time and became a long process of attrition. This was partly because in most cases church leaders ceased to rally political opposition to communist rule and also because the costs to the communist authorities in foreign policy, internal popular discontent, and ideological embarrassment outweighed any need to liquidate the "religious problem" through precipitate means. The ideological embarrassment was related to the fact that Marx and Engels had taught that religion was a symptom of oppression, an "opium" to dull the workers' outrage and convert their revolutionary zeal into passivity, manifested in the dream of happiness in the next world rather than in this one. Theoretically, religion should have withered away naturally in a socialist society where the workers ruled.

The communists were always ready to take active measures to "help nature along," and the religious arena was no exception. As a practical matter, the Soviet authorities developed three long-range strategies designed to sap the church's vitality: interrupt the church's cycle of regeneration, confine the church to rites performed in church sanctuaries out of sight, and indoctrinate the people in atheism.

The church, like all human institutions, must renew itself with each new generation. The communists believed that the interruption of this process would ultimately eradicate religious practice and belief. One might use the analogy of a disease that the authorities wished to wipe out. This is not the way the communists expressed themselves, and they never did develop a wholly satisfactory rationale for the persistence of religion in socialist society.[23] The analogy of disease, however, may clarify what the communist authorities were trying to accomplish. Take a disease-producing organism that passes through various environments and stages in its life cycle. If one can interrupt its regeneration at any point, the malady can be overcome.[24] For example, one can spray ponds with oil to kill the larvae of malaria-carrying mosquitos rather than attempt to catch the insects on the fly.

The communist authorities tried to interrupt the cycle of religious regeneration in analogous ways. In a series of laws and decrees issued between 1918 and 1924, they forbade the organized teaching of religion to persons under the age of eighteen.[25] Let the old—or even the adults in society—go to church until they die, the communists reasoned, but save tomorrow's generation from reactionary belief. The early Soviet experiments in collective institutional child-raising—away from parental and grandparental influence—were part of this effort. The communists closed all the Orthodox seminaries and theological academies.[26] Let the priests grow older, they reasoned, until they die off without replacement. The publication of new copies of scripture and liturgical books was terminated in the late 1920s, with the result that the books and scriptures of every confession were ultimately reduced to "a few old, worn, torn relics."[27] Church-run shops making new liturgical garments, vessels, and other supplies were closed, and the communists waited hopefully for celebrants' robes to become threadbare tatters.

A church building does not quickly wear out, but the population moves, and a ban on new church construction could be the equivalent of closing churches. The Soviets took pride in the fact that the great industrial city of Magnitogorsk was built from the ground up in the 1930s without a single church. Demographic change worked against the church. Urbanization negatively affected Orthodox practice, as workers migrated from the traditional Orthodox culture of the Soviet countryside to the "godless" cities. No less a figure than Metropolitan Kirill (Gundyaev) of Smolensk acknowledged this problem in 1988.[28] If they could immobilize the churches, the communists believed, society might grow away from religion.

This poses the question of theological growth—a difficult subject. The Russian Orthodox Church asserts the immutability of doctrine, expressed in the duty of the church to preserve the faith. The Orthodox do, however, recognize the need to reinterpret church teaching for a new generation. Some even understand faith as an ever-expanding concept, like the expanding universe created around us. Nevertheless, when beleaguered, churches tend to defend themselves by resisting experimentation. The time when a rampart is being stormed is not the time for reckless innovation. It might be, however, that the short-term value of resisting debilitating change will exact a long-term price in terms of arrested development. For these reasons, the communists may have preferred an immobile church. Emelyan Yaroslavski, the founder of the League of the Militant Godless, asserted that a reformed, modernized religion might become more dangerous than the old one. Soviet officials were wary of religion "in new, refined forms."[29]

The Marxists' second long-term strategy was to limit the churches to the performance of the rites within the walls of the sanctuary. Again, one might use the analogy of disease. The human body may combat an invading parasite or microbe by enclosing it in a cyst, thus isolating it and protecting the surrounding organism. Encased in this shell, the parasite may live for years, or die, or become calcified, while the body continues to live.[30] In a certain sense the communists tried to do the same thing, confining religion behind the doors of the churches and isolating church life from society at large.

In 1924 the communists proscribed religious assemblies and processions.[31] This action affected some of the oldest and most treasured practices of the church. For example, there is an ancient tradition of going to the rivers on Epiphany to bless the waters. On this solemn occasion the faithful would build great ice crosses and tables on the frozen surface of the river, after which the bishop might cast a decorated cross into the hole in the ice, and intrepid youths would plunge into the frigid currents and rescue the cross as an act of piety and fortitude.

On April 8, 1929, the authorities decreed the dissolution of lay organizations and banned church-run charitable activities, including relief of the needy. The authorities closed Orthodox medical institutions, orphanages, and homes for the mentally ill, disabled, and the old.[32] In particular, Article 17 of the decree outlawed the use of church premises for activities beyond worship, thereby prohibiting libraries, organized religious education, prayer meetings for women and young people, religious study groups, and even sewing circles. The same decree mandated that clergy do their work only on the premises of the church society employing them, meaning that it was unlawful for a priest to serve two parishes or to celebrate the sacraments in nonchurch institutions (except to aid the sick or dying). It reaffirmed that churches lacked juridical rights. Central church organs were forbidden to establish bank accounts for the deposit of free-will offerings. The decree was largely a codification of earlier dispositions, and the rigor of its enforcement varied with the times, but it stood on the books for sixty years, consistently inhibiting church activities.[33]

Priests and other religious persons were prohibited from wearing their habits in public places, a measure that removed a visual reminder of the church.[34] In 1932 priests were forbidden to live in the cities.[35] In 1929 a scrap metal drive for industry resulted in the communists' seizing most church bells, thereby silencing them. The remaining bells were stilled by decree.[36] The atheists used these tactics to remove the sight and sound of religion from the streets of cities and the byways of the countryside. These measures were also designed to foster a perception of the church as a place where rituals were mechanically performed, and nothing more.

The abolition of religious holidays in 1923 and the institution of Sunday morning "voluntary" secular activities, such as work brigades and sporting events, were part of an effort to separate religion from the world of daily life. In 1929 the government introduced a rotating six-day workweek. This work schedule gave the people Sunday off only once in every six weeks. The new workweek fostered the isolation of the religious communities, which were depicted as consisting mostly of pensioners and the incapacitated. Orthodox priests adjusted their service times, but the impact was real—and resented.[37]

A third long-range strategy to weaken religion was the communists' propaganda for atheism. Beyond the secularization of schools and the prohibition of organized religious education of the young, the government amended the Russian constitution in 1929 to outlaw proselytizing. The constitution of 1918 had given both atheists and believers the right to propagate their beliefs, but the 1929 amendment gave the right of propaganda to the atheists and allowed the believers only the opportunity to profess their beliefs and engage in worship. The 1936 Stalin constitution gave them only the right to worship.[38]

In the early years the thrust of atheist propaganda tended to be crude and political, although early Marxist leaders such as Anatoli Lunacharski and Lenin himself were intellectually impressive men. Lunacharski and other antireligious leaders were not afraid to engage clerics in open debate in those optimistic, uninhibited, and experimental days of the communist movement. Nevertheless, militant godless propagandists were more often blunt and coarse. In their enthusiasm, Bolshevik governmental leaders ordered the opening of reliquaries on March 1, 1919, and in August of 1920 ordered "the complete liquidation of the cult of corpses and mummies" by transferring these relics to state museums. The atheists tried to expose the "incorruptible" remains of saints as mere rotting bones and wax figures. In one museum showcase they exhibited the relic of a saint side by side with a mummified rat.[39]

In the early 1920s the communists tried to prove that the Russian Orthodox Church was the instrument of a corrupt, reactionary, and treacherous clergy. They accused priests and bishops of usury, black marketeering, and seditious collaboration with the anti-Bolshevik White Guards in the civil war. On a personal level, priests were depicted as licentious, sadistic, and depraved. A few clerics truly were immoral, of course, but not many raped small girls or sodomized altar boys as the propaganda would have had one believe.[40]

By the mid-1920s the propaganda began to change. With Tikhon's "confession" and Sergi's declaration of loyalty in 1927, the church's open defiance of communist power essentially came to an end. For their part, communist leaders began to discourage mocking parades and carnivals as counterproductive. Competition between priest-blessed and scientifically seeded grain plots became more characteristic of the atheists' efforts than actions to force open reliquaries. After complaints in the antireligious press that the believers made the unbelievers look foolish in debates, open confrontations of this kind mostly ceased.[41]

The wave of violence in 1929 and 1930 and the famine that ensued produced a reversion. The League of the Militant Godless pushed its membership up to 5.5 million by 1932. The league's magazine, *Bezbozhnik* [The Godless], was supplemented by an array of atheist publications, traveling cinemas, antireligious "universities," godless shock brigades, godless collective farms, and proliferating antireligious museums. Mocking plays, songs, and carnivals reappeared.[42] The school curriculum, which had previously been essentially secular, became sharply antireligious.[43]

As the 1930s progressed, godless propaganda evolved into the form it retained until the late 1980s. Public attention was directed to the medical hazards said to be caused by religious practice, including the spreading of disease through drinking from a common spoon and cup in communion and by kissing icons.[44] For example, in 1972 a U.S. apologist for the official Soviet position described the scene at the Trinity-Sergius monastery in Zagorsk as follows: "With a rag the priest periodically wipes the spittle from the pure silver coffin [of St. Sergius] . . . as pilgrims, mostly older women and mothers with their children, continue passionately to kiss the coffin."[45] The Soviet press recounted stories of babies dying of pneumonia after baptism by immersion.[46]

Even so, there was a trend away from ridiculing believers. Some observers believe that the avoidance of provocative, flamboyant, antireligious acts caused the ideological campaign to sink into gray formlessness. The antireligious museums came to emit a distinct air of boredom.[47] Despite its dissemination of at least 100 million copies of antireligious literature, the League of the Militant Godless lost almost two-thirds of its membership between 1932 and 1938.[48]

The third great wave of church closings began in 1936 at the time of the great purges. The official crackdown was given additional impetus by the discovery, jolting to atheist leaders and propagandists, that religious belief was not dying away as Marxist doctrine predicted that it must. The 1937 census had a question on religion, and the results, which were leaked to informed circles and the West, showed that over half the people in the country—two-thirds of the population in the villages and a third of the urban population—still considered themselves believers. Stalin had decreed in 1932 that the church was to be eradicated in five years, which would have been in 1937, and yet the census had revealed a "deplorable" persistence of belief. The authorities' reaction was to intensify repression.[49]

The archives of the Soviet government's Council for Religious Affairs provide fragmentary data on the rising numbers of church closings in 1937 and 1938, then a slackening of the intensity of the antireligious drive between 1939 and 1941.[50] William Fletcher also noted that the 1937–1938 attack became a bit more relaxed after 1938, at least with respect to underground religious activity.[51] One must add, however, that the easing in the number of church closings after 1938 may simply have reflected the fact that there were so few churches left to close.

Like the earlier two waves of church closings, the 1936–1938 campaign was very much a part of the general upheaval in society, which had ripped away all veneer of normalcy and restraint. The terror, the executions, and the growth of the labor camps in Siberia and in European Russia (i.e., Russia west of the Urals) were felt by everyone.

It may be remembered that on December 1, 1934, a shot in the back had killed the Leningrad Communist Party chief, Sergei M. Kirov. The circumstances of the murder lent credence to the probability that it was Stalin himself who had inspired the deed. Nevertheless, while "investigating" the crime, Stalin had the secret police interrogate and torture an ever-widening circle of people. Of the members of the Central Committee of the Communist Party elected at the 1934 congress, more than two-thirds had perished by 1938. In the great purge trials, the towering figures of Lenin's time were forced to confess treasonous crimes, and most were executed. The commander in chief of the army, every officer who commanded a military district or an army corps, almost every division commander, and close to half of the 75,000 Red Army officers were arrested or shot. An estimated 19 million Soviet citizens died in the terror. The police (NKVD) became the largest employer in the USSR, responsible for a sixth of all new construction in the country.[52]

An understanding of the suffering inflicted on the whole citizenry of the USSR truly does help make clear what the Russian Orthodox Church was also going through and why there were no longer mighty armies of peasants able to hold off the militant godless as they tried to close the churches. And close the churches they did—and arrest the priests and incarcerate the bishops and exile the believers to the GULAG Archipelago. By the late 1930s, 80,000 Orthodox clerics, monks, and nuns reportedly had lost their lives at the hands of the Bolsheviks. This figure represents about half the total number of clerics, monks, and nuns serving before the 1917 revolution.[53]

In the late 1930s, there were only four active bishops in the USSR.[54] In addition to Metropolitan Sergi, the church's acting head, there were Metropolitan Aleksi (Simanski) of Leningrad, his suffragan, Nikolai (Yarushevich), and Metropolitan Sergi (Voskresenski). Anatoli Levitin-Krasnov, the Orthodox dissident writer, described Aleksi's and Nikolai's situation:

Aleksi's suffragan, Bishop Nikolai of Peterhof (the future Metropolitan), used to keep by him at home a small bag with two changes of clothes, two sheets and a towel—in case he was arrested. I think Metropolitan Aleksi also had a similar bag at home. Every two or three months brought some kind of unpleasant surprise—the arrest of a group of priests. By 1937 there were only fifteen of them left in the whole of the Leningrad region, whereas in 1930 they had numbered more than a thousand. In the spring of 1937 the metropolitan was turned out of his rooms . . . and found shelter for himself in the bell tower of the Prince Vladimir Cathedral in the cramped and gloomy accommodation formerly occupied by the caretakers. Metropolitan Aleksi took church services along with Archdeacon Verzilin, the only deacon left in Leningrad. After Verzilin's death in 1938 he celebrated without a deacon. . . . I remember once, as I was walking along Nevsky Prospect . . . I noticed the metropolitan clad in civilian garb. A threadbare light-weight overcoat, galoshes, an ordinary grey cap—all this, in conjunction with his aristocratic face and subtle elegance of gesture, gave him the appearance of a bankrupt landlord. As I passed I made him a deep bow and the metropolitan acknowledged it with a slight nod. He was very resigned.[55]

The church was perilously close to demise, given the canonical need for an unbroken apostolic succession—bishops were essential for the continuation of both a line of hierarchs and of priests. The police might have carried off the remaining openly functioning bishops in a single night. Why did Stalin not order the police to do so? Probably he had some concern for the likely international reaction and some desire to maintain the facade of freedom of worship, as declared in the "Stalin constitution" of 1936. In any case, those four bishops were spared.

What about church premises? There were about 50,000 churches before the Bolshevik revolution—or close to 80,000 functioning church establishments if one counted chapels, convent churches, institutional prayer houses, and so on.[56] According to journalist Walter Kolarz, "By July 1937 not a single church remained open in Byelorussia."[57] Yuri Degtyarev, an authoritative spokesman of the Soviet government and Communist Party, wrote that there were no open churches at all in more than a third of the seventy-odd regions (oblasts) of the Russian Federated Republic; in another third, each region had no more than five churches.[58] Six regions in Ukraine had no open churches at all, and three regions had only one church each.[59] In 1939 those nine regions constituted most of the Ukrainian Soviet Socialist Republic. A well-known specialist on Ukrainian churches, Bohdan R. Bociurkiw, confirmed Degtyarev's range of numbers; he reported fewer than a dozen Orthodox parishes intact in the whole of Ukraine before World War II.[60] In the great Ukrainian diocese of Kiev, which had more than 1,600 churches before the 1917 revolution, the occupying Germans found two churches that had been functioning under the Soviets, one at the edge of the city of Kiev and one in the countryside.[61] One church was said to be open in the Ukrainian diocese of Zhitomir.[62] The Germans found one church in the city of Odessa, where there had once been forty-eight churches.[63]

Nikita Struve, another expert on Russian Orthodox religion, described the situation in the diocese of Rostov-on-Don, just east of Ukraine:

> Its archbishop, Seraphim (Silichev), had been exiled to the far north in 1930, where he soon died. Shortly afterwards, his Vicar, Mgr. Nicholas Ammasisky, was sent to the steppes of Astrakhan to graze a flock of sheep. In 1938 he was again arrested and this time shot, but miraculously recovered from his wounds. Meanwhile, the authorities continued to close the churches. In Rostov itself, even the former Cathedral of St. Nicholas was transformed into a zoo; the new Cathedral of St. Alexander Nevsky was razed to the ground; the huge Church of All Saints turned into a workshop, and the Greek Church became an antireligious museum. . . . Throughout the whole province, one single church, served by a very old priest, was still functioning in a village close to Taganrog.[64]

In the northern territories near Leningrad, an Orthodox mission team from Latvia followed the advancing Germans in 1941 and found only two functioning churches in that immense and populous territory.[65]

In the whole of the Soviet Union in 1939, there were only 200–300 open churches.[66] This figure has been compiled from reports of no churches open in Byelorussia (Kolarz) and "less than a dozen" in Ukraine (Bociurkiw). There were fifteen to twenty churches in the city of Moscow, five in Leningrad, and a few more in the hinterlands of the two capitals, for a total of 150–200 in the Russian republic (Degtyarev's figures).[67] There were, in addition, a few Russian Orthodox churches in Central Asia and in the Caucasus. This adds up to 200–300 churches nationwide.

The situation of the priests was little better. The Germans found three active priests in the two functioning churches in the diocese of Kiev (compared to 1,435 priests before the revolution).[68] In the Ukrainian city of Kamenets-Podolski, the advancing Germans found one aged priest holding services, and the mission team from Latvia found two priests "reduced to complete impoverishment" in the area south of Leningrad.[69]

To complete this description of the church's travail, I recount the story of Metropolitan Sergi's removal from Moscow after the German invasion in 1941. As Hitler's armies approached, Stalin decided to evacuate most of the leaders of the religious communities, no doubt fearing that they might defect, or that the Germans could turn the Soviet churchmen to their own political purposes if they were captured. In fact, the decision to evacuate these men rather than kill them may have been sheer luck, as the Soviets in retreat had frequently executed people in such circumstances. Reportedly Sergi drew up a will on October 12, two days before he was sent east from Moscow.[70]

On October 14 the authorities rounded up Metropolitan Sergi and the other leaders of religious communities and—as A. Krasnov of the Renovationist church described it—crowded them all into a railroad carriage. There were Renovationist church hierarchs with some family members, a bearded old gentleman with one eye who was the Old Believer archbishop of Moscow and All Russia, some modestly dressed leaders of the Baptist community, and then "into the compartment came a medium-tall, old man with a broad, thick, grey beard, gold pince-nez, and a facial tic. He was dressed in a cassock and wore a monastic skull-cap." It was Sergi, the head of the Russian Orthodox Church, seen off by Nikolai and accompanied by Archpriest N. F. Kolchitski.[71]

About 600 kilometers east of Moscow, during a trip that had already lasted days, Sergi became quite sick. As Wassilij Alexeev described it, Sergi developed a fever of 104° and drifted in and out of delirium. According to Krasnov, some medical people examined Sergi and had the railroad car redirected to Ulyanovsk rather than to the original destination of Orenburg, which was 600 kilometers still farther to the east. Somewhat later, a violent quarrel broke out between two of the sons of a Renovationist hierarch, and all the sick old metropolitan could do was to press himself still deeper into a corner of the compartment.[72]

Finally the train reached Ulyanovsk, which Krasnov described as "for two years the Russian Vatican, the religious capital" of the country. It was a quiet, sleepy town, "with almost no factories, no tram lines, and automobiles one could count on one's fingers."[73]

According to Alexeev, "Sergi was met . . . only by the chairman of the local Orthodox parish society. . . . Not even a group of believers met him. . . . There was no place for him to live . . . and he stayed for a few days in a railroad car. . . . Sergi sent . . . to a neighboring town to get church keys, organize a church society of twenty persons and start services. . . . When Sergi arrived, church activity had been virtually suspended."[74]

Krasnov's description was similar: "There was one little cemetery church, hardly more than a chapel, at which a young monastic priest of doubtful reputation and uncertain ecclesiastical loyalty was serving. It became the first 'pitiful outpost' of the Moscow Patriarchate in the region. Sergi did not even have a place to stay." Kolchitski and others "began feverish efforts to find a suitable church." Krasnov continued:

> It was not so easy. In Ulyanovsk, once rich in churches, there were not then even church grounds. Where the cathedral once stood, on the highest ground in the city, there was now a gigantic statue of Lenin. A town square had been made on the spot where the ancient Ascension Church once stood. There were two city churches still standing . . . but long in disuse. They had deteriorated to the point of being beyond

any quick restoration to tolerable condition, particularly in wartime circumstances. ... Finally [Kolchitski and the others] took over the former Roman Catholic parish church with an auxiliary premises where the parish priest had once lived. Soon the little church was opened under the imposing name of the Kazan Cathedral, and [Sergi] ... moved into the former apartment of the priest.[75]

It is said that Sergi had very little disposable income. The story is told that on one occasion Sergi wanted to give money to someone in need but could find none, so he gave his watch instead.[76]

The light of the "candle in the wind" of the Russian Orthodox Church still shone forth to Soviet people and to the world, but for all too many Soviet citizens who were far from any church or priest it must have flickered in the distance, beckoning elusively from afar, with the ever-present danger that the flame might be extinguished by a single order from that former seminarian, Joseph Stalin.

2

The Turnaround

WHATEVER HARM the 1939 Molotov-Ribbentrop Pact between Germany and the Soviet Union did to Europe and the world, it rescued the institution of the Russian Orthodox Church. Hitler's deal with Stalin allowed the Soviets to occupy eastern Poland, and 1,200 Orthodox parishes were incorporated into the Soviet Union as a result.[1] Then, in mid-June of 1940, the Soviets occupied Estonia, Latvia, and Lithuania, among whose 6 million people were almost a half million traditionally Orthodox persons who worshiped in about 300 Orthodox churches.[2] Later in the same month the Soviets compelled the Romanians to cede Bessarabia and northern Bukovina with their 4 million people, 3 million of them traditionally Orthodox. There were between 2,000 and 2,500 parishes in these formerly Romanian lands. These annexations brought the Russian Orthodox Church more than 6 million traditionally Orthodox people and 3,500–4,000 churches with active priests, as well as many monasteries and nunneries, some bishops and seminaries, and other resources. The institutional strength of the church must have increased fifteenfold.

The communists soon started closing churches and arresting priests and lay Christians in the newly acquired lands, but they also understood that the Russian Orthodox Church could be an instrument of assimilation and of Soviet control.[3] It was no accident that two of the only four surviving active Russian Orthodox bishops were sent to the annexed territories. Metropolitan Sergi (Voskresenski) was sent to Riga, and Nikolai (Yarushevich), Aleksi's former suffragan in Leningrad, was sent as exarch for western Ukraine and Byelorussia.[4] The communists soon began the process of Russifying defiant separatist religious communities and suppressing Ukrainian, Byelorussian, and Baltic nationalists allied with non-Soviet church hierarchs. In this sense the interests of the beleaguered church and the Soviet authorities had elements in common. The result was that the draconian Soviet attack on all religious manifestations, which was still going on in the "old" Soviet territories, was only partially extended to these newly acquired western lands, and religious institutions in those areas largely survived.

In August of 1941 the Soviet embassy in London released exact figures on the number of functioning churches in the Soviet Union on the eve of Hitler's June attack. Apparently the Soviets did this to counter criticism of Soviet religious suppression voiced by their newly acquired British allies, but the press release backfired because Westerners were impressed with the paucity of the numbers rather than their magnitude. Little did they know how low pre–September 1939 figures would have been.

The figures for the Orthodox and Renovationists (mostly the Living Church) were 4,225 churches and 37 convents (monasteries and nunneries).[5] The separatist Renovationists had already been much reduced by 1941, and almost all those remaining rejoined the patriarchal church over the next several years. Therefore, the 4,225 churches could effectively be regarded as Orthodox, and over 90 percent of them were in the lands annexed in 1939–1940.[6]

When Hitler launched his invasion, German forces advanced with great speed along a thousand-mile front stretching from the Baltic Sea to the Black Sea. As already described, Orthodox priests came in their wake and opened churches, to the joy and gratitude of believers. Initially the German soldiers were welcomed by many in the populace with the traditional bread and salt of hospitality, and Stalin apparently began to fear that Orthodox Christianity might become a weapon of the invaders against a reeling, staggering Soviet defense. Metropolitan Sergi had been quick to rally believers to the defense of the motherland, however, and the Nazi Germans' arrogance and brutality soon began to alienate the peoples in the Wehrmacht's path.[7]

Long-occupied lands experienced a much greater religious revival during World War II than those briefly occupied or close to the front lines. For example, the advancing Germans found one church in each of the cities of Kiev and Kharkov. In Kiev, occupied three years and generally far behind the lines, believers opened twenty-five churches during the course of the occupation. In Kharkov, always close to the battle lines and much fought over, believers opened only two churches.[8]

Life for the surviving Orthodox people in areas under continuing Soviet rule remained extremely hard, particularly in the blockaded city of Leningrad. During the siege, the priest and deacon at the Transfiguration Church lived in the church's cellar. At the Cathedral of St. Nicholas, an eyewitness reported:

> Metropolitan Aleksi courageously walked in procession with an icon around the church even during air raids. . . . In the meantime the members of the Cathedral choir were dying, one-by-one, until the choirmaster himself collapsed and died in the middle of a church service. . . . The three surviving women in the choir grew so weak that they could no longer climb to the choir loft, but they continued to sing as best they could from a low platform in the sanctuary (the *kliros*). . . . Aleksi himself was wasting away, looking increasingly waxy. A novice monk named Yevlagi foraged just enough food to keep the Metropolitan alive. . . . Another witness, Nikolai Uspenski, reported passing by the Cathedral one day. He saw an older man strug-

gling to clear enough snow to make a walkway to the church. It was Aleksi. Nikolai joined in to help, and Aleksi invited him to reestablish the choir, which by then had expired. . . . The last remaining deacon in Leningrad continued to serve until he, too, died. Thereafter Aleksi celebrated the liturgy alone.[9]

Soviet government policy toward the Russian Orthodox Church was changing, albeit slowly. Antireligious propaganda stopped, and the League of the Militant Godless was dissolved in September of 1941. A small number of churches were reopened in late 1941 around Ulyanovsk where Metropolitan Sergi had set up church headquarters after his evacuation from Moscow. Soon bishops were consecrated and a few churches opened in Saratov, Orenburg, Kuibyshev, and other places east of Moscow.[10] This was not a large-scale development; Alexeev estimated that no more than a few dozen churches were able to open their doors.[11] In the spring of 1942 the church leadership consisted of three metropolitans—Sergi (Stragorodski), Aleksi (Simanski) and Nikolai (Yarushevich)—and eight active diocesan bishops.[12] In January of 1943 Sergi obtained Stalin's written permission to open a bank account to handle the church's collections in support of the Red Army. The church's fortunes continued to improve, and in March of 1943 Bishop Luka (Voino-Yasenetski) happily wrote his son that a church had been opened in the distant Siberian city of Krasnoyarsk, where the bishop, who was still technically a religious detainee, was serving as chief surgeon at a military hospital.[13]

On September 4, 1943, Stalin received Metropolitans Sergi, Aleksi, and Nikolai in the Kremlin. A Soviet writer with access to the record of the meeting reported that Stalin met earlier in the day with Georgi Malenkov, Lavrenti Beria, and Georgi G. Karpov, an NKVD general who would later become head of the Soviet government's Council for Russian Orthodox Church Affairs.[14] Stalin wanted to ensure that the church would not stray from government control, and he had asked whether he should receive the three church hierarchs. His aides endorsed the idea, and the churchmen responded to the summons that same day. Stalin was accompanied at the meeting by Vyacheslav Molotov and Karpov.

Stalin assented to Sergi's request for a church council to elect a patriarch. When the clerics proposed a date weeks later, Stalin asked, "Why so slow?" Stalin ultimately offered some transportation and financial support to solve the church's severe logistical problems.[15] Four days after the meeting, a national church council of nineteen bishops elected Sergi as patriarch.[16] At the meeting with Stalin, Aleksi and Sergi also requested permission to organize theological courses for priests, the aim being later establishment of seminaries and academies. Stalin said: "Go straight to seminaries and academies—but it's your business!" The churchmen asked for permission to set up shops and candle factories, to publish a monthly journal, to open new churches, to consecrate bishops, and to ordain more priests. Stalin assented. The churchmen sought authorization for a part of parish and diocesan receipts to be given to the central church administration and for the inclusion of priests in parish executive organs. Stalin did not object. The hierarchs then turned to less "convenient" questions, including the fate of imprisoned hierarchs and clergy and the seizure of the living quarters of arrested priests. Stalin told the churchmen to make lists of cases and said Karpov would look into these matters. Finally Malenkov suggested that a photographer be brought in to take a photograph. Stalin responded that it was already two o'clock in the morning and "we'll do it another time." During the remaining ten years of Stalin's life, there never was another time.[17]

Why did Stalin receive the hierarchs, and why did he do so when he did, more than two years after Hitler's invasion? The probable explanation starts with his limited amelioration of church policy in 1941, which was in reaction to the renaissance of church life behind German lines and his evident fear that the yearnings of Soviet believers would make them anti-Soviet activists. In the desperate months of the initial Soviet retreat and in the renewed retreats of 1942, Stalin's energies were concentrated on survival and military strategy; he probably concluded—to the extent that he thought about Sergi and his church—that additional concessions would have little effect on Sergi's already supportive public stand. By 1943, however, Stalin was thinking more about politics, and Red forces were liberating areas where newly opened Orthodox churches abounded. Soviet social control in these formerly occupied areas was partial at best, and Stalin may have felt that an indiscriminate closure of Orthodox churches would be difficult to enforce. Some sort of policy was clearly necessary, and Sergi's church was an instrument of Soviet dominance over unsubmissive Ukrainian and Byelorussian Greek-Catholics, sects, and other religious forces that had collaborated in varying degrees with the Germans. A softer policy toward the Russian Orthodox Church could reduce the incentive to organize a religious underground, which Stalin clearly did not want, and diminish unrest. Moreover, Stalin's own atheism was probably as much political and pragmatic as profoundly held.[18]

In addition, as William Fletcher suggested, Stalin may have been willing to elevate Sergi to the patriarchal office in order to strengthen Sergi's hand in his struggle with the separatist Ukrainian Autocephalous Orthodox Church of Metropolitan Polykarp (Sikorski). The last thing Stalin wanted was a vigorous, independent Ukrainian church that was ready to help political nationalists longing for a non-Soviet Ukraine. The same national church council in Moscow that elevated Sergi also excommunicated Polykarp.[19]

Foreign policy may also have entered into Stalin's calculations. Stalin was hoping for loans and other help from the West, and he undoubtedly was aware of Western sensitivities regarding the persecution of religion in the USSR. Stalin wanted the West to open a second front in France, and his natural political allies in England included the dean of Canterbury, Hewlett Johnson, and the archbishop of York, who was planning to lead a church delegation to Moscow. The

Tehran summit meeting of Stalin, Roosevelt, and Churchill was in the offing. Moreover, the Russian Orthodox Church might prove useful in furthering Soviet ambitions in the Balkans and the near east after the war. Reportedly Stalin had quizzed Malenkov, Beria, and Karpov about the patriarchates of Constantinople and Jerusalem and the Orthodox churches of Romania, Bulgaria, and Yugoslavia when he held his preparatory meeting on September 4, 1943. In fact, Russian Orthodox hierarchs were subsequently employed in the pursuit of Stalin's goals in those areas.[20]

According to Russian Orthodox Church sources, after Patriarch Sergi was enthroned in September 1943, "the number of churches began to increase in both the cities and villages."[21] The fact that church sources were explicit in saying that the number "began" to increase in late 1943 would tend to confirm that Metropolitan Sergi had been able to open only a very few churches during his two previous years of residency in Ulyanovsk. Even after the meeting, the Soviet government hardly rushed to authorize new parishes. According to one well-placed source, Vyacheslav Molotov instructed Karpov to delay authorizing the registration of new church societies until the situation could be surveyed, recommendations submitted, and clearance obtained. Molotov was quoted as saying: "We will have to open churches in some places, but the policy is to keep the process slow."[22]

Sergi lived for eight months after his historic meeting with Stalin. During that time regular dioceses were established in Soviet territories behind the war zones, and more bishops were consecrated. An official Soviet report dated March 15, 1944, listed twenty-nine functioning bishops besides the patriarch.[23] The *Journal of the Moscow Patriarchate* resumed publication.[24]

Metropolitan Sergi died on May 15, 1944, and Metropolitan Aleksi of Leningrad became acting head of the church. The opening of churches continued, as did the consecration of new bishops and the ordination of pious laymen as priests. Priests in hiding or detention increasingly were able to return to their clerical duties. Many priests who had opened churches under the German occupation continued to serve.

A pastoral school and theological institute opened in Moscow in June 1944, a development that reversed the total prohibition of such institutions that had been in effect since the beginning of the 1930s. In August of 1944 Karpov stated that the number of Orthodox churches exceeded the prewar figure. By that time Soviet troops had already pushed the Germans out of pre-1939 Soviet territories and were fast reconquering the lands annexed in 1939 and 1940. Most of the functioning parishes were in these formerly occupied lands. In late November of 1944 Aleksi reported to a council of bishops that "over two hundred churches" had been opened in the USSR in the year after Sergi had been enthroned; no doubt he was referring to churches in the Soviet heartland. Two Soviet government decrees, one at the end of 1944 and another in mid-1945, authorized the turning over of 300 more churches to the Orthodox.[25]

On January 31, 1945, a national church council convened in Moscow and unanimously elected Aleksi as the new patriarch. Of the forty-two bishops then in the country, forty-one were in attendance; Archbishop Luka (Voino-Yasenetski), then of Tambov, was not invited as a consequence of his objection to the uncanonical presentation of a single candidate for patriarch.[26]

A Soviet government decree of August 22, 1945, implemented Stalin's 1943 decision to grant the church significant attributes of a "legal person." The church could thereafter lease, construct, and purchase houses (but not the land under them), own and operate vehicles, and establish shops for the manufacture of candles and religious objects. Local authorities were instructed to provide the church with necessary materials for building and repair, and the ban on ringing church bells was eased.[27] By April of 1946 the church's hierarchy consisted of a patriarch, four metropolitans, twenty-one archbishops, and thirty-six bishops, a total of sixty-two.[28]

By that April, two and a half years after Stalin received Sergi, the continuity of the patriarchate had been reaffirmed and a patriarchal residence and central administration in Moscow had been reestablished.[29] A church governing a handful of dioceses in the central USSR had grown to more than fifty sees spread throughout the country; a few dozen churches had become a few thousand; the supply of priests had increased greatly; the Renovationist schism had disappeared; seminaries and theological academies had reopened; and convents in annexed territories and some reconstituted under German occupation had been able to renew the cloistered life of monks and nuns in the USSR. In some ways the church remained beleaguered, but the contrast between its situation in 1939 and its condition in 1946 was immense.

The recovery and expansion of the church's institutional strength continued until 1948, a year that marked a high point for the immediate postwar period. There were six components of the church's institutional strength in 1948. The first of them consisted of the 200–300 churches and the beleaguered company of priests and hierarchs that had survived the persecutions of the first decades of communist rule. The second source of renewed strength was the government-permitted opportunity to open churches in territories never occupied by the Germans. An inspector of the Council for Russian Orthodox Church Affairs reported that 1,270 churches were opened in these lands between 1944 and 1947, most of them in the Russian Federated Republic.[30] Thus 1,600–1,700 churches must have been functioning in these areas in 1947.[31] Most of the clergy who staffed these churches were priests obliged to take secular employment in the 1930s, clerics forced into hiding or taken to labor camps, and pious laymen with experience as psalmists or readers who could be ordained as deacons and priests.

The third component in Orthodox institutional strength consisted of the resources acquired in the 1939–1940 annexations. The Soviets lost these lands, churches, priests, and people in the weeks that followed the German invasion in 1941, but they reacquired the territories, most of the churches (those not destroyed), some of the priests, and most of the people before the end of 1944. Of the 3,500–4,000 parishes acquired in the 1939–1940 annexations, 3,000–3,200 seem to have survived into the postwar period as functioning churches. Over half of the convents that emerged from the war were located in the annexed lands. In fact, almost a quarter of the convents in the USSR after the war were located in the single diocese of Kishinev (Moldavia).

The fourth major source of renewed strength came from the prewar Soviet territories occupied by the Germans, where churches were reopened in large numbers. In the diocese of Kiev alone, between 700 and 800 parishes had opened in the 1941–1943 period.[32] An inspector for the Council for Russian Orthodox Church Affairs gave the figure of 7,547 churches opened in the occupied territories between 1941 and 1945.[33] Not all of these newly opened churches stayed open, but most did. Perhaps as many as 6,000–6,200 of them survived the immediate postwar upheavals.

The fifth source of augmented strength for the Russian Orthodox Church was in territories first annexed after World War II.[34] Transcarpathia, with a population approaching 1.5 million, was ceded by Czechoslovakia to the USSR on June 29, 1945. The Greek-Catholics in Transcarpathia were obliged to submit to patriarchal authority in a process that lasted several years and was characterized by widespread violence, including the assassination of the ruling Greek-Catholic bishop.[35] The Russian Orthodox Church thereby became the only large overt religious community in that territory; there were 559 Orthodox churches, 407 of them former Greek-Catholic parishes. Transcarpathia emerged from the World War II period with two monasteries, four nunneries, and twelve small hermitages.[36]

The forced incorporation of the Greek-Catholics in Galicia was the sixth important augmentation of the church's institutional resources in the postwar period. Under conditions of great intimidation and after the arrest of the Greek-Catholic hierarchy in western Ukraine, a Russian Orthodox Church council assembled in Lvov in March of 1946. In a memorandum to Stalin dated March 15, 1945, Karpov had complained about Orthodox passivity in the "fight with Catholicism," and Stalin no doubt made the decision personally to convene the council. Soviet government and NKVD agents organized the meeting.[37] The result was the forced conversion of almost 2,500 Greek-Catholic parishes to Russian Orthodoxy.[38] Virtually all of these were incorporated into what are now the dioceses of Lvov, Ternopol, and Ivano-Frankovsk. In addition, the few remaining Greek-Catholic parishes in Byelorussia were absorbed into the Russian Orthodox establishment.[39] Orthodox spokesmen subsequently gave the figure of "about 3,000" Greek-Catholic parishes as the number joining Orthodoxy in Byelorussia and western Ukraine, including Transcarpathia.[40]

The total for these six components of Russian Orthodox Church strength is a median figure of slightly more than 14,000 churches in January of 1947. This correlates closely with figures declassified in the late 1980s from the official archives of the Soviet government's Council for Religious Affairs. The council recorded 14,039 registered church societies or parishes on January 1, 1947. Its figure in early 1946 was 10,504 registered church societies.[41] The difference reflects the almost 3,000 Greek-Catholic parishes added to the Orthodox rolls in 1946 and the continuing, although slackening, registration of new church societies throughout the country.

For January 1, 1945, the council recorded 14,100 church societies, or roughly 3,500 more than in January of 1946. There are several reasons for the apparent decline in 1945. First, the January 1945 figure was rounded, whereas other council figures over the years were invariably expressed in exact numbers. The council's commissioner for Ukraine submitted a report during this period in which he stated candidly that his records were unreliable and incomplete. The central authorities in Moscow were also estimating the number of rural churches and priests in the country in the 1945 period.[42] The 1945 figure can therefore be considered a rough estimate that was corrected in the course of 1945.

Moreover, some churches opened during the German occupation were denied registration and had to close after the war. Many hundreds of priests had fled with the retreating Axis troops, leaving parishes vacant. Both Soviet regulations and Orthodox canons denied standing to a church without a priest, and the authorities deregistered quite a number of parishes on this basis. The Soviet government also decreed that arrangements made under the German occupation were invalid. Churches opened under the Germans fell under this proscription, which was enforced in some cases. As already mentioned, the Ukrainian Autocephalous Church of Archbishop Polykarp, which had opened about 500 churches in Ukraine, came under heavy Soviet government and Russian Orthodox attack as a "Fascist" body; some of its churches were closed (and others were turned over to the Orthodox).[43] Further, a council inspector noted that less than half of the churches in Poltava oblast under the German occupation in 1941 and 1942 were registered by the council after the war because the other communities of believers failed to get the "necessary documents."[44] The council's records contain frequent notations that churches were closed because there was "no priest," because the church was "not active," or because the church society was unable to collect the required "documents" of eligibility to remain open.

New registrations continued on a reduced scale under more restrictive ground rules through 1947 and into 1948. The number of officially registered parishes in January 1948 was 14,329, an increase of about 300 registered parishes over the previous year.[45] The 1949 figure of 14,421 parishes documented an additional increase of slightly fewer than 100, these concentrated almost entirely in Ukraine and Byelorussia. Most communities of believers had to submit repeated petitions before getting registration.[46] An indication of the degree to which authorizations were cautiously handled and reluctantly approved was a report by a council inspector in early 1948 who noted that the believers in a town he was visiting had submitted fifteen petitions to register their parish in the period since the war.[47]

As for the priests, the Russian Orthodox Church emerged from the war with an acute shortage of clerics in the western lands, which is where most of the churches were. The *Journal of the Moscow Patriarchate* reported that for two years after the Soviet expulsion of the Germans from Moldavia in August 1944, the bishop of Kishinev dedicated his full efforts to filling parishes left vacant by priests who had fled or to finding worthy priests for parishes led by canonically unqualified persons. In those two years, approximately half the parishes were successfully supplied with qualified priests.[48] The same reality was identified by the Council for Russian Orthodox Church Affairs, which in April 1946 recorded 269 registered priests for the 582 churches in Moldavia.[49] The Baltic states had a similar problem, even if on a smaller scale. Had there been enough priests available in the western lands between 1944 and 1947, 1,000–2,000 parishes that were denied registration after the war might have remained open.

The image that emerges from the foregoing description is a Russian Orthodox Church rescued from its institutional agony by the infusion of resources after the Soviet Union's territorial annexations and by the religiously permissive policies of the German occupation forces, which in turn caused the Soviet government to become more permissive. Forces set in motion between 1939 and 1943 caused a great strengthening of the church. Nevertheless, the material institution of the church still fell far short of the resources and strength it had commanded before the Bolshevik revolution or even during the 1920s and early 1930s.[50]

The imbalances in terms of nationality and geography made the anomaly of the church's situation striking. The Russian Orthodox Church had become a predominantly Ukrainian institution, as almost two-thirds of its parishes were in Ukraine. If the parishes in Byelorussia, the Baltic states, and former Romanian Bessarabia are included, more than 80 percent of church parishes were in western lands annexed in 1939 and 1940 or occupied by the Germans during World War II. As one of the council's inspectors noted, in January of 1948 Ukraine had 78 percent of the churches located there in 1914; the Russian republic had 5 percent.[51] The geographic imbalance was similar in terms of monks, monasteries, nuns, and nunneries. Moreover, 20 percent of the Russian Orthodox parishes in the USSR had been seized from the Ukrainian Greek-Catholics. There were more formerly Greek-Catholic churches in the Russian Orthodox Church institution than there were Russian Orthodox churches over the length and breadth of the immense Russian Federated Republic. About half of the churches in the country were in territories that had not been part of the Soviet Union in early 1939. This increased the usefulness of the church to the Soviet government as an instrument of Russification, but it also increased the church's vulnerability. Inevitably it would find itself in the cross fire as tensions over nationality grew. One can understand why Orthodox hierarchs have been so sensitive when Ukrainian Greek-Catholics and Catholics throughout the world have pressed the issue of religious liberty and the right of Ukrainian Greek-Catholics to the same opportunity to worship that the Soviet constitution extended to other religious communities.

In 1948 Stalin's apparent benevolence turned once again to official hostility. What Bohdan Bociurkiw described as a "golden era" of Russian Orthodox Church expansion came to an end.[52]

3

Stalin's Last Years
and the
Early Khrushchev Period

IN THE PAGES that follow, an examination of the number of functioning Orthodox churches in the USSR in the late 1940s and 1950s forms a considerable part of
the material I present. Why have I emphasized what are, in the last analysis,
bricks, stones, mortar, wood, and nails? The answer is that the performance of
the liturgy in a physically extant church is crucially important in Orthodoxy. The
rite is the Russian Orthodox Church's glory. A thousand years ago, as the earliest
Russian Chronicle tells it, Prince Vladimir sent emissaries to observe the Muslim
Bulgars, the Catholic Germans, and the Orthodox Greeks. His delegates returned
with unflattering comments about the Bulgars and the Catholics, but when they
worshipped with the Orthodox Greeks, "we knew not whether we were in heaven
or on earth. For on earth there is no such splendor nor such beauty."[1]

Contemporary Orthodox people have the same view. Metropolitan Vladimir
(Sabodan) described a Christian's experience in church: "For us believers our
presence in church is truly an encounter with God, a meeting with the saints,
represented visibly in the form of icons. . . . The very architecture of the church,
the brightly burning candles, and the painting on the walls in clear and clean
tones, call forth . . . joy and hope, and . . . radiant reflections."[2]

Fathers Nikolai Eshliman and Gleb Yakunin described the Orthodox church
building as "indeed the house of God, the focal point of church life, the spiritual
table which feeds the faithful with the incorruptible gifts of divine grace."[3] Anatoli
Levitin-Krasnov said: "Every church is the most precious thing in the whole world,
it is washed with the believers' tears."[4]

The transcending importance of the physical church and of the liturgy celebrated there constitutes both a strength and a vulnerability. When the churches
are closed, the loss is all the greater. Soviet sociologists reported that Orthodox
believers who migrated to towns that had no church found their commitment

weakening and ultimately dissipating.[5] No doubt the observers were biased, but it is nevertheless critical for the Orthodox believer to be able to get to a church, at least occasionally.

With characteristic eloquence, Aleksandr Solzhenitsyn described Russia's closed churches:

> They nod to each other from afar. . . . They soar to the same heaven. . . . You are never alone: the head of some bell tower will beckon to you. . . . But when you get into the village you find that not the living but the dead greeted you from afar. The crosses were knocked off the roof or twisted out of place long ago. . . . Weeds grow . . . in the cracks in the walls. . . .
>
> On the porch there are barrels of lubricating oil. . . . Or else a truck has smashed into the church doorway to pick up some sacks. . . .
>
> People were always selfish and often unkind. But the evening bells used to ring out, floating over villages, fields and woods. Reminding men that they must . . . give their time and thought to eternity. These bells . . . raised people up and prevented them from dropping down on all fours.
>
> Our forefathers gave their best; all their understanding of life they put into these stones, into these bell towers.
>
> Ram it in, Vitka, give it a bash, don't be afraid!
>
> Film show at six, dancing at eight.[6]

The film *Repentance* closes with an old woman asking the film's heroine if the road they are on leads to the church. On being told that it does not, the old woman answers as she trudges off: "Oh, what good is a road if it doesn't lead to the church?"[7]

Between 1948 and 1953, during Stalin's last five years of life, the aging dictator's policies shifted back toward repression. By January of 1954 the Russian Orthodox Church had lost about 1,000 of the slightly more than 14,400 registered parishes it had in January of 1949. Data from the archive of the Soviet government's Council for Religious Affairs are as follows for the years between January of 1947 and January of 1954, which was a little less than ten months after Stalin's death:[8]

Russian Orthodox Churches in the USSR

1947	14,039
1948	14,191
1949	14,421
1950	14,273
1951	13,867
1952	13,740
1953	13,508
1954	13,422

The Soviet government cut back sharply on new church registrations in 1948 and—except for Transcarpathia—had altogether stopped registering new churches and parishes by 1949.[9] The *Journal of the Moscow Patriarchate* lacked any report of a new parish church consecration between January of 1949 and mid-December of 1952.[10] Also in 1948, the authorities started deregistering previously accepted parishes at an increasing rate. From 1944 to 1948, deregistration of church buildings recorded in the council's archive had never exceeded 20 in a single year. In 1948 deregistrations jumped to 73; they rose to 400 in 1950 and only began to ease off in 1953, the year Stalin died. The country lost about 7 percent of its parishes.[11] In 1948 the council began to record the number of churches being demolished to make the materials available for other construction. The council also began to record the conversion of church buildings to factories, workers' clubs, shops, and movie houses. Ukraine, which had about two-thirds of the churches in the whole country in 1948, accounted for approximately two-thirds of the deregistrations.

Serious problems continued in western Ukraine. In 1945 Ukrainian nationalist forces under the leadership of Stepan Bandera, a Greek-Catholic priest, had retreated to the wooded hills and battled the Red Army and Soviet security forces in a guerrilla war that lasted for several years. On September 20, 1948, supporters of the nationalist and Greek-Catholic cause assassinated Archpriest Gavriil Kostelnik, a principal organizer of the 1946 Lvov council that had forced the Greek-Catholics to join Orthodoxy.[12] Declaring the merger of the Greek-Catholic and Orthodox churches had been easier than accomplishing it, and many formerly Greek-Catholic churches ended up closed and locked. There were also numerous reports of Greek-Catholic believers and priests going secretly to these churches to use them for religious services.[13]

The factors that might have caused disproportionately high church closings in Ukraine as a whole were counterbalanced by relative leniency toward the Orthodox in formerly Greek-Catholic areas. More than a third of the churches in Ukraine were located in these territories, but only about a quarter of the Ukrainian deregistrations occurred there. The authorities continued to carry a large number of locked and shuttered churches on the books as registered Orthodox religious communities even though they had no priest and were inactive.

In the years after the Lvov council, the Orthodox leadership was notably permissive about what it regarded as continuing "Roman" or Latin deviations in the practices of formerly Greek-Catholic clerics. In 1950, however, Archbishop Makari (Oksiyuk) of Lvov started an "Orthodoxisation" drive, issuing a pastoral letter designed to eliminate aberrations.[14] The ensuing controversy and struggle resulted in the resignation or dismissal of additional priests and the closure of some churches. The number of registered churches in Ukraine dropped by almost 300 in 1950, more than in any other year between 1949 and 1954.[15]

There were greater relative losses in central and eastern Ukraine than in the formerly Greek-Catholic territories. Most central and eastern oblasts lost 10–15

percent of their Orthodox parishes (compared to 7 percent in the whole country). Poltava oblast declined from 326 functioning churches in early 1944 to 262
after Stalin's death, a loss of about 20 percent.[16] In comparison, functioning
churches in the Russian republic dropped from 3,228 in January of 1948 to 2,980
in January of 1954, a loss of 8 percent.[17]

Not a single new bishop was elevated to that office in the USSR between April
of 1950 and the end of 1952. Sixteen of the eighty-five monasteries and nunneries
functioning in 1948 were closed down. The blessing of the waters at Epiphany,
which had been permitted for a few years after the end of the war, was forbidden
in 1949.[18] Publicly announced new church periodicals in Estonia and Moldavia
failed to materialize.[19]

Why did Stalin move again toward repression during the last five years of his
life? In the first place, Hitler was defeated, the war was over, and the need for
Orthodox Church support was no longer what it had been. Besides, the regime
had reestablished the essentials of its pervasive prewar social control and was re-
asserting its hold on the life of the people.[20] During these years there was a broad
reversion to earlier policies, and Stalin did not exempt the church. Many Soviets
had thought that the postwar period would bring a happier time when a grateful
leader would strive to reward his long-suffering people for the sacrifices endured.
Such false hopes disappeared as Stalin sank deeper into a mood of suspicion and
bitterness. Those years of cultural suppression became known as the Zhdanov-
shchina (after Andrei A. Zhdanov, who was point man in the campaign against
intellectuals, artists, and writers). In foreign policy, they spanned the communist
coup in Czechoslovakia, the Berlin crisis, the Western airlift, and the Korean War.
No sensitivity to Western opinion could have acted as a great element of restraint
during those times. In 1952 the fabricated Jewish doctors' plot (in which nine
physicians, most of them Jewish, at the Kremlin were accused of killing Zhdanov
and other Soviet leaders) and Stalin's apparent decision to launch another great
purge made a liberal religious policy even less likely.

Interestingly, the crackdown against the Orthodox Church apparently did not
last in full force until the day of Stalin's death. A bishop was consecrated on
March 1, 1953, four days before Stalin died, and the meeting of the Holy Synod
that named this bishop reportedly was held in January of 1953. What appears to
have been a new Orthodox prayer house was also consecrated on December 12,
1952; work on its foundation supposedly started the previous June.[21] One prayer
house does not make a spring thaw, of course, and these small indications do not
reveal whether the old man's hands were loosening. Another possible explanation
might be connected to the work of the Orthodox Church in organizing a countrywide conference of Soviet religious leaders in May of 1952 at the Trinity-
Sergius monastery in Zagorsk, at which time an intensified defense-of-peace
campaign was launched. Some of the tiny church groups heard from there may
have been given the chance to organize their leadership from scratch as part of

the conference preparations. Perhaps the Orthodox had also been thrown a concession or two.

The fortunes of the Russian Orthodox Church brightened considerably in the period after Stalin died. Nikita Struve described it as a time of "relative freedom" that peaked in 1957 and ended in 1958.[22] In those years the Orthodox were able to publish a half dozen liturgical books, including a prayer book and a Bible.[23] The church was allowed to consecrate eight bishops in 1953, and the number of bishops increased over the next few years and reached a high of seventy-three in 1957.[24]

Antireligious propaganda actually intensified for a time after Stalin's death; the peak came in the summer of 1954.[25] In November, however, a resolution of the Central Committee of the Communist Party, signed by Nikita S. Khrushchev as first secretary, resulted in the toning down of the propaganda campaign. Its key passage was as follows: "Administrative measures of any kind and insulting attacks . . . can only do harm, can only lead to strengthening and even intensifying the religious convictions" of believers.[26] This was not the first time such a caveat had been uttered: After the 1922 campaign the Communist Party had stated that "it is necessary to liquidate all attempts to uproot religion by administrative measures, such as the closing of churches."[27] After the 1929 wave, a decree was issued stating that "the closing of churches was effected by local authorities against the will of the people" and ordering the cessation of such practices.[28] Likewise, in 1939 the use of coercion in 1937 and 1938 was deplored, and party organs were advised to avoid offending the sensibilities of believers.[29] As we shall see, 1954 would not be the last such word, just as it was not the first.[30]

The Twentieth Communist Party Congress of February 1956 and Khrushchev's Secret Speech recounting Stalin's crimes produced a faltering of dedication to Stalin's memory and to Stalinism that opened the door to a renewal of faith and a renaissance in religious commitment. Commissioners of the Council for Russian Orthodox Church Affairs began noting in their secret reports that more worshipers were going to church.[31] Moreover, Khrushchev's amnesties declared for millions of prisoners from the GULAG facilitated a religious boom as large numbers of clerics and dedicated believers were released from the camps and returned home. There was hardly a family in the Soviet Union that failed to experience the beneficent effects of the emptying out of the camps. It was a great emancipation of suffering millions, which reverberated throughout society. In addition, Khrushchev's liberalization of the pension system allowed many older believers to retire and worship without fear for their livelihood.[32] Religion was not dying out by itself, and it was continuing to interest considerable numbers of young people. These developments alarmed the communists. It was immediately clear to them that the revival of belief and practice contradicted the party's declared approach to communism, and some communist leaders argued that eradicating "religious prejudices" by closing churches would be easier than providing the material abundance necessary to build communism without coercion.[33]

Data from the archive of the Council for Religious Affairs indicate a remarkably stable number of registered church societies in the USSR for the period 1955–1958:[34]

Russian Orthodox Churches in the USSR	
January 1955	13,376
January 1956	13,417
January 1957	13,430
January 1958	13,415[35]

The figures reflect an almost even balance between the registration of new parishes and parish deregistrations. Between 1954 and 1958, 121 new registrations were recorded, 60 percent of them in western Ukraine, despite the fact that less than half of the existing churches in the formerly Greek-Catholic dioceses had a regularly assigned priest. The politically motivated desire to Russify the area and provide an Orthodox alternative to the Greek-Catholics continued to rule policy. Individual inspectors of the Council for Russian Orthodox Church Affairs cited the fact that Eastern Rite Catholics were worshiping without permission as a justification for authorizing the registration of an Orthodox church in one or another of the towns they visited.[36]

Table 3.1, shown at the end of the chapter, presents the number of churches recorded in each diocese on January 1, 1958, just before Khrushchev's antireligious drive gathered force.[37] Thirty-one dioceses, or almost half of those in the country, were in lands that the Germans never occupied. These dioceses had 1,757 churches. Thus 13 percent of the churches were in what was most of the territory of the country, an area containing roughly half of the traditionally Orthodox population. Except for the 200–300 churches that had survived through the 1930s, these were churches the Soviet government had reluctantly allowed to open, mostly between 1943 and 1947. The twelve dioceses in the Russian republic that had fallen under German occupation in World War II had 1,307 churches in 1958, almost as many as in the vastly more populous and extensive territories never occupied. Byelorussia, with over 8 million people, had 967 churches; Moldavia, with about 2.5 million traditionally Orthodox people, had 546 churches. Estonia, Latvia, and Lithuania, with about 2.5 million traditionally Orthodox people, had 301 churches. Central Asia and Kazakhstan had 128. Thus fourteen of the fifteen constituent republics of the USSR had 5,006 registered church societies, or 37 percent of the churches in the country. Ukraine had the rest. Of the roughly 8,500 registered church societies in Ukraine in January 1958, about 3,000 were formerly Greek-Catholic churches.[38]

The Orthodox hierarchs gave some statistics about the number of functioning churches. In a November 1945 interview, Metropolitan Nikolai (Yarushevich) stated that the Orthodox Church had 30,000 parishes.[39] At about this same time the head of the Council for Russian Orthodox Church Affairs was saying that the church had only about half that number.[40] In the 1945–1946 period, Patriarch Aleksi was quoted as claiming about "25,000" churches.[41] The figures were always in round thousands, as I myself pointed out in a dissertation completed in the spring of 1960.[42] I also calculated then that the Orthodox had many thousands of churches less in the 1950s than they were claiming publicly.[43] Public claims were "20,000" to "25,000."[44] The patriarchate avoided putting numbers in writing, although it did occasionally quote a foreign cleric giving a number.[45] For their part, Soviet commentators tended to quote the Orthodox hierarchs, thereby dissociating themselves from the figures' accuracy. Occasionally, they contradicted church leaders, as Aleksandr Veshchikov did in 1962 when he said: "Now there remain, according to the testimony of Churchmen themselves, about 20,000" church buildings, "though these data are very exaggerated."[46]

In April 1961 the Russian Orthodox Church formally applied for membership in the World Council of Churches and was asked to list the number of its churches in the application papers. It listed "20,000 churches."[47] By then, the government's secret archives indicated that there were no more than about 11,000 functioning churches in the country. The application also claimed 30,000 clergy, whereas government archives indicated 10,411 priests in January of 1961. Including deacons would have brought the total to only about 1,000 more.[48] Metropolitan Nikodim (Rotov) was by then in charge of the church's international relations. One has to wonder what sensations the metropolitan had in the pit of his stomach when he was obliged to list such figures in print, in a statement so formal and so official.

Why did the church hierarchs allow themselves to be drawn into these inflated claims? Metropolitan Nikodim was wont to acknowledge cheerfully that truthfulness was not the highest consideration with him when the welfare of the Russian Orthodox Church was in the balance.[49] Nikolai, who had earlier been forced by his relationship to the Soviet government to distort the truth on occasion, must have felt that some inflation of figures was defensible.[50] Besides, one could count all chapels and consecrated altars in a church as "churches" and find other ways to manipulate the figures. There was considerable confusion in the 1940s and 1950s about the distinction between the number of registered Orthodox Church societies and the number of registered societies of all faiths, cults, and denominations. It was easy for an Orthodox spokesman to slip into a failure to correct such confusions and ultimately slide into an affirmation of them. The correction of them would not only have undermined the church's position, but it might also have enraged the Soviet government when the inevitable Western denunciation of Soviet persecutions ensued. In Stalin's time, virtually all Soviets knew that dissembling was the price of institutional and personal survival. One should not too readily cast stones.

In any case, the first four years of Khrushchev's time in power were years of respite for the church. The institutional losses suffered in Stalin's final years were not made up, but the religious situation stabilized. The church was gathering spiritual and human strength against the communists' ideological discomfiture after de-Stalinization and the cracking of the monolith of Soviet power in Eastern Europe and China. The communists' god was failing, although the reality of that loss of communist faith would not become wholly clear for another third of a century.

TABLE 3.1　Number of Registered Orthodox Communities in each Diocese on January 1, 1958

Alma Ata	60	Odessa	392
Arkhangelsk	33	Olonets	6
Astrakhan	16	Omsk	20
Cheboksary	41	Orel	97
Chelyabinsk	29	Orenburg	23
Chernigov	360	Penza	60
Chernovtsy	362	Perm	63
Dnepropetrovsk	286	Poltava	262
Gorki (Nizhni Novgorod)	48	Pskov	107
Irkutsk	18	Riga	123
Ivano-Frankovsk	646	Rostov-on-Don	213
Ivanovo	56	Ryazan	76
Izhevsk	29	Saratov	45
Kalinin (Tver)	91	Simferopol	48
Kaluga	38	Smolensk	54
Kazan	31	Stavropol	158
Khabarovsk	13	Sumy	219
Kharkov	158	Sverdlovsk (Yekaterinburg)	46
Khmelnitski	393	Tallin	123
Kiev (Kyyiv)	582	Tambov	48
Kirov	80	Tashkent	68
Kirovograd	255	Tula	40
Kishinev (Chisinau)	546	Ufa	41
Kostroma	80	Ulyanovsk	19
Krasnodar	208	Vilnyus	55
Kuibyshev (Samara)	19	Vinnitsa	598
Kursk	288	Vladimir	65
Leningrad (St. Petersburg)	57	Vologda	17
Lvov	2071	Volyn	792
Minsk	967	Voronezh	111
Moscow	212	Voroshilovgrad (Donetsk)	306
Mukachevo	512	Yaroslavl	143
Novgorod	41	Zhitomir	295
Novosibirsk	56		
		Total	13,415

Source: Tsentralny Gosudarstvenny Arkhiv, Fond 6991s, Opis No. 2, Vol. I, delo Nos. 206, 253.

4

Khrushchev's Attack

"WE'LL TAKE GOD by the beard," Nikita Khrushchev said in speeches, and he spoke of showing the last Christian on television by 1980.[1] Why did Khrushchev say these things, and why did he launch the great antireligious drive? The best answer seems to be that Khrushchev really did dream of leading the USSR to full and true communism by 1980.[2] He promised as much at the Twenty-first Communist Party Congress at the beginning of 1959, and atheist writers confirm that he launched the antireligious drive with this hope in mind.[3] Moreover, Khrushchev had never shrunk from coercing people.

Khrushchev's education in atheism went back a long way. As he described it, his mother and maternal grandfather had been religious, and he was brought up to kneel and pray. His favorite teacher in school was a revolutionary and an atheist, however, and she taught the boy Nikita well. He read Emile Zola and *Pravda,* and his youthful convictions stuck with him throughout his life.[4] Interestingly, Khrushchev hardly mentioned religion, other than the comments about his boyhood just described, in the thousand-plus pages of his memoirs and gave no account or explanation of his antireligious drive. Yet he was said to have had a "constant preoccupation" with religion and a personal "hatred" of it, although this judgment was disputed by at least one well-informed Soviet official.[5] My own guess would be that Khrushchev's vision of a breakthrough to communism is a better explanation of his actions than the presumption of a personal loathing of religious manifestations. Sometimes crude, intrinsically optimistic, and an advocate of direct action, Khrushchev may really have believed that he would be the man to lead his people to the society of his dreams. Then, later, as he sat in his country house outside Moscow recording his memoirs in gloomy retirement, I can understand why he had no stomach for describing or analyzing the reasons for his antireligious crusade.

The question of when Khrushchev's drive to close churches by the thousands really started is relevant because there are those who contend that the Russian Orthodox Church brought the church closings upon itself by a series of defiant acts in late 1959 and early 1960. The story begins in 1956, the year Khrushchev denounced Stalin's crimes. Anatoli Levitin-Krasnov, the dissident Orthodox author, asserted that Soviet ideology received a "fatal blow" at that time, even though Khrushchev himself did not realize what he had done.[6] This can be argued, but the events of 1956 certainly did bring soul-searching in Communist Party circles and also brought slashing attacks from the People's Republic of China on Soviet revisionism and ideological laxity. In addition, a new generation of Soviet communists needed a battle cry.[7] Khrushchev was soon under heavy pressure to reassert ideological leadership.

In June of 1957 Khrushchev bested his opponents in the Communist Party Presidium, branding them members of an "anti-Party group." Some observers noted that two of his adversaries, Malenkov and Bulganin, had become protective of the churches.[8] Reportedly, Malenkov became a practicing Christian at the end of his life.[9] It may also have been the case that Khrushchev's victory over his rivals freed him to pursue his ideological objectives with less restraint.[10] There were reports of a secret party meeting in Moscow in August of 1957 at which 350 theorists and activists discussed the ongoing influence of religion in the country and the party's shortcomings in antireligious education and propaganda.[11]

The emphasis of the communist leadership from late 1957 through 1958 was principally on ideological work, especially among the youth, and on mobilizing and training antireligious forces.[12] The focus did not include any mass closing of churches, although the authorities began withholding permission for new episcopal consecrations. Persuasion and pressure on individual clerics resulted in the defection of some priests to the atheist cause, and these priests would play a great role in the propaganda campaign that was to come.[13] In 1958 the authorities eliminated military service deferments for seminary students.[14] On October 16, 1958, the Council of Ministers of the Soviet government directed its two councils for religious affairs to study and make recommendations within six months for reducing the number of functioning convents.[15] On April 2, 1959, Georgi Karpov, head of the Council for Russian Orthodox Church Affairs, advised the patriarch that the Soviet government contemplated closing twenty-eight convents and hermitages, or almost half of those functioning at the time. Soon thereafter the patriarch was obliged to instruct diocesan bishops not to allow persons under thirty years of age to enter a convent. In fact, the authorities moved against the convents somewhat earlier than they acted massively against the parish churches. Also in 1959, the authorities put the convents under heavy financial pressure by discontinuing tax exemptions on convent buildings and agricultural landholdings, a concession granted in 1945. Income taxes on convents' receipts and on diocesan enterprises, in particular shops manufacturing candles, were sharply increased. The prices at which candles could be sold were frozen. The result was a financial crunch affecting candle shops, the central administration of the church, and local parishes' ability to pay clergy, psalmists, and professionals in choirs.[16]

The first slight dip in the number of registered church societies was documented in 1958. In January of 1959 there were 13,325 registered societies, 90 fewer than in the year before. This was the largest drop since 1954, not very significant but an omen.[17]

After the plenum of the Central Committee of the Communist Party in November 1958, the media attack on religion intensified.[18] Although religion was not publicly castigated at the party's twenty-first congress in January and February of 1959, it was rumored that Khrushchev had pushed through a secret resolution calling for the elimination of religious "survivals" during the forthcoming seven-year plan.[19] Another account indicated that the decision was made by the Presidium just after the congress.[20] In any case, in February of 1959 the emphasis in the propaganda campaign began to shift from the exposition of atheist arguments to pointed accusations by name against church hierarchs.[21] A few subsequent episcopal transfers had the look of being punitive. For example, a rising star in the hierarchy, Bishop Mikhail (Chub) of Smolensk, was transferred to Izhevsk, a small diocese west of the Urals.[22] The taxation affecting convents and diocesan enterprises also resulted in some bishops losing their episcopal residences, which were seized by the authorities after the dioceses failed to keep current on tax obligations.[23] Moreover, the authorities began taxing individual priests as members of the "liberal professions" rather than as workers, driving up their taxes to the point that the government took most of their income.[24]

An editorial in *Pravda* on August 21, 1959, signaled a shift from ideological and atheistic propaganda to legislative and administrative methods.[25] Toward the end of 1959, there were signs that financial pressures were resulting in the closure of parish churches.[26] According to Council for Religious Affairs records, the number of registered church societies dropped by 361 churches in 1959 to bring the total down to 12,964 in January of 1960.[27]

The mass deregistrations of church societies in 1959 were concentrated in territories in Ukraine that had long been Soviet-ruled, were traditionally Orthodox, and had been subjected to extended German occupation in World War II. Dnepropetrovsk diocese lost 16 percent of its parishes in that single year. In the Russian republic, Rostov-on-Don lost twenty-six registered church societies, more than 10 percent of the total in that diocese. In September the archbishop of Rostov wrote Patriarch Aleksi and lamented increased official efforts to bar priests from carrying out prayers in private homes, force both parents to give written permission for a child's baptism, and bar those under eighteen from attending church.[28] Throughout the Ukrainian and northern Caucasian dioceses, the shortage of priests in the late 1950s was serious, and Khrushchev's antireligious activists turned these shortages to their own purposes in deregistering churches that lacked priests.

In December of 1959 the storm broke in full force. *Pravda* carried an article on December 6 by a priest who was a professor of Old Testament theology at the Leningrad theological academy, Aleksandr A. Osipov. In it, Osipov renounced his religious conviction and went to the side of atheism.[29] As luck would have it— and churchmen believed the timing was deliberately chosen to embarrass the church—a senior delegation from the World Council of Churches was visiting the USSR to explore the possibility of the Russian Orthodox Church joining that body.[30] On December 30, 1959, an outraged Holy Synod excommunicated Osipov and other priests and laymen "who had reviled the Name of God." This excommunication could have been interpreted as including the antireligious forces in general and Khrushchev himself.[31] The church was fighting back.

In early January 1960, the Central Committee of the Communist Party called for still more intensive antireligious propaganda.[32] Shortly thereafter, the Communist Party's Central Committee adopted a measure to curtail "illegal" housing for parish priests and the provision of vehicles for their use.[33] On January 27, *Pravda* announced that the Society for the Dissemination of Political and Scientific Knowledge (which had inherited the responsibilities of the League of the Militant Godless) had held a congress attended by at least four of Khrushchev's most senior colleagues.[34] Even so, the February issue of the *Journal of the Moscow Patriarchate* dared to publish the church's excommunication of Osipov and other apostates. Well-informed observers knew that Karpov must have been in a position to see and stop the excommunication announcement before the *Journal* was distributed; perhaps he was not as alert as he should have been.[35]

On February 16, 1960, Patriarch Aleksi delivered a speech at a Kremlin peace and disarmament conference that further enraged senior Soviet leaders. In the text, apparently drafted by Metropolitan Nikolai (Yarushevich), Aleksi claimed credit on behalf of the Russian Orthodox Church for Russia's heroic past, its glorious culture, and its leadership for peace. He decried the insults and attacks to which the church was being subjected and quoted Jesus' statement that the gates of hell shall not prevail against the church.[36] On February 21, 1960, *Izvestiya* announced that Karpov had been replaced as head of the Council for Russian Orthodox Church Affairs and that Vladimir A. Kuroedov, a party functionary with no previous direct connection with church affairs, had succeeded him.[37]

Four days after Karpov's removal was made public, Patriarch Aleksi observed his patron saint's day and also the fifteenth anniversary of his enthronement. Nikolai eulogized the patriarch for his and the church's achievements in Russia and abroad, omitting the usual obeisance to the great role of the Soviet state. In his reply, Aleksi made pointed reference to the "griefs" inflicted on the church by the "enemies of God."[38]

The authorities continued their administrative measures against the church, perhaps both as part of their accelerating antireligious campaign and in retribution for Nikolai's and Aleksi's perceived defiance. The cathedral in the city of

Perm was closed in February with the explanation that the crowds milling outside the church constituted a traffic hazard.[39] Believers were harassed at Easter
services in a number of cities.[40] It also became unlawful to have baptismal chapels in buildings separate from the parish churches.[41] The theological seminary at
Kiev was notified that it must close.[42]

On June 15, 1960, Kuroedov reportedly told the patriarch that the church's passivity on the international front was reprehensible. According to Soviet government archives, he said: "In recent years the patriarchate has not carried out a single powerful initiative to unite other Orthodox churches around the Russian
Church"—in marked contrast to the pope's reactionary activities and the slanderous propaganda elaborated abroad about the religious situation in the USSR.
Kuroedov particularly blamed Metropolitan Nikolai for inaction and suggested
that the patriarch remove him.[43]

On June 21, 1960, the Holy Synod duly relieved Metropolitan Nikolai of his
duties as head of the church's Office of Foreign Religious Affairs.[44] Then, on September 19, 1960, the Holy Synod "accepted" Nikolai's "request" to retire from his
functions as metropolitan of Krutitsy and Kolomna.[45] Shortly thereafter Nikolai
wrote to a leader of the international peace movement and described his situation as "forced inaction. . . . I shall no longer be able to take part in any activity,
or celebrate the liturgy, or publish anything." Apparently he was living under virtual house arrest and was kept from contact with believers on those few occasions
when he was allowed to celebrate the liturgy. Fifteen months after his removal,
Nikolai died at Botkin hospital in Moscow. For the last three or four weeks of his
life he was under the care of a state-assigned physician. His friends, his fellow
churchmen, and even his sister, who was an Orthodox nun, were barred from the
hospital room. According to Nikita Struve, after his death "his naked body was
left unattended in the mortuary for more than thirteen hours," and rumors that
he was murdered have persisted ever since.[46]

Nikolai was not the only hierarch targeted by the authorities. Archbishop Iov
(Kresovich) of Kazan was arrested, tried, and sentenced for swindling and em-
bezzlement in mid-1960. Church sources maintained that the real reason for the
archbishop's incarceration was his defiance of pressures on him to close churches
in his diocese.[47] Parish priests were also increasingly brought before the courts.
Science and Religion reported in September of 1960 that twenty-six priests faced
court proceedings in Orenburg oblast alone.[48]

Three months after Kuroedov had proposed Nikolai's removal, it was reported
in the council's archives that "the patriarch accepted the recommendation of the
Council that the Russian Orthodox Church enter into membership of the World
Council of Churches." Apparently, representatives of the community of autocephalous Orthodox churches had met in Moscow in 1948 and had declared that
the purposes and orientation of the international ecumenical movement were

not entirely compatible with Orthodox understandings and principles. In April of 1959, Patriarch Aleksi had informed the World Council that the Russian Orthodox Church wished to strengthen its ties with that organization and send observers to its meetings but still did not favor actual membership. Nevertheless, Metropolitan Nikodim, Nikolai's successor, was an enthusiast of ecumenism, and his influence reinforced the Soviet government's inclinations. The church did join the World Council of Churches, over the opposition of the Russian Orthodox Church Abroad (the Karlovcians) and some other Orthodox leaders.[49]

Reports proliferated of church closings in Ukraine, Byelorussia, and the recently annexed western lands. *Pravda Ukrainy* reported that seventeen churches (over 20 percent of the parishes) had closed in the Ukrainian oblast of Zaporozhe between January and June of 1960 as a result of "individual meetings with believers."[50] Various Western reports of developments in Cherkassy oblast in Ukraine gave figures of forty to seventy churches closed before the end of 1960.[51] The journal *Philosophical Sciences* reported in March of 1961 that "over 500 Orthodox churches" had been closed in Ukraine.[52] Communist authorities in Moldavia noted with pride in December 1960 that eighteen of twenty-five churches had been closed in one raion (roughly a small county) and six of fourteen churches had been closed in another.[53] Official figures were that 168 churches in Moldavia were deregistered in 1960, approximately a third of the total number (541) in that republic.[54] There were 212 church societies deregistered in Byelorussia, down from 944 in January 1960.[55]

For the Soviet Union as a whole, an Italian journal with Vatican connections gave one of the earlier Western reports of the developing Khrushchev drive in February 1961, reporting—correctly—that "500 churches" had been closed.[56] It also noted increasing pressure on priests and seminarians.[57] Walter Kolarz had already written at Christmastime in 1960 that "several hundred" Orthodox churches had been closed.[58] In a letter written in September of 1961, Francis House of the World Council of Churches noted that the propaganda drive launched "two years ago" had become an "administrative action" involving arrests and the closure of churches in the "last few months."[59] These Western reports of church closings reveal that information was indeed filtering to the West, although most Western observers were ignoring the signs.

The year 1960 witnessed a greater drop in the number of officially registered church societies than at any time since 1945. In the Soviet Union as a whole, 1,400 churches were deregistered, a drop of about 11 percent of the total at the beginning of the year.[60] More than half of the deregistrations took place in Ukraine, although its relative loss, 9 percent, was less than in the Soviet Union as a whole.[61]

The aggregate figures for Ukraine disguise the considerable variation among subregions. The formerly Greek-Catholic oblasts lost 114 churches, only 3.5 percent of the 3,200 parishes there. Eastern Ukraine, with fewer than half of the re-

public's parishes, bore the brunt of the Ukrainian church closings. Of 3,871 registered church societies in January of 1960, eastern Ukraine suffered the loss of 529
parishes, or 14 percent of those functioning at the beginning of the year.[62] Clearly,
the authorities were continuing to be lenient with the former Greek-Catholics. In
1960 the formerly Greek-Catholic oblasts incorporated about 2 percent of the
population of the USSR and about a quarter of the Orthodox churches in the
country.

In early 1961 Soviet writers on atheism and official spokesmen began to use
figures ranging between 11,000 and 12,000 for the number of functioning Orthodox churches in the USSR. Volodymyr K. Tancher stated in a book published in
Kiev that there were "over 11,000" Orthodox churches at the time he wrote. He
seems to have completed his text at the end of 1960 or early in 1961.[63] Nikolai I.
Yudiń gave the figure of 11,500 Orthodox churches in a book that went to print in
1961.[64] A year or so later the atheist publication *Science and Religion* also gave the
figure of "11,000 Orthodox churches" for 1961.[65] Council archives reveal an official
figure of 11,571 registered church societies on January 1, 1961.[66]

The year 1961 brought even greater trials for the Russian Orthodox Church. A
new instruction on the application of the USSR statutes for religious cults was
issued on March 16, 1961, and it forbade central church authorities from offering
financial help to local parishes that could not support themselves fully.[67] Under
this pressure, the church issued an instruction that parishes that could not pay
their way should amalgamate with neighboring churches. The authorities then
stepped in to deregister financially weak rural parishes.[68]

The authorities also ruled that only one church could remain open in a single
village, that churches in the cities and towns must be substantially separated in
distance from one another, and that a single priest would not be able to serve
more than one church. The enforcement of all of these measures resulted in the
closing of churches on a large scale.[69] Moreover, the authorities took further advantage of the old decree that invalidated arrangements made under the German
occupation and used it as an instrument to shut down quite a few churches
opened during World War II in Ukraine and the western lands.[70]

The authorities put resisting priests and bishops under great pressure.
The best-known case in 1961 was that of Archbishop Andrei (Sukhenko) of
Chernigov, who strongly opposed the closing of churches and convents in his diocese. He was arrested and sentenced to eight years imprisonment on the charge
that he had engaged in religious propaganda among some miners and had
avoided paying taxes.[71] The Soviet authorities also closed down the Chernigov
cathedral and other churches in the city, leaving the diocese with its episcopal
seat in a small suburban church.

On March 31, 1961, Kuroedov of the Council for Russian Orthodox Church Affairs called in the patriarch and three other church hierarchs, denounced the "dic-

tatorial power" of parish priests, and asserted that the lay executive authority in a parish must rule.[72] In April of 1961 the Holy Synod, under official duress, drew up recommendations for a revision of church statutes that would transfer administrative and financial authority from the parish priest to the laity.[73] The revision was then presented to a hastily convened council of bishops, which met at the Trinity-Sergius monastery on July 18, 1961. The meeting was organized in such a way as to minimize the opportunity for dissent, and the revision was approved without openly expressed opposition.[74]

The change in parish governance made the closure of churches easier, as the authorities could sometimes rely on compliant churchwardens to overcome priests' opposition. Moreover, a "reregistration" of priests was initiated after the meeting of the council. Clerics who refused to sign an agreement to uphold the revised statutes were denied renewed authorization to function.[75] Government authorities then took advantage of Soviet regulations and church canons denying standing to a church without a priest and closed many churches where the priests had not been reregistered, had been removed, or—as already noted—had been serving the parish from another church as a second responsibility.[76]

At the Twenty-second Communist Party Congress in October of 1961, Nikita Khrushchev asserted the central importance of emancipating Soviet people from the "dreadful power" of "religious prejudices and superstitions."[77] The congress duly issued a call for "scientific atheist education which would . . . prevent the spread of religious views."[78]

The campaign to close churches accelerated further, with most forcible closings still taking place in Ukraine, Byelorussia, and the recently annexed western lands.[79] *Science and Religion* reported that 880 parishes lost their registration between July and December of 1961 with 216 of these deregistrations taking place in December alone.[80] The total for 1961 was 1,585.[81] In Ukraine the total number of deregistrations throughout 1961 was 997.[82]

In 1961 there was a further crackdown on church activities such as works of charity, pilgrimages to holy places, the ringing of church bells, and the teaching of religion to children, including the children of active parishioners.[83] At a Young Communist League (Komsomol) congress in 1962, the denial of parental rights to bring up children as religious believers was reiterated and given ideological justification.[84]

In 1962 Soviet government regulations were changed again to make the registration of a new church society even more difficult, if not virtually impossible, and to facilitate the authorities' efforts to close churches. The opportunity to appeal a church closing was effectively eliminated. Church closings in Ukraine reached their peak in 1962 with 1,144 church societies deregistered.[85]

At about this time, public assistance commissions were established to assist local officials in enforcing regulations limiting the practice of religion. Members of these commissions were supposed to monitor and investigate religious activities and activists, including reporting absences of workers from their jobs in order to attend church, the appearance in a parish of a priest from another place, and infractions of the rules against a priest receiving unreported income or payment in kind for performing weddings, baptisms, or funerals.[86] Parish leaders were made personally responsible if adolescents below the age of eighteen were recruited for church work.[87] The teaching of the catechism to young people was declared a violation of law.[88] Ceremonies for the sick in private homes were rigorously suppressed.[89]

The drive to close churches affected quite a number of cathedral churches. The bishops' cathedrals in Orel, Kishinev, Riga, and Vinnitsa were closed in 1962.[90] Over the course of the Khrushchev drive, at least a dozen cathedral churches were closed.[91] It was almost as if Khrushchev had told his people to get the big Orthodox churches out of the centers of the great cities and into inconspicuous corners or distant suburbs. Besides, in Khrushchev's view, it would not hurt the believers to walk a few miles or take a long trolley ride.

The first sign of a slackening in the fury of the church-closing campaign appeared in early 1963. For example, only one church in Chernovtsy diocese (northern Bukovina) was closed in 1963, whereas almost 100 churches had been deregistered there in the course of the three previous years.[92] In Ukraine as a whole, 526 churches were closed in 1963 (a number representing fewer than half the 1,144 churches closed in 1962), and 239 churches were closed in 1964.[93]

The slowing of Khrushchev's campaign was noted in the West and discussed in émigré publications. An article in *Posev* in early 1965 commented that churches had been closed by the thousands during the first several years of the antichurch drive, but they had been closed by the hundreds in 1964.[94] The reasons *Posev* gave for the slowing tempo were believers' opposition, general popular disapproval, Western protests, and, in particular, criticism from Western communists like Palmiro Togliatti of Italy, who were politically embarrassed by the evident abuse of Soviet believers. Savelii Tuberozov, writing in the *Eastern Churches Review* at the end of the 1960s, estimated correctly that approximately 2,000 churches had been closed between 1962 and 1964.[95]

Soviet authorities also supplied quite accurate figures in public, although not until much later. For example, in 1987 the chairman of the Council for Religious Affairs, Konstantin Kharchev, stated that 4,219 Orthodox societies lost their registration between January 1, 1961, and January 1, 1966. Other Soviet government and atheist commentators revealed similar results in 1989.[96]

One should not conclude that the slackening pace of church closings signified a reduction in efforts to promote atheism. In fact, atheist educational efforts were intensified. By 1963 children and teenagers under the age of eighteen were being prevented, even more systematically than previously, from entering and attending church services.[97] Leonid Ilichev, who had been leading the antireligious campaign, wrote an authoritative article in the January 1964 issue of *Kommunist* that urged even greater exertions, particularly against Muslims and Baptists, who were by then organizing nonregistered religious communities on an increasing scale.[98] In that same year the scientific atheists organized an All-Union Seminar Conference on Socialist Ceremonies, where they discussed substitute rituals, such as emotionally satisfying marriage ceremonies at wedding palaces, reverential visits to the Lenin mausoleum, and socialist funerals.[99]

The losses were grievous for the institutional strength of the Russian Orthodox Church. Five of the eight theological seminaries operating in 1959 had been closed. Over two-thirds of the monasteries and nunneries were closed.[100] A net figure of four out of every ten priests functioning in 1958 had retired, died, or lost authorization to serve in a parish.[101]

Table 4.1 lists the number of churches still functioning in each diocese, the number of church societies deregistered in each diocese in the eight-year period between January of 1958 and January of 1966, and the losses in each diocese expressed as a percentage of the registered church societies functioning on January 1, 1958.[102] There were 13,415 church societies in the country in 1958 and 7,466 in 1966; thus deregistrations over the eight-year period reached a total of 5,949, or 44 percent of the church societies functioning in 1958.[103]

As had been true early in the drive, the central and eastern parts of Ukraine were the areas where the Russian Orthodox Church suffered its greatest losses. Ten dioceses lost over half their churches, and two dioceses lost over three-fourths of them. In the formerly Greek-Catholic lands of western Ukraine, the deregistration of parishes was under the average for the whole country.[104] The relative immunity of these lands from church closure had dissipated as the Khrushchev drive progressed, but the crackdown was still somewhat less severe than it was in eastern Ukraine, no doubt for the same reasons that had previously dictated leniency. Ukraine as a whole emerged from the drive with 61 percent of the churches in the country, down slightly from 63 percent in 1958. The Russian Orthodox Church remained a mostly Ukrainian community.

The phenomenon of draconian church closings spilled over into the once German-occupied lands north of the Caucasus: Krasnodar and Rostov-on-Don dioceses lost over half of their churches. Moldavia and Byelorussia had been occupied early by the Axis powers and abandoned late in the war, and these constituent republics also lost more than half their churches. It was said that the communist authorities in Byelorussia vowed to make their republic a churchless one, and during the years of the Khrushchev drive they made considerable advances in this direction.[105]

In the Russian republic, besides Krasnodar and Rostov-on-Don, the greatest

TABLE 4.1   Number of Registered Orthodox Communities in each Diocese on January 1, 1966

	1966 Total	Change Since 1958			1966 Total	Change Since 1958	
		No.	Percent			No.	Percent
Alma Ata	46	−14	−23	Odessa	144	−248	−63
Arkhangelsk	23	−10	−30	Olonets	4	−2	−33
Astrakhan	17	+1	+6	Omsk	12	−8	−40
Cheboksary	37	−4	−10	Orel	65	−32	−33
Chelyabinsk	15	−14	−48	Orenburg	13	−10	−43
Chernigov	160	−200	−56	Penza	46	−14	−23
Chernovtsy	264	−98	−27	Perm	41	−22	−35
Dnepropetrovsk	35	−251	−87	Poltava	62	−200	−76
Gorki (Nizhni Novgorod)	46	−2	−4	Pskov	91	−16	−15
Irkutsk	16	−2	−11	Riga	95	−28	−23
Ivano-Frankovsk	374	−272	−42	Rostov-on-Don	73	−140	−66
Ivanovo	44	−12	−21	Ryazan	59	−17	−22
Izhevsk	18	−11	−38	Saratov	32	−13	−29
Kalinin (Tver)	54	−37	−41	Simferopol	14	−34	−71
Kaluga	28	−10	−26	Smolensk	38	−16	−30
Kazan	24	−7	−23	Stavropol	104	−54	−34
Khabarovsk	12	−1	−8	Sumy	142	−77	−35
Kharkov	77	−81	−51	Sverdlovsk (Yekaterinburg)	30	−16	−35
Khmelnitski	140	−253	−64	Tallin	90	−33	−27
Kiev (Kyyiv)	216	−366	−63	Tambov	41	−7	−15
Kirov	34	−46	−57	Tashkent	51	−17	−25
Kirovograd	111	−144	−56	Tula	32	−8	−20
Kishinev (Chisinau)	223	−323	−59	Ufa	19	−22	−54
Kostroma	71	−9	−11	Ulyanovsk	12	−7	−37
Krasnodar	77	−131	−63	Vilnyus	43	−12	−22
Kuibyshev (Samara)	18	−1	−5	Vinnitsa	350	−248	−41
Kursk	197	−91	−32	Vladimir	54	−11	−17
Leningrad (St. Petersburg)	45	−12	−21	Vologda	17	0	0
Lvov	1,201	−870	−42	Volyn	489	−303	−38
Minsk	423	−544	−56	Voronezh	80	−31	−28
Moscow	172	−40	−19	Voroshilovgrad (Donetsk)	160	−146	−48
Mukachevo	428	−84	−16	Yaroslavl	86	−57	−40
Novgorod	25	−16	−39	Zhitomir	173	−122	−41
Novosibirsk	33	−23	−41	Total	7,466	−5,949	−44

Source: Tsentralny Gosudarstvenny Arkhiv, Fond 6991s, Opis No. 2, Vol. I, delo Nos. 206, 208, 263; Fond 6991s, Opis No. 4, Vol. I, delo Nos. 573, 574, 575; Kharchev, "Garantii svobody," p. 23.

losses were in the Urals area—Chelyabinsk, Sverdlovsk, and Ufa—and in the diocese of Kirov (46 percent), where the church's losses were eloquently chronicled by the great dissident Orthodox layman Boris Talantov. Lower than average losses were to be found in the middle Volga area (Cheboksary, Gorki, Kostroma, and Kuibyshev), in eastern Siberia, and in dioceses like Vologda, where the number of churches was very small even before Khrushchev's antireligious drive.

Talantov described the closing of the church in Korshik in the oblast of Kirov, one of thousands of such episodes:

> On 21 March 1963 a workers brigade, headed by . . . [village soviet chairman Sergei] Ponomarev, visited Korshik. They began by drinking up the church wine. Fortified by it, they began to tear down the icons, hack the highly artistic carved iconostases with axes, and they used mallets to smash the precious chandeliers and other holy vessels. All the icons, the iconostases of the two side chapels of the winter church, the gonfalons and all the ancient liturgical books were burnt. . . . Vestments, linen, flour, candles, holy oil and other valuables were simply stolen. . . . Ponomarev appropriated the green paint . . . laid in . . . for painting the roof of the church. Feeling beyond retribution, Ponomarev painted his own house outside and in, so that the act of theft is irrefutably visible to all even now. . . . On 27 September 1963 he and the director of the oil factory sawed off the crosses from the top of the domes. . . . The stoves were broken, the window bars were sawn off and holes were knocked through the outside.[106]

In a 1988 lecture to teachers of the Higher Communist Party School, Council for Religious Affairs Chairman Konstantin Kharchev described the closing of another church where the local authorities had loaded the icons on a truck, got mired in the mud, and used the icons to try to wedge and lever the wheels of the truck out of the muck, all in plain view of outraged villagers. Kharchev noted somewhat ruefully that such displays did not help the image of the authorities or of the party.[107] Kharchev was right. Acts of this kind perpetrated throughout the USSR in the years of Khrushchev's antireligious drive left a sickening residue in the hearts of many in the population, including some who were not believers themselves.

Yet the church presented an essentially unchanged face to the passing foreign visitor in Moscow or to the casual observer of church affairs. The celebration of the liturgy at the patriarchal Cathedral of the Epiphany was as beautiful, solemn, and resplendent as ever. The patriarch was as dazzlingly vested, deeply reverent, and inscrutable as always. Great operatic performers of the Bolshoi Theater continued to slip over to the cathedral to sing in its choir. Except for an ugly incident in 1964 when the Church of Saints Peter and Paul on Transfiguration Square was demolished to make way for a planned subway expansion, Moscow's churches— and Leningrad's churches—were little affected in any visible way. The Trinity-Sergius monastery northeast of Moscow continued to welcome pilgrims and foreign visitors with dignity, beauty, and faith. The international role and influence of the Russian Orthodox Church continued to grow. As its institutional resources at home languished, largely out of sight, its light in the world shone ever more intensely. It was a strange time.

5

The Period of Stagnation

THE 1964–1982 BREZHNEV era in the USSR was called the "period of stagnation." Yuri Andropov's year and three months in power between November of 1982 and February of 1984 revealed stirrings of change, but Konstantin Chernenko then returned to most of the policies of Brezhnev, and stagnation again settled across the land, lasting until Chernenko's death in March 1985. In Soviet society as a whole the Brezhnev period was characterized by corruption, cronyism, slowing economic growth, ideological rigidity, a creeping return to Stalinist attitudes, an atmosphere of cynicism, and recurring cycles of dissident activity and repression.

As the Brezhnev years slipped by, a new generation of church leadership came of age. The older generation, including the patriarch, the metropolitans, and the senior bishops, had experienced the desperate years at the edge of organizational extinction prior to World War II. These men had lived through the war, and they had led the church through the travail of Khrushchev's antireligious assault. For the most part, the rising prelates had not been obliged to face these tests, but both generations shared the dilemmas of church administration under a hostile government. Pressures to collaborate with KGB and Communist Party authorities pervaded local church, diocesan, and patriarchal offices. It was difficult for a bishop, or even a parish priest, to know the boundary line between effectiveness in bringing the sacraments to the people and the faithlessness of lost personal integrity. Divisions in the church grew, as many dissidents came to believe that a corrupted hierarchy was beginning to accept personal and psychological comfort at the cost of prophetic mission.

The period of stagnation brought slow erosion of the church's institutional resources. It was an era free of large-scale church closings and without the agonies of the Khrushchev attack, but the losses of the Khrushchev attack were not reversed and additional losses accumulated. Between January 1966 and January 1971, the number of registered Orthodox church societies fell by approximately 250, or fifty parishes a year.[1] Gerhard Simon, a well-informed observer of Russian Orthodoxy, wrote that about fifty-five churches may have opened between 1965 and 1970, or a little more than ten a year, and the *Journal of the Moscow Patriarchate* did carry scattered reports of church openings.[2] One might calculate that approximately ten new communities per year were registered, and approximately sixty communities a year lost registration, almost all of the latter in the western lands annexed after World War II.

The Soviet government's policy between 1965 and 1971 was driven more by events in which the Russian Orthodox Church was only tangentially involved than by the situation of the Orthodox themselves. A large segment of the Baptist community had moved to an illegal, nonregistered existence in 1961–1962. The Khrushchev campaign had led many Baptists, Muslims, Roman Catholics, and others to reject a policy of docility and compliance with repressive, secret, antireligious decrees. Khrushchev's fall from power had interrupted this tendency, but by late 1965 the Baptist initiative group—which became the Reform Baptists—had become disenchanted with the prospects for any true change in policy under Brezhnev. Elements in other religious communities did the same, but the Baptists became the main problem in the eyes of the Soviet authorities.[3] In order to improve internal coordination and strengthen the government's control over the situation—and perhaps for other internal political and bureaucratic reasons—the Soviet authorities merged the Council for Russian Orthodox Church Affairs with the Council for the Affairs of Religious Cults.[4]

Reacting to the increase in nonregistered churches, the Soviet authorities enacted several new regulations in 1966. The first imposed fines on members of religious associations who were avoiding registration, holding unauthorized meetings and processions, and organizing forbidden youth activities. The others modified Article 142 of the penal code, mandating punishment for arousing "religious superstition" (evangelizing), for duress used in collecting moneys (asking payments for baptisms, funerals, and the like), for disregard of regulations on church registration (meeting informally), and for teaching religion to minors under the age of eighteen. Although these new measures were primarily inspired by Baptist actions, they affected the Orthodox as well.[5]

The Central Committee of the Communist Party passed a resolution on August 14, 1967, calling for intensified atheistic propaganda. Efforts to enhance the effectiveness of education in scientific materialism continued through the remaining years of the Brezhnev era and into the Andropov and Chernenko periods.[6]

Nevertheless, the situation of the Russian Orthodox Church in the late 1960s was better than it had been under Khrushchev. A commentator writing for *Posev* early in 1968 reported that forcible church closings had stopped. It is clear from data discussed previously that inactive parishes in the western lands were still being deregistered, but the *Posev* commentary appears largely correct. The *Posev* reporter noted also that the authorities no longer persecuted priests indiscriminately and had ceased canceling their registrations. If a priest was needed in a diocese and wanted to go, the authorities would register him—although this situation changed for the worse in subsequent years. Further, the practice of keeping children from attending church had eased off, but priests were still barred from baptizing children outside church premises and still had to record both parents' internal passport data, thereby exposing them to harassment and reprisal. The commentator added that priests did go to people's homes to perform baptisms. They were afraid, but they went.[7]

The 1968 "Prague Spring" in Czechoslovakia affected the Russian Orthodox Church because the Czechoslovak authorities restored the Catholic Church of the Eastern Rite in that country, and this move inspired the Ukrainian Greek-Catholics in the Soviet Union to renew their efforts to obtain legal recognition.[8] After the Soviet invasion of Czechoslovakia in August of 1968, however, Orthodox Church leaders and the Soviet authorities moved to suppress the surviving Ukrainian Greek-Catholics and other suspected nationalist elements in western Ukraine. Much of the leadership for this renewed drive came from Metropolitan Filaret (Denisenko) of Kiev, the first true Ukrainian to occupy that post since World War II. In western Ukraine, at least, the lull described by the *Posev* commentator was short-lived.[9]

To put this 1965–1970 period into the larger context of Soviet politics and dissent, the time was characterized by a seesaw battle between the emerging forces of liberty and the efforts of the KGB authorities to suppress these stirrings. The open and defiant human rights movement in the USSR was born in a public demonstration held in Moscow's Pushkin Square on December 5, 1965. Later in December two Orthodox priests, Nikolai Eshliman and Gleb Yakunin, wrote the Soviet chief of state, Nikolai Podgorny, asking that the Soviet government cease its interference in church affairs. They also wrote Orthodox leaders asking for the repeal of the 1961 revision of church statutes that had curtailed the authority of parish priests.[10] A Social Christian Union in Leningrad under the leadership of Igor Ogurtsov had already become active in 1964.[11] The hand-to-hand dissemination of forbidden information (samizdat) was soon increasing markedly, as were writings spirited abroad to be published in the West and then broadcast or infiltrated back into the USSR (tamizdat). In April of 1968 the *Chronicle of Current Events* put out its first issue. This samizdat publication reported political arrests and dissident activities, and Andrei Sakharov later hailed it as the greatest achievement of the human rights movement. In the same year a fund was established to send food, warm clothes, writing materials, books, and money to political and religious prisoners. In November of 1970 Andrei Sakharov and several other leading dissidents in Moscow founded the Committee for Human Rights in the USSR. This was the initial flowering of the human rights movement.[12]

The KGB was not idle during these years. What one well-qualified observer, Ludmilla Alexeyeva, called "coordinated arrests" began in 1965. In what was later characterized as "a declaration of war on samizdat," Andrei Sinyavski (pen name

Abram Terts) and Yuli Daniel (Nikolai Arzhak) were arrested in September. A reexpansion of the labor-camp system followed.[13] In 1966 Fathers Eshliman and Yakunin were suspended from their priestly functions. In 1967 the Leningrad Social Christian Union was "exposed," and most of its members were sent to the camps. Also in 1967, Vladimir Bukovski, who later documented Soviet use of psychiatric hospitals for the incarceration of political and religious prisoners, was sentenced to a prison camp. In 1969 the authorities arrested Boris Talantov, who had revealed the devastation of Khrushchev's antireligious drive in Kirov province, and they also arrested Anatoli Levitin-Krasnov, another brilliant lay Orthodox writer. In the same year the founder of the *Chronicle of Current Events* was apprehended. These were but a few of the arrests and trials in those years. By the end of the 1960s, according to Alexeyeva, "the KGB leadership supposed that the human rights movement was finished."[14]

The human rights movement was not finished, however; nor were open religious dissidence, unauthorized religious action, religious samizdat and tamizdat, and underground worship. There was a dynamic process of action and reaction at work that drove both state policy and political and religious dissent. Repression was the authorities' reaction to dissidence, whether political or religious, and repression then drove dissent and worship underground.

In April of 1970 Patriarch Aleksi died at the age of ninety-two, and Metropolitan Pimen (Izvekov) was elected as his successor at a national church council held in late May and early June of 1971. Pimen was known to be pious and traditional and an impressive celebrant of the liturgy. He had a reserved personality, however, and was not intellectually powerful or widely regarded as strong. He had been incarcerated during the 1930s and 1940s and had served as an army officer in World War II, perhaps doing political work and concealing his monastic past. It is said that the discovery of this anomaly resulted in his removal from the army and his second incarceration. Other accounts have it that he was framed and tried for desertion, even though he had committed no crime. It is also said that Pimen's sufferings left him with a residue of vulnerability to official pressure, which was one reason the authorities supported his elevation in 1971. Nevertheless, he was the church's senior prelate and an obvious choice. Despite the criticisms of Pimen, the depth of his religious faith was not seriously questioned.[15]

Between 1971 and 1975 churches continued to be closed. Newly opened churches were no more than a handful.[16] At the beginning of 1975, the leaked V. G. Furov report gave a figure of 7,062 registered Orthodox religious societies.[17] This would represent an average net decline of about thirty-five Orthodox societies a year from January 1971 to January 1975.[18]

To reconcile the various statistics for churches in the Soviet Union during the

Brezhnev era, it is necessary to distinguish between registered church societies and active, functioning parishes with regularly established church premises and a priest even intermittently available. Reports of operating churches rather consistently showed 300–400 fewer churches in the country than registered societies.[19]

Moreover, there has always been a large difference in the western lands between churches that hold daily services with a regularly assigned priest, and churches that hold services less often because of the extreme shortage of priests. Furov's figures for Ivano-Frankovsk at the beginning of 1975 are indicative. He wrote that only half of the 364 registered parishes in the diocese held services daily (as an Orthodox church is supposed to do), 126 held services once or twice a week, 23 held services no more than four to five times a year, and 33 parishes did not hold services at all.[20] In an observation consistent with Furov's data, Dimitry Konstantinov reported that only 4,000 churches in the USSR were open all the time in 1975, when there were about 7,000 church societies registered.[21]

Although it was a time of few basic policy changes, some additional antireligious actions were taken by the Soviet government in the 1973–1975 period. In July of 1973 an educational law was passed by the USSR Supreme Soviet that placed an obligation on parents "to bring up their children in a spirit of high Communist morality." This would theoretically have obliged believing parents to raise their children as atheists, although this interpretation seems never to have been enforced.[22] Nevertheless, the official Furov report noted eighteen months later that members of parish executive committees in Byelorussia were being fined for permitting teenagers to act as godparents. The Byelorussian authorities were also fining priests for baptizing children in private homes.[23]

Further amendments to the 1929 law on religious associations were enacted in 1975; they mostly codified changes made by regulations issued over the Khrushchev and Brezhnev years. The only positive effect was to increase the opportunities for religious societies to own vehicles and other movable property.[24] Additionally, the powers of the Council for Religious Affairs were enhanced, and the discretion of local soviets and other local authorities was reduced. Explicit prior permission of the council was required to register or deregister a church society, and the council acquired the power to remove even elected members of local church organizations and committees by summary action.[25]

In the early 1970s, the Soviet authorities continued to try—but nevertheless failed—to quench the fires of dissidence. In 1972 the authorities searched the houses of political and religious activists in Moscow, Leningrad, Kiev, Vilnyus, and other cities, making numerous arrests. In those years, an eloquent priest in Moscow, Father Dmitri Dudko, was becoming widely known for his bold sermons, and in 1973 he began to conduct hugely popular question-and-answer sessions after Saturday vespers. Although transferred out of Moscow in 1974 and later transferred again, he continued his activities throughout the 1970s.[26]

The *Chronicle of Current Events* was forced to stop publication at the end of

1972, and the Committee for Human Rights in the USSR also fell silent. Solzhenitsyn was expelled from the country in February of 1974. In November 1974, Vladimir Osipov, the founding editor of the Orthodox nationalist journal *Veche* [Assembly], was arrested. As Alexeyeva wrote, in 1973 and 1974 both enemies and well-wishers spoke of the human rights movement "in the past tense."[27] Once again, this judgment was premature, however, and the survivors fought on. The greatest of them was Andrei Sakharov, who led the human rights movement in Moscow for the next half dozen years.

In May of 1974 the *Chronicle of Current Events* resumed publication and the human rights movement began to recover. The 1975 Helsinki Conference on Security and Cooperation in Europe gave great impetus to the dissidents' activities. Alexeyeva suggested that the publication in August 1975 of the Final Act of the Helsinki Conference, including its humanitarian articles, opened the eyes of Soviet activists to the government's international obligations. Yuri Orlov, backed by Andrei Sakharov, announced the formation of the Moscow Helsinki Watch Group. In 1976 two Orthodox laymen, Aleksandr Ogorodnikov and Vladimir Poresh, founded a Christian seminar, which united young people from a number of cities in essentially nonpolitical religious and philosophical dialogue. In December 1976 the Christian Committee for the Defense of the Rights of Religious Believers in the USSR (Christian Committee), led by Father Gleb Yakunin, released its first document.[28]

In the mid-1970s the Soviet government seemed to retreat somewhat reluctantly from its policy of refusing permission for young people with a higher education to enter theological schools and become priests. The Soviet authorities had no doubt found this prohibition difficult to explain in a period when the *Chronicle of Current Events* was once again publishing accounts of human rights abuses, when the Helsinki Conference was pressing the Soviet Union to demonstrate greater observance of international norms, and when watch groups in the USSR were monitoring compliance. According to Dimitry Pospielovsky, the influx of highly educated young men into the seminaries resulted in a "new type" of bright young Orthodox priest coming from the intelligentsia and commanding a distinctive respect.[29]

The overall reaction of the authorities to the resurgent dissident movement was an intensification of repression. Yuri Orlov, Aleksandr Ginzburg, and other Helsinki Watch Group members were arrested in February of 1977.[30] Anatoli Shcharanski was arrested in March. Aleksandr Ogorodnikov was arrested in 1978, and the arrest of other members of the Christian seminar, including Vladimir Poresh, followed. Father Gleb Yakunin was arrested on November 1, 1979, and Father Dmitri Dudko was arrested in January of 1980. During the same month Andrei Sakharov was exiled from Moscow to virtual house arrest in Gorki. Repression continued through Brezhnev's last years in office.[31]

Father Sergei Zheludkov, the saintly priest and dissident writer from the outskirts of Pskov, was a voice the Soviet authorities had long tried to still but had failed to silence. Driven from his parish but not intimidated, Father Sergei remained active until shortly before he died of cancer following surgery in a Moscow hospital on the night of January 29–30, 1984.[32]

In the five years between 1976 and 1981, the number of registered Orthodox societies stabilized. This did not mean that church closings in the western lands stopped, but closings there were partially counterbalanced by the registration of new communities in the rest of the country. Overall, about sixty church societies were deregistered in those years and thirty new societies were inscribed.[33]

The 1978–1980 period was the best time during the 1970s and early to mid-1980s for the authorization of new Orthodox communities, and the Soviets were most benevolent in Siberia and Central Asia and to a lesser extent the Volga region.[34] Probably the reason Soviet authorities were modestly responsive to believers' desires in the remote regions of Asia was to accommodate Russian settlers and to promote Russification in politically and strategically sensitive non-Russian areas.[35]

Various observers have noted that defiant or underground religious activity gives the authorities an incentive to ease up on overt, tractable religious institutions. It is likely that the activities of nationalist religious movements, the Helsinki Watch Group, and the Orthodox dissident movement stimulated the modest 1978–1980 change in policy that permitted Russian Orthodox Church societies to be registered in greater numbers once again after the hiatus of the earlier 1970s. In any case, official Soviet policy toward the church did soften during those years.[36]

In 1980 the Russian Orthodox Church leadership began to think seriously about commemorating the millennium of the baptism of Rus in 988. In December of 1980 the Holy Synod founded a Jubilee Committee, and the authorities were modestly supportive.[37] In January of 1981 the rate at which clergy were taxed on their income was cut slightly.[38] During Brezhnev's last months of life in 1982, the sick and aging leader authorized the Council for Religious Affairs to turn over to the church the historic Danilov monastery complex so it could be rehabilitated to become the central headquarters of the patriarchate during the celebration of the Millennium.[39] This did not mean, however, that the repression of dissidents stopped. If anything it intensified in the early 1980s. As a Leningrad religious activist put it, "The first half of the 1980s was distinguished by the harsh repression of all dissenters, including the believers."[40]

Ambiguities reflecting a Soviet leadership in flux characterized the early 1980s. The authorities tightened up once again on authorizations for new Orthodox Church communities, and deregistrations increased. During the first half of the

1980s, an average of two new church societies were registered each year, most of them east of the Urals. Deregistrations were running at about 40 per year, almost all of them in the western lands, and net losses were approximately 200 between January 1981 and January 1986.[41] In contrast to the ongoing police repression of religious dissidents and the continuing administrative measures directed against the church, antireligious propaganda languished. The cadre of atheist writers got progressively older, and few competent new authors appeared. After the mid-1970s party ideologues relied increasingly on translations from abroad, reprints of articles written during the 1960s, and reminiscences of doddering heroes of the atheist movement. *Science and Religion* and other antireligious publications gave a dwindling readership esoteric articles on obscure religious and mythological phenomena and mildly sympathetic exhortations to protect believers' legal rights and respect their sensibilities. Doctrinal atheism as an intellectual vehicle in motion was running out of gas.[42]

Brezhnev caught his death of cold—literally—standing in the bitter chill atop Lenin's mausoleum on November 7, 1982. Three days later he was dead. His successor, Yuri Andropov, had long headed the KGB and was no kinder to the religious communities than Brezhnev had been. Keston College researchers concluded that the treatment of these people became "even harsher," as Orthodox laypersons who possessed Christian literature or met in study and discussion groups were repressed.[43] In February 1984 Andropov himself died, succumbing to kidney disease and other ailments. At his funeral his wife was observed making the sign of the cross over the coffin.[44]

Konstantin Chernenko, an even more elderly and infirm leader, succeeded Andropov. He had been Brezhnev's dedicated lieutenant and staff officer for many years and was a living embodiment of the era of stagnation. In July 1984, *Pravda* called for a more active battle against religion and the "prejudices and fraud that are the weapons of the church."[45]

The retirement in late 1984 of the aged chief of the Soviet government's Council for Religious Affairs, Vladimir Kuroedov, portended no perceptible change in policy. His successor, Konstantin Kharchev, a former party secretary in the Soviet maritime provinces and then ambassador in Guyana, had little previous experience in religious or even antireligious work.[46] He told an interviewer later that he was unacquainted with the Bible when he assumed office, although it must be said for Kharchev that renewed work on a law to regularize church-state relations began at about the time he took up his duties.[47]

Chernenko's infirmities worsened. For the last few months of his public life he had to be supported by aides as he stood, and his last public appearance was in December of 1984, less than a year after his accession to office. He made two more appearances on television, probably staged in a hospital, and died on March 10, 1985.

The country was ready for change and vigorous leadership, and a few in power even wondered whether the church might have some role in the moral and ethical restoration of a nation clearly gone astray.

Table 5.1 shows the number of registered Russian Orthodox Church societies in each diocese on January 1, 1986, at the end of the era of stagnation.[48] Increases

TABLE 5.1   Number of Registered Orthodox Communities in each Diocese on January 1, 1986

	1986 Total	Change Since 1966			1986 Total	Change Since 1966	
		No.	Percent			No.	Percent
Alma Ata	57	+11	+24	Odessa	121	−23	−16
Arkhangelsk	21	−2	−9	Olonets	5	+1	+25
Astrakhan	17	0	0	Omsk	13	+1	+8
Cheboksary	37	0	0	Orel	55	−10	−15
Chelyabinsk	15	0	0	Orenburg	12	−1	−8
Chernigov	110	−50	−31	Penza	46	0	0
Chernovtsy	258	−6	−2	Perm	41	0	0
Dnepropetrovsk	33	−2	−6	Poltava	52	−10	−16
Gorki (Nizhni Novgorod)	45	−1	−2	Pskov	86	−5	−5
Irkutsk	17	+1	+6	Riga	87	−8	−8
Ivano-Frankovsk	334	−40	−11	Rostov-on-Don	64	−9	−12
Ivanovo	44	0	0	Ryazan	53	−6	−10
Izhevsk	18	0	0	Saratov	31	−1	−3
Kalinin (Tver)	49	−5	−9	Simferopol	14	0	0
Kaluga	24	−4	−14	Smolensk	37	−1	−3
Kazan	26	+2	+8	Stavropol	101	−3	−3
Khabarovsk	16	+4	+33	Sumy	92	−50	−35
Kharkov	61	−16	−21	Sverdlovsk (Yekaterinburg)	32	+2	+7
Khmelnitski	138	−2	−1	Tallin	82	−8	−9
Kiev (Kyyiv)	182	−34	−16	Tambov	38	−3	−7
Kirov	32	−2	−6	Tashkent	50	−1	−2
Kirovograd	80	−31	−28	Tula	32	0	0
Kishinev (Chisinau)	198	−25	−11	Ufa	17	−2	−11
Kostroma	64	−7	−10	Ulyanovsk	9	−3	−25
Krasnodar	76	−1	−1	Vilnyus	41	−2	−5
Kuibyshev (Samara)	18	0	0	Vinnitsa	266	−84	−24
Kursk	172	−25	−13	Vladimir	51	−3	−6
Leningrad (St. Petersburg)	44	−1	−2	Vologda	17	0	0
Lvov	1,076	−125	−10	Volyn	455	−34	−7
Minsk	370	−53	−13	Voronezh	75	−5	−6
Moscow	175	+3	+2	Voroshilovgrad (Donetsk)	142	−18	−11
Mukachevo	422	−6	−1	Yaroslavl	78	−8	−9
Novgorod	25	0	0	Zhitomir	155	−18	−10
Novosibirsk	38	+5	+15	Total	6,742	−724	−10

Source: Tsentralny Gosudarstvenny Arkhiv, Fond 6991, Opis No. 6, delo Nos. 3129–3140.

and decreases in the number of parishes in each diocese during the twenty years after January 1, 1966, are also shown. During those two decades, 724 church societies, net, were deregistered; this number reduced the total Orthodox parishes by about 10 percent. Roughly half of the losses were in the historically Orthodox regions of Ukraine, and an additional quarter of them were in regions of western Ukraine where Eastern Rite Catholics had predominated prior to the Lvov council of 1946. Most of the rest were in dioceses south of Moscow occupied by the Germans in World War II, in Byelorussia (Belarus), in Moldavia (Moldova), and in the Baltic states. There were scattered increases in the number of functioning parishes in Siberia, Kazakhstan, and a few other places, but these were more than offset by scattered losses throughout the Russian republic.

Table 5.2 is a list of the average number of traditionally Orthodox people served per church, diocese by diocese.[49] Table 5.3 shows the same data displayed by region. It is almost as if the USSR had a geological tilt from east to west—the country's modest supply of churches collected in the west, the vast stretches of Siberia virtually high and dry. The five immense dioceses in the Russian republic east of the Urals were averaging 250,000–400,000 traditionally Orthodox people per parish. In Central Asia an average parish served 75,000–100,000 traditionally Orthodox people, and in European Russia the average was about 70,000. In central and eastern Ukraine—except for Dnepropetrovsk and Simferopol, which suffered Draconian church closings in the Khrushchev drive—the dioceses were serving fewer than 50,000 people per parish, and in formerly Greek-Catholic areas of western Ukraine an average parish was serving fewer than 4,000 people. The extreme variation from east to west was consistent and dramatic.

As the Millennium approached, 59 percent of all the parishes in the USSR were still to be found in Ukraine. If the other western lands (Byelorussia, the Baltic states, and Moldavia) are included, the total rises to over 70 percent. Only slightly more than 2,000 functioning churches could be found in all of the vast Russian republic and in Central Asia and Kazakhstan. The legacy of World War II still lingered, and functioning Orthodox churches in territories never occupied by Hitler's armies remained few and far between. The era of stagnation remained generally in the pattern of earlier times.

For two decades and more, the period of stagnation in the country, mostly under Leonid Brezhnev's sclerotic hand, was reflected in apparent stability. The situation of the church was not so stable as it looked, however, as a slow, inexorable erosion of its position was continuing. The Brezhnev era began as Khrushchev's all-out assault was ending, so additional losses were registered against that already drastically lowered condition. Continuing population shifts were leaving

TABLE 5.2   Average Number of Traditionally Orthodox People Served by Diocese, mid-1980s

Alma Ata	127,000	Odessa	31,000
Arkhangelsk	143,000	Olonets	148,000
Astrakhan	56,000	Omsk	345,000
Cheboksary	35,000	Orel	18,000
Chelyabinsk	235,000	Orenburg	179,000
Chernigov	14,000	Penza	54,000
Chernovtsy	3,400	Perm	75,000
Dnepropetrovsk	170,000	Poltava	34,000
Gorki (Nizhni Novgorod)	45,000	Pskov	9,900
Irkutsk	254,000	Riga	29,000
Ivano-Frankovsk	3,900	Rostov-on-Don	64,000
Ivanovo	30,000	Ryazan	24,000
Izhevsk	85,000	Saratov	170,000
Kalinin (Tver)	33,000	Simferopol	140,000
Kaluga	43,000	Smolensk	30,000
Kazan	81,000	Stavropol	40,000
Khabarovsk	384,000	Sumy	16,000
Kharkov	50,000	Sverdlovsk (Yekaterinburg)	177,000
Khmelnitski	11,000	Tallin	18,000
Kiev (Kyyiv)	31,000	Tambov	35,000
Kirov	52,000	Tashkent	75,000
Kirovograd	31,000	Tula	69,000
Kishinev (Chisinau)	20,000	Ufa	179,000
Kostroma	13,000	Ulyanovsk	147,000
Krasnodar	65,000	Vilnyus	17,000
Kuibyshev (Samara)	177,000	Vinnitsa	7,700
Kursk	16,000	Vladimir	32,000
Leningrad (St. Petersburg)	147,000	Vologda	78,000
Lvov	3,500	Volyn	4,800
Minsk	26,000	Voronezh	49,000
Moscow	82,000	Voroshilovgrad (Donetsk)	56,000
Mukachevo	2,700	Yaroslavl	19,000
Novgorod	27,000	Zhitomir	10,300
Novosibirsk	345,000		

Sources: Gosudarstvenny komitet po statistike, informatsionno-izdatelski tsentr [State Committee for Statistics, Information-Publishing Center], Itogi, Vsesoyuznoi perepisi naseleniya 1979 goda [Results of the All-Union Population Census of 1979] (Moscow: Goskomstat SSSR, 1989), Vol. 1, Tables 5 and 6, pp. 28–55. Adjusted for mid-1980s in John L. Scherer, ed., and subsequently Alan P. Pollard, ed., *USSR Facts and Figures Annual,* Vols. 9–12 (Gulf Breeze, Fla.: Academic International Press, 1985–1988), demographic tables. The number of registered Orthodox communities in each diocese appears in Table 5.1.

more and more areas without churches, including burgeoning industrial cities where new churches were being neither authorized nor built.

The number of priests had declined by almost a thousand between 1966 and 1985; the number of monks, nuns, and novices, already reduced to about 1,300 at the end of the Khrushchev drive, had dropped by about 100. Church attendance slowly declined. Intellectual life in the church seemed to languish, focusing on the distant past and devoting little attention to current issues and contemporary

57

TABLE 5.3 Regional Breakdown of Average Number of Traditionally Orthodox People Served by Diocese, mid-1980s

People per Church	Siberia and Asia	European Russia	Central and Eastern Ukraine	Non-Ukrainian Western Lands	Western Ukraine
400,000	Khabarovsk Novosibirsk Omsk				
300,000	Irkutsk Chelyabinsk				
200,000		Orenburg Ufa Kuibyshev Sverdlovsk Olonets Leningrad Ulyanovsk	Dnepropetrovsk		
	Alma Ata	Arkhangelsk	Simferopol		
100,000		Izhevsk Moscow Vologda			
	Tashkent	Perm Tula Krasnodar Rostov-on-Don			
50,000		Astrakhan, Penza Kirov Voronezh, Gorki Kaluga, Stavropol Tambov	Voroshilovgrad Kharkov		
		Cheboksary Kalinin, Vladimir	Poltava Kiev, Odessa Kirovograd		
		Smolensk, Ivanovo Novgorod Ryazan, Yaroslavl Orel Kursk Kostroma Pskov	Sumy, Chernigov Khmelnitski Zhitomir Vinnista	Riga, Minsk Kishinev Tallin, Vilnyus	
					Volyn, Lvov Ivano-Frankovsk Chernovtsy Mukachevo
0					

Sources: Gosudarstvenny komitet po statistike, informatsionno-izdatelski tsentr [State Committee for Statistics, Information-Publishing Center], Itogi, Vsesoyuznoi perepisi naseleniya 1979 goda [Results of the All-Union Population Census of 1979] (Moscow: Goskomstat SSSR, 1989), Vol. 1, Tables 5 and 6, pp. 28–55. Adjusted for mid-1980s in John L. Scherer, ed., and subsequently Alan P. Pollard, ed., *USSR Facts and Figures Annual,* Vols. 9–12 (Gulf Breeze, Fla.: Academic International Press, 1985–1988), demographic tables. The number of registered Orthodox communities in each diocese appears in Table 5.1.

social concerns. The published minutes of the Holy Synod gave the impression of excruciating attention to foreign delegations and international church politics and of little visible attention to internal church problems and the possibility of vigorous action to meet them. Those looking for patriarchal leadership perceived a vacuum. Aleksi had been in his late eighties when Brezhnev took power, and his private secretary was alleged to have run the church in the last years before the patriarch died.[50] Pimen grew more removed, less vigorous, and more clearly infirm as the nineteen years of his patriarchal service progressed.

The smell of collaboration with the communist authorities, if not submission to them, hung over the church's episcopal administration. Many of the most courageous dissident priests and Orthodox laymen were in prison camps, driven from the country, or dead. The underground church was feeling the brunt of intense KGB suppression. Religious division and dissension in Ukraine were rising.

The accumulated impact of the foregoing developments was an impression that the era of stagnation was becoming a creeping threat to the church's continuing institutional viability. The slow process in motion was designed ultimately to destroy the church, and—unless arrested—it might have done so. The 1980s did not have the stark drama of the church's crisis of survival in 1939, but the trend lines pointed down. One had to wonder, as in the case of an endangered species in the animal kingdom, when the critical aggregation, or level of viability, might be passed, below which the dynamic of life would work against survival rather than for it.

6

The Millennium

A SECOND DRAMATIC turnaround in the fortunes of the Russian Orthodox Church occurred during the Gorbachev era. By the close of 1988, the millennial year, over 800 newly opened parishes had been registered; new monasteries and nunneries had been established; seminaries, theological training institutes, and schools for psalmists, choir directors, and church administrators had opened. After six decades of suppression, Sunday schools, church-run charitable activities, and overt Christian study groups had reappeared. Bishops, priests, and faithful could once again march down to the rivers on Epiphany Day to bless the waters and hail the baptism of Christ.

Why did government policy change? Mikhail Sergeevich Gorbachev played the leading role, although he did not act alone. Changes in Soviet society and the Communist Party had left fewer dedicated atheists anywhere in party ranks. Gorbachev himself was a pragmatist, never the ideological fighter Khrushchev had been. As for Gorbachev's personal convictions, he confirmed publicly in 1989 that both he and his wife had been baptized as infants. His comment was "I think that's quite normal."[1] There was also a widely publicized story that Gorbachev's mother was a believer.[2] Whatever the reason, Gorbachev, the master of the moving bottom line, was never locked into atheistic militancy and had a relatively benevolent attitude toward the church.

Early in his incumbency, Gorbachev was searching for allies to make perestroika work. He understood that his country needed a moral reawakening if the corruption and cronyism that prevailed during the Brezhnev era were ever to be curbed. A population sodden with alcohol and devoid of a work ethic could not implement perestroika. Glasnost, in Gorbachev's original conception, was less freedom of speech than it was the license to speak up and to denounce the wrongdoer and the evil done. All these goals would require higher ethical standards, and the church could help.

Even before Gorbachev assumed power, there had been an understanding in the government that the Millennium would attract immense worldwide attention. There was a touch of national pride in the attitude of communist leaders toward it. Gorbachev was seeking international approval, renewed leadership in the world peace movement, and an international impression of religious freedom in the USSR. Changed perceptions abroad might also bring much needed economic support, investment, loans, and help in building a liberalized economy. Besides, visitors to the Millennium celebrations would bring a large infusion of foreign currency. The hope of benefits from abroad resulting from changed religious policies was fused with a desire to harness religious forces at home to the wagon of perestroika and renewal.

Gorbachev took office in March of 1985, but changes in religious policy came neither right away nor in a clear line of action. New Orthodox parish registrations that year totaled exactly three, as compared to two new registrations the previous year.[3] Deregistrations outnumbered new parishes in both years, and the total number of Orthodox communities in the country continued to sink. In April of 1985, however, the party directed members not to permit the "violation of believers' feelings."[4] According to the head of the Council for Religious Affairs, Konstantin Kharchev, government policy on religion began to change significantly at the end of the year.[5] Some pro-Christian literary works were successfully published in the 1985–1986 period; several pro-church speeches were given at the Eighth Writers' Union Congress in June of 1986; and the church was praised publicly for its generous response to the Chernobyl tragedy.[6]

In January of 1986 the *Journal of the Moscow Patriarchate* stated that clergy were once again permitted to officiate in parishes not their own and to call on the sick when the need arose, without the special permission previously required. Children aged ten and older could be voluntary participants in religious rites, whereas formerly one had to be eighteen. Religious societies would again be recognized as "bodies in law," a status giving them the right to own movable property. Religious associations could also draw their legal minimum of twenty members from a region broader than a single village; this made it easier for people in scattered rural communities to qualify for registration.[7]

By some accounts, Gorbachev took church leaders aside at a Kremlin reception in November 1986 and asked that the church help the Communist Party raise the moral level of the people and assist in controlling alcoholism.[8] In the same month, however, Gorbachev called for "a decisive and uncompromising struggle" against religion and for the strengthening of atheistic work.[9] In 1986 only ten Orthodox religious societies were registered, and the pattern was—as previously—to register a few new societies in remote towns in Siberia or Central Asia.[10]

The Orthodox Church, for its part, prepared for the Millennium by launching a series of international conferences. The first, held in Kiev during July of 1986, discussed the history of the church. A conference in Moscow during May 1987 focused on mission, theology, and spirituality, and the third, in Leningrad during January of 1988, addressed liturgical life and church art. This series had significance beyond the subjects addressed because of the wide international participation the conferences attracted; the openness of Orthodox theologians to the discussion of subjects previously regarded as sensitive, such as the views of émigré scholars and critics; and the presence, active participation, and scholarly contributions of Soviet intellectuals and establishment leaders not previously willing to involve themselves in church-sponsored meetings.[11] There were those in both East and West who dared to hope that Eastern spirituality, suffering, piety, conviction, and sense of history might be combined with Western theological inquiry, including the reconciling of scientific thought and religious faith, to create a new force. As on Russia's great rivers in the springtime, the thaw came, and the ice began to move.

The gradual opening of more intensive contacts with the West had additional dimensions. As Soviet opposition to the importation of foreign religious literature softened, Bibles, New Testaments, and other liturgical, theological, and religious books were imported in increasing numbers, ultimately becoming a flood. As Soviet opposition to material help from abroad changed to receptivity, the world responded with building supplies, bells, crosses for the tops of cathedrals, and all manner of other practical and financial contributions. Europeans, particularly the Germans, were at least as supportive as Americans in this regard, probably more so. As barriers to foreign volunteer efforts and visitors' exchanges slowly lowered, increasing numbers of Westerners, including U.S. college students, went to work in individual Orthodox parishes, helping and building.

After a telephone call from Gorbachev in December of 1986, Andrei Sakharov was permitted to leave internal exile in Gorki and return to Moscow. The following month Gorbachev made his celebrated openness, democratization, and perestroika speech, saying that the restructuring of Soviet society was possible only through democracy and "free thought in a free country." He said this meant the "promotion of non-Party comrades to leading work." In February 1987 news came of the release from labor camps of 51 prisoners of conscience, including 9 known religious believers. A few days later it was announced that 140 prisoners had been pardoned and that the sentences of 140 more were under review. Father Gleb Yakunin and the Christian layman Aleksandr Ogorodnikov were both freed. Yakunin subsequently received a parish assignment.[12]

As 1987 passed, reformist publications such as *Moscow News, Ogonëk* [Little Fire], *Literaturnaya Gazeta* [The Literary Gazette], and even *Izvestiya* and *Vechernaya Moskva* [Evening Moscow] began writing sympathetically about believers' rights and publicizing their struggles to have churches returned to them. Permission to publish scriptures and liturgical books in the USSR was becoming easier to obtain. Publicly expressed Soviet governmental attitudes were sounding more tolerant.[13]

The spring of 1987 brought the optimism that accompanied these developments, but it also brought signs of renewed division within the Christian community. In April of 1987, on the first anniversary of the Chernobyl nuclear disaster, Marina Kazin, a girl in the little Ukrainian town of Grushevo (Hrushiv), reported that she had seen a vision of the Virgin Mary on the balcony of a former Ukrainian Greek-Catholic chapel in the village.[14] Tens of thousands of people assembled, and many of them also claimed to have seen the Mother of God and to have heard the sounds of the Holy Mass coming from the empty chapel. There were also visions reported in nearby towns. Peasant folk interpreted the little girl's vision as a sign of the Virgin's concern for her suffering Catholic people and interpreted the Chernobyl disaster as a divinely ordained punishment for the forcible incorporation of the Greek-Catholics into Orthodoxy in 1946. Allegedly a half million people made the pilgrimage to the Ukrainian village in the weeks and months that followed. Greek-Catholic bishops and priests increasingly risked appearing in the open and professed their ongoing loyalty to the Holy Father in Rome. A public campaign to obtain recognition of Catholic institutions in western Ukraine steadily built strength but encountered unbending opposition from Russian Orthodox hierarchs.[15] This was not the only episode of this kind in western Ukraine after 1946, but it marked the beginning of a Catholic-Orthodox crisis that would grow in magnitude in subsequent years.[16]

The record regarding new Orthodox Church societies remained unimpressive. Yuri Degtyarev of the Council for Religious Affairs reported that sixteen new Orthodox societies were registered in 1987, and other sources reported that ten church structures were turned over to believers.[17] As before, most of the new parishes were in dioceses like Novosibirsk, Sverdlovsk, and Alma Ata, although a few new church societies were authorized in European dioceses such as Kirov, Leningrad, and Smolensk. Public agitation by *Moscow News* and other periodicals was a key factor in forcing reluctant local authorities in Kirov and elsewhere to act.[18] Deregistrations still outnumbered new registrations. As was consistently true over the years, estimates of the number of functioning churches ran several hundred below the estimates for registered church societies. For example, Paul A. Lucey gave a figure of 6,500 functioning churches in 1986–1987; the official figure for registered church societies was 6,742 in January 1986.[19]

Toward the end of 1987, two monastery complexes were returned to the church, to the deep joy of the Orthodox. These were the Tolga Presentation of Mary nunnery in Yaroslavl diocese and the Optina Presentation men's hermitage in Kostroma diocese. The latter, closed in 1923, had been an inspiration to some of Russia's greatest literary figures in the nineteenth century.

Kharchev's subsequent accounts indicated that he was encountering recalcitrance from hard-liners at the Central Committee offices of the Communist Party. At the end of 1987, according to Kharchev, party propaganda director Sklyarov strongly contested Kharchev's position that the Millennium celebrations should be national in scope and tried, unsuccessfully at the time, to get Kharchev removed. Kharchev supported the church's desire to build a great new church in Moscow commemorating the Millennium, but Yegor Ligachev, then the senior party secretary for ideology, opposed him. Gorbachev supported Kharchev and overruled Ligachev.[20]

The great Millennium celebrations were scheduled for June of 1988, and, as the year was beginning, the public statements of Soviet government officials sounded increasingly accommodating. For example, in a January interview, Yuri Smirnov, head of the International Department of the Council for Religious Affairs, said that the Soviet authorities recognized past errors in dealing with the churches and were trying to rectify them under Gorbachev's leadership. He acknowledged that communist leaders had earlier "tried to force the masses away from religion. . . . Much has changed. The needs of believers . . . are being regarded more calmly and attentively." During the same month Kharchev spoke of a "new interpretation of the principle of freedom of conscience" and a religious policy "cleansed of all elements of bureaucracy."[21]

In late March 1988 a meeting of Orthodox bishops was informed that the Soviet government had abolished the requirement that both parents publicly register their passports when baptizing their children.[22] Some dioceses and the patriarchate's publishing department received enlarged offices. Additional buildings were provided for the Moscow seminary, the Leningrad theological academy, and the nuns at Korets and Pyukhtitsa. The Sofrino manufacturing shops were given a parcel of land, and it was announced that the revered chapel of St. Kseniya of St. Petersburg had been returned to the church. In addition, the Easter liturgy at the patriarchal Epiphany Cathedral was broadcast live on Soviet television, apparently for the first time. The Communist Party's authoritative monthly journal, *Kommunist,* ran an article in its April 1988 issue softening the line on religion and admonishing party members that they should not regard the registration of a new church society as an ideological defeat.[23]

In early April of 1988, Patriarch Pimen gave a controversial interview to an

Izvestiya correspondent. Although he praised the attitude of the Soviet central authorities, he sharply criticized local officials for continuing to obstruct the registration of new Orthodox communities. He observed that some "progress" was being made, noting that "sixteen" new Orthodox societies had been registered in 1987.[24] This last statement must have been a deliberate effort to put pressure on the authorities, as nobody in the USSR or in the world could have believed that sixteen new church societies in the vastness of the Soviet Union could be regarded as great progress. As previously discussed, that number of new societies would not even counterbalance the number of parishes still being closed down.

Crosscurrents in communist attitudes toward the church continued, but Gorbachev remained determined in his desire to enlist Orthodox hierarchs, priests, and lay believers in support of his program. He made clear to the patriarchate that the Soviet government wanted the help of all sectors of society, including the church.[25]

On April 29, 1988, Gorbachev received Patriarch Pimen and five metropolitans who were members of the Holy Synod and talked with them for ninety minutes in the Kremlin.[26] Gorbachev thanked the church leaders for the Russian Orthodox Church's patriotism and material contributions during World War II and for the leaders' participation in the fight for peace and against nuclear destruction. He acknowledged that Stalin and, by indirection, Khrushchev had mistreated the church and believers, and that they, like other Soviet citizens, deserved the benefits of democratization and glasnost. He also took credit on behalf of the Soviet government for the return of the Danilov, Tolga, and Optina convents and for government assistance in planning the millennial celebration.[27]

In his reply, Pimen somewhat pointedly added to the list of benefits that he hoped might be extended by the Soviet government, mentioning restoration of the church societies closed in the 1960s, the registration of new church societies, the opening of church edifices closed down, and the building of new churches. He further noted additional issues that still needed resolution, including the restoration of the nine dioceses closed in the 1960s, authorization for an increase in the number of monks and nuns and facilities for them, permission to expand training programs for priests, psalmists, and other church servers and to open new seminaries in Byelorussia and other constituent republics, the return to the church of the monastery of the Caves in Kiev, an increase in the allowed print runs of Bibles and other church literature, and a revision of state legislation regulating churches and cults.[28] Pimen blessed Gorbachev and his labors for the welfare of the motherland. Gorbachev promised to refer the patriarch's specific requests and concerns to his colleagues for resolution. In truth, Gorbachev's government responded to the church's appeals in all of these areas.

Other accounts of the church's list of requests to Gorbachev indicate that church leaders also asked for permission to do charitable work, particularly to care for the sick and old, and requested the return of revered icons and relics from state museums.[29] After the meeting, government attitudes toward church assistance to the sick, old, and infirm shifted markedly, and reports were heard from widely separated localities of priests, monks, nuns, devoted laywomen, and others performing works of mercy in clinics, hospitals, and other institutions. In some places church workers began agitating for the right to open their own religiously sponsored homes for pensioners and others who required nursing.[30] The authorities returned some church treasures.

Church leaders also hoped for permission to conduct seminars and discussion groups in church, open publicly accessible church libraries, and have access to the state-owned mass media.[31] Clergymen did begin to appear on television. Metropolitan Aleksi (Ridiger) of Leningrad, who was elected in 1989 to the Congress of People's Deputies with Pimen and two other clerics, was able to address that assemblage and the greater Soviet public, which watched the televised proceedings from one end of the country to the other. I was in Kishinev at the time and remember the electrifying sight of the metropolitan passing down the aisle in full ecclesiastical garb to reach the podium and appeal to the nation to let the Russian Orthodox Church play its crucial role in the moral restructuring of Soviet society.[32] The patriarchate, with West German assistance, also produced a film depicting the role of the Russian Orthodox Church through the course and sweep of the country's history. In addressing the Stalinist period, the film included photographs of church martyrs and the destruction of churches. Dramatic footage showed the 1931 dynamiting of the Cathedral of Christ the Savior in Moscow with the huge dome crumbling and the immense edifice falling into dust and rubble. *Khram* [The Church], another film that showed the Orthodox in a highly favorable light, was shown on television, also in 1988.[33]

At the end of May 1988, the bishops of the church met again, this time at the Novodevichi monastery in Moscow. They gave final approval for the celebration of the Millennium and decided on the canonization of nine new saints, including Grand Prince Dmitri Donskoi, the Russian victor over the Tatars in 1380.[34]

The pace of new Orthodox Church society registrations began to increase after the Pimen-Gorbachev meeting, although it was hardly a stampede. Sixty-some societies were registered between January of 1988 and the end of May—almost all of them after April 29.[35] On June 7, 1988, Metropolitan Vladimir (Sabodan) gave the exact figure of 6,893 for the total number of Russian Orthodox parishes, including those located within the USSR and those located abroad.[36] Thus there were slightly fewer than 6,800 registered parishes in the country in the spring of 1988.[37]

At roughly the same time, Metropolitan Filaret (Denisenko) of Kiev announced that the Soviet authorities had agreed to return the Far Caves and related grounds and churches of the monastery of the Caves in Kiev, and that the church would reestablish its ancient monastery there.[38] Earlier, the church had publicly expressed its expectation that the entire monastery would be returned, so the dividing of the grounds and caves was widely hailed but actually some-thing of a disappointment.[39]

June 1988 was the month of the celebrations. In colorful procession, Christian leaders from all over the world gathered in Moscow, Zagorsk, Kiev, and other great Orthodox centers in the USSR. On June 5 a liturgy in the patriarchal cathedral in Moscow opened the festivities, and a national council of the Russian Orthodox Church convened on June 6 at the Trinity-Sergius monastery in Zagorsk. A new church statute was adopted that restored the parish priest-in-charge to his position as head of the parish community and chairman of the parish meeting, to which the parish council would be accountable. Although application of the statute would depend on new legislation being drafted by the Soviet government, it was the first step in undoing the 1961 curtailment of the parish priest's authority. In discussing the new church statute, Metropolitan Vladimir (Sabodan) gave an example from a parish in Pskov diocese where the senior church warden had managed to get rid of twenty-five priests-in-charge in the course of his incumbency.[40]

On June 10, 1988, the Soviet government conferred decorations on the patriarch and other church leaders in the Kremlin, and the Bolshoi Theater was made available in the evening for a televised concert of church music. Raisa Gorbachev sat on the dais. The next day church leaders met with USSR president Andrei Gromyko in the Kremlin. Other publicized church services followed, including the ceremonial laying of the cornerstone of a great new church in Moscow—the one Gorbachev had authorized over Ligachev's objections. There were also commemorations in Kiev and other cities. These celebrations had a public impact never before countenanced in the seventy years of communist rule. The release of prisoners of conscience also continued.[41]

In the second half of 1988, the registering of new Orthodox societies accelerated. According to Degtyarev, 809 Orthodox church societies were registered in the course of 1988, and virtually all of the registrations took place after the April 29 Pimen-Gorbachev meeting.[42] On January 1, 1989, there were reported to be 7,549 registered church societies in the country.[43] This was about the same number of registered parishes as there had been at the end of the Khrushchev antireligious drive.

Degtyarev made clear in June 1989 that new registrations of Orthodox church societies were heavily concentrated in Ukraine, Byelorussia, and Moldavia. They were not new societies but parishes closed in the 1959–1964 drive or after it.[44] Nikolai Kolesnik, the chairman of the Council for Religious Affairs in Ukraine, confirmed Degtyarev's breakdown, reporting that in 1988 more than 430 Orthodox churches had been turned over in Ukraine alone, the "overwhelming majority" of them in the formerly Ukrainian Greek-Catholic areas.[45] Some of these churches given over to the Orthodox were buildings where the Greek-Catholics had continued after 1946 to hold services without authorization.[46]

Official sources reported that throughout the country 528 church buildings had been turned over in 1988 and 44 permits for new church construction had been issued, for a total of 572 buildings—237 units short of the 809 new parish societies registered during the same period.[47] The discrepancies were becoming larger between the number of registered societies and truly functioning parishes with available buildings and priests.

From the end of World War II through late 1990, a religious community followed a prescribed path in obtaining its registration, as it did in losing it, and the benevolence or hostility of the authorities always made a great difference at every stage. In the establishment of a new religious society, the basic legal unit responsible was an association of at least twenty laypersons, a *dvadtsatka*. This entity had to apply to its town (or raion) executive council for registration. The papers then passed through district authorities, constituent republic councils of ministers, and oblast or republic commissioners of the Council for Religious Affairs.[48] Finally they reached the USSR Council for Religious Affairs for approval.

In 1988 and 1989, as already indicated, central governmental attitudes became more benevolent, but many local officials retained their personal animus against the believers and clerics they had fought for so long. Many were "conservative" apparatchiks, unenthusiastic about Gorbachev and perestroika. According to Degtyarev, the central authorities had to overturn negative recommendations of local governmental organs in fully a sixth of the applications submitted in 1988 and had to reverse between a quarter and a third of the applications from Lvov oblast (formerly Greek-Catholic territory). In many cases local officials simply sat on the applications month after month. Four-fifths of all applications in 1988 were to reopen rural churches, and nine-tenths of the applications in Ukraine were for village parishes.[49]

When a society was registered, it might or might not get a crumbling or half-ruined former church turned over to it or get a permit to build a new one. Waiting for a church could take months or years, and reconstruction and repair of a returned church structure could take more years. In the meantime, once a religious community was registered, it could usually meet in a peasant cottage or some sort of prayer house—if a priest could be found to lead it. Raising the money to repair a church was never easy, even if the bishop contributed diocesan funds, which were always in extremely short supply—although the prohibition against transferring such funds to individual parishes was no longer being enforced.

After the Millennium celebrations, the pace of beneficent change quickened. The authorities relaxed their ban on ringing church bells, which had been in effect since 1961.[50] Although this is getting ahead of the story, on Easter of 1994 even the bells of the Kremlin's churches and towers pealed out over Moscow. Raisa Gorbachev continued to demonstrate a friendly interest in the Russian Orthodox Church. She visited the Far Caves of the Pecherskaya Lavra in Kiev on February 20, 1989, and planted a tree on the grounds, a symbolic act of support for the church.[51]

As reports proliferated during 1989 of faithful Orthodox people doing charitable work in hospitals, mental institutions, old people's homes, and prisons, the hierarchs of the church embraced the cause.[52] In a press interview in March 1989, Patriarch Pimen observed that the possibility of the church's resuming charitable service was "particularly significant." Metropolitan Yuvenali (Poyarkov) of Krutitsy took up the cause, and Archbishop Kirill (Gundyaev) of Smolensk urged each diocese, convent, and large parish to organize a home for those who needed assistance and then to undertake broader programs of charity. He observed that the existing law did not authorize such activity but made his appeal anyway, anticipating new legislation.[53] Everywhere, Orthodox activists were beginning to organize their own charitable activities and institutions.[54]

In late 1988 and early 1989, reports spread of church Sunday schools and catechism classes. They were still legally forbidden but now were tolerated. Children began to be taught from the age of five. In some cities, including Moscow, clerics organized classes in religion at public schools. Even atheist observers remarked on the dedication and fervor with which these works were undertaken.[55]

As the critical reevaluation of the Stalin era progressed apace, Orthodox leaders began, albeit hesitantly, a process of reappraisal and self-examination. In April of 1989 the Holy Synod established a commission to examine materials and documents concerning the rehabilitation of clergy and laypersons repressed in Bolshevik times. Metropolitan Vladimir (Sabodan) of Rostov chaired the committee.[56] In one sense the establishment of the commission was an act of repentance on the part of church hierarchs who had themselves demonstrated less courage than had the martyrs awaiting rehabilitation and honor. Confronting the past would soon play a role in the church similar to the historical truth-seeking in secular politics and society.

Over 900 new societies were registered between January 1, 1989, and April 29, 1989, more than had been registered in all of 1988. Over 1,700 new societies were registered in the single year after the Pimen-Gorbachev meeting.[57]

It was spring, when blossoms and new growth break forth and the grip of snow and ice loosens—Eastertide, 1989. Easter is the great holy day of Orthodoxy, even more so than it is for the Western churches. It is the day of triumph for the faith. In one sense, Easter of 1989 also marked the triumph of the church, the first anniversary of the fateful meeting of Pimen and Gorbachev, a day when the suffering of the past was transcended and the road ahead could be surveyed with confidence. The sunlit avenues toward the future beckoned with particular warmth and clarity on that Easter Day. Opportunities for service closed to the church since Lenin's time were opening. Institutional resources were multiplying. The ranks of the clergy and of monks and nuns were filling out. Even famous atheists deplored the persecutions of the past and hailed the cultural and political contributions of Orthodoxy to the development of the Russian spirit. Although there were a few small clouds visible above the horizon, the sun shone brightly in the blue heavens.

7

Squalls and Tempests

BETWEEN THE SPRING of 1989 and the end of 1991, the Russian Orthodox Church successfully continued the recovery of its institutional strength. Over 2,000 new Orthodox parishes were registered. Freedom-of-conscience laws put the changes begun in 1988 on new legal foundations, and after the death of its aged and ailing patriarch, the church elevated a man of high intelligence and vigor to the patriarchal throne.[1]

The church's ongoing life was not trouble-free, however, as the smallish storm clouds on the horizon gradually became larger and more menacing. The Russian language has a special word for a storm cloud, *tucha,* perhaps because blue skies so regularly darken into thunderclouds in that long-suffering land.

In June of 1989 Konstantin Kharchev's enemies in the Communist Party, in the Soviet government, and in some sectors of the church hierarchy caught up with him, and he was relieved of his duties as chairman of the Council for Religious Affairs. In an interview with Aleksandr Nezhny of *Ogonëk,* Kharchev described his troubles and presented himself as a reformer attacked by hard-line adversaries.[2] He asserted that he had tried to eliminate KGB dominance of the council and to dismiss a hard-line, KGB-affiliated deputy chairman.[3] He claimed that he had favored democratically organized, multicandidate patriarchal elections.[4] He also said he had incurred the enmity of local communist officials by supporting the return of churches to believers.[5]

Kharchev's interview aroused much interest in church circles, particularly because of his willingness to wash dirty linen in public. Kharchev's comments were unquestionably self-serving. He had given the church's leaders cause to regard him as a busybody, inserting himself into church matters he should have left to the bishops. Nevertheless, his dismissal was a setback for church reform and a success for the clerical "old-boy network" and its attempts to sweep past collaboration under the rug.

Kharchev's successor was Yuri Nikolaevich Khristoradnov, another Communist Party functionary with no more experience in religious affairs than Kharchev had possessed when he assumed the position in 1984. Aleksandr Nezhny described Khristoradnov as having imposed "one more humiliation" on the infirm patriarch. Apparently Khristoradnov insisted that Pimen come to his government office to conduct business, despite the fact that the patriarch was by then unable to walk. Church aides brought Pimen to Khristoradnov in a chair rigged as a litter. Khristoradnov then read previously prepared remarks and directives from a sheet of paper. The patriarch silently nodded acquiescence; his aides then carried him away.[6]

The expansion of the range and scope of the church's activities continued. The first Orthodox religious work camp was organized in summer 1989 with young Finnish volunteers working with students at the St. Petersburg theological schools. The Council of Russian Orthodox Bishops, which met in October 1989, called for the countrywide development of charity work, education of the laity, and the establishment of diocesan publications and church libraries. The bishops also agonized over the issue of participation in the country's political life; the horns of this dilemma were an activism that compromised pastoral authority or an abstinence that led to irrelevance and a failure to be heard. A few days after the council adjourned, representatives of the church met with U.S. experts in a seminar to develop strategies to deal with pervasive alcohol abuse and the less pervasive but growing problem of drug addiction in the USSR.[7]

Internal divisions were appearing. According to Serge Keleher, the first public effort to revive the Ukrainian Autocephalous Orthodox Church was initiated by a priest of the patriarchal church serving in Lithuania, Father Bohdan Mykhailechko. The Autocephalists had been active during the 1920s prior to Stalin's suppression of them as Ukrainian separatists. They had reappeared under the German occupation of Ukraine during World War II and had been suppressed again as Nazi "collaborators" at the end of the war. On August 19, 1989, the priest-in-charge and most of his parishioners at the Church of Saints Peter and Paul in Lvov passed over to the Autocephalists, and on October 22, 1989, the Orthodox bishop of Zhitomir, Ioann (Bodnarchuk), proclaimed the reestablishment of the Autocephalous Orthodox Church throughout Ukraine and was officially excommunicated by the Russian Orthodox Church Holy Synod in consequence.[8]

In January of 1990 a council of 168 priests and 204 Orthodox laypersons met in Ivano-Frankovsk in western Ukraine and declared their adherence to the newly reestablished church.[9] Scattered additional adhesions were reported, and *Novoe Vremya* [New Times] reported in February 1990 that "over 100 parishes" had abandoned their Russian Orthodox Church allegiance.[10] In June of 1990 the Autocephalists held a church council in Kiev. It was attended by seven bishops, over 200 priests, and several hundred lay representatives. In elections for a new patriarch, the delegates chose Metropolitan Mstyslav (Skrypnyk), the aged archbishop of Philadelphia, Pennsylvania, and primate of the Ukrainian Autocephalous Orthodox Church in the diaspora. Because Mstyslav was denied a Soviet visa and was unable to assume his duties, Ioann was elected metropolitan and acting head of the church in Ukraine.[11]

The beleaguered Orthodox faced challenges on all sides. The Ukrainian Greek-Catholics campaigned vigorously to obtain official recognition and to recover their former churches. On September 17, 1989, 150,000 Ukrainian Greek-Catholics gathered publicly to attend open-air services in Lvov. As darkness fell over the city, citizens placed burning candles in their windows to commemorate the victims of Stalinism and to observe the "fiftieth anniversary of the Soviet occupation of western Ukraine." On October 29, 1989, Ukrainian Greek-Catholics took control of the Transfiguration Church in Lvov, symbolically important to both Ukrainian Greek-Catholics and Orthodox because it had been the church of Father Gavriil Kostelnik, the chief clerical organizer of the 1946 Lvov council and the victim of assassination in 1948. On November 26 there was another mass demonstration of more than 100,000 believers in Lvov. In the months that followed, most of the remaining churches in Lvov and many parish churches throughout western Ukraine were occupied by Ukrainian Greek-Catholics. Each side accused the other of resorting to threats, intimidation, violence, and even religiously motivated murder.[12] In truth, both sides engaged in violence.

The dilemma posed by the activism of the Ukrainian Greek-Catholics developed into a delicate issue in foreign policy, for both the church and the Soviet Union. Archbishop Kirill (Gundyaev) of Smolensk replaced Metropolitan Filaret (Vakhromeev) of Minsk as head of the Office of Foreign Church Relations in mid-November.[13] Filaret, a courageous prelate, had just been named exarch of Byelorussia and was facing the difficult task of opening hundreds of new parishes and multiplying the number of dioceses in that republic.[14] There were also negative factors that may have contributed to the advisability of moving Filaret aside. It was the eve of Gorbachev's scheduled visit to Pope John Paul II in Rome, and Filaret had urged the pope in August to ask the Ukrainian Greek-Catholics to accept reintegration into the Russian Orthodox Church, a proposal that the pope must have found unwelcome. Moreover, Filaret was reported by various sources as having taken an extremely hard line with respect to the Autocephalists. Apparently it was only with extreme difficulty that Kirill and other advisers had convinced Filaret that a public excommunication of all the Autocephalists would only advertise the Russian Orthodox Church's difficulties.[15] Last, there was a report that Filaret had suffered a psychological breakdown.[16] Kirill, on the other hand, was regarded as flexible, agile and strong—the most able of the younger bishops and highly experienced in foreign affairs.[17]

Gorbachev's historic meeting with Pope John Paul II took place on December 1, 1989. While attending the Millennium celebrations in June of 1988, Agostino Cardinal Casaroli had presented Gorbachev with a letter from the pope expressing concern about the welfare of Catholics in the USSR. In partial response, the Soviet authorities returned the Roman Catholic cathedral in Vilnyus to believers in February 1989. In April they permitted the restoration of the Lithuanian hierarchy, and in July they authorized the consecration of a Catholic bishop in Byelorussia. A central question from the Vatican's point of view, however, was legalization of the Ukrainian Greek-Catholic Church and the return of the churches seized in 1946. For his part, Gorbachev was attracted to the prestige of talking and cooperating with the pontiff and to the possibility of a papal visit to the USSR. A visit with the pope would open virtually the last closed door blocking full international acceptance. Gorbachev may also have hoped that the pontiff would convince the world that the persecution of religion in the USSR was a thing of the past, and international support and approval would then flow in.

Gorbachev probably miscalculated, not realizing the cost of the policies he agreed to before visiting the pope. Some observers believed he was asking for the pope's help in calming tensions in Ukraine and restraining the Ukrainian Greek-Catholics from "pushing for a separate Ukrainian state."[18] If this was his intention, he got the opposite result. Other observers speculated that Gorbachev and his advisers thought, at least until shortly before the actual meeting, that it would not be necessary to legalize the Ukrainian Greek-Catholic Church as a condition for the meeting and for the establishment of relations with the Holy See.

The Vatican negotiators did get a commitment from Gorbachev to legalize the Ukrainian Greek-Catholics and to register their congregations, although there was no Soviet commitment to return the churches seized in 1946. Apparently Gorbachev made his final decision only a week before meeting the pope, and it was announced on the day they met.[19] Metropolitan Yuvenali (Poyarkov) of Krutitsy went to Italy shortly before Gorbachev's trip and stated publicly that the Russian Orthodox Church was unilaterally postponing scheduled talks with the Catholics because of what the Orthodox described as the violent "seizure" by Ukrainian Greek-Catholics of the Church of the Transfiguration in Lvov.[20] This Orthodox stand did not derail Gorbachev's commitment, however, and the registration of Ukrainian Greek-Catholic religious communities commenced in 1990, although with delay and initially small numbers.[21] The Russian Orthodox Church establishment found itself odd man out, and felt the sting.

Throughout 1989 Soviet officials continued to release statistics on new Orthodox registrations. About 2,560 new Orthodox Church societies were registered in the course of the year to bring the total up from about 7,550 registered parishes on January 1, 1989, to 10,110 on January 1, 1990.[22] This reflected a quickening pace at which new parishes were being founded, an average of over 200 a month. The equivalent figure for late 1988 was a little over 100 a month.

As 1990 began, patriarchate and Vatican representatives met to discuss the Orthodox–Greek-Catholic crisis.[23] Held in Moscow, the meeting lasted from January 12 to January 17. Toward the end of the sessions, Ukrainian Greek-Catholic and western Ukrainian Orthodox prelates joined in the talks. The participants agreed to establish a commission, composed of the four parties just mentioned, to decide on the disposition of churches in dispute.[24] According to the Russian Orthodox Church, the rule of thumb was to be that in towns where there were two churches and a population divided between Greek-Catholics and Orthodox, one church would be given to each religious community. Where there was only one church, it would be given to the community with more adherents.[25]

At the end of January a bishops' council of the Russian Orthodox Church issued an appeal deploring the violence in western Ukraine and calling for a peaceful resolution of the religious conflict there. In a move to blunt the appeal of the Autocephalists and Ukrainian Greek-Catholics among nationalists and independence-minded believers in the western lands, the council also decided to set up separate—but not totally independent—Ukrainian and Byelorussian Orthodox churches. The council also liberalized rules for the use of the Ukrainian and Byelorussian vernacular in church services.[26]

In the meantime, both sides mobilized their supporters in Ukraine. Ivan Gel (Hel'), who had long been incarcerated for his beliefs, became chairman of the Committee for the Defense of the Ukrainian Catholic Church. Members of the nationalist Ukrainian People's Movement (RUKH) were winning governmental and legislative positions in Ukraine and mostly supported the Ukrainian Greek-Catholics and the Autocephalists. District and village authorities increasingly turned over Orthodox churches to their rivals and cast a blind eye to anti-Orthodox demonstrations and the invasion of Orthodox premises. Patriarch Pimen appealed to Gorbachev to "calm" the interchurch conflict. Gorbachev already had troubles enough and did nothing. In March the Republic Committee for the Defense of the Rights of Believers of the Ukrainian Orthodox Church was formed in Kiev by delegates from Lvov, Ternopol, Ivano-Frankovsk, and Transcarpathia. Their declaration deplored the activities of "national-religious Black Hundredism," a reference to the infamous persecutions of Jews and dissidents in late czarist times.[27]

The joint Catholic-Orthodox commission met in Kiev and Lvov March 6–13, 1990. According to the Orthodox, the disposition of a number of individual churches was agreed to without opposition, but suddenly, on the last day of the meeting, Archbishop Vladimir Sternyuk, the Ukrainian Greek-Catholic prelate, plugged in a tape recorder and announced his dissatisfaction with the proceedings, declared all decisions invalid, and withdrew. According to the Greek-Catholic side, the Orthodox discussed the disposition of a few church buildings but otherwise stalled and refused to address issues of substance. Reportedly the archbishop's withdrawal was in protest against the patriarchate's refusal to discuss the return of the Cathedral of St. Yuri (St. George) in Lvov, to acknowledge the invalidity of the 1946 Lvov council, to recognize the canonical, corporate nature of the Ukrainian Greek-Catholic Church, and to stop accusing the Greek-Catholics of unprovoked violence. Furthermore, the Orthodox allegedly had manipulated schedules and locations to prevent believers from talking to Catholic delegates.[28] A subsequent statement by the Greek-Catholics called for a Russian Orthodox Church commitment to support the rehabilitation of the Greek-Catholic Church or, in another variant, to accept the liquidation of Orthodoxy in traditionally Catholic areas of western Ukraine.[29]

There were indications that the Greek-Catholics were not satisfied with the support they received from representatives of the Holy See who had come from Rome to join the talks. In fact, the Greek-Catholics reportedly asked the two Vatican delegates to withdraw, and a deputy in the Ukrainian parliament publicly criticized one of them, Archbishop Stephen Sulyk of Philadelphia.[30] Echoes of dissatisfaction regarding positions taken by Vatican representatives resurfaced at a meeting in West Germany several months later of the Mixed Commission for Orthodox–Roman Catholic Theological Dialogue.[31]

The Ukrainian Greek-Catholics continued to seize churches. The Ivano-Frankovsk authorities decided to transfer the Resurrection Cathedral there to the Greek-Catholics, and the Lvov City Council transferred the Cathedral of St. Yuri. The Orthodox in Lvov resisted this transfer with great passion for a number of months, but it was effected on August 19, 1990, and was celebrated with a procession in which 300,000 faithful were said to have participated.[32]

Although the popularity of the Greek-Catholics in western Ukraine was unmistakable, there was also evidence that some support for Orthodoxy, even the Orthodoxy of the patriarchal church, persisted among rank-and-file believers. Between March and June of 1990, an institute of the Soviet Academy of Sciences conducted a poll in the three traditional Greek-Catholic districts of Lvov, Ivano-Frankovsk, and Ternopol. About a third of the respondents reportedly favored the Orthodox, about a fifth supported the Greek-Catholics, about a seventh endorsed the Autocephalists, and almost a third were indifferent or atheist.[33] Considering the fact that by mid-1990 over 90 percent of the Orthodox churches in Lvov and Ivano-Frankovsk oblasts had been seized or transferred to the Greek-Catholics or Autocephalists, it is probably fair to say that Ukrainian nationalist pressures were pushing the de facto situation somewhat further away from the Ukrainian Orthodox position than popular sentiment would have supported.

Orthodox-Catholic talks resumed in Moscow from September 11 to September 14, 1990. On this occasion it was the Orthodox who broke off the talks, as they were turned down in their request that the Church of the Transfiguration in Lvov, the metropolitan's chapel in Lvov, and the Resurrection Cathedral in Ivano-Frankovsk be returned to them.[34]

Despite the fact that the Vatican was less hard-line than local Greek-Catholics, relations between the Holy See and the Orthodox markedly deteriorated. Metropolitan Filaret (Denisenko) of Kiev publicly questioned whether the Orthodox–Roman Catholic Theological Dialogue should continue, and the Holy Synod of the Russian Orthodox Church posed this issue officially after the September 1990 talks in Moscow. Subsequently, the Russian Orthodox leadership decided to restrict future activity in the dialogue, at least initially, to the question of "Uniatism." A meeting of Eastern Orthodox patriarchs in Istanbul in March 1992 condemned Catholic "proselytism," which was said to include "material enticement" and violence in the occupation of churches.[35]

For its part, the Soviet government continued to develop a warmer relationship with the Greek-Catholics and the Vatican. The long-exiled head of the Ukrainian Greek-Catholic Church, Myroslav Cardinal Lubachivsky, was permitted to return to Lvov on March 30, 1991. He was met by waving, weeping crowds and "forests of blue-and-yellow Ukrainian flags."[36]

With the problem of the Ukrainian Greek-Catholics and the Ukrainian Autocephalists representing two fissures in the structure of Orthodoxy, a third fissure was appearing once again. This was a response from within the USSR to the Russian Orthodox Church Abroad.[37] Under the new conditions, scattered Orthodox clerics and laity who were struggling against hierarchs they perceived as unjust, venal, oppressive, or compromised became aware of the church hierarchy outside the USSR. The Russian Orthodox Church Abroad became an alternative jurisdiction to which disaffected and politically affronted priests might turn.

According to patriarchal church leaders, May 1990 was the beginning of the movement toward the Russian Orthodox Church Abroad.[38] It was then that Archimandrite Valentin (Rusantsov) of the Emperor Constantine Church in Suzdal appealed to Metropolitan Vitali (Ustinov), the head of the Russian Orthodox Church Abroad, to accept him and his parish into its jurisdiction. Reportedly Father Valentin, a popular priest, had refused to submit police reports on his conversations with foreigners and had run for the Suzdal city soviet without his bishop's permission. Archbishop Valentin (Mishchuk), his diocesan superior, was stiff-necked in his handling of the matter. The archbishop first transferred Father Valentin to a distant parish in the Vladimir district and then forbade him to serve in Suzdal when Father Valentin refused to move. Parishioners demonstrated with signs demanding that Father Valentin stay and Archbishop Valentin be transferred, and the uproar attracted national press attention. Father Valentin was duly accepted into the Russian Orthodox Church Abroad and was soon elevated to episcopal rank. Somewhat later, the Moscow patriarchate transferred Archbishop Valentin to become archbishop of Korsun with jurisdiction over a handful of Western European churches.[39]

Since May of 1990, dissident clerics and their followers have passed over to the Russian Orthodox Church Abroad in at least two dozen scattered dioceses ranging from the Baltic states in the west to Khabarovsk and the Pacific maritime province.[40] By January of 1991 almost forty parishes had changed allegiance.[41] According to spokesmen in the United States, just over fifty parishes and communities were adhering to the Russian Orthodox Church Abroad in early 1992; at the end of 1992 at least seventy functioning church societies were claimed.[42] By latter 1994 the number of claimed parish communities approached 100, but many of these held services irregularly in rural cottages or in a room of a small city apartment. Apparently more parishes have been newly established or have passed over than have priests, a difference adherents of the movement explain as motivated by fear and by extreme financial stringencies that prevent defecting priests from earning more than a fraction of the income they had received in the patriarchal church.[43]

Bishops of the Russian Orthodox Free Church, the branch within the former USSR territories of the Russian Orthodox Church Abroad, are Archbishop Lazar (Zhurbenko) of Tambov (now resident outside Odessa), Bishop Valentin (Rusantsov) of Suzdal, and Bishop Veniamin (Rusalenko) of the Black Sea and the Kuban.[44] Two or three bishops from Western and Central Europe have also been active in what is now the former Soviet Union. Territorial diocesan demarcation lines have come slowly, and defecting parishes have been relatively free to appeal to one or another of the bishops for acceptance.[45] Although many cases of transferring parishes have involved personality conflicts between unsubmissive clerics and arrogant or maladroit bishops, an underlying issue has been widespread distrust of church hierarchs' record of collaboration with a godless regime and their perceived cowardice in failing to defend Christian rights. Without these issues of principle, the scattered cases of insubordination would have been of marginal consequence, but deeper troubles lay beneath the surface.

Journalists and commentators sympathetic to the Russian Orthodox Church

Abroad have accused the patriarchate of manipulating its ties to Soviet and post-Soviet authorities in order to enlist police aid, bring force to bear, and inspire legal sleight of hand in obtaining the expulsion of Russian Orthodox Free Christians from church buildings. These allegations have no doubt been true in some cases.[46]

Some spokesmen of the patriarchal church have been gracious in their references to the Russian Orthodox Church Abroad, and the Holy Trinity monastery in Jordanville, New York, has been generous in providing books to patriarchate-run theological schools.[47] Nevertheless, a reconciliation is highly unlikely, as the conditions of the Russian Orthodox Church Abroad could hardly be met by the patriarchate. These demands include (1) canonization of the "new martyrs" of Russian Orthodoxy, including Czar Nicholas II; (2) repudiation of Metropolitan Sergi's loyalty declaration and the legitimacy of Sergi's leadership of the church; (3) renunciation of membership in the World Council of Churches and ecumenical dialogue; and (4) public repentance for past collaboration with the atheist communist state and the exposure and removal of the church's most compromised clerics.[48]

Not all developments in Soviet national life were signaling troubles for the church. There were also positive changes. For example, two new laws were adopted by the Supreme Soviet of the USSR in early 1990 that gave the church significant property rights. The first of these gave religious organizations the right to tenure of land, which could be used for agriculture or forestry. This was important because—in pre-Soviet times—churches and convents had depended heavily on agricultural operations. Under the second law religious organizations could own buildings or other facilities "essential to their activities." The implementation of these two laws did not go forward unambiguously, however, and later compromises made in connection with the freedom-of-conscience bill left the status of religious property somewhat murky. Still, the two laws were a step ahead.[49] In due course, the Soviet government also abolished its requirement that priests be approved and registered by commissioners of the Council for Religious Affairs before they could serve a parish.[50]

The year 1990 saw further development of the church's charitable work. Orthodox activists were able to establish church-run hospitals, clinics, nursery schools, social service schools, and additional homes for the poor. A contemporary version of the historic charitable society of Mary and Martha, the Christian Brotherhood of Believing Doctors, and the spiritual-evangelical society Radonezh (named after St. Sergius) were organized in Moscow. A priest in Riga established a "hot line" for people contemplating suicide, and the Brotherhood of John the

Baptist established an equivalent service in Russia.[51] The newly established Union of Orthodox Brotherhoods convened a congress in October and adopted an ambitious program for religious-moral education and charitable work. At the end of the year the Holy Synod ratified these plans and mandated staff and budgetary support for the union at the national, diocesan, and parish level. The church also planned bookstores, lecture halls, libraries, and polyclinics. Individual churches were told to develop Sunday schools, nursery schools, libraries, almshouses, kitchens for the poor, and interparish temperance brotherhoods.[52]

Patriarch Pimen (Izvekov) died on May 3, 1990. Archimandrite Sergi (Toroptsev) described Pimen's last days:

> The Patriarch was weak and lay in bed during the Easter service. . . . When we came to him for his blessing, there were tears in his eyes. . . .
>
> In the evening of May 2 it was decided to give His Holiness communion. . . . Consecrated bread was brought. . . . I did not leave the old man until 3 A.M., observing his troubled sleep (he was breathing heavily) interrupted every fifteen minutes by coughing. At 8 o'clock in the morning Bishop Aleksi [Kutepov] began the liturgy. . . . When we came to the bedside His Holiness . . . took communion. . . . I raised him on his pillow and gave him a few sips of warm water.
>
> The Patriarch had blessed the convening of the Holy Synod on May 3. . . . At 12 noon I dressed His Holiness. He lay quietly, looking with a concentrated gaze into the distance. He agreed to have tea. The first sip went well, but the second one made him cough. . . . Dinner with the Holy Synod was set for 3 P.M. . . . I helped him up and helped him into a chair by the bed. I was still holding him when suddenly his face went white and his eyes went blank. He breathed deeply three times and became quiet. Peacefully, in that way the fourteenth Patriarch went to his Lord and Maker.[53]

Pimen had been very isolated. As he confided once to friends, he had lived in a "golden cage," but his taciturnity had contributed to this seclusion.[54] On occasion he had been criticized for being lazy, prone to luxury, and inactive, a clerical embodiment of the stagnation of the Brezhnev era. Allegedly he had sung in "symphony" with the country's communist regime.[55] He was credited, however, with having saved the church from a "modernism" reminiscent of the Renovationist schism of the 1920s and a "pseudo-ecumenism" that would have embraced international Protestant "illusions" leading to "unwise" and "precipitate" theological reforms. In short, he "preserved the faith."

With his experience as a choirmaster, Pimen sustained the monastic style of church singing. Even as an old man, he had a rare voice and an "absolute musical ear." He served in church with great feeling and sustained a deep spiritual bond with the faithful.[56] He was a gifted poet, whose verses radiated spirituality.[57] As

Aleksandr Nezhny described the dichotomy, two natures coexisted within the man. One was the believing, praying, grieving pastor; the other was the cool, helpless, hardened witness to the "methodical torture" of the church.[58]

After Pimen's death the Holy Synod chose Metropolitan Filaret (Denisenko) of Kiev as *locum tenens,* or interim head of the church.[59] It set June 6, 1990, as the date for a preliminary meeting of bishops, which would select three recommended candidates, and set June 7–8 for a national church council, which would make the final selection in secret balloting.

Some outspoken priests and journalists criticized the process for selecting delegates and the hasty convocation of the council, as it would occur even before the end of the forty-day period of mourning for Pimen.[60] The principal reason given for calling the national council so soon was to put the church in a position to deal quickly with the schismatic tendencies in the church.[61] A second reason was concern for stability in the face of ethnic tensions throughout the country and the uncertain political situation in the USSR, characterized by the fierce struggle between conservative hard-liners and democratic reformers.[62] This split was reflected within the church's leadership. The conservative tendencies found expression in the view that the church not only should be free but also should have a privileged status as the national church, as of old. The reformist tendency favored a true church-state separation, sometimes described as a "free church in a free state." A third suggested reason for the rapid calling of the council was fear that the perusal of Pimen's personal archives after forty days might reveal compromising documents that could be exploited in subsequent maneuvering for and against particular candidates for the patriarchal office.[63]

The identity of the principal candidates was clear. The main ones were Metropolitan Filaret (Denisenko) of Kiev, Metropolitan Vladimir (Sabodan) of Rostov, and Metropolitan Aleksi (Ridiger) of Leningrad.[64] Despite his being the ranking prelate and *locum tenens,* Metropolitan Filaret had significant opposition. In the first place, he had just been elevated to become head of the Ukrainian Orthodox Church, and the patriarchate was straining to give that church the appearance of virtual independence from Moscow.[65] Moreover, Filaret was widely regarded as having mishandled the Ukrainian Greek-Catholics by inflaming passions over the years. Also, Maksim Sokolov published an article in the weekly journal *Kommersant* shortly before the council met, saying that it was "no secret" that Filaret was a "good family man," which is "not altogether becoming for a monk subject to the vow of chastity, and still less becoming for a patriarch."[66]

Metropolitan Vladimir of Rostov was the candidate of the reformers. As the respected chief of administration for the patriarchate, Vladimir was an activist. He had been a good rector of the Moscow academy and seminary. He had only been appointed to the Holy Synod in 1982 and was thus less tainted by collaboration than some other senior hierarchs. He was the most junior of the principal candidates, however, and the bishops, who had great influence in council voting, were mostly conservatives—as were many of the other delegates.[67]

The last of the major candidates was Aleksi of Leningrad. Aleksi had been a successful bishop of Tallin for three decades and head of the great Leningrad see for five years. He was highly experienced in central patriarchal administration and international work. He was known to be intelligent, energetic, hardworking, systematic, perceptive, and businesslike. In the weeks leading up to the national council, Aleksi was described in press stories as essentially "apolitical" and a guarantor of a desirable "quietness" and "peace" within the church. Others, particularly those fearing the possible election of Metropolitan Filaret of Kiev, described Aleksi as the "lesser evil." Aleksi had a reputation as a conciliator, "a person who can find common ground with various groups in the episcopate."[68]

Among Aleksi's possible drawbacks as a candidate was the fact that he was not wholly Russian. He grew up as the son of a prominent Orthodox priest in Tallin and was of mixed ancestry and of Estonian nationality.[69] Another liability was the reverse of the coin with respect to his strength of experience. For thirty years he had operated in the context of church-government politics, accommodating the demands of the Council for Religious Affairs and the KGB. In 1987 the dissident magazine *Glasnost* had published some KGB reports of Aleksi's meetings with council representatives in the late 1960s. Aleksi came across in the documents as candid and sensible but prepared to talk with considerable openness to the KGB and willing to pass on unflattering tales about his fellow clerics. Vice Chairman Furov of the Council for Religious Affairs had characterized Aleksi in 1975 as loyal, patriotic, and not overly zealous—the most compliant of the three categories into which Furov placed the church's bishops.[70]

On June 6, 1990, the council of bishops met. There was some discussion of choosing the patriarch by lot in order to have the choice made by the hand of God, as had been done when Tikhon was selected in 1917, but this proposal did not carry. In the first round of voting by the bishops Aleksi received 37 votes, Vladimir received 34, Filaret received 25, and Metropolitan Yuvenali (Poyarkov) of Krutitsy received 25. In the second round of voting, Filaret was chosen over Yuvenali, and the bishops had their three candidates to recommend.[71]

At the meeting the following day of the national church council, there were ninety bishops (two were sick), ninety-two lower ranking clerics, eighty-eight lay delegates (thirty-eight women), thirty-nine representatives from the church's convents, and eight representatives from the theological schools, for a total of 317. Forty of the delegates were from the church's jurisdictions abroad, and a few of the lay delegates were young people under twenty-five years of age.[72] Although additional prelates could be nominated from the floor, and four were, none of these candidacies survived to compete against the bishops' council's three nominees.[73] In the first ballot Aleksi received 139 votes, Vladimir 107, and Filaret 66. In the runoff vote Aleksi received 166 of 309 valid votes, and Vladimir received 143. Aleksi was declared elected. The strength of liberal and reformist support for Vladimir and the poor showing of Filaret surprised some observers.[74]

Aleksi was enthroned on June 10, 1990, and received by Gorbachev, along with the permanent members of the Holy Synod, on June 12, 1990. According to an interview Aleksi gave *Izvestiya* on June 16, the new patriarch raised the question with Gorbachev of the Greek-Catholics in western Ukraine and the inroads made by the Russian Orthodox Church Abroad.[75]

Commentators writing after Aleksi's elevation seemed to give the new patriarch the benefit of the doubt, looking toward the future of the church with optimism. Many were impressed with the modesty of Aleksi's posture and the fact that he did not bring a great retinue of personal followers to Moscow. A few also pointed out, however, that Aleksi was a hierarch who carried the baggage of past church-state collaboration. For these reformers, who had hoped for a fresh start with a patriarch untainted by a record of compromises and deals, Aleksi's elevation was a disappointment. One could not altogether forget Father Gleb Yakunin's prediction before the national council that, if one of the "people of the past" were elected, a church schism would become inevitable.[76]

Even the final passage on October 1, 1990, of the long-heralded Soviet Law on Freedom of Conscience and on Religious Organizations spelled some continuing trouble for the church.[77] The bill had been in gestation for years, and action had repeatedly been put off.[78] The Council for Religious Affairs had consulted the church communities in February of 1989, and in its response the Russian Orthodox Church had emphasized the need to make the church's central administration and all its parts a single "juridical person," to reduce exorbitant taxes, and to secure the church's property rights and its opportunity to carry on religious instruction, charity work, and publishing.[79] After the consultation with the religious communities, the draft legislation went to the ideological commission of the Communist Party's Central Committee staff. According to Kharchev, many in the party merely wanted to change the facade of government-church relations without changing the substance, but the party ideologues were only in a position to delay but not to sabotage implementation of the Politburo's decision.[80]

About a year later both the chairman of the responsible parliamentary committee and the church's Holy Synod were expressing concern about the apparent lack of progress.[81] No doubt as a result of these pressures, the Presidium of the USSR Council of Ministers reviewed the draft law on April 11, 1990.[82]

After a first reading of the draft law in the Supreme Soviet on May 30, 1990, the text was finally published in early June and enacted four months later.[83] Clarified and somewhat improved from the church's point of view, the June text nonetheless continued to draw criticism and pointed commentary from observers.[84] The most controversial question, still unresolved when the USSR collapsed, was whether religious instruction would be permitted on the premises of the nation's schools.

In the meantime, several republics, including the Baltic states, Ukraine, Georgia, and the Russian republic, were drafting their own legislation on religious freedom. These laws would prove to be more liberal than the USSR text but less radically so than some people had expected. The Russian republic enacted its legislation on October 25, 1990, slightly less than a month after the all-USSR legislation had been enacted.[85] The Ukrainian law was passed in April 1991 and went into force in June.[86] The question of primary jurisdiction for all-USSR or republic legislation remained unresolved for more than a year—until the breakup of the USSR at the end of 1991 settled the issue in favor of the republics.

The all-USSR legislation improved the situation of the religious communities in several ways.[87] An individual religious community was relieved altogether of the legal obligation to register, although unregistered communities had limited rights beyond the opportunity to conduct worship in private premises. Religious denominations received the right to proselytize, publish freely, import literature, and have access to the media. Atheists were barred from using government funds or official facilities to propagandize or educate people in unbelief.[88] Religious instruction of children of any age in private premises was authorized.[89] The draft article permitting religious classes in public schools on a voluntary basis during nonschool hours was struck from the bill, but the alternative draft article explicitly forbidding such instruction was also removed, which left the situation ambiguous. This was particularly true in the Russian republic, where legislation authorized optional religious instruction in preschools and teaching institutes, and religious teaching "bearing an informational character," without the performance of religious rituals, was permitted in state schools.[90] Religious communities were authorized to own property, establish charitable institutions, and engage in manufacturing for religious purposes.

Clergy and church employees were taxed on the same basis as employees of any public institution, and they became eligible for social security and pensions. Taxes on religious organizations were reduced. Like other students, seminarians were deferred from military service. Clergymen were permitted to be active in politics, but religious organizations were not. Military conscripts received the right to attend religious services when not on duty, but alternative service for conscientious objectors was not mandated by the all-USSR legislation.[91]

As Orthodox hierarchs pointed out, the resolution of a number of issues remained unsatisfactory. Although an individual church community, a convent, or even a diocesan or patriarchal office could register as a juridical person with the right to appeal to the courts, the nationwide institution of the church did not become an all-embracing legal entity. This meant, for example, that the property of a local church community that ceased to exist would not necessarily pass to the central Russian Orthodox institution. Another sticky question was registration of a local church community. It was not clear that the authorities were obligated—lacking legal grounds for refusal—to register a community promptly. Nor was it clarified whether local functionaries had to provide reasons to applicants in writing if registrations were denied.[92]

As Aleksandr Nezhny complained, the procedure for handing over church buildings to the church was "virtually unchanged." There was no legal requirement that previously confiscated church buildings be turned over, and even such premises as the Danilov monastery were not passing into full church ownership. The church also wanted but failed to get full ownership of churches repaired at the expense of believers and relief from rental payments.[93]

The USSR Council for Religious Affairs survived for a time as an organization of "informational, consultative and expert" character. Most registration functions were now to be performed by republic and local authorities. The all-USSR provisions became almost a dead letter when the Soviet Union ceased to exist at the end of 1991—"almost" because Russia and other republics have not been entirely consistent in repudiating USSR legislative provisions. On occasion they enforce the Soviet laws that suit them. In any case, the Council for Religious Affairs passed from the scene because legislation of the Russian republic explicitly stated that "no executive and administrative organs of state power . . . assigned for the resolution of questions connected with the realization of the right of citizens to freedom of belief may be established on the territory" of the Russian republic.[94]

In October of 1990 the Ukrainian Autocephalous Orthodox Church patriarch, Mstyslav (Skrypnyk), returned to Kiev from the United States and held services outside St. Sofia Cathedral and at St. Andrew's Church (still museums). The new Russian Orthodox patriarch, Aleksi II, also announced his intention to celebrate at St. Sofia. The Ukrainian People's Movement (RUKH) tried without success to dissuade Aleksi from celebrating in this formerly Autocephalist church. On October 27–28, 1990, Autocephalists gathered, as did Orthodox faithful. Militia, riot police, and KGB troops set up barricades and battled protesters. The patriarch was escorted into the cathedral by a back door on October 28. Aleksi bestowed the title of His Beatitude on Metropolitan Filaret (Denisenko), consonant with the elevation in status of the patriarchal Ukrainian Orthodox Church.[95] After the incident, interconfessional resentments continued to smolder.

Increasing political diversity presented the Russian Orthodox Church with difficult choices in serving Soviet citizens of every political sympathy while avoiding the embrace of right-wing monarchist and nationalist forces in the country, some of which were anti-Semitic.[96] At the time of Aleksi's elevation, Aleksandr Nezhny asserted that the new patriarch was taking over a church "in the body of which is the poison of chauvinism" and recalled the heroic priests in Old Russia who saved Jews at the time of the pogroms and rejected the anti-Semitism of that era. In early 1989 a seminarian at the Moscow theological school, writing about his life there, asserted that hard-line communist infiltrators and "those from Pamyat [Memory]," the rightist organization, were recognizable when they inscribed themselves as seminarians and did not genuinely "learn here." According to an Orthodox worker at the Tolga nunnery, when Pamyat members came to help in the restoration work, "they didn't behave themselves." They would "rarely help in the manual labor," and when they did, "they always had a photographer with them." A commentator writing in the *Moscow Church Herald, Weekly* alleged that the supporters of Pamyat were ready to wave imperial flags but were not interested in "true worship." Nevertheless, a few priests became prominent in monarchist and right-wing political organizations; the movement to canonize Czar Nicholas II gained strength; Orthodox priests and laymen carried pictures of the executed czar at demonstrations; and a mixed Orthodox-patriots conference was held in late 1990 at which delegates called for the restoration of the monarchy.[97]

On Sunday September 9, 1990, Archpriest Aleksandr Men was murdered outside his home in Zagorsk. Born into an intellectual Jewish family, Father Aleksandr had been brought up as an Orthodox Christian by his mother. He became a prominent liberal theological force in Russian Orthodoxy, writing for publications of the Moscow patriarchate and via manuscripts smuggled abroad. Hard-line elements in the Brezhnev security establishment had perceived him as a threat and had harassed him with interrogations and the confiscation of books.[98] At the end of January 1990, I attended a program in a sports stadium in Moscow where approximately 15,000 people heard Father Aleksandr explain his convictions and answer questions.[99] In answer to one question about anti-Semitic organizations, Father Aleksandr quoted then Metropolitan Aleksi in urging Orthodox faithful not to fall into bigotry, intolerance, and chauvinism.[100]

Soon after Men's death, *Ogonëk* published an article disputing police speculation that Men had been the victim of a drunken assailant or solitary robber. The assassin had smashed Men's skull with an axe at 6:30 A.M. as he was walking from his home to the railroad station on the way to his parish church. This would not have been a usual time for a drunk or robber to attack the priest. Men's briefcase was taken and his glasses, which he used only for reading, were found splintered and smashed underfoot, which perhaps suggested that the assailants had asked Men to read something. At a press conference in early 1991, Men's friends asserted that police investigators had been given the license number of a car that trailed Men on the day before his death, and a man seen on a deserted path near Men's home that day had been identified from photographs, but the police had not followed up either lead.[101] Plausible suspects in the Men killing would appear to have been hard-line communists, the KGB, or right-wing chauvinists.[102] The author in *Ogonëk* compared Men's murder with the assassinations of President Kennedy in the United States and Father Popieluszko in Poland, noting the profound psychological and political impact of those two killings. He then lamented that "our country" did not so much as shudder when Father Men, the saintly priest, was axed down. This commentary may have been unfair, however, as the crowd that assembled at Father Men's funeral was immense.

Another strange event occurred on December 19, 1990, that appeared to be an effort by hard-line forces to draw Patriarch Aleksi into supporting their law-and-order position. On that day an appeal was distributed at the Soviet Congress of People's Deputies, which was meeting in the Kremlin. It was an open letter calling on Gorbachev to take urgent measures, including a state of emergency and presidential rule in zones of conflict, to prevent "the breakup of the state." This appeal preceded the January violence perpetrated by state-controlled organs in Vilnyus and Riga and was interpreted as anticipating and justifying such acts. The appeal was issued over the names of fifty-three prominent national figures, including the most senior generals and admirals, the minister of culture, and— alone as the only religious leader—Patriarch Aleksi.[103] *Agence France Presse* checked with Aleksi later on the same day, and the patriarch—who was ill and in the hospital—denied having signed the appeal.[104] According to one report, the authors of the letter phoned the patriarch and gave him a distorted representation of its contents, after which Aleksi assented to the use of his name.[105] In any case, his disavowal was immediate. The incident further illustrated the delicacy of the church's position.

The registration of new Orthodox religious societies continued throughout 1990. Yuri Degtyarev of the Council for Religious Affairs reported 759 new societies inscribed in the first five months of 1990 and only 1 deregistered.[106] This was an impressive average of about 150 registrations a month, even though it was down slightly from the average of 210 registrations a month in 1989. Degtyarev acknowledged the slowing tempo, attributing it to more nearly "satiated" demand for new congregations on the local level and efforts by local authorities to deal with new registration requests themselves, not always favorably, rather than referring them to the central offices of the Council for Religious Affairs. Degtyarev recorded only 5 Ukrainian Greek-Catholic congregations registered in western Ukraine at the end of May, obviously many fewer than the number of Greek-Catholic congregations active there. He blamed local authorities for dragging their feet in recording changes in the actual situation on the ground.[107]

Official figures soon began to surface indicating that losses to the Ukrainian Greek-Catholics and the Autocephalists in western Ukraine had been massive. Degtyarev's statistics for January 1, 1991, reflected a total of 1,809 registered Ukrainian Greek-Catholic church societies, 952 Ukrainian Autocephalous Church societies (almost all of them in western Ukraine), and about 10,000 registered Russian Orthodox Church societies (down almost 2,000 from the end-of-September figure of 11,940).[108] Besides these losses, there should also be counted the parishes in the USSR that went over to the jurisdiction of the Russian Orthodox Church Abroad.

Table 7.1 lists the number of registered Russian Orthodox Church societies in each diocese on January 1, 1991. Increases and decreases in the number of registered parishes since 1986 are also shown.[109] It should be noted, however, that these official figures were still lagging behind the situation on the ground in western Ukraine, as there were not as many as 704 functioning Russian Orthodox parishes in Lvov and Ternopol dioceses at that time. Nevertheless, the figures were beginning to catch up, as they did, for example, reflect the loss of more than 90 percent of the Orthodox parishes in Ivano-Frankovsk.

More than 4,000 new parishes had been established during and after the Millennium. About 1,600 of these were in Russia, and 1,700-plus were in Ukraine, offset in part by the officially recorded loss of almost 700 parishes in Ivano-Frankovsk, Lvov, and Ternopol and a few more losses in Mukachevo (Transcarpathia) compensated by new parishes opened there. In Ukraine the least impressive gains were in Chernovtsy (northern Bukovina) and in the Russian-speaking territories of the east and north. The greatest gains were in the south of the republic and around Kiev (despite the loss of more than 20 parishes evacuated after the Chernobyl disaster in 1986).[110] Of the 10,000 parishes in the country, 5,031, or almost exactly 50 percent, were in Ukraine. By 1991 there had been 452 new parishes established in Kishinev diocese; 240 in Byelorussia; about 40 in Central Asia and Kazakhstan; and fewer than 15 in the Baltic states.

When the violence in Vilnyus exploded in mid-January 1991, Aleksi criticized both sides, suggesting that the Lithuanians had overstepped the limits of moderation and respect for the rights of others, and the Soviet leadership had made "a great political mistake—in church language a sin" in using military force against

TABLE 7.1   Number of Registered Orthodox Communities in each Diocese on January 1, 1991

	1991 Total	Change Since 1986 No.	Percent		1991 Total	Change Since 1986 No.	Percent
Alma Ata	80	+23	+40	Odessa	249	+128	+106
Arkhangelsk	50	+29	+138	Olonets	11	+6	+120
Astrakhan	30	+13	+76	Omsk	43	+30	+231
Cheboksary	75	+38	+103	Orel	100	+45	+82
Chelyabinsk	25	+10	+67	Orenburg	34	+22	+183
Chernigov	197	+87	+79	Penza	90	+44	+96
Chernovtsy	360	+102	+40	Perm	79	+38	+93
Dnepropetrovsk	102	+69	+209	Poltava	87	+35	+67
Gorki (Nizhni Novgorod)	120	+75	+167	Pskov	105	+19	+22
Irkutsk	30	+13	+76	Riga	90	+3	+3
Ivano-Frankovsk	30	−304	−91	Rostov-on-Don	112	+48	+75
Ivanovo	80	+36	+82	Ryazan	107	+54	+102
Izhevsk	35	+17	+94	Saratov	65	+34	+110
Kalinin (Tver)	100	+51	+104	Simferopol	40	+26	+186
Kaluga	51	+27	+113	Smolensk	62	+25	+68
Kazan	50	+24	+92	Stavropol	250	+149	+148
Khabarovsk	36	+20	+125	Sumy	129	+37	+40
Kharkov	87	+26	+43	Sverdlovsk (Yekaterinburg)	99	+67	+209
Khmelnitski	398	+260	+188	Tallin	83	+1	+1
Kiev (Kyyiv)	362	+180	+99	Tambov	50	+12	+32
Kirov	125	+93	+291	Tashkent	66	+16	+32
Kirovograd	139	+59	+74	Tula	57	+25	+78
Kishinev (Chisinau)	650	+452	+228	Ufa	40	+23	+135
Kostroma	97	+33	+52	Ulyanovsk	31	+22	+244
Krasnodar	145	+69	+91	Vilnyus	50	+9	+22
Kuibyshev (Samara)	48	+30	+167	Vinnitsa	427	+161	+60
Kursk	200	+28	+16	Vladimir	99	+48	+94
Leningrad (St. Petersburg)	86	+42	+95	Vologda	25	+8	+47
Lvov	704	−372	−35	Volyn	800	+345	+76
Minsk	610	+240	+65	Voronezh	144	+69	+92
Moscow	250	+75	+43	Voroshilovgrad (Donetsk)	225	+83	+58
Mukachevo	447	+25	+6	Yaroslavl	106	+28	+36
Novgorod	43	+18	+72	Zhitomir	248	+93	+60
Novosibirsk	73	+35	+92	Total	10,118	3,376	+50

Sources: Reports of provincial commissioners of the Council for Religious Affairs in the Central State Archive, now of the Russian republic, supplemented by Russian Orthodox, Soviet, and Western data. See Chapter 7, note 109.

fellow citizens of the Soviet Union.[111] Aleksi, himself from the Baltic states, must have been under great pressure to prove himself representative and worthy of the ancient Russian Orthodox Church.

On the night of February 1–2, 1991, a third priest in the Moscow area was murdered. Besides Men, the second had been Hegumen Lazar (Solnyshko), killed on December 26, 1990. Father Lazar was said to have been a member of a church commission investigating Men's killing, but church spokesmen denied it. It was also alleged that homosexuality might have had a role in Hegumen Lazar's death, but this too was disputed by the murdered priest's friends. The third cleric to meet a violent death was a monastic priest, Father Serafim (Shlykov), the pastor of a recently reopened church in Moscow. Politics was clearly a motive in Serafim's murder, as it had been in the murder of Men. Serafin had found himself trying to cope with a deeply split parish community, including a militant, anti-Semitic splinter of the Pamyat organization opposing his pastorate. Allegedly he had received at least one hate letter accusing him of having sold himself to the Jews.[112]

In early March 1991, Aleksi met with the heads of the various religious communities in the USSR, and the group issued a public statement urging a "yes" vote on Gorbachev's March 17 referendum on renewing the Soviet multinational federation. Gorbachev received the assemblage of religious leaders on March 13. Aleksi was involving himself increasingly in politics. Within the previous two months he had not only made a pronouncement on the violence in the Baltic states but had also expressed himself publicly on the Persian Gulf war and the danger that Soviet citizens might be sent to fight there.[113]

In June, on the first anniversary of his elevation to the patriarchal throne, Aleksi gave an interview to *Izvestiya* in which he made a public explanation and apology for his past collaboration with the Communist Party and government:

> Defending one thing, it was necessary to give somewhere else. Were there any other organizations, or any other people among those who had to carry responsibility not only for themselves but for thousands of other fates, who in those years in the Soviet Union were not compelled to act likewise? Before those people, however, to whom the compromises, silence, forced passivity or expressions of loyalty permitted by leaders of the church in those years caused pain, before these people, and not only before God, I ask forgiveness, understanding and prayers.[114]

Aleksi accepted responsibility for the past. He said that Metropolitan Sergi had signed his 1927 loyalty declaration under threat by the authorities that over a hundred bishops in custody would be shot if he refused. He explained that Sergi wanted to save the church. As for the stand of the Russian Orthodox Church Abroad, Aleksi charged that body with support for Hitler in World War II and for Lyndon Johnson in Vietnam, but "we did not do the same thing in Afghanistan." When the *Izvestiya* interviewers reminded Aleksi that Vice Chairman Furov of the Council for Religious Affairs had categorized him as among the most compliant hierarchs in 1975, Aleksi defended his record, noting that while he was bishop of Tallin in 1961, he resisted the communist authorities' efforts to make the Alexander Nevsky Cathedral in the city a planetarium (which, in truth, they did do elsewhere in the Baltic states) and to convert the Pyukhtitsa Dormition nunnery to a rest home for miners. He then asserted with pride that in his years as a bishop there was not one case of the administrative closing of a church, and the Pyukhtitsa nunnery grew in numbers from 80 in 1961 to 160 in 1988. (The official statistics for Tallin diocese do not quite support these claims.)[115]

In July 1991, Aleksi attended the inauguration of Boris Yeltsin as the freely elected president of the Russian republic. He blessed the new president and spoke eloquently about their "gravely ill" country.[116] Aleksi and Boris Yeltsin were developing a relationship of mutual regard.

When the putsch attempt began on Monday, August 19, 1991, the patriarch did not of course know how things would turn out, and he bore an immense responsibility for defending the church's institutional position. Reportedly, Yeltsin sent his vice president, Aleksandr Rutskoi, to see the patriarch early on Monday morning, and Aleksi at first declined to receive Rutskoi, citing illness.[117] Apparently Aleksi relented, and Rutskoi was able to deliver Yeltsin's appeal to the patriarch to condemn the coup publicly.[118] At 10 A.M. the patriarch celebrated the liturgy in the Dormition Church in the Kremlin, and people at the service reported later that the patriarch omitted the usual prayer for Gorbachev's or anybody's government.[119] By the time the service was over, tanks were in the nearby streets.

According to Paul D. Steeves, the patriarch withdrew from the city of Moscow on Monday in the middle of the day, presumably to avoid being drawn into the political struggle.[120] Some other senior Orthodox hierarchs were less circumspect and supported the coup. Reportedly, Metropolitan Filaret of Kiev, Metropolitan Pitirim of Volokolamsk, and Metropolitan Yuvenali of Krutitsy were among them. Pitirim was reported to have called on Minister of Interior Boris Pugo, a main activist in the putsch, on Wednesday, August 21.[121] The patriarch said in the Soviet parliament that he personally opposed the coup but had delayed speaking out immediately because of the differing views of other senior hierarchs.[122] A journalist of *Moscow News* later described relations within the Holy Synod as follows:

> The Synod tried to convince the public that it had remained united during the days of the August coup. The harder they tried, the more dubious this looked. One might suppose that the Synod members managed to convince the Patriarch that an open rupture within the Synod was fraught with highly undesirable consequences for him.[123]

On Tuesday, Yeltsin made a public appeal to Aleksi to speak out.[124] Before that day was over, he did so, questioning the junta's legitimacy and calling for restraint by the military, demanding that Gorbachev be allowed to address the people, and calling on the Supreme Soviet to take charge.[125] Shortly after midnight he made a second appeal to armed civilians and soldiers not to commit the "grave sin" of fratricide and "bloody acts." This statement was amplified over loudspeakers to the troops outside the Russian "White House" half an hour before the major attack was expected and the first bloodshed did in fact occur.[126] Later, he anathematized the plotters.[127]

Other priests, both of the patriarchal and émigré churches, moved faster than Aleksi did to rally to Yeltsin and the defenders of the White House, but they were less answerable for the safety of the whole Russian Orthodox Church.[128] History proved Aleksi's judgment essentially sound during the August 1991 coup attempt, at a time when countless leaders in the nation jumped the wrong way. The central issues of the coup were glasnost, liberalization, democratization, constitutionalism, self-determination, and a market economy on the one hand, and preservation of the Soviet Union as a cohesive state under a socialist system on the other. The price of preserving the USSR had become repression, the instrument that had preserved czarist Russia so often over the centuries. The price of upholding the democratic path had become the fragmentation of the Soviet Union. Schism in the patriarch's church would be an inevitable ultimate result of such a political disintegration.

As 1991 progressed, the church continued to expand its educational endeavors, youth activities, and charitable operations. In the city of Moscow alone, thirty-two parish Sunday schools were teaching over 10,000 pupils in the late winter of 1991. As always, the main problem was to find enough qualified instructors. By late summer of 1991 the second Orthodox high school (*gimnaziya*) in Moscow was in operation. The Russian Orthodox Youth Movement began a scouting program and launched its own publication.[129] The All-Church Orthodox Youth Movement was founded early in the year and held its first congress at Moscow State University in late January.[130]

With the coldest months of winter upon them, church workers focused on distributing food to institutionalized children; this aid effort depended largely on relief supplies provided by German donors. The church did not find it easy to get organized, and quantities supplied did not fully meet needs.[131] Patriarch Aleksi's trip to the United States in November had a clear purpose of encouraging greatly increased monetary and material support. The church was a natural channel for such efforts, as it was and is morally committed and relatively free of the wholesale corruption and black marketeering sweeping through the former Soviet Union. The church was slow, however, in its efforts to step into the breach, and some Protestant Christians moved more quickly than the Orthodox and on a larger scale.[132]

Mikhail Gorbachev's attempts to preserve a reduced-profile Soviet federation ended in December 1991 when Boris Yeltsin met the Ukrainian and Byelorussian presidents in Minsk and agreed to form what became the Commonwealth of Independent States (CIS). Within days, Yeltsin was in Rome promising John Paul II that all believers in Russia would enjoy constitutionally guaranteed equal rights.[133] On December 26, Gorbachev arrived at the door of his Kremlin office to find a brass plaque bearing the name of Boris Nikolaevich Yeltsin by the door. The red flag with the hammer and sickle was soon lowered from atop the Kremlin and the Russian tricolor took its place. The Union of Soviet Socialist Republics was no more.

Governmental authorities had reported approximately 10,000 Russian Orthodox Church societies in January 1991, and there were probably no more than 10,800 registered societies a year later, in January 1992.[134] The Ukrainian Greek-Catholics in western Ukraine claimed 2,176 churches in December 1991, or almost 400 more than the official registrations reported at the beginning of the year.[135] The Autocephalists were estimated to have 1,400–1,600 parishes in late 1991, also an increase in the course of the year.[136] The Russian Orthodox Church Abroad continued to claim just over 50 parishes and communities throughout the country.[137]

Between the spring of 1989 and the end of 1991, a number of dangerous problems became visible. In Ukraine—where most of the parishes of the church were located—Ukrainian Greek-Catholics and Ukrainian Autocephalists had seized between a third and a half of the parishes in the republic. Despite Aleksi's strong opposition to anti-Semites, chauvinists, and neofascists, some Orthodox clerics and believers were making common cause with these forces. Freedom-of-conscience legislation disappointed Orthodox Christians in significant respects.

Not everything was going badly, of course. The sun was still shining on the Russian Orthodox Church's revival. Patriarch Aleksi, despite the flaws in his record, was known by all to be a vast improvement in effectiveness over his predecessor, "the hermit of Chisty pereulok [the patriarchal headquarters]."[138] The freedom-of-conscience laws in the various republics represented an immense advance over the regressive legislation of the Soviet era, and the atmosphere of religious liberty was a blessing. Institutional expansion advanced apace.

To change the metaphor, the edifice of the institutional church had been a bit like an old mansion opened up after the death of the aged person who inhabited it, who had kept the windows and blinds securely shut. Everything looked so much better after a spring cleaning, a little paint, and some refurbishing. Everyone felt so much better after open windows let fresh air, optimism, bustle, and energy blow through the long-shuttered rooms. Only later did structural problems with the beams and troubles with the roof become visible. Whether they too could be fixed with patience and hard work was the central question as the Year of Our Lord 1992 commenced.

8

Accusations and Schisms

IF STORM CLOUDS gathered against the Russian Orthodox Church in 1990 and 1991, gales of hurricane force struck it in 1992. In January, the long-brewing tempest over episcopal collaboration with the KGB broke over the heads of church leaders. Soon Metropolitan Filaret (Denisenko) and his followers, supported by President Leonid Kravchuk of Ukraine, defied patriarchal authority and advanced tumultuously in the direction of complete independence for the Ukrainian Orthodox Church. This added another schismatic movement to the ecclesiastical divisions that had already appeared in Ukraine, where almost half of the parishes of the Russian Orthodox Church were still located even after the loss of between 3,500 and 4,000 churches to the Ukrainian Greek-Catholics and Autocephalists.[1]

The Greek-Catholics marched forward in what the Orthodox had come to fear was an expansionism that set its sights beyond western Ukrainian Galicia to the heartland of Orthodoxy. Some Autocephalists maneuvered to join with Filaret if he could enforce Ukrainian autocephaly and positioned themselves to profit from his failure if he could not. The Russian Orthodox Church Abroad and its associated movements—the Russian Orthodox Free Church, the "catacomb" church, and the True Orthodox—continued to pick up scattered parishes. Free Orthodox churchmen ever more loudly accused the patriarchal church of ecclesiastical imperialism and collusion with former communist authorities in the persecution of their adherents and parishes. Some political leaders and priests who had battled the godless authorities made common cause with the breakaway churches. A number of Orthodox priests and a few hierarchs drifted more visibly toward alliances with hard-line chauvinists, anti-Semites, and nationalist agitators. Sectarians and Asiatic cults increasingly threatened the beleaguered Orthodox, or so Orthodox leaders perceived the trends to be.

In the meantime, loyal Orthodox priests and workers labored in the vineyard, building churches, performing works of charity, teaching the essentials of the faith, and developing the infrastructure for new successes. It was not easy, however, to concentrate on the patient work of institution building amid the squalls.

Accusations that church leaders collaborated with the secret police, the Bolshevik government, and Communist Party organs were not new. They had been heard in the months after Lenin seized power, and the politics of the Renovationist schism and Patriarch Tikhon's efforts to combat it were directly related to the authorities' efforts to use collaboration as a wedge to divide the church and as an instrument to control it. Metropolitan Sergi's 1927 loyalty declaration and his subsequent perceived collaboration with the authorities had led to further assaults from the Karlovci Synod and the Russian Orthodox Church Abroad. In 1980, the émigré press in Paris obtained and published the 1975 secret report of V. G. Furov to the Central Committee of the Communist Party of the Soviet Union in which he contrasted the "loyal" and "patriotic" stance of all too many hierarchs with the actions of less cooperative bishops. In 1987, as previously noted, the dissident journal *Glasnost* published secret police accounts of KGB meetings with Pimen, Aleksi, and other senior clerics in which they purportedly had passed on sensitive information about fellow churchmen and internal church administration. In 1990, former KGB Major-General Oleg Kalugin publicly stated that some of the top hierarchs of the Russian Orthodox Church—whom he did not name—were "on the payroll of the KGB."[2]

What was different as 1991 drew to a close was that the USSR was breaking up, the Soviet KGB was passing into limbo, and the KGB's files were becoming available to parliamentary commissions of inquiry and other investigators. Three experts on Orthodox Church politics undertook the task of culling the files and fitting the KGB's code names to the actual identities of collaborating bishops. These researchers were Father Vyacheslav Polosin, chairman of the Russian Supreme Soviet's Committee on Freedom of Conscience, Father Gleb Yakunin, deputy of the Russian Supreme Soviet and a famous dissident priest, and Aleksandr Nezhny, the journalist.[3] Their findings were reported in large-circulation periodicals in January 1992.[4] The most prominently revealed KGB "agents" were Metropolitan Filaret (Denisenko) of Kiev, code-named "Antonov," Metropolitan Yuvenali (Poyarkov) of Krutitsa, code-named "Adamant," Metropolitan Pitirim (Nechaev) of Volokolamsk, code-named "Abbat," and Metropolitan Mefodi (Nemtsov) of Voronezh, code-named "Pavel."[5] It was said that Patriarch Aleksi, code-named "Drozdov," was also an agent, but he largely escaped denunciation, perhaps because the investigators did not quite want to accuse the head of the church.[6]

Archbishop Chrysostom of Vilnyus, known as an intrepid and honorable priest, introduced a sensible perspective into the matter with his comments to Mikhail Pozdnyaev, published in *Russkaya Mysl* in Paris:

Yes, we—I, at least, and I say this first about myself—I worked together with the KGB. I cooperated, I made signed statements, I had regular meetings, I made reports. I was given a pseudonym—a code-name as they say there—"Restorer." I knowingly cooperated with them—but in such a way that I undeviatingly tried to maintain the position of my Church, and, yes, also to act as a patriot, insofar as I understood, in collaboration with these organs. I was never a stool pigeon, nor an informer.[7]

In defending his credentials for courage in resisting co-optation, Chrysostom mentioned that he had ordained Georgi Edelshtein (the celebrated dissident) when other bishops would not and had defended Edelshtein for five years. "Nobody touched him." For his resoluteness in this and other cases, Chrysostom had been removed from Kursk, the largest diocese in the Russian republic after Moscow, and had been sent off to distant Irkutsk to preside over a sixth of the parishes he had administered in Kursk.

Chrysostom was right. If the bishops wished to defend their people and survive in office, they had to collaborate to some degree with the KGB, with the commissioners of the Council for Religious Affairs, and with other party and governmental authorities. Courageous former dissidents remained critical, however, and the media were flooded with denunciatory articles, roundtable debates, and unflattering analyses of the hierarchs' past conduct. Church leaders reacted in outrage against their tormentors and the press.[8] Reportedly church representatives tried, successfully after a time, to convince the authorities to curtail the investigators' search of the KGB archives.[9] Polosin, Yakunin, Nezhny and Edelshtein went from talk show to interview to lecture hall.[10]

Church leaders nursed their wounds, although most of the accused hierarchs escaped any formal sanction. The exception was Bishop Gavriil (Steblyuchenko) of Khabarovsk, but he was removed more for arrogance toward his priests and people than for his record of collaboration. The bishops' council of the Russian Orthodox Church met from March 31 to April 5, 1992, and did establish a commission, however, to make an "objective investigation" of the charges of past collaboration.[11] Bishop Aleksandr (Mogilev) of Kostroma was named to chair it. Not yet thirty-five years old when he was named to the commission and consecrated bishop only two and a half years before, Aleksandr was untainted by past acts of episcopal venality, and he enjoyed a good reputation, even among dissident priests like Edelshtein.[12] He would have needed to be courageous indeed, however, to do very much under the circumstances.

As USSR People's Deputy Sergei Averintsev had said earlier, "The laity believes that men of weak character have been elevated to the episcopacy," and "open atheists" were among "the Brezhnev episcopate." According to Averintsev, they were unrepentant of their sins. Father Edelshtein characterized the Moscow patriarchate as the "last Soviet institution." Others sneeringly dubbed it the Metropolitburo.[13]

Averintsev and Edelshtein were partly correct but only partly so. There is little doubt that almost all of the bishops were and are believers. They are anguished by their acts of past collaboration, and most are deeply conscious of their sin. Although their attitudes echo the old order to some degree, they are not a "Soviet institution."

❋   ❋   ❋   ❋   ❋

In early November of 1991 a council of bishops of the Ukrainian Orthodox Church requested that the Moscow patriarchate grant it full autocephaly. The patriarchate had granted the Ukrainian church administrative autonomy in 1990, but canon law requires that autocephaly be granted by the parent church with the concurrence of other Orthodox national communities. Consequently, the November 1991 action was a petition, not a notification. The request presented the following justifications: First, autocephaly would strengthen the unity of Orthodoxy in Ukraine, would liquidate the Autocephalist schism, and would check Greek and Latin rite Catholic expansion. Second, autocephaly would serve the interests of the Ukrainian nation. The petition added that an independent church in an independent nation was both canonically justified and historically inevitable.[14] In late November an interconfessional forum was organized in Kiev (Kyyiv) to which Ukrainian president Leonid M. Kravchuk declared: "For an independent state—an independent church."[15] Partisans of the patriarchal church noted, however, that he did not apply the same standard to the Ukrainian Greek-Catholics.[16]

At the end of December the Holy Synod of the Russian Orthodox Church decided that a plenary council of bishops would have to consider the Ukrainian church's petition. The Ukrainian bishops met again and sent the patriarchate another petition for autocephaly. Three bishops of the Ukrainian church opposed this action, and Metropolitan Filaret forthwith stripped them of their diocesan jurisdictions.[17]

The Moscow patriarchate soon began to report "thousands" of letters and telegrams from clerics and laypeople throughout Ukraine entreating Moscow to resist Filaret's plans. Believers in the Donets basin were quoted as protesting Filaret's "dictatorial regime" and asking that their former bishop Alipi (Pogrebnyak) be returned to them. The bishop who had replaced Alipi in Donetsk found the strain more than he could bear and had to be relieved at the end of January. He died seven weeks later. Laypeople in Kiev diocese reportedly told Moscow that some clergy silenced by their clerical superiors had approached representatives of the Russian Orthodox Church Abroad with the thought of joining the "catacomb church." Some parishes stopped mentioning Filaret at the place in the liturgy where senior hierarchs are named in prayer.[18]

On February 4, 1992, Aleksi II telegraphed Filaret admonishing him to desist from canonical sanctions against clergy who opposed his position, at least until a

Holy Synod meeting scheduled for February 18–19 could discuss the situation. In reply, Filaret advised Aleksi not to interfere in the internal life of the Ukrainian Orthodox Church. On February 19, Aleksi and the Holy Synod sent a formal message to Filaret deploring pressure on Ukrainian priests to sign statements favoring autocephaly and condemning Filaret's punitive sanctions.[19]

The planned conclave of the council of bishops of the Russian Orthodox Church (with the Ukrainian bishops' participation) met from March 31 to April 5, 1992, at the Danilov monastery in Moscow. Most of the bishops opposed autocephaly. Some bishops in eastern Ukraine, where Russians are numerous, reported that priests and laypeople in their dioceses had told them: "If you support autocephaly in Moscow, don't show your face here again!" Metropolitan Mefodi (Nemtsov) of Voronezh reported that priests in eastern Ukraine were coming to him to see if they could slip across the border to his neighboring diocese to escape the "pressure." The bishop of Alma Ata, Archbishop Aleksi (Kutepov), pointed out that minority Orthodox believers in Muslim Central Asia would be fragmented by internal divisions if Russian and Ukrainian Orthodoxy split. The council's conclusion was that western Ukraine favored autocephaly, but the majority of hierarchs, clergy, and believers in central and eastern Ukraine did not. Nevertheless, the bishops decided that the next national council of the Russian Orthodox Church—scheduled for 1995—should consider the question.

Under great pressure, Filaret promised to present his resignation as head of the Ukrainian Orthodox Church to a council of bishops in Kiev and accept transfer to a lesser see. On April 6, the day following the last session of the Moscow council, an expanded meeting of the Holy Synod of the Ukrainian Orthodox Church, meeting in Kiev, rescinded Filaret's summary transfers of the three bishops who had opposed him.[20]

Filaret returned to Kiev and disavowed his promise to resign. In a press interview on April 14, 1992, he asserted that the bishops' council in Moscow had violated church statutes because it had disregarded the Ukrainian Orthodox Church's already recognized autonomy, and he could not, in conscience, step down. On May 6–7, 1992, the Holy Synod of the Russian Orthodox Church met again. Filaret had been invited but did not appear. Moscow lamented that, when Filaret had renounced his April promise to resign, he had repudiated an oath made with his hands placed on the Cross and the Gospels. The Holy Synod forbade Filaret to act as head of the Ukrainian Orthodox Church except to convene a bishops' council to present his resignation; if he failed to comply by May 15, Filaret would be summoned before an ecclesiastical court. On May 7, Aleksi and the Holy Synod also sent a message to the bishops, clergy, and laity of the Ukrainian Orthodox Church asserting that the majority of Orthodox in Ukraine clearly did not wish to separate from Moscow but reaffirming that a national Russian Orthodox Church council would further consider the question.[21]

Later in May, the patriarch gave interim responsibility for the Ukrainian church to Metropolitan Nikodim (Rusnak) of Kharkov, the senior Ukrainian hierarch after Filaret, who convened a council of Ukrainian bishops for May 27–28. Eighteen of the twenty-two Ukrainian bishops met in Kharkov and elevated Metropolitan Vladimir (Sabodan) to head the church. Vladimir had until then presided over the Russian see of Rostov and had been in charge of patriarchal administration, not functions closely associated with an autonomous Ukrainian Orthodox Church. Nevertheless Vladimir was the runner-up to Aleksi in the patriarchal election of 1990. Vladimir was also a born Ukrainian and had been a student, instructor, and rector at the Odessa seminary, bishop of Pereslavl-Khmelnitski (vicar of the Ukrainian exarch), bishop of the Ukrainian see of Chernigov, and editor of the Ukrainian exarchate's journal, *Pravoslavny Visnyk*. The Kharkov council reiterated the Ukrainian bishops' November 1991 petition for canonical autocephaly.[22]

The Ukrainian government's Council for Religious Affairs issued a statement after the Kharkov council declining to recognize the validity of Vladimir's election, asserting that there had been violations of the officially registered Ukrainian church statute, including a provision in it requiring that the head of the church be a bishop serving on the territory of Ukraine. The government's council expressed continuing support for Filaret.[23]

On June 11, 1992, a bishops' council of the Russian Orthodox Church charged Filaret with flagrant insubordination, "cruel and arrogant" treatment of bishops in his jurisdiction, the creation of a schism, and unworthy personal conduct. Filaret was demoted to the status of a simple monk.[24] Somewhat later, the ecumenical patriarch, Bartholomeos I, endorsed the bishops' action against Filaret and the election in May of Vladimir as head of the Ukrainian Orthodox Church.[25]

A joint church council of Ukrainian Orthodox loyal to Filaret and representatives of the Ukrainian Autocephalous Orthodox Church convened on June 25, 1992. The unification of the two churches was proclaimed the next day under the name Ukrainian Orthodox Church–Kiev Patriarchate (UOC-KP). Patriarch Mstyslav (Skrypnyk) of the Autocephalists, aged ninety-four, was proclaimed head of the unified church, and Filaret was chosen as Mstyslav's deputy. The Autocephalist negotiators were led by Metropolitan Antoni (Masendich), thirty-one, Mstyslav's chief of administration in Kiev. Mstyslav was in the United States; Antoni reported that he had failed to reach the aged patriarch to consult him, and Mstyslav thus was not informed prior to the unification action. The *Ukrainian Weekly,* published in Jersey City, New Jersey, did reach Mstyslav and quoted the patriarch as follows: "If [the union] is with the remnants of the Church headed by Filaret, then I cannot imagine that we could cooperate or unite with him. It would be beneath my dignity to cooperate with Filaret."[26] The heads of the western Ukrainian autocephalous dioceses, where most of the autocephalous parishes were located, also failed to endorse the unification.[27] In fact, hostile local believers in northern Bukovina all but mobbed Filaret when he visited there.[28]

On July 1, 1992, Mstyslav flew to Kiev, ostensibly to enforce his decision to repudiate the union with Filaret. Once Mstyslav was in Kiev, however, the Ukrainian government pressed him to relent, and he was reported to have issued an ambiguous statement to the effect that anyone who wished to join his church was welcome. Mstyslav then flew back to the United States.[29] There the patriarch's opposition to Filaret became clear again, and his office later announced the removal of Metropolitan Antoni because of Antoni's collaboration with Filaret (Antoni did not obey the removal order). Later, on December 15, 1992, a church council of the merged church met in Kiev, reaffirmed the June merger, and took the position that Mstyslav—for church matters in Ukraine—was under the jurisdiction of the church authorities in Kiev.[30]

On June 11, 1993, Mstyslav, by then ninety-five, died in Canada, where he was visiting relatives. The authorities in Kiev of the merged church retained Metropolitan Filaret as patriarchal deputy and elevated Metropolitan Vladimir (Romanyuk) (Volodymyr in Ukrainian), sixty-seven, a hero of resistance to Soviet power who had been confined in the camps in Siberia for ten years, to act as head of the church until an all-Ukrainian Autocephalous Orthodox council, scheduled for October 21, 1993, could choose a new patriarch.[31]

Relationships among the Autocephalists became even more complicated when a bishops' council of the anti-Filaret group met in Lvov in July of 1993 and selected Archbishop Petr (Petro, Petrus) of Lvov to become their candidate for the patriarchal throne left vacant after Mstyslav's death. Petr had opposed the union of June 25–26, 1992, remaining steadfastly loyal to Mstyslav. A church council of this anti-Filaret faction assembled in Kiev on September 7, 1993, and selected Archbishop Dmitri (Demetriy) of Pereyaslav and Sicheslav as patriarch (rather than Petr of Lvov). Dmitri, a seventy-seven-year-old priest (Petr or Petro Yarema), had taken monastic vows and had been consecrated bishop a few weeks earlier. He was enthroned on October 14, 1993, at the Church of Our Savior in Kiev.[32]

For its part, the merged Ukrainian Orthodox Church–Kiev Patriarchate (UOC-KP) convened its council on October 21, 1993, as scheduled and selected Vladimir (Romanyuk), already acting head of the church, as patriarch. The result was that the Autocephalists became an overtly divided body with two rival patriarchs competing for authority. Metropolitan Constantine of the Ukrainian Autocephalous Orthodox Church in the United States appealed to leaders of both groups on July 12 and on August 21, 1993, to resolve their differences, name a unification commission, and end the new schism.[33]

In December 1993 five bishops of the UOC-KP broke with Filaret (Denisenko) and declared obedience to Metropolitan Vladimir (Sabodan) of the Ukrainian Orthodox Church (Moscow patriarchate). The most prominent of them was

Metropolitan Antoni, who had been a principal moving force in the unification with Filaret on June 25–26, 1992, and had harbored ambitions to become patriarch instead of Vladimir (Romanyuk). Antoni handed over his own church, St. Feodosi, and was demoted from the rank of metropolitan to that of bishop. He was then placed on medical leave in Russia.[34]

In the struggle between Metropolitan Vladimir (Sabodan) and Metropolitan Filaret (Denisenko), Vladimir appealed to President Kravchuk of Ukraine on August 19, 1992, protesting the favoritism of Ukrainian authorities toward the UOC-KP. According to Vladimir, there were a dozen instances of violence during the summer of 1992, when armed groups seized cathedrals, diocesan offices, and monasteries under Vladimir's jurisdiction, most of them in western Ukraine.[35] Reportedly the Ukrainian National Self-Defense Guard (UNSO), a Ukrainian nationalist militia, forcibly occupied Ukrainian Orthodox churches and turned them over to Filaret's people. UNSO deployed its irregular troops to defend Metropolitan Filaret's residence in Kiev and to secure Filaret's possession of St. Vladimir's Cathedral. UNSO troops also tried to storm the monastery of the Caves, but monks, novices, and seminarians there contained the initial assault, and special military detachments of the Ukrainian Ministry of Interior (OMON Black Berets) later went into action against UNSO to the surprise of combatants on both sides. Metropolitan Vladimir arrived in Kiev on June 20, 1992, and set up his residence at the monastery.[36] Nevertheless, Kravchuk, some leaders of the Ukrainian parliament, and elements in the Ukrainian political movement RUKH continued to support Filaret, and Ukrainian authorities continued to withhold governmental recognition of Vladimir's church.[37]

Official Ukrainian statistics published in early 1993 listed 5,658 Orthodox parishes under Vladimir and the Moscow patriarchate, 1,665 parishes of Filaret and the Autocephalists allied with him, 10 Russian Orthodox Free Church parishes (under the Russian Orthodox Church Abroad), and 2,759 Greek-Catholic parishes.[38] Despite their losses, the Orthodox affiliated with Moscow had apparently gained a net of 500–600 parishes in Ukraine during the two years after January of 1991, virtually all of them newly established Orthodox communities.[39] (The number of parishes adhering to Moscow in 1994 will be discussed at the end of the chapter.)

When Filaret broke with Moscow and joined the Autocephalists in 1992, he brought with him little more than St. Vladimir's Cathedral in Kiev and a few scattered parishes, although forcible seizures carried out by UNSO and transfers of jurisdiction sanctioned by Ukrainian governmental authorities resulted in accretions in strength. In early 1993 it appeared Filaret had 250–300 parishes of his own (not Autocephalist ones).[40] According to commentators close to the Moscow patriarchate, the height of Filaret's campaign—abetted by the Ukrainian authorities—was in the summer of 1992. Filaret also was in control of considerable

Ukrainian Orthodox Church wealth.[41] Moreover, in the autumn of 1992 he opened a trans-Dniester diocese, appealing to Slavs in conflict with the Moldovan authorities.[42] Reports in late 1993 indicated that Filaret and the UOC-KP might have made some additional gains at the expense of the anti-Filaret Autocephalists and Vladimir's Ukrainian Orthodox associated with Moscow. At the end of 1993, the UOC-KP claimed 3,000 congregations with 2,500 churches and priests. This was no doubt an exaggeration, but this church, by then headed by Patriarch Vladimir (Romanyuk) and Filaret, clearly had greater Autocephalist strength than Patriarch Dmitri (Yarema) had. The anti-Filaret Autocephalists claimed 1,500 parishes but had only about 300 priests.[43]

The Greek-Catholics continued steadily to increase the numbers of their parishes in western Ukraine from the 1,912 they had in January of 1991 to almost 3,000 in the spring of 1994 (with 2,200 church buildings). In the eastern regions of Ukraine the Greek-Catholics had close to 40 parishes.[44]

In Latvia, the entry of Orthodox priests from Russia became more difficult after Latvian independence was recognized following the August 1991 putsch. Nevertheless, a diocesan meeting of clergy and laity on November 11, 1992, voted to preserve the Latvian Orthodox Church's canonical ties with Moscow, and on the following day, Metropolitans Yuvenali (Poyarkov) and Kirill (Gundyaev) and the archbishop of Riga, Aleksandr (Kudryashov), met with Latvian government representatives and worked out a formula of autonomy—but not autocephaly—for the Latvian Orthodox Church with church properties to be under Latvian jurisdiction, ownership, and control.[45] Not all Latvian political and religious leaders were satisfied with the arrangement, however, and local Orthodox clerics predicted a fragmentation of the church, with some of the ninety parishes in the country remaining in canonical union with Moscow, some adhering to the Latvian Orthodox Church Abroad, and some adhering to the Russian Orthodox Church Abroad (three parishes had passed over to this last jurisdiction by late 1992).[46]

As for Estonia, the Holy Synod of the Russian Orthodox Church decided in August of 1992 to give the Estonians independence in administration, church management and instruction. The Estonian synod would own church properties and be supreme in civil matters. This status conformed to Patriarch Tikhon's dispositions made in July of 1920.[47] In the spring of 1993 the patriarchate went a step further, granting the Estonian church independence in all but canonical relations with Moscow—the same status given the Orthodox in Ukraine and Belarus.

With respect to the 150 sisters of the Pyukhtitsa nunnery, most of them Russian, the authorities took the position that the nuns could remain as "guests."

Patriarch Aleksi's Estonian origins have given the nunnery and Estonian priests a degree of visibility and perhaps some protection. Even so, about twenty of the eighty-three parishes in the country have returned to obedience to the ecumenical patriarch at the Phanar (as during the interwar period) and call themselves the Autonomous Estonian Orthodox Church. On August 16, 1993, the Estonian authorities recognized their synod as the sole legitimate successor of the prewar Orthodox Church, despite the fact that three-fourths of the parishes still adhere to the Moscow patriarchate. Russian-speaking parishes side with Moscow, while most Estonian-speaking orthodox parishes have broken away.[48]

In Lithuania, Archbishop Chrysostom's known courage and moral strength, his outspoken pro-Lithuanian stand after the January 1991 massacre in Vilnyus, and the overwhelming Catholic strength in the country have combined to make the situation of the small Russian Orthodox Church community more acceptable and less threatening than in the other Baltic states. Apparently Chrysostom has so far managed to hold his diocese together and retain considerable independence of action.[49]

In late December of 1992, Radio Bucharest announced that the Romanian Orthodox Church had decided to reincorporate Kishinev (Chisinau) diocese as a metropolitan see. A Moldovan (formerly Moldavian) delegation headed by Bishop Petr (Peduraru) of Beltsy (vicar of the diocese of Kishinev) had made the request. Evidently, Petr had displayed pro-Romanian and anti-Muscovite tendencies as 1992 had progressed. On September 8, 1992, three months before the bombshell announcement in Bucharest, a diocesan meeting of Moldovan clergy disciplined Petr and forbade him to conduct services. To forestall defections, the Russian Orthodox Holy Synod had granted the Moldovan church self-administration on October 5, 1992. The synod also raised Archbishop Vladimir (Cantareanu) to the rank of metropolitan. Vladimir's Moldovan church submitted its statute—which had been approved by the Holy Synod—to the Moldovan government for registration. At about the same time, Bishop Petr, who evidently had received some advice and assistance from the Romanian patriarchate, submitted a statute for the "Bessarabian metropolitanate," a body to be under the authority of the Romanian church. The Moldovan government declined to register either statute, urging the two sides to work things out. Metropolitan Vladimir convened a meeting of bishops, priests, and parish representatives from most of the churches in the diocese and obtained their "overwhelming majority vote" in favor of retaining the church status granted by Moscow in October.[50]

Moldovan governmental authorities invited the two sides to a meeting on December 16, 1992, at which encounter Metropolitan Vladimir urged Petr to accept

Moscow's authority. Petr refused and walked out. On December 20, 1992, Metropolitan Vladimir learned that Bishop Petr and his delegation had been received by Patriarch Feoktist of Romania.[51]

Feoktist and the Romanian synod appointed Petr acting head of the Bessarabian metropolitanate and invited Moldovan priests to pass over to the jurisdiction of the Romanian Orthodox Church. According to Metropolitan Vladimir, only 7 of the 715 church servers in Moldova became sympathizers or open supporters of Petr.[52] In mid-1994, the large majority of Moldovan priests and parishes were continuing to adhere to Vladimir and the Moscow patriarchate. How long this will remain true, however, is problematical. If the bulk of Moldova's 650 parishes should ultimately pass over to Romanian jurisdiction or should break with Moscow, about 7 percent of the total number of parishes in the Russian Orthodox Church community in the former USSR would be removed from Moscow's authority.[53]

What is emerging is the piece-by-piece, stage-by-stage detachment of Orthodox communities in former Soviet republics outside of present-day Russia. Moscow's position is buttressed by the historical Orthodox canonical requirement that autocephaly requires consent and by the relationship Aleksi II has established with Bartholomeos I, the ecumenical patriarch. Nevertheless, the drift of events must be recognized as negative in the long term for the Russian Orthodox Church.

Two problems for the Russian Orthodox Church had roots deep in Russia's past and greatly increased in magnitude as 1992 and 1993 passed into history. The first was the growth of religious sects and quasi-religious movements competing with Orthodoxy for the soul of Russia. The second was the effort by Russian nationalists, many of them right-wing extremists, to enlist Russian believers in their cause.

The sectarians ranged from evangelical Protestant denominations, supported by volunteers and massive infusions of money from abroad, to occult Asian sects and even to avowedly pagan movements.[54] Siberia and the Pacific maritime provinces have been particularly at risk from the Orthodox point of view because merciless suppression of Orthodoxy over the years resulted in the creation of what many Orthodox churchmen have described as a desert of spiritual ignorance and indifference. When I talked with Bishop Arkadi (Afonin) of Magadan in the summer of 1992, he lamented a large Protestant missionary "invasion" from Alaska with a million dollars to spend, a well-financed Presbyterian proselytizing effort among Korean immigrants, and a Baha'i incursion onto Sakhalin

Island. This was not to speak of the efforts of Evangelical Christians, Baptists, and other homegrown Russian Protestants.

I proceeded to Yuzhno-Sakhalinsk in 1992 and discovered that a wealthy Iranian Baha'ist had indeed financed the establishment of a thriving Baha'i religious community. In 1992, the city of Yuzhno-Sakhalinsk (population about 200,000) had seven churches, one of them Orthodox and the remaining six of them sectarian. Not long before, Hegumen Ambrosi (Yepifanov) of Vladivostok reported that the sectarian movement was "very aggressive," whereas "we have only two or three clerics in the diocese with a seminary education. People as yet know very little—they don't know what the Russian Orthodox Church is, what its structure is, who the bishop is, still less who the Patriarch is."[55]

The spread of sectarianism is by no means confined to the Russian far east. In Ukraine, the John Guest evangelistic team conducted a month-long crusade in Kiev in 1991.[56] Mission Volga brought the gospel message to "over 120,000 people" in the summer of 1992.[57] The great Olympic Stadium in Moscow has been used repeatedly for evangelical mass meetings, including Billy Graham's crusade of October 23–25, 1992.[58] Western televangelists like Robert Schuller, Pat Robertson, and others are also active.[59] According to *Orthodox Russia*, more than 700 Western organizations are working to evangelize the Russians, and over 2,000 Protestant preachers are preparing themselves to work in Russia.[60]

During my travels in Russia each year, I have found Western evangelical missionaries everywhere. In the summers of 1993 and 1994, for instance, I visited Archangel, Kostroma, Minsk, Perm, Petrozavodsk, Smolensk, Syktyvkar, Tula, Yaroslavl, and Yekaterinburg and found that U.S. Christian witnessing groups were or had just been to every one of those cities. These committed men and women suffer the disadvantages of not speaking fluent Russian—although Russian evangelicals interpret for them—and not staying in any city long enough to become part of a Christian community. They have the advantages of evident sincerity and of resources, including large numbers of Russian-language Bibles to distribute as gifts and sometimes medicines, clothing, and food. A woman who had gone to one of their meetings told me that the U.S. lay preacher asked the crowd at the end of his presentation who in the throng had found Christ. An older woman rose and answered: "Those of us who were Christians when you came are Christians still." Yet the evangelicals are making gains.

The reaction to Western proselytizing of Orthodox and other religious leaders in Russia has been deep concern. On April 20, 1993, President Boris Yeltsin received the patriarch, the mufti responsible for European Russia and Siberia, the head of the Council of Evangelical Christian and Baptist Churches, and other Russian church and parliamentary leaders. As Yeltsin's press chief described the meeting, Aleksi II said relatively little, but other church leaders complained about the misuse of tourist visas to mount proselytizing campaigns, expansionist activity by Roman Catholic missionaries, and foreign-sponsored Islamic penetrations. In an action taken apart from the meeting, the patriarch seems to have sent confidential letters to Yeltsin and Supreme Soviet president Ruslan Khasbulatov urging them to restrict foreign missionary activity on Russian territory.[61]

In July 1993 the Russian Supreme Soviet passed a bill requiring foreign religious organizations to attach themselves to Russian religious bodies or seek accreditation, which might be denied if the foreign body acted against the interests of the Russian state or undermined "social concord." After opposition was expressed by the Roman Catholic Church, foreign Protestants, sects such as Hare Krishna, and Russian champions of religious liberty, President Yeltsin withheld his signature and returned the bill to the parliament. At the end of August the Supreme Soviet backed off from the proposed restrictions. When the fate of the bill was still hanging in the balance—in July—the patriarch publicly deplored the "massive" western pressure on Yeltsin to veto it. Reportedly, "President" Aleksandr Rutskoi actually signed it on October 4, during that crisis. There is continuing speculation that the idea of the bill lives on.[62]

On the personal level, Russian Orthodox people resent the perceived assumption of foreign Protestants that Russia is a pagan land without its own Christian community, which must be won for Christ. An article in the *Moscow Church Herald, Weekly* characterized Billy Graham's crusade as a grandiose, self-satisfied, immodest "show," which treated the Russians as if they were natives of New Guinea without authentic religious roots, faith, or culture.[63]

Nevertheless, Russians often publicly and privately acknowledge their sense of religious emptiness and then express interest in knowing more about some Asian sect. I have frequently been approached by young people selling copies of books by these mystics. It is easier to learn the teachings of the guru Shree Shmiman in Moscow than in New York.

In mid-1991 church publications had already been musing about the possibility of a "25–50-year moratorium" on foreign proselytizling, and the Holy Synod examined the question of heretical and occult movements in December of that year. The bishops' council of March–April 1992 discussed "movements from the East," theosophists, and mystical sects. Orthodox Church publications have carried exposés of Hare Krishna activities, telesorcery, extrasensory influences, witchcraft, black magic, and devil worship.[64]

There are movements and sects that add nationalistic and militaristic politics into the mix. In 1984, Father Ioann (Bereslavski) of the "True Orthodox Church" began receiving "revelations" of the Word of the Mother of God. Allegedly he represented the Mother of God as urging that new money be printed with her likeness and that of Nicholas II.[65] After Father Ioann and a colleague, Petr Bolshakov, organized the Mother of God Center, the movement began to enjoy "ever increasing popularity."[66] The center held a meeting in a Moscow movie house in May 1993 at which 1,600 people were said to have been present. With a staff of several score persons, the center claims the adherence of "thousands" in Russia. Quite a few "fanatical" supporters are teenagers, and an organization of outraged mothers has charged that many of these young people were recruited through misrepresentation and extortion.[67]

In 1992 a retired army major reported receiving a letter from the Mother of God Center inviting him to become a priest of the catacomb church. The letter asserted it had been revealed to Father Ioann that Russia would be redeemed by military officers. The major was invited to sign a "white charter" and take part in a "great liturgy" that would commit him to the movement. In a similar vein, the *Moscow Church Herald, Weekly* reported on meetings held in late 1991 and early 1992 at the Central Museum of the Armed Forces in Moscow, one of which was attended by no less a figure than Aleksandr Rutskoi, then vice president of Russia. Apparently these meetings included representatives of the True Orthodox Church, among them Father Ioann, and veterans from the Soviet campaigns in Afghanistan. It was asserted there that Russia would be saved by the army, and an astrologer predicted which dates would be propitious for armed action. Combat flags were blessed.[68]

Another cult movement, the Great White Brotherhood, also tried to attract teenagers away from their families, allegedly using hypnosis and mind-altering drugs to do so. In 1990, cult founder Yuri Krivonogov (Kryvonohov) proclaimed himself the reincarnation of the Apostle Peter, the Prophet Isaiah, and John the Baptist. He further proclaimed his wife, Marina Tsvigun, to be Maria Devi Christos, the incarnation of Jesus, who would be crucified and rise from the dead on Judgment Day in November 1993 at the great St. Sofia Cathedral in Kiev. Cult leaders boasted of 150,000 followers, who would die with their crucified messiah. In the summer of 1993, I saw Maria Devi posters on church doors as far away as Archangel on the White Sea, and other notices were reported from Moldova to Moscow. Ukrainian police arrested at least 600 cultists when the fateful November arrived. Many of them soon began hunger strikes in detention and had to be force-fed. Yuri, Maria, and about sixty followers were arrested inside St. Sofia on November 10, 1993, after battling police with fire extinguishers seized in the cathedral. Observers variously blamed the cult manifestation on alleged Muscovite attempts to discredit the Ukrainian authorities and the "spiritual vacuum" young people were experiencing.[69]

Laymen doing works of charity and religious education and the Union of Orthodox Brotherhoods that unites them have been influenced on occasion by nationalistic elements. In particular, the Union of Christian Renovation and the St. Sergius Brotherhood of Sergiev Posad have campaigned against "Jewish-Masonic" plots, have held prayer vigils to protest the church's continuing failure to canonize Nicholas II, have organized cells of like-minded individuals for semipolitical purposes, and have noisily criticized the patriarch. At the union's third congress in St. Petersburg in June 1992, "patriotic" Orthodox delegates objected strenuously to conciliatory interfaith remarks Aleksi made to a meeting of rabbis in New York during the patriarch's visit to the United States in November 1991.

Some church hierarchs have also expressed nationalistic and occasionally even anti-Semitic sentiments. In particular, Metropolitan Ioann (Snychev) of St. Petersburg has become a strident champion of some of these views. He has publicly given credence to "the Protocols of the Elders of Zion," the anti-Semitic forgery concocted by czarist intelligence agents, and has denounced or denigrated the Masons, Western evangelical missionaries, the "almighty dollar," the breakup of the Soviet state and army, Roman Catholic popes, and "Russophobes." In early 1993 representatives of the patriarchate were obliged to disavow an article the metropolitan had written, noting that the opinions expressed there and elsewhere were "personal views" and not positions of the church.[70]

As 1994 progressed, the rift between "modernists" and "traditionalists" widened. Archpriest Georgi Kochetkov became a focal point of the controversy, as he had introduced gospel readings in vernacular Russian and had edited the church Slavonic texts at other places in the liturgy to make the service more readily understandable to ordinary Russians. Advocates of church renewal additionally favored acceptance of the western Gregorian calendar, reformist political activism, enhanced ecumenical dialogue with Roman Catholics, Protestants, and Jews, and sympathetic understanding of women attending church in slacks and with heads uncovered. The conservatives, led by the Union of Orthodox Brotherhoods and hierarchs like Metropolitan Ioann of St. Petersburg, accused Kochetkov and his "neo-Renovationist" allies of arrogance and a desire to debase the language of the traditional liturgy. Underlying the controversy was the disdain of some traditionalists for "Yeltsin's Jews and western lackeys" and the conservatives' support for what appeared to be messianic religious and political imperialism.

For their part, the modernists, who were clearly in a minority among the clergy, raised the specter of a return of the activities of the "Black Hundreds," who had persecuted Jews and liberal thinkers during the last years of the Czar. The patriarch, struggling to prevent the rift from becoming a new church schism, tried to silence Kochetkov and transferred him from the great Moscow church of the Vladimir icon of the Mother of God to a small, not yet functional church. Caught between the contending factions, Aleksi delayed Kochetkov's transfer for several months. The patriarch's formal position was that revisions in the liturgy should be approved by a church council, and an individual priest or group should not introduce changes without comprehensive debate and full authorization. Kochetkov reluctantly submitted to patriarchal authority, but the struggle between conservatives and reformers is far from over.[71]

In April 1992, the *Moscow Church Herald, Weekly* published an open letter from thirty Moscow priests to Metropolitan Vitali (Ustinov) of the Russian Orthodox Church Abroad characterizing the canonization by Vitali's church of Nicholas II and his family in 1981 as "a gift of God to all Russia." The Patriarchate, while not yet moving to canonize the Czar, took the occasion of the 75th anniversary of his murder to declare national repentance.[72] At the end of the same month Patriarch Aleksi II conducted funeral services in St. Petersburg for Grand Duke Vladimir Kirillovich, until then head of the Russian imperial house. The services were carried out with great deference and ceremony but in an essentially nonpolitical way. The same issue of the *Moscow Church Herald, Weekly* also carried a letter from a student at the Minsk seminary who advocated "an Orthodox monarchy" as the best form of governance for Russia and who looked forward to a time when catechisms for young people would once again proudly say "For Faith, Czar, and Fatherland—God, Czar, Russia." It was less significant that the seminarian felt as he did than that the *Moscow Church Herald, Weekly* published his letter.

As indicated in chapter 7, the Freedom of Conscience Laws left the relationship between the church and military service only partially resolved. The church confessed that it did not have enough trained priests experienced in military service to assign as chaplains. Nevertheless, the Russian minister of defense, Pavel Grachev, called on the patriarch at his residence in March 1994—to the annoyance of some nonorthodox religious leaders not so favored—and an agreement on cooperation and the training of chaplains was reached. In an earlier speech to the Humanities Academy of the Armed Forces the patriarch had spoken of a "spiritual vacuum" in the army, and had emphasized the deleterious effects of the vicious hazing practiced against new recruits and ethnic minorities, of the high incidence of suicides in the armed services, and of the criminality, drug addiction, alcohol abuse, and boredom all too evident in military life. The patriarch also exalted the nonpolitical, neutral function of the defense forces and warned that soldiers must not allow themselves to become "toys" of either the left or the right.[73]

On September 21, 1993, President Boris Yeltsin suspended the Russian Congress of People's Deputies and ordered new parliamentary elections on December 11–12. At midnight on the same day the parliament voted to depose Yeltsin and declared Vice President Aleksandr Rutskoi acting president. Authorities loyal to Yeltsin soon cut most telephone and electric lines and prevented heating fuel, water, and supplies from reaching the parliament building (the White House). Patriarch Aleksi, who had been in the United States on a visit to mark the bicentennial of Orthodoxy in North America, cut short his U.S. tour and returned to

Moscow on September 28, offering to mediate between the two sides. He talked with Yeltsin in the Kremlin, with Constitutional Court chairman Valery Zorkin, and with two envoys from the parliament. He nearly succeeded in brokering an agreement under which lawmakers and their supporters would have surrendered most of their arms, government authorities would have restored some services to the building, and both sides would have cooperated in patrolling the premises. Opposition deputies in the White House rejected the agreement, however, and violence erupted on the streets of Moscow on October 2.

On October 3 pro-parliament forces, urged on by Rutskoi, stormed the offices of the mayor of Moscow and carried out a bloody but ultimately unsuccessful assault on Moscow's Ostankino television complex. Aleksi was reported to be suffering heart problems. On October 4 Yeltsin ordered and army troops executed an assault on the White House, bombarding the building, forcing its defenders to surrender, and overcoming snipers in the vicinity. The officially acknowledged dead numbered 187, the heaviest toll from fighting in Moscow since the Bolshevik revolution of 1917. If Aleksi could have pulled off his mediation, he and his church would have emerged as national saviors. As it was, the outcome was very sad. Aleksi had repeatedly prayed for the avoidance of bloodshed and national fratricide, but it was not to be.[74]

Table 8.1 shows the number of registered Russian Orthodox communities adhering to the Moscow patriarchate in each diocese on January 1, 1994. The total is approximately 12,800, or 2,700 more than in 1991 (about 700 more than in January 1993). The Russian republic increased from about 3,500 parishes in 1991, to 4,600 in 1993, and to 5,200 in 1994. There were notable gains in Siberia and some areas in the Urals. Ukraine increased from about 5,000 parishes in 1991, to 5,590 in 1993, and to 5,700 in 1994. Great losses were suffered in western Ukraine as the Greek-Catholics and Autocephalists acquired formerly Orthodox churches, and considerable losses were registered around Kiev as Metropolitan Filaret captured churches with the help of the Ukrainian National Self-Defense Guard (UNSO). Compensating gains in other regions of Ukraine resulted in modest overall accretions of strength for the Moscow-affiliated Orthodox. Belarus increased by 240 parishes between 1991 and 1994; Kazakhstan and Central Asia increased by about 60; and the Baltic states increased by about 10.[75]

Since mid-1992, church hierarchs have begun to use a figure of "about 15,000 parishes" when speaking of the Russian Orthodox Church's strength.[76] One has to wonder whether the preceding figures are truly thousands of parishes off the mark. I believe the discrepancy is really a difference in definition, as church leaders give figures for the number of churches or parishes in a jurisdiction and then

TABLE 8.1   Number of Registered Orthodox Communities in each Diocese on January 1, 1994

	1994 Total	Change Since 1991			1994 Total	Change Since 1991	
		No.	Percent			No.	Percent
Alma Ata	102	+22	+28	Odessa	330	+81	+33
Arkhangelsk	63	+13	+26	Olonets	27	+16	+145
Astrakhan	36	+6	+20	Omsk	65	+22	+51
Cheboksary	75	—	—	Orel	149	+49	+49
Chelyabinsk	56	+31	+124	Orenburg	22	−12	−35
Chernigov	280	+83	+42	Penza	175	+85	+94
Chernovtsy	370	+10	+3	Perm	79	—	—
Dnepropetrovsk	145	+43	+42	Poltava	130	+43	+49
Gorki (Nizhni Novgorod)	90	−30	−25	Pskov	180	+75	+71
Irkutsk	50	+20	+67	Riga	87	−3	−3
Ivano-Frankovsk	14	−16	−53	Rostov-on-Don	200	+88	+79
Ivanovo	133	+53	+66	Ryazan	75	−32	−30
Izhevsk	36	+1	+3	Saratov	187	+122	+188
Kalinin (Tver)	155	+55	+55	Simferopol	50	+10	+25
Kaluga	48	−3	−6	Smolensk	114	+52	+84
Kazan	84	+34	+68	Stavropol	250	—	—
Khabarovsk	83	+47	+54	Sumy	170	+41	+32
Kharkov	130	+43	+49	Sverdlovsk (Yekaterinburg)	111	+12	+112
Khmelnitski	500	+102	+26	Tallin	63	−20	−24
Kiev (Kyyiv)	210	−152	−42	Tambov	79	+29	+58
Kirov	122	−3	−2	Tashkent	100	+34	+52
Kirovograd	210	+71	+51	Tula	50	−7	−12
Kishinev (Chisinau)	650	—	—	Ufa	96	+56	+140
Kostroma	97	—	—	Ulyanovsk	70	+39	+126
Krasnodar	199	+54	+37	Vilnyus	82	+32	+64
Kuibyshev (Samara)	34	−14	−29	Vinnitsa	610	+183	+43
Kursk	242	+42	+21	Vladimir	75	−24	−24
Leningrad (St. Petersburg)	199	+113	+131	Vologda	59	+34	+136
Lvov	262	−442	−63	Volyn	1,120	+320	+40
Minsk	850	+240	+39	Voronezh	150	+6	+4
Moscow	746	+496	+198	Voroshilovgrad (Donetsk)	320	+95	+42
Mukachevo	510	+63	+14	Yaroslavl	200	+94	+89
Novgorod	51	+8	+19	Zhitomir	340	+92	+37
Novosibirsk	176	+103	+141	Total	12,823	+2,705	+27

Sources: Reports of local authorities to the Ministry of Justice of the Russian republic, supplemented by Russian Orthodox, Western, and official data of the authorities of the republics of the former Soviet Union. See Chapter 8, note 75.

state frankly that a large proportion of the churches are not yet repaired, in some cases not yet reclaimed from secular institutions and personal tenants, and not yet holding services. In Moscow, for example, Aleksi II stated in December 1992 that the patriarchate had 225 churches but added that services were being conducted in only 132 of them.[77] In Rostov diocese church leaders spoke in early 1993 about organizing icon-painting shops to supply "over 600 churches in the district" but noted that two-thirds of the churches were still awaiting restoration "to life."[78] In Saransk (Penza) diocese, church leaders reported that "in the past year the number of Orthodox parishes in Mordvinia reached seventy-seven" but churches for these parishes "have been turned over without roofs, with obliterated paintings and smashed iconostases."[79] In light of the foregoing, it is not difficult to understand why a diocese-by-diocese listing of functioning churches would diverge considerably from global figures mentioned by Russian Orthodox Church hierarchs.

Compared to the "stable" figures of the Brezhnev time before the Millennium, the number of functioning church societies in Kazakhstan, Central Asia, and Russia east of the Urals more than trebled in the period 1986–1994, from about 240 to more than 740. Russia west of the Urals achieved lesser but impressive relative gains, increasing from approximately 1,800 parishes in 1986 to over 4,600 parishes in 1994. Active parishes under Moscow's jurisdiction in Ukraine, about 5,700, accounted for about 45 percent of the parishes in the Russian Orthodox Church establishment, a marked shift from almost a half century of the parishes in Ukraine constituting about 60 percent of the total.

For a numerical listing of Orthodox societies between January 1945 and January 1994, see Table 8.2; for a graphical rendering of the same data, see Figure 8.1.[80]

TABLE 8.2   Number of Russian Orthodox Church Societies in the USSR or former constituent republics, 1945–1994 (beginning of year figures)

Year	Number	Year	Number
1945	14,100	1963	8,269
1946	10,504	1964	7,600
1947	14,039	1965	7,500
1948	14,191	1966	7,466
1949	14,421	1971	7,210
1950	14,273	1972	7,200
1951	13,867	1975	7,062
1952	13,740	1976	7,000
1953	13,508	1981	6,960
1954	13,422	1985	6,754
1955	13,376	1986	6,742
1956	13,417	1988	6,740
1957	13,430	1989	7,549
1958	13,415	1990	10,110
1959	13,325	1991	10,118
1960	12,964	1992	10,800
1961	11,571	1993	12,100
1962	9,986	1994	12,800

Source: The Central State Archive of the USSR for statistics to 1991, and the archives of the former republics of the USSR after 1991. See Chapter 8, note 80 for explanatory comments.

FIGURE 8.1
Russian Orthodox Church Societies in the USSR
or former constituent republics, 1945–1994

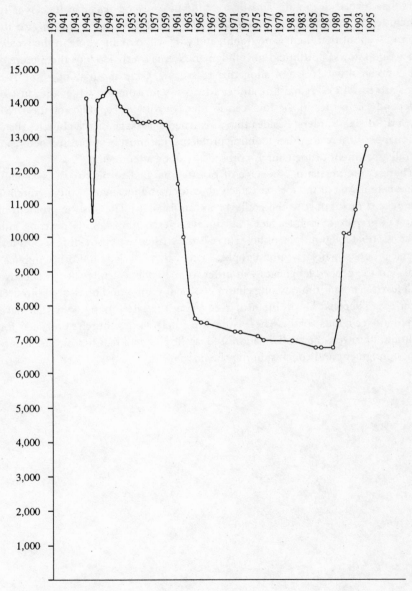

Aleksandr Nezhny, the famous commentator on Russian Orthodox Church affairs, has turned deeply pessimistic over the past several years. In June 1992 he
concluded in an article for *Russkaya Mysl* that the church "is crashing to the
ground—about that there is no doubt; and who will remain whole in the wreck-
age—God knows."[81] Although this judgment seems overly gloomy, the picture of
the church's situation is not altogether reassuring. Only about 5,000–5,500 parishes are certain of remaining under Moscow's jurisdiction when the dust of
independence settles in the fourteen former constituent republics of the USSR
beyond Russia's borders. Besides this threatened shrinkage of the church's institutional base, there are other looming problems that must be addressed before an
overall assessment of the church's prospects can be attempted.

There is the persisting shortage of priests qualified to fill parish vacancies.
There is the issue of the former catacomb church and its anger at the hierarchy's
long record of support to the godless communist state. There is the problem of
trying to prepare church leaders and educate priests, monks, nuns, deacons, and
other essential religious personnel. There is the challenge of providing scriptures,
liturgical books, scholarly monographs, catechistic materials, and other publications—in the needed languages—in order to make the teaching church effective
at all levels. There is the yawning chasm of absent money and unassured physical
resources. There is the problem of recovering the laity, many of whom have
drifted into religious apathy. These issues are crucial to the church's prospects for
health and growth; they will be addressed in the chapters that follow. Then, perhaps, a judgment and conclusion may be possible.

9
Russian Orthodox Clergy

SINCE WORLD WAR II, the Russian Orthodox Church has lacked a sufficient supply of clergy to staff its parish churches and meet the needs of Orthodox people in their long struggle to preserve their faith. The church emerged from the war with about 2,000 fewer priests than churches. This deficit has varied between approximately 1,000 and 3,000, and has been most in evidence in the western lands. Moreover, a large proportion of priests ordained in Soviet times have been the product of informal instruction and service as readers and psalmists rather than graduates of formal theological courses at seminaries and academies. The continuing deficit has deeply affected the nature and scale of cloistered monastic life, the nature and scale of theological education, and the church's ability to maintain a supply of deacons.

To set the stage, there were more than 50,000 Orthodox priests before the Russian Revolution; by mid-1939 there were no more than 300–400, although several thousand "laicized priests" were working in secular jobs after having been driven from their clerical positions.[1] In 1941 the Soviet government stated publicly that there were 5,665 serving priests of the Orthodox tradition.[2] Nearly all were clerics who had been absorbed in 1939–1940, along with their parishes, in what was then Estonia, Latvia, Lithuania, northern Bukovina, Bessarabia, and eastern Poland.

After Hitler's 1941 invasion, Orthodox priests came in behind the Germans from Poland, Romania, and other places. Some priests who had escaped to the West during Stalin's 1939–1940 annexations began to trickle back to their old homes, now occupied by the Wehrmacht. Others came out of hiding or resumed their calling, and new priests were consecrated from among psalmists and other church servers. As the Germans retreated, however, many priests from these lands fled with them.[3] On the Soviet side of the front lines, in the never-occupied territories, a relatively small number of priests had resumed their vocation.

After the Soviet annexation of Transcarpathia in 1945, about 100 priests of the formerly Czechoslovak Orthodox diocese of Mukachevo joined the Russian Orthodox Church, but this number of priests could not fully staff the 152 traditionally Orthodox parishes acquired at the same time; some of the priests in this territory had also fled. In early 1946, as the archives of the Council for Religious Affairs later revealed, there were an estimated 8,500 Orthodox priests in the country serving in 10,500 registered church societies, a shortfall of 2,000.[4]

The Council for Religious Affairs compiled statistics on the education, age, and time of ordination of Orthodox clergy in early 1946. Of the priests and deacons, only 3.5 percent had a university or theological academy degree; 39 percent more had graduated from a high school–level seminary, a ten-year public school, or a comparable high school; 57 percent—more than half—had not advanced beyond a basic primary school education. Eight percent of the priests and deacons were under forty-one years of age; 16 percent were forty-one to fifty; 31 percent were fifty-one to sixty; 33 percent were sixty-one to seventy; and 12 percent were over seventy. More were over seventy than under forty-one. Forty-six percent of the priests had been ordained before 1917, 30 percent had begun serving during World War II, and 24 percent had either been ordained in the interwar period or after World War II. Almost half of the clergy had been ordained before the Bolshevik revolution. Of the 264 priests and deacons in the Russian republic who had begun their clerical service during World War II, over 90 percent had been ordained in the occupied territories, and less than 10 percent, or twenty-four persons, had actually been ordained in the Soviet hinterland before the end of the war.[5]

In March 1946, when the Lvov council incorporated 2,500 Ukrainian Greek-Catholic parishes into Orthodoxy, only 1,000 Greek-Catholic priests became even nominally Orthodox. The total number of Orthodox priests in the country on January 1, 1948, was 11,800.[6] Despite the continuing efforts of Orthodox hierarchs to ordain devout laymen and close the gap, the increase in parishes was outpacing the ordination of priests, and the overall deficit of priests was about 2,400.

By 1949, with the forced incorporation of the Ukrainian Greek-Catholic Church in Transcarpathia, 400 more parishes had become part of the Russian Orthodox Church, but only about 100 priests had. Official figures indicate that on January 1, 1950, there were approximately 12,000 priests in the whole country and 14,300 Orthodox parishes; the deficit was 2,300.[7]

What areas suffered from this deficit? There was a shortfall of about 500 priests in eastern and central Ukraine, about 1,800 in western Ukraine (counting both former Greek-Catholic and Orthodox clerics), close to 150 in the Baltic states, and 250–300 each in Byelorussia and Moldavia. The shortfall in these areas was approximately 3,000, or 700 more than the nationwide deficit of 2,300. The deficit was lower at the national level because Moscow, for example, had at least 50 more priests than parishes. The extra priests worked in large churches, in the patriarchate's central offices, and in the academy and seminary at Zagorsk. In fact, most of the dioceses where theological schools were located had more priests than churches.[8] It was clear enough that the principal shortfalls were in the western lands annexed at the time of World War II and in other territories that had been occupied by the Germans.

The council's figures for the number of priests in the country dropped by almost 1,000 in 1950, to roughly 11,200. Stalin's decision to renew repression was in full swing by 1950, and many of these priests had either lost their authorizations to serve or had been arrested. Aged priests also continued to die, and new ordinations were being restricted. Some of those who ceased to be active were no doubt Greek-Catholics unwilling on reflection to serve under the Orthodox. The figures for western Ukraine dropped by 500 priests, half of the overall loss. In January of 1951 the overall deficit of priests in the country stood at 2,700, and the deficit in Ukraine alone stood at 2,800.[9]

Stalin died in March of 1953, and the number of priests in the country reached a low point of approximately 10,700 at the end of the year. In 1954 there was a modest turnaround, and by January of 1958 the authorities reported about 11,100 priests in the country—about 400 more priests than there had been on January 1, 1954.[10] Khrushchev's amnesties of the mid-1950s, which caused the release of a considerable number of clerics from Siberian camps, no doubt contributed to this increase.[11] Because the number of churches had held steady, the deficit dropped to 2,300—still a significant shortfall, of course, and concentrated as always in the western lands. There were only about four priests for every ten parishes in formerly Greek-Catholic areas.[12]

The council's statistics for January of 1958 for the entire Soviet Union revealed that 3,648 priests and deacons served in 1,491 city churches, 610 clergy served in 559 churches in factory towns, and 7,911 clergy served in 11,363 rural churches, for a shortfall of almost 3,500 priests and deacons in the village parishes. This meant that a third of the rural village churches in the USSR had no priest. It also meant that the city churches had an average of 2.4 priests and deacons per church.[13]

Between January of 1958 and January of 1960 the number of priests in the country declined by almost 900; three-fourths of the decline took place during 1959 as the Khrushchev antireligious drive was gathering momentum. The militant atheists were assiduously enticing priests to abandon their calling. Despite their efforts, informed Western scholars estimated that only about 200 priests joined the atheists in the half dozen years of the Khrushchev drive.[14] In January of 1960, 64 bishops, 10,236 priests, and 782 deacons were serving in 12,964 churches, for an overall deficit of 2,700 priests.[15] Thus the gains made between the time of Stalin's death and January 1958 had been wiped out, and the gap was again at the 1951 level.

The next half dozen years saw the ranks of priests in the USSR (including bishops) decline by about 3,400, from 10,200 in 1960 to 6,800 in January 1966; they were serving in about 7,500 churches.[16] The gap had been reduced to approximately 700, but only because about 2,000 more churches than priests were deregistered during those years of the Khrushchev antireligious drive. As described in Chapter 4, thousands of parishes in Ukraine that had no priest in 1960 were removed from the Soviet government's rolls of registered church societies permitted to hold services. Over half of the more than 3,000 priests deregistered after January of 1960 had been serving in Ukraine, and the persisting deficit was still concentrated there.[17] Because the surplus in 1958 of clergy over churches in cities and industrial towns was about 2,200, it must have been true even after the Khrushchev drive that the deficit of priests in village parishes was close to 2,000. In January 1966 there were only 1,327 priests to serve 2,267 parishes in the five Western Ukrainian oblasts of Lvov, Ternopol, Ivano-Frankovsk, Chernovtsy, and Transcarpathia.[18]

In central and eastern Ukrainian territories, about 60 percent of the churches were closed between 1958 and 1966, but the deregistration of priests was even more unsparing. The number of registered priests (including bishops) dropped from 2,446 to 865, a loss of about two-thirds. In Dnepropetrovsk oblast, of 167 priests ministering in 1958, 30 remained in January 1966; in Zaporozhe 9 of 92 priests remained; in Poltava 57 of 221 priests remained. These were not mere statistics; they represented immense human tragedy. In Zaporozhe province, where nine out of ten priests were driven from their vocation to dig ditches, sweep streets, or beg, most parishioners in the province were left with neither a priest nor a church.[19]

For every priest who retired in more normal times during the 1950s and after 1964, I calculated that 1.9 priests retired in 1960, 3.2 retired in 1961, 3.0 retired in 1962, 1.3 retired in 1963, and 1.2 retired in 1964.[20] This is consistent with the evidence that the Khrushchev drive peaked in overall intensity in 1961 and slackened during his last year in power.

In the five years between January of 1966 and January of 1971, the number of priests in the entire country declined by 100–150 a year to a level of 6,200 priests (and 600 deacons) in 1971. Between early 1971 and early 1975 the number declined at about half that rate, 60 a year, to 5,994 priests (and 594 deacons) at the beginning of 1975.[21] The rate of decline in the number of priests was close to the rate of church deregistrations, and the net deficit of priests for the country continued to range between 500 and 1,000.[22]

Between 1975 and early 1988 the number of priests held steady, hovering around 6,000. The number of churches continued to decline at the average rate of about 35 a year, and thus the net deficit of priests compared to churches was reduced to approximately 500. However, because of the city churches with several priests, clerics in the patriarchal administration, and priests in theological schools, 1,500–2,000 village churches must still have lacked priests, most of them as always in the western lands. For example, the bishop of Mukachevo stated in mid-1988 that 287 priests were serving in the 420 parishes of Transcarpathia.[23]

The numbers of seminary and academy graduates have not been sufficient over the years to replenish the ranks of the clergy, at least according to the statistics already given. But what do the graduation statistics reveal? Archbishop Aleksandr (Timofeev) stated on June 8, 1988, that 9,957 students had completed seminary between 1971 and 1988.[24] This would represent close to 600 graduates a year, and a credible estimate is that about 250–300 new Russian Orthodox priests with a theological school education entered the system each year between 1965 and 1988.[25]

Priests were leaving the system each year by retirement, death, or other reasons. Obituaries published in the *Journal of the Moscow Patriarchate* indicated that 100–200 priests were dying each year.[26] A considerable number of priests were retiring during the period between 1965 and 1988. The church had been relying since World War II on aged priests ordained before the revolution, on priests trained in Poland, Romania, and other lands not part of the USSR in the interwar period, and on church servers elevated without seminary training, many of them older men. Between 1965 and 1988 these men were retiring in large numbers. There was also a small outflow of priests deregistered by the Soviet government, although this was a trickle after the Khrushchev drive. Still, voluntary and involuntary retirements and deaths between 1965 and 1988 should have been balanced by the 250 educated priests entering the system and the numbers of devout laymen being ordained each year without formal training.

The overall body of the clergy was getting younger—a favorable development. The median age of the clergy peaked just before the Khrushchev antireligious drive and went steadily down until 1988. In 1930 the median age of the clergy had been about fifty, and the median age advanced to almost sixty in 1946.[27] By 1958, the median age had advanced still further, to sixty-three.[28] In 1975, however, it was once again just under sixty, and by 1988 it had dropped to forty-seven.[29] Loyal, aged priests carried the burden of the church through the postwar era, making up for the fact that the seminaries had been closed altogether between 1930 and 1944 and the opportunity for private instruction and learning at the altar had been virtually eliminated. Then, after the Khrushchev drive, seminary education slowly began to recover, as did informal instruction. If the conditions of the mid-1980s had continued without other variables entering the picture, the gap between the overall number of churches and priests would have closed.

Where were the graduates going? As already observed, many of the most ambitious ones were finding jobs in the patriarchal offices (particularly the Office of

Foreign Church Relations), in the seminaries and academies, or in the large city churches. Others became assistants to the great hierarchs, were assigned abroad, or started up the ladder to episcopal office (if they were monastics and academy graduates). Nevertheless, seminary graduates tended to go back to their home diocesees; if a bishop or his predecessor had not actively recruited young men to go to seminary, few graduates would return. ·

In early 1975 V. G. Furov, the vice chairman of the Council for Religious Affairs, informed the Central Committee of the Soviet Communist Party that just over 40 percent of the 5,994 priests in the country had no theological education (compared to 57 percent in 1946). Just under 40 percent had seminary training and 18 percent had academy training (compared to 3.5 percent in 1946).[30]

Some dioceses consistently have had greater or lesser percentages of seminary and academy graduates than the overall averages. Among the dioceses with a higher percentage of educated priests have been Moscow, St. Petersburg, Kiev, and Odessa and dioceses in the western lands, including Lvov, Ternopol, Ivano-Frankovsk, Chernovtsy, and Kishinev.[31] Furov cited the traditionally Greek-Catholic diocese of Lvov in particular, quoting the Council for Religious Affairs commissioner for Lvov oblast:

> The diocesan administration suffers from a great shortage of priests. . . . The clergy tries to resolve the shortfall by enticing young men to study in theological seminaries. Their attempts in that direction are not unsuccessful. In 1974 they were able to recruit forty-seven persons, i.e., about 30 percent of those in the Ukraine who expressed a desire to study in seminaries.[32]

As a matter of fact, Lvov has had more regular priests (*svyashchenniki*) who graduated from seminary than any other diocese, including even Moscow. Lvov has had about 15 percent of the country's seminary graduates but only about 7 percent of the country's priests. Furov reported that the council "took steps to restrict admissions to theological institutes from the western provinces of the Ukraine," although he noted that young men from Lvov oblast sometimes moved and found jobs in places as distant as Archangel in order to get around the restrictions.[33] Despite the council's punitive measures, almost half of the regular priests cited by the *Journal of the Moscow Patriarchate* as seminary graduates are from the six dioceses of western Ukraine.

These trends strengthen the conclusion that the Russian Orthodox Church has—at least until the early 1990s—lacked an effective system of allocating human resources; the church has failed to move priests (whether monastic clerics or regular priests graduating from seminary) to places where they are most needed. The diocesan bishops effectively run the church; if they are skillful, aggressive, and lucky, they may do well. Archbishop Chrysostom (Martishkin) of Kursk in the 1970s and Metropolitan Filaret (Vakhromeev) of Minsk in the 1980s virtually eliminated their huge deficits of priests, although they did it by ordaining devout laymen rather than by attracting large numbers of seminary graduates to their dioceses.

Senior clerics from widely separated locations have complained loudly over the years about not receiving substantial numbers of seminary and academy graduates and of grievous shortages of priests. The supply of such young clerics appears to have been particularly small in Siberia, Central Asia, eastern Ukraine and many of the historically renowned territories of the Russian republic. For example, in 1974 Archbishop Antoni (Vakarik) of Chernigov said: "In the past year . . . the Education Committee of the Moscow Patriarchate had not assigned a single priest to our diocese." He lamented that there were "no priests in forty-nine of the 148 congregations" in his diocese. Bishop Chrysostom (Martishkin) of Kursk complained that the theological schools "cannot supply clergy for the parishes"; Bishop Feodosi (Dikun) of Poltava was making a similar complaint in 1977.[34] More recently, in 1989, Archbishop Feodosi (Protsyuk) of Omsk bemoaned the fact that "in the past two years not a single graduate of the theological schools has come to us to serve. . . . I consecrate devout laymen as clerics in the thought that they can then study theology in the correspondence division."[35]

For a diocesan bishop who has almost half his parishes lacking a priest, seminary training clearly cannot be relied upon to solve the problem, no matter how assignments are managed. It takes about six years for a newly recruited student to apply to and finish seminary and to return to serve a parish. This was true in 1988, and since 1988 the personnel crisis has become all-encompassing. Nevertheless, improved management of assignments could help.

In 1990 the patriarchate finally moved to strengthen the church's authority to assign seminary and academy graduates to places where the need was greatest. With Patriarch Aleksi's approval, Archbishop Aleksandr (Timofeev) of Dmitrov, the head of the Holy Synod's committee on instruction and rector of the Moscow theological schools, asserted the right to assign seminary and academy graduates as the church's situation required. He noted that the practice until 1990 had been to return graduates to their home dioceses but that in future the seminaries and theological training institutes, which desperately needed competent instructors, would have first call on academy graduates. A resolution establishing central authority in assignments was signed on August 27, 1990. Diocesan bishops, who had previously not fully "understood" the problem, would be obliged to accommodate themselves to the new arrangement.[36]

I should say another word about the indomitable old men who continued to serve as active priests through their eighties and even nineties. The *Journal of the Moscow Patriarchate* printed the obituaries of one old gentleman who died, still on active service, at the age of ninety-four and of another who retired at the age of ninety-seven. Another venerable archpriest served in the same parish fifty-two years and was credited with having inspired over fifty of his parishioners to enter church service.[37] There is something marvelous about the visages of the ancient clerics pictured now and then in the *Journal* with the notation that they celebrated the liturgy on the day they died or even that they collapsed in the sanctuary in the act of glorifying the name of God.

The fortunes of the church began to improve as the millennial year progressed. The number of priests in the country increased at an accelerating pace after the Gorbachev-Pimen meeting in April of 1988. On June 7, 1988, Metropolitan Vladimir (Sabodan) of Rostov reported that there were approximately 6,600 bishops and priests in the USSR—about 600 more than at the start of the year.[38] In the 1988–1989 period the deficit of priests compared to parishes began to increase again, however, particularly in the western lands. Numerous societies were being registered and churches were being turned over by the authorities, but the church did not have the priests to staff them. It was a time of benign turmoil. In Moldavia, the number of registered Orthodox societies had tripled to almost 600 by September of 1989, compared to a figure of slightly under 200 registered societies before the Millennium. The diocese had only about 370 "church workers" in September of 1989, however, and many of them were not ordained priests.[39] In early October 1989, the Russian Orthodox Church had a net deficit of approximately 2,450 priests, as compared to 7,150 priests actually serving.[40] Thus almost 4,000 village churches were once again without a priest.

There were significant developments in the late 1980s in the Greek-Catholic areas of western Ukraine. Estimates vary of how many nominally Orthodox priests returned to their Catholic obedience when they had the chance in late 1989 and early 1990, but the number appears to have been approximately 350 in January 1990 with considerable additional numbers passing over in subsequent months.[41] Moreover, by the spring of 1990 several hundred priests had defected to the Ukrainian Autocephalous Orthodox Church, and hundreds more transferred their allegiance as the year progressed. Defections of Orthodox clerics to the Russian Orthodox Church Abroad, although not significant numerically, were also occurring. At the end of 1990 there were approximately 6,000 Russian Orthodox priests in service, compared to more than 7,000 a year earlier.[42] On the other hand, even greater losses of parishes to the Russian Orthodox Church's competitors in western Ukraine produced—in a way not in the least desired by the patriarchal church—a mitigation of the deficit in the number of priests.

Many of the roughly 2,000 Russian Orthodox priests brought into active service in 1988 and 1989 were retired clerics. I can attest to this fact from my visits to churches and from conversations with priests. In June of 1988, Metropolitan Vladimir stated that 4,007 church servers were receiving a pension.[43] My estimate is that 2,500 of these pensioners were ordained priests, and perhaps half of these retired priests had the strength and vigor to return to service. The available pool of such willing and able retirees was probably almost empty, however, by late 1989.

Over the years I have recorded the names and locations of roughly 5,500 living priests and 2,800 deceased priests whose obituaries have appeared in the *Journal of the Moscow Patriarchate*. These data provide information on about two-thirds of the presently serving priests and on most of the retired priests or those who have died in the past thirty years. These statistics indicate that slightly over 10 percent of the priests serving in the dioceses are monastic clergy.

Metropolitan Nikolai (Yarushevich) once explained to Francis House of the World Council of Churches that the paucity of cloistered monastic priests and the greater number of monastic priests working out in the parishes "was partly because so many congregations preferred monks to married priests."[44] If this was a part of the explanation, it was a very small part of it, as the shortage of regular parish clergy was what forced the monastic clergy into parish work. Of the monastic clergy in the dioceses, 15–20 percent hold the episcopal office, 20–25 percent have the rank of archimandrite, 25–30 percent have the rank of hegumen, 20–25 percent are monastic priests (*ieromonakhi*), and less than 5 percent are monastic deacons or simple monks. Of the nonmonastic priests, about 3 percent are mitered archpriests, 48 percent are nonmitered archpriests, and 49 percent are simple priests. About 20 percent of the deacons are archdeacons in rank.

Church publications occasionally have referred to a priest serving two or more parishes at the same time, mostly in the western lands and Ukraine. This practice continued in those areas throughout the postwar period—except during the Khrushchev drive—even though the decree of April 8, 1929, had made such dual service illegal. The reason for this double duty was the shortage of priests.

Even in places where the parish has a full-time priest, the man is often stretched very thin. A correspondent for the *Moscow Church Herald, Weekly* interviewed a number of young Pentecostals who had come from Orthodox families. Their explanations for having become sectarians revolved around the fact that the Pentecostal presbyter of a relatively small community knew everybody, had time for all, and was available to respond to any question. In contrast, even though the Orthodox sanctuary was more beautiful and the service more affecting, the priest was always surrounded by hundreds of the faithful and physically unable to give his attention to the concerns and doubts of young people seeking answers. According to these converts, it was difficult even to get close enough to the priest in the throng to talk to him.[45]

There is also a widespread phenomenon of commuter priests—priests who do not live in their parishes but commute from more distant places to celebrate the liturgy and perform other services. For example, Archpriest Georgi Studenov was reported in the spring of 1990 to have been commuting every day for over a year to his newly opened church in southwestern Moscow from Zagorsk (now Sergiev Posad), seventy-five kilometers northeast of the city.[46] Evidently he could not find suitable housing or get the necessary permission to live in the capital. He must have spent several hours a day, at least, getting back and forth. Priests serving rural parishes may also commute because there is no house available in the village or, by choice, because the amenities are better in a larger community, because there is work for their wives, because there is adequate schooling for their children, or for other reasons.

In a confidential lecture given in March of 1988 to the Communist Higher Party School in Moscow, Konstantin Kharchev noted with satisfaction that a "new type" of Russian priest was coming to the fore who was "not tied to his flock," who came "from a different place," who was often "of a different nationality," and who "drives to church once a week."[47] Orthodox spokesmen described the same phenomenon with less satisfaction: "The rural pastor who lives with the people and among the people is a type that is, alas, rapidly disappearing," said one.[48] Another observer, Archpriest Vladimir Rozhkov of Moscow, commented:

> The clergy is not altogether ready for service in the new conditions. Often priests live far from the church, even outside the city, and hurry home when services are over. In truth, half of the clerics in Moscow come from outside the city. At the same time many priests who live in Moscow serve in the suburbs and even in the Kalinin [Tver], Kaluga, Vladimir and other dioceses. . . . This is not conducive to the strengthening of the parish.[49]

As already observed in connection with seminarians, most priests and deacons return to their dioceses after being sent abroad or on interdiocesan assignments. A few priests do move from diocese to diocese permanently, either on their own initiative or to meet a need elsewhere, but few priests who are in good standing with their bishops and the authorities do so. Monastic clergy serving in the parishes do not move around much either. Perhaps the governmental authorities, at least in the Soviet era, discouraged or forbade such transfers. In any case, the dioceses with large deficits of priests do not seem to have larger than average numbers of monastic clergy. The priest-starved diocese of Ivano-Frankovsk, for example, had an extraordinarily small number of monastic clergy serving there even before the upheaval led by the Greek-Catholics.

The Russian Orthodox clergy working abroad are a mixture of priests sent out on assignment by the patriarchate and priests of the host country's nationality. In Latin America priests bear such names as Sanchez, Chacon, and Duran; U.S. priests are named Shinn, Odell, and Waters. There are not enough nationals of the various host countries to staff the Russian Orthodox parishes located abroad, however, and considerable numbers of priests must be sent out.

The surnames of Orthodox priests in Russia reflect the fact that whole extended families are in the priesthood, generation after generation. There are Dzichkovskis, Kolyadas, Gogolushkos, and Protsyuks by the score, clearly with sons, brothers, cousins, nephews, and grandsons in the priesthood. It may have been a strength of the Russian Orthodox Church that the regular priesthood is not celibate, as religion always set a young man apart in the former Soviet society, and the sons of priests may have grown up accustomed to the special pressures and ostracism in the lives of the religiously committed.

This separateness of the priests has often manifested itself in a kind of diffidence, a protective shell that Russian Orthodox priests carried with them and perhaps still do. Many a time I have watched a priest walk by, even in church, clearly avoiding eye contact. Observers have written that perestroika left priests responding "like moles thrust into daylight." Michael Bourdeaux commented in the mid-1960s: "I did not meet as many priests as I had intended, because they seem to be the most elusive individuals in the Soviet Union. . . . It was almost impossible to engage monks in conversation." Interestingly, authors in the church's own publications have echoed the same judgment, even in recent years: "Seminary graduates are timid and notoriously guarded in their contacts with the secular world."[50] It is hardly surprising, of course, that Russian Orthodox priests schooled themselves in caution.

Despite the diffidence mentioned here, priests have also demonstrated great courage and impressive public presence. *Moscow News* reported in late 1990 that 192 Orthodox priests had succeeded in being elected as people's deputies at some level of government in the previous two years.[51] The roster of courageous, fearless priests is long. Some, like Father Nikolai Eshliman, have died; others, like Deacon Vladimir Rusak, have emigrated; but many remain and the list is growing. They have included men who will surely someday be recognized as saints, such as Fathers Tavrion (Batozski), Sergi Zheludkov, and Aleksandr Men, Archbishop Luka (Voino-Yasenetski), and many others.

Figure 9.1 traces the trend lines for the number of priests and parishes in the USSR and successor states between 1945 and 1993 and shows the gap, or deficit of priests, as it widened, narrowed, and widened again over the years. The reality in the east of the Russian republic has been a population spread out over immense spaces with almost no churches, but in the western lands it has been a relative abundance of churches and an immense deficit of priests.[52]

FIGURE 9.1

Trends in the Number of Churches and Priests in the USSR and Successor States

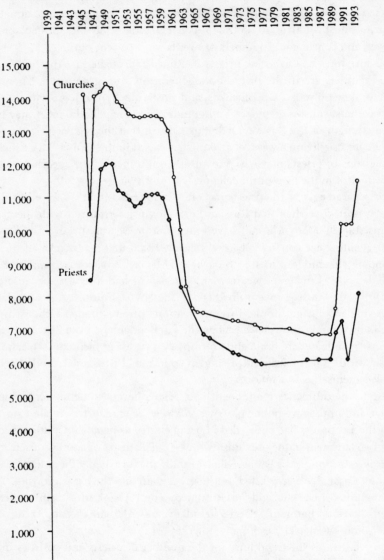

Sources: Reports of provincial commissioners of the Council for Religious Afairs in the Central State Archive, now of the Russian republic, supplemented by other reports of local authorities, Russian Orthodox hierarchs' statements, Western data, and other Soviet and Soviet successor state reporting. See Chapter 8, notes 75 and 80, and Chapter 9, note 52.

10

Illegal and Underground Orthodox Religion

FRANCIS HOUSE, a distinguished student of Russian Orthodoxy, estimated that there were 48 million clandestine Christians in Brezhnev's time.[1] A Russian Orthodox priest in Moscow, Father Sergi Popov, expressed a different view about the Brezhnev era: "The 'catacomb' Church, thanks to the diligent 'work' done by the KGB . . . is practically non-existent."[2]

One reason for the immense difference in these perceptions lies in what is meant by clandestine religion. In one sense, when two Christians in the former USSR met and shared their discontents, that could have been regarded as an underground. I asked a young Komsomol leader I met in Murmansk in 1987 whether he had ever been to church. He smiled and said: "Yes. I went to church when I was on vacation last year on the Black Sea." In its way, that was concealed religion. The practice of Soviet citizens slipping into church in a strange town to attend services among strangers was widespread, at least until the millennial year. It was so common, in fact, that the authorities stationed agents in the churches in resort towns to maintain surveillance. My wife and I went into the Alexander Nevsky church in Yalta in June of 1985 and were approached by a woman who was clearly working for the KGB. Her interest in us was so pointed, her effort to draw us into an illegal currency transaction was so obvious, and her attempt to follow us was so crude that we had to recognize her as an agent. The attitude of the faithful babushkas replacing candles and cleaning the church floor was also too contemptuous to leave any doubt.

Whole parishes have subsisted "out of discipline" at various times in the past. After Sergi's loyalty oath of 1927, numerous local churches continued to function as part of the regular Russian Orthodox establishment but did not commemorate Sergi or the national authority in the liturgy.[3] After World War II the *Journal of the Moscow Patriarchate* made occasional references to "disorganizers" of discipline and to persons who "are called only by themselves Orthodox Christians."

Patriarch Aleksi (Simanski) rebuked believers "who take it upon themselves to judge their appointed shepherds."[4] Such churches and priests were in various degrees of rebellion against the patriarchal church and the communist state, but they existed overtly and were not a "catacomb" church in any real sense.

Between the mid-1960s and the mid-1980s, considerable numbers of lay intellectuals participated in religious discussion groups, seminars, and prayer circles.[5] Some of these were informal, spontaneous meetings. In the Brezhnev era the authorities issued KGB warnings and exerted other pressures to curb such activities. Sometimes the intimidation would work and the meetings would stop. Other gatherings were not so quickly discovered nor their members so easily cowed, and they developed into organized groups, which disseminated religious materials, sent protest letters, and distributed samizdat. People following this road, such as Anatoli Levitin-Krasnov, Aleksandr Ogorodnikov, and Vladimir Poresh were arrested and spent years in prison or the labor camps. Boris Talantov and many others died there. Although the line may have been unclear at the margin between groups of Christians meeting informally and the underground church, there is no question that Ogorodnikov's and Poresh's Christian seminar and similar groups became part of a catacomb church. Such religious activities were mostly a phenomenon of the cities, where there were concentrations of urban intellectuals.

In rural areas, village life went on largely unseen, and in the hundreds of thousands of communities in the country that lacked a church there were many pious Christians who maintained an Orthodox religious practice as best they could. They relied on family, believing neighbors, icons that had been preserved or procured, and such other religious materials as they could obtain. I remember talking in the spring of 1990 with a young physicist working at Akademgorodok outside Novosibirsk. He told me he had grown up spending his summers with his grandparents in the village of Lebyazhe, Kurgan oblast, where his grandmother was a devout believer. The nearest church was forty kilometers away, but his grandmother did works of charity in town and sheltered Christians passing through, sometimes for as long as a month. The result was that the physicist's grandparents lost their pensions. "Life was hard," he said.

The hidden practice of religion, as opposed to a formal underground church, may also include duly registered clergy who work in legally recognized parishes but who perform weddings in absentia, blessing a wedding ring sent by mail from afar, or who perform funeral services over a bit of earth taken from a grave and then returned to it.[6] William C. Fletcher cited Soviet academic studies indicating that the majority of funerals in some communities were performed in this fashion in the Brezhnev era.[7] That official Soviet statistics reflect this fact somewhat vitiates the impression that this form of religion was truly hidden from scrutiny.[8] Soviet government sources frequently complained that "older, more conservative and fanatical priests" traveled to outlying churchless areas to minister to believers' needs and to perform rites in private dwellings.[9]

In the mid-1950s I conducted a modest interview program among Russians who had just departed the Soviet Union. The descriptions of three of those interviewed follow:

> My father died and was given a civil burial. After a few days, through a friend, I arranged to meet a priest on a street corner. A nondescript man came up and said, "I think you wanted me" and walked on in silence to the cemetery. A third person followed at some distance. At the cemetery the priest opened his coat and showed that he was in clerical robes. The third man came up and assisted him in the service. After the service I paid the priest and we parted. . . .
>
> I approached an old woman in the cemetery where my mother was buried. She found me a priest who frequented the place for such purposes. . . .
>
> A government inspector came to a collective farm I was visiting. He turned out to be a priest and he baptized a group of children there.[10]

These were not dramatic stories; they were part of normal life, and such events still occur in places where churches are lacking. Pospielovsky commented that the "catacomb" church may include citizens who disagree with the policies of the patriarchate yet accept the sacramental validity of its clergy and turn to "pastors of the official church whom they personally trust."

The priests who served this great private "congregation" during the Soviet era had varied backgrounds. During and after the Khrushchev antireligious drive, thousands of priests were deprived of the official registration that enabled them to function legally in their vocation. Such a priest's first recourse was to go to another diocese and see if the bishop would give him a parish and whether the local commissioner of the Council for Religious Affairs would let him be registered. If the commissioner of the priest's previous district pursued him with papers that became a blackball, the priest would then be outside the law, and many such priests became "wandering priests" visiting faithful where there were no churches and performing rites without reporting them. This often suited the needs of laypeople afraid of being revealed as believers. In this way a large semi-underground church was formed. Most of the priests remained in good ecclesiastical standing with the bishops and the patriarchate. Some of them even settled down in the locality where their parish church had been closed and opened a prayer house, and carried on more or less as before.[11]

There also were priests who, for one reason or another, had to divorce themselves from their bishops or the patriarchal church hierarchy. This resulted later in some attempts by priests to shift allegiance to the Russian Orthodox Church Abroad, claiming the catacomb heritage of the True Orthodox Church and the True Orthodox Christians.

The authorities usually were quite well informed about unauthorized religious

activity in this semiunderground. Many of the sources of information about unregistered priests were Soviet officials or scholars publishing openly in the USSR.
In the mid-1940s, inspectors of the Soviet government's Council for Russian Orthodox Church Affairs began to report matter-of-factly on unregistered priests
conducting services in homes and unregistered church societies commencing activities without authorization.[12] Local commissioners of the council sometimes
gave statistics on illegal church societies in their districts.[13] The *Handbook of the
Propagandist and Agitator* printed countrywide statistics and descriptive material
on unregistered religious societies.[14] Konstantin Kharchev, the former chairman
of the council, spoke frankly in interviews about illegal church activities and "underground" religious communities.[15] Father Petr Bolshakov wrote in 1990 that
the local police very often knew about the existence of the underground church:
"Some tried to root it out; others looked the other way." According to Bolshakov,
young monks were made to get jobs, but the authorities were more tolerant of
old men, even in the Brezhnev era.[16] The *Journal of the Moscow Patriarchate* even
reported in print on unregistered priests serving illegally in unregistered parishes
with the sure knowledge of local authorities who must have acquiesced or closed
an eye.[17] Consequently, it cannot be assumed that illegal activities, priests, communities and parishes were necessarily truly secret and unknown to the Soviet
authorities.[18] Apprehension, arrest, and public exposure of the activists sometimes depended on pressures, moods, politics, and strategies within the Soviet
government.

By the late 1980s the dissident unregistered Baptists had existed overtly for a
quarter of a century, at some periods even outnumbering the legal registered
Baptist communities. The famous Orthodox dissident priest Gleb Yakunin once
proposed that the Orthodox embark on a similar course. He made a clear distinction between unregistered communities and catacomb or underground ones,
pointing out that parishes refusing registration "do not hide themselves from the
state."[19]

The prisons and labor camps long constituted a setting for unauthorized religious activity, different in kind from the various forms of overt, defiant or
semiclandestine religious practice described in the preceding section. William
Fletcher, Aleksandr Solzhenitsyn, John Noble, Michael Bourdeaux, and many
others told poignant tales of courageous prisoner-priests holding whispered services in three-man railroad cages, freezing barracks, rock quarries, the bottoms
of mine shafts, and abandoned coal galleries.[20] Andrei Sinyavski (Abram Terts)
spoke of "many shades of Orthodoxy" in the camps in the 1970s.[21] Dimitry
Pospielovsky described a Kolyma camp prisoner's encounter with four priests in
the mines:

One day three of the priests were driven away in a lorry. Fear . . . spread among the remaining inmates . . . who included regular criminals. It was then that Father Sergi spoke to them all for the first time.

And all the bandits and murderers listened to his every word in utter silence. He spoke on the futility and poverty of our life, on the eternal blessedness that awaits those who will repent. All this was so new and unusual to the audience, that it appeared as if someone else was speaking through his lips.

Of the other three priests only one, Father Rafail, returned. He said they [the priests and two laymen] had been taken to a hut and asked one by one to deny Christ or else they would be shot. Not one of them agreed. . . . All except Father Rafail were shot in his presence. Father Rafail was told to bury them and then, for some reason, taken back to the camp.[22]

Whether the authorities had cause for serious concern about the Orthodox religious underground in confinement is arguable, as the prisoners of conscience who were inmates were already perceived to be deviant and had been removed from normal pursuits. Religious detainees were not wholly insulated from the general population, however, as some imprisoned bishops and priests successfully maintained contact with members of their flock at liberty.[23] Moreover, priests in the camps influenced other inmates, and these prisoners were sometimes released. Sooner or later some of the surviving priests were themselves released.

The prison camps constituted important recruiting grounds for Christian converts. Ivan M. Andreev noted that worship services and the sacraments were more frequently available to the prison population than to members of free society in the late 1930s.[24] John Noble, who was an inmate at the Vorkuta camp, observed that many prisoners first learned of Christianity in the camps.

By the time the believing camp inmates returned to society, they had learned a great deal about concealment. Fletcher described how the camps served as a sort of "theological seminary" for underground Orthodoxy:

> Living conditions in the labour camps necessitated the use of clandestine techniques. . . . Thus the mechanics of underground religious practices—services held in secret, methods which could be used to avoid detection, production of items necessary for divine services from materials at hand, independent organization of religious life in the absence of a functioning hierarchy, etc.—were learned by every active believer in the prison population. Experience in the camps could be applied directly to the organization of underground religious life upon release from confinement.[25]

The camps taught believers self-reliance. The experience also taught interconfessional cooperation in conditions of common adversity. There is some evidence that the inmates from the western lands—Poles, Ukrainians, and those from the Baltic states—were "more bold" than prisoners from the Soviet heartland in organizing worship.[26] This would support the conclusion that the added decades of Soviet rule in the old and never-occupied regions of the USSR had taken their toll in constricting religious life.[27]

Another aspect of the prison camp phenomenon was that a large proportion of the inmates, when they were released, were confined to internal exile in far corners of the USSR, often close to the camps and in inhospitable living conditions. These colonies of former camp inmates manifested a high number of adherents of outlawed sects, dissident True Orthodox believers, and illegally operating Orthodox parishes.[28]

The third sector of underground religion in the former Soviet Union is the classically defined Orthodox underground—illegal, secret, vigorously dealt with when apprehended, and separated entirely from the patriarchal church. Even under this definition, however, there is still a distinction between the integrated, coordinated, fully organized national movements with extensive communications and systematic leadership structures and the more amorphous, isolated, cellular, informal, flexibly organized communities.

In *The Russian Orthodox Church Underground, 1917–1970*, William Fletcher characterized the True Orthodox Church as representing the structured pattern and the True Orthodox Christians as representing the more flexible one. This is an oversimplification of Fletcher's analysis, but the distinction has validity.[29] Fletcher's description is notable for showing that the highly structured, nationally organized True Orthodox Church was effectively destroyed in the years after Stalin reverted to a harsh antireligious policy in 1948. Fletcher concluded: "By the early fifties it would appear that the True Orthodox Church no longer existed as an organized movement in the USSR. . . . The organized, disciplined True Orthodox Church was defunct." In contrast, the True Orthodox Christians benefited in a relative sense from their nonhierarchical organizational arrangements in their struggle for survival. Their movement has endured through the years until the present day, even though the True Orthodox Christians lost about half their numerical strength in the antireligious drive of Stalin's last years.[30]

Both branches of the True Orthodox movement developed in reaction to Metropolitan Sergi's 1927 loyalty declaration to the Soviet state. Neither branch was heretical or doctrinally schismatic by intention; the True Orthodox were simply outraged at Sergi's "sinful" political submission to the godless.[31]

Their political orientation led the True Orthodox down a hazardous road. Effectively, it allied them with political forces that sought to overthrow the Soviet state. Patriarch Tikhon had avoided this course of action, despite the furious church-state struggles that characterized the period between 1917 and 1925. Moreover, there is an important difference between a political resistance movement and an underground church, and the True Orthodox did not always observe it. As time went on, however, the True Orthodox oriented themselves more strictly to religious practice, although they tried to separate themselves from membership in collective farms, work in state-run industry, service in the military, and participation in public schooling above the earliest grades.[32]

The True Orthodox Christians turned to lay pastors when the supply of underground priests dwindled, both in the 1930s and as the Khrushchev drive gained force in the 1950s. The fact that the children of clergy had been legally barred from higher education until the promulgation of the constitution of 1936 meant that a natural supply of lay pastoral leadership was available, as these often talented people were both religiously oriented and alienated from the general society and its opportunities.[33]

Some of the offshoot communities of the True Orthodox Christians withdrew to live as hermits in the deep forest (the *skrytniki*); others took vows of silence in order not to betray their faith to the forces of the Antichrist (*molchalniki*); still others renounced life itself and committed suicide. The most active offshoot became that of the True Orthodox Christian Wanderers (*stranniki*)—itinerant, apocalyptic religious pilgrims whose practices and rites stand somewhere between the traditions of the Orthodox and the Old Believers. In fact, the similarities are striking between the mutations in practice characteristic of certain Old Believers in the periods of extreme persecution after the great schism of 1667 and the changes in Orthodox practice adopted by the True Orthodox Christians. They include (1) a certain antimodernism, or freezing of doctrinal belief; (2) priestless leadership, including lay administration of the Eucharist, dictated by necessity and contrasting with the conservatism just noted; (3) the renunciation of marriage, caused in part by the vulnerability of children to state reprisal and by apocalyptic expectations; (4) a tendency to adopt somewhat aberrant practices, including some of those associated with the Khlysty; and (5) an increase in the role of women, characteristic of both branches of the True Orthodox and also seen in the patriarchal church itself in its most beleaguered times.[34]

Several commentators have described the divisions within the contemporary True Orthodox community. To review a bit of history, Patriarch Tikhon (Belavin) secretly ordained Bishop Serafim (Pozdeev) in early 1925. In 1956, after more than thirty years in the camps, Serafim settled in Buzuluk, now Orenburg oblast, and consecrated Bishop Gennadi (Sekach) shortly before Serafim's death in 1971. Serafim had obtained the written agreement of another True Orthodox bishop, Alfei, before performing the ordination. Gennadi was later elevated to the dignity of metropolitan by Georgian and True Orthodox prelates at Christmas services in the underground vaults of a prison in Tbilisi.

Gennadi spent much of his life as a wandering prelate, reportedly founding twelve secret monasteries and consecrating over 500 monks. He consecrated his

nephew Grigori as a bishop, and Grigori subsequently was elevated to the rank of
metropolitan. Grigori was said to be cordial, simple, and pure in heart. His singing was exquisitely beautiful, as if inspired by the angels. Metropolitan Gennadi
also consecrated another monk, Feodosi, as bishop, and he was also elevated to
the dignity of metropolitan. In the Brezhnev era the three metropolitans lived in
a secluded house and grounds protected by a high fence. Faithful wanderers came
from afar, some of them very simple folk but others highly educated, even hold-
ers of doctoral degrees.

When the metropolitans left their fenced-in quarters, they disguised themselves as women, wearing skirts and shawls. Even so, the authorities harassed
them and on one occasion a local newspaper published a slanderous article
about them. Metropolitan Gennadi died in 1987, and his nephew also died, leaving Metropolitan Feodosi and another senior True Orthodox prelate, Metropolitan Yepifani, as leaders of this branch of the church.[35]

True Orthodox services were and are usually held in private homes, and the
strength of this branch is largely concentrated in the Kuban, the Urals area,
Belarus, and Ukraine. It has an ascetic tradition that recalls the spiritual dedication of the Optina hermitage. This branch of True Orthodoxy is also said to pre-
dominate in the Mother of God Center in Moscow, although that religious-
nationalist establishment has its roots in direct "revelations" made to Father
Ioann (Bereslavski).

A subgroup of Metropolitan Gennadi's branch of True Orthodoxy apparently
broke away in the summer of 1990. Without the blessing of other True Orthodox
prelates, two True Orthodox bishops, Isaaki and Antoni, consecrated Harion and
Afanasi as vicar-bishops to represent Isaaki. Bishops Isaaki and Antoni were de-
frocked in consequence, and their two consecrations were pronounced invalid by
a council of four bishops and several priests meeting in Belarus on January 15,
1991.[36]

Commissioners of the Council for Religious Affairs were reporting small-scale
activity in the 1980s on the part of the True Orthodox. For example, the commissioner for the Altai in Siberia reported two recognized Orthodox communities in
1986 and three additional communities of True Orthodox Christians, who were
engaged in what he described as "increased activity." In Kazakhstan, the commissioner reported a single True Orthodox Christian community in Turgai. In
Ukraine and European Russia, on the other hand, commissioners reported True
Orthodox activity decreasing as the 1970s ended and the early 1980s passed.[37]

Even now, however, scattered parishes and True Orthodox communities are
known to exist throughout the territories of the former USSR. A group of about
ten True Orthodox priests ordained by Bishop Antoni (Golynski), who died in
1976, is said to have some large parishes. In addition, there is a group of "pass-
portless" True Orthodox, who refuse to carry internal identity documents; they

are reported to number some thousands scattered in Russian provinces west of the Urals and in Siberia. Their bishop, Feodosi (Bakhmetev), died in 1986; he was succeeded by Bishop Guri, a Chuvash monk in his mideighties who was consecrated in Boston, Massachusetts, on July 28, 1991, by prelates of a branch of the True Orthodox Church in Greece.[38]

As described in previous chapters, there have been cases when priests and faithful have broken with arrogant or maladroit diocesan bishops, transferring their obedience to the Russian Orthodox Church Abroad. Some of these dissident communities classify themselves as True Orthodox, although most of them now say they are members of the Russian Orthodox Free Church. Other True Orthodox have sought ties with the Ukrainian Autocephalists and Greek-Catholics, usually unsuccessfully.[39]

According to Vladimir Moss, in 1976 the Russian Orthodox Church Abroad began to shift its support from the historical underground True Orthodox to the dissident priests who had broken away from the patriarchal church or had become disaffected. Moss reported that the authorities of the Russian Orthodox Church Abroad rejected the legitimacy of the ordination of a long list of catacomb priests in August of 1990, and that this caused "distress and division" among True Orthodox communities throughout the Soviet Union.[40]

There is little question that the True Orthodox are fragmented. There are monarchists among them who long for a restored Romanov czar; there are young "Westernizer" bishops; and there are Slavophiles in the tradition of Aleksei Khomyakov, Konstantin Aksakov, and Aleksandr Solzhenitsyn, the thundering voice of Great Russian nationalism in our time.

One religious community has made a great witness to the ability of an underground church to survive. The Ukrainian Greek-Catholic Church has been able to consecrate a shadow hierarchy in secret, celebrate the mass in abandoned and concealed churches, organize small monasteries and nunneries in the deep forests, and sustain the loyalty of millions of faithful. Does this mean that there might exist and have long existed an Orthodox catacomb church just as powerful, operating throughout the length and breadth of the USSR and subsequently in its successor states? Might the reality be that the rest of the world simply did not and does not even now know of it?

This is somewhat unlikely, as the Ukrainian Greek-Catholics (Uniates) are special in a number of ways. They are part of Roman Catholicism, a great, worldwide institution, which has helped sustain the Ukrainian Greek-Catholics in adversity despite extreme difficulties and some ambivalence over policy in Rome.[41] They are also located in the lands annexed by the USSR at the time of World War II and did not endure over seventy years of communist antireligious action as did the Orthodox in the Russian heartland. Other religious communities in the western lands have also withstood Bolshevik pressures better than the religious communities in the territories never occupied by the Germans. Moreover, since 1945 the Ukrainian Greek-Catholics have stood as a continuing symbol of Ukrainian nationalism against perceived Russian imperial rule, and that nationalism has become a powerful force.

A fully developed underground church did not simply rise to aboveground status in 1990. The impressive Ukrainian Greek-Catholic institutional structure seen in the 1990s had not been the reality in the days of most extreme repression. Vasyl Markus described the situation in 1984:

> The followers are organized informally around unregistered priests, itinerant monks or nuns, and activist lay people. . . . Secret bishops have their eparchial territories, although they may live as workers or pensioners in a small village. . . .
>
> Soviet sources report on "secret seminaries," that are in reality no more than private training courses. . . . A great deal of pastoral work is done by the nuns. They usually live in small communities and earn their living as factory workers, medical personnel, or workers on collective farms. Their identities are, in most cases, known to the authorities. Because they do exemplary work . . ., they are harassed but usually tolerated. Still, from time to time arrests do occur. The priests are watched, called to police stations, fined, and even arrested. . . .
>
> It seems that there is a tacit understanding on the local level that if religious activities of the recalcitrant Uniates are not provocative, are not widely known, and are conducted semiprivately (e.g. celebration of the Holy Mass at a private home), they can be overlooked. Periodic imprisonments, searches, trials, public "unmaskings" of illegal activities serve to compel, or at least encourage, the Uniates to restrict themselves to low-key and subdued religious work.
>
> Along with the moderate underground Uniate church, there are more radical followers to Uniatism . . . whose fanatical spokesmen disagree with the . . . hierarchical Uniate church . . . anathematizing Rome for its cooperation with "Antichrist."[42]

It is reminiscent of the plight of the Orthodox in the 1920s that the Greek-Catholics, too, had their breakaway dissidents who were outraged at the "soft" stance toward the Soviet regime of Greek-Catholics in western Ukraine and Catholic authorities in Rome. It was not that the Greek-Catholics actually were "soft," but their hierarchs did have to suffer criticism from more militant coreligionists. More broadly, the foregoing excerpts are notable for their believable descriptions of the apparent state of affairs in 1984; for their intimations that the Ukrainian Greek-Catholic underground was somewhat comparable to other catacomb churches in the USSR in earlier times; and for their indications that the authorities had considerable knowledge of what was going on and did tolerate it to some degree. Even in the 1950s, commissioners of the government's Council for Russian Orthodox Church Affairs had some information about Greek-Catholic religious life. They used the prevailing situation as an argument, in fact, for permitting the registration of additional patriarchal Orthodox churches.[43]

The well-organized Ukrainian Greek-Catholic institution that was revealed to the world in 1990–1991 was organized in substantial degree during and after Soviet governmental attitudes gradually changed. Gorbachev's policies of democratization, glasnost, legality, and perestroika were already taking shape in the 1986–1987 period. The days when Ukrainian Greek-Catholics were being condemned to years of confinement in prison camps had by then passed.[44] Soviet authorities progressively eased off on the arrest and imprisonment of Greek-Catholic priests and lay leaders who participated in forbidden religious services, imposing fines instead of the GULAG.[45] In 1987 Greek-Catholics began appearing in the open and overtly pursued the work of organizing their community.[46] By 1989 they were carrying out immense mass demonstrations and recapturing churches. All in all, it would appear that the experience of the Greek-Catholic underground church, impressive as it is in demonstrating survival in extreme adversity, is not an argument for overturning the cautious judgments expressed by many authors about the size and organizational strength of the Orthodox Church underground over the years of extreme persecution.

Observers have seen a close connection between the rising and falling levels of official persecution of overt religion and the fortunes of underground Orthodoxy. It has seemed to be a triangular relationship connecting the former Soviet state, the overt patriarchal church, and the underground movement. The atheist state periodically cracked down on overt religion. The crackdown then stimulated the growth of the religious underground. The increased effectiveness of the catacomb church put pressure on the authorities to become more tolerant of legally recognized religious organizations in order to avoid a more powerful catacomb church. The easing of restrictions on aboveground churches then stimulated secret believers to come out from under cover. Relaxed conditions also encouraged intrepid religious activists to test the boundaries of official tolerance. The state's reaction was repression, and the cycle started again. Put another way, the overt and covert religious forces may have been like riders on a seesaw, with the government standing behind the overt rider within reach, pushing the rider down in repression or letting the rider back up again when the level of covert religion rose dangerously high.[47]

There is another possible set of relationships, however, that tends to contradict the seesaw effect just described. If repression is crushing and merciless enough, it may push both overt and covert religion down, leaving both "riders" prostrate. Such all-encompassing repression may also drive the underground religious communities to aberrant practices, inflexible doctrines, and priestless existence, as was the case in the history of some Old Believers in past centuries and some True Orthodox worshippers in more recent times.

Conversely, if government policy relaxes, both overt and covert religion may benefit from eased conditions and both may develop and grow. In fact, the relationship between aboveground and underground religion has seemed to be more centrally affected by the degree of public "collaboration" articulated by the overt church than by the mix of tolerance or repression experienced by the overt church. Perceived surrender to the Antichrist may stimulate underground religion regardless of any favors the state may grant or withhold from the overt communities.

It remains true, however, that increases in underground church activity repeatedly induced the communist state to grant concessions and ease up on the overt religious communities. The Baptists after 1965 and the Orthodox at the end of the 1970s are but two examples. Konstantin Kharchev, the chairman of the Council for Religious Affairs, stated candidly in March 1988 to a closed communist meeting: "We favored the registered sects because we feared they would go underground, and we would lose control."[48] Gerhard Simon observed in 1973: "Administrative suppression . . . increased the danger of some of the dissolved congregations going underground—a development which the Soviet authorities fear and try as far as possible to prevent." He went on to assert that dissident attacks on legal church leaders caused the authorities to soften their policies affecting the overt church, again for fear of further defections to underground religion.[49] The other side of this coin was that collaborationist statements forced out of overt churchmen by communist authorities stimulated the growth of the religious underground.[50]

A look at the phases through which the overt patriarchal church and the underground church have passed under varying state policies may clarify these relationships. The persecution of the 1920s and 1930s produced a sharp increase in underground activity. The revulsion of many believers at Sergi's perceived capitulation in 1927 intensified this development, feeding the increasingly significant True Orthodox movements. Draconian Stalinist repression seems to have driven even the underground church to desperation by 1939, however, although thousands of deregistered priests and millions of resentful believers populated both the prison camps and society at large.

Western Orthodox clerics who followed the Germans into the occupied territories in 1941 did find an underground church but not a large one. For example, the autonomous (Orthodox) bishop of Smolensk found only 8 to 10 clandestine churches operating in the Smolensk region (compared to 819 openly functioning churches in 1912, 548 in 1925, and about 200 in 1936).[51] The huge numbers of baptisms performed by priests in the German-occupied territories were an additional indication that the Orthodox religious underground had not previously been able to reach and serve most people desiring that sacrament.[52]

The German occupation resulted in a great resurgence of religious activity in the south of the USSR and in the western lands, as previously discussed. The liberal period in government policy between 1943 and 1947 saw thousands of priests and believers pass over from underground observance and frustrated isolation to the overt religious establishment. According to Fletcher, the 1943–1947 period was also one of underground renaissance, as the two branches of the True Orthodox extended their activities throughout the country; other observers have been more cautious about the extent of this growth in True Orthodox activity, but growth surely occurred.[53]

The increase in the size of the True Orthodox communities during the postwar period of expansion for overt religion may stem from the fact that Sergi's 1927 loyalty declaration was recent enough to weigh heavily in the minds of priests and lay believers. These believers took advantage of unsettled conditions, relative official permissiveness, and incomplete communist social control to build True Orthodox institutions. The end of the war also left a residue of thousands of priests and lay believers in the USSR who had collaborated with the Germans, had formed the Ukrainian Autocephalous Orthodox Church, had supported other separatist or nationalist tendencies, or had otherwise run afoul of the authorities and the patriarchal church hierarchy. Except for those who fled west with the Germans, these people had nowhere to go but underground.[54] There had also been such an explosion of religious activity during the war in the western and occupied territories that religious people were able to press forward with both the aboveground and underground religious revivals.[55]

The period between 1948 and 1953 saw both a Stalinist crackdown against the overt patriarchal church and an intense campaign against the True Orthodox. As already noted, William Fletcher reported that the True Orthodox Church was destroyed and the True Orthodox Christians lost half their adherents.[56] Even in the early 1990s descriptions of these suppressions were cropping up. For example, in 1992 Aleksandr Soldatov noted how believers had fled the

> mince-meat grinders of collectivization and Stalin's torture chambers to establish hermitages and religious communities in the deep Taiga forests. But those the authorities couldn't hunt down and destroy in the Thirties, they hunted down in the Fifties. Small groups of Catacomb Christians remained only in the great cities, where the system of conspiracy was well developed, and in the mountains of Eastern Siberia, where local communities still survive, rather like those of the Priestless Old Believers.

Soldatov noted that some "Catacombists" had recently surfaced in the Novosibirsk parish of the Russian Orthodox Free Church.[57]

In the mid-1950s the fortunes of the patriarchal church brightened, but the number of functioning parishes in the country did not significantly increase. Fletcher reported that the True Orthodox Christians "revived," although the extent of the revival is not clear. He did say that periods of relaxation in state policy, such as the time between 1953 and 1957, were "marked by great proliferation of the activities of the underground Orthodox organizations," for the "relaxation of police and investigatory pressure" gave them "immensely amplified opportunities for activity." Khrushchev's amnesties in the mid-1950s, when large numbers of religious inmates of the prison camps returned to society at large, also helped the True Orthodox Christians.[58]

The subsequent Khrushchev antireligious drive gravely wounded the overt patriarchal church. Fletcher reported that it also drove the underground church to some of the aberrant practices already mentioned.[59] He asserted that the drive forced new thousands of priests and believers into the underground, which was undoubtedly true. He made a particular point that the closing of monasteries drove monastics into the catacomb church, and some monks from the beleaguered Pochaev Lavra apparently became True Orthodox Christian Wanderers. I would guess, however, that more priests and monastics went into itinerant ministry or unauthorized parish work on their own than into the True Orthodox Christian movement. Most of these men retained some connection to the patriarchal church, and many church hierarchs sympathized with them and helped them.[60]

The Brezhnev era, or the period of stagnation, was an extension of the Khrushchev policy in the sense of a continuing erosion of the overt patriarchal church's institutional strength. It is probably also fair to say that the same erosion was eating away at the strength of the underground church, as the KGB was very active in suppressing dissent, including illegal religious activity. A 1990 article in the *Moscow Church Herald, Weekly* stated that Christian intellectuals in Leningrad managed to meet and hold a few seminars during the 1975–1980 period, but KGB repression between 1980 and 1985 suppressed this underground activity, at least until the end of the Brezhnev era.[61] The conclusion that this period was one of net erosion of underground religious strength may have to be qualified, however, as there are perceptive and well-informed observers who assert that a whole new generation of underground religious dissenters emerged. These people, "sickened" by the Khrushchev drive, reacted against both the Soviet government's violations of legality and the patriarchate's failure to mount an effective defense of the church or raise a determined protest against the regime's actions.[62] This development would appear reminiscent of the post-1927 period.

With Gorbachev's dramatic change in policy, the overt Orthodox began opening churches, organizing new seminaries, ordaining new priests, bringing clerics out of retirement, consecrating bishops, opening convents, and rebuilding Orthodox religious life on every front. The underground movements and, perhaps more important, unregistered priests forced from their vocation, as well as Orthodox lay activists, came to the surface and resumed overt religious work. Fletcher predicted in 1970 that this might happen: "If an abrupt termination of pressure should occur, the underground movements would be able to supply important human material for the reorganization of the seriously weakened structure of Russian Orthodoxy."[63]

A note of caution is advisable before concluding that the recent passage of catacomb Christians into overt activity is a flood and not a trickle. In its publications, the Russian Orthodox Church Abroad reports on formerly underground communities and True Orthodox Christians who have become affiliated with it as Russian Orthodox Free Church members. *Pravoslavnaya Rus* [Orthodox Russia] presents poignant and moving narratives of the experiences of hidden communities, faithful nuns, and intrepid priests. What emerges from these accounts, however, is an impression of quite scattered, small-scale activity during the long years of persecution.[64]

If there has been any time when the seesaw effect has been evident, it is probably now, in the postmillennial Orthodox Church revival. The renaissance of the overt church is absorbing the talent, commitment, time, energies, human resources, and money of believers to the point that I have difficulty believing much is left over for a simultaneous renaissance of the underground church. Besides, if the prison camps were once a vast training establishment for the underground religious movements, and Khrushchev's church-closing campaign created, as Fletcher put it, "a vast and fertile field for practitioners of underground Orthodoxy," then the closing of the camps and the recent opening of churches may perhaps have relieved, if not reversed, these influences. Perhaps Fletcher's "immensely amplified" opportunities for underground church proliferation, which can be expected to accompany "periods of relative relaxation in state policy," are finding their expression once again in the present benign circumstances. However, the overt Orthodox and overt Free Church renaissance is so all-pervasive that I somewhat doubt it.[65]

The driving force that pushed Christian believers into the underground in the first place was communist state policy and action (and what was perceived as an unworthy church response). Oppression confirmed the underground believers' sense of persecution, but there was never any theological or ecclesiological reason for these Orthodox Christians to separate themselves from the overt church. The collapse of the communist state may have washed away many of these incentives for remaining in the underground.[66]

One can argue that the Orthodox and the Catholics, as highly structured, hierarchical institutions, have found it particularly difficult to sustain underground church organizations, whereas flexibly organized groups have had an easier time.[67] Some support for this idea may also be found in the history of the Old Believers, as the movement split into hierarchical, priested Old Believers and priestless ones who rejected structure and hierarchy. It is difficult to see how either tendency manifested in the practices of the Old Believers decisively contributed to successful survival, however, and neither branch is thriving today in the historic Russian heartland.[68] Both the Ukrainian Greek-Catholics and the Orthodox have been quite successful over the years in training and ordaining priests privately and informally. Both communities have managed to consecrate bishops in secret. There are dramatic reports of funerals where mourners were surprised to see the deceased lying in the coffin arrayed in the full regalia of an Orthodox bishop or archbishop. In one case the dead man had been a famous scientist who had successfully concealed his religious faith and activities from the world.[69]

To conclude, the question of underground Orthodox religion is peculiarly difficult to address successfully. There are those who say the evidences of a highly developed, ubiquitous underground church organization are like the resplendent new clothes of the emperor in Hans Christian Andersen's fairy tale—clothes visible only to those disposed to see them or say they see them. They assert that the relative paucity of visible evidence of underground religion reflects the real absence of it. Others say that evidences of underground Orthodoxy are few because its activities and institutional arrangements are secret and meant to be. Underground Orthodoxy has been extremely important at various times in the history of the church-state struggle. Depending on one's definition of them, unauthorized, illegal religious activities were widespread during crucial periods of Soviet history. In the post-Soviet era, however, I would have to conclude that underground Orthodoxy, including the movements growing out of "True Orthodoxy," are subsisting at the margins of the country's religious life and are not likely to move center stage unless or until official policy should turn sharply hostile once again.

11

Monks, Nuns, and Convents

THE RUSSIAN ORTHODOX CHURCH has a profound tradition of asceticism, mysticism, and reclusion. Monasticism has always played an immense role in Russian Orthodox piety, not merely among the ordained clergy but also among the laity. Throughout history devout Christians have made pilgrimages to monasteries and nunneries and have sought out monastic holy elders, *startsi*, to listen, learn, and find spiritual renewal. In many ways the convents are the heart of the Russian Orthodox Church.[1]

Moreover, the monastic clergy provides the only source from which candidates to episcopal office can be drawn; priests with wives who are living cannot aspire to become bishops. Nuns and nunneries have an equally significant place in the devotional tradition of Orthodoxy. Holy women have been leaders over the centuries in works of charity, mercy, and healing.

A young man faces a profound and irrevocable choice as he progresses through seminary. He may marry and enter the parish clergy, but he must do so before he is ordained a deacon. If he does not marry before ordination, he is expected but not obliged to take monastic vows. A parish priest may not marry after ordination, may not divorce and remarry, and may not remarry if a widower. However, a priest who has lost his wife may take monastic vows, and most of the bishops consecrated during the renaissance of church life during World War II were in fact bereaved priests. These rules have created resentment among some married priests in the past, a sentiment that played a role in the Renovationist schism in the 1920s. The Russian Orthodox Church is a conservative body, however, and the exclusion of married priests from the episcopacy is unlikely to change soon. A secular priest may, of course, have duties entailing high responsibility, such as heading one of the great seminary-academy complexes of the church, running an important office in the patriarchal administration, or administering a diocesan headquarters. An archpriest may also be honored by the granting of a miter, which makes his physical appearance as he celebrates the liturgy quite similar to that of a bishop. Nevertheless, monastic clergy lead the church.

The exigencies of life under communism made it difficult for monastics to maintain the ascetic, withdrawn, contemplative pattern of the cloisters characteristic of past centuries, even before the monasteries and nunneries were closed altogether in 1929. As already described, the shortage of priests forced monastic clerics into parish work from one end of the country to the other. For similar reasons most lay brothers were encouraged to accept ordination as deacons and priests, although the great monasteries even now have gardeners, custodians, artisans, icon painters, and others who lead dedicated lives as monks. One Marxist observer who wrote a dissertation for Moscow State University in 1989 on contemporary Orthodox monasticism stated that the patriarchate rethought the role of monks, and concluded that the church should put less emphasis on monastic separation from the world at large and what he termed "social uselessness." He spent two months at the Zhirovitsy monastery in Byelorussia in 1987 and did nevertheless observe a "new asceticism."[2] In fact, the Orthodox tradition of seeking holiness in removal from the world is slowly being renewed.

A man enters a monastery as a novice and has the opportunity to withdraw if the life does not suit him. After some years he may adopt a saint's name and take vows as a monk. After many years, usually at the end of a long life of monastic devotion, a monk may assume the *mega schema* (angelic habit) and change his name again, committing himself to a life even more ascetic than the life led under lesser degrees of monastic profession, and he will become even more deeply devoted to prayer and meditation.[3] Some communist writers alleged that this hierarchy in a monastery is oppressive and creates a system of "bondage." It is more likely, however, that when abusive leadership has occurred, it has originated with the father superior. Archimandrite Gavriil (Steblyuchenko) allegedly was such a man when he headed the monastery of the Caves near Pskov from 1975 to 1988.[4]

There is considerable variation in the kinds of men attracted to the various monasteries. The Optina hermitage, as already mentioned, was a beacon of intellectual and literary brilliance in the nineteenth century. It shows signs of resuming that role, and its novices include a majority of young, educated men, among them an architect, a physicist, a doctor, and a university student. Nina Chugunova of *Ogonëk* described how a high government functionary was observed in the early 1970s going to church. He was called in by the party bosses and told that he could keep his position and his perquisites if he would promise never again to darken the door of a church. In an act of courage he forfeited his comfortable position, and a decade and a half later, he was a novice at Optina.[5]

After taking vows, a man may be ordained a monastic deacon (*ierodyakon*). He may then be ordained a monastic priest (*ieromonakh*) and later become the head of a small monastery, or a hegumen (*igumen*), a title that has effectively become a rank. The head of a large monastery is an archimandrite, a title that has also become a rank. Next, the man may receive consecration as a bishop, elevation to archbishop, elevation to metropolitan, and the possibility of election as patriarch.

Women follow a similar path to the rank of hegumen (abbess), serving as novices before taking vows as nuns. Communist writers alleged that some nunneries, including the Pyukhtitsa nunnery in Estonia, deliberately keep women many years as novices in order to get more labor out of them, as the balance shifts away from work and toward even greater prayer and devotion when a woman takes the veil. The mother superior at Pyukhtitsa answered, however, that a woman needs to be sure of her vocation before she renounces the world. Some nunneries will not accept novices under thirty and will sometimes have them wait for up to two decades before taking vows.[6]

Mothers superior may also examine prospective candidates over the course of many interviews and do not make admission easy.[7] In a 1988 interview the mother superior at Korets expressed pride in her strict standards and even more in the fact that no woman had left the nunnery after admission.[8] There is some variation in the educational and intellectual level of novices in the various nunneries; Korets and Pyukhtitsa have reputations as being attractive to young professional women.[9] Even in a place like Pyukhtitsa, however, some secular observers detect a quality of shyness and timidity in the sisters, as if they had sought the security of the cloister as a refuge. The allegation is made that most of the sisters are from broken homes, although this is no doubt an exaggeration.[10]

Since World War II government officials have noted that quite a few nunneries are nonresidential.[11] Even now, many nuns attach themselves to individual churches, performing myriad tasks in support of the local parish in which they work.

A large portion of the activity cloistered monks and nuns engage in is devotional, and some convents maintain extremely rigorous schedules. The nunnery of St. Florus follows the ancient rule of Constantinople; the nuns rise at 2:30 A.M. and the offices can occupy sixteen hours of the day. Other nunneries are somewhat less severe but hardly lax. In the nunnery of the Protection of the Veil of the Mother of God in Kiev, the sisters gather in church at 5 A.M. for prayers. The holy liturgy begins at 7, and the nuns breakfast at 10. Evening services begin at 5 P.M. and last four hours and sometimes longer. Monks and nuns do not eat meat in order "to discourage sinful thoughts."[12]

The monks and nuns also engage in economic activity to earn income, to feed themselves, and to help meet the needs of the church. Before the religious houses were closed in the 1930s and in the more tolerant days between World War II and the Khrushchev antireligious drive, the convents had considerable lumbering, small-scale manufacturing, and agricultural operations on adjacent lands. The Pyukhtitsa nunnery engaged in commercial-scale mushroom and berry picking. The Soviet government's reports on the monasteries and nunneries after World

War II concentrated, with a highly critical slant, on the convents' economic activities, obviously worrisome to the Marxists. One of the first objectives of the Khrushchev drive was to clip the wings of the religious communities' enterprises.[13] Out of this ultimately came, in some cases, arrangements between convents and nearby collective farms, state farms, and even factories under which monks and nuns worked for the farms and enterprises for pay. For example, a church publication described how the novices at the Korets nunnery worked in an agricultural brigade of a neighboring state farm. The chairman was described as "happy, because they are good workers."[14]

Virtually all the convents paint icons, make sacramental vessels, produce candles, fashion birth crosses, embroider vestments, sew altar cloths, paint Christmas cards, or bake bread for communion and for blessing and distribution (*prosfory*).[15] In 1980 the church established a shop complex at Sofrino, outside Moscow, to do manufacturing on a large scale, but the convents still do much of the work, to the great benefit of the church and the economic sustenance of the religious houses.[16]

In a few of the most celebrated convents, the communities receive enough free-will offerings from pilgrims and parishioners to sustain themselves, but most convents have had to maintain some productive activity to survive. After the easing of governmental attitudes under perestroika, the convents began somewhat cautiously returning to the conduct of their own economic activities. The Korets nunnery, for example, was given back its old orchard and garden area.[17]

There were 1,025 functioning convents, both monasteries and nunneries, in 1914; the last of them was closed by 1929.[18] The annexations of 1939–1940 resulted in the absorption into the USSR of 64 functioning convents and hermitages, and 40 more were opened under the German occupation during World War II, for a total of 104 when the Red Army liberated the western territories.[19] In 1945 the Soviet authorities recorded 101 functioning convents and hermitages.[20] There were 2 open convents in the Russian Federated Republic (the Kursk nunnery and the monastery of the Caves near Pskov), 68 in Ukraine, 24 in Moldavia, 3 in Byelorussia, 2 in Lithuania, 1 in Latvia, and 1 in Estonia.

In 1946 there were 99 convents and hermitages open; 2 had been closed down in Ukraine, 1 had been closed in Moldavia, and a monastery had been reopened in the Russian republic. The one reopened was the Trinity-Sergius Lavra in Zagorsk (Sergiev Posad), forty-five miles northeast of Moscow. This ancient, celebrated convent and fortress, constructed on the site where St. Sergius Radonezh had established a hermitage, was the only monastery in the never-occupied lands turned over to the church in the postwar period prior to 1983. It had been made available in 1944 but only opened as a monastery in 1946.[21]

In October of 1947 the Soviet authorities recorded 96 convents and hermitages in the country, a reduction of 2 more in Ukraine and 1 in Moldavia. At that time 41 of the convents were monasteries and 55 were nunneries. By January of 1948, another 11 had been closed.[22]

As was the case for churches and priests, the last years of Stalin's life were difficult for monks and nuns because the authorities intensified their repressive measures. Almost a fifth of the operating convents were obliged to close their doors; this left 69 in the country in 1953.[23] After Stalin died the numbers held steady for several years, but by 1956 the closing of convents had resumed. In January of 1957 there were 64 convents and hermitages, 5 fewer than in 1953.[24]

As mentioned in Chapter 4, Khrushchev's campaign to close convents preceded his main drive to close churches. Almost a third of the convents and hermitages were liquidated in 1959, and only 44 were operating in January of 1960. In January of 1961 there were 33; a year later there were 22. Among the convents closed in 1961 was the celebrated monastery of the Caves in Kiev, allegedly because the premises were unsafe. By the end of the Khrushchev drive there were 18; over five-sixths of the 104 convents that emerged from World War II had been closed down.[25]

Even the convents that survived found their garden plots confiscated or drastically reduced in size. Taxes on the convents were raised, younger monks and nuns were expelled, and organized pilgrimages were forbidden. The militia harassed monks, nuns, and individual pilgrims, many of whom nevertheless continued to make their way to the great convents to visit the shrines and talk with revered elders.[26]

One convent that survived the Khrushchev drive was the Dormition monastery at Pochaev in western Ukraine. Its continuance was a near thing, however, and achieved at great human cost.[27] In 1959 the local authorities confiscated the monastery's ten-hectare farm plot, fruit garden, and bee hives. They also closed the hermitage of the Holy Ghost, located about two miles from the principal monastery complex, where about fifty of the 130–140 monks and novices at Pochaev had resided in the early postwar period.[28] In 1960 Soviet representatives forbade the acceptance of new monks or novices, seized the monastery's trucks and car, and began arresting pilgrims. In 1961 the militia seized a number of shops and a dormitory and declared several monks mentally disturbed, sending some to a psychiatric ward—where several died—and sending others to their home villages, canceling their internal passport registrations for Pochaev. The dormitory for pilgrims became an insane asylum, and the shrieks of deranged patients could be heard during services in the church. By early 1962 over half of the 140 monks and novices had been forced from the convent, some sent to hospitals for treatment of dysentery and other maladies "diagnosed" by the authorities, and others conscripted into construction battalions headed for the extreme north of the USSR. Senior administrators were arrested and removed. Pogroms were carried out against devout villagers who supported the monks.

According to a protest letter from the monastery's spiritual council to Soviet president Nikolai Podgorny, "drunken KGB agents and militiamen went around at night armed with clubs and guns and began thrashing the pilgrims, who scattered helter-skelter in terror. Then they were picked up one by one, robbed, beaten and thrown into a mental hospital." The protest letter continued:

> Abbot Iosif (Golovatyuk) was a venerable old man of seventy who had nearly all his life followed an occupation in the monastery and did not want to leave it. However they might torment him, he wanted to end his days there. Sixteen militia and KGB men came to him in his cell, grabbed the old man and dragged him out; . . . he nearly died. . . . He was taken to the mental hospital at Budanov. . . . His hair and beard were shaven off and every day he was forced to have some kind of injection in very large doses. As a result his whole body, especially his legs, swelled up and became as stiff as a board; his skin nearly burst from fluid which the doctors kept injecting. . . . Only after petitions and protests . . . was he discharged . . . to a nephew . . . [on] condition that he would never again appear in the monastery.[29]

At the end of the Khrushchev drive there were thirty to thirty-five "old and weak" monks at Pochaev, which was about a quarter of the monastery's population six years earlier.[30] It is believed that widespread international protest and publicity saved the monastery from extinction.[31]

The eighteen convents in the USSR that survived the Khrushchev drive have remained open until the present day.[32] The authorities resumed their harassment of cloistered monks and nuns during the late 1970s and early 1980s, however, and the most notable victims again were the monks at Pochaev. Dimitri Pospielovsky characterized the renewed campaign as a reaction to a religious revival in the country inspired by the "islands of true spirituality" in the convents, which strongly attracted those trying to find their way toward God.[33]

For almost four decades, not a single new convent had been allowed to open or reopen its doors. Only in May 1983 was the Danilov monastery complex turned over to the church in anticipation of the Millennium celebrations five years later.

The number of cloistered monks declined precipitately during the years of the Khrushchev drive, as might be expected. Some monks did manage to move from their former monasteries to the ones that remained open, but most of them—those who were not detained, at least—went into secular work or went to live with relatives. For example, in Moldavia there were over 300 monks in seven monasteries in 1959, and every monastery was closed. Few of these men could go, or perhaps even wanted to go, to the two remaining Ukrainian monasteries or the single remaining Byelorussian one. The Council for Religious Affairs recorded 893 cloistered monks and novices in the USSR in 1957, and there were 325–350 after the Khrushchev drive.[34] Before the Bolshevik revolution there had been about 21,000 monks and novices in the country, so less than 2 percent of monks and novices serving in imperial times were living in cloisters during the late 1960s.[35]

During the period of almost twenty-five years between the end of the Khrushchev drive and the Millennium, the number of cloistered monks and novices in the six open monasteries in the country remained quite stable. Many of these monks were not young enough to be vigorous, however, particularly if one considers the fact that aging bishops and monastic priests tend to retire to monasteries when their active days are over. There were 900–1,000 monastic priests in the whole country; about a third of them were resident in the convents and about two-thirds of them were in parish or diocesan work or otherwise living in the world.[36] Listed in approximate order of size, the six monasteries open between 1964 and 1983 were as follows:

1. *The Holy Trinity–St. Sergius monastery at Zagorsk (Sergiev Posad), Moscow oblast.*[37] This *lavra* (monastery of the highest rank) had eighty-three monks and novices in January 1956, and in January of 1966, after the Khrushchev antireligious drive, it was down to sixty-two.[38] By 1987 the number had reportedly risen to 123.[39]

2. *The Holy Dormition monastery of the Caves, about thirty-five miles west of Pskov.* In 1957 the monastery had about fifty monks and novices. In 1958 seven monks who had fled the USSR and settled in Finland decided to return, and some novices were also accepted; these additions resulted in sixty-five monks and novices in 1958. The Khrushchev antireligious campaign apparently left the monastery relatively unaffected, as there were sixty-three monks and novices in 1966.[40] The numbers held steady at about sixty through the next decade and crept up to about seventy-five in the early to mid-1980s.[41] By January 1, 1991, the numbers had dropped back to sixty-seven, of whom seventeen were under thirty years of age and twenty-four were over sixty.[42]

3. *The Holy Dormition monastery at Pochaev, Ternopol oblast, western Ukraine.* The vicissitudes of this *lavra* during the Khrushchev antireligious campaign have been described. Nevertheless, the historic *lavra* did slowly recover from the government's assaults. During the five years prior to 1970, the number of monks and novices had increased by about a dozen to reach a figure of forty-five.[43] The campaign against the *lavra* resumed with great intensity in 1980. The anger and frustration of local communist authorities at their earlier failure to close the monastery were said to have contributed to the violence of the renewed drive. Leading monks were expelled and beaten, to the point that one of them died and another lost his sanity. Drunken militiamen were observed by foreign visitors kicking worshipers. A farm worker at the monastery who had repeatedly been sent to a psychiatric hospital had both arms broken.[44]

The reemergence of the Ukrainian Greek-Catholics in the western Ukraine means that the Pochaev Lavra has become an embattled outpost of Orthodoxy once again. According to two bishops who visited Pochaev in mid-1992, both the Greek-Catholics and the Autocephalists were pressing the authorities to transfer the *lavra* to them. In January 1991 the monastery had forty-seven monks and novices.[45]

4. *The Holy Dormition monastery at Odessa.* Before the Khrushchev antireligious drive, there were fifty to sixty monks and novices in residence. In 1965, after the drive, there were about thirty-five.[46] By 1970 the number had increased to thirty-nine, and it remained at about forty for the following decade and beyond. In 1991 the monastery had forty-four monks and novices.[47]

5. *The Holy Dormition monastery at Zhirovitsy, Grodno oblast, Belarus (Byelorussia).* Monks and nuns live in the same premises, despite monastic rules to the contrary. According to a Soviet government inspector, the monastery emerged from World War II with twenty-eight monks and novices, of whom thirteen were "unable to work." In January of 1959 there were thirty-one. That was the year the Khrushchev drive was unleashed, and in early 1960 only twenty-three monks and novices remained in residence. By 1981 the number had dropped to a total of fifteen, and there were seventeen in 1986.[48]

6. *The monastery of the Holy Ghost, Vilnyus, Lithuania.* There are both monks and nuns here, as the authorities have been unwilling to make separate premises available. In 1957 it had twelve monks and one novice. By January 1966 enough new novices had been admitted to bring the monastery's total to fifteen, despite the death of four monks in the interim. Through the 1980s the total stood at about ten monks and novices.[49]

The Russian Orthodox Church emerged from the Khrushchev antireligious drive with twelve nunneries. There was not a single one in the huge Russian Federated Republic, although the Pyukhtitsa nunnery in Estonia was and is in a Russian-populated area; there were seven in Ukraine; there was one in each of the Baltic states; there was one in Moldavia; and there was one in Byelorussia. All twelve were nunneries that had been functioning under the German occupation in World War II and had been permitted to remain open when the Red Army recaptured the western territories. In approximate order by region and size, the twelve were as follows:

1. *The Pyukhtitsa Dormition nunnery at Iykhvi-Ukarty, just west of Narva, in Estonia.* This is currently the largest of the nunneries in the successor states of the USSR. In 1955 there were 106 nuns and novices in residence. The numbers slowly but steadily increased over the next five years, but these gains were lost in the Khrushchev drive. The nunnery resumed its slow growth in about 1970, reaching a total of 148 nuns and novices in 1987.[50]

2. *The Holy Trinity nunnery at Korets, Rovno oblast, Ukraine.* During and immediately after the German occupation in World War II, there were about 135

nuns and novices here.[51] By 1958, after the early Khrushchev drive had forced the merger of the Trinity and nearby Resurrection nunneries, this community had 172 nuns and novices.[52] Forty-five sisters from Dnepropetrovsk and Zhitomir oblasts were also moved to Korets in 1959, bringing the total to 211.[53] During the half dozen years after the drive, the nunnery declined by about seventy nuns and novices to a total of 144, and by 1990 the numbers were down to 110.[54] In January 1991 the nunnery had 114 nuns and novices.[55] The mother superior of the nunnery stated in an interview in February 1989 that the obstacle to admitting more novices was the attitude of the local authorities, as "many women are willing to take the veil." In a later interview in early 1991, however, the mother superior said that the authorities' restrictions had eased, and the effective limit on the number of sisters had become physical space, as the nunnery could accommodate only 136 women. In the meantime, the Resurrection nunnery complex, which had been turned into a commercial center, burned almost to the ground, and the authorities gave it back to the Trinity nunnery rather than rebuild and restore it.[56]

3. *The nunnery of the Protection of the Veil of the Mother of God in Kiev.* The nunnery emerged from the German occupation period with 245 nuns and novices.[57] It was said that a novice was not allowed to take the vows and veil of a nun at an age younger than fifty.[58] The nunnery emerged from the Khrushchev antireligious drive with 215 nuns and novices.[59] The Presentation of the Mother of God nunnery in Kiev, which had 142 nuns and novices before the Khrushchev drive, was closed in the course of it, so the nuns and novices in the Protection nunnery after the drive reflected a consolidation of those religious houses and a loss of approximately 180 sisters.[60] The Soviet authorities recorded 168 nuns and novices in the Protection nunnery in 1970, or a loss of almost 50 more. Apparently many aged nuns died during those years. In 1979 a Western observer gave the figure of 105, for an additional loss of 60 sisters.[61] In the early 1980s the numbers given by reliable observers very slowly declined and leveled off at 90–95 during the 1980s. In January 1991 there were 112.[62] Thus the number of sisters in the nunnery was little more than a quarter of the number residing in the Protection and Presentation nunneries prior to the Khrushchev drive.

4. *The St. Florus nunnery in Kiev.* The nunnery had 250 nuns and novices during and just after the German occupation.[63] Over the next dozen years the nunnery grew modestly in overall numbers, but it started to decline in 1958 and had lost about a hundred sisters by the end of the Khrushchev drive. By 1988 about fifty-five nuns and novices were in the nunnery, although the numbers grew again to eighty-one in January 1991.[64] The decline over the years can no doubt be explained in part by the agedness of the sisters in the community throughout the postwar years and the great rigor of the nunnery's regimen.

5. *The Protection of the Veil of the Mother of God nunnery at Krasnogorsk (Zolotonosha), Cherkassy oblast, Kiev diocese.* There were approximately 250 nuns and novices at the two nunneries in Cherkassy oblast prior to the Khrushchev antire-

ligious drive. Krasnogorsk nunnery, then the only nunnery in Cherkassy oblast, emerged from the drive in 1966 with eighty-six nuns and novices, all but three of whom were reported by the authorities to be over fifty years of age. In 1986 the number of nuns and novices was sixty-five, almost 200 fewer than the number of sisters in the Cherkassy region in the late 1950s. In January 1991 the number was seventy.[65]

6. *The Birth of the Mother of God nunnery near Aleksandrovka, Odessa oblast.* This nunnery is located in the Bolgrad-Izmail district of the oblast, close to Moldavia (Moldova) and Romania. The nuns of St. Michael's nunnery in Odessa joined the nuns at Aleksandrovka when their own nunnery was closed in the Khrushchev antireligious drive. According to Michael Bourdeaux, the nuns at St. Michael's were forced out by the government's insistence that the sale of their needlework for vestments and altar cloths was henceforth illegal and they would have to go to work in industry "or starve."[66] The negotiated solution was that they join the nunnery at Aleksandrovka. The combined community emerged from the Khrushchev drive with about forty-five nuns and novices.[67] In 1987 there were thirty-two nuns and fourteen novices, a total of forty-six. In January 1991 there were sixty-one.[68]

7. *The St. Nicholas (Mirlikiski) nunnery under Chernechei Mountain near Mukachevo, Transcarpathia.* The nunnery's history after World War II was much influenced by the absorption of Transcarpathia into the USSR from Czechoslovakia and the forced conversion of the previously dominant Greek-Catholics into Orthodoxy in the 1947–1949 period. Soviet authorities reported 321 cloistered women in the oblast in 1958, of whom 64 were too old and infirm to work.[69] By 1960 the number was down to 278, no doubt because some aged nuns passed away. After the closure of the Lipcha nunnery and other communities, most of the religious women from these places moved to the St. Nicholas nunnery.[70] The Khrushchev antireligious drive hit the St. Nicholas nunnery hard, and it was reported that the nuns had to earn their living by working in local factories. The nunnery emerged from the drive in 1966 with 124 nuns and no novices.[71] In 1979 "about 100" were reported; and "100 sisters" was still the figure given in 1990.[72]

8. *The Holy Ascension nunnery at Chumalevo.* This second nunnery in Transcarpathia has never been large, despite the fact that nuns from other nunneries were transferred there during the Khrushchev antireligious drive. In particular, the nuns of the John the Evangelist hermitage in Kopashnevo were sent there in 1960.[73] The Soviet authorities recorded thirty-eight nuns and no novices there in January of 1966. In January 1986 thirty-five nuns and novices were recorded in official records, none of them under forty years of age.[74]

9. *The Holy Trinity–St. Sergius nunnery in Riga, Latvia.* The nunnery includes the satellite Transfiguration hermitage, near Yelgava. The revered *starets*, Archimandrite Tavrion (Batozski), preached at the hermitage for almost a decade until

he died at the age of eighty in 1978. He attracted hundreds of pilgrims a day in summertime and tens of thousands through the course of his ministry. He was a great orator, able to give his listeners "the fire of the Spirit," as one pilgrim described it, "a torrent of life-giving wisdom . . . baring the secrets of the conscience but bathing the heart with the great love and tenderness of the heavenly Father. . . . His sermons . . . [were] evangelical judgment on contemporary reality." Father Tavrion had been in labor camps or exile from 1928 to the Khrushchev amnesty of 1956, and his life is celebrated as an expression of the highest Russian Orthodox monastic tradition.[75] In the 1950s, prior to the arrival of Father Tavrion, a Moscow theological academy professor had noted with regret that no special discipline, such as silence, was maintained at the nunnery because the sisters were not spiritually equal to it.[76] Such was Father Tavrion's power for change.

There were ninety-one cloistered women at the nunnery in 1959 and seventy nuns and novices in 1966, at the end of the Khrushchev antireligious drive.[77] As aged women died, the nunnery reached a low point in 1968 with about thirty nuns and novices, about twenty in Riga and about ten in the hermitage. Father Tavrion arrived soon thereafter, and the population of the nunnery and hermitage almost doubled with an increase of twenty-five sisters in the 1968–1970 period. In 1980 a Western observer stated that there were fifty nuns and novices there ranging in age from twenty-four to ninety. At the end of 1991 there were reported to be seventy sisters.[78]

10. *The St. Mary Magdalene nunnery in Vilnyus, Lithuania, located on the grounds of the Holy Ghost monastery.* The nunnery had twenty-eight religious women in residence on January 1, 1955. The numbers declined during the years of the Khrushchev drive, and the number seems to have fluctuated between a dozen and sixteen during the following two decades.[79]

11. *The Ascension nunnery at Zhabka, Moldova (Moldavia), Kishinev diocese.* In September 1945, with nine nunneries in the republic, the Soviet authorities recorded 246 nuns and 156 novices in cloisters and 859 nuns and 481 novices living in noncloistered quarters, a total of 1,742.[80] By April of 1946 these numbers had dropped by more than a third.[81] The numbers changed very little over the next thirteen years; there were 1,027 nuns and novices in January 1959 living in seven nunneries. Three nunneries were closed in the course of 1959, and the number of nuns and novices dropped by almost a half, to 537.[82] Three more nunneries were closed between 1960 and 1965.[83] After the Khrushchev drive, the sole nunnery in the republic, Zhabka, emerged with 38 nuns and 38 novices, a total of 76.[84] Noncloistered nuns continued serving in individual churches when possible or earned a living as best they could in secular occupations. In 1986 45 nuns and novices were reported to be in Zhabka.[85]

12. *The nunnery of the Birth of the Mother of God at the Holy Dormition monastery at Zhirovitsy, Grodno oblast, Belarus (Byelorussia).* The nunnery was estab-

lished at Zhirovitsy in the middle of the Khrushchev antireligious campaign, 1963–1964, when the nuns and novices of the Birth of the Mother of God nunnery at Grodno and the St. Yevfrosiniya nunnery at Polotsk were transferred to the grounds of the Zhirovitsy monastery and obliged to resettle their communities there.[86]

In January 1957 there were 106 nuns and novices in the two nunneries that were later consolidated at Zhirovitsy.[87] The repercussions of the coerced transfers and the inroads of the Khrushchev drive reduced the community by half, and the authorities recorded 36 nuns and novices in 1986.[88] In October of 1989 the St. Yevfrosiniya nunnery in Polotsk was permitted to reopen, and the nuns living on the Zhirovitsy grounds were transferred to Polotsk a few months later. About 20 nuns made the move back to Polotsk.[89]

Do the figures add up? Summary Table 11.1 shows the number of monks and nuns, including novices, in each of the eighteen monasteries and nunneries in the middle to late 1980s.

On June 7, 1988, Metropolitan Vladimir (Sabodan) of Rostov, the chief of administration of the patriarchate, gave the figure of 1,190 monks, nuns, and novices in twenty-two convents.[90] Vladimir's figures included the Gorny nunnery in Jerusalem and the three convents turned back to the church in anticipation of the Millennium. The four convents had perhaps as many as seventy-five monks,

TABLE 11.1   Monks and Nuns in Convents, Middle to Late 1980s

Monasteries		*Nunneries*	
1. Zagorsk	123	1. Pyukhtitsa	148
2. Pskov	75	2. Korets	120
3. Pochaev	80	3. Kiev (Protection)	90
4. Odessa	40	4. Kiev (Florus)	55
5. Zhirovitsy	15	5. Krasnogorsk	65
6. Vilnyus	10	6. Aleksandrovka	46
		7. Mukachevo	100
Monasteries, total	343	8. Chumalevo	35
		9. Riga	12
		10. Vilnyus	12
		11. Zhabka	45
		12. Zhirovitsy	33
		Nunneries, total	761
	Convents, total	1,104	

Sources: Statistics recorded in the Archive of the Council for Religious Affairs, amplified and explained in notes 38–41, 43, 45–55, 57, 59–65, 67–69, 71–72, 74, 77–85, and 87–91 of Chapter 11.

nuns, and novices resident in 1988, and if one subtracts that figure from Metro-politan Vladimir's 1,190, the result is quite close to the total reached by addition in Table 11.1.[91] These figures for 1988 represented a decline of about eighty-five sisters from the number of nuns and novices in the USSR in the late 1960s, which even then was after the depradations of the Khrushchev antireligious drive.[92]

With the Pimen-Gorbachev meeting of April 29, 1988, and the celebration of the Millennium, the door opened wider to the reopening of convents. As just re-counted, there were twenty-one functioning convents in the USSR in June of 1988. In late 1989 Metropolitan Vladimir (Sabodan) reported that there were thirty-five functioning convents.[93] At the end of September 1990, the Novosti Press Agency reported twenty-five monasteries and thirty-one nunneries, a total of fifty-six. Late in 1991 Patriarch Aleksi asserted that there were 121 convents, and in late 1992 the patriarchate said there were 150 of them. In late 1993 the patriarch reported that there were 213 convents plus eleven convent missions (*podvorya*).[94] Figure 11.1 is a graph showing the number of open convents in the USSR and successor states in the post–World War II period. It is notable that about fifty of the church's functioning convents are in the Russian republic, ranging from the Solovetski Islands in the White Sea to other far corners of Russia. As already de-scribed, there was only one monastery (Trinity-Sergius) and not a single nunnery in the vast territory of the Russian republic in the years between 1929 and 1983.

How are the Orthodox managing to find monks and nuns to restore religious life in these convents? Most of the new convents are small, and many have been established with no more than a handful in residence.[95] In some cases aged men and women who lived a secular life for years have returned. I talked to one old monk in 1989 at the monastery of the Caves in Kiev, and he told me he had been a member of the community until the monastery was closed in 1961, at which time he went to live with relatives and made a living as best he could. When the mon-astery was reopened in 1988, he returned.

The established convents have been sending monks and nuns to the newly es-tablished ones. For example, eleven sisters, including the new mother superior, came to Shamordino from the Trinity-Sergius nunnery in Riga in order to rees-tablish that celebrated convent near the Optina hermitage, where Leo Tolstoy's sister served and lies buried. This represented about a fifth of the entire popula-tion of the Riga nunnery, although the convent soon admitted eleven additional novices. To take another example, monks from the Danilov monastery in Mos-cow have gone to help in the reconstitution of the Optina hermitage and some other convents.[96] Moreover, the church taps senior monastic priests regularly for elevation to the episcopate. The result of all of this has been that many of the

FIGURE 11.1
Number of Convents

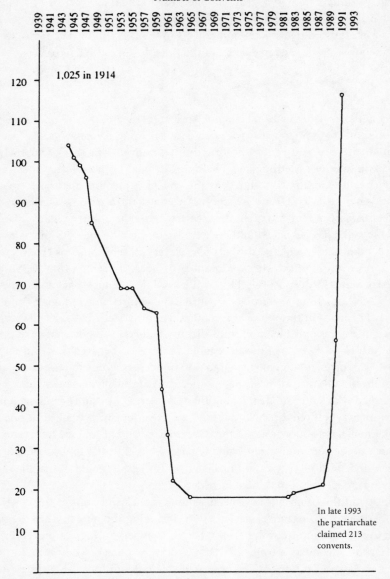

1,025 in 1914

In late 1993
the patriarchate
claimed 213
convents.

Source: Statistics recorded in the Archive of the Council for Religious Affairs, statements by Russian Orthodox hierarchs, and data given by Soviet, Soviet successor state, and Western observers. See Chapter 11, notes 18–25, 91, 93–94. For late 1993 see *Zhurnal Moskovskoi Patriarkhii* (Journal of the Moscow Patriarchate), No. 2 (February), 1994, p. 9.

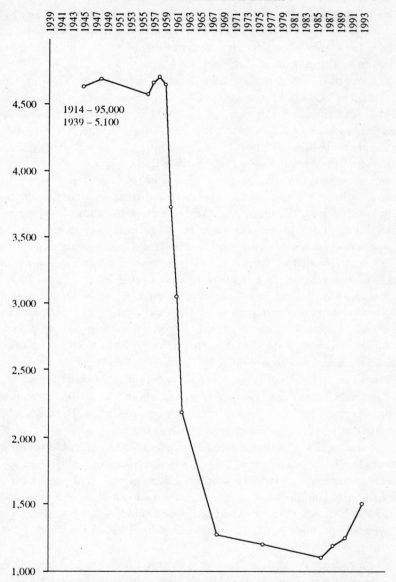

FIGURE 11.2
Number of Monks and Nuns in Cloisters

1914 – 95,000
1939 – 5,100

Sources: Statistics recorded in the Archive of the Council for Religious Affairs, statements by Russian Orthodox hierarchs, and data given by Soviet, Soviet successor state, and Western observers. See Chapter 11, note 98.

established convents have been struggling to maintain their ranks at premillennial levels, let alone to build up numbers.

Despite the problems, dedicated laypeople are volunteering to spend long months and sometimes years in the difficult and demanding work of reconstructing the convents and churches. Some of them find vocations and become novices and ultimately monks, monastic priests, and nuns.

The ranks of cloistered monks and nuns seem to have been increasing slowly since 1988. The Novosti Press Agency published the figure of 677 monks and nuns in Ukrainian convents in late 1990.[97] That would represent an increase of about 50 over the 630 monks and nuns in Ukrainian convents in the mid-1980s (which was slightly more than half the total in the country). Using data from a number of individual convents throughout the former USSR, one can estimate that the number of cloistered monks, nuns, and novices in 1994 was approximately 1,500. Figure 11.2 shows the numbers in the USSR and successor states in the post–World War II period.[98] Figures 11.1 and 11.2, taken together, show that the number of functioning convents is greater now than at any time since World War II, but the number of cloistered monks, nuns, and novices is hardly more than a third of the numbers recorded between 1945 and 1959. The church has had much more success in recovering its former premises and opening formerly closed convent buildings than it has had in finding large supplies of worthy men and women with vocations; to the church's credit, it has upheld rigorous standards even at the cost of numbers. Many years are needed to form and educate dedicated persons. It is difficult to imagine the church easily producing instant new cadres of committed, prepared, and effective nuns, brothers, and monastic priests.

I cannot close this discussion of Russian Orthodox monasticism without a word about the astonishing beauty of vespers in a monastic chapel, where ancient monks produce a music of worship that cannot be described. There must be an out-of-self inner peace as a monk or nun drags the body out of a cot to shiver through matins. There is a sense of belonging and exaltation and of community that is marvelously present—and tragically absent from most of modern life. To look into the cragged, gnarled, and sublime faces of the monks and nuns who have donned the angelic habit of the *mega schema* is to have a sense of approaching the Lord's design. Our present, frenetic world could use a few medieval saints, and we may find them in the monasteries and nunneries of the Russian Orthodox Church.[99]

The attitude of the authorities, although still a problem in a few places, is probably no longer an important obstacle to a renaissance of convent life. If not always benign, officials are often helpful or at least indifferent. The twin problems of human resources and money to repair and rebuild the institutions of the church have moved center stage. Both shortages will be excruciatingly difficult to overcome.

12

Theological Education

"AFTER LOVE, EDUCATION." These were the words of St. John Chrysostom, the golden-tongued saint of Orthodoxy, writing nearly sixteen centuries ago. He was describing the formation of a good pastor.[1] Through the long history of Russian Orthodoxy, there has never been any question that superior clerical training and education is vital to the well-being and future of the church.[2] How effective are the church's schools? Are perceptive and deeply knowledgeable professors successfully preparing intelligent and motivated students to become the future leaders of Russian Orthodoxy? Is the spiritual atmosphere in the schools conducive to the deepest commitment, faith, and Christian love?

The church provides an array of institutions and arrangements to train priests. At the exalted heights, the theological academies provide a university-level degree and are home to the scholars of the church. There are three academies, one in Kiev organized in 1991–1992 and two academies reopened just after World War II. These are the academy at the Trinity-Sergius monastery northeast of Moscow and the academy in the heart of St. Petersburg. The academies offer the *candidat* degree, which consists of three years of university-level study plus a thesis year.[3] After graduation as a *candidat,* a student may study three additional years at the Moscow academy and become an *aspirant.* Finally, as a bridge to a permanent career at the theological schools, a student may continue at one of the academies as a professorial scholar. The central task of the academies is to prepare highly qualified men for episcopal office and other crucial leadership positions. Academy and seminary students, like all college-level students in the former Soviet Union, paid nothing for instruction, room, and board; they received stipends according to a sliding scale that reflected academic excellence.[4]

The theological seminaries are technically regarded as secondary schools. They have maintained a four-year program since the World War II period and for a time had a fifth year during which students were expected to write a thesis.[5] The seminary curriculum is highly demanding despite a focus in the classroom on recitation, often by rote. Those who cannot complete the course may withdraw and become deacons, psalmists, church readers, or sometimes priests. Only about 2 percent of seminary students actually fail their course work in any given year, but another 2–3 percent who are doing badly appear to leave of their own accord. Others fall sick, and still others leave for personal reasons.[6] Attrition averaged about 10 percent a year in the 1950s and after 1965. During the Khrushchev drive, numerous seminarians were drafted into the army and whole seminaries were closed. After 1965 most students entered seminary after completing military service.

Some seminary students are ordained priests when they embark on their studies. For example, a fifty-five-year-old archimandrite who had been ordained for twenty-eight years graduated from the Odessa seminary in 1962. The more usual opportunity for such priests, however, is to enroll in the church's correspondence courses, either for seminary education or at the academy level. In October 1989 the Russian Orthodox bishops' council decided to have all seminaries and academies offer correspondence courses and also to organize an external studies department under which students, particularly those working in central church offices, could study independently and take examinations on their accomplishments.[7] Due to the shortage of parish priests, church authorities are loath to see an ordained cleric leave his flock to enter seminary.

The correspondence schools offer the same academic programs as the academies and seminaries. The Russian Orthodox culture fosters strong correspondence programs, in large part because they are closely monitored, hands-on, and demanding. During each of three sessions a year, correspondence students must attend two weeks of exams and intensive study on campus.[8] Eligible applicants greatly outnumber available places, and the church imposes a quota system in allocating slots.[9]

The third method of educating priests is a brief pastoral-theological course offered to devout men who normally have served for years as psalmists, readers, or deacons.[10] After World War II, the church organized these courses in many of the western lands of the USSR. The last method is that men can be ordained after devoted service at the altar and private instruction from experienced priests. The majority of the priests ordained in the Russian Orthodox Church since World War II have been church servers who have not had the benefit of extended formal theological education.

In addition to these four routes to the priesthood, the church has a variety of specialized training institutions for church servers. Laypeople may enter programs of up to three years in preparation for service as choir directors, deacons, psalmists, readers, and administrative workers (four years for the icon painting course). Unlike the seminaries and academies, which focus on the all-male priesthood, many of these institutions offer religious education and training to both women and men.

A measure of the magnitude of the church's educational effort is the number of schools and the number of students studying in each of them. In the 1930s Stalin closed all religious educational institutions. The situation changed, however, as World War II brought a loosening of the noose around the throat of the church and authorization in 1943 to reestablish formal training.

The long hiatus in institutional theological education made recovery very difficult. In 1943 Orthodox leaders spoke optimistically of establishing seminaries throughout the dioceses, as had been the case with the fifty-eight seminaries operating prior to the revolution.[11] In actuality, church leaders decided in late October 1943 to open a three-year theological institute program in Moscow and short pastoral-theological courses elsewhere. The Moscow institute, located at the former Novodevichi convent, was inaugurated on June 14, 1944. Due to the vicissitudes of the times, only half of the original thirty-six students completed their first academic year. In part, this reflected the church's difficulties in housing out-of-town students. Even in the autumn of 1945, 40 percent of the seventy-four students came from Moscow and lived at home. Late that year church authorities started organizing pastoral-theological courses in Leningrad, in the Ukrainian cities of Odessa and Lutsk, and in Byelorussia. Except for Leningrad, these places had been occupied by the Germans, and Orthodox Christians had been able to organize some sort of religious instruction during the occupation.[12]

By 1946 the church had opened full-fledged seminaries in Moscow, Leningrad, Lutsk, Minsk (Zhirovitsy), and Stavropol. During the following year seminaries began instruction in Kiev, Odessa, and Saratov. Saratov was the last to open, and Georgi Karpov, the chairman of the Soviet government's Council for Russian Orthodox Church Affairs, pointedly informed foreign correspondents that the state had given the church permission to open the Saratov seminary in early 1944; he claimed that the three-year delay was not "the fault of the state," indicating that it reflected the church's inefficiency. By 1946, advanced theological academies were operating in Leningrad and Moscow.[13] In 1948, the Moscow academy and seminary moved to the grounds of the Trinity-Sergius monastery at Zagorsk (Sergiev Posad). The monastery is located in Moscow oblast, and the theological schools there continue to this day to call themselves the Moscow academy and seminary.

During this period, the church also established programs to educate priests already serving in the parishes. In 1948, the Leningrad seminary and academy established correspondence programs to upgrade the education of priests unable to commute to their studies. Originally, the programs served only priests from the metropolitan of Leningrad's jurisdiction, which extended 1,000 kilometers from the edge of the Kola peninsula in the north to the Valdai hills south of Novgorod. In the 1950s, both the Moscow and Leningrad academies also ran evening courses for priests and deacons living within commuting distance.[14] According to Orthodox officials, a total of about 200 such students were enrolled in the two schools in 1956.[15]

In those early postwar years, Orthodox leaders encountered many additional obstacles as they tried to organize theological education. Some observers described a "desert," from which institutions were built from nothing and instructors assembled from a void. There were insufficient facilities, a paucity everywhere of sleeping quarters for students, a virtual absence of needed books, and some degree of disorganization and timidity. Dimitry Pospielovsky recounted a tale about Archbishop Vasili (Ratmirov) of Minsk, who successively refused three sites offered, including the former Lubomirski palace, for fear of the costs of restoration and the upkeep of the palace's beautiful gardens and vast buildings. He finally settled on excessively modest premises on the rural Zhirovitsy monastery grounds.[16] Nevertheless, most of the immediate postwar difficulties were slowly overcome, and the two academies and eight seminaries in the country lived through more than a decade of relative stability and improving effectiveness.

Although the postwar years were a period of growth, the state seems to have limited the student population, imposing an unpublicized but enforced ceiling of 200 students (counting both the seminary and the academy) at Moscow and the same number in Leningrad. As seminary students finished their course, and as some of them began graduate work at the academies, the number of academy students increased steadily at both institutions. For a year or two, the Leningrad schools could absorb the increase because they had not yet reached their ceiling. The Moscow schools seem to have pared the entering seminary classes, which allowed the academy to continue growing without exceeding the cap. Enrollment figures for the Moscow seminary's entering classes in the late 1940s illustrate this phenomenon: seventy-nine new students in 1946; fifty-seven in 1947; and forty-three in 1948. Seminary officials pointed to "higher academic and medical standards" to explain why they had accepted so few of the applicants, but they were actually making necessity a virtue.[17] In 1948, the Soviet government recorded 562 students at the eight seminaries and two academies in the country.[18] By the 1950–1951 school year enrollment had increased to a total of 730.[19]

Sometime after Stalin's death the ceilings for the Moscow and Leningrad schools apparently were raised to 300 each and for the six other seminaries to 150 each. Zhirovitsy in Byelorussia and Odessa in Ukraine briefly exceeded the cap, but the student populations at the other seminaries ranged between 72 (Stavropol in 1955) and 148 (Lutsk in 1957).[20]

By 1955 the Leningrad correspondence schools were serving students throughout the Soviet territories, and their numbers had grown from 200 to approximately 400.[21] There were a few more students in the correspondence academy course (147) than the number studying full-time and in residence at the two academies (142).[22] In the autumn of 1956 the Council for Russian Orthodox Church Affairs recorded the ecclesiastical ranks of the correspondence students at all levels and the places from which they came. Over 75 percent were parish priests, about 10 percent were deacons, and about 3 percent were monastic clergy; about half were from Ukraine, and 90 percent were from the western territories taken as a whole.[23] The Soviet government recorded enrollments in each institution for the fall of 1955 as follows:

Academies		Seminaries	
Moscow	79	Moscow	149 [24]
Leningrad	63	Leningrad	100
	142	Kiev	72
		Minsk (Zhirovitsy)	104
		Odessa	124
		Saratov	84
		Stavropol	72
Correspondence study		Lutsk	113
Leningrad	403		818
All students		1363 [25]	

Numbers increased over the following several years. As the 1958–1959 school year started, the number for all students had increased to over 1,700.[26] In the late 1950s there were close to 1,100 full-time seminary students in the country, about 160 full-time academy students, and almost 500 seminary and academy correspondence students.

The Khrushchev antireligious drive hit the church schools hard. One of the drive's first measures, taken in 1959, was to exclude seminarians from draft deferments normally given to college-level students.[27] On May 4, 1960, Vladimir Kuroedov, the new head of the Council for Russian Orthodox Church Affairs, summoned Patriarch Aleksi I and told him he should close the Kiev, Stavropol, and Saratov seminaries. Interpreting Kuroedov's "proposal" as an order, the patriarch acquiesced. According to Dimitry Pospielovsky, Metropolitan Ioann (Sokolov) of Kiev and Metropolitan Antoni (Romanovski) of Stavropol "rushed" to close their seminaries "without waiting for the secular authorities to put pressure to bear on them."[28]

The denial of draft deferments to seminarians was having an even greater impact on seminary enrollments than the closing of the Kiev and Stavropol schools. By January of 1961, the figure for total enrollment in the country had already dropped to 667 resident academy and seminary students, about 500 fewer than the number of resident students enrolled in 1959–1960.[29]

The authorities obliged the Leningrad correspondence schools to stop accepting students in 1961.[30] Saratov closed later in the year. In Odessa, the seminary was forced to relinquish its premises, but local church leaders moved the students to the Dormition monastery grounds at the edge of the city, where Patriarch Aleksi had his summer residence, and thereby saved the school. By early 1962, the authorities were recording 561 resident academy and seminary students; this represented a drop of about 100 in resident enrollment in two years.[31]

According to Father Sergi Gordun of the now-reborn Minsk seminary, that institution had been blocked from recruiting a new entering class after 1959 and had only five remaining upperclassmen in August of 1963, at which time the seminary ceased to function. The patriarch never agreed to its closing nor to the later closing of the Lutsk seminary.[32] Lutsk taught its last courses in 1964 and closed down, having been reduced, like the Minsk seminary, to five upperclassmen in the summer of 1963.[33] Lutsk almost survived the Khrushchev drive, and with a little more luck, it might have stayed open. Caprice and personality played a great role in these matters, as mighty cathedrals and village churches also succumbed or survived on what was almost a roll of the dice. By the autumn of 1963, the church had obtained permission to open a four-year correspondence seminary program and a four-year correspondence academy program based in Moscow (Zagorsk), which compensated somewhat for the ban on new admissions to the Leningrad correspondence programs.[34] In September of 1964, just before Khrushchev fell, there were 211 resident seminary students and 207 resident academy students in the country.

After the Khrushchev drive, the church emerged with three functioning seminaries—Moscow, Leningrad, and Odessa—and with its two academies. Resident enrollment at the academies had been sustained far better than at the seminaries, partly because the church gave the academies top priority as the source of future bishops and intellectual leaders, partly because the authorities cared less about these aging clerics, perhaps knowing more about them, and partly because conscription affected the academies less. The Moscow schools suffered the least from Khrushchev's antireligious assault; their combined resident seminary and academy enrollment dropped from roughly 300 before the drive to about 250.[35] In Leningrad, the combined resident seminary and academy enrollment dropped from about 270 in 1956 to 150 Soviet students in 1965.[36] The Odessa seminary had been forced to halve its pre-1960 enrollment of 150. Whereas there had been slightly more than 1,200 full-time academy and seminary students in the country in the late 1950s, there were about 475 in 1965. The Moscow correspondence school emerged from the Khrushchev drive with about 300 combined seminary and academy students, about 200 fewer than had been studying by correspondence at the Leningrad school in 1958–1959.[37] The Moscow correspondence school grew steadily, however, and reached a student population of about 400 by 1968–1969.[38] Between 1958 and 1965 total figures for academy and seminary students dropped from roughly 1,700 to about 800.

In the decades between the end of the Khrushchev antireligious drive and the Millennium, the number of religious educational institutions for priests remained constant. The enrollment figures, however, grew slowly throughout this period.

The Moscow schools' resident student population reached what was probably a combined seminary-academy ceiling of 300 by 1973, 400 between 1978 and 1980, and 500 between 1980 and 1988. The ceilings during this period may have reflected both the government's restrictions and the capacity of the schools' residential facilities. A Western observer explained the increased enrollments by noting that the Moscow complex had raised its intake "by packing the students in 'like herrings in a box.'"[39] In the 1984–1985 academic year at Moscow there were 412 resident seminary students and 113 resident academy students, a total of 525.[40]

The Leningrad schools seem to have crept back to a ceiling of 200 resident academy and seminary students in the period between 1965 and 1972–1973. In 1977 the authorities gave the seminary and academy two more buildings and apparently increased the ceiling to 300. In the early 1980s the ceiling was probably raised to 400, not counting foreign students or a few commuters from the city. In 1988 the Leningrad academy received more space and the opportunity to expand further.[41]

The Odessa seminary crept up to about 100 students at the beginning of the 1970s. In 1975 the seminary expanded further, opening two parallel sections for its first-year class. By the 1975–1976 school year the seminary was serving about 140 students. In 1976 the authorities allowed the seminary to rebuild its facilities. Francis House recounted the story: "The Rector, who was described as 'a very clever administrator,' obtained permission to restore the old and cramped seminary building. But it 'fell down'—and was then rebuilt with double the accommodation. Government officials accepted the *fait accompli*."[42] In 1988 the student body consisted of 240 students.[43]

During the 1974–1975 academic year, the number of residential students at the church's five schools exceeded the countrywide 1948 enrollment figures by 5 men and the 1965 figures by about 100, for 567 full-time students.[44] By 1988 the number of full-time students had grown by 450 more, to a total of 1,029.[45] By 1977 enrollment at the Moscow correspondence schools approached 800 and remained at about that level until the Millennium.[46] Thus, by the Millennium, the church's theological schools had worked their way back up to a full-time enrollment of about 200 fewer than in 1959 and to a correspondence school enrollment of about 300 more than in 1959.

Although the number of theological school graduates is one measure of success in the creation of an educated clergy, the adequacy of professorial staff and the quality of instruction are also crucial factors. In 1947–1948 the Moscow establishment had a faculty of eighteen and a faculty-student ratio of about one to ten, a ratio that has not changed significantly since then. In 1964, after Moscow took on the correspondence school function, there were about thirty-five on the faculty.[47] In 1973–1974 there was a teaching staff of fifty-three, of whom seven were in subjects like music and art. In 1984 there were about sixty faculty members.[48]

In Leningrad there were ten faculty members in 1946 and twenty-five in 1956.[49] In 1982 the teaching staff totaled forty-three men and women.[50] A dozen to fifteen faculty members taught at the Odessa seminary in the late 1960s and early 1970s, maintaining a faculty-student ratio of about one to ten.[51] By the end of the 1970s the faculty had increased to twenty-two, after which the numbers leveled off.[52]

Judging the quality of instruction is more difficult than counting the teaching staff. Instruction and scholarship at the church's schools can be regarded as sound but not innovative. The Russian Orthodox seminary curriculum is quite similar to that of Orthodox seminaries in the West—St. Vladimir's in New York, for example. Russian Orthodox students spend about thirty-six hours a week in class, compared to about twenty-five in New York, and their program requires Greek and Latin, which are not required in New York. St. Vladimir's has a semester of Christian education, which was omitted from the curriculum for most of the Soviet period, but the Gorbachev-era laws on freedom of conscience and the reforms opened the door to this important subject.[53]

The curriculum of the Moscow and St. Petersburg (formerly Leningrad) academies is similar to that of the seminaries but on a more advanced level. Some students write dissertations on semipolitical subjects, but most write in the field of church history or the writings of the church fathers. The academies also teach a number of subjects not offered in the seminaries, including logic, canon law, Byzantology, archaeology, and Hebrew.[54]

Western observers consistently note the paucity of philosophical inquiry and instruction on contemporary social issues in the Russian Orthodox schools. William C. Fletcher commented some years ago:

> The theological research done at these schools, so far as is known, has assiduously avoided any attempt at the risky business of answering the challenges of present Soviet society. Instead, the theological schools have been devoting the bulk of their attention to such matters as patristics and dogmatics, or to ecumenical research. Neither of these fields seems to promise particular benefit in increasing Orthodoxy's ability to relate to modern society, for the former areas are in many respects antiquarian, while the latter deal with events more applicable outside the USSR than within contemporary Soviet society.[55]

Fletcher was right. The Soviet authorities suppressed the study of philosophy and non-Marxist social studies at both the seminary and academy levels.[56] Until the USSR collapsed, the delicacy of the church's position in a Marxist society explained these failings, although Soviet churchmen offered other explanations. In the mid-1950s the rector of the Moscow theological seminary and academy stated: "The Academy does not bother with rationalism or philosophical systems. . . . If a rare preacher preaches a philosophical sermon, our people say: 'We can get that elsewhere, tell us about Christ.'"[57]

Nikolai K. Gavryushin, an instructor at the Moscow academy, echoed Western scholars' criticisms in a broadside published by the *Moscow Church Herald, Weekly* in September 1990. Gavryushin blamed the "sad state" of the Moscow academy on the predominance of "scholastic" forms of thought (rather than creative and insightful ones). The theological schools emerged after World War II with "barracks discipline" and a "bureaucratic leadership." Gavryushin asserted that Soviet theologians had not kept up with work being done abroad. (When I visited the Valaam monastery in May 1994, I conversed with one of the senior monastic priests there, an academy graduate, and found that he had never heard of Paul Tillich or Reinhold Niebuhr.) Gavryushin said that the Moscow and Leningrad academies did not even exchange copies of dissertations. He charged that some correspondence students could not even answer simple questions put to them. At least until the late 1980s, the academy curriculum largely repeated the seminary course, and "not on a new level." The textbooks were old. Independent thinking was not encouraged; students' *candidat* dissertations were compilations. *Magister* dissertations emphasized bulk. According to Gavryushin, the theological schools needed ties with the secular universities, better language facilities, and most important, an atmosphere of scholarly association and creative cooperation. There was a consciousness among junior instructors of being "disenfranchised hired hands." A theological bulletin was planned for the end of 1990, but Gavryushin expressed the fear that it would end up suffering from church-imposed censorship.[58]

Maksim E. Kozlov wrote an answering article that appeared a few weeks after Gavryushin's critique. Kozlov defended the scholarship of the theological schools, although he used a 1948 example in doing so; he also defended the psychological atmosphere of the Moscow schools, asserting that a committed religious community needed rigor. Kozlov acknowledged the Moscow instructors' unfamiliarity with international scholarship, explaining that "until recently," internal conditions got in the way (meaning official Soviet governmental interference). He expressed gratitude for the gifts of books coming from the Russian Orthodox Church Abroad, which contributed to improvements in the schools' programs. The editor of the *Moscow Church Herald, Weekly* closed the exchange with the affirmation that the wounded, struggling church needed an open dialogue to diagnose its maladies and added that it should be in the pages of its own publications, not simply in *Ogonëk* and *Kommersant*.[59]

The church hierarchy had already voiced some of the same concerns Gavryushin expressed with such passion. In 1988 Archbishop Aleksandr (Timofeev), the rector of the Moscow schools, called for theological journals, more contact between the Moscow and Leningrad academies, and a scientific-theological center for the Russian Orthodox Church. In a report of October 1989, Archbishop Aleksandr emphasized the need to strengthen seminary instruction in philosophy, history, literature, and languages. So far as the academies were concerned, he called for the deepening of scholarship in Biblical and theological sciences, liturgics, church history, canon law, and ancient and modern languages. He acknowledged the problem of overlapping in the instruction offered by the seminary and academy courses and cited the need for better coordination with the newly opened seminaries and theological training institutions. He recognized the need for more "practical" efforts to prepare pastors to feel responsible for the "spiritual condition, fate, joys and sorrows" of their flock, putting behind them the idea that it was enough to perform the cult. Last, Archbishop Aleksandr noted that increased financial resources would be necessary to cure the ailments of the church's educational system.[60]

Even in the aftermath of World War II, A. V. Vedernikov, the first postwar inspector of the Moscow theological school, had written as follows: "It was necessary to lift the [students] ... to a higher understanding of Christianity. ... This meant first of all a struggle with the tendency of the majority ... to learn theological truths by rote."[61] Vice chairman Furov of the Council for Religious Affairs noted lax academic standards at the Moscow academy in the mid-1970s; in 1974 the academy even awarded the degree of *candidat* to four students who had failed to submit the required thesis. One man studying to become an *aspirant,* on the other hand, submitted a dissertation of 3,235 typed pages, most of it simply retyped documents.[62]

As for improving ties with secular universities, Patriarch Aleksi II discussed collaboration with the rector of Moscow State University in 1991, and cooperative, integrated instruction has ensued. With regard to "barracks discipline," there is no gainsaying that the daily schedule at the schools is rigorous. Morning prayers start the day at 5:30 A.M., and studies, homework, chores, choir, meals, and evening prayers fill the hours until bed at 11 P.M. Only on Sunday is discipline relaxed to the point of showing a movie.[63]

If the folklore is to be believed, there are fundamental differences between the Moscow and St. Petersburg theological schools. Foreigners have reported that the latter have "a more worldly atmosphere and ... a somewhat more Western outlook," whereas the Moscow schools are "more conservative."[64] The 1975 Furov report quoted Archbishop Yermogen (Orekhov) of Kalinin as follows:

> Our clergy is divided into two categories—representing the graduates of the theological schools in Zagorsk and in Leningrad. Among the former are, unfortunately, many obscurantists, fools for God and fanatics. Soberly thinking individuals predominate among the latter. Much can be explained by the atmosphere [at the two

schools]. Human psychology cannot remain unaffected by living four and, in some cases, eight years within the walls of the [Trinity-Sergius] monastery.[65]

The Soviet commissioner to whom Yermogen made the foregoing remarks agreed that "fanatics, persons with unwholesome attitudes and lawbreakers are most common among the graduates" of the Moscow schools. In other words, the Moscow graduates were notably zealous and committed, both "fanatical" traits from the communist point of view. The Moscow schools lie, as Yermogen observed, within the walls of Russian Orthodoxy's greatest monastery, removed from the influence of the city of Moscow, whereas the St. Petersburg school lies in the center of the most western of Russia's great cities.

Although both Moscow and St. Petersburg enjoy the leavening and broadening influence of a considerable contingent of foreign students, the St. Petersburg academy is particularly blessed in this regard. There have been times when the St. Petersburg schools have had about fifty enrolled foreign students.[66] The city's academy has also lived under the strong influence of Metropolitan Nikodim (Rotov) and his disciple, Metropolitan Kirill (Gundyaev), head of the church's Office of Foreign Church Relations and formerly rector of the Leningrad schools. Nikodim resided on the premises of the Leningrad schools when he presided over the Leningrad see (1963–1978). He was a modernist, an ecumenist, and a friend of Catholics and Protestants, causing some to believe he would lead Russian Orthodoxy toward a new Renovationist schism. His and Kirill's influence unquestionably brought liberalizing and reformist currents of thought to Leningrad.

As for Odessa, its retired rector, Archpriest Aleksandr N. Kravchenko, worked at the seminary for forty years as assistant inspector, acting inspector and inspector, and as rector for a quarter century. A strong, wily, and effective administrator, he made the school prosper as the only Ukrainian theological school during Brezhnev's era of stagnation. Because it has no academy, Odessa has largely avoided the theological controversies that have characterized the life of the schools at Moscow and St. Petersburg. The school has become a beacon for the intellectual aspirations of Ukrainian priests.

The church overextends all the schools' human and material resources. The name of an overworked professor is on the roster of almost any international delegation of the Russian Orthodox Church. When foreign visitors come, and a great many do, professors often conduct them around. The theological schools work in tandem with the Office of Foreign Church Relations, and one sometimes has to wonder whether the professors are left with any time to teach, let alone think. The professors are the shock troops of the patriarchate.

The schools' libraries are similarly stretched to the limits. Even the established schools possess relatively small and outdated libraries, and the newly opened seminaries struggle painfully to obtain books. Raymond Oppenheim reported in the mid-1970s that the library at Moscow had 270,000 volumes, half of them predating the 1917 revolution and about 15 percent foreign. By 1982 the library had almost 300,000 volumes and has modestly increased its holdings since then.[67]

The Leningrad theological schools' library had 10,000 volumes in 1946.[68] It was later able to reacquire some 80,000 books of the old St. Petersburg theological academy, and its collection had grown to 200,000 volumes by the autumn of 1956.[69] I did some work in the library during the summer of 1991 and estimated its holdings at 300,000 volumes. The library occupies a small suite of rooms on the second floor of the seminary and academy building.[70] A Dutch student at the Leningrad academy between 1974 and 1977 described the library's holdings as follows:

> The books in Russian, as far as they concern theology, are in general pre-revolutionary. Book[s] which have appeared in Russian in the West after 1917 are rare. . . . Books on subjects in history are still the best ones, especially if they are about long-distant times. . . . Textbooks in Russian are either pre-revolutionary or do not exist. With great zeal and love, textbooks are replaced by hard-covered bound sheets, typed (with some sheets of carbon paper one can make three or four copies, the last one of course of a terrible quality) by typists in the academy.[71]

The Odessa seminary was reported in 1976 to have a library containing 25,000 books.[72] Even in the late 1980s, students there had to share textbooks. Archbishop Aleksandr (Timofeev) publicly expressed his concern in 1989 at the lack of books in the newly opened theological schools, noting that the Moscow and St. Petersburg libraries were generously "helping" by giving books. Because of the paucity of resources in those principal libraries, the new schools must be encountering immense difficulties.[73]

The quality of the students ultimately determines an educational institution's success. According to Dimitry Pospielovsky, "the new generations of priests produced by the postwar seminaries are of incomparably higher spiritual and moral caliber" than the "impudent, fattened, slipshod priests of Stalin's vintage."[74] Yet Pospielovsky also said:

> It is generally recognized in church circles that, owing to the close control of the seminaries by the CRA [Council for Religious Affairs]—which includes rejection of so-called religious fanatics, constant KGB attempts to recruit seminarians, and . . . subservience . . . of the seminary administration and some professors—the priests graduating from the seminaries are on the average less dedicated to their vocation than those who prepare for ordination outside any institutional framework, under the guidance of a bishop or a priest.[75]

Other observers also asserted that the "truest priests are those consecrated directly, not the seminary graduates."[76]

One cannot deny that the Council for Religious Affairs and its local commissioners investigated and rejected seminary applicants throughout the postwar era until 1988. The KGB consistently tried to recruit and "turn" seminarians and systematically infiltrated the administrative and teaching staffs of the seminaries and academies. Nonetheless, most of the seminary and academy graduates turned out to be committed Christians. Some priests were more courageous than others, but most were not voluntary tools of the Soviet organs of control. In any case, the manipulative, subversive, and repressive capacities of the Council for Religious Affairs and the KGB had diminished greatly even before the passage of the freedom-of-conscience legislation in late 1990 and the events of August 1991.

The foregoing does not invalidate assertions by Pospielovsky and others that the priests trained privately are the best ones, but priests trained at the seminaries and academies are also required. The leaders of the church have labored greatly to find loyal sons of the church among those who serve at the altar, yet it also needs educated sons.

Statistics on the percentage of applicants accepted for the seminaries and academies abound. Unfortunately, all too often the trends have reflected factors unrelated to the desire of applicants to pursue a priestly vocation. Reportedly there was an easing in harassment of prospective seminarians in 1967 that caused more to apply.[77] As already mentioned, in the mid-1970s, the Soviet government began allowing graduates of secular universities to be accepted at the seminaries. For most of the postwar Soviet era, at least twice as many young men sought entrance to the seminaries as had the chance to go, and there were times when the ratio was three or four applicants for every place.[78] The academies were somewhat less selective, partly because eligibility was principally established by a student's grades in seminary and because quite a few young men married and chose to go out and serve in the parish ministry without further delay.[79] Overall, the schools attracted a talented and committed group of students.

A large proportion of the young men who have entered the priesthood are sons or close relatives of priests. Clearly, others have been deeply influenced by committed, believing women in their families or close to them. Nevertheless, a seminarian at the Moscow school estimated that half of his fellow students were from nonreligious families; one seminarian even found his way to faith after he was assigned to carry out surveillance in church as a Komsomol spy. Another had hidden out in friends' cellars and in the forest for a summer in the 1960s to avoid being apprehended and thereby prevented from matriculating. In the 1950s the Council for Religious Affairs recorded some figures on the number of entering seminarians who came from church-related families. The statistics confirmed that about half of those who applied from Moscow were from church-related families, and about a quarter of the applicants from western Ukraine were from such families. The majority of the applicants were from rural communities in both cases, although some were intellectuals who found their own path to Christian belief.[80] In late 1989 the *Moscow Church Herald, Weekly* published vignettes of eight young men who were new seminarians at Moscow. Here are a few snatches of the descriptions:

> . . . ex-Komsomol. Parents became Christians. Turned to reading the Gospels. Baptized in 1986. Father Nikolai Vedernikov of Moscow had a great influence.
>
> . . . After high school went to military school because of family tradition. Turned to reading Dostoyevski. Got faith in the army.
>
> . . . Grew up in Lithuania. Parents believers.
>
> . . . Ukrainian. Grew up in a believing family. Army officers knew of belief, but the army experience was "normal." Became a sexton. The bishop and the parish priest had a great influence.
>
> . . . From Ivano-Frankovsk in western Ukraine. Father read the Bible. Wife from a family of believers. Applied Moscow seminary in 1981. Application filed too late. Applied again in 1982, but was not selected. Now, in 1989, accepted.
>
> . . . Studied at the Marxist-Leninist University in Odessa. A fellow student talked about religion and taught it man to man. Baptized when in the army.
>
> . . . Son of a priest. From Ukraine.
>
> . . . From the Urals. Parents not believers. Thought about the meaning of life.[81]

Although the seminary and academy courses form the backbone of formal religious education, the Russian Orthodox Church also sponsors specialized schools for choir directors. In the late 1960s, Moscow, Leningrad, and Odessa opened three-year choir directors' courses for students who were musically gifted.[82] This did not much swell the supply of choir directors, however, as musical training was an add-on for young men already preparing for the priesthood. In the late 1970s, however, the choir directors' courses were opened to laypeople, including women.[83] By 1988 there were 60 students at the Moscow choir school, and 240 young men and women completed the course at one of the three institutions offering it in the seventeen years between 1971 and 1988.[84] I should add that competent choir direction in an Orthodox church is immensely important work.

As it did for so many other aspects of church life, the Millennium greatly changed the church's theological education. The number of students at the established seminaries increased markedly. For the 1988–1989 school year the first two classes of the Moscow seminary were split into four parallel streams.[85] The Moscow seminary took in an entering class of 200 in the late summer of 1991 (out of 400 applicants); the entire seminary had had only 500 students prior to the Millennium.[86] According to its rector, the St. Petersburg seminary had 480 students in the spring of 1991. If St. Petersburg's resident academy students are included, this would be at least 100 more students than there were prior to the Millennium.[87] The Odessa seminary had 282 students in early 1991, compared to 240 in 1988. The school also opened a new three-story dormitory complex.[88] The Holy Synod authorized the reestablishment of the seminaries at Kiev and Minsk (Zhirovitsy) in early 1989, and both were functioning by autumn. The Kiev seminary had 159 students in early 1991.[89] A new seminary at Tobolsk (Tyumen oblast) in Siberia was reported to have commenced operations before the close of the 1989 calendar year.[90]

In early October 1989, Metropolitan Vladimir (Sabodan) of Rostov reported 2,948 students in what were then the church's nineteen schools. Of these students, 750–850 were resident seminary students at Moscow and Leningrad; slightly over half of them were at Moscow. The Odessa, Kiev, Minsk, and Tobolsk seminaries had about 450–550 more resident students, half of them at Odessa. The Moscow seminary correspondence school division would add 650–750 students. The Moscow and Leningrad resident academies would add 200 resident students, 60 percent of them at Moscow, and 220 Moscow academy correspondence students. Five new theological training institutes for psalmists, readers, and choir directors (at Chernigov, Kishinev, Novosibirsk, Smolensk, and Stavropol) had a total in that category of about 200. The Moscow and Leningrad choir schools, taken together, had about 200 students, divided fairly evenly between the two schools. The Moscow school for the postgraduate *aspirantura* degree would add about twenty more. The total enrollment for the nineteen schools just mentioned is close to the metropolitan's figure of 2,948.[91]

By late 1990 one new seminary and ten new theological institutes had opened.[92] Student enrollment at fifteen of the nineteen schools existing in late 1989 had gone up by less than 3 percent, to a total of about 2,700. The institutes added about 200–250 students to this figure, and a new icon-painting school established at Moscow added another 20 students.[93] The total number of students in late 1990 thus was 2,900–2,950.[94]

In the course of the 1990–1991 academic year the Leningrad academy and seminary, the Odessa seminary, and the newly opened seminaries in Kiev and Minsk (Zhirovitsy) implemented the church's directive, to open correspondence divisions. The Odessa seminary reported "over 100" enrolled correspondence students; the Minsk seminary correspondence division, which opened November 26, 1990, reported 31.[95] In the autumn of 1991 the Moscow seminary and academy correspondence schools had 815 students enrolled, a decline from 915–920 in the autumn of 1990.[96]

In the autumn of 1991 the Moscow choir school had grown to 164 enrolled students, both men and women, or roughly 50 more than in the autumn of 1989. The Moscow icon-painting school had grown to 44—double the enrollment of the year before. The number of resident students at the Moscow seminary had grown in the two years between late 1989 and late 1991 from slightly over 400 to close to 500, and the number of resident students at the Moscow academy had grown from about 120 to about 150. In late 1993 the patriarch reported that the church's establishments for educating priests and other church workers consisted of three academies (Moscow, St. Petersburg, and Kiev, which—after some initial faltering—were in operation); thirteen seminaries (an increase of five over the eight functioning in late 1989); and twenty-two theological institutes for the training of church workers and in some cases priests.[97]

In March 1992 the St. Tikhon Orthodox Theological Institute began operations, first as a part-time enterprise, then in September 1992 as a full-time activity, and in 1993 it added a correspondence school. Headed by Archpriest Vladimir Vorobev, it claims 1,000 students, among whom about 100 are studying for the priesthood. Its various programs include music, icon painting, secular arts, architecture, museum work, and theological study and research. The institute uses Moscow State University classrooms and facilities but hopes to acquire its own premises.[98]

A new Russian Orthodox University of St. John the Evangelist, located on the Zaikonospasski monastery grounds near Red Square in Moscow, opened its doors to students in February 1993. The university planned a five- to six-year course with three academic departments: philosophy and theology, Bible studies and patristics, and history, languages, and philosophy. Rigorous study of ancient and modern languages was announced as a requirement. Hegumen Ioann (Ekonomtsev) was named the rector and the announced purpose of the institution is to unite scientific thought and religious values, principally for lay people working in the world. The university claims 2000 students—mostly part-time—and some at the secondary-school level. In addition to the university just described, there is also an Open Orthodox University in Moscow named after Father Aleksandr Men and a Humanitarian Christian University in St. Petersburg.[99]

Figure 12.1 reflects the number of students in the seminaries and academies between 1944 and the 1992–1993 academic year and enrollments in all the church's long-term theological training institutions during the same period.[100]

Why were not all five seminaries that perished during the Khrushchev antireligious drive promptly reopened? Until 1988, there was undoubtedly resistance on the part of the authorities to such a restoration. The patriarchal authorities were resourceful enough, however, to expand their operations and facilities to almost predrive levels. After the Millennium, church leaders perceived the need for auxiliary church servers to be so great that they turned in that direction. For

FIGURE 12.1
Number of Students in All Theological Schools

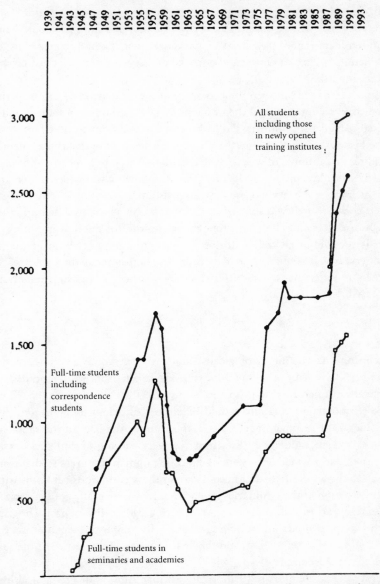

Sources: Statistics recorded in the Archive of the Council for Religious Affairs, statements by Russian Orthodox hierarchs, and data given by Soviet, Soviet successor state, and Western observers. See Chapter 12, notes 12, 17–22, 25–26, 29–31, 34–38, 40, 43–46, 83–84, 86–89, 91, 93–97, and 100.

example, rather than reopening as seminaries, Saratov and Stavropol initially organized training institutes for psalmists and choir directors.[101] Smolensk, Chernigov, and a number of other dioceses moved in the same direction.[102] Obviously, Kiev and Minsk, seats of newly "autonomous" churches, could not be without seminaries, and these institutions were among the first reopened in 1989. Siberia had its pride as a region and also had an extraordinarily activist group of clerics in Tobolsk.[103]

In general, however, the central leadership of the church seemed to be turning its most urgent efforts toward the development of the human resources so long neglected—deacons, psalmists, choir directors, and administrative workers. In fact, the bishops' council that met in October 1989 explicitly stated that theological training institutions "of a new type"—schools for church servers—should be accorded "special attention." At its meeting the following June, the council articulated the hope that every diocese have an institute.[104]

Whether the church will succeed in eliminating the grievous deficit of church servers at the altar and choir directors in the choir loft is another question. The answer is probably that they will not, because a large proportion of the new church servers will sooner or later be ordained as priests, as their predecessors have been, in order that the still overwhelming shortage of parish priests can be ameliorated.

In conclusion, the existing theological schools have overcome the blows received in the Khrushchev antireligious drive and are graduating greater numbers of theologically trained men than in the late 1950s. The output was then "almost enough." Seminary graduations would be almost sufficient today if conditions were stable, if the number of parishes in the country were about the same as in early 1988, if most graduates of the seminaries were sent out to staff parishes, and if the church had an effective system of allocating human resources so that priests would go to the areas of greatest need. None of these conditions yet holds true.

The instruction at the seminaries and academies is essentially good, despite an excess of rote learning and a preoccupation with the long-distant past. The young men who go to seminary are in their great majority people one can admire. Even now, it is not easy to be a priest, and the dedication and intelligence of the seminarians of today are impressive.

Whether the academies are turning out seminal thinkers or theological innovators is another matter. There is a real question whether they should be doing so, or whether they should be concentrating on the training of future bishops who are gifted pastors. It is difficult in any case to know the well-springs of creativity in any society or in any academic institution anywhere. Perhaps the Florovskys, Florenskys, Bulgakovs, and Berdyaevs of tomorrow are already waiting in the wings, and they may break free, regardless of the conservative, traditional character of the academies in the present age. It is difficult ever to know where the borderline between constructive innovation and destructive experimentation lies.

The canons of the church admonish the church's leaders and faithful that their first duty is "to preserve without distortion and innovation that faith passed on to us."[105] The church's leadership and the church's educational institutions have preserved the faith, and that is no mean accomplishment.

13
Publications and Finances

St. John's Gospel begins "In the beginning was the Word." Although Jesus proclaimed the Word by means of voice, acts, and example, Christian disciples soon needed holy scriptures to teach the faith to new generations. Church servers need liturgical books; Christian scholars need publications and journals; the Russian Orthodox community needs printed materials to bind it together and enlighten its thought. Publishing is crucial to the health of the Russian Orthodox Church.

In 1926, the Soviet authorities withheld all authorizations to publish Bibles and other religious materials; this was part of the Bolsheviks' effort to suffocate the church. Not until thirty years later, in 1956, did they grudgingly permit an edition of 25,000 Bibles.[1] According to Deacon Vladimir Rusak, who worked in the publishing department of the patriarchate, only 10,000 of these copies were distributed to parishes in the USSR. Of the remaining 15,000, the theological schools received 3,000, the patriarchate kept 2,000 as a reserve, and the authorities sent 10,000 Bibles abroad.[2] The Four Continents Book Shop in New York received fifty of these volumes, while millions of believers in the Soviet Union went without.[3] The state did not permit another edition until 1968, when the church published 40,000 Bibles; two years later it published an additional 30,000 copies. The patriarchate had to share these Bibles with the Baptists. Rusak stated that ten Bibles were distributed to each Moscow church, but many village churches received none.[4] The 1970s brought some loosening of government restrictions, and the church published 220,000 copies of the Bible between 1976 and 1983. In sum, roughly 300,000 Bibles were printed in a fifty-seven-year period.[5]

Until 1988, however, the slight relaxation of restriction on printing did not affect the ban on importing Bibles. A foreigner could take only one copy of the Bible into the USSR, and had to register it on his or her customs declaration to ensure that the Bible was taken back out. I well remember leading a group of students on a train from Helsinki in May of 1985. The woman on duty in the railroad car interrogated me about the possibility that the students were bringing in Bibles; she ended her admonitory lecture by saying that it would be a far, far better thing, indeed, for the students to cast their illegal Bibles out of the train window before the border than to be apprehended with those forbidden books.

According to reports that filtered to the West over the years, these restrictions created a thriving black-market trade in Bibles; they were sold for 100–160 rubles (then $200), a large sum for a Soviet worker or pensioner in those days. Observers speculated that customs inspectors and personnel of the Council for Religious Affairs enriched themselves by supplying this black-market trade.[6]

The prohibition against importing Bibles began to crack in March 1988, when the Soviet authorities announced an easing of the customs ban. Apparently, the new rules allowed a private citizen to receive by mail two religious texts per calendar year.[7] In November of the same year, the customs authorities at the border relaxed their vigorous searches for contraband Bibles.[8] The Soviet government allowed the Russian Orthodox Church to accept 100,000 copies of the Bible in Ukrainian from the United Bible Societies and 150,000 copies of A. P. Lopukhin's three-volume interpreter's Bible as a gift from Christians in the Nordic countries.[9]

The patriarchate published 100,000 copies of the Russian-language Bible in 1988.[10] In 1989, *Izvestiya* reported that 9,000 Bibles in Ukrainian were to be printed and 200,000 Ukrainian Bibles were expected from abroad.[11] In March, *Komsomolskaya Pravda* reported that the entire print run of 100,000 Russian-language Bibles authorized for the Millennium had been sold, and another 50,000 were to be run off the presses.[12] In October, however, Metropolitan Pitirim (Nechaev) acknowledged that he could not obtain the necessary supplies of paper.[13]

In 1990 and 1991 there was a significant expansion in both the publishing and importation of Bibles. The ecumenical North-West Bible Commission in Leningrad was reported to be printing over 200,000 copies of the Bible at the end of 1990 and in 1991. In early 1991, the church established a commission in Cheboksary to update a 1911 translated edition of the Bible in the Chuvash vernacular, and a Chuvash New Testament was published in 1992. The patriarchate also developed plans to provide the Belorussian victims of the Chernobyl nuclear accident with Scriptures; Belorussian clerics were translating the New Testament into that language. In 1993 the Stockholm Institute for Bible Translation presented an edition of 50,000 Uzbek Bibles, had completed translations into Tadzhik and Kirghiz, and was working on Kazakh, Tatar, and Turkmen editions. Ukrainian church officials arranged for an additional 240,000 Bibles in Ukrainian. The United Bible Societies also sent 30,000 Bibles in Moldovan to the Moldovan Interconfessional Bible Society and reported that a total of 1.2 million Scriptures had been distributed in the USSR in 1990; by late 1991 they had delivered 2.5 million copies and had plans to provide 17 million more by 1994.[14] Despite these efforts, however, the process of rendering Scriptures in non-Russian minority languages had commenced late and was advancing only too slowly.

The supply of New Testaments and Gospels has, hardly surprisingly, paralleled the publication and importation of full copies of the Bible. In 1947 the American Bible Society sent the Russian Orthodox seminaries about 100,000 Gospels and 500 Greek New Testaments, and it planned to send almost 2 million Bibles the following year.[15] The strictures on church life that began in 1948, however, and perhaps the Soviet government's reaction at that early time to the project's scale, prevented its realization. Between 1956 and 1979, the Soviet authorities allowed the patriarchate to publish about 150,000 New Testaments, but most of these volumes, it was alleged, were actually sold abroad.[16] Early in 1988, the church published the New Testament in Ukrainian.[17] In August, the Soviet authorities gave the patriarchate permission to accept 1 million New Testaments in Russian from Open Doors International, and by early 1989 the Taize monastic community in France had sent the church an additional 1 million. The Greek Orthodox monastery of the Paraclete supplied each of the church's theological students with a copy of the New Testament in Russian and Church Slavonic, printed in parallel.[18] The Evangelical Christian Publishers Association, which was represented at the Moscow Book Fair for the first time in September 1989, handed out 10,000 copies of the New Testament to huge queues at its exhibit.[19] In 1990 the Holy See made a gift of 100,000 New Testaments to the Moscow patriarchate.[20]

These supplies were dramatically insufficient, and as a partial remedy, various Soviet publications began to serialize publication of the Bible. The Ukrainian Orthodox monthly published the Gospels with commentary over a period of years. The Russian journal *In the World of Books* began serializing the New Testament in 1988, interrupted the series in the first several months of 1989, and resumed in April of that year.[21] Even the illustrious *Literary Gazette* began publishing a concordance of the synoptic Gospels in April of 1990.[22] There is no question that the increased accessibility of the Scriptures is helping the Russian Orthodox Church significantly in its effort to re-Christianize Rus.[23]

In addition to the holy texts, the church has had a grievous lack of the publications that support the clergy. Nevertheless, liturgical publishing has gained strength over the years. In the first decade after World War II, only a few small service books were published. The situation improved in the mid-1950s. During and after the Khrushchev drive this publishing languished, but it picked up again in the 1970s and flowered in the 1980s.[24] With the advent of the Millennium, the church modestly extended its small-scale efforts to reach the community of believers, publishing 75,000 copies of a prayer book and psalter and importing 400,000 more from West Germany.[25] The patriarchate produced a Moldovan-language prayer book in 1986–1987, and Father Aleksandr Kudryashov edited a

Latvian prayer book in 1989. In 1990 the diocese of Krasnodar, which managed to establish its own printing press, published 100,000 prayer books. Other dioceses followed suit, establishing their own presses and modest printing facilities in the years between 1990 and 1994.[26]

In a similar vein, the annual eighty-page, illustrated church calendar—a publication more important than it may sound—provides a reference book on the church's feasts and fasts, saints' days, organization, and history. Calendars have been published in editions of 40,000–50,000 copies each, although the Soviet authorities apparently used to take a large proportion of them for their own uses. At candle desks in churches I have very occasionally been able to pick up copies of the church's pocket calendar, published in Magnitogorsk. A calendar in Estonian has been published since 1975, one in Latvian has been published since 1983, and one in Ukrainian has been published since 1985.[27]

The liturgical books and calendars met some of the clergy's needs, but the church also sought to provide academic support for its theologians through a scholarly journal. Church authorities began planning the journal in the late 1940s, but the first issue of *Theological Works* did not appear until 1960. During and after the Khrushchev antireligious drive, the church averaged one issue every two years; the frequency of issues rose to about two a year after 1970. Over the years, the journal has had a circulation of 3,000 copies per issue. Most observers agree, however, that its contents are not very original or creative—dull in fact. The journal concentrates on liturgical and historical subjects.[28]

The final category of church publications consists of the church's house organs, the periodicals that unite the Russian Orthodox community and communicate the concerns of the hierarchy. The *Journal of the Moscow Patriarchate*, the flagship periodical of the church, has acted as the journal of record and the promulgator of the church's internal and international policies. At one point the subscription price in U.S. dollars was actually carried in the magazine.[29] Since 1971 a slightly abridged English-language edition of the *Journal* has also been published.

The *Journal* began publication in 1931, was snuffed out in 1935, and resumed publication on the day of Patriarch Sergi's enthronement in 1943.[30] Like all religious publications during the Soviet era, the *Journal* operated under special rules, and it continues even now to do so, perhaps as a result of momentum. Other books and periodicals carry identification and authorization data, a price, and a notation of the copies printed.[31] After a brief period of conforming to these regulations during World War II, the patriarchate ceased doing so, undoubtedly under governmental instructions. Clearly, the Soviet authorities did not want the world to know how few copies of the *Journal*, the Bible, and other religious publications were seeing the light of day. The lack of price information also served the church, as it permitted candle desks in parish churches to sell printed materials at a markup, although only about 2–3 percent of parish churches had copies to sell prior to 1988.[32]

The print run of the *Journal* appears to have been 10,000–15,000 copies in Russian from the 1940s through most of the 1960s.[33] The print run was then raised to 20,000, although several thousand copies were consistently being sent abroad.[34] By 1988 the print run was increased to 30,000, and in early 1991 it was increased again to 33,000 copies in Russian and 4,000 copies in English.[35] At about the same time, the vicissitudes of enterprise in the crumbling Soviet Union became visible in the *Journal,* as its paper quality declined and the center section of colored photographs became intermittent. The collapse of the ruble and of orderly arrangements for the exportation of publications in 1991–1992 resulted in the *Journal* becoming almost unattainable for a time in the West.

For many years, the *Journal* had a "Church Life" section, which chronicled official initiatives, appointments, activities of the theological schools, the convents, and bishops' visits to parishes and also carried obituaries of clerics. During the middle years of the Khrushchev antireligious campaign, this segment was drastically reduced and even the obituaries were sharply cut back. It was as if the church leadership or the authorities were afraid that these chronicles would reveal too much about what was actually happening. They were right; Western scholars, including me, learned quite a bit from these sections. A renewed period of curtailment of these materials came in the early 1990s, perhaps because the church's leadership was appalled by what they might reveal about the situation in Ukraine and about the church's vicissitudes in general.

The *Journal* also carries sermons, which no doubt help priests compose their own. These sermons are highly traditional, although some are luminous with faith. Another category of articles was the "Defense of Peace" section, renamed in April of 1989 "For Peace and the Living Together of Humanity," and discontinued altogether in 1991. Before Gorbachev's time the "Defense of Peace" section was shameless Soviet propaganda, and I doubt that many subscribers to the *Journal* bothered to read it.

An ecumenical section criticized the ecumenical patriarch at the Phanar when relations were strained, but its usual contents were inter-Orthodox news and descriptions of meetings with representatives of the World Council of Churches. The *Journal* also used to fulminate against the Vatican and glorify the reunification with Orthodoxy of Ukrainian Greek-Catholics. There were also a theological section and a practical liturgical section. Often the *Journal* closed with book reviews and poetry (including that of Boris Pasternak, even before it was altogether risk-free to disseminate his works).

Over the years the *Journal* has conveyed the views of the holy fathers about fasting, confession, the Eucharist, and other timeless subjects. It has gradually improved the quality and depth of its theological and historical articles, uniting the saints of the past with the Christians of today. However, the *Journal* has always had a musty air. In 1965, the former responsible editor of the *Journal*, A. V. Vedernikov, published a report on the state of the church as it emerged from the Khrushchev antireligious drive, in which he had the grace to be apologetic about the stodgy content of the *Journal*.[36] In October 1989, the chief editor, Metropolitan Pitirim (Nechaev), again acknowledged that the *Journal* overemphasized outdated reports and uninteresting accounts of clerics' trips abroad. He promised improvements. Minor changes did ensue, and roundtable discussions of current problems did appear, but the essential character of the *Journal* remained the same. Dimitry Pospielovsky observed that Metropolitan Pitirim is not regarded as an intellectual. He quoted the joke current in the 1980s that the *Zhurnal Moskovskoi Patriarkhii* (commonly abbreviated as Zh.M.P.) is referred to as the *Zhalkie Mysli Pitirima* (also Zh.M.P.—translated as The Pitiful Thoughts of Pitirim). Pitirim has been criticized sharply in church meetings over the years—and with reason—for failing to meet the needs of the dioceses.[37]

Although the *Journal of the Moscow Patriarchate* is the church's flagship, the Ukrainian branch of the church also started publishing the *Orthodox Herald*, or *Pravoslavny Visnyk*, after the March 1946 Lvov council that produced the involuntary union of the Greek-Catholics with Orthodoxy. Protopresbyter Gavriil Kostelnik, famous—or infamous—for his role in the council, took a leading role in editing the journal, which was variously called the *Lvov Church Journal*, the *Lvov Herald*, and the *Diocesan Herald*.[38] The name was changed to the *Orthodox Herald* in February of 1948; the price was five kopecks, and the print run was reported to be 3,000 copies. After Father Kostelnik's assassination in September of 1948, direction of the *Orthodox Herald* passed into the hands of less obviously controversial prelates. The church would not accept foreign subscriptions and used the journal as an instrument to try to strengthen Orthodoxy among former Ukrainian Greek-Catholics.[39] Other than the *Journal of the Moscow Patriarchate* and Ukraine's *Orthodox Herald*, no Orthodox ecclesiastical monthlies were permitted in the entire country until 1988. Ukraine's special treatment reflected the importance of the forced union of 1946 and the extreme sensitivity of Russian Orthodox leaders and the Soviet authorities to the discontent prevailing in western Ukraine.

As the Khrushchev antireligious drive gained momentum, the fortunes of the *Orthodox Herald* became less certain. The editors normally published monthly issues of thirty-two pages, but they printed a single twenty-nine-page issue for August to December of 1960. In January of 1961, there was a polemical article against the Vatican, but the regular obituaries and parish life sections were omitted. In February of 1961, the *Herald* published an odd, quite candid article about

Orthodox relations with the Greek-Catholics. There were April and May–June issues, after which the *Orthodox Herald* ceased publication.[40] It resumed publishing in August 1968 with a single issue for August–December. The journal was printed in Kiev, but the editorial offices remained in Lvov until 1971, at which time they too were moved to Kiev.[41] The print run in the 1950s had been 10,000 or fewer; the commissioner for Ukraine revealed in 1989 that the print run of the *Orthodox Herald* had been "doubled" in 1988.[42]

In the 1970s the *Orthodox Herald* underwent a transformation from a journal focusing on the sensitivities and discontents of the formerly Greek-Catholic community in western Ukraine to become the house organ of the Ukranian Orthodox Church.[43] When the church split in 1992, Metropolitan Filaret (Denisenko) managed to seize control of the *Orthodox Herald* and has continued to publish infrequent issues (four in 1993).

Since the easing of restrictions at the time of the Millennium, religious publications have become more common and the church has heightened efforts to communicate with the faithful and the larger population. It has also increased its efforts to improve its worldwide public relations. The result has been a series of newly founded publications, some of which have folded. In 1987, in anticipation of the Millennium celebrations, the patriarchate started to issue a slick-paper monthly in five languages, the *Moscow Church Herald*. In March of that year, the Soviet government's Novosti [News] Press Agency—which had close KGB connections—launched a monthly bulletin aimed at foreigners and printed in seven languages. During and after the millennial year it published some quite revealing statistical compilations. Novosti's periodical, *Religion in USSR,* stopped publication in December 1991.

In 1988, the Russian Orthodox also began publishing journals aimed at local audiences. Dioceses, monasteries, hermitages, and various religious associations have launched gazettes and journals, some of them published as often as weekly and others with print runs of up to 15,000 copies.[44]

One of these newer publications directed at Russian Orthodox believers is the *Moscow Church Herald, Weekly,* which was founded in April 1989. Apparently Metropolitan Pitirim (Nechaev) allowed a group of younger clerics to launch this journal of news and commentary, which proved to be of impressive quality. Its articles after Patriarch Pimen's death commenting on his leadership, its descriptions of the church's troubles with the Ukrainian Greek-Catholics, and its discussions of the situation in the church's academies and seminaries were candid to a degree not seen before. Published approximately every other week (despite its title), the journal was distributed to churches throughout the country and even managed to break into distribution channels at secular news kiosks in Moscow (outlets of Soyuzpechat, the press merchandising organization that supplies news kiosks throughout the country). Reportedly it has had a print run of 200,000.[45]

In late 1990, the articles in the *Moscow Church Herald, Weekly* became less daring, and I wonder whether the new patriarch drew in the reins. In any case, the *Herald* became the principal vehicle of communication with the lay community of Orthodoxy, a shift that left the *Journal of the Moscow Patriarchate* increasingly a periodical of official record. In 1993 the *Herald* died; it was reborn at the end of April 1994 as an occasional insert in *Vechernaya Moskva* (Evening Moscow), the popular evening newspaper in the capital, which has a print run of 400,000 copies. The second insert of the *Herald* appeared six weeks after the first (on June 10) despite the restoration of "Weekly" to the masthead.

The patriarchate has also issued recordings of church music, films, slide collections, traveling exhibits, collections of photographs, and other materials for a wider audience. Since 1988, Soviet Television, now Russian Television, has increasingly given the church access to a nationwide audience.[46] Religiously inspired stage performances are becoming more frequent, and Orthodox bookstores have also opened in Moscow and other cities.[47]

The publications department of the patriarchate has achieved substantial results, but it is also easy to understand why church leaders and priests across the land have been critical of Metropolitan Pitirim's administration of this activity. In 1989 and 1990, two church councils issued formal calls for the establishment of a synodal printing press and printing establishments in all the dioceses and theological academies; nevertheless, progress has been slow. As already noted, this is particularly true in the effort to publish Scriptures and other religious materials in national languages other than Russian. Metropolitan Pitirim himself observed in October 1989 that tensions among the nationalities in the USSR might have been less severe if translation and publication of religious materials had been pursued earlier and more vigorously.[48] Although the metropolitan was probably exaggerating the potential influence of Russian Orthodox publishing on the Soviet nationality question taken as a whole, the future strength and strategic position of the church in the former USSR have surely been weakened by the failures Metropolitan Pitirim acknowledged.

To conclude this discussion of church publishing, more effective work in this area has the potential to change the church's contemporary situation in fundamental ways. The Scriptures are becoming available to a people hungry for access to the Bible, largely thanks to massive consignments of Bibles, New Testaments, and Gospels provided by Bible societies and others throughout the Western world. These materials have consistently sold at prices that work a hardship on would-be purchasers, but just when increased supplies were beginning to bring prices down, even for black-market sales, inflation sent all prices skyrocketing.

Children's Bibles, materials for religious instruction, textbooks, and theological materials are still in woefully short supply. The collapse of the Soviet state eliminated many restrictions and created great opportunities, but the effectiveness of the patriarchate's publishing department continues to be, at best, mediocre. In fairness to Metropolitan Pitirim and his department, one must add that the church's failure to solve its problems more effectively has been due in large part to a grievous lack of funds.

For many years, the Russian Orthodox Church had more than enough money to support the activities authorized by the Soviet state. According to official figures, church income through the 1950s more than tripled, reaching a figure well in excess of 700 million rubles, or $175 million (see Table 13.1).[49]

It is not surprising that Ukraine had an income almost twice that of the Russian republic in 1948, as two-thirds of the churches were located there, and much of the area emerged from the war with a vigorous parish life. The Russian republic soon surpassed Ukraine in receipts, however, as Ukraine's little parish churches were struggling to make ends meet, and a priest-in-charge might have earned about the same income as a pensioner or invalid.[50] In contrast, the patri-

TABLE 13.1   Church Income for 1948, 1955–1959 (millions of rubles)

	1948[a]	1955	1956	1957	1958[b]	1959[b]
Byelorussia	4.3	7.9	9.8	12.6	14.0	13.0
Russia	68.6	182.7	397.0	433.0	481.0	490.0
Ukraine	107.4	118.2	139.9	167.4		
Estonia				2.4	2.7	
Latvia		5.0[c]	3.1	3.4		
Lithuania			0.4	0.4		
Moldavia		13.5	16.4	18.7		
Kazakhstan		10.3	11.4	12.4	14.0	14.0
Kirghizia		2.4	2.8	2.8		
Uzbekistan		12.5	13.0	14.0		
Total (estimates in parentheses for 1948, 1958, and 1959)	(200)	353	596	667	(720–730)	(730–740)

[a] The data for 1948 are incomplete because the data on file at the Council for Religious Affairs were incomplete (as they were for 1958 and 1959). The data given for 1955, 1956, and 1957 make clear, however, that close to 90 percent of all income came from the three Slavic republics where data were recorded. One may conclude that the church's income was about 200 million rubles in 1948.

[b] Ratios of 1956 and 1957 indicate that the three republics where data are complete represent about 70 percent of overall receipts. One may estimate, therefore, that the church's income was about 720–730 million rubles in 1958 and 730–740 million rubles in 1959.

[c] In 1955, church income from the Baltic states totaled roughly 5 million rubles, a figure included in the year's total.

Source: Archive of the Council for Religious Affairs. See Chapter 13, note 49.

archal cathedral in Moscow, the Trinity-Sergius monastery churches, St. Nicholas and Trinity in Leningrad, and the other great churches of Russia collected millions of rubles a year.[51] Reportedly, a priest at the patriarchal cathedral declared an income in 1946 about fifty times greater than the salary of the Ukrainian parish priest just mentioned.[52] Cemetery churches also had (and have) large incomes, as their priests not only officiated at funerals but also received gratuities for remembrance services (and still perform these functions).

Proceeds from the sale of religious items, particularly candles, have always constituted the bulk of the church's officially reported income. The Council for Religious Affairs itemized income in the Russian republic for 1959 as follows:

	Millions of Rubles
Sale of candles	293
Blessed bread (*prosfora*)	52
Cult objects (crosses, icons)	25
Loose plate offerings	37
Charges for rites	31
Funerals	30
Other	22
Total	490

The council also estimated that the clergy received an additional 100 million rubles in "personal income" in 1959, presumably money for unregistered services.[53]

For a Western religious community of comparable size, the income just described would be grossly insufficient. During most of the Soviet period, however, Soviet state policy barred the church from educating children, sponsoring charities, publishing for a mass readership, and engaging in the normal activities carried on by churches elsewhere. When asked in the 1960s to describe his greatest problem, a Russian Orthodox bishop reported: "We have too much money. . . . People are beginning to say: the clergy live on the fat of the land. . . . The present financial position of the church creates many pastoral problems and temptations."[54] At the time bishops were riding in chauffeured sedans, and priests often had cars—features that still exist and are a manifestation of affluence in the former USSR even today. A British monk described the patriarch's country house on the Black Sea as "a very imposing dacha, too, overlooking the sea, and with a private funicular for the hierarchy, the monks and their guests [leading] down the cliff to a delightful, secluded little bay."[55] The church also regularly provided transportation, luxurious living accommodations, banquets, and substantial bundles of spending money for foreign ecclesiastical guests.[56]

The Khrushchev antireligious campaign reduced church income severely—both countrywide and at the church's central offices. Not only were taxes on the clergy sharply increased, leaving parish priests and church societies in dire straits, but almost 45 percent of the churches were deregistered, and as they disappeared, so did their contributions to the patriarchal establishment in Moscow.

The church's financial troubles were exacerbated by the unevenness of income sources. As was previously discussed, during and after the Khrushchev drive the Soviet authorities constrained the patriarchate and the diocesan offices from moving funds around to rescue drowning parishes. These constraints slowly loosened, but they continued to inhibit the church's freedom of action. As the annual income of St. Nicholas Cathedral in Leningrad went up from 1 million rubles in 1977 to 1.3 million rubles in 1981, the added revenues did the hardest-pressed parishes little good.[57]

The financial situation of the convents also reflected this problem of unevenness. Reportedly, three or four convents—Trinity-Sergius at Zagorsk, Pochaev, and the two nunneries in Kiev—received close to half of the total income of the church's eighteen cloistered communities in 1970, which left extremely little income among the remaining convents.[58] To take another example, the Cathedral, monastery, and nunnery in Vilnyus—all on the monastery grounds—received almost half of the income of the whole diocese in 1982–1983, which consisted of forty-one parishes at the time.[59] In contrast, in 1970 the two nunneries in Transcarpathia received only 47,000 rubles for 123 sisters at Mukachevo and 5,093 rubles for 41 sisters at Chumalevo.[60] This would provide only 124 rubles a year for each sister at Chumalevo (1,240 rubles prior to the 1961 currency reform), an inadequate amount even in light of the nunnery's modest agricultural operations.

In the middle to late 1980s, annual church income appears to have ranged between 250 million and slightly over 300 million rubles, with approximately 250 million rubles the likely figure for 1987. It is difficult to compare these figures with those for the 1950s, as currency reform and an erosion of purchasing power had changed the situation almost beyond recognition in the intervening thirty years. It can probably be said that the church's finances recovered modestly compared with the situation at the end of the Khrushchev antireligious drive. The commissioners' figures also throw additional light on the sources of the church's acknowledged income and the distribution of diocesan expenditures. Income in 1985 came mostly from the sale of candles, small icons, neck crosses, and other items sold at the candle desks of parish churches. Between two-thirds and three-fourths of the dioceses' total income came from these sources, and candles accounted for over half of receipts. Income from services performed—funerals (mostly by correspondence), marriages, baptisms, and so on—accounted for 14–18 percent of income (17 percent of income in Ukraine). Loose plate offerings accounted for roughly 10–15 percent of income, although far less—3 to 4 percent—in the Pacific maritime regions.[61]

With respect to expenditures, priests' and other church servers' salaries accounted for about 15 percent of expenditures in 1985. Wages of sextons and charpeople totaled about 12 percent. Choir directors and paid singers received about 7 percent of total income. I might add that Dimitri Pospielovsky reported that there were 41,000 permanent members of church choirs in 1970, of whom roughly 23,000 were volunteers and 18,000 were paid. "Leadership expenses"— presumably the bishop's car and other such outlays—accounted for another 1 percent of expenditures. This would make personnel costs about 35 percent of all disbursements.[62]

In 1985, repairs and property costs accounted for about 15 percent of all expenditures, divided into land rent (2–3 percent), utilities (4 percent), and actual repairs (8 percent). The patriarchate was also spending some money for the repair and reconstruction of churches and convents (particularly the Danilov monastery), even in 1985. In early 1988, *Science and Religion* estimated that the church was spending 45 million rubles for reconstruction of functioning churches, many of which were cultural monuments; in these cases the church and the Soviet government split the costs of restoration.[63] In addition, the church reluctantly contributed 5 million rubles annually to the Fund for the Preservation of Cultural Monuments, many of which were churches converted to become museums, concert halls, or other secular structures. About 4 percent of expenditures in Ukraine went into this fund, although the percentages averaged only 1–2 percent in the Russian republic.[64]

Science and Religion reported in 1988 that the church was contributing 30 million rubles a year to the governmentally sponsored Peace Fund. For many years the church had played a conspicuous role in the international peace movement and had drawn criticism from some Western political and religious observers for collaboration with the atheist authorities and "slavish" conformity to Soviet international positions.[65] Commissioners' reports put diocesan and parish contributions to the Peace Fund at approximately 13 percent of total expenditures.[66]

Manufacturing of candles and other objects for sale accounted for approximately 20 percent of total expenditures in 1985, which meant that these operations were quite profitable because half to two-thirds of church income was derived from the sale of these items.[67] Last, the parishes sent about 15 percent of expendable funds to the "center."[68] This would represent a sum of more than 30 million rubles, no doubt divided between diocesan headquarters and the central offices of the patriarchate. As discussed later, the patriarchate's operating budget in 1989 (15 million rubles) and various earmarked obligations totaled well over 30 million rubles, but its special sources of income accounted for at least part of the difference.

With the Millennium came extraordinary new opportunities that created heavy new financial demands. Believers regained thousands of church buildings in excruciatingly bad physical condition, and the patriarchate received permission to open new convents, seminaries, and theological training institutions and to catechize both young and old. Charity work, homes for the incapacitated and sick, and all manner of good works in the world became possible. On the income side the church was losing ground, as parishes in western Ukraine, including some very prosperous ones, passed over to Ukrainian Greek-Catholic obedience. Moreover, older believers on fixed income could no longer contribute as they had in past years.

After the Millennium, the church took the opportunity presented by glasnost and perestroika to curtail its "voluntary" contributions to the Peace Fund and the international peace movement.[69] The head of the church's Office of Foreign Church Relations, Archbishop (now Metropolitan) Kirill (Gundyaev), obtained the Holy Synod's agreement in January 1990 to cut the church's foreign relations budget by a half million rubles and recommended that these moneys be redirected to the construction and renovation of churches and convents.[70] This was undoubtedly a popular move, as the offerings of the faithful had long been squandered on foreigners, to the dismay of many Russian Orthodox believers.[71] In August 1990, Patriarch Aleksi II (Ridiger) announced that the church was discontinuing its contributions to the officially sponsored Soviet funds for culture and charity, as the church itself would carry on these activities.[72] In 1991, the church withdrew from the World Peace Conference in Prague.

The church's business office, under the leadership of Metropolitan Mefodi (Nemtsov), moved to tap supplies of hard currency through exports of religious objects and contributions by sympathetic Christians in the West. The church has also taken steps to organize banking operations in partnership with Greeks, Cypriots, and U.S. bankers. Church administrators said they were looking toward a revolving credit fund of two billion rubles in 1994 and thirty million dollars in foreign exchange capitalization.[73] Hard currency may ease the church's increasingly crushing financial problems, but all this takes time, governmental acquiescence, sophisticated organization, and deft management as the situation inside the country continues to develop and change.

In October 1989, Metropolitan Vladimir (Sabodan) of Rostov gave figures for the budget and finances of the patriarchate, the church's central offices. The patriarchate's operating budget for the calendar year 1989 was 14.7 million rubles, including planned capital projects. Through September, the central offices had received 2.6 million rubles from the dioceses, 4 million rubles from its workshops, about 750,000 rubles from the Moscow churches, and about 500,000 rubles from sales of the *Journal of the Moscow Patriarchate*. The total of about 7.8–7.9 million rubles indicated that during the first three quarters of the year, the operating budget had a deficit of roughly 3 million rubles.

On the outlay side, the budget contained 6.2 million rubles for the patriarchate's Office of Foreign Church Relations (cut the following January by 0.5 million rubles); 4.5 million rubles to support the church's theological schools; 2.7 million rubles to build and restore the medical clinic at the Trinity-Sergius monastery; and 1.3 million rubles for maintenance of patriarchal residences, library, administration, and "patriotic and charitable measures" (contributions to the Soviet Peace Fund and culture and charity funds, discontinued in 1990). Outlays to support the theological schools and to help restore churches had grown much faster than income, and the patriarchate closed the gap with surpluses from earlier years. The church also diverted the earnings of the Sofrino workshops away from the patriarchate's operating budget in order to continue construction of a 200-bed hotel-dormitory at the Danilov monastery in Moscow, completed in 1992.[74]

A special fund to build the great new church in Moscow commemorating the Millennium received almost 9 million rubles between January and September 1989, a sum that raised the total collected for this church to 16 million rubles. Almost nine-tenths of the 9 million came from the sale of Bibles and other religious literature donated from abroad. These proceeds were also used to restore half-ruined churches, to build new churches, to support theological students, and to succor the poor.[75] A third special fund of the patriarchate was earmarked for the restoration of the Optina hermitage, and a fourth, the "Holy Synod" fund (5 million rubles), was set aside, not to be spent except in dire emergency.[76] If the church has not managed by now to convert this fund to hard currency or physical assets, it has no doubt lost virtually all of its value.

In October 1989, Archbishop Aleksi (Kutepov), the head of the patriarchate's administration of shops, construction, and manufacturing activities, reported that pending construction and workshop renovation projects would cost at least 15–20 million rubles, and no funding was in sight.[77]

The activities and finances of the Sofrino workshops deserve some additional explanation. Located fifty kilometers from Moscow, these shops produce a large proportion of the candles (manufacturing ten tons of them a day), small icons, baptismal crosses, communion vessels, vestments, and other church articles used throughout the dioceses of the church. Church authorities are encouraging diocesan bishops to establish such shops in each diocese, and the convents help manufacture these supplies, but the bulk of the mass-produced items still comes from Sofrino. The workshops suffer from worn-out and antiquated machinery, poor services for the double shifts of workers who commute two to three hours each way from Moscow, and insufficient raw materials, such as paraffin, lamp oil, fabrics, and sheet metal. Nevertheless, the operation produces immense quantities of church supplies and is profitable. Before the Millennium, Sofrino had 345 workers and gross sales of 23 million rubles a year. In 1988 the workforce grew to 1,000, and sales reached almost 59 million rubles, of which wages, salaries, raw materials, and other operating expenses consumed 18 million rubles and government taxes and levies consumed another 29 million, which left about 12 million rubles profit.[78] In 1989 sales reached approximately 100 million rubles, and in

1990 they were running at about 140 million rubles. The patriarchate hired 300 more workers, in part to produce for export, although the church had not yet been able to get governmental authorization to retain the foreign currency for its own use.[79]

Pensions for retired priests and other church workers are an additional expense for the church. In October 1989, Metropolitan Vladimir stated that the church had paid nearly 2.7 million rubles to 4,000 religious pensioners. He reported that a retired priest who had worked for twenty-five years would receive an average of fifty rubles a month, and the widow or orphaned child of a church worker might receive only half that amount. The metropolitan added that the situation was particularly bad for psalmists and choir people and that one couldn't live on a sum so small. In July 1990, the Holy Synod increased the minimum pension to seventy rubles, to be paid by the local dioceses.[80] That increased sum was also insufficient, and adjustments in pensions since then have utterly failed to compensate for the sinking value of the ruble.

In February 1992, the Holy Synod of the Russian Orthodox Church discussed the dire financial straits of the central church administration. The estimated deficit of the patriarchate was projected at 15 million rubles in February 1992 prices. The Holy Synod decided in consequence to ask each diocesan administration to pay 10,000 rubles a year for every resident student from the diocese studying in the theological schools and institutions. The balance of 2,000 to 5,000 rubles a year for each student and the cost of correspondence students would continue to be borne by the church's central administration. Income from the Sofrino shops, church publications, and the 200-bed hotel-dormitory at the Danilov monastery would be used to help meet the patriarchate's needs. The government of the city of Moscow stepped forward to assume the costs of constructing the new church on the outskirts of Moscow commemorating the Millennium. These last-mentioned dispositions must have helped, but they surely did not close the gap.

Since the late 1980s the lack of money to repair and restore church buildings returned to believers has virtually overwhelmed church administrators at every level. The patriarchate has helped pay restoration costs in some cases, and diocesan administrations have also paid what they could, but many parishes have had to raise the necessary money themselves. The result has been the publication of poignant entreaties in church publications like the *Moscow Church Herald, Weekly* and even in the daily newspapers of Moscow and other cities. Walls outside churches are plastered with these appeals. Often earnest women will stop visitors outside churches to implore them to contribute. Some resourceful parishes with good connections even set up tables and booths at the entryways of historical monuments and tourist attractions and sell religious items. When my wife and I visited the restored palace of Pavlovsk outside Leningrad (now St. Petersburg) in 1990, a pleasant man from the St. Sofia parish in Pushkin had such a table and was selling attractive Easter cards. As an indication of the sums needed, however, the patriarchate estimated in late 1988 that the restoration of the Tolga nunnery in Yaroslavl diocese would cost 14 million rubles, of which a little over 1 million had been raised.

An anguished appeal in March 1994 for foreign help from the rector of the Smolensk theological institute illustrates the church's financial predicament:

> To our deepest misfortune, a threat has come to hang over our theological institute in most recent times. From the moment of its founding, it was financed almost entirely by the parishes of the diocese of Smolensk. Today the situation in the parishes is so difficult that one can characterize it as catastrophic. Galloping inflation ever more decisively curtails the scope of donations. Simply put, we have no means of feeding our students.

The rector's letter appeared in *Russkaya Mysl,* the Russian-language newspaper published in Paris, and gave a bank credit transfer address and another address to which money, food or clothing might be sent.[81]

The collapse of the ruble, food shortages, and the economic and political crisis throughout the former Soviet Union are placing the church in even more dire straits than before. Inflation has thrown the patriarchate's finances into turmoil and has destroyed the value of its financial reserves. Widows and pensioners, whose mites have sustained the church for so long, can no longer keep their own bodies and souls together without help and charity. With supplies of vital necessities so short, pressures on the church to feed, clothe, and heal the destitute are multiplying. Western aid channeled through the church may help it to meet these needs, but there are also dangers of diversion and malfeasance. The church is not always efficient, nor will it always be perceived as being evenhanded and uncorrupted, regardless of the justice or injustice of accusations against it. It already stands indicted by some for selling supplies and literature donated from abroad and diverting the proceeds to its own profit, if not to the hierarchs' personal gain.[82]

The Russian Orthodox Church faces an appalling lack of financial and organizational resources, insufficient transport, and all manner of obstacles to effectiveness. As William C. Fletcher put it to me in 1993, "The church is broke, in a country that's gone broke; God help them both." Lack of money has moved center stage as an obstacle to religious renewal. The shortage of qualified priests and the church's financial straits are two of its greatest problems as it seeks to carry out its mission.

14

The Laity

ON JULY 2, 1986, in the great hall of the Leningrad theological schools, the rector, Archpriest Nikolai Gundyaev, was fielding questions from insistent foreign clergymen. One from the United States pointedly inquired why the Russian Orthodox Church was not pressing the Soviet authorities harder for permission to open additional churches in Leningrad to serve the people. Archpriest Nikolai responded: "You go out to our Leningrad churches. We have a subway, and transportation is good in our city. The people can reach our sixteen churches in the city and can come here to our seminary church. Go into our churches on Sunday morning. You will see that there is room enough for all who come."[1]

Archpriest Nikolai was right. Except for special occasions and high holy days like Easter, Christmas, and Trinity Sunday, Russian Orthodox churches are not badly overcrowded if one bears in mind that worshipers normally stand.[2] In the 1980s and 1990s I have attended services from the coast of the Pacific Ocean to the Baltic Sea and from Murmansk and Yakutsk in the north to Yalta, Stavropol, and Dushanbe in the south.[3] Normally there is room enough for the devout old women to creak down onto their knees and genuflect to the floor.

Such adequacy of space was not always the reality. When I lived in Moscow in the mid-1950s, I traveled throughout the country and went to a different church every Sunday. In those days, winter and summer, one could hardly press one's way through the church doors. I remember thinking that I could lift my feet and be carried across the sanctuary by the press of the surging throng. This difference is even more striking given that there were almost twice as many churches in the country in the mid-1950s as there were when the rector spoke in 1986.

Rural communities may be different, of course. Traditional society in the villages encourages attendance at church, and religious practice has survived better than in urban places.[4] However, in Siberia and the rural heartland east of Moscow, churches are few and far between. Someone living in the city can normally find sufficient public transportation to go to church if he or she is willing to spend time and endure inconvenience. The task is more difficult in much of the countryside.

In any case, rural churchgoing has also declined, and rural churches do not often seem terribly overcrowded. Former Soviet journals sometimes described how the writer visited a village and found the church half empty or closed altogether. In one case, an old woman explained: "The priest doesn't serve every Sunday, because few people come."[5] Another observer, a priest himself, wrote in late 1991 that in the villages one sees "almost no young people praying."[6] In May 1990, I spent a weekend in a small village about an hour's walk plus a ninety-minute boat ride from Kotelnich in Kirov oblast. The villagers, carrying luggage and shopping bags and commenting audibly about their plans, clearly were not taking the boat to attend services at the nearest church, in Kotelnich. An old woman died in the village while I was there. I asked whether a priest might conduct the funeral. The villagers answered that the priest would charge thirty rubles to make the round-trip. No doubt the arrangements and the travel required to accomplish them were as much a problem as was the money. In any case, the old woman was buried without benefit of clergy, a practical decision made often in churchless villages.

Russian Orthodox dissident activists and clerics tend to confirm the foregoing observations. Mikhail Meerson-Aksënov, the courageous Orthodox layman who was arrested, condemned to prison camp, and finally emigrated after his release, commented in 1986: "An overall sharp decline in religious consciousness during the Soviet period is characteristic of all religious groups. The net effect of sixty-seven years of an atheistic regime has been religious estrangement."[7] Kirill Golovin wrote in *The Samizdat Bulletin* in 1987: "According to the priests themselves the attendance at religious services has gone down in comparison with the preceding decades due to the change in generations that has occurred."[8] Writing in *Religion in the USSR* in 1987, Father Innokenti asked his readers to remember the "sea of black kerchiefs in the Moscow churches during lenten services in the early 1960s." He described the subsequent decline in the number of worshipers, noting that during regular Sunday services in Moscow and Leningrad, the congregation, on average, filled three-fourths of the sanctuary, and even during holiday services in a large church, a worshiper could freely enter. He continued:

> At the end of the 1960s and the beginning of the 1970s there was a clear generational change. Among the believers, the number of those who had formed their religious personalities in the pre-revolutionary time significantly decreased. . . . This brought a diminution in the overall number of Orthodox believers, principally in the central and eastern districts of the country.[9]

Father Innokenti pointed out that churches in the western lands that became communist only in the 1940s were better attended. In those territories, he said, there were still large numbers of people whose religious formation occurred before Soviet rule brought an end to church schools and catechization.

Set against these judgments is the oft-repeated aphorism that "the grandmothers never die." It is true that observers noted the great preponderance of
tottering old women shortly after the Bolshevik revolution and have noted the
same phenomenon ever since. At the end of the 1920s, an Orthodox observer
noted: "You are struck by the emptiness of the churches. Women and old men are
almost the only ones who go to church."[10] Still earlier, in 1922, an Orthodox priest
had predicted that in ten years the falling away of the younger generation would
result in "a spiritual desert where we shall be surrounded by beasts."[11] More than
six decades later, a Russian Orthodox priest reminded a U.S. delegation of the
church's staying power: "Lenin argued that once the grandmothers died, nobody
would remember that there had been a church in Russia. But now Lenin is long
dead, and the church is still full of grandmothers who were children when he was
alive."[12] Although there is an element of truth in the phoenix like self-renewal of
the faithful, it is both truly sad and sadly true that atheism took away millions in
the 1920s and 1930s.[13] Even Metropolitan Nikolai (Yarushevich), who was wont to
put the best public face on the church's situation, acknowledged in the late 1950s
that "worship in the Soviet Union has fallen by nearly three-fourths from pre-
Revolutionary days."[14]

How many Orthodox people really do go to church on a Sunday morning in
the territories that comprised the USSR? Francis House reported an estimate of
30 million churchgoers, or one-sixth of the population of European Russia.[15]
Gerhard Simon reported an estimate of 0.3 percent of the population in the cities
as being regular worshipers (approximately 500,000 people).[16] It is a considerable
understatement to note that these two estimates are far apart. My own estimate,
with a description of the logic that brought me to it, follows.

As previously discussed, the Council for Religious Affairs made a breakdown
of the number of churches of each size and category in the country in 1958. There
were roughly 13,400 churches at that time. Although almost half of them were
closed in the Khrushchev antireligious drive, the number returned to a figure
close to the 1958 number, and most of the churches opened since 1988 have been
parishes closed in the 1959–1964 period. As a result, the 1958 breakdown may provide a fair indication of the size and type of churches operating in the mid-1990s.
The council recorded 1,491 city churches. From my visits to city churches, during
which I counted congregations or counted worshipers in sectors of the throng, I
estimate that fifty of these churches draw an average of 2,000 people each for the
late service on a normal Sunday morning. These fifty large churches include the
patriarchal cathedral and Trinity Church at the Danilov monastery in Moscow,
St. Nicholas Cathedral and Trinity Church in St. Petersburg, and St. Vladimir's
Cathedral in Kiev, among others.[17] A few immense churches in outlying places
also fit this category.[18]

Roughly 1,440 other city churches are in the mix. Some in Moscow, like
Bolshaya Ordynka Church and Resurrection Church, are very large, almost in a

class with the "top fifty." Some much smaller churches balance these large ones, however, and among the city churches not in the top fifty, attendance at the late Sunday morning service averages fewer than 250 worshipers.[19] In the roughly 560 industrial towns recorded by the Council for Religious Affairs, attendance on a normal Sunday averages at most 150. In the remaining village churches, attendance on Sunday morning averages about 50.[20] The sum of these figures is about 1.1 million worshipers.

This total includes only one service each week in each of the Russian Orthodox churches. In the cities, churches frequently offer an early Sunday morning service and a Sunday evening service. Some churches in both the city and the countryside also hold weekday services, although many of the devout worshipers at them may be the same people who attend on Sunday. Judging from attendance figures I recorded for these other services, I estimate that approximately 2 million separate individuals—1 percent of the traditional Orthodox in the former USSR—now attend services in one of the roughly 12,000–13,000 Russian Orthodox churches during the course of a normal nonholiday week. By a similar calculation, I estimate that 1.0–1.5 million people attended church in a normal week prior to the Millennium, when there were about 7,000 churches in the country. This would have represented somewhere between 0.5 percent and 0.75 percent of the traditionally Orthodox population.

As already explained, the foregoing are figures for people in church on a nonholiday week. Many people, even those who are regular churchgoers, do not attend church every single week of the year. Therefore, it might be reasonable to double the weekly attendance figures to reach a number of 4 million churchgoers, or roughly 2 percent of the traditionally Orthodox population.

Many more people attend services on great religious holidays like Easter; others attend for funerals, baptisms, and marriages; others attend perhaps two or three times a year for some special reason. It is difficult, however, to substantiate or confirm a regular church attendance at normal Sunday or weekday services of more than about 4 million individuals, despite higher figures often given by Western observers and Russian Orthodox spokesmen. By comparison, pollsters report that between three and four of every ten Americans say they attend church on any given Sunday.[21] Reportedly only 3 percent of the English regularly are present at Anglican services, however, and about 11 percent of the French are said to go to mass regularly.[22]

Who are these 4 million Orthodox churchgoers? Are they women or men, young or old, urban intellectuals or rural workers? As indicated in the preceding section, rural worshipers compose close to 50 percent of the worshipers served by all the churches in the former Soviet territories during the main service on Sunday morning.[23] The urban population exceeded 60 percent of the total population in the late 1970s and is now close to two-thirds, which indicates that per capita church attendance in the countryside exceeds that in the cities.

The most obvious feature of a typical congregation, however, is the overwhelming proportion of women. Christel Lane and William Fletcher examined Soviet publications in the late 1970s for figures on the predominance of women in the congregations and found data ranging between 65 percent and 97 percent. Their research indicated that women probably constituted slightly over 80 percent of those attending church, at least during the two decades before the Millennium. For weekday services Fletcher gave an estimate of "more than 90 percent" women.[24] According to my own count, taken in thirty-five churches during late Sunday morning services between 1983 and 1990, 86 percent of the worshipers were women.[25] The count for services at other times, including weekday services, was 87 percent, which also conforms to Fletcher's findings.[26]

To count gender differences for purposes of writing my dissertation in the 1950s, I used photographs for earlier years. The results were 95 percent women in 1937; 93 percent women in 1942; 82 percent women in 1944; and 83 percent women in 1955–1958.[27] The 1944, 1955–1958, and 1983–1990 figures ranged between 82 percent and 86 percent, which is a statistically insignificant variation. Men at the front lines, casualties, and prisoners of war in World War II reduced the percentage of men at services in 1942; the terror and the GULAG, where men constituted most of the victims, had produced a similar effect in 1937.

The whole post–World War II period has witnessed a large gender imbalance in the population at large. Immediate postwar Soviet demographic statistics revealed an overall preponderance of women over men of about two to one in virtually every age group, so roughly 85 percent female attendance at church after the war would be a less extreme imbalance of male-female propensity to go to church than it might appear. As the years have passed, however, this gender imbalance in the population at large has worked its way up through the age spread; by the end of the 1980s, only the population over sixty-five years of age had two women for every man, whereas the younger population was close to a fifty-fifty split. However, a large proportion of churchgoers in the former Soviet Union are indeed people over sixty-five years of age.[28] It is also true, of course, that U.S. churches, particularly those not in the suburbs, have a preponderance of older women.

Age does bring increased religious observance in most societies. Perhaps maturity brings faith because people think about the eternal as they come closer to death, as youthful ambition for worldly success fades, or as the reality of this world as a vale of tears sinks in. In any event, it is a fact. A U.S. visitor to the Soviet Union in the 1950s remarked: "Take away the permanents, the lipsticks and the make-up from the women of your own congregations, and they wouldn't look so good either."[29]

Both Lane and Fletcher examined Soviet literature for reflections of the age imbalance during the Soviet era and reported that "old or middle aged" people constituted between 80 percent and 96 percent of those attending a normal Orthodox service.[30] On church holidays the percentage of young worshipers was consistently higher. I have tried to generate figures on this phenomenon. It is difficult because one has to estimate a person's age by looking at his or her face and appearance. During my 1983–1994 visits, I found that roughly 90 percent of the women were older or old, a figure comparable to statistics from 1937, 1944, and 1955–1958.[31]

In contrast, over half of the men I saw in the churches appeared to be young or at least youngish. I was surprised again and again by observing this fact during church visits. Of course, only about 15 percent of the people in church were men of any age. But it was a clearly observable phenomenon, one also noted by priests of the Russian Orthodox Church. For example, in 1987 Father Innokenti remarked on the number of young and younger men, particularly between the ages of eighteen and thirty, who were beginning to appear in church.[32]

Since the 1980s the number of young people of both sexes going to church has significantly increased. As early as 1980, Protopresbyter Vitali Borovoi said:

> A new movement has begun among the educated youth, the coming of the young generation into Church, a generation which . . . gained its conversion to Christ on its own, by way of the most profound reflections and inner trials. This is not to our credit. . . . It is to the credit of our believing people . . . for whom there is no road and yet they come to the Church by many different ways. . . . This often results in the break-up of families, educational and professional sacrifices . . . and we now have hundreds and thousands of such concrete living examples. . . . This is what is new in our Church.[33]

A poll conducted in 1987 by the Young Communist League confirmed the development, reporting young people's "growing fascination, especially among the well-educated, with religious literature and service."[34] Part of the increased youthful attendance can be explained by a lessening of intimidation, as the terror and the GULAG were not part of most young people's personal experience, and as atheist sanctions at the workplace were losing steam.

I have seen these young people in church. By their dress, their style of hair and beard if they have one, and their demeanor, some young men hint at incipient religious vocations. Other young men and women, very appealingly, show signs of inner turmoil, hesitating before they present themselves for the sacraments but nevertheless demonstrating their faith. Yet one should not be deceived by such images. The Trinity Church on Sparrow Hills (Lenin Hills), a few hundred yards from the Moscow University dormitories that house 8,000 students, finds a half dozen to a dozen identifiable students in its congregation on a Sunday morning. Scores of students assemble within a few feet of the church to catch buses to athletic events, but few go in.

Ignorance is widespread. Among the young people I have talked to during my visits, some have not known what Christmas stands for. In May 1992, I was talking to older teenagers at the edge of a soccer field in Yuzhno-Sakhalinsk. I asked one of the young men if he was a believer. He said yes, but it developed that he had never been inside a church. I asked the other. He shrugged but later told me he had been in a church—once, at least, during the time he was old enough to remember. A young Soviet adult said to me in 1991: "I am not a believer, but perhaps God exists. It would be awful to know he did not."

Similar remarks have been made quite consistently over the years. Marcus Bach observed in the 1950s that nine out of ten students he talked to had "never been inside a church."[35] Another clergyman who visited the Soviet Union in the 1950s, Nils A. Dahl, said that among young people, "ignorance of the church is nearly complete."[36] Interviewed in the 1950s, a young émigré said: "Among the youth, nobody believes. It is not a question which is asked anymore; it doesn't come up. . . . We young people are brought up in the 'Devil's Spirit'; we don't believe."[37] Nevertheless, caution is necessary because such generalizations about nearly universal atheism, made by young people in the 1950s and the 1990s, often refer to people other than themselves. When talking about their own beliefs, many say they do not know, or they indicate some sort of semiagnostic, semiconvinced belief.[38]

Ignorance, although most widespread among the young, touches other ages as well. I remember having supper with several Russian teachers in February of 1990 after my wife and I had seen Chekhov's *Anyuta* at the Bolshoi Theater. I described how Modest, Anyuta's priggish, villainous, aging husband, sat down on his bed in his nightgown and crossed himself with a great exaggerated gesture as a titter went through the audience in the theater. One of the teachers, a woman in her sixties, then crossed herself somewhat pensively, getting it backward for an Orthodox person. I asked her if she was Catholic. She answered that she wasn't really anything but then described how she loved to hear the churchmen on television. As the conversation developed, it became clear she did not know that the patriarch was head of the Russian Orthodox Church. Nicholas Timasheff stated that "many, especially among the younger generation, . . . look for something better than the official Marxist line but do not yet know the way to Christ."[39] Timasheff wrote this in 1944, but it is still true, despite the collapse of the "official Marxist line."

On the educational level of Orthodox people of all ages and sexes, Fletcher reported the findings of Soviet researchers that "there is indeed an immense [inverse] correlation between religiousness and educational level in the general population." He quoted a table prepared by a Soviet researcher in Voronezh showing a spectacular gradient among people claiming to be religious. The results ranged from 69 percent of illiterate persons asserting their belief to 1.4 percent of high school graduates and 0.15 percent of people with at least some university education.[40] Of course, among the educated, fear for one's career has always played a large inhibiting role. During the late 1980s Orthodox commentators like Father Innokenti were quoting Fletcher and accepting his findings, although they pointed out that the church was by then attracting academics, world-famous artistic figures, and specialists in a variety of fields. He estimated that at least a third of regular attenders in church are people who have been converted as adults. Innokenti explained that mothers and grandmothers believe but do not give intellectual expression to their belief and do not teach religion effectively. These women are dismissed by younger persons as conservative, ignorant, and irrelevant.[41] Anatoli Levitin-Krasnov commented that the Russian Orthodox Church attracts "both the most educated and the most backward sections of the population. Those who fall between these two groups have mostly left the church." He also said that the church appeals to "urban, intellectual youth."[42] Vladimir Zelinsky, a Russian Orthodox lay theologian, described young churchgoers as "almost entirely from the intelligentsia . . . Almost none of them are young working class people." Zelinsky explained that young workers have neither the high level of intellectual awareness of young intellectuals nor the religious roots of the grandmothers and consequently fall into an intermediate sector largely uninfluenced by the church.[43] He asserted that even some young intellectuals, attracted by the church's music, ritual, icons, and rich Christian culture, tend to lack intellectual depth and doctrinal understanding.[44] In the past, such tendencies may have been accentuated by the church's lack of active proselytizing and instruction, due in part to the Soviet state's prohibitions in this regard but also in part to an attitude that the church, as the repository of the faith, can rely on the inherent devotion of the believers and limit itself to serving those who come through its doors.

It was true during the Soviet era that believers tended to become separated from Soviet society, even in areas of life unconnected with religion. Practicing one's faith typically required both courage and a willingness to forgo many of life's secular rewards and opportunities. Perforce, this meant that religious commitment had a special, high place in such a person's priorities and set the young believer apart in all aspects of life. Zelinsky mentioned that "the emphasis in our society is on the young, the healthy, the attractive, the successful. Where is there room for the forgotten, the old, the sick, whose lives have not been a success?"[45]

Thus, not only in the former USSR, but also across the world, the church has provided solace for the old, the halt, the uneducated, the misfits, and those in the back eddies of life. That was the gospel Jesus preached, and that is a role the church is playing in the former Soviet republics. The beggars are back at the doors of the churches, as the authorities have abandoned their efforts to shoo them away or lock them up. The passage of the freedom-of-conscience laws made it possible for the church once again to carry out acts of charity and mercy, constrained only by its own abilities and its human and material resources.

Although church attendance is a measure of commitment in action, commentators have also tried to measure the subjective, inner realities of belief and unbelief in the population at large. To be sure, the millions of people living in communities without churches make attendance an inadequate measure of adherence. Belief is especially difficult to measure, but government researchers, polling organizations, and Orthodox leaders have provided a mass of data on the subject. Moreover, glasnost and democratization reduced the fear that so inhibited reliable polling and scholarly inquiry in previous eras.

Even prior to 1985, the authorities had considerable information, some of it quite reliable despite the pervasive intimidation that prevailed. Anatoli Lunacharski examined a number of regional surveys conducted in the late 1920s and concluded that roughly 80 percent of the population believed in God.[46] By the mid-1930s the Soviet government estimated—no doubt exaggerating its antireligious successes—that half of the people were believers.[47] The leaked census results of 1937 reported a figure of 55–60 percent believers in the country.[48]

World War II and its aftermath brought the annexation of territories with about 10 million Orthodox, and the postwar religious revival increased the ranks of believers significantly.[49] However, continuing antireligious propaganda, intimidation, and the Khrushchev antireligious drive took a toll. The country emerged from the Khrushchev drive with Soviet atheistic researchers and the Soviet authorities variously estimating 20–30 million Orthodox believers in the country, or roughly 15–20 percent of the traditionally Orthodox population.[50] Church leaders tended to accept these figures, or at least not to dispute them.[51] In the early to mid-1970s, the estimates for the number of Orthodox believers varied between 30 million and 50 million.[52]

According to Dimitry Pospielovsky, Soviet researchers abruptly stopped publishing survey results on religious belief in the mid-1970s. No doubt the results failed to conform to their hopes. Then, in 1984, one Soviet source published an estimate of 26 percent of the whole population as believers, a figure that dovetailed with the data published in the 1970s and contradicted the atheists' predictions of a steady decline in belief.[53] As a figure for believers of all confessions, it probably represented close to 40 million Orthodox believers.[54] In a 1984 interview with Bishop Sergi (Fomin) of the patriarchate, a Western journalist noted that outside observers estimated the number of Russian Orthodox believers at

40–50 million. The bishop indicated that the lower of those two figures was accurate.[55] According to the *Los Angeles Times,* in 1990 the Central Intelligence Agency estimated that 20 percent of the Soviet population, or almost 60 million people, were Orthodox believers.[56]

The ambiguous meaning of "believers" renders these figures extremely imprecise, although some polls have tried to refine and clarify the data. In 1989, a poll reported that 32 percent of Muscovites said religion played a part in their lives—a very great part, 4 percent; quite important, 9 percent; and not very important, 19 percent. Seven percent of Muscovites believed in life after death; 10 percent were sure God exists; 13 percent of the intelligentsia said religion played a "very great role," and 8 percent of Muscovites over sixty years of age agreed.[57] The thrust of these findings is that intensive, sure, committed belief was characteristic of relatively few of the citizens of Moscow; a vague, diffuse religious attachment was more widespread.

Another poll, taken countrywide in early 1990, found that 8 percent of the respondents gave religion high priority in their scale of values, and 5 percent asserted that they had an active involvement in religion. Father Vsevolod Chaplin of the Patriarchate's Office of Foreign Church Relations wrote in April 1994: "In reality, 5 percent of Russians participate in church life—and that's a maximum."[58] These low percentages reflect an erosion of active religious observance, including participation in confession and communion, fasting, and a systematic regimen of prayer and home devotions at the icon corner.[59] Roughly 15 percent of the sample affirmed a somewhat amorphous religious connection; almost half professed some sort of belief but not at the level of a recognizably committed witness.

Still another poll taken countrywide in early 1990 reported that 8 percent of the population placed religious values first—as did the poll just described—and were prepared to bring their children up as believers. The magazine *Ogonëk* (Little Fire) reported in January 1994 on a poll of teenagers that asked why they were afraid of premarital sex. Of the girls, 14 percent answered that it was morally wrong—the eighth of ten possible answers. Of the boys, 6 percent said it was morally wrong—the tenth of ten possible answers. The newspaper *Moskovskie Novosti* (Moscow News) reported in polling results in January 1994 to the following question: "What does Russia need this coming year?" Five percent of respondents referred to a "revival of religion and faith," tenth in rank among answers given, trailing long after "stabilization of the economy" (60 percent) and "action against the Mafia and corruption" (47 percent).[60] In another poll taken countrywide in December 1989, only 0.3 percent said they were members of a parish society.[61] More polling reported that the percentage of countrywide respondents who described themselves as believers increased from 19 percent in December of 1989 to 33 percent in April of 1990.[62] My guess is that this dramatic rise in acknowledged belief over a period of only four months reflected the rapid disintegration of communist ideological authority during that period and the decrease in career-related fear of expressing one's opinion. I was in Moscow during the period straddled by these polls and can confirm the radical change in public psychology occurring at that time. A poll conducted in Belarus in 1992 reported 60 percent "Orthodox" and 33 percent "atheist."[63]

On a deeper level, what does it all signify? It seems to mean what has been known all along: People are a complex mixture of contradictory, unpredictable, and inconsistent feelings and reactions, and polling results are treacherous by their nature. All the polls tend to confirm that focused, informed belief is found among relatively few in the population, whereas vague, uninformed religious sentiment is quite widespread. A U.S. visitor to the Soviet Union during the 1950s once recounted a poignant conversation with his Intourist guide about her mother's faith:

> American: She doesn't belong to church now or go to church anymore?
> Guide: No. All this was years ago.
> American: Before the war?
> Guide: Before the war. . . .
> American: Did the war destroy your mother's faith in God?
> Guide: I really don't know. You see, when you say "God" and ask about God, I really do not know what you mean. The war destroyed many things. I suppose it could destroy what you call "faith," too. But as for Mother, she just gradually stopped saying her prayers and making the sign of the cross. She has not done any of that for years. If she had any reason for stopping, I do not know about it. We do not discuss such things.[64]

I wonder how Mother would be classified in a poll. Would she be a believer, a waverer, or what? If she were polled now, my guess is that she would respond that she was a believer, and her voice might well be firm in making the affirmation.

Poll results confirm many of the regional and demographic trends discussed in the preceding section. In 1988, a researcher surveyed the populations in Kemerovo oblast, the heart of Siberia's great coal-steel complex in the Kuznetsk basin, and in Lvov oblast in western Ukraine. Both regions have roughly 3 million people, although the Siberian oblast had 11 churches compared to 600 in Lvov in 1988. Siberia reported a low incidence of belief: Only 2 percent of those surveyed said they were believers compared to 34 percent in Lvov; 21 percent were "waverers" compared to 36 percent in Lvov; 77 percent were indifferent to religion, nonbelievers, or atheists compared to 30 percent in the Ukrainian oblast. Yet the percentage of "convinced atheists" was not so different—8 percent of the population in Kemerovo and 7 percent in Lvov.[65] Later data in Lvov oblast indi-

cated still higher—and rising—assertions of belief. In September 1989, the head
of the ideological department in the communist headquarters in Lvov reported
that 40 percent were convinced believers in the region, up 6 percent over the previous year, and poll figures for late 1989 showed 77 percent believers and waverers, up from 70 percent in 1988.[66] Changes in fashion and loss of fear were
undoubtedly elements in these shifts in reported opinion, as they were in the
countrywide polls previously described. In any case, the immense difference between "godless" Siberia and western Ukraine was dramatically reflected.

The profile of the believing Orthodox population reflected in polling is very
similar to the profile of the churchgoers—a very heavy concentration of old
women, no more than about 15 percent of all believers in their twenties, no more
than about 5 percent in their teens, about twice the percentage of rural people
asserting belief as city folk, very few workers, and a small but significant percentage of intellectuals professing belief.[67] Those intellectuals who during polling asserted their belief tended to be vocal and influential.[68] The striking difference between believers and churchgoers is in numbers: Only about 5 percent of the
self-described believers attended church in a typical nonholiday week; a very
large mass of believers did not regularly attend church, even in the postmillennial
era.

As for believers' motivations, Bohdan Bociurkiw cited a late 1960s poll in
Ukraine indicating that 61 percent of respondents who were believers came to be
so as a result of family upbringing, 26 percent as a result of personal misfortunes,
and 9 percent because of "religious propaganda." This was Ukraine, where family
religious influences remain strong, particularly in the west. Respondents also indicated the attractions of religion for them: Twenty-six percent were attracted by
the church's moral teachings, 22 percent by personal salvation, 19 percent by con-
solation in grief, and 6 percent by the aesthetic qualities of religious rites. Not
surprisingly, a more than proportional number of believers were reported to be
single people, many of them widows.[69]

Polling has turned up considerable evidence indicating what people think
about religion, as distinguished from the question of their own belief. These results throw light on the relative importance people think religion has in society
and the role people think religion should play. One poll in 1989 found that 44
percent of respondents thought more religious activity (evangelizing) would
benefit society, and 8 percent thought it would not. The rest thought that it
would not make much difference or that it was "hard to say." Two-thirds of the
respondents said priests should have access to television and radio (1 percent said
no), and the same preponderance favored the return of seized churches to believers. A majority favored religious education in the schools, religious publications,
and church efforts to help solve international conflicts and to help with relief
after natural disasters.[70]

Polls in 1989 and 1990 asked respondents to indicate which of nine organizations enjoyed their "full confidence" and which enjoyed their trust but not in a total sense. "Religious organizations" or the "church" started out in early 1989 ranking seventh in full confidence (with the Supreme Soviet and the media first and second). By mid-1990 the church ranked first in full confidence, followed by the media, the environmental movement, and the armed forces. The church was trusted completely or in essence by almost two-thirds of the respondents, whereas the judiciary, the militia, and the Komsomol were trusted only by approximately a quarter of them.[71]

Another poll in early 1990 asked about respondents' aspirations, listing nine choices. Of the respondents, 38 percent put the securing of material welfare in first place, followed by the establishment of "fairness without special privileges." Renewing the "moral foundations" of the society ranked sixth—not a very impressive emphasis.[72]

Another poll taken in early 1990 asked about the reasons for widespread premarital sex among young people. The principal reason given (41 percent) was the overall moral decline in society and the lack of moral education. A "lack of religious upbringing" ranked only sixth (13 percent) out of nine choices. Earlier physical development of boys and girls (15.5 percent) and the imitation of the Western style of life (15 percent) outranked the "lack of religious upbringing" as causes.[73]

Still another poll in early 1990 asked respondents what bothered them. Low income, high prices, insufficient food, low-quality food, housing problems, and the lack of manufactured products led the list. "Lowered morals" ranked eighth, just after under-the-table payments.[74] A poll in late 1990 asked essentially the same question and got similar results, with bread-and-butter issues, the environment, technological backwardness, bureaucracy and organized crime the dominant concerns. The "destruction of morality" was cited by 16 percent and "loss of religious faith" by 10 percent.[75] Still another poll in 1990 asked respondents who inspired their pride. After a father, mother, son, daughter, or a "specialist," a "believing person" ranked tenth (8 percent).[76]

This additional polling indicates that the public appears to have an amiable, benevolent, and welcoming attitude toward the religious institutions in the country, but people do not seem to make the church central to their own existence. Some do, of course, but most do not.

Birth, death, and marriage are life's great milestones, and baptism, a religious funeral, and a wedding in the church express the religious component of these transcending personal events. Baptism may be one's own or that of an offspring.

It may reflect the views of others through infant baptism or of one's own belief through adult baptism, an act that in the past carried concomitant risks. Infant baptism may not even reflect the beliefs of one's parents; a grandmother may slip off with the baby without the parents' knowledge. Over the years, Soviet sociological studies reported that many nonbelieving parents, by some accounts the majority of them, baptized their children out of consideration for older family members. Other factors were respect for tradition, social custom, and a semisuperstitious desire to take out "insurance" for the child "just in case" the Christians should be right.[77]

Through the latter half of the 1920s about 60 percent of children born in Moscow were baptized, and higher percentages no doubt were baptized in the countryside, at least in the areas with churches.[78] After the war, according to one Soviet source, "the majority" of the people in rural Byelorussia still baptized their children. Russian Orthodox church officials said in the mid-1950s that about half the children in Moscow were being baptized and that in Sverdlovsk, the great industrial city in the Urals, 20 percent to 30 percent were baptized.[79]

The Council for Religious Affairs collected figures on baptisms in the Russian republic in 1959, just before the Khrushchev antireligious drive reached full force. The records show that 553,000 children were baptized in the entire Russian republic; these represented slightly over 30 percent of the children born. The oblasts with high percentages of children baptized, ranging down from 62 percent, were mostly in old European Russia; those with particularly low percentages were mostly in Siberia, the Pacific maritime provinces, the central Urals industrial zone, and other oblasts with few and very widely scattered churches. In Sverdlovsk, the figure was 14 percent (note that church officials said it was 20–30 percent in the mid-1950s).[80] If Ukraine and the western lands are included, the percentage of babies baptized would be higher. Two atheist researchers estimated that 40–50 percent of all children born in the USSR were being baptized at the end of the 1950s and the beginning of the 1960s.[81]

In 1959–1960 the Khrushchev antireligious drive struck. Over the next several years regulations requiring the consent of both parents to baptize a child were progressively tightened to force both parents to attend in church, to present internal passports, and to provide a written permit to the father issued by the local authorities. The baptism was then registered in a book open to inspection. In December of 1964 the patriarch—under governmental pressure—decreed very strict requirements, making registration of all baptisms obligatory under church rules and forbidding the carrying out of sacraments in private living quarters outside church premises.[82]

The council recorded the percentages of newly born children baptized in 1965, after the Khrushchev drive, and the figures reflected the drive's results. In the traditional Russian Orthodox heartland, many oblasts recorded a continued high incidence of baptism, although it was lower than in 1959. Siberia and the Pacific maritime provinces registered very low percentages.[83] There were also official figures for baptisms throughout the country; they indicated that 20–25 percent of children were baptized in 1965 and annually thereafter through the remainder of the decade.[84] This was a substantially lower percentage than the 40–50 percent reported before the Khrushchev drive.

By 1972 at least one Soviet sociologist claimed that baptisms had declined to 20 percent of births, and official figures also showed them at about 20 percent through the mid-1970s.[85] Ukraine accounted for 32 percent of all baptisms in 1975, even though Ukraine had only 19 percent of the country's total population; about a third of newborn children in Ukraine were being baptized.[86] There was a slight decline in baptisms nationwide in the early 1980s, to about 18 percent of traditionally Orthodox children.[87] Another official source gave the figure of 16.4 percent of newborn children baptized in 1984–1985.[88] The decline occurred in Ukraine, where officially recognized baptisms fell from 259,000 in 1975 to 155,000 in 1985. Baptisms in the remainder of the USSR actually increased, from 549,000 in 1975 to 620,000 in 1985. The churches closed in western Ukraine, the shortage of priests there, unrecorded secret baptisms, and the continuing suppression of the Greek-Catholics may help explain what happened.[89] In 1987 official figures indicated that baptisms represented about 18 percent of traditionally Orthodox births.[90]

Metropolitan Vladimir (Sabodan), in his report to the national council of the church in June of 1988, stated that 30 million people had been baptized between 1971 and 1988. This would be almost 2 million a year, or about twice the official figures of the Soviet government. One's first thought might be that the difference represented adult baptisms, but the Council for Religious Affairs included these in its totals, indicating that 20,000–30,000 adults were baptized each year in the 1970s and 45,000–55,000 adults were baptized each year in the 1980s.[91] Alternatively, the church may have maintained independent records for unregistered or "illegal" baptisms, which would mean that about half the baptisms performed by the church were unregistered. The church would have been very courageous, however, if not foolhardy, to have kept such records and publicized them in June 1988. As a final alternative, the church may have pulled together unsystematic and somewhat optimistic estimates from the various dioceses in arriving at the 30 million figure, which would then be somewhat inflated. This is the most likely explanation.[92]

In 1988, as already described, the government abolished the requirement that parents register their internal passports in order to baptize a child. This reform lifted a considerable burden of fear, although the government still required a record of the child's birth certificate.[93] The baptismal statistics reflected this increased sense of freedom. Official statistics recorded that a third of newborn children were baptized in 1988. In 1989 Western observers reported that 46 percent of newborn children received the sacrament.[94] In June 1990, Patriarch Aleksi II stated that christenings had increased threefold, which would indicate the baptism of half or slightly more than half of traditionally Russian Orthodox infants.[95]

Who brings the children for baptism—other than the devout grandmothers? Apparently, working-class families will baptize their babies, whether or not they believe. Most intelligentsia will baptize their children only when they believe. About a third of the military will baptize a child, although 60 percent were baptized themselves.[96] The frequency of baptism has fluctuated as fear and repression have fluctuated, with many—or even most—families having wanted to give their children this initial opportunity for salvation.

A religious funeral, like baptism, offers little indication of the survivors' belief in God. After all, Stalin himself gave his first wife a Christian burial.[97] Usually, the survivors request a religious funeral when they believe the deceased would have wanted one. It should be added that the widespread practice of sending a bit of earth to a priest or church for a funeral by "correspondence" distorts the official figures, although the authorities included these rites in absentia, at least those they were aware of, in their official reports.

During the 1920s, official Soviet statistics indicated that 57–59 percent of all burials were religious in the mid-decade years, and 66–67 percent were religious in the 1927–1928 period after the New Economic Policy was in full swing, Sergi had made his loyalty declaration, and fear had receded.[98] Official statistics indicated that a third of all funerals in the Russian republic were religious in 1959; in contrast, one Soviet scholar said 60 percent of funerals throughout the country were religious in 1961.[99]

By the end of the Khrushchev drive the reported nationwide figures had dropped to about 40 percent with the incidence of religious burials lowest in Siberia and the Pacific maritime provinces.[100] By 1971–1972 the percentages had increased, perhaps to about 45 percent once again.[101] Through the 1970s and mid-1980s official statistics for the number of religious funerals of all denominations rose at a little more than 1 percent a year.[102] Kharchev singled out Moldavia as a place with a particularly high percentage of religious funerals.[103] There were indications that the number of religious funerals increased dramatically in 1988 and 1989, perhaps rising to 60–70 percent of the deceased.[104]

The third great milestone of life reflected in a religious rite is marriage. Neither in the former Soviet republics nor in the United States does a religious marriage carry the same importance as the other two rites; consecrating a union has neither the psychological nor ecclesiastical significance associated with baptism and a religious interment. In the United States, 97 percent of marriages in 1849 were in church; by the 1990s the percentage had fallen to the 60–70 percent range—indeed, many people were forgoing any marriage formality at all. In the former

USSR, young people were notably deterred during the Soviet era because they were vulnerable to reprisal and career disadvantage. In addition, they could not evade the fact that a church wedding was their own voluntary act. Besides, baptism was easier, as a priest might come to a village once every few months and baptize the children all at once.[105]

In the late 1920s, the incidence of church weddings fell steadily from 21 percent of all marriages in 1925 to less than 10 percent in 1929.[106] Estimates of 10 percent or less continued into the 1950s, and the statistics of the Council for Religious Affairs indicated that in 1959 there were 37,632 religious weddings in the Russian republic out of 900,000 total, or 5 percent. If Ukraine and other western lands are included, the total would be much higher.[107]

The Khrushchev antireligious thrust affected religious marriages as it did other rites, driving the percentage of church weddings down even further. Council figures for 1965 in a number of oblasts and krais of the Russian republic indicated that religious weddings represented 1 percent or less of all marriages in many oblasts, particularly in Siberia.[108] In western Ukraine and western Byelorussia, on the other hand, reports for the 1970s indicated that a majority of young people continued to marry in church. Overall figures for the country in 1965 for all confessions were 60,516 religious marriages, or about 3 percent of the total.[109] These figures did not, of course, include church weddings performed in secret. Over the next decade and a half official figures for religious marriages for all confessions went up to approximately 80,000 in 1985. This represented about 4 percent of all marriages.[110] In June 1990, Patriarch Aleksi II spoke of a tenfold increase, which would presumably have brought church weddings up to the 40 percent range.[111]

Where do all these statistics leave the Russian Orthodox Church's laity in terms of belief and practice? Although a society "against God" seems not to have won the support of the people, a society functioning "without God" seems to have come close to becoming a reality, at least in the long period of persecution that preceded the Millennium.[112] With the political changes in the country during the years that followed the Millennium, new opportunities quickly opened up. However, church hierarchs also found a de-Christianized wasteland in all too much of society. Repressive legislation and restraints on church activity had left their baneful legacy, and internal problems continued to impede the church's efforts to revitalize lay activity, participation, and belief.

There were at least three impediments to a renaissance of lay Christians' religious commitment. First, some bishops and many priests still harbored a lingering attitude that the church serves the believers who find their own way to faith and practice; they did not seem to see a proselytizing, evangelizing church at the heart of things. Of course, the church has long been an institution bringing the liturgy and the sacraments, solace, marvelous beauty, community, and personal salvation to those who enter in of their own accord. In 1967, Nikita Struve wrote:

> The people pray together as a community and individually as persons. Every face is spiritually withdrawn, lips are gently murmuring: a human person is gently speaking to the personal God. And then, during the litanies, the doxologies, and the more important moments of the canon of the Eucharist, all make the sign of the Cross and bow deeply. This creates a rhythm of adoration. But this rhythm is no hindrance to a wide freedom of personal behavior. It does not prevent the worshipper from feeling at home in God's house. He takes his candles to it, he venerates its icons.[113]

Only slowly has the church begun to carry out its mission to change the world, not only to lead the unbelievers back to Christ but also to build the kingdom of God in the world. Lay Orthodox Christians like Yevgeni Barabanov and Mikhail Meerson-Aksënov saw this problem clearly in the 1970s. As Barabanov said, it was not sufficient for the church simply to *be*, waiting for the secular realm to come to it. The church had a duty to go to the world, bringing it the gospel, transforming it.[114] The church is learning and changing but more slowly than many lay intellectuals within its ranks would like.

Second, Russian Orthodox clerics seem to have sometimes failed to recognize and accept lay opinion and leadership. According to one article in the *Moscow Church Herald, Weekly*, they fear losing "prestige." Sometimes parish priests ignore or try to suppress lay groups. They may withhold information about church income and expenditures. *Sobornost*, the Orthodox tradition of governance by meeting, consultation, and consensus, requires an informed laity participating in the decisionmaking.[115] Whether reluctant clerics fear being second-guessed or want a sense of power, the problem seems real.

Third, the laity distrusts the bishops' past collaboration and present perceived unrepentance. For example, Sergei Averintsev, the chairman of the Soviet parliamentary committee that had jurisdiction over religious legislation, asserted in May 1990 that the laity believed men of weak character had been elevated to the episcopacy. The state authorities had used infiltration and corrupting inducements to "educate" bishops or episcopal candidates. The bishops became compromised by their way of life. There were even "open atheists" among the Brezhnev-era clerics elevated to episcopal sees.[116] Although Averintsev's assertions were exaggerated, he represented the views of a sizable portion of the laity.[117]

The church has a serious problem with lay opinion and lay unruliness. The problem for Russian Orthodox hierarchs is similar to the problem in other churches throughout the world, only aggravated by the priests' and bishops' relative passivity in evangelism, antipathy to lay involvement in decisionmaking, and resistance to a truly self-critical review of the Soviet past.

15

Conclusion

It destroyed churches . . . , it degraded all Christian officials. Presently it ordered that the clergy should be imprisoned. The attack was once more on the organization. . . . The intelligence of [the ruling power] . . . refrained from re-inspiring enthusiasm by martyrdoms. Christendom was to expire from lack of nutrition; churches, documents, sacraments, were to be removed; . . . the Faith was to be flung back on solitude, poverty, ignorance, inconvenience, suspicion and contempt.[1]

These words were written to describe the Tenth General Persecution in the fourth century A.D. under Emperor Diocletian in Rome. The author of them went on to describe how, after some time, the emperor became sick, and persecution under his successor took a different and less calculating form. The kaleidoscope of history turned—and it has also turned for the Bolsheviks. The study of history is a study of continuities and discontinuities, crimson threads woven through the fabric of all time and cloth rent asunder, where the weaving has had to commence anew.

Where were the great discontinuities in Soviet, Russian, and Russian Orthodox Church history? There were certainly three, one affecting the communists, one transforming the situation of the church, and one changing the nation as a whole.

As for the communists, it would have been relatively easy to follow the thread of communist policy concerning religion between 1917 and 1988. The communists displayed great constancy and patience and could claim a considerable degree of destructive success. From the start, the communist state grasped the reality of the church as a refuge for independent thought and a fortress for those who believed in a philosophy incompatible with the communists' creed. Their sentiments were all too clear. Marx had asserted that "the abolition of religion, as an illusory happiness of the people, is a requisite of their real happiness."[2] Engels wrote: "We wish to make a clean sweep. . . . We have then declared war once and for all on religion."[3] Lenin said:

> Every religious idea, every idea of god, even every flirtation with the idea of god is unutterable vileness . . . of the most dangerous kind, "contagion" of the most abominable kind. Millions of sins, filthy deeds, acts of violence and *physical* contagions are . . . less dangerous than the *subtle,* spiritual idea of a god decked out in the smartest "ideological" costumes.[4]

Nevertheless, despite Lenin's views, antireligion was never a primary element in the communists' program. Organized religion was not one of Lenin's "commanding heights." The communists never considered the religious problem as being of immediate and overriding urgency. They repeatedly chose to pursue short-range political objectives even at the cost of their long-range goals. Their resolve varied according to time, circumstances, and place. When the government could afford to assert its authority internally or establish ideological hegemony, the church was one of the victims, as was true at times with Lenin, Stalin, Khrushchev, and Brezhnev. Nevertheless, even Lenin waited until after the civil war before ordering Communist Party members to break with religion.[5] Whenever the state was in serious trouble, antireligious activity languished.

As the years went by, party members' ideological fervor waned and atheist militancy diminished, probably even faster than overall ideological dedication. In the conclusion of my 1960 dissertation, I wrote:

> There is little question that the communists have been suffering a decline in ideological militancy within the areas they control. A case can be made, in fact, for the proposition that the atheistic roots of communist doctrine are shallower than sometimes supposed. . . .
>
> Another possibility is that there will be a continuing ideological decline in the communist movement, until little is left of atheism as a creed. One could conceive of some future day when a . . . Soviet chief of state . . . might feel a personal compulsion to make his peace with the church. Having done so, the Soviet inner circle might find not only that nobody seemed to care, but that it was expedient to use this fact abroad as a demonstration of religious freedom and liberality. It would not be so long a step from this to an official government agnosticism; and ultimately the party might conceivably declare that religion in a classless society is a matter of conscience, even for the party's own members. There is already a tactical accommodation between the Soviet regime and religious forces, and such arrangements tend to settle imperceptibly into permanence.[6]

Although true, these comments must strike today's reader as banal. The communists reached the condition described, and their own disintegration then went further, resulting in the dissolution of their state after the failure of the three-day coup in 1991.

In the 1970s the samizdat journal *Veche* published the following comment: "Atheism is the dark side of faith. Do you remember the first years of the Revolution? With what religious fervor they destroyed everything! They destroyed—and now we sit on the ruins."[7] Seventeen years later the communist principal at Raisa Gorbachev's old high school told a U.S. journalist: "Everyone has to believe in something. In your country you believe in God. In ours we had some kind of faith in a bright future. Now we have lost this belief and found nothing to replace it."[8] In April of 1991 another U.S. journalist described the Easter service at the patriarchal cathedral: "Boris Yeltsin . . . and Prime Minister Valentin Pavlov were among a gaggle of senior officials who stood gamely, if somewhat sheepishly, at the front of the church, occasionally bowing and fiddling with candles in an attempt to show that they were not totally unfamiliar with the Orthodox rites."[9] A poll conducted in the spring of 1989 by the Soviet Institute of Sociology reported that half of all Communist Party members in the institute's sample even then said religious believers could also be members of the party.[10]

Since the late 1980s, Yeltsin has become progressively friendlier to the church. On a trip to Paris in February 1992, Yeltsin said: "We treasure religion. . . . The church feels freer in our country. When you see the Russian president at a service in church, do not think that this is for propaganda purposes. In church you become cleaner in your soul."[11] Yeltsin apparently was himself baptized as an infant, as Gorbachev was—not that either of them had any part in the decision.[12] Yeltsin almost drowned.[13]

There are still a few of the godless around. Gorbachev was asked about his religious convictions during a joint television appearance with Yeltsin on September 5, 1991. He answered straightforwardly that he was still an atheist. There are former communist chieftains, some of them still atheists, governing oblasts, autonomous republics, and even many of the newly independent states that once formed the USSR. Like chameleons, the communists have changed their skin color from red to green, in some cases Islamic green, and altered their public faces, but some of them keep to Lenin's opinion. Not many of them are giving antireligion high priority as they maneuver for survival, but it is doubtful that many of them have become dedicated believers either.

Also still surviving are local apparatchiks who have battled and hated the believers for years, people like the Communist Party chief in Ivanovo who was defeated in his bid to become a people's deputy because he showed no mercy to Christian women demonstrators.[14] There are still bureaucrats who are trying to hang on to churches converted into concert halls, museums, clubs, offices, and apartment buildings; there are a few ossified professors unable to teach anything besides diluted or disguised dialectical materialism; there are a few former watchdogs of the KGB and the army; and there are ordinary people who believed in and still believe in communism and the motherland's achievements and who resent the loss of everything they sacrificed for over a lifetime.

The thread of continuity and the progressive decline in communist dedication are traceable through the pages of this book and in the reality of events. At a certain point, as the communists used to put it, cumulative, quantitative change became transforming, qualitative change. This happened to the Communist Party. The ideological structure collapsed, most of all in that alcove named antireligion. Discontinuity became disaster. Communism lost both ideological force and political power.

The second great discontinuity that affected the church occurred in 1989 when President Gorbachev visited the pope, and the change became evident in the new freedom-of-conscience laws passed in 1990. Over the long centuries, going back beyond the Mongol conquest, the church had played a central role in holding the Russian people together, a unifying force against invaders from East and West. In the course of this history, the church became a tool of state policy, but it also enjoyed a degree of state protection and support.

Even in the Soviet period there was a backhanded symbiotic relationship between church and state. Legally and officially, Lenin disestablished the church, but that did not make Soviet power neutral or uninvolved. After Tikhon's and Sergi's loyalty declarations, the Soviet government altered policy each time, and this enabled the church to counter and finally eliminate the Renovationist schism. It was Soviet power that suppressed the Autocephalous Orthodox Church in Ukraine in 1930 and again in 1944–1945. It was Soviet power that opened the door to Orthodoxy in the territories annexed by the USSR in 1939 and 1940 with Stalin using the church to Russify and help absorb these populations while cynically continuing to persecute the church in Old Russia. When Hitler invaded the USSR in 1941, the church rallied to support the motherland, as it had done on countless other occasions.

Stalin's policies toward Orthodoxy softened, at least for a time. Between 1946 and 1949 in western Ukraine, Stalin forced 3,000 Ukrainian Greek-Catholic parishes and the priests who could be rounded up with them to incorporate themselves into Orthodoxy, additions that increased the number of Russian Orthodox churches in the country by almost a third. It was not that Stalin loved the Orthodox; he hated the Vatican more. He detested the reach of an ecclesiastical power he could not control and saw the Vatican, wrongly, as a tool of Western imperialism. However tormented, persecuted, and reduced, Russian Orthodoxy was the national church. Stalin used it and—in his peculiar way—favored it. Khrushchev and Brezhnev used the church to make life easier for Russian settlers living among Muslims and other alien peoples in Siberia and other distant places. The authorities put a thumb on the Orthodox side of the scales when Baptists and other sectarians competed for adherents in strategically sensitive outposts. In addition, Soviet power made the public accession of scattered parishes in the USSR to the Russian Orthodox Church Abroad both impractical and inconceivable.

For reasons one can admire, Gorbachev moved in 1989 to make neutrality among confessions and freedom of religion a reality. Glasnost, democratization, and new thinking in foreign policy combined to induce the Soviet president to discontinue the status of the Russian Orthodox Church as the protected church of the state—in the odd and repressive way it had previously been favored. This signified that the church's strange and unlovable shield against religious challenge and schism was removed. The church lost its defense against the efforts of the Greek-Catholics to recover their freedom, properties, and position. The church also lost its protection against the Ukrainian Autocephalists; it lost its protection against Protestant evangelists; it lost its protection against schism everywhere.

Resurgent nationalism entered the mix and became a mighty force against Russian Orthodoxy in Ukraine and a growing force in Byelorussia (Belarus). The Russian Orthodox had been wise enough to let the Georgian Orthodox go in 1944, but Ukraine is too big for that. Between 1946 and 1988, two-thirds of the Russian Orthodox churches in the nation were located there.

Meanwhile, there was growing danger of schism in the heartland. Many observers said that if large-scale religious dissidence came, it would be a reaction against unrepentant hierarchs' collaboration with the communist authorities and sycophantic behavior toward them. Some priests and separatist church communities denounced what they regarded as the abjectly submissive record of the patriarchal administration, including the new patriarch, and of all too many diocesan bishops. Activists warned that attempts to carry on as before and avoid true repentance would aggravate lay discontent and bring massive division to the church. The Russian Orthodox Church Abroad and the Russian Orthodox Free Church would be among the beneficiaries. Other Russian Orthodox Christians, however, were no doubt deterred from breaking away by the "tragic" historical memory of the Old Believers' schism in the seventeenth century and that of the Renovationists in the 1920s. Many of the religious intellectuals who could lead a separatist movement were viscerally and instinctively supportive of Orthodox history and tradition.[15]

Moreover, even some of the sharpest critics of the collaborating hierarchs and priests acknowledged them as Christian believers. Anatoli Levitin-Krasnov, the celebrated Christian dissident, approvingly quoted a priest he knew: "I have known negligent priests, lecherous, drunken ones, but I have never met a single nonbelieving priest."[16] It was said of Patriarch Aleksi (Simanski) that a bishop complained to him in the 1960s about the "catacomb congregations" in his diocese. Reportedly Aleksi replied: "You should thank God that there are so many courageous Christians in your diocese who have not bowed their backs to the atheists as we have done."[17] In June 1964, the same Aleksi was reported to have been called to the Kremlin by Nikita Khrushchev, who tried to inveigle the patriarch into agreeing to close fourteen additional churches in Moscow, where church connivance would be politically important. Aleksi reportedly answered: "Close my churches by force if you will, but you will have to take my head from my shoulders before you use my authority to take the crosses off the cupolas of our churches."[18] Dimitry Pospielovsky recounted that Patriarch Aleksi II (Ridiger) sank to his knees facing the huge crowd of worshipers in the patriarchal cathedral on Forgiveness Sunday in 1991 and asked the faithful for forgiveness.[19]

When the freedom-of-conscience laws were passed in 1990, the disestablishment of Orthodoxy, already asserted by Gorbachev in Rome, became a consummated reality. The new legislation declared that every legitimate religious community was free to go its own way.[20] The Russian Orthodox Church at least temporarily lost a position it had occupied, for better or for worse, over a period of 1,000 years, including the years of communist power.

The third great discontinuity of the times has changed the whole Soviet Union. Beyond schism in the church, there has been the fragmentation of the country.

Until 1989, it was not widely doubted that the Soviet Union would endure within its existing boundaries and under an approximation of its prevailing system of communist rule. Then came the elections for the Congress of People's Deputies in the spring of 1989, not wholly democratic but largely so. Communist Party chiefs in great cities lost in the elections and lost power. Opposition figures like Boris Yeltsin won in the elections and gained power. Abroad, the Brezhnev Doctrine was disavowed, and communist positions in Eastern Europe crumbled. At home, glasnost and democratization, and the example of Eastern Europe, swept away the bonds of fear that had so long bound together the Soviet multinational empire and the Russian empire before it. Lithuania declared its independence in March of 1990, and Moscow failed to crush the Lithuanians' spirit of defiance. Other republics followed Lithuania's lead, some cautiously and some boldly. The Russians, who had pushed out beyond the natural ethnic, cultural, and religious boundaries of their land, were paying the price. The dismantling of the USSR's command economy was moving faster than the emplacement of a market system, and production, supply, and distribution spiraled down. Inflation spiraled up, and the economic crisis merged with the nationality crisis to become a general crisis. The alliance of liberal reformers and nationalist separatists transformed the drive for freedom and democracy into a motor of devolution for the nationalities previously bound together.

What are the possible outcomes? One possibility is that liberalizing forces will ultimately prevail. The result in terms of the nationality question has already become the dissolution of the state. In western Ukraine the forces of nationalism are drawing the Greek-Catholics' triumphant battle chariot, and it is doubtful that any Russian Orthodox leadership could have stopped this movement, whether reformist or conservative, whether untouched by or deeply involved in past collaboration. It was Gorbachev's change in policy in 1989 that undid the forced union with Orthodoxy, and nothing short of sweeping repression could have changed the outcome.

The future of the Autocephalists—whether or not their partial union with Metropolitan Filaret (Denisenko) endures—is intimately connected to the Ukrainian assertion of nationhood and independence. The Russian Orthodox Church's hold is slowly but inexorably loosening. The fortunes of Moscow's "autonomous" surrogate, the Ukrainian Orthodox Church led by Metropolitan Vladimir (Sabodan), are also ultimately clouded and uncertain. One cannot assume, however, that the fractured Autocephalists and their allies will inherit Ukrainian Orthodoxy. During the German occupation in World War II, the Autocephalists were in a distinct minority, and most Orthodox faithful frequented and supported the Ukrainian Autonomous Orthodox Church, which continued to recognize the canonical authority of Moscow. If the Moscow patriarchate should play its cards astutely enough in the political breakaway of Ukraine, it might be able to prevent an en bloc hostile ecclesiastical separation. It will be necessary, however, to infuse the present "autonomous" Ukrainian Orthodox Church—still part of the patriarchal establishment—with the full substance of independence and ultimately to grant autocephaly. The other alternative, of course, would be the ultimate political reincorporation of Ukraine into a restored Great Russian state—a bloody enterprise.

Similar hard choices are materializing in the formerly Romanian territories of Moldova (Bessarabia) and Chernovtsy (northern Bukovina). As described in Chapter 8, some Moldovan Orthodox have already passed over to the Romanian Orthodox Church's jurisdiction. So far as the Orthodox establishment in Chernovtsy diocese is concerned, its situation is complicated by the fact that northern Bukovina has become an oblast integrally part of Ukraine, and the Ukrainian government is likely to resist, by force if it comes to that, any loss of territories to Romania.

As Belarus (Byelorussia) consolidates its independence, the "autonomous" Byelorussian Orthodox Church will have to follow the path indicated for Ukrainian Orthodoxy. "Autonomy" will have to be infused with substance, and ultimately the Belarusans—assuming that Belarus remains independent and is not reabsorbed by the Russians—will no doubt press for autocephaly.[21] As the Baltic republics consolidate their independent positions, local political forces are already pressing the Orthodox to separate from Moscow. This result occurred in the interwar period, and it is beginning to happen again.

The Orthodox Churches in Central Asia and Kazakhstan are less likely than the religious communities in other parts of the former Soviet Union to break away from Moscow. Except in Kazakhstan, they represent beleaguered Slavic Christian communities in an Islamic sea. It is quite possible, however, that Ukrainian Orthodox communities will sever their ties to the Moscow hierarchy and cleave to their own church if and when it emerges in some sort of consolidated form.

All this leaves a reduced but still immense Russian federated republic of 150 million people spread across eleven time zones. In that republic the Russian Orthodox Church may have 5,200–5,500 parishes, even with the churches that have opened since 1988. It will have vast churchless spaces and towns, approximately a fifth of the formerly predictable vocations to the priesthood, and perhaps a million believers attending church on a Sunday morning.[22] The church will no longer be an "imperial" institution reaching out to unite and "Russify" non-Russian peoples in non-Russian republics.[23] Its tasks will be simplified in some ways, but it will be a very different church.

Since the aborted putsch of August 1991, the old order has been destroyed, but there is still a haunting possibility that glasnost, democratization, liberalism, self-determination, perestroika, and a working market economy may perish in the years ahead and thus make way for reaction and counterreform. Vladimir Zhirinovsky probably will not be the ultimate standard-bearer of these forces, but would-be successors to his mantle will surely appear. This has been the story of Russian history ever since the incipient democratic institutions of Kievan Rus, Novgorod, and Pskov were swept aside by the emerging autocratic Muscovite state. Political theorists advise us that revolutions in the world normally sweep out the moderates and idealists who start them and usher in the extremists and despots who finish them. In France, the cry of liberty, equality, and fraternity became the terror and the guillotine. A growing number of Russians believe that their country needs a man on a horse—or at least a leader who is truly strong.[24] Will a Russian Bonaparte appear on the scene? After all, Napoleon was a mere colonel of artillery when the French Revolution was sweeping that nation. It is a good question, however, whether even the strongest leadership could reconstruct the USSR or reverse the rolling economic debacle. But Ivan did; Peter did; Lenin did.

In another great crisis of prerevolutionary Russian history, the Time of Troubles, the church had a central role in saving Russia. Two patriarchs were principal actors. In 1608 Yermogen (Yermolaya) fed the people of Moscow from the church's last stores of grain. He inspired the monks to defend the besieged Trinity-Sergius monastery; he rallied the people in defense of the motherland. Seized by the Poles, he nonetheless refused in 1611 to validate Russia's submission to a Polish monarch and renewed his call to resist. Incarcerated by the Poles in the Chudov monastery in Moscow, he starved to death in early 1612, martyred for his Orthodox faith and patriotism. Inspired by Yermogen's blessing and marching in the shadow of the Kazan icon of the Mother of God, Russian soldiers defeated their enemies the following October. A council of the Russian land then elected Michael Romanov czar, and Michael's father, soon to become Patriarch Filaret (Romanov-Yurev), ruled as cosovereign with his teenaged son, providing strength and wisdom to guide the Russian state out of its Time of Troubles.[25] Russians call the post-Soviet epoch the Second Time of Troubles.[26]

The church was also instrumental in preserving the Russian nation during the long years of degradation under the Mongol yoke. It rallied the Russian people against pagans, Muslims, and all manner of other invading armies and faiths from the East. St. Sergius Radonezh blessed and inspired Dmitri and his men to win Russia's first victory against the Tatars in 1380. In struggles against the West, the church played the same role, mobilizing Russian courage against Teutonic Knights, Poles, Lithuanians, Frenchmen, Swedes, Germans, and many others. The church was born in Ukraine, in Kherson and Kiev, and was a unifying force for Ukrainians, Russians, Byelorussians, Cossacks, and dozens of converted, non-Slavic peoples. In most of Russia's crises, the church has been a powerful voice for justice, mercy, and national salvation. During the post-Soviet travail, neither restive patriots nor church leaders can have forgotten this history.

As the breakup of the Soviet empire continues, ethnic conflicts are being carried down to the second tier: In the Russian republic, struggles continue with Chechens, Ingush, north Ossetians, Kazan Tatars, Yakuts, and others; in Georgia with south Ossetians, Abkhazians, and Adzharians; in Moldova with trans-Dniester Russians and Gagauzi; in Lithuania against Poles; in Azerbaidzhan against Armenians; and so on. As the economic crisis deepens, nationalist and separatist forces are gaining strength.

Against the centrifugal forces just mentioned there are opposing centripetal ones straining to pull the former constituent republics, Russia's "near abroad," back into Moscow's zone of power. Russian politicians and military commanders, some with clear direction from the center and some without it, are already attempting to assert a degree of Russian control in the trans-Dniester area of Moldova, in Ukraine, in the Caucasian republics, and in Central Asia.

Forces seeking national salvation, some of them with pure and some with impure motives, will make renewed attempts to co-opt the church.[27] Attempts to draw the patriarch into rightist appeals for national preservation have mostly been clumsy and quickly disavowed, but there will be more such attempts. Hardline communist survivors are allying themselves with chauvinist, anti-Semitic, and neofascist movements in the attempt to "save" Russia. If things go really badly, all sorts of ugly phenomena are possible. The pressures on the church are immense, and the patriarch will need all the sagacity he can muster and all the moral strength he can find within himself. There are forces emerging in Russia that are prepared to bring back the old imperial slogan "Nationality, Orthodoxy,

Autocracy." The church is already seen by many as a ready instrument for Russification, discipline, control, and order.

It has always been hazardous to assume that benign and liberalizing changes in Russia are irreversible. Stalin's abandonment of the New Economic Policy and his repression did not simply draw on an existing undercurrent of ideological opposition to liberalism. He created his own context—terror—and nourished his own malignant growths, which ultimately fed upon themselves. Repeatedly in Russian and Soviet history, the waves of destruction that crashed over the church were at the same time washing away normal society and engulfing church institutions almost as a coincident result of the deluge. But these are among the less imminent perils. The closer danger is that a repressive nationalist leadership might install itself in the Kremlin in the aftermath of political and economic disaster and press the patriarch and other church leaders to join a holy or unholy alliance to save the nation at the cost of liberty.

The Russian Orthodox Church, whether in its current form or reduced to being the church of the Russian heartland, faces the challenge of reaching an immense, religiously inactive population. Both the communist and religious tides have receded, leaving a larger and larger ideologically inert human mass between them. It is not clear whether this belief-empty population will remain, like a tide-washed slough, until a new wave comes or whether, like a vacuum, it will strain to be filled.[28] Patriarch Aleksi II said in 1991: "When militant atheism planted itself in our society, a vacuum was formed in the souls of the people."[29] In another interview the patriarch said: "The new generation has forgotten everything. . . . People live with emptied souls."[30] Metropolitan Vladimir (Sabodan), now of Kiev, was even more direct: "The most serious and difficult problem of all is the necessity of re-Christianization, of bringing the Church to the population, a population which estranged itself from the Church of God. Much ability and readiness for this enterprise was lost among the clergy over the past seventy years, and in places the fire went out altogether."[31] In the *Journal of the Moscow Patriarchate,* Vladimir Semenko appealed to the laity to become missionaries "in the ocean of neopaganism which surrounds us."[32] For his part, Metropolitan Kirill (Gundyaev) of Smolensk observed that "it is well known that for some decades the prophetic voice of the church was heard by few of our fellow citizens."[33]

Bishop Vadim (Lazebny) of Irkutsk described the situation in Siberia in even more anguished terms:

> Some simply lose heart. The reason for this can be found in a lack of true spirituality. . . . Religiousness among our contemporary sybarites now and then takes non-Orthodox forms—even entirely nonconfessional ones. Sometimes this is sim-

ply the religiousness of every-day, arising from superstition. Not very many here regularly go to church.

Of the thirty clerics in Irkutsk diocese . . . seven are sybarites, born and raised in the same surroundings as their parishioners. The rest come from outside. It would be possible to open a theological training institute. But whom could one teach there? You see, it takes more than one generation of devout lay men and women to form priestly vocations, and these lay people also need spiritual formation. . . .[34]

The church has a new problem. It has become fashionable to be a superficial Christian. The children of privilege in Moscow wear neck crosses and Christian symbols as earrings.[35] It is becoming unnecessary to sacrifice for one's belief, and that fact alone is eroding dedication. With the church's return to respectability and influence, many of the problems and dilemmas facing churches in the West are arising in the East. Factions are more visible, power games more tempting, and the challenges of preserving the unity of the church more daunting.

Lay commentators have noted the church's failures in outreach. Vladimir Poresh observed: "The years of totalitarian terror did their job," threatening the church with "spiritual paralysis."[36] Poresh then quoted other Orthodox lay critics: "The Church's weakness and the distortion of its influence" also lie in the inadequacy of the church's word addressed to the world and the undeveloped nature of Orthodox dogma "when it is required to reach out beyond the inner, sacramental borders of the Church and address itself to people who live a secular life, giving unbelievers a contemporary explanation of its teaching. . . . The Church today has not found an authentic, appropriate form of existence outside the church building." Hiding its confusion, it "reveals itself as an archaic" moralizer.[37]

Clerics find themselves under increasing pressure to demonstrate leadership and an activism beyond their abilities. In former times it was an act of courage to perform the rites, and doing so with dignity and conviction was all that seemed essential. Now the church is reaching out in social action and religious instruction, but not always successfully. All too often laypeople perceive the priests as "too busy" to know their names or their needs.[38] As in the West, priests and lay believers are finding that honest efforts and good motives are not always enough.[39]

Even if the people do, indeed, draw to faith as if pulled by a vacuum, it is not necessarily preordained that the Russian Orthodox Church will be the religious body to fill that void. As already described, the Baptists, other evangelicals, and a variety of sects are attracting throngs of new believers.[40] Church publications also describe, condemn, and bemoan people's belief in poltergeists, occult appearances, interplanetary aliens, pseudoreligion, and paganism.

Nevertheless, one should not read too much into these phenomena. The historical faith of Russia is Orthodoxy, and Orthodoxy is deeply embedded in the Russian soul. It defines a Russian's sense of nation, history, and identity, even when the individual is not devout. I have heard many Russians say that they are not believers, but they do know which the true faith is.[41]

Russians are returning to the church and becoming both believers and practitioners once again. The work of the clergy, of the teaching and catechizing laymen, of the sisters of charity, and of the grandmothers is not easy, but it is being done, and the baptism of Rus is being repeated, soul by soul. In the 1950s, a U.S. traveler described a conversation with a Soviet citizen in what is now Volgograd who spoke of Orthodoxy and predicted that, when a return to faith took hold of the Russian masses, "we Americans would be shamed by their devotion and embarrassed by their demonstration of religious fervor."[42]

History has a way of deceiving those who think they can guess its course. This study began with the observation that the churches have material dimensions as well as spiritual ones, and that philosophers and theologians, with the gift of flight, may neglect to walk. Much of the introduction to this book was an appeal for understanding that material realities do matter. Facts—such as the number of churches, where they are, and how long a walk it is to get to one—do have their real importance. The "mundane" literally refers to what is of the earth, and even for the church of God, it is real. It is no part of the purpose of this study, however, to deny the importance or the power of spiritual truth and the great work of those who affirm its transcending reality. It would be as myopic to view the churches only in their dimensions on the ground as to view only their spiritual ones. The shroud of fog and smoke remains. Perhaps the city stands the way cities of spires sometimes do, with a low-lying fog bank hugging the ground, leaving the city darkened and obscured only for those walking in the streets, close to the earth. In these cases, the tops of the spires sometimes rise up to reach the open air and brilliant sunshine, so that those who fly are able to see more clearly.

Notes

Introduction

(Pages xv–xviii)

1. If we believe God acts in history, then all history must be the product of God's will. For a discussion of some of the issues raised here, see James J. Lorence and James G. Grinsel, "Amen: The Role of Religion in History Teaching," *Perspectives,* American Historical Association Newsletter, Vol. 30, No. 7, October 1992, pp. 20–23.

2. "Religion," *Webster's New International Dictionary* (Springfield, Mass.: G. and C. Merriam Co., 1931).

3. *Zhurnal Moskovskoi Patriarkhii* [Journal of the Moscow Patriarchate], No. 10 (October), 1991, p. 6. For the lack of churches causing severe damage to religious faith and practice in the U.S.S.R., see William C. Fletcher, *The Russian Orthodox Church Underground, 1917–1970* (London: Oxford University Press, 1971), pp. 270–271. The word Aleksi used in the quoted passage as a place in Asia Minor was "Kaledoniya," but it is unlikely that he meant Caledonia. Gregory the Illuminator was raised and lived at times in Caesarea in Cappadocia. Basil the Great was bishop of Caesarea, and I wonder if Caesarea or Cappadocia might have been what Aleksi was referring to. As another possibility, Calchedon, or Chalcedon, in Asia Minor comes close to a transliteration of Aleksi's word.

4. I am indebted to Joseph G. Brennan for reading and commenting on this text. His comment on this passage was: "The flower may be very different from the earth in which it grows, but it does need that earth for its roots."

5. Daniel Jenkins, *The Strangeness of the Church* (Garden City, New Jersey: Doubleday, 1955), p. 117.

6. Georg Wilhelm Friedrich Hegel, as quoted by Edward Rogers, *A Commentary on Communism* (London: The Epworth Press, 1951), p. 65.

7. Lin Yutang, as quoted in *The World's Great Religions,* the editors of *Life* (New York: Time, Inc., 1957), p. 89.

8. Ruth Benedict, "Religion," *General Anthropology,* ed. Franz Boas, (New York: D. C. Heath and Co., 1938), pp. 628–629. In order to make sure that Benedict's generalization has not been overturned by subsequent scholarship, I consulted with Professors Sharon Parks and Wilfred Cantwell Smith of Harvard and Professor Clifford Geertz of the Institute for Advanced Study at Princeton. They indicated that scholarship in anthropology and religion has moved away from the examination of such generalizations, but no one disputed the continuing acceptance of Benedict's assertion. Its reaffirmation appears in most general textbooks on anthropology, for example, Carol R. and Melvin Ember, *Cul-*

tural Anthropology, 6th ed. (Englewood Cliffs, New Jersey: Prentice Hall, 1990), pp. 280–283.

9. Benedict, pp. 632–633.

10. Paul Tillich, *The Protestant Era* (Chicago: University of Chicago Press, 1948), p. 254.

11. John C. Bennett, *Christianity and Communism* (New York: Hadden House Associated Press, 1948), pp. 33–34. See also Nicolas Berdyaev, *The Origin of Russian Communism* (London: Geoffrey Bles, 1948), p. 10.

12. Benedict, p. 630.

13. Albert Boiter, *Religion in the Soviet Union* (Beverly Hills, Calif.: Sage Publications, 1980), p. 21.

14. Nathaniel Davis, *Religion and Communist Government in the Soviet Union and Eastern Europe,* dissertation, The Fletcher School of Law and Diplomacy, June 1, 1960, pp. 37–39. The text has been slightly edited and shortened, and tenses have been recast.

15. For a description of the origins of the red Easter egg, said to have been presented to Tiberias by Mary Magdalene, see the *Moskovski Tserkovny Vestnik, Yezhenedelnik* [Moscow Church Herald, Weekly], No. 5, April 1991, pp. 4–5. There actually have been two patriarchate publications called the *Moskovski Tserkovny Vestnik* [Moscow Church Herald]. The first was a slick-paper monthly magazine designed for overseas readers. It was first published in 1987 and continued publication through 1989, when *Pravoslavnoe Chtenie* [Orthodox Readings] replaced it. The second *Moskovski Tserkovny Vestnik* began publication in spring 1989. The masthead called it a "Yezhenedelnik" [weekly], but it was actually published approximately biweekly. The "Yezhenedelnik" was dropped from the masthead starting with issue number 8 of 1990, but restored in April 1994. My citations list it as *Moskovski Tserkovny Vestnik, Yezhenedelnik,* for consistency and to distinguish it from the slick-paper monthly.

16. The photograph was published in the *Zhurnal Moskovskoi Patriarkhii,* No. 9 (September), 1967, inside the back cover.

17. Father Vitaly Borovoi. See Dimitry Pospielovsky, *The Russian Church Under the Soviet Regime, 1917–1982,* 2 Vols. (Crestwood, New York: St. Vladimir's Seminary Press, 1984), p. 459.

Chapter 1

1. Wassilij Alexeev, *Russian Orthodox Bishops in the Soviet Union, 1941–1953,* text in Russian (New York: Research Program on the U.S.S.R., Mimeographed Series No. 61, 1954), pp. 84–85. See also Wassilij Alexeev, "The Russian Orthodox Church 1927–1945: Repression and Revival," *Religion in Communist Lands,* Vol. 7, No. 1, Spring 1979, p. 30. In the latter account Alexeev mentioned two nuns who slept out of earshot in the attic.

2. Alexeev, *Russian Orthodox Bishops,* pp. 14, 84.

3. Dimitry Pospielovsky, *The Russian Church Under the Soviet Regime, 1917–1982,* 2 Vols. (Crestwood, New York: St. Vladimir's Seminary Press, 1984), pp. 29–31.

4. Pospielovsky, pp. 31–32, 37.

5. A. Vvedenski, *Tserkov i gosudarstvo* [Church and State] (Moscow: Mospoligraf "Krasny Proletari," 1923), p. 115.

6. John Shelton Curtiss, *The Russian Church and the Soviet State, 1917–1950* (Boston: Little, Brown and Co., 1953), p. 52.

7. W. Bruce Lincoln, *Passage Through Armageddon: The Russians in War and Revolution, 1914–1918* (New York: Simon and Schuster, 1986), p. 149.

8. Mikhail Heller and Aleksandr Nekrich, *Utopia in Power,* trans. Phyllis B. Carlos (New York: Summit Books, 1986), p. 117.

9. Fletcher wrote that Tikhon was willing to give up valuables not consecrated to religious usage, but the Soviet government declared the confiscation of all valuables except vessels actually necessary to the conduct of religious worship. William C. Fletcher, *The Russian Orthodox Church Underground, 1917–1970* (London: Oxford University Press, 1971), p. 27. See also Pospielovsky, p. 93.

10. The Vatican and others, including local hierarchs and laity, offered to ransom the Orthodox Church's sacred objects for money if the authorities would spare them from confiscation. Nicholas S. Timasheff, *Religion in Soviet Russia, 1917–1942* (London: Sheed and Ward, 1944), p. 29. Heller and Nekrich, p. 137, reported 8,100 priests, monks, and nuns executed in 1922.

11. Pospielovsky, p. 38, stated that at least twenty-eight bishops were killed between 1918 and 1920. An order to open reliquaries and place the remains of saints in museums had already produced violent struggle, arrests, and the forcible closing of churches. Pospielovsky, p. 39.

12. Pospielovsky published large excerpts of the text, taken from the *Vestnik Russkogo Studencheskogo Khristianskogo Dvizheniya* [Herald of the Russian Student Christian Movement], published in the West in 1970. In 1964 in the forty-fifth volume of the *Sobraniya sochineni V. I. Lenina* [Collection of the Works of V. I. Lenin], there had been an abbreviated reference to the document. In the Moscow weekly of the Komsomol, *Sobesednik* [Interlocutor], *Komsomolskaya Pravda* Supplement, No. 16, April 1990, p. 7, a discussion of the history of the matter and considerable excerpts of Lenin's memorandum were published. I was in Moscow at the time and was told by a number of former communists that they had resigned from the party as a direct consequence of the revelation. They could believe that Stalin might have written such a document, but they were distressed that Lenin could have acted in this way.

13. Pospielovsky, pp. 22–24, 43–92. Walters asserted that Trotsky was in charge of the campaign to seize church treasures and favored having the patriarch shot, but Lenin did not want to create so prominent a martyr. Philip Walters, "A Survey of Soviet Religious Policy," *Religious Policy in the Soviet Union,* ed. Sabrina Petra Ramet (New York: Cambridge University Press, 1993), pp. 8, 9.

14. Pospielovsky, pp. 51–61; Fletcher, p. 32.

15. Pospielovsky, pp. 59, 148; Matthew Spinka, *The Church in Soviet Russia* (New York: Oxford University Press, 1956), pp. 37–41; Nikita Struve, *Christians in Contemporary Russia,* trans. Lancelot Sheppard and A. Manson (New York: Charles Scribner's Sons, 1967) pp. 38–40; Paul B. Anderson, *People, Church and State in Modern Russia* (New York: The Macmillan Co., 1944), p. 66. According to Francis House, there was pressure for Tikhon's release from the archbishop of Canterbury and from Western governments, including some from which the Soviet authorities wished to buy grain. Francis House, *The Russian Phoenix* (London: SPCK, 1988), p. 59.

16. Pospielovsky, pp. 61–62; Fletcher, pp. 32–33.

17. Curtiss, p. 183; Spinka, p. 65.

18. Struve, p. 44; Spinka, p. 66; Pospielovsky, p. 109. As Sergi was later to point out, Russian grammar makes clear that the antecedent of "joys and successes" was the feminine "motherland" and not the masculine "Soviet Union."

19. Pospielovsky, pp. 114–158; Heller and Nekrich, p. 177.

20. Heller and Nekrich, pp. 237, 242; Nikita S. Khrushchev, *Khrushchev Remembers,* ed. and trans. Strobe Talbott (Boston: Little, Brown and Co., 1970), p. 74.

21. Pospielovsky, p. 168.

22. Nathaniel Davis, *Religion and Communist Government in the Soviet Union and Eastern Europe,* dissertation, The Fletcher School of Law and Diplomacy, June 1, 1960, pp. 128–309.

23. The communist authorities spoke of subversive infiltration from abroad as a justification for atheist failures in Stalin's time and even into the 1980s.

24. Schistosomiasis is an example. The blood flukes that produce the disease have a distinct life cycle, from human blood and urine, to fresh water, to water-dwelling snails, to fresh water again, and to human skin that can be penetrated to reach the bloodstream. In combating the disease in Africa, public health workers concentrated on the snails and the fresh-water environment.

25. Spinka, p. 93; Curtiss, p. 294.

26. Two seminaries operated secretly for a time, and an Orthodox theological institute was allowed to function between 1927 and 1929. Pospielovsky, pp. 31, 41 (note 38), 110.

27. David I. Golovensky, "An American Rabbi in Russia," *Congress Weekly,* Vol. 23, No. 25, November 15, 1956, p. 8.

28. Pospielovsky, p. 342; Metropolitan, then Archbishop, Kirill (Gundyaev) of Smolensk, "Pravoslavnoe bogosluzhenie i problemy prikhodskoi zhizni [The Orthodox Service of Worship and Problems of Parish Life]," *Religiya v SSSR* [Religion in the USSR], No. 3 (March), 1988, p. IT1.

29. Curtiss, p. 153; Vladimir Gsovski, ed., *Church and State Behind the Iron Curtain* (New York: Frederick A. Praeger, 1955), p. xii. See also Jane Ellis, *The Russian Orthodox Church: A Contemporary History* (Bloomington, Indiana: Indiana University Press, 1986), p. 279, and note 62, p. 487.

30. Trichinosis is a disease that the body seeks to isolate in the fashion described.

31. Pospielovsky, p. 102.

32. Harvey Fireside, *Icon and Swastika: The Russian Orthodox Church Under Nazi and Soviet Control* (Cambridge, Mass.: Harvard University Press, 1971), p. 33; J. B. Barron and H. M. Waddams, *Communism and the Churches, a Documentation* (London: SCM Press, Ltd., 1950), pp. 18, 61.

33. Enforcement of a number of the provisions of the decree was relaxed toward the end of World War II and in the immediate postwar period. It should also be noted that the authorities did not consistently enforce the technical prohibition against manufacture of candles for sale. The decree was rigorously enforced during the Khrushchev antireligious drive. The decree was issued by the Russian republic, not by the USSR authorities. Other republics then followed suit. The text appears in Barron and Waddams, pp. 17–20.

34. Albert Galter, *The Red Book of the Persecuted Church* (Westminster, Maryland: The Newman Press, 1957), pp. 437–438.

35. Fireside, p. 33; House, p. 64.

36. Curtiss, p. 238; Timasheff, p. 39; Robert Tobias, *Communist-Christian Encounter in East Europe* (Indianapolis, Indiana: School of Religion Press, 1956), p. 261.

37. Timasheff, pp. 37, 40, 144; Curtiss, pp. 211, 214. The six-day workweek was discontinued in June of 1940. Spinka, p. 81.

38. Fireside, p. 33.

39. Timasheff, p. 59; Curtiss, pp. 85–86, 199; Pospielovsky, p. 39; Gsovski, p. xix; Galter, p. 33.

40. Curtiss, pp. 66, 88, 115, 235.

41. Curtiss, pp. 199, 203, 207, 211–212, 215; Timasheff, p. 34–35, 103.

42. Curtiss, pp. 205–210, 217, 226, 239–241, 250–251, 255; Spinka, p. 76; Pierre Van Paasen, *Visions Rise and Change* (New York: The Dial Press, 1955), p. 294.

43. Curtiss, pp. 213–214; Timasheff, p. 44. A kind of "cultural revolution" dominated the educational scene for several years. The 1928–1931 period saw the relative ascendancy of Yaroslavsky over Anatoli Lunacharski, and Lunacharski was dismissed as commissar of education in September 1929. Andrei Bubnov replaced Lunacharski, but a more traditional, essentially nonreligious curriculum was reinstituted in 1931. In 1937 there was a spasm of renewed antireligious instruction. Nevertheless, Bubnov was arrested in October of that year and shot in 1938. Teachers were never comfortable or confident indoctrinating pupils in the essentially negative concept of antireligion, and the instruction did not work very well. Larry E. Holmes, "Fear No Evil: Schools and Religion in Soviet Russia, 1917–1941," *Religious Policy in the Soviet Union,* Sabrina Petra Ramet, ed. (New York: Cambridge University Press, 1993), pp. 138–146.

44. Georges Bissonnette, A.A., *Moscow Was My Parish* (New York: McGraw-Hill Book Co., 1956), p. 248.

45. Howard L. Parsons, *Christianity in the Soviet Union,* Occasional Paper No. 11 (New York: The American Institute for Marxist Studies, 1972), p. 50.

46. House, p. 87.

47. Zinaida Schakovskoy, *The Privilege Was Mine,* trans. Peter Wiles (New York: G. P. Putnam's Sons, 1959), p. 256.

48. Membership of the League of the Militant Godless fell to 2 million in 1938, even though 22 million dues-paying members by 1937 were planned. Pospielovsky, p. 178.

49. Heller and Nekrich, p. 265; William C. Fletcher, "Introduction: The State of Soviet Sociology of Religion," *U.S.S.R., Western Religion: A Country by Country Sociological Inquiry,* ed. Hans (J. J.) Mol (The Hague, Paris: Mouton, 1972), pp. 577–578; Fireside, p. 35.

50. In 1947, the Council for Russian Orthodox Church Affairs (later the Council for Religious Affairs) initiated a practice of sending an inspector to the site of a proposed parish registration to report on its advisability. These reports often recorded when the church had been closed in the 1930s. When collated, the data show modest numbers through 1935, a slight increase in 1936, numbers several times the previous levels in 1937 and 1938, and a slackening off in 1939, 1940, and 1941. Tsentralny Gosudarstvenny Arkhii Oktyabrskoi Revolutsii [Central State Archive of the October Revolution], Vysshikh Or-

ganov Gosudarstvennoi Vlasti i Organov Gosurdarstvennogo Upravleniya S.S.S.R. [of the Higher Organs of State Government and Organs of State Administration of the U.S.S.R.], Soviet po delam religii pri Sovete Ministrov [the Council for Religious Affairs attached to the Council of Ministers], Fond 6991s, Opis No. 2, Vol. I, delos 1–86. The "s" in 6991s stands for *sekretny* (secret).

51. Fletcher, *The Russian Orthodox Church Underground,* p. 102; Fletcher, "Introduction," pp. 567–569. In the latter work Fletcher gave numerical estimates of functioning Russian Orthodox churches through the 1920s and 1930s.

52. See Roy A. Medvedev, *Let History Judge: The Origins and Consequences of Stalinism* (New York: Vintage Press, 1973), pp. 157–239, 281–282. See also Anton Antonov-Ovseyenko, *The Time of Stalin: Portrait of a Tyranny* (New York: Harper and Row, 1982).

53. Serge Schmemann, "Patriarch's Church Revives, but Will Spirituality?" *The New York Times,* November 9, 1991, p. 2. There were about 50,000 priests, 15,000 deacons, and 95,000 monks and nuns (including novices) in Russia before the 1917 revolution, a total of approximately 160,000. There were about 44,000 psalmists and lay readers in addition. Pospielovsky, pp. 174–175, quoted a figure of 42,000 clerics killed. From his discussion, he was counting both priests and deacons, but not nuns or unordained monks. For the pre-revolutionary figures, see Wassilij Alexeev and Theofanis G. Stavrou, *The Great Revival: The Russian Church Under German Occupation* (Minneapolis: Burgess Publishing Co., 1976), pp. 7, 29; Serge Bolshakoff, *The Christian Church and the Soviet State* (London: Society for Promoting Christian Knowledge, 1942), p. 56; Curtiss, p. 91; Pierre Fontanieu, "Le problème religieux en U.R.S.S. [The Religious Problem in the U.S.S.R.]." *Christianisme Social* [Social Christianity], Vol. 63, Nos. 1–2 (January–February), 1955, pp. 60, 61; Nicholas S. Timasheff, "Urbanization, Operation Antireligion and the Decline of Religion in the U.S.S.R.," *The American Slavic and East European Review,* April 1955, p. 228; Tobias, p. 225.

54. Alexeev, *Russian Orthodox Bishops,* p. 5. The Soviet government's Council for Russian Orthodox Church Affairs confirmed the number of bishops. See Tsentralny Gosudarstvenny Arkhiv, Fond 6991s, Opis No. 2, Vol. I, delo No. 4, report of April 1, 1946, p. 1.

55. Michael Bourdeaux, *Patriarch and Prophets: Persecution of the Russian Orthodox Church Today* (Oxford: A. R. Mowbray and Co., 1975), p. 291.

56. The figures were for the number of churches and chapels in the imperial territories prior to the territorial losses suffered between 1918 and 1921. John Meyendorff, *The Orthodox Church,* 3d ed. (Crestwood, New York: St. Vladimir's Seminary Press, 1981), p. 155; Bolshakoff, *The Christian Church,* p. 1; Nikolai I. Yudin, *Pravda o Peterburgskikh "Svyatynyakh"* [The Truth About the Petersburg "Shrines"] (Leningrad: Lenizdat, 1962), p. 117; *Vsepoddanneishi otchet ober-prokurora svyateishago sinoda pravoslavnago ispovedaniya za 1911–1912* [Comprehensive Report of the Over-Procurator of the Holy Synod of the Orthodox Confession for 1911–1912] (Sanktpeterburg: Synodalnaya Typ., 1913), p. 11.

57. Walter Kolarz, *Religion in the Soviet Union* (New York: St. Martin's Press, 1961), p. 125. See also Alexeev and Stavrou, p. 112.

58. Yuri Degtyarev, "Neukosnitelno soblyudat zakon [To Observe the Law Strictly]," *Religiya v SSSR,* No. 6 (June) 1989, p. 3. Tambov oblast, for example, had two functioning churches in 1939. Pospielovsky, pp. 29–31; Bohdan R. Bociurkiw, "The Orthodox Church

and the Soviet Regime in the Ukraine, 1953–1971," *Canadian Slavonic Papers,* Vol. XIV, No. 2, Summer 1972, p. 191.

59. Degtyarev, p. 3. For the single church in Kharkov (as cited by Degtyarev), see also Wassily (Wassilij) Alexeev, "L'Église Orthodoxe Russe sous l'occupation allemande, 1941–1944 [The Russian Orthodox Church Under the German Occupation, 1941–1944]," *Irénikon,* Vol. 29, 1956, p. 257.

60. Bociurkiw, p. 191.

61. Friedrich Heyer, *Die Orthodoxe Kirche in der Ukraine von 1917 bis 1945* [The Orthodox Church in Ukraine from 1917 to 1945], Vol. III of *Osteuropa und der Deutsche Osten* [East Europe and the German East] (Köln-Braunsfeld: Rudolf Müller, 1953), p. 206.

62. Bociurkiw, p. 191.

63. Nikita Struve, "Tserkov v Sovetskoi Rossii [The Church in Soviet Russia]," *Vestnik Russkogo Studencheskogo Khristianskogo Dvizheniya,* No. I, 1955, p. 191. For the prerevolutionary figure in Odessa, see Alexander Dallin, *Odessa, 1941–1944: A Case Study of Soviet Territory Under Foreign Rule* (U.S. Air Force Project Rand, RM-1875, ASTIA Doc. No. AD 123552, The Rand Corp., February 14, 1957), p. 232. See also Pospielovsky, p. 175, for an explanation of why Stalin allowed the single church in Odessa to remain open but with no regular priest. Apparently it was a concession to Academician Filatov, the great eye doctor, who had treated Stalin and had asked the favor that at least one church in Odessa remain open. As the story goes, the priests and deacons who volunteered to perform the rite there were successively arrested until only laymen were left to pray in the church. See also Andrew Sorokowski, "Church and State, 1917–64," *Candle in the Wind: Religion in the Soviet Union,* eds. Eugene B. Shirley, Jr., and Michael Rowe (Washington, D.C.: Ethics and Public Policy Center, 1989), p. 40.

64. Struve, *Christians in Contemporary Russia,* p. 57. Alexeev and Stavrou, p. 193, quoted a local inhabitant as saying that there was one functioning church in Rostov at the start of World War II. They also indicated that Novocherkassk had one functioning cemetery church (p. 195).

65. One of these churches was in Gdov. Sources differ as to whether the second church was also in Gdov or in Pskov. See Pospielovsky, p. 229; Alexeev and Stavrou, pp. 100, 101, 144, 207; Alexeev, "L'Église Orthodoxe Russe," p. 257.

66. For a figure of 300, see Schmemann, p. 2.

67. Pospielovsky, p. 174. Struve, *Christians in Contemporary Russia,* p. 70, spoke of five parishes in the "immediate approaches to Leningrad." Monastic Priest Innokenti, in "O sovremennom sostoyanii Russkoi Pravoslavnoi Tserkvi [About the Present Situation of the Russian Orthodox Church]," in *Religiya v SSSR,* No. 8 (October), 1987, p. VS5, noted that two of these five churches were Renovationist. Anatoli Levitin-Krasnov also mentioned five churches in Leningrad and gave a somewhat higher figure of thirty to forty churches for Moscow in the "early 1940s," and several other sources listed figures in the range of eighteen to forty, some including the countryside around Moscow. House, p. 64, reported five churches in Leningrad and fifteen in Moscow. Levitin-Krasnov described a cemetery chapel in Ryazan, one functioning church in Astrakhan, and a tiny church in the suburbs of Novosibirsk. Anatoli Levitin-Krasnov, "Religion and Soviet Youth," *Religion*

in Communist Lands, Vol. 7, No. 3, Autumn 1979, p. 232. The Council for Religious Affairs recorded twelve functioning churches in Orel oblast and seven churches in Krasnodar oblast prior to the German invasion in 1941. Tsentralny Gosudarstvenny Arkhiv, Fond 6991s, Opis No. 2, Vol. I, delo No. 16, reports of April 25, 1944, and February 6, 1944.

    68. Heyer, p. 260.

    69. Alexeev, "L'Église Orthodoxe Russe," p. 257, 271.

    70. William C. Fletcher, *A Study in Survival* (New York: The Macmillan Co., 1965), p. 103.

    71. A. Krasnov, "Zakat Obnovlenchestva [The Sunset of Renovationism]," *Grani* [Facets], No. 87–88, 1973, p. 248.

    72. Alexeev, *Russian Orthodox Bishops,* p. 7; Krasnov, p. 249.

    73. Krasnov, p. 249.

    74. Alexeev, *Russian Orthodox Bishops,* p. 7.

    75. Krasnov, p. 250.

    76. Fletcher, *A Study in Survival,* pp. 107, 153 (note 65).

Chapter 2

    1. Soviet-occupied eastern Poland had a population of almost 4 million Ukrainians, over 1 million Byelorussians, and 150,000 Russians. The Ukrainians and the Byelorussians were divided between Greek-Catholics and Orthodox. Berthold Spuler, "Die Orthodoxen Kirchen [The Orthodox Churches]," *Internationale Kirliche Zeitschrift* [The International Church Journal] (Bern), No. 30, April–June 1940, p. 94; Wassilij Alexeev, "The Russian Orthodox Church, 1927–1945, Repression and Revival," *Religion in Communist Lands,* Vol. 7, No. 1, Spring 1979, p. 30.

The Greek-Catholics are also called Catholics of the Eastern Rite (not preferred in the community since 1991), "Uniates (not preferred)," and in Ukraine, Ukrainian Greek-Catholics or Ukrainian Catholics. This community became Catholic in the Union of Brest in 1596 when western Ukraine was under Catholic Polish rule. The Holy Mass, or liturgy, has remained similar, although not identical, to the Orthodox liturgy over the years, and secular priests can be married, as they can under the discipline of the Eastern churches. An unlearned person attending a church service might not recognize it as Catholic until prayers were offered for the pope in Rome rather than for the Orthodox patriarch in Moscow.

    2. Alexeev and Stavrou gave a figure of 440,000 traditionally Orthodox people in the three Baltic states. "Traditionally Orthodox people" would include all members of families, regardless of age, belonging to a community or national group where the religious tradition and adherence were historically Orthodox. The Russian Orthodox Church has never made a sharp distinction between "members" and nonmembers within the Orthodox communities. "Traditionally Orthodox people" would exclude Lutherans and Roman Catholics in the Baltic states; Muslims in Central Asia, Tatarstan, Bashkiria, Azerbaidzhan, and the Caucasus; Buddhists in the Buryat and Kalmyk lands; Armenian Christians; and so on. Wassilij Alexeev and Theofanis G. Stavrou, *The Great Revival: The Russian Orthodox Church Under German Occupation* (Minneapolis: Burgess Publishing

Co., 1976), pp. 73, 76. Alexeev gave the figure of 300 Orthodox churches in the Baltic states in "The Russian Orthodox Church, 1927–1945," p. 30.

In the dictated peace that ended the Winter War with Finland in March 1940, the Soviet Union acquired territories on the Karelian isthmus, on the shores of Lake Ladoga, and in Lapland. Almost all the Finns left these territories, however, and the annexations provided little in terms of Russian Orthodox population or institutional resources for the church.

3. Nicholas S. Timasheff, *Religion in Soviet Russia, 1917–1942* (London: Sheed and Ward, 1944), p. 130; "Killing of Priests in Poland Related," Associated Press (AP), *The New York Times,* October 12, 1939, p. 8; Serge Keleher, "Church in the Middle: Greek-Catholics in Central and Eastern Europe," *Religion, State and Society,* Vol. 20, Nos. 3 and 4, 1992, p. 293; Wassily (Wassilij) Alexeev, "L'Église Orthodoxe Russe sous l'occupation allemande, 1941–1944 [The Russian Orthodox Church Under the German Occupation, 1941–1944]," *Irénikon,* Vol. 29, 1956, p. 249.

4. William C. Fletcher, *Nikolai: Portrait of a Dilemma* (New York: The Macmillan Co., 1968), p. 34.

5. Statistics released by the Soviet embassy in London and published in *Soviet War News,* August 22, 1941. They are reproduced in Stanley Evans, *Churches in the U.S.S.R.* (London: Corbett Publishing Co., 1943), pp. 87–89.

6. There is no evidence of churches being opened between 1939 and 1941 within the USSR's interwar boundaries. The figure in the 1941 Soviet press release for the Armenian churches functioning in the country is revealing—only nine were listed.

7. Dimitry Pospielovsky, *The Russian Church Under the Soviet Regime, 1917–1982,* 2 Vols. (Crestwood, New York: St. Vladimir's Seminary Press, 1984), pp. 194–195; Nikita Struve, *Christians in Contemporary Russia,* trans. Lancelot Sheppard and A. Manson (New York: Charles Scribner's Sons, 1967), pp. 59–61.

8. Gleb Rar (also Rahr), "Skolko v Rossii pravoslavnykh khramov? [How many Orthodox Churches Are There in Russia?]" *Posev,* January 1974, pp. 39–44; Alexeev and Stavrou, p. 164. Friedrich Heyer, *Die Orthodoxe Kirche in der Ukraine von 1917 bis 1945* [The Orthodox Church in Ukraine from 1917 to 1945], Vol. III of *Osteuropa und der Deutsche Osten* [East Europe and the German East] (Köln-Braunsfeld: Rudolf Müller, 1953), p. 209; Nikita Struve, "Tserkov v Sovetskoi Rossii [The Church in Soviet Russia]," *Vestnik Russkogo Studencheskogo Khristianskogo Dvizheniya* [Herald of the Russian Student Christian Movement], No. I, 1955, p. 19; *Zhurnal Moskovskoi Patriarkhii* [Journal of the Moscow Patriarchate], No. 10 (October), 1946, p. 23.

9. V. Kononenko, "Pamyat blokady [A Remembrance of the Blockade]," *Nauka i Religiya* [Science and Religion], No. 5 (May), 1988, pp. 10–11.

10. Pospielovsky, p. 196; Struve, *Christians in Contemporary Russia,* pp. 61–62, 64; Wassilij Alexeev, *Russian Orthodox Bishops in the Soviet Union, 1941–1953,* Text in Russian (New York: Research Program on the U.S.S.R., Mimeographed Series No. 61, 1954), pp. 7–8; *Zhurnal Moskovskoi Patriarkhii,* No. 6 (June), 1953, p. 61; No. 3 (March), 1987, p. 28; No. 4 (April), 1988, p. 23.

11. Alexeev, "L'Église Orthodoxe Russe," p. 250.

12. Metropolitan Sergi (Voskresenski) had chosen to remain in Riga when the Germans took the city.

13. Pospielovsky, p. 200, 203.

14. Karpov was said to have the military rank of major general of the NKVD (National Comissariat of Internal Affairs). Francis House, *The Russian Phoenix* (London: SPCK, 1988), p. 79; *Soviet Affairs Notes,* No. 186, March 28, 1956, p. 4; Sergi Gordun, "Russkaya Pravoslavnaya Tserkov v period s 1943 po 1970 god [The Russian Orthodox Church in the Period from 1943 to 1970]," *Zhurnal Moskovskoi Patriarkhii,* No. 1 (January), 1993, p. 39.

15. Gordun, p. 40.

16. Struve, *Christians in Contemporary Russia,* p. 66. A *pomestny sobor* is sometimes translated as a "local council," but it is local only in the sense that it is national and not ecumenical or international in scope.

17. Gordun, p. 40; Mikhail Odintsov, "Drugogo raza ne bylo . . . [There Never Was Another Time . . .]," *Nauka i Religiya,* No. 2 (February), 1989, p. 9. Odintsov had served as deputy chairman of the Council for Religious Affairs of the Soviet government.

18. D. A. Volkogonov rejected the idea that Stalin's policy shift in 1943 represented any changed conviction about God, saying it was strictly political and practical. He also noted that Stalin, in choosing books for his own personal library, specified that he wanted "no atheistic trash (*makulatury*)." I. Nikolaeva, "Triumfi i tragediya [Triumph and Tragedy]," interview of D. A. Volkogonov, *Nauka i Religiya,* No. 2 (February), 1989, p. 11.

19. William C. Fletcher, *The Russian Orthodox Church Underground, 1917–1970* (London: Oxford University Press, 1971), p. 168.

20. Gordun quoted V. Alekseev in connection with the foregoing arguments. Gordun, pp. 39–40, 42; House, p. 75.

21. "Sorok let vozrozhdennogo Patriarshestva [Forty Years of the Reborn Patriarchate]," *Zhurnal Moskovskoi Patriarkhii,* No. 12 (December), 1957, p. 42.

22. Yuri Degtyarev, "Stalin and the Russian Orthodox Church," *Religion in USSR,* No. 12 (December), 1991, p. 61. According to Father Sergi Gordun, the cabinet decree regulating the opening and registration of new church societies was No. 1325 of November 28, 1943, issued almost three months after Stalin's meeting with Sergi. Gordun, p. 42.

23. Tsentralny Gosudarstvenny Arkhiv Oktyabrskoi Revolutsii [Central State Archive of the October Revolution], Vysshikh Organov Gosudarstvennoi Vlasti i Organov Gosurdarstvennogo Upravleniya S.S.S.R. [of the Higher Organs of State Government and Organs of State Administration of the U.S.S.R.], Soviet po delam religii pri Sovete Ministrov [the Council for Religious Affairs attached to the Council of Ministers], Fond 6991s, Opis No. 2, Vol. I, delo No. 4, report of March 15, 1944, p. 5.

24. Pospielovsky, pp. 203–207. The Georgian Orthodox Church was also given its ecclesiastical independence, or autocephaly, at about this time.

25. Pospielovsky, p. 204; John Shelton Curtiss, *The Russian Church and the Soviet State, 1917–1950* (Boston: Little, Brown and Co., 1953), p. 294; Robert Pierce Casey, *Religion in Russia* (New York: Harper and Bros., 1946), p. 186; *Zhurnal Moskovskoi Patriarkhii,* No. 12 (December), 1944, p. 6; Robert Tobias, *Communist-Christian Encounter in East Europe* (Indianapolis, Indiana: School of Religion Press, 1956), p. 260.

26. Pospielovsky, pp. 209–210; Struve, *Christians in Contemporary Russia,* pp. 81–82.

27. Bohdan R. Bociurkiw, "Church-State Relations in the U.S.S.R.," *Religion and the Soviet State: A Dilemma of Power,* eds. Max Hayward and William C. Fletcher (London:

Pall Mall Press, 1969), p. 91. Odintsov wrote in late 1991 that the Council of People's Commissars passed this measure in secret. It was rescinded at the time of Khrushchev's antireligious drive. Mikhail Odintsov, "The Soviet State and Laws on Religion," *Religion in USSR*, No. 12 (December), 1991, pp. 56–57.

28. Tsentralny Gosudarstvenny Arkhiv, Fond 6991s, Opis No. 2, Vol. I, delo No. 4, Sidirov report, p. 1.

29. The patriarchate was given the former residence of the German ambassador in Moscow, in Chisty Pereulok. Gordun, p. 40.

30. Tsentralny Gosudarstvenny Arkhiv, Fond 6991s, Opis No. 2, Vol. I, delo No. 263, report of May 6, 1961, by Inspector Pashkin, p. 46.

31. The 1,600–1,700 figure is reached by adding the 200–300 surviving churches in 1939, the few score opened between 1941 and 1943, and the 1,270 churches opened between 1944 and 1947.

32. The ecclesiastical mission from Latvia reportedly opened between 200 and 300 parishes south of Leningrad. About 1,250 churches were opened during the occupation in Byelorussia. Slightly over 200 of these churches apparently were denied registration, as the highest postwar figure for registered church societies in Byelorussia was 1,040 in January 1949. Pospielovsky, pp. 242, 346; Alexeev, "The Russian Orthodox Church, 1927–1945," p. 32; Alexeev and Stavrou, pp. 101, 102; Struve, *Christians in Contemporary Russia*, p. 71; Tsentralny Gosudarstvenny Arkhiv, Fond 6991s, Opis No. 2, Vol. I, delo No. 180.

33. The inspector's figure of 7,547 churches opened would not include open churches annexed in 1939–1940. Tsentralny Gosudarstvenny Arkhiv, Fond 6991s, Opis No. 2, Vol. I, delo No. 263. Data from Western scholars indicate something quite close to this figure. See Struve, "Tserkov v Sovetskoi Rossii," No. I, 1955, p. 19; Alexander Dallin, *Odessa, 1941–1944: A Case Study of Soviet Territory Under Foreign Rule* (U.S. Air Force Project Rand, RM-1875, ASTIA Doc. No. AD 123552, The Rand Corp., February 14, 1957); Pierre Fontanieu, "Le problème religieux en U.R.S.S. [The Religious Problem in the U.S.S.R.]," *Christianisme Social* [Social Christianity], Vol. 63, Nos. 1–2 (January–February), 1955, p. 61; Heyer, pp. 206, 207, 208, 209, 211; Alexeev, "L'Église Orthodoxe Russe," pp. 272, 273.

34. Two territories annexed by the USSR late in World War II are not treated here because the impact of their annexation on the church's institutional strength was negligible. Tuva, on the Mongolian border, was absorbed in October 1944, and two churches, part of the diocese of Novosibirsk, were opened there 1945–1946. The Kurile Islands and the southern half of Sakhalin Island were annexed from Japan at the end of World War II. They became part of the diocese of Khabarovsk, but the first church society registered there, in Yuzhno-Sakhalinsk, was not inscribed until 1988.

35. *Keston News Service*, No. 376, May 30, 1991, p. 4. The last formalities of the union with Orthodoxy were completed in August 1949. *Pravoslavny Visnyk* [Orthodox Herald], No. 1 (January), 1990, p. 13.

36. Tsentralny Gosudarstvenny Arkhiv, Fond 6991s, Opis No. 2, Vol. I, delo Nos. 80, 206.

37. P. Vasilev, "Uniaty [Uniates]," interview of Mikhail Odintsov, *Argumenty i Fakty* [Arguments and Facts], No. 40 (469), October 7–13, 1989, p. 7. Yuri Degtyarev recounted that Stalin had instructed Karpov in early 1945 to prepare an analysis of Soviet-Vatican

relations, and Karpov reported that "pro-Fascist" elements had leadership roles in the Vatican and the Greek-Catholics were instruments for Catholicizing the Ukrainian population in western areas of that republic. Protopresbyter Gavriil Kostelnik, who emerged as a leader of the Lvov council, was defended by Degtyarev as having advocated considerable autonomy for the Greek-Catholics, a gradual process of union, and the release of imprisoned Greek-Catholic hierarchs. Degtyarev credited Kostelnik with saving the lives of a considerable number of Greek-Catholic priests and noted that Patriarch Aleksi proposed noncoercive diocesan meetings in western Ukraine with Greek-Catholic clergy desiring to join Orthodoxy. Aleksi's proposals were rejected. Yuri Degtyarev, "Greko-Katolicheskaya tserkov v S.S.S.R. i Perestroika [The Greek-Catholic Church in the U.S.S.R. and Perestroika]," *Religiya v SSSR* [Religion in the USSR], No. 5 (May), 1990, pp. 4–5.

According to Georgi Rozhnov of *Ogonëk,* in 1944 Red Army, NKVD, and other Soviet government representatives asked Metropolitan Andrei (Sheptitski) of the Ukrainian Greek-Catholic Church to appeal to anti-Soviet guerrillas and insurgents to lay down their arms. The metropolitan refused, and Stalin's reaction was reportedly an order to liquidate the Greek-Catholic Church. *Ogonëk* [Little Fire], No. 38, September 16–23, 1989, pp. 6–8, as reported in *Keston News Service,* No. 338, November 16, 1989, p. 9.

38. The exact number in the records of the archive is 2,491 Greek-Catholic churches. Tsentralny Gosudarstvenny Arkhiv, Fond 6991s, Opis No. 2, Vol. I, delo No. 263, report of May 6, 1961, by Inspector Pashkin, p. 46.

39. Harvey Fireside, *Icon and Swastika: The Russian Orthodox Church Under Nazi and Soviet Control* (Cambridge, Mass.: Harvard University Press, 1971), p. 140.

40. Metropolitan Filaret (Denisenko) of Kiev said in a 1989 interview that "about 3,000 parishes" of the Eastern Rite Catholics joined the Orthodox Church after World War II. *Religiya v SSSR,* No. 6 (June), 1989, p. 22. Osyp Zinkewych and Taras R. Lonchyna, "Ukraïnska Kat. Tserkva [The Ukrainian Catholic Church]," Vol. II of *Martirologiya Ukraïnskikh Tserkov* [The Martyrdom of the Ukrainian Churches], eds. Osyp Zinkewych and Olexander Voronym, 4 Vols. planned (Toronto: V. Symonenko Smoloskyp Publishers, 1987), pp. 56–57, gave 1943 figures of 2,635 parishes and 3,874 churches for western Ukraine and Mukachevo.

41. Tsentralny Gosudarstvenny Arkhiv, Fond 6991s, Opis No. 2, Vol. I, delo Nos. 180, 183, 209, 263. The 1946 figure was for April 1, 1946.

42. Tsentralny Gosudarstvenny Arkhiv, Fond 6991s, Opis No. 2, Vol. I, delo No. 60, report of P. Khodchenko, p. 1; delo Nos. 54, 183, 209, 263.

43. John A. Armstrong, *Ukrainian Nationalism, 1939–1945* (New York: The Columbia University Press, 1955), p. 200.

44. Tsentralny Gosudarstvenny Arkhiv, Fond 6991s, Opis No. 2, Vol. I, delo No. 16, report of October 9, 1944.

45. Tsentralny Gosudarstvenny Arkhiv, Fond 6991s, Opis No. 2, Vol. I, delo No. 263, report of May 6, 1961, by Inspector Pashkin, p. 46. Other council reports indicated 14,190 churches in January of 1948, but the 14,329 figure probably is accurate.

46. Tsentralny Gosudarstvenny Arkhiv, Fond 6991s, Opis No. 2, Vol. I, delo No. 70, Leningrad oblast inspector; delo Nos. 183, 209, 263.

47. Tsentralny Gosudarstvenny Arkhiv, Fond 6991s, Opis No. 2, Vol. I, delo No. 19, Teploklyuchenki village, Kirghizia.

48. *Zhurnal Moskovskoi Patriarkhii,* No. 8 (August), 1947, p. 42.

49. Tsentralny Gosudarstvenny Arkhiv, Fond 6991s, Opis No. 2, Vol. I, delo No. 60, report of Commissioner Romenski, April 1, 1946, p. 2.

50. In 1933 the patriarchal church still had almost 23,000 houses of worship. M. I. Odintsov, "Khozhdenie po mukam [Purgatory]," from *Nauka i Religiya,* Nos. 5–8, 1990, and No. 7, 1991, translated and reproduced in *Russian Studies in History,* guest ed. Edward E. Roslof, Fall 1993, p. 64.

51. Tsentralny Gosudarstvenny Arkhiv, Fond 6991s, Opis No. 2, Vol. I, delo No. 263, report of May 6, 1961, by Inspector Pashkin, p. 46.

52. Bociurkiw, p. 96. See also Struve, *Christians in Contemporary Russia,* pp. 93–94. Mikhail Odintsov confirmed in late 1991 that the "development of relations between the state and the church ceased" in 1948 with the number of registered church societies reduced and new registrations discontinued. Odintsov, "The Soviet State," pp. 56–57.

Chapter 3

1. The Russian Primary Chronicle, or the Chronicle of Nestor (who lived in the eleventh century), began with the deluge, and continued with the arrival of the Varangians in Russian lands, the founding of Kiev, and other events of the ninth, tenth, and eleventh centuries. Nestor, the reputed author, probably drew on earlier Slavonic chronicles, now lost, and poetic legends, which no doubt embellished historical facts. For an excerpted text, see Thomas Riha, ed., *Readings in Russian Civilization,* Vol. I (Chicago: The University of Chicago Press, 1964), pp. 27–28.

2. Metropolitan Vladimir (Sabodan), "Soedinyaya veka [Uniting the Centuries]," *Moskovski Tserkovny Vestnik* [Moscow Church Herald], No. 9 (September), 1988, p. 7. For the significance of the physically standing church, see also *Zhurnal Moskovskoi Patriarkhii* [Journal of the Moscow Patriarchate], No. 8 (August), 1978, p. 11, quoting Patriarch Pimen (Izvekov); No. 8 (August), 1989, p. 12; No. 2 (February), 1990, p. 9.

3. Orthodox dissident priests Nikolai Eshliman and Gleb Yakunin, quoted in Michael Bourdeaux, *Patriarch and Prophets: Persecution of the Russian Orthodox Church Today* (Oxford: A. R. Mowbray and Co., 1975), p. 198.

4. Jane Ellis, *The Russian Orthodox Church: A Contemporary History* (Bloomington, Indiana: Indiana University Press, 1986), p. 29.

5. Christel Lane, *Christian Religion in the Soviet Union: A Sociological Study* (Albany, New York: State University of New York Press, 1978), pp. 57, 59, 65.

6. *The Samizdat Bulletin,* No. 100, August 1981; Bourdeaux, pp. 154–155.

7. Tengiz Abuladze, *Pokayanie* [Repentance] (Tbilisi: Gruziafilm, 1987).

8. Technically, the figures are identified as for registered churches and prayer houses in the USSR, although later statistics refer to registered Orthodox church societies. All data are for January 1 of the year in question, except for 1950, when the figure was actually recorded for December 1, 1949. Georgian churches have been subtracted from the totals when the totals have included them. Tsentralny Gosudarstvenny Arkhiv Oktyabrskoi Revolutsii [Central State Archive of the October Revolution], Vysshikh Organov Gosudarstvennoi Vlasti i Organov Gosurdarstvennogo Upravleniya S.S.S.R. [of the Higher Organs of State Government and Organs of State Administration of the U.S.S.R.], Soviet

po delam religii pri Sovete Ministrov [the Council for Religious Affairs attached to the Council of Ministers], Fond 6991s, Opis No. 2, Vol. I, delo No. 263. A table of these data appears on page 56 in the folio, but the documents are not a continuous text and are sometimes out of order. Similar data with a few additions are presented in Opis No. 2, Vol. I, delo Nos. 156, 180, 181, 182, 183, 206, and 209.

9. Most of the 407 former Greek-Catholic parishes in Transcarpathia that were forcibly incorporated into the Russian Orthodox Church in the 1946–1949 period (see Chapter 2) were no doubt included in the increase of 400 parishes between January 1947 and January 1949. The addition in 1949 of the last former Greek-Catholic Transcarpathian parishes no doubt offset some of the 220 deregistrations recorded in 1949, as the total number of registered church societies dropped by only 148 rather than 220, and registrations of new church societies throughout the country had altogether stopped. See also Aleksandr Trofimovich Veshchikov, "Etapy bolshogo puti [Milestones of a Great Journey]," *Nauka i Religiya* [Science and Religion], No. 11 (November), 1962, p. 60; an English translation appears in *Religion in Communist Dominated Areas*, No. 149, December 24, 1962, p. 7. Yuri Degtyarev, "Neukosnitelno soblyudat zakon [To Observe the Law Strictly]," *Religiya v SSSR* [Religion in the USSR], No. 6 (June), 1989, p. 3; William C. Fletcher, *The Russian Orthodox Church Underground, 1917–1970* (London: Oxford University Press, 1971), pp. 198, 230.

10. The only church consecration that might have been considered a new church was the Novye Senzhary prayer house in Poltava diocese (consecration October 22, 1950). However, the parish priest conducted regular services on the eve of the consecration, so it would appear that the church was reconsecrated after reconstruction. *Zhurnal Moskovskoi Patriarkhii*, No. 5 (May), 1951, p. 65. In an article reflecting the church's false hopes, the Journal had optimistically noted in 1946 that St. Sophia Cathedral in Kiev was "still closed for services," as it was "under repair;" in fact, the cathedral remained a state museum. *Zhurnal Moskovskoi Patriarkhii*, No. 10 (October), 1946, p. 3.

11. The 7 percent loss is a net figure. In 1949 there were 220 deregistrations, in 1951 about 150; and in 1952 about 230; in 1953, the year Stalin died, they eased to 86 and in 1954 to 56. Ukraine had 9,176 churches in January of 1949 and 8,506 in January five years later, a loss of 670, or 7 percent, as was true in the country as a whole. Tsentralny Gosudarstvenny Arkhiv, Fond 6991s, Opis No. 2, Vol. I, delo Nos. 180, 263.

12. As for Kostelnik's death, there is even now some question whether Eastern Rite Catholic militants or Lavrenti Beria's NKVD subordinates carried out the deed. See Walter Kolarz, *Religion in the Soviet Union* (New York: St. Martin's Press, 1961), pp. 238–239.

13. Vasyl Markus, "Religion and Nationality: The Uniates of the Ukraine," *Religion and Atheism in the U.S.S.R. and Eastern Europe*, eds. Bohdan R. Bociurkiw and John W. Strong (London: The Macmillan Co., 1975), p. 109; Ivan Hvat, *The Catacomb Ukrainian Catholic Church and Pope John Paul II* (Cambridge, Mass.: Ukrainian Studies Fund, Harvard University, 1984), pp. 283–287.

14. Vasyl Markus, *Religion and Nationalism in Soviet Ukraine After 1945* (Cambridge, Mass.: Ukrainian Studies Fund, Harvard University, 1985), p. 107.

15. During the period between 1949 and 1954, the formerly Greek-Catholic areas of

western Ukraine lost 164 registered churches. Tsentralny Gosudarstvenny Arkhiv, Fond 6991s, Opis No. 2, Vol. I, delo Nos. 156, 180, 206, 209.

16. Tsentralny Gosudarstvenny Arkhiv, Fond 6991s, Opis No. 2, Vol. I, delo Nos. 18, 156. Poltava's losses were exceptionally severe between 1944 and 1965. For Bishop Feodosi (Dikun) of Poltava's anguished letter on this subject to Leonid Brezhnev of October 26, 1977, see Arkadi Zhukovski, "Ukraïnska Pravoslavna Tserkva, dokumenti, materiyali Khristiyanski samvidav Ukraïni [The Ukrainian Orthodox Church, Documents and Christian Materials of the Samizdat of Ukraine]," Vol. I of *Martirologiya Ukraïnskikh Tserkov* [The Martyrdom of the Ukrainian Churches], eds. Osyp Zinkewych and Olexander Voronym, 4 Vols. planned (Toronto: V. Symonenko Smoloskyp, 1987), pp. 779–808. Bishop Feodosi indicated in his letter that there had been 340 churches in Poltava diocese in 1958 before the Khrushchev drive. He was mistaken in this statement. He had not, of course, been in Poltava himself as ruling bishop prior to the drive. Somebody had probably told him that there had been 340 churches in the diocese (there were 326 in 1944). The council's records indicate that the number of churches in the diocese remained unchanged at 262 from 1954 until January 1959. Between 1959 and 1965, the oblast lost 76 percent of its registered church societies. Bishop Feodosi was correct in his anguished description of the misfortunes of the diocese.

17. Byelorussia dropped from 1,040 churches in 1949 to 966 in 1954, a loss of 7 percent. Moldavia dropped from 612 in 1948 to 544 in 1954, a loss of 11 percent. Losses in Central Asia and the Baltic states were no more than a handful in any republic. The losses in individual constituent republics total more than the 998 churches lost in the USSR as a whole because the losses for each republic are figured from the peak year, which in some cases was January of 1948 and in some cases was January of 1949. Tsentralny Gosudarstvenny Arkhiv, Fond 6991s, Opis No. 2, Vol. I, delo Nos. 180, 209.

18. *Zhurnal Moskovskoi Patriarkhii,* No. 3 (March), 1948, p. 54; No. 2 (February), 1949, p. 22; *Moskovski Tserkovny Vestnik,* No. 7 (July), 1989, p. 3.

19. *Zhurnal Moskovskoi Patriarkhii,* No. 4 (April), 1945, p. 4; No. 8 (August), 1947, p. 42.

20. Fletcher, p. 196.

21. *Zhurnal Moskovskoi Patriarkhii,* No. 3 (March), 1953, pp. 11, 13, 19; No. 2 (February), 1953, p. 49.

22. Nikita Struve, *Christians in Contemporary Russia,* trans. Lancelot Sheppard and A. Manson (New York: Charles Scribner's Sons, 1967), p. 94.

23. *Zhurnal Moskovskoi Patriarkhii,* No. 9 (September), 1956, p. 78. See also *The New York Times* of August 17, 1956.

24. Leu Haroska (Haroshka) in Boris I. Ivanov, *Religion in the U.S.S.R.,* trans. and ed. James Larkin (Munich: Institute for the Study of the U.S.S.R., Munich Series 1, No. 59, July 1960), p. 18.

25. *Pravda,* July 24, 1954. See also Max Hayward and William C. Fletcher, eds., *Religion and the Soviet State: A Dilemma of Power* (London: Pall Mall Press, 1969), p. 96.

26. *Pravda,* November 11, 1954. William C. Fletcher suggested that the November 10, 1954, resolution—the first that bore Khrushchev's signature alone as first secretary— served to demonstrate his ascendancy over Malenkov and to quash Malenkov's "Hundred Days Campaign" against religion. Under this interpretation the resolution would have

been closely tied to Kremlin politics, and religious policy would have been a less important motivation for its promulgation. Besides, the resolution heavily emphasized the need
to prepare cadres for atheist propaganda and might even then have foreshadowed
Khrushchev's subsequent antireligious campaign. For Malenkov's campaign, see Kolarz,
pp. 66–67; Joshua Rothenberg, "The Legal Status of Religion in the Soviet Union," and
Donald A. Lowrie and William C. Fletcher, "Khrushchev's Religious Policy, 1959–1964," in
Aspects of Religion in the Soviet Union, 1917–1967, ed. Richard H. Marshall, Jr. (Chicago:
University of Chicago Press, 1971), pp. 84–85, 131; and Philip Walters, "A Survey of Soviet
Religious Policy," *Religious Policy in the Soviet Union,* Sabrina Petra Ramet, ed. (New
York: Cambridge University Press, 1993), p. 19.

27. E. M. Yaroslavski, *Na anti-religioznom fronte* [On the Antireligious Front] (Moscow: Krasnaya N., 1924), pp. 49–52.

28. Nicholas S. Timasheff, *Religion in Soviet Russia, 1917–1942* (London: Sheed and
Ward, 1944), p. 45.

29. Timasheff, pp. 96–97.

30. An echo of the November 10, 1954, resolution of the Central Committee appears to
have been heard in a Central Committee resolution of October 4, 1958. It is likely, however, that this was a ritual incantation that preceded substantive antireligious directives.
See John Anderson, "The Archives of the Council for Religious Affairs," *Religion, State and
Society,* Vol. 20, Nos. 3 and 4, 1992, p. 400.

31. Sergi Gordun, "Russkaya Pravoslavnaya Tserkov v period s 1943 po 1978 god [The
Russian Orthodox Church in the Period from 1943 to 1970]," *Zhurnal Moskovskoi Patriarkhii,* No. 1 (January), 1993, p. 48.

32. Dimitry Pospielovsky, *The Russian Church Under the Soviet Regime, 1917–1982,* 2
Vols. (Crestwood, N.Y.: St. Vladimir's Seminary Press, 1984), pp. 323, 355.

33. Dmitri Radyshevski, "Gonimye za veru [Persecuted for Their Faith]" *Moskovskie
Novosti* [Moscow News], No. 18, May 6, 1990, p. 16.

34. Tsentralny Gosudarstvenny Arkhiv, Fond 6991s, Opis No. 2, Vol. I, delo Nos. 180,
206, 263.

35. The council also gave this figure as 13,462, but that figure included parishes of the
Georgian Orthodox Church. Tsentralny Gosudarstvenny Arkhiv, Fond 6991s, Opis No. 2,
Vol. I, delo Nos. 206, 263.

36. Tsentralny Gosudarstvenny Arkhiv, Fond 6991s, Opis No. 2, Vol. I, delo Nos. 98,
125, 206.

37. For reasons of comparability of figures, the dioceses are listed as they stabilized
during the almost thirty-five-year period between the Khrushchev drive and 1988. This
means, for example, that Byelorussia is treated as a single diocese even though there were
a number of Byelorussian dioceses before the Khrushchev drive and about a dozen in the
1990s. Moscow is treated as a single diocese even though administration of the churches in
the city and in Moscow oblast outside the city is distinct.

38. Archive data show 8,537 churches in Ukraine. In another set of records the figure is
8,525 churches, or 12 fewer. Tsentralny Gosudarstvenny Arkhiv, Fond 6991s, Opis No. 2,
Vol. I, delo Nos. 206, 208.

39. *The New York Times,* November 28, 1945, p. 25.

40. Georgi G. Karpov, interviewed by C. L. Sulzberger of *The New York Times* on June

7, 1945, described by David J. Dallin, *The Changing World of Soviet Russia* (New Haven, Conn.: Yale University Press, 1956), p. 282.

41. John L. Strohm, *Just Tell the Truth* (New York: Scribner and Sons, 1947), p. 175. See also Lowrie and Fletcher, pp. 151–152. Lowrie and Fletcher quoted my dissertation with eighteen different citations giving various numbers, all in round thousands, for the functioning Orthodox churches in the USSR over the years. Fletcher gave additional data in his 1972 book chapter. See William C. Fletcher, "Introduction: The State of Soviet Sociology of Religion," *U.S.S.R., Western Religion: A Country by Country Sociological Inquiry,* ed. Hans (J. J.) Mol (The Hague, Paris: Mouton, 1972), pp. 572–573.

42. Matthew Spinka, in *The Church in Soviet Russia* (New York: Oxford University Press, 1956), p. 119, noted in the mid-1950s that the patriarchate's statistics were in round numbers "and therefore not statistics at all." He also expressed skepticism that the patriarchate's figure of 22,000 churches in 1946 was not inflated. Aleksandr A. Bogolepov, in *Tserkov pod vlastyu kommunizma* [The Church Under Communist Rule] (Munich: Instit. po izucheniya S.S.S.R., 1958), p. 52, also noted that the number of churches, always rounded off in thousands, might be exaggerated.

43. Nathaniel Davis, *Religion and Communist Government in the Soviet Union and Eastern Europe,* dissertation, The Fletcher School of Law and Diplomacy, June 1, 1960, pp. 357–364, 488–550.

44. For 25,000, see Nicholas S. Timasheff, "Urbanization, Operation Antireligion and the Decline of Religion in the U.S.S.R.," *The American Slavic and East European Review,* April 1955, p. 233; *Newsweek,* October 18, 1954, p. 31. For 20,000, see Joseph H. Jackson, *The Eternal Flame* (Philadelphia, Penn.: The Christian Education Press, 1956), p. 64; Paul B. Anderson, "Churchmen Visit Russia," *Christian Century,* April 18, 1956, p. 480.

45. For example, the *Zhurnal Moskovskoi Patriarkhii,* No. 8 (August), 1957, p. 32, quoted Bishop Paul of Finland as saying that there were 22,000 Orthodox churches in the USSR.

46. Veshchikov, p. 57.

47. J. A. Hebly, *The Russians and the World Council of Churches* (Belfast: Christian Journals Limited, 1978), p. 114. William Stroyen made the following comment on the statement the church presented to the World Council of Churches: "It is improbable that the statement cited above can be readily accepted in view of what the *Zhurnal* reflects in its pages." William B. Stroyen, *Communist Russia and the Russian Orthodox Church, 1943–1962* (Washington: The Catholic University of America Press, 1967), p. 80. See also Fletcher, "Introduction," p. 573.

48. Tsentralny Gosudarstvenny Arkhiv, Fond 6991s, Opis No. 2, Vol. I, delo No. 263.

49. Francis House, *The Russian Phoenix* (London: SPCK, 1988), p. 94.

50. For example, Nikolai was on the official Soviet commission investigating the Katyn massacre and must have had some understanding that the commission's report was false.

Chapter 4

1. "Tserkov v S.S.S.R. posle Khrushcheva [The Church in the U.S.S.R. After Khrushchev]," *Posev,* January 15, 1965, p. 2; Patriarch Aleksi (Ridiger) quoted in *Zhurnal Moskovskoi Patriarkhii* [Journal of the Moscow Patriarchate], No. 4 (April), 1991, p. 34.

2. Dimitry Pospielovsky, *The Russian Church Under the Soviet Regime, 1917–1982,* 2

Vols. (Crestwood, New York: St. Vladimir's Seminary Press, 1984), p. 351; *Russia Cristiana Ieri e Oggi* [Christian Russia Yesterday and Today], No. 14, February 1961, p. 18; Trevor Beeson, *Discretion and Valor* (Philadelphia, Penn.: Fortress Press, 1974 and 1982), p. 71; Gerhard Simon, *Church, State and Opposition in the U.S.S.R.* (London: C. Hurst and Co., 1974), p. 69; Alexander Nezhny, "Law and Conscience," *Moscow News*, No. 33, 1987, translated by *Religion in Communist Dominated Areas*, Vol. XXVI, No. 2, Spring 1987, p. 41.

3. Pospielovsky, p. 351; Konstantin M. Kharchev, "Religiya i perestroika [Religion and Perestroika]," speech to the instructors of the Higher Communist Party School, Moscow, end of March 1988 (transcribed by memory and abridged), *Russkaya Mysl* [Russian Thought], No. 3725, May 20, 1988, p. 4; Yuri Degtyarev, "Neukosnitelno soblyudat zakon [To Observe the Law Strictly]," *Religiya v SSSR* [Religion in the USSR], No. 6 (June), 1989, p. 3; Viktor Ivanovich Garadzha, director of the Institute of Scientific Atheism, "Pereosmyslenie [Rethinking]," *Nauka i Religiya* [Science and Religion], No. 1 (January), 1989, p. 3. See also P. Makartsev in the same issue of *Nauka i Religiya*, p. 8, and Yuri Khristoradnov in *Nauka i Religiya*, No. 1 (January), 1990, p. 2.

4. Nikita S. Khrushchev, *Khrushchev Remembers*, ed. and trans. Strobe Talbott (Boston: Little, Brown and Co., 1970), pp. 22–23.

5. Walter Kolarz, *Religion in the Soviet Union* (New York: St. Martin's Press, 1961), p. vii; "Tserkov v S.S.S.R. posle Khrushcheva," p. 2. Konstantin Kharchev, who became head of the Council for Religious Affairs in 1984, told Aleksandr Nezhny in a 1988 interview that Khrushchev held no ill feeling toward the church and was motivated by the desire to build a communist society. Aleksandr Nezhny, "Sovest svobodna [A Free Conscience]," *Ogonëk* [Little Fire], No. 21, May 1988, pp. 26, 28.

6. Anatoli Levitin-Krasnov, "Religion and Soviet Youth," *Religion in Communist Lands*, Vol. 7, No. 3, Autumn 1979, pp. 232ff.

7. Nikita Struve, *Christians in Contemporary Russia*, trans. Lancelot Sheppard and A. Manson (New York: Charles Scribner's Sons, 1967), pp. 292–293.

8. Dimitry Pospielovsky, "The Soviet State Versus the Russian Orthodox Church, 1959–1988," *Religion in Communist Dominated Areas*, Vol. XXVII, No. 4, Fall 1988, p. 105; Kolarz, pp. 67–70, 173; Mesrob K. Krikorian, "The Armenian Church in the Soviet Union, 1917–1967," *Aspects of Religion in the Soviet Union, 1917–1967*, ed. Richard H. Marshall, Jr. (Chicago: University of Chicago Press, 1971), p. 252; Struve, p. 106. According to Kolarz, p. 70, Georgi Zhukov also tried to protect the church.

9. Dimitry V. Pospielovsky, *Soviet Studies on the Church and the Believer's Response to Atheism*, Vol. 3 of *A History of Soviet Atheism in Theory and Practice, and the Believer* (New York: St. Martin's Press, 1988), p. 237.

10. V. Stanley Vardys, "Catholicism in Lithuania," *Aspects of Religion in the Soviet Union, 1917–1967*, ed. Richard H. Marshall, Jr. (Chicago: University of Chicago Press, 1971), p. 387.

11. Struve, p. 293.

12. Vardys, p. 388; Struve, p. 293.

13. Struve, p. 294; Pospielovsky, *The Russian Church*, p. 317.

14. *Zhurnal Moskovskoi Patriarkhii*, No. 8 (August), 1989, p. 16; Pospielovsky, *The Russian Church*, p. 343. Gordun identified this as Cabinet Decree 2215 of August 29, 1945. Sergi

Gordun, "Russkaya Pravoslavnaya Tserkov v period s 1943 no 1970 god [The Russian Orthodox Church in the Period from 1943 to 1970]," *Zhurnal Moskovskoi Patriarkhii*, No. 1 (January), 1993, p. 47 (continued in February).

15. Walter Sawatsky, "Secret Soviet Lawbook on Religion," *Religion in Communist Lands*, Vol. 4, No. 4, Winter 1976, p. 30. A Marxist scholar, V. V. Pashkov, mentioned this Council of Ministers decree, No. 1159 of October 16, 1958, noting that the objective was to build a true communist society. See Vladimir Vasilevich Pashkov, *Monastyri v S.S.S.R.: Ideologiya i deatelnost* [Monasteries in the U.S.S.R.: Ideology and Activity], dissertation for candidate's degree, full abstract (Moscow: Moscow State University named after Lomonosov, 1989), p. 13.

16. Gordun, *Zhurnal*, No. 2 (February), pp. 11–12.

17. Tsentralny Gosudarstvenny Arkhiv Oktyabrskoi Revolutsii [Central State Archive of the October Revolution], Vysshikh Organov Gosudarstvennoi Vlasti i Organov Gosurdarstvennogo Upravleniya S.S.S.R. [of the Higher Organs of State Government and Organs of State Administration of the U.S.S.R.], Soviet po delam religii pri Sovete Ministrov [the Council for Religious Affairs attached to the Council of Ministers], Fond 6991s, Opis No. 2, Vol. I, delo No. 263.

18. Bohdan R. Bociurkiw, "Church-State Relations in the U.S.S.R.," *Religion and the Soviet State: A Dilemma of Power,* eds. Max Hayward and William C. Fletcher (London: Pall Mall Press, 1969), p. 96.

19. Donald A. Lowrie and William C. Fletcher, "Khrushchev's Religious Policy, 1959–1964," *Aspects of Religion in the Soviet Union, 1917–1967,* ed. Richard H. Marshall, Jr. (Chicago: University of Chicago Press, 1971), p. 132.

20. Pospielovsky, *The Russian Church,* p. 356.

21. William Stroyen, *Communist Russia and the Russian Orthodox Church, 1943–1962* (Washington: The Catholic University of America Press, 1967), p. 93.

22. *Zhurnal Moskovskoi Patriarkhii*, No. 4 (April), 1959, p. 6; Pospielovsky, *The Russian Church*, pp. 325, 327, 396; Jane Ellis, *The Russian Orthodox Church: A Contemporary History* (Bloomington, Indiana: Indiana University Press, 1986), pp. 205, 217, 218.

23. Simon, p. 84.

24. Struve, pp. 296–297. Struve asserted that taxes increased to as much as 83 percent of income under Article 19 of the finance law, and that in 1962 the authorities mandated a fixed salary for priests so that they could not support themselves by contributions of the faithful and thereby avoid taxation.

25. *Pravda*, August 21, 1959. See also Max Hayward and William C. Fletcher, eds., *Religion and the Soviet State: A Dilemma of Power* (London: Pall Mall Press, 1969), p. 97.

26. Struve, pp. 296–299. An example of a church closed in 1959 might be St. Nicholas church in Rusanovka, Sumy diocese. A priest was assigned there on January 19, 1959, and finished his duties there on November 16, 1959. See *Pravoslavny Visnyk* [Orthodox Herald], No. 3 (March), 1979, p. 10. The church was next referred to thirty years later in the *Zhurnal Moskovskoi Patriarkhii*, No. 8 (August), 1987, p. 41.

27. Tsentralny Gosudarstvenny Arkhiv, Fond 6991s, Opis No. 2, Vol. I, delo No. 263.

28. John Anderson, "The Archives of the Council for Religious Affairs," *Religion, State and Society,* Vol. 20, Nos. 3 and 4, 1992, p. 400.

29. William C. Fletcher, *Nikolai: Portrait of a Dilemma* (New York: The Macmillan Co., 1968), pp. 184–186. Osipov's wife had gone to the West during World War II, and Osipov had married again after she divorced him. This was a direct violation of the canons of the Russian Orthodox Church, as priests may marry only before ordination and only once.

30. *Russia Cristiana Ieri e Oggi,* No. 21, September 1961, p. 4.

31. *Zhurnal Moskovskoi Patriarkhii,* No. 2 (February), 1960, p. 27. In addition to Osipov, a priest named Pavel Darmanski (one of those who defected to the atheists in 1958) and a layman named Evraf Duluman (who had been an instructor at the Saratov seminary) were specifically mentioned.

32. Lowrie and Fletcher, p. 133; Beeson, p. 71.

33. Gordun, *Zhurnal,* No. 2 (February), p. 12.

34. Lowrie and Fletcher, p. 133. See also Francis House, *The Russian Phoenix* (London: SPCK, 1988), p. 87.

35. Father Sergi Gordun reported that every issue of the *Journal* required the agreement of the state organs. Gordun, *Zhurnal,* No. 1 (January), p. 47.

36. Pospielovsky, *The Russian Church,* pp. 333–335; Fletcher, p. 188; B. Lyubimov, "Moi dom—moya tserkov [My Home—My Church]," *Moskovski Tserkovny Vestnik, Yezhenedelnik* [Moscow Church Herald, Weekly], No. 22, October 1990, p. 8.

37. Lowrie and Fletcher, p. 133; Anderson, p. 400.

38. Fletcher, pp. 189–193.

39. Michael Bourdeaux, *Opium of the People* (Indianapolis, Indiana: The Bobbs-Merrill Co., 1966), p. 208.

40. "Chronicle," *Kirche im Osten* [The Church in the East], Vol. 4, 1961, p. 152.

41. Simon, p. 82.

42. Struve, p. 310.

43. Gordun, *Zhurnal,* No. 2 (February), p. 23.

44. *Zhurnal Moskovskoi Patriarkhii,* No. 7 (July), 1960, p. 6. Anderson alluded to the June 1960 meeting between the new chairman of the Council for Russian Orthodox Church Affairs, Vladimir Kuroedov, and Patriarch Aleksi at which Kuroedov "recommended" that Nikolai be replaced. Anderson, p. 400.

45. Fletcher, p. 200.

46. Struve, pp. 313–315; Fletcher, p. 201; Simon, p. 72. Anderson referred to an anonymous letter in the Council for Religious Affairs archive that came into the hands of council chairman Vladimir Kuroedov and was forwarded to the KGB. The letter alleges the involvement of leading Orthodox hierarchs in Nikolai's murder. Anderson, p. 403.

47. Struve, p. 312; Bourdeaux, p. 214. See also Michael Bourdeaux, *Patriarch and Prophets: Persecution of the Russian Orthodox Church Today* (Oxford: A. R. Mowbray and Co., 1975), pp. 69–73.

48. *Nauka i Religiya,* No. 9 (September), 1960, p. 50. The antireligious publication *Nauka i Religiya* had been launched in the late 1950s as part of the Khrushchev campaign. See also Pospielovsky, "The Soviet State," p. 106; House, p. 87. In the Khrushchev drive the number of functioning priests in Orenburg diocese dropped from forty-seven to nineteen and the number of parishes dropped from twenty-three to thirteen. Tsentralny Gosu-

darstvenny Arkhiv, Fond 6991s, Opis No. 2, Vol. I, delo No. 263, and Opis No. 4, Vol. I, delo No. 573.

49. Gordun, *Zhurnal,* No. 2 (February), p. 24.

50. V. Slovodchenko, "Vse shire sfera vliyaniya [Ever-Widening Sphere of Influence]," *Pravda Ukrainy* [Truth of Ukraine], October 20, 1960, p. 3. During 1960, twenty-five of the seventy-nine churches in Zaporozhe oblast were deregistered. Tsentralny Gosudarstvenny Arkhiv, Fond 6991s, Opis No. 2, Vol. I, delo No. 263.

51. Struve p. 300; Pospielovsky, *The Russian Church,* p. 346; *Posev,* No. 45 (1016), November 5, 1965; *Russia Cristiana Ieri e Oggi,* No. 16, April 1961, p. 28, quoting *Agitator,* No. 3 (March), 1961, p. 55. According to archive records, 50 of the 204 churches in Cherkassy oblast were closed in 1960. Tsentralny Gosudarstvenny Arkhiv, Fond 6991s, Opis No. 2, Vol. I, delo Nos. 206, 208, 263.

52. *Filosofskie Nauki* [Philosophical Sciences], No. 3, 1961, p. 16.

53. Lipkan and Kotov raions, Struve, p. 300, quoting *Sovetskaya Moldavia* [Soviet Moldavia], December 13, 1960.

54. Tsentralny Gosudarstvenny Arkhiv, Fond 6991s, Opis No. 2, Vol. I, delo No. 263.

55. Tsentralny Gosudarstvenny Arkhiv, Fond 6991s, Opis No. 2, Vol. I, delo No. 263.

56. "Prova di forza tra Chiesa Ortodossa e Regime nell' U.R.S.S.? [A Test of Strength Between the Orthodox Church and the Regime in the U.S.S.R.?]" *Russia Cristiana Ieri e Oggi,* No. 14, February 1961, p. 116. See also No. 18, June 1961, p. 17. A. Bisesti, "Attività religiosa clandestina nell' U.R.S.S. [Clandestine Religious Activity in the U.S.S.R.]," *Russia Cristiana Ieri e Oggi,* No. 18, June 1961, p. 17.

57. *Russia Cristiana Ieri e Oggi,* No. 14, p. 116; No. 18, p. 17. The journal noted that popular priests were being transferred away from parishes where they were loved, and young women were being pressured not to marry seminarians.

58. Kolarz, p. 71.

59. J. A. Hebly, *The Russians and the World Council of Churches* (Belfast: Christian Journals Limited, 1978), p. 106.

60. Tsentralny Gosudarstvenny Arkhiv, Fond 6991s, Opis No. 2, Vol. I, delo No. 263. The Russian republic lost 258 of its 2,842 parishes in 1960.

61. Tsentralny Gosudarstvenny Arkhiv, Fond 6991s, Opis No. 2, Vol. I, delo No. 263. Archive records list 745 of 8,207 Ukrainian church societies deregistered in 1960.

62. The historically Orthodox areas in western Ukraine encompass Volyn, Rovno, and Chernovtsy, where 102 of 1,133 parishes were closed. Tsentralny Gosudarstvenny Arkhiv, Fond 6991s, Opis No. 2, Vol. I, delo No. 263.

63. Volodymyr Karlovych Tancher, *Osnovi ateizmu* [The Foundations of Atheism] (Kiev: Vydavnytsvo Kyivskogo Universytetu, 1961), p. 181. Tancher's figure was embedded in other material that described "seven" functioning seminaries, which would suggest that the passage was written after the Kiev seminary was closed in 1960 and before the process of closing the Saratov and Stavropol seminaries was launched in the early months of 1961. *Russia Cristiana Ieri e Oggi,* No. 14, February 1961, p. 16, had already reported the closing of the second seminary. Moreover, Tancher cited several contemporary newspapers and periodicals, the last of which is dated December 7, 1960.

64. Nikolai I. Yudin, *Pravda o Peterburgskikh "Svyatynyakh"* [The Truth About the Petersburg "Shrines"] (Leningrad: Lenizdat, 1962), p. 8. Yudin's book was consigned to the printer on October 12, 1961.

65. *Nauka i Religiya,* No. 11 (November), 1962, p. 60.

66. Tsentralny Gosudarstvenny Arkhiv, Fond 6991s, Opis No. 2, Vol. I, delo No. 263. In 1987, the head of the Council for Religious Affairs, Konstantin Kharchev, published figures indicating 11,742 registered Orthodox religious societies in January of 1961. Konstantin M. Kharchev, "Garantii svobody [Guarantees of Freedom]," *Nauka i Religiya,* No. 11 (November), 1987, pp. 23.

67. Sawatsky, p. 28; *Religion in Communist Dominated Areas,* Vol. X, Nos. 19–24, October–December 1971, p. 160; Pospielovsky, *The Russian Church,* p. 342.

Gordun, *Zhurnal,* No. 2 (February), pp. 18–19. Gordun described a provision of Decree No. 263 of March 16, 1961, delegating action to register and deregister church societies as a maneuver to shift blame for unpopular deregistrations to the local authorities without the central authorities relinquishing actual control. The cabinet-level decree also extended the applicability of increased income taxes to all church workers, not just parish clergy, and it encouraged local authorities to curtail the ringing of church bells once again. The council's implementing instructions outlawed charitable work, pilgrimages to holy places, financial help to local parishes, meetings without special permission, religious instruction (except in the authorized academies and seminaries), the conduct by church servers of funerals in cemeteries, rites in homes, and the publishing of religious propaganda except as specifically authorized. The instructions also stated that the seizure of prayer buildings was permitted "if the building is needed for state or social purposes." See *Moskovski Tserkovny Vestnik, Yezhenedelnik,* No. 4, 1993, p. 15. In essence the decree and instructions returned the status of permitted religious activity to that permitted under the decree of April 8, 1929, when that decree was being rigorously enforced.

68. Pospielovsky, *The Russian Church,* p. 342. Pospielovsky also pointed out that ongoing urbanization resulted in population declines in central Russia, the Volga, the Urals, and parts of Siberia, which made it progressively more difficult for rural churches in those areas to make ends meet.

69. Struve, pp. 296–297. According to Gordun, the commissioner for the Council for Russian Orthodox Church Affairs in Kalinin oblast was already enforcing a rule in 1959 against priests and deans (*blagochinnye*) serving outside their own parishes. Gordun, *Zhurnal,* No. 2 (February), p. 13.

70. Struve, p. 296; Pospielovsky, *The Russian Church,* p. 206.

71. Bourdeaux, *Opium of the People,* pp. 213–214.

72. Gordun, *Zhurnal,* No. 2 (February), p. 19.

73. House, p. 89.

74. Ellis, pp. 53–69. According to *The Samizdat Bulletin,* No. 180, p. 10, the patriarch opposed the revision of church statutes in unpublicized meetings with Soviet authorities.

75. Dimitry Konstantinov, *The Crown of Thorns* (London: Zarya, 1979), p. 267. Gordun put the timing of the "reregistration" as the "end of 1961" and emphasized that it included an inventory of movable and immovable property. He added that the reregistration facil-

itated the blocking of church construction and repair and led to the confiscation of considerable numbers of vehicles and trucks. Gordun, *Zhurnal*, No. 2 (February), p. 19.

76. Father Nikolai I. Eshliman and Father Gleb P. Yakunin, "Declaration," *Religion in Communist Dominated Areas*, Vol 5, Nos. 9–10, May 15–31, 1966, Items 842–852, pp. 76, 78.

77. Lowrie and Fletcher, pp. 133–134.

78. Bourdeaux, *Patriarch and Prophets*, p. 38. See also Lowrie and Fletcher, p. 141.

79. Pospielovsky, *The Russian Church*, p. 206, note 26.

80. *Nauka i Religiya*, as quoted by *Keston News Service*, No. 322, March 30, 1989, p. 17.

81. Gordun, *Zhurnal*, No. 2 (February), p. 20.

82. Tsentralny Gosudarstvenny Arkhiv, Fond 6991s, Opis No. 2, Vol. I, delo No. 263.

83. Pospielovsky, *The Russian Church*, p. 344; *Zhurnal Moskovskoi Patriarkhii*, No. 6 (June), 1989, p. 26; Lowrie and Fletcher, p. 144; William C. Fletcher, *The Russian Orthodox Church Underground, 1917–1970* (London: Oxford University Press, 1971), p. 259; House, p. 90; Aleksandr Nezhny, "Zakon i sovest [Law and Conscience]," *Ogonëk*, No. 50, December 1988; Gordun, *Zhurnal*, No. 2 (February), pp. 18–19.

84. Lowrie and Fletcher, p. 146. Fletcher reported that the authorities deprived True Orthodox Christian parents of parental rights in 1959. Fletcher, *Russian Orthodox Church Underground*, p. 228.

85. Walter Sawatsky, "Secret Soviet Lawbook," pp. 24–34; Tsentralny Gosudarstvenny Arkhiv, Fond 6991s, Opis No. 2, Vol. I, delo No. 263.

86. Albert Boiter, *Religion in the Soviet Union* (Beverly Hills, Calif.: Sage Publications, 1980), pp. 50–51. See also Michael Bourdeaux, *Religious Ferment in Russia* (London: The Macmillan Co., 1968), pp. 14–15.

87. Hayward and Fletcher, pp. 97–98.

88. Fletcher, *Russian Orthodox Church Underground*, p. 259.

89. Sawatsky, p. 26. The 1929 decree made an exception to the prohibition against a priest offering the sacraments in a private home when a sick or dying person was being served.

90. *Zhurnal Moskovskoi Patriarkhii*, No. 2 (February), 1987, p. 23; No. 5 (May), 1976, p. 15; No. 11 (November), 1959, p. 41; No. 4 (April), 1969, p. 66; and No. 2 (February), 1975, p. 32; Pospielovsky, *The Russian Church*, p. 346; Struve, p. 300; Konstantinov, p. 249.

91. The cathedral churches in Chelyabinsk, Chernigov, Chernovtsy, Kishinev, Minsk, Novgorod, Orel, Perm, Poltava, Riga, Sverdlovsk, and Vinnitsa were closed.

92. Tsentralny Gosudarstvenny Arkhiv, Fond 6991s, Opis No. 4, Vol. I, delo No. 574.

93. After Khrushchev's fall registration of new church societies apparently was resumed on a very small scale. Tsentralny Gosudarstvenny Arkhiv, Fond 6991s, Opis No. 4, Vol. I, delo Nos. 574, 575.

94. "Tserkov v S.S.S.R. posle Khrushcheva," *Posev*, January 15, 1965, p. 2. See also "Chronicle," *Kirche im Osten*, Vol. 8, 1965, p. 146.

95. Savelii Tuberozov, "News and Comment," *Eastern Churches Review*, Vol. II, 1968–1970, p. 285.

96. The figure Kharchev gave was 7,523 societies on January 1, 1966 (and 11,742 in 1961). See Kharchev, "Garantii svobody," p. 23. Figures in council archives (Georgian Orthodox parishes excluded) were 11,571 in January of 1961 and 7,466 in January of 1966, or a net

deregistration of 4,105 church societies. Tsentralny Gosudarstvenny Arkhiv, Fond 6991s, Opis No. 2, Vol. I, delo No. 263; Fond 6991s, Opis No. 4, Vol. I, delo Nos. 574 and 575. It is not altogether clear why Kharchev's 1966 figure is 57 higher than the archive number. Failing to subtract the Georgian parishes would account for a discrepancy of about 45 registered church societies.

Yuri Degtyarev wrote in 1989 that "over 40 percent" of the churches were closed from 1960 (a year earlier than Kharchev's 1961 figure) to 1966. Forty-two percent of 12,964 churches on January 1, 1960, would equal 5,445 churches closed, or 7,519 remaining on January 1, 1966, a figure extremely close to Kharchev's 1966 figure of 7,523. Degtyarev, p. 3.

The figures given publicly in 1989 by V. Garadzha of the Institute of Scientific Atheism were that an average of 420 churches a year were closed between 1950 and 1964. Garadzha's figures obscure the devastating effects of the Khrushchev drive by including the stable numbers of the mid-1950s in the calculation. If one multiplies 420 by 15 (January 1, 1950, to the end of 1964) the result is 6,300. The figure of 14,273 churches in January of 1950 minus 6,300 gives a figure of 7,973 at the end of 1964. A few more churches were closed in 1965, to reach a total fairly close to Kharchev's figure. See Garadzha, p. 3, and Tsentralny Gosudarstvenny Arkhiv, Fond 6991s, Opis No. 2, Vol. I, delo No. 180.

97. Fletcher, *Russian Orthodox Church Underground,* p. 259; House, p. 90.

98. Bourdeaux, *Religious Ferment,* p. 93; Bourdeaux, *Patriarch and Prophets,* pp. 39–41. See also Philippe Sabant, "Religion in Russia Today, Part I," *The Tablet* (London), Vol. 234, No. 7279, January 12, 1980, p. 31; House, pp. 107–110.

99. Mikhail Heller and Aleksandr Nekrich, *Utopia in Power,* trans. Phyllis B. Carlos (New York: Summit Books, 1986), p. 677.

100. According to council archives, there were thirty-six nunneries, six hermitages for women (*skits* or sketes), twenty monasteries, and one hermitage for men on January 1, 1958. Tsentralny Gosudarstvenny Arkhiv, Fond 6991s, Opis No. 2, Vol. I, delo Nos. 206, 263. Foreign scholars, usually quoting church sources, reported sixty-seven to sixty-nine functioning convents of both sexes in 1958. During the post-Khrushchev period the number of convents stabilized at twelve nunneries and six monasteries.

101. See Chapter 9.

102. Astrakhan was the only diocese that gained church societies in the course of the Khrushchev drive. This was because the remnants of the Kalmyk people, whom Stalin had deported to Siberia, were allowed by Khrushchev to return to their historical lands. In the course of their resettlement, the Orthodox among them were allowed to open two churches. One of the sixteen churches in the remainder of the diocese was closed down.

103. The data given in Table 4.1 are most subject to error for the Sverdlovsk diocese. The reports of commissioners to the Council for Russian Orthodox Church Affairs from which these figures for January 1, 1966, are taken had no report for Sverdlovsk oblast, although there was a report from the commissioner in Kurgan oblast, which was also part of the diocese of Sverdlovsk. Therefore, it was necessary to interpolate the figures for the number of church societies in Sverdlovsk oblast on January 1, 1966, from other data.

104. Lvov and Ivano-Frankovsk lost 42 percent. Mukachevo diocese seems to have been relatively sheltered and lost only 16 percent of its parishes.

105. Pospielovsky, *The Russian Church,* p. 441.

106. Bourdeaux, *Patriarch and Prophets,* pp. 135–136.

107. Kharchev, "Religiya i perestroika," p. 4.

Chapter 5

1. Konstantin Kharchev reported 7,523 Orthodox religious societies in January 1966 and 7,274 societies in January 1971, for a net loss of 249 parishes over five years. He failed to subtract Georgian Orthodox parishes. Corrected figures would be 7,466 in 1966 and 7,210 in 1971. Konstantin M. Kharchev, "Garantii svobody [Guarantees of Freedom]," *Nauka i Religiya* [Science and Religion], No. 11 (November), 1987, p. 23.

2. Gerhard Simon, *Church, State, and Opposition in the U.S.S.R.* (London: C. Hurst and Co., 1974), p. 88. Simon gave the figure of 1 percent of those closed in the Khrushchev drive, which would be fifty-five churches. Simon published the German edition of his book in 1970, so the figure would cover about five years after 1965. Specific mention in the *Journal of the Moscow Patriarchate* to new churches opened included Saratov, Stavropol, Vologda, and Voroshilovgrad (Lugansk). *Zhurnal Moskovskoi Patriarkhii* [Journal of the Moscow Patriarchate], No. 5 (May), 1967, p. 35; No. 4 (April), 1966, p. 20; No. 11 (November), 1964, p. 22; No. 1 (January), 1970, p. 22; No. 10 (October), 1967, p. 13. In 1965, ten church societies were registered in Ukraine and thirty-two societies were deregistered. Tsentralny Gosudarstvenny Arkhiv Oktyabrskoi Revolutsii [Central State Archive of the October Revolution], Vysshikh Organov Gosudarstvennoi Vlasti i Organov Gosurdarstvennogo Upravleniya S.S.S.R. [of the Higher Organs of State Government and Organs of State Administration of the U.S.S.R.], Soviet po delam religii pri Sovete Ministrov [the Council for Religious Affairs attached to the Council of Ministers], Fond 6991s, Opis No. 4, Vol. I, delo Nos. 574, 575.

3. Michael Bourdeaux, *Religious Ferment in Russia* (London: The Macmillan Co., 1968), p. 21; Max Hayward and William C. Fletcher, eds., *Religion and the Soviet State: A Dilemma of Power* (London: Pall Mall Press, 1969), p. 103; Ludmilla Alexeyeva, *Soviet Dissent: Contemporary Movements for National, Religious and Human Rights* (Middletown, Conn.: Wesleyan University Press, 1985), pp. 203–214.

4. Albert Boiter, *Religion in the Soviet Union* (Beverly Hills, Calif.: Sage Publications, 1980), pp. 46–47; Dimitry Pospielovsky, *The Russian Church Under the Soviet Regime, 1917–1982*, 2 Vols. (Crestwood, New York: St. Vladimir's Seminary Press, 1984), p. 343. The merger was announced in December 1965 and carried out in 1966.

5. Vladimir Kuroedov, "Lenin's Principles of Freedom of Conscience in the U.S.S.R.," *Nauka i Religiya,* No. 6 (June), 1968, as translated in *Religion in Communist Dominated Areas,* Vol. VIII, Nos. 7–8, Item 1436, April 1969, p. 70; Boiter, pp. 36–37, 60. The modifications to the penal code were to the codes of the Russian republic, but other republics took parallel action.

6. Dimitry Pospielovsky, "The Soviet State Versus the Russian Orthodox Church, 1959–1988," *Religion in Communist Dominated Areas,* Vol. XXVII, No. 4, Fall 1988, p. 105.

7. "A. S.," *Posev,* Vol. XXIV, No. 5 (1132), May 1968, p. 7.

8. Serge Keleher, "Church in the Middle: Greek-Catholics in Central and Eastern Europe," *Religion, State and Society,* Nos. 3 and 4, 1992, p. 294–296.

9. Vasyl Markus, "Religion and Nationality: The Uniates of the Ukraine," *Religion and Atheism in the U.S.S.R. and Eastern Europe,* eds. Bohdan R. Bociurkiw and John W. Strong (London: The Macmillan Co., 1975), pp. 108–109; Vasyl Markus, *Religion and Nationalism in Soviet Ukraine After 1945* (Cambridge, Mass.: Ukrainian Studies Fund, Harvard University, 1985), pp. 113–115.

10. Several other priests wrote the 1971 national council of the Russian Orthodox Church urging the repeal of the 1961 revision of church statutes. Jane Ellis, *The Russian Orthodox Church: A Contemporary History* (Bloomington, Indiana: Indiana University Press, 1986), pp. 292, 303; Alexeyeva, pp. 249–250.

11. Ellis, pp. 291–292; Alexeyeva, pp. 435–438; Trevor Beeson, *Discretion and Valor* (Philadelphia, Penn.: Fortress Press, 1974 and 1982), p. 82. The full title of Ogurtsov's organization was the All-Russian Social Christian Union for the Liberation of the People (Russian acronym VSKhSON).

12. Donald W. Treadgold, *Twentieth-Century Russia,* 6th ed. (Boulder, Colo.: Westview Press, 1987), pp. 464–467, 473–482; Alexeyeva, pp. 9, 16, 249–250, 285, 288, 293.

13. William C. Fletcher, *The Russian Orthodox Church Underground, 1917–1970* (London: Oxford University Press, 1971), p. 126.

14. Alexeyeva, pp. 11, 35, 43, 89, 250, 274–279, 310–311, 335.

15. Pospielovsky, *The Russian Church,* pp. 112, 391–394, 421; Ellis, pp. 225–226, 229–233; Beeson, pp. 80–81; S. Belavenets, "Pamyati Patriarkha Pimena [Recollections of Patriarch Pimen]," *Zhurnal Moskovskoi Patriarkhii,* No. 9 (September), 1991, p. 30; *Glasnost* (Moscow), No. 13, December 1987, pp. 2–6. Purported KGB documents printed in *Glasnost* quoted Aleksi, now the patriarch, as passing on rumors that Pimen had children living in Rostov-on-Don and saying that Pimen had relations with women in Moscow. *Glasnost,* No. 13, December 1987, pp. 2, 4. Sergei Belyaev, in "Pamyati svateishego [Recollections of a Saintly Man]," *Literaturnaya Rossiya* [Literary Russia], May 12, 1990, p. 2, described Pimen as serving in military communications during World War II and once protecting his men with his own body when bombed, which resulted in permanent injury to his spine. The *Moskovski Tserkovny Vestnik, Yezhenedelnik* [Moscow Church Herald, Weekly], No. 10, 1990, pp. 3–7, made some candid obituary comments about Pimen, mentioning his collaboration with the authorities and his false assertion during Brezhnev's time that church-state relations were "absolutely normal."

16. The *Journal of the Moscow Patriarchate* noted two new churches, one in Voronezh diocese (south of Moscow) and one in Moldavia, although the latter case seems to have been the handing over of a substitute church to compensate for a church demolished in a street reconstruction. *Zhurnal Moskovskoi Patriarkhii,* No. 4 (April), 1975, p. 16; No. 4 (April), 1975, p. 17.

17. V. G. Furov, "Cadres of the Church and Legal Measures to Curtail Their Activities: A Secret Report by the Council on Religious Affairs," *Religion in Communist Dominated Areas,* Vol. XX, Nos. 1–3, 1981, p. 4.

18. For the beginning of 1976, Kharchev gave a figure of 7,038 societies, or a reduction of 24 in 1975. Kharchev, p. 23. Subtracting Georgian churches, the figure would be 6,990–7,000.

19. In 1967, when there were 7,300–7,350 Orthodox religious societies registered, Dim-

itry Konstantinov reported Orthodox contacts as saying that there were fewer than 7,000 churches open. Dimitry Konstantinov, *The Crown of Thorns* (London: Zarya, 1979), p. 248. In 1972, when there were about 7,200 Orthodox societies, Dimitry Pospielovsky reported 6,850 churches. Pospielovsky, *The Russian Church,* p. 401. In May of 1976, when there were about 7,000 Orthodox societies registered, Furov estimated that there were about 6,500 open churches.

20. Furov gave the figure of 182 fully active parishes, or exactly half of the 364 registered societies. If the 33 totally inactive parishes are subtracted from the 364 registered societies, the resulting figure of 331 is very close to the 334 registered societies on January 1, 1986 (see Table 5.1). Furov, p. 5.

21. Dimitry Konstantinov, *Stations of the Cross: The Russian Orthodox Church, 1970–1980* (London: Zarya, 1984), p. 15.

22. Ellis, pp. 308–309.

23. V. G. Furov, "Cadres," *Religion in Communist Dominated Areas,* Vol. XX, Nos. 4–6, 1981, p. 65.

24. Paul A. Lucey, in "Religion," *The Soviet Union Today,* ed. James Cracraft (Chicago: Bulletin of the Atomic Scientists, 1983), p. 295.

25. Ellis, p. 24; Pospielovsky, *The Russian Church,* pp. 449, 493–500; Boiter, p. 39.

26. Alexeyeva, pp. 8, 66, 112–116, 251–253; Beeson, pp. 86–88. Father Dudko later recanted, to the distress of many human rights activists.

27. Alexeyeva, pp. 316–317, 320–321, 438–441; Beeson, p. 82.

28. Alexeyeva, pp. 16–17, 255–259, 327–328, 335–336, 340, 450–451; Beeson, pp. 84–86. In 1975 Yakunin and Lev Regelson had appealed to the World Council of Churches to help the believers in the USSR. Regelson later recanted. Deacon Vladimir Rusak made a similar appeal to the 1983 meeting of the World Council of Churches.

29. Dimitry V. Pospielovsky, "Intelligentsia and Religion: Aspects of Religious Revival in the Contemporary Soviet Union, the Orthodox Church," *Religion and Communist Society,* ed. Dennis J. Dunn (Berkeley, Calif.: Berkeley Slavic Specialties, 1983), pp. 33–35. See also Archbishop Makari (Svistun), "The Contemporary Status of Religion in the U.S.S.R.," Chapter 2, *Christianity and Russian Culture in Soviet Society,* ed. Nicolai N. Petro (Boulder, Colo.: Westview Press, 1990), p. 17.

30. Alexeyeva, p. 263.

31. Alexeyeva, p. 53, 253, 257, 342, 344, 359–360, 368; Beeson, p. 83. After Yakunin's arrest Father Nikolai Gainov and Father Vasili Fonchenkov attempted for a time to lead the Christian Committee. Alexeyeva, p. 258; Ellis, pp. 301, 303, 379–381.

32. Beeson, p. 78; Ellis, p. 328; Simon, p. 129; *The Samizdat Bulletin,* No. 130, February 1984, pp. 1–2.

33. Kharchev's figures for 1976 were 7,038 registered Orthodox societies and for 1981 7,007 registered societies—or a net loss of 31 societies between 1976 and 1981. Because Georgian churches were still being carried in the overall totals, there were about 6,960–6,965 registered Russian Orthodox societies in January 1981. Konstantin Kharchev, "Sovetskoe gosudarstvo i tserkov [The Soviet Government and the Church]," *Religiya v SSSR* [Religion in the USSR], No. 10 (December), 1987, p. KKh3. Kuroedov reported 30 new Orthodox societies registered between 1977 (January) and 1982. Catherine P. Henry,

"Registration of Churches in the Soviet Union," *Religion in Communist Dominated Areas*, Vol. XXVI, No. 1, Winter 1987, p. 19. See also Yuri Degtyarev, "Neukosnitelno soblyudat zakon [To Observe the Law Strictly]," *Religiya v SSSR*, No. 6 (June), 1989, p. 4.

34. Philippe Sabant, in "Religion in Russia Today, Part II," *The Tablet* (London), Vol. 234, No. 7280, January 19, 1980, p. 55, gave the figure of a score of churches opened between 1977 and 1980. In addition to churches in Siberia, Central Asia, and the Volga region, one or two were authorized in the oblasts of Kiev, Minsk, Moscow, Rostov-on-Don, and Vladimir. *Zhurnal Moskovskoi Patriarkhii*, No. 3 (March), 1978, p. 24; No. 6 (June), 1978, p. 19; No. 8 (August), 1978, p. 11; No. 2 (February), 1979, p. 18; No. 6 (June), 1980, p. 18; No. 8 (August), 1980, p. 20; No. 11 (November), 1980, pp. 12–14; No. 4 (April), 1981, p. 22; No. 5 (May), 1981, p. 30; No. 5 (May), 1982, p. 25; No. 9 (September), 1983, p. 18; No. 6 (June), 1984, p. 23. See also *Moskovski Tserkovny Vestnik* [Moscow Church Herald], No. 4 (April), 1988, p. 8.

35. See Henry, pp. 14, 20; Pospielovsky, *The Russian Church*, p. 406; Ellis, p. 22.

36. Fletcher, p. 289.

37. Patriarch Pimen (Izvekov) *Religiya v SSSR*, No. 5 (May), 1988, p. 4. See also *Zhurnal Moskovskoi Patriarkhii*, No. 1 (January), 1982, p. 5.

38. The *Keston News Service*, No. 336, October 19, 1989, p. 6.

39. Michael Warder, "Soviet Image-Building Through a Church Anniversary," *Religion in Communist Dominated Areas*, Vol. XXVIII, No. 2, Spring 1989, p. 61. The complex was actually turned over in May of 1983.

40. E. Pazukhin, "Poiski puti [In Search of the Way]," *Moskovski Tserkovny Vestnik, Yezhenedelnik*, No. 9, April 1990, p. 4.

41. James Moss, "The Russian Orthodox Church, 1986–1988," *Religion in Communist Dominated Areas*, Vol. XXVIII, No. 2, Spring 1989, p. 48; Henry, p. 19; Degtyarev, p. 9; Kharchev, "Garantii svobody," p. 119.

42. I am indebted to William C. Fletcher for the observations made in the latter part of this paragraph.

43. Philip Walters, ed., with Keston College researchers, *World Christianity: Eastern Europe* (Monrovia, Calif.: Missions Advanced Research and Communications Center, 1988), p. 39.

44. Treadgold, pp. 499–500. Other Soviet leaders' relatives were also said to have been religious. Brezhnev's mother was one. Stalin's daughter, Svetlana Alliluyeva, was baptized when she was living in the Kremlin. Khrushchev's son Sergei is reported to be a practicing Orthodox Christian. Anatoly Dobrynin's mother was reported by her son, the ambassador, to be a loyal believer. "Tserkov v S.S.S.R. posle Khrushcheva [The Church in the U.S.S.R. After Khrushchev]," *Posev*, January 15, 1965, p. 2; Francis House, *The Russian Phoenix* (London: SPCK, 1988), p. 116.

45. Seth Mydans, "In Soviet, Religion Ceases Outside Church Doors," *The New York Times*, July 15, 1984, p. 10.

46. Ellis, p. 453; Pospielovsky, *The Russian Church*, pp. 340, 395; Simon, pp. 81, 83, 86.

47. Aleksandr Nezhny, "Treti razgovor s Kharchevem [Third Conversation with Kharchev]," *Ogonёk* [Little Fire], No. 44, 1989, p. 9; Mikhail Odintsov, "The Soviet State and Laws on Religion," *Religion in USSR*, No. 12 (December) 1991, p. 58.

48. For 1966 figures, Tsentralny Gosudarstvenny Arkhiv, Fond 6991s, Opis No. 4, Vol. I, delo Nos. 572–575. Gleb Rar (also Rahr), "Skolko v Rossi pravoslavnykh khramov? [How Many Orthodox Churches Are There in Russia?]" *Posev,* January 1974, p. 39, gave correct figures for about fifteen dioceses. Sabant, Ellis, Pospielovsky, James Moss, and others reported accurate statistics for some individual dioceses.

49. Greek-Catholics are counted as Orthodox for the purposes of Tables 5.2 and 5.3 because the Greek-Catholic churches existing before and during World War II in western Ukraine were under Orthodox jurisdiction in 1986 (or closed or used clandestinely), and most Greek-Catholics worshiping overtly were attending Orthodox churches. In contrast, the populations of Lutheran, Roman Catholic, Muslim, Buddhist, Armenian, and other historically non-Orthodox religious communities have been subtracted from demographic totals in making up the tables.

50. Aleksi's private secretary, Daniil Ostapov, exercised great influence on the aging and infirm patriarch. Father Georgi Edelshtein quoted Archbishop Ioann of Pskov in this regard in "The Election of a Patriarch: Crossroads or Dead-End?" *Religion in Communist Lands,* Vol. 18, No. 3, Autumn 1990, p. 269. Allegedly Archbishop Ioann said: "Once a lay brother simply knew the patriarch and carried chamber pots to him; now he directs the church." Ostapov had been deeply loyal to Aleksi over the years of tribulation but was regarded by many in the church as authoritarian, unresponsive, rigid, and unimaginative. His manner had become peremptory, and some thought him downright arrogant.

Chapter 6

1. *Keston News Service,* No. 330, July 20, 1989, p. 10.

2. William Pfaff, "Sweeping Soviet Retreat on Religion?" *Los Angeles Times,* May 5, 1988, Part I, p. 9; *Time,* December 21, 1987, p. 18; January 4, 1988, p. 29. The story about Gorbachev's mother went on to assert that she regularly attended church in Gorbachev's native village, Privolnoe, but these accounts are apocryphal. I visited Privolnoe in June 1991. The village church was destroyed many years ago, and there was no Orthodox house of prayer there, although the villagers were planning to build a new church and had already called in a priest to bless the plot of land where it was to be built. The nearest church was in Krasnogvardeisk, fifteen miles down the road toward Stavropol. Mrs. Gorbachev was reported by local people to have difficulty walking, and it is most unlikely that she walked to and from Krasnogvardeisk. Local people readily described Mrs. Gorbachev's other arrangements, including a special telephone line so her elder son could call her without difficulty, but I heard no indication that a special car was ever provided to take her to church.

3. *Nauka i Religiya* [Science and Religion], No. 1 (January), 1990, p. 2.

4. George W. Cornell, "Analysts See Hopeful Stirrings of Improvements for Soviet Churches," *Los Angeles Times,* May 3, 1986, Part II, p. 5.

5. Aleksandr Nezhny, "Treti razgovor s Kharchevem [A Third Conversation with Kharchev]," *Ogonëk* [Little Fire], No. 44, 1989, p. 9.

6. Dimitry V. Pospielovsky, "Religious Themes in the Soviet Press in 1989," *Religion in Communist Lands,* Vol. 18, No. 4, Winter 1990, p. 319; Dimitry V. Pospielovsky, *Soviet*

Studies on the Church and the Believer's Response to Atheism, Vol. 3 of *A History of Soviet Atheism in Theory and Practice, and the Believer* (New York: St. Martin's Press, 1988), pp. 135–145; Valery Petrochenkov, "Christian Patterns in Contemporary Soviet Prose," *Christianity and Russian Culture in Soviet Society,* ed. Nicolai N. Petro (Boulder, Colo.: Westview Press, 1990), pp 130–142.

7. *Zhurnal Moskovskoi Patriarkhii* [Journal of the Moscow Patriarchate], No. 1 (January), 1986, p. 80.

8. Kirill Golovin (a pseudonym), "The Day Will Come . . . ," *The Samizdat Bulletin,* No. 174, October 1987, p. 11; Philip Walters, ed., with Keston College researchers, *World Christianity: Eastern Europe* (Monrovia, Calif.: Missions Advanced Research and Communications Center, 1988), p. 106; *KC [Keston College], The Right to Believe,* No. 2, 1987, p. 1. Reportedly Gorbachev made another private overture to church leaders during a conference called "For a Nuclear-Free World; For the Survival of Humanity" in early 1987. Archbishop Makari (Svistun), "The Contemporary Status of Religion in the U.S.S.R.," Chapter 2, *Christianity and Russian Culture in Soviet Society,* ed. Nicolai N. Petro (Boulder, Colo.: Westview Press, 1990), p. 19.

9. Gorbachev's Tashkent speech of November 26, 1986. Kent R. Hill, *The Puzzle of the Soviet Church: An Inside Look at Christianity and Glasnost* (Portland, Oregon: Multnomah Press, 1989), pp. 93–94; and Philip Walters, "Gorbachev: Is This the Breakthrough?" *Frontier,* March–April, 1987, p. 5. Walters noted that Gorbachev's Tashkent speech was not carried by the central Soviet news agencies and asserted that it was intended for a local audience only. Gorbachev probably was more concerned about a spillover of Islamic fundamentalism than he was about any gains of Russian Orthodoxy.

Yegor Ligachev, then the senior ideologist of the Communist Party, was reported to have attacked those who "talk about the need to tolerate religious ideas" in late 1986. William Safire, "Flirting with God," *The New York Times,* December 25, 1986, p. 31.

10. Yuri Degtyarev, "Neukosnitelno soblyudat zakon [To Observe the Law Strictly]," *Religiya v SSSR* [Religion in the USSR], No. 6 (June), 1989, p. 9; *Zhurnal Moskovskoi Patriarkhii,* No. 1 (January), 1987, p. 22; No. 1 (January), 1987, p. 24.

11. Metropolitan Vladimir (Sabodan), "Sovremennoe sostoyanie Russkoi Pravoslavnoi Tserkvi [The Present State of the Russian Orthodox Church]," *Religiya v SSSR,* No. 10 (October), 1988, p. MV9; *Zhurnal Moskovskoi Patriarkhii,* No. 1 (January), 1990, pp. 79–80. The Very Reverend Leonid Kishkovsky, later president of the U.S. National Council of Churches, made the point in a lecture given in Claremont, California, on March 8, 1989, that the great significance of the church's three international conferences was that they brought Soviet religious and secular scholars together in dialogue.

12. Walters, "Gorbachev: Is This the Breakthrough?" pp. 4–6; Francis House, *The Russian Phoenix* (London: SPCK, 1988), p. 103; Bill Keller, "Atheist Preaches Glasnost, so a Priest Has Hope," *The New York Times,* June 8, 1987, p. A4.

13. James Moss, "The Russian Orthodox Church, 1986–1988," *Religion in Communist Dominated Areas,* Vol. XXVIII, No. 2, Spring 1989, p. 50; *Religiya v SSSR,* No. 9 (September), 1987, p. NG1; Zachary T. Irwin, "Moscow and the Vatican," *Religion in Communist Dominated Areas,* Vol. XXIX, No. 2, Spring 1990, p. 40.

14. In Ukrainian, Marina's name and that of the town are Mariika Kizin of the town of

Hrushiv, near Drogobych in western Ukraine. A question arises about whether to render Ukrainian names in a transliteration of Ukrainian or a transliteration of the Russian equivalent. As most of the data in this volume are taken from Russian-language sources, names are rendered in Russian when the sources are Russian. When the source is Ukrainian, the name is transliterated from Ukrainian.

15. V. Kharazov, "Chudesa v Grusheve [Miracle in Grushev]," *Nauka i Religiya*, No. 5 (May), 1988, pp. 21–23, 47–48; *Religiya v SSSR*, No. 8 (October), 1987, p. NT1. Serge Keleher pointed out that two Greek-Catholic bishops from Ukraine "managed to go to Moscow and meet Cardinals Casaroli and Willebrands" at the time of the millennial celebrations. Serge Keleher, "Church in the Middle: Greek-Catholics in Central and Eastern Europe," *Religion, State and Society*, Vol. 20, Nos. 3 and 4, 1992, p. 297.

16. In Serednia, a Carpathian village in Ivano-Frankovsk oblast, a woman had a vision of the Mother of God in 1954. The "miracle of Serednia" inspired thousands of pilgrims and caused the formation of a radical separatist Ukrainian Greek-Catholic sect that opposed the underground, Vatican-supported Ukrainian Greek-Catholics. These separatists were called Ihnativtsi, after their leader, Father Ihnatii Soltys, and later called Pokutnyky (Penitents). Vasyl Markus, *Religion and Nationalism in Soviet Ukraine After 1945* (Cambridge, Mass.: Ukrainian Studies Fund, Harvard University, 1985), pp. 71–72.

17. Degtyarev, p. 9. For churches turned over to believers, see Francis X. Clines, "Bells Are Ringing as Soviets Return Churches to Faithful," *The New York Times*, April 16, 1989, pp. A1, A18.

18. *Zhurnal Moskovskoi Patriarkhii*, No. 11 (November), 1987, pp. 38–39; No. 11 (November), 1988, pp. 17, 21; *The Samizdat Bulletin*, No. 173, September 1987, p. 11; Moss, pp. 47–48.

19. Paul A. Lucey, "Religion," *U.S.S.R. Facts and Figures Annual*, ed. Alan P. Pollard (Gulf Breeze, Florida: Academic International Press, 1988), p. 318. There were two registrations in 1984, three in 1985, ten in 1986, sixteen in 1987.

20. Nezhny, p. 10; *Keston News Service*, Vol. 30, No. 339, 1989, pp. 16–17.

21. Mark J. Porubcansky, "State Tolerance Increases as Russian Christianity Marks 1000th Year," *Los Angeles Times*, January 9, 1988, Part I, p. 6; Irwin, p. 40.

22. *Religiya v SSSR*, No. 4 (April), 1988, p. AK2. In actuality, the abolition of the requirement that parents of baptized children register their passports did not make it impossible for party authorities to trace the identity of such parents, although it made such verification more time-consuming.

23. *Religiya v SSSR*, No. 4 (April), 1988, p. AK2; *Los Angeles Times*, April 11, 1988, Part I, p. 5; "Sotsializm i religiya [Socialism and Religion]," *Kommunist*, No. 4 (April), 1988, pp. 115–123. John B. Dunlop of the Hoover Institution expressed skepticism about the liberalizing thrust of the *Kommunist* article. See Dunlop, "The Russian Orthodox Church and Nationalism After 1988," *Religion in Communist Lands*, Vol. 18, No. 4, Winter 1990, p. 293.

24. Charles P. Wallace, "Orthodox Head Assails Soviet Religious Curbs," *Los Angeles Times*, April 9, 1988, Part I, p. 3.

25. Michael Bourdeaux, "Glasnost and the Churches: Developing a Perspective," recording of Keston U.S.A. seminar, Dallas, Texas, May 6, 1989, Side A.

26. *Zhurnal Moskovskoi Patriarkhii*, No. 7 (July), 1988, pp. 2–6; *Moscow News*, No. 19, May 8, 1988, p. 4. Kharchev stated, however, that the patriarch and the metropolitans in

the Holy Synod requested the interview, Kharchev supported the request, and "Gorbachev made it happen." Nezhny, p. 10.

27. Bourdeaux stated that Gorbachev promised a "new deal" in return for the hierarchs' loyal support of perestroika and talked of the "common cause" between religion and communism. Michael Bourdeaux, "Patriarch Aleksi II: Between the Hammer and the Anvil," *Religion, State and Society,* Vol. 20, No. 2, 1992, p. 234.

28. Metropolitan Vladimir (Sabodan), p. MV12; Aleksandr Nezhny, "Zakon i sovest [Law and Conscience]," *Ogonëk,* No. 50, December 1988. Some accounts of the meeting suggested that the church's list of requests was presented to the government after the face-to-face meeting and not during the course of it. See Victor S. Potapov, "The Celebration of the Millennium of the Baptism of Rus in the U.S.S.R.," *Religion in Communist Dominated Areas,* Vol. XXVII, No. 4, Fall 1988, p. 113.

29. Bourdeaux asserted that at the meeting Gorbachev invited the church to "plunge headlong into charitable work." Bourdeaux, "Patriarch Aleksi II," p. 234.

30. Jim Forest of the International Fellowship of Reconciliation, quoted in *Surviving Together,* Summer 1988, p. 32; Potapov, p. 114; Natalya Buldyk, "Rushitsya barer neponimaniya [The Barrier of Incomprehension Crumbles]," *Religiya v SSSR,* No. 1 (January), 1989, p. 12; Anatoli Leshchinski, "Tserkov v Tropareve: Posle osvyashcheniya [The Church in Troparev: After Its Consecration]," *Religiya v SSSR,* No. 4 (April), 1989, p. 24; Clines, p. 1; Vs. Chaplin, "Khabarovskaya Yeparkhiya [The Khabarovsk Diocese]," *Moskovski Tserkovny Vestnik* [Moscow Church Herald], No. 5 (May), 1989, p. 3; V. Lebedev, "Da svetit svet vash [May Your Light So Shine]," *Moskovski Tserkovny Vestnik,* No. 6 (June), 1989, pp. 1–2.

31. Potapov, p. 114.

32. Metropolitan Pitirim of Volokolamsk and Archpriest Petr Buburuz of Kishinev were also elected.

33. The film, *Pod blagodatnym pokrovom* [Under Beneficent Protection], was produced for the Moscow Patriarchate by the Central Studio of Documentary Films together with the West German firm Noviteks. For *Khram* [The Church], see Kirill Golovin (a pseudonym), "Same Homeland, Different Future," *Sobornost,* No. 2, October (10), 1988, p. 13.

34. *Zhurnal Moskovskoi Patriarkhii,* No. 6 (June), 1988, p. 3.

35. Metropolitan Vladimir (Sabodan) stated on June 7, 1988, that "over sixty" new societies had been registered between January 1 and the end of May 1988. *Zhurnal Moskovskoi Patriarkhii,* No. 9 (September), 1988, p. 15. See also Degtyarev, p. 4; Moss, p. 51.

36. *Zhurnal Moskovskoi Patriarkhii,* No. 9 (September), 1988, pp. 14–15. The figure for the exact number of parishes includes churches abroad because Metropolitan Vladimir (Sobodan) listed a series of exact statistics, and the figures for dioceses, bishops, convents, and so on clearly did include those abroad. A text of his speech less edited than the *Zhurnal* version was published in *Religion in the USSR,* and it explicitly quoted the metropolitan as saying there were seventy-four bishops and "of those, seven work abroad." Metropolitan Vladimir (Sabodan), p. MV2. The metropolitan also said that there were twenty-two convents, which had to include convents abroad. (For some reason the later text in *Religion* quoted Vladimir as saying there were "twenty-one" convents. Perhaps someone realized before *Religion* went to press that the Russian Orthodox monastery on Mount Athos in Greece is actually under the jurisdiction of the Greek Orthodox Church.)

So far as churches abroad were concerned, *Nauka i Religiya,* No. 6 (June), 1988, pp. 16 and 57, gave figures of "over 120" and "130" parishes in twenty-nine countries. These figures are consistent with my records of Russian Orthodox parishes outside the USSR.

37. Kharchev, p. 119; Degtyarev, p. 9; Golovin, "Same Homeland," pp. 15, 17. Kharchev gave the figure of 6,800 registered religious societies in March of 1988. See Konstantin M. Kharchev, "Religiya i perestroika [Religion and Perestroika]," speech to the instructors of the Higher Party School, Moscow, end of March 1988 (transcribed by memory and abridged), *Russkaya Mysl* [Russian Thought], No. 3725, May 20, 1988, p. 4. *Nauka i Religiya,* No. 6 (June), 1988, p. 16, gave the same figure.

38. Michael Parks, "Talks Set on Ukraine Church Status," *Los Angeles Times,* June 5, 1988, Part I, p. 13; *Zhurnal Moskovskoi Patriarkhii,* No. 9 (September), 1988, p. 18.

39. Metropolitan Filaret (Denisenko), "O podgotovke Pomestnogo Sobora Russkoi Pravoslavnoi Tserkvi i yubileinogo torzhestva v tselom [About the Preparation of the National Council of the Russian Orthodox Church and the Celebration of the Jubilee in Its Totality]," *Religiya v SSSR,* No. 4 (April), 1988, p. AK3. The monastery of the Caves had been closed in 1929, reopened under the German occupation in World War II, and closed again in 1961. *Religiya v SSSR,* No. 4 (April), 1988, p. IT2. See also Aleksandr Nezhny, "Sovest svobodna [A Free Conscience]," *Ogonëk,* No. 21, May 1988, p. 26. In that interview Kharchev had himself expressed the expectation that the church would be given back both the Near and Far Caves.

40. Moss, p. 59; *Zhurnal Moskovskoi Patriakhii,* No. 2 (February), 1990, p. 14.

41. Michael Parks, "Soviet Rights Group Urges Release of Jailed Believers," *Los Angeles Times,* August 10, 1988, Part I, p. 6.

42. Degtyarev, pp. 4, 7. *Zhurnal Moskovskoi Patriarkhii,* No. 4 (April), 1989, p. 6; No. 5 (May), 1989, p. 22; Leshchinski, p. 24. Degtyarev added that 60 percent of the total of new registrations for all denominations in 1988 were authorized during the last three months of the year, and over three-fourths of them were Orthodox societies. Kharchev told an interviewer in mid-December of 1988 that "over 600" church societies had been registered in 1988 up to that time. O. V. Serkora, interview, *Foreign Broadcast Information Service,* December 16, 1988, pp. 68–69.

43. If there were 6,740 registered church societies on January 1, 1988, and 809 societies were added and no societies deregistered, the total would become 7,549. In February 1990, Metropolitan Vladimir (Sabodan) said there were, in fact, 7,549 registered parishes at the end of 1988. The metropolitan in this case probably was given the figure by the Council for Religious Affairs, which did not count parishes outside the USSR. *Zhurnal Moskovskoi Patriarkhii,* No. 2 (February), 1990, p. 9.

44. Degtyarev, pp. 4–6.

45. *Foreign Broadcast Information Service,* February 10, 1989, pp. 67–68. See also the Ukrainian Catholic Center, Rome, March 2, 1989, reported in K. Fotiev, "Russkaya Pravoslavnaya Tserkov posle Yubileya [The Russian Orthodox Church After the Jubilee]," *Posev,* No. 4 (April), 1989, p. 56. In November of 1988 *Argumenty i Fakty* reported 300 new Orthodox societies registered. *Argumenty i Fakty* [Arguments and Facts], No. 47, November 1988. Undoubtedly many additional societies were registered in November and December after the aforementioned statistics were compiled. Throughout the years the

council worked frenetically at the end of the year, in the weeks before the reporting period ended, registering and deregistering church societies, depending on the instructions of official higher-ups at the time.

46. Serge Keleher, "Out of the Catacombs: The Greek-Catholic Church in Ukraine," *Religion in Communist Lands,* Nos. 3–4, Winter 1991, p. 251.

47. *Nauka i Religiya,* No. 1 (January), 1990, p. 2.

48. Commissioners were also called "plenipotentiaries." The procedures described here were modified by the freedom-of-conscience law passed in late 1990.

49. Degtyarev, pp. 5, 8.

50. Clines, pp. 1, 18.

51. *Pravoslavny Visnyk* [Orthodox Herald], No. 3 (March), 1989, pp. 19, 24. *Zhurnal Moskovskoi Patriarkhii,* No. 6 (June), 1989, p. 5; No. 11 (November), 1990, p. 12. Monks at the monastery of the Caves proudly showed me the tree in June of 1989.

52. *Moskovski Tserkovny Vestnik, Yezhenedelnik* [Moscow Church Herald, Weekly], No. 8, August 1989, p. 1.

53. *Zhurnal Moskovskoi Patriarkhii,* No. 7 (July), 1989, p. 3; No. 8 (August), 1989, p. 52.

54. *Moskovski Tserkovny Vestnik, Yezhenedelnik,* No. 11, September 1989, p. 4; *Foreign Broadcast Information Service,* March 8, 1989, pp. 73–74.

55. *Nauka i Religiya,* No. 9 (September), 1989, p. 17; *Moskovski Tserkovny Vestnik, Yezhenedelnik,* No. 2, May 1989, p. 8, and No. 15, November 1989, p. 1; *Ekspress-Khronika* [Express Chronicle], No. 46, November 12, 1989, p. 3; *Chas Pik* [Rush Hour], March 26, 1990, p. 8; *Religiya v SSSR,* No. 3 (March), 1990, p. 6; *Literaturnaya Gazeta,* No. 14, April 1, 1990, p. 2.

56. *Zhurnal Moskovskoi Patriarkhii,* No. 7 (July), 1989, p. 12.

57. *Moscow News* of April 9, 1989, stated that 1,244 new Orthodox societies were registered between April 1, 1988, and April 1, 1989. *Keston News Service,* No. 323, April 13, 1989, p. 2; Clines, p. 18; *Nauka i Religiya,* No. 5 (May), 1989, p. 46; No. 9 (September), 1989, p. 3; *Moskovski Tserkovny Vestnik, Yezhenedelnik,* No. 3, May 1989, p. 3; Patriarch Pimen (Izvekov), *Zhurnal Moskovskoi Patriarkhii,* No. 8 (August), 1989, p. 7. Parish deregistrations had by this time effectively ceased. Registrations have been calculated by figuring 20 societies registered in the first four months of 1988 and thus 789 new societies registered in the last eight months of 1988 (809 − 20 = 789). Subtracting 789 from 1,700 gives the figure of approximately 910 societies registered in the first four months of 1989. *Keston News Service,* No. 325, May 11, 1989, p. 8; No. 348, June 22, 1989, p. 11; *Moskovski Tserkovny Vestnik, Yezhenedelnik,* No. 3, May 1989, p. 3; No. 5, June 1989, p. 4; Pimen quoted in the *Zhurnal Moskovskoi Patriarkhii,* No. 8 (August), 1989, p. 7.

Chapter 7

1. Patriarch Aleksi II's vigor and good health are marred by reported heart problems that have resulted in his hospitalization at crucial times of national political trouble.

2. Aleksandr Nezhny, "Treti razgovor s Kharchevem [Third Conversation with Kharchev]," *Ogonëk* [Little Fire], No. 44, 1989, pp. 9–11.

3. Boris Yeltsin, in confirmation hearings for government ministers in 1989, criticized

the KGB for excessive involvement in church matters. In addition, allegations became widespread in the late 1980s and early 1990s of KGB officers enriching themselves by misappropriating church funds. Jane Ellis, "Hierarchs and Dissidents: Conflict over the Future of the Russian Orthodox Church," *Religion in Communist Lands*, Vol. 18, No. 4, Winter 1990, pp. 313–314.

4. Kharchev's advocacy of multicandidate patriarchal elections was unpopular among some church leaders who preferred the old system used in 1945 and 1971. Jane Ellis reported that a delegation of the Holy Synod did go to the Supreme Soviet to complain about Kharchev (with Pimen's acquiesence), and this complaint was the final straw that caused his dismissal. She added that Kharchev had unsuccessfully tried to have an interview published in April 1989 criticizing the church leadership over financial irregularities, perhaps connected to KGB misappropriation of funds. Ellis, p. 313, and Jane Ellis, "Some Reflections About Religious Policy Under Kharchev," *Religious Policy in the Soviet Union*, Sabrina Petra Ramet, ed. (New York: Cambridge University Press, 1993), p. 98.

5. Kharchev also claimed to have supported Pimen against jealous hierarchs in making appointments, to have tried—unsuccessfully—to shift authority over religious affairs to the Soviet parliament, and to have supported the legal registration of previously persecuted Hare Krishnas. Yuri Degtyarev, "Religioznye obedineniya v S.S.S.R. [Religious Societies in the U.S.S.R.]," *Religiya v SSSR* [Religion in the USSR], No. 5 (May), 1990, p. 2. As for local communists, Kharchev claimed he had acted against party bosses in Kirov who had violated the law in harassing local believers, including several women who had gone on a hunger strike. In retaliation the Kirov bosses accused Kharchev of having accepted graft when furnishing his apartment. Nezhny, p. 10; *Newsweek*, December 4, 1989, p. 90.

6. Aleksandr Nezhny, "Sudba Patriarkha [The Fate of the Patriarch]," *Ogonëk*, No. 27, June 30–July 7, 1990, p. 32.

7. *Zhurnal Moskovskoi Patriarkhii* [Journal of the Moscow Patriarchate], No. 1 (January), 1990, p. 62; No. 2 (February), 1990, p. 10; No. 5 (May), 1990, p. 15; No. 7 (July), 1990, p. 7; *Moskovski Tserkovny Vestnik, Yezhenedelnik* [Moscow Church Herald, Weekly], No. 6, March 1990, p. 4; No. 22, October 1990, p. 7.

8. The first Ukrainian Autocephalous Apostolic Orthodox Church of the Greek-Ukrainian Rite was established in October 1921. Its archbishop, V. K. Lipkovski, had not been consecrated under apostolic succession, and the church resembled the later Renovationists in sanctioning married bishops and lay preachers and supporting Soviet rule. Despite its political support of the Bolsheviks, the church's Ukrainian separatist convictions resulted in its being suppressed by late 1930. The Ukrainian Autocephalous Orthodox Church under Metropolitan Polykarp (Sikorski) reappeared under the German occupation in World War II. Its episcopate was fully canonical, and it was a more ecclesiastically conservative body than Lipkovski's church. William C. Fletcher, *The Russian Orthodox Church Underground, 1917–1970* (London: Oxford University Press, 1971), p. 165–166. *Religiya v SSSR* [Religion in the USSR], No. 2 (February), 1990, p. 1; Serge Keleher, "Out of the Catacombs: The Greek-Catholic Church in Ukraine," *Religion in Communist Lands*, Nos. 3–4, Winter 1991, pp. 253–254; *Zhurnal Moskovskoi Patriarkhii*, No. 3 (March), 1990, p. 8.

9. *Keston News Service*, No. 346, March 22, 1990, p. 13. Orthodox sources reported that

about 190 Orthodox clergy went over to the Autocephalists "after December 1989." *Pravoslavny Visnyk,* No. 4 (April), 1991, p. 48. Keleher, whose sympathies were with the Greek-Catholics, asserted that the Soviet government and the KGB favored the Autocephalists in an attempt to divide the Ukrainian nationalists and limit the influence of the Greek-Catholics. As evidence, he noted that Archpriest Vitali Politylo, "a notorious sycophant of the government and the Communist Party," passed over to the Autocephalists in late 1989. Keleher, pp. 254–255. See also David Little, *Ukraine: The Legacy of Intolerance* (Washington, D.C.: United States Institute of Peace Press, 1991), pp. 50, 69.

10. *Novoe Vremya* [New Times], No. 7, February 9, 1990, p. 38. See also R. Vadimov, "Khranit apostolskie zavety [Preserve Apostolic Precepts]," *Moskovski Tserkovny Vestnik, Yezhenedelnik,* No. 4, February 1990, p. 2; S. Geruk, "Vremya Yedineniya, a ne rozni [The Time for Unity, Not Dissension]," *Moskovski Tserkovny Vestnik, Yezhenedelnik,* No. 9, April 1990, p. 3; *Ekspress-Khronika* [Express Chronicle], No. 46, November 12, 1989, p. 3; No. 7, February 13, 1990, p. 3; No. 16, April 17, 1990, pp. 2, 3.

11. John B. Dunlop, "The Russian Orthodox Church and Nationalism After 1988," *Religion in Communist Lands,* Vol. 18, No. 4, Winter 1990, p. 297.

12. *Moskovski Tserkovny Vestnik, Yezhenedelnik,* No. 16, November 1989, p. 7; No. 17, December, 1989, p. 6; No. 1, January 1990, p. 7; No. 4, February 1990, p. 2; No. 8, April 1990, pp. 6–7; No. 11, May 1990, p. 1; Bohdan R. Bociurkiw, "The Re-emergence of the Eastern Catholic Church in Ukraine," *Ecumenism,* No. 107, September 1992, pp. 14, 15; Keleher, p. 252; *Novoe Vremya,* No. 7, February 9, 1990, p. 38; *Ekspress-Khronika,* No. 7, February 13, 1990, p. 1.

13. *Zhurnal Moskovskoi Patriarkhii,* No. 2 (February), 1990, p. 4.

14. *Keston News Service,* No. 338, November 16, 1989, p. 11; No. 339, November 30, 1989, p. 8; *Religiya v SSSR,* No. 2 (February), 1990, p. 2.

15. *Keston News Service,* No. 339, November 30, 1989, p. 8.

16. James R. Moss, "The Russian Orthodox Church, 1988–1990," *Religion in Communist Dominated Areas,* Vol. XXIX, No. 1, Winter 1990, p. 12, note 9.

17. *Keston News Service,* No. 339, November 30, 1989, p. 8.

18. *Newsweek,* December 4, 1989, p. 88.

19. *Keston News Service,* No. 340, December 14, 1989, pp. 7, 8; R. Vadimov, "Eto agressiya [This Is Aggression]," *Moskovski Tserkovny Vestnik, Yezhenedelnik,* No. 1, January 1990, p. 7. See also Myroslav Tataryn, "The Re-emergence of the Ukrainian (Greek) Catholic Church in the U.S.S.R.," *Religious Policy in the Soviet Union,* Sabrina Petra Ramet, ed. (New York: Cambridge University Press, 1993), pp. 299, 302–304, 316. Tataryn noted that the decision to allow registration of the Greek-Catholic Church was probably made in the late summer or early fall of 1989.

20. A delegation consisting of Metropolitan Filaret (Denisenko), Metropolitan Filaret (Vakhromeev), and Metropolitan Yuvenali (Poyarkov) had been received by the pope on August 25, 1989. Ostensibly the purpose of the visit had been to thank the pope for the distinguished Catholic presence at the celebrations of the Millennium, but Russian Orthodox concerns about the resurgence of the Ukrainian Greek-Catholic Church had already emerged. *Zhurnal Moskovskoi Patriarkhii,* No. 1 (January), 1990, p. 34. For the Catholic Orthodox talks, see Serge Keleher, "Church in the Middle: Greek-Catholics in Central

and Eastern Europe," *Religion, State and Society,* Vol. 20, Nos. 3 and 4, 1992, pp. 296–297. Keleher asserted that a video crew of the Canadian Broadcasting Company was present in the Church of the Transfiguration when it passed over to the Greek-Catholics, and there was no violence. Keleher, "Out of the Catacombs," pp. 252–253.

21. Over 600 applications for registration were reported by December 21, 1989, and 300 Greek-Catholic parishes were said to be functioning. Two hundred priests previously registered as Russian Orthodox clerics were said to have applied for transfer and to have been accepted by the Greek-Catholics. Marco Bojcun, "Ukrainian Catholics Reject Orthodox 'Violence' Claims," *Keston News Service,* No. 341, January 11, 1990, pp. 21–22.

22. Exact figures were 2,564 new church societies registered in 1989 and 3 societies deregistered. *Nauka i Religiya* [Science and Religion], No. 1 (January), 1990, p. 2; Degtyarev, pp. 2, 3. Metropolitan Vladimir (Sabodan) of Rostov gave a figure of 9,734 for the number of parishes in the Russian Orthodox Church at the end of September 1989 (including parishes outside the USSR). *Zhurnal Moskovskoi Patriarkhii,* No. 2 (February), 1990, p. 9. Bohdan Bociurkiw asserted that over 700 of these parishes were shuttered Greek-Catholic churches that the authorities encouraged the Orthodox to register in order to preempt the Greek-Catholics. Bociurkiw, p. 14.

23. Keleher, "Church in the Middle," pp. 297–298.

24. *Religiya v SSSR,* No. 1 (January), 1990, pp. 5–6; No. 2 (February), 1990, pp. 4–5.

25. *Pravoslavny Visnyk,* No. 7 (July), 1991, p. 7.

26. *Moskovski Tserkovny Vestnik, Yezhenedelnik,* No. 4, February 1990, p. 2; *Keston News Service,* No. 343, February 8, 1990, p. 3; *Zhurnal Moskovskoi Patriarkhii,* No. 4 (April), 1992, pp. 8–10. A bishops' council meeting of October 9–10, 1989, authorized a study of the situation of the Ukrainian and Byelorussian exarchates. The study commission's report was presented to the Holy Synod on December 28, 1989, and the Holy Synod submitted the findings to the bishops' council that met January 30–31, 1990. The national church council of June 1990 accepted and endorsed the findings; the Ukrainian Orthodox Church established its own synod in July. A Russian Orthodox bishops' council meeting October 25–27, 1990, ratified the Ukrainian church's new status, and Patriarch Aleksi signed the act establishing the almost independent Ukrainian Orthodox Church on October 27, 1990. On October 28, 1990, Aleksi presented Metropolitan Filaret (Denisenko) with the appropriate credentials.

27. *Ekspress-Khronika,* No. 7, February 13, 1990, p. 1; *Moskovskie Novosti* [Moscow News], No. 17, April 29, 1990, p. 5; *Moskovski Tserkovny Vestnik, Yezhenedelnik,* No. 4, February 1990, p. 2; No. 8, April 1990, pp. 6–7; Aleksandr Annin, "Uzniki svobody [Prisoners of Freedom]," *Nedelya* [The Week], No. 22, 1990, p. 5; *Keston News Service,* No. 344, February 22, 1990, p. 11; *Novoe Vremya,* No. 7, February 9, 1990, p. 38; *Pravoslavny Visnyk,* No. 6 (June), 1990, pp. 30–31.

28. *Keston News Service,* No. 346, March 22, 1990, p. 5; Little, p. 64; Tataryn, p. 307. For specific churches on which the Orthodox reported that agreement was reached, see *Moskovski Tserkovny Vestnik, Yezhenedelnik,* No. 22, October 1990, p. 3.

29. *Moskovski Tserkovny Vestnik, Yezhenedelnik,* No. 8, April 1990, p. 6; *Komsomolskaya Pravda,* March 24, 1990, p. 1; *Izvestiya,* April 13, 1990, p. 6. Jane Ellis was reported to have questioned the Orthodox leadership's commitment to the March talks in western

Ukraine, noting that the patriarchate only appointed one delegate of "questionable character" to represent Moscow instead of the two delegates permitted it. The man in question was Metropolitan Mefodi (Nemtsov) of Voronezh. Little, p. 94 (note 27); Moss, p. 10.

30. *Keston News Service,* No. 346, March 22, 1990, p. 7; Little, pp. 94–95 (note 27); Keleher, "Church in the Middle," pp. 293–300.

31. *Moskovski Tserkovny Vestnik, Yezhenedelnik,* No. 17, August 1990, p. 7; Keleher, "Church in the Middle," pp. 296–299.

32. *Religiya v SSSR,* No. 4 (April), 1990, pp. 5–6; *Moscow News,* No. 6, 1990, p. 5; *The New York Times,* August 23, 1990, p. A7.

33. Institute of Sociology of the U.S.S.R. Academy of Sciences, "Analytical Report: The State of Interconfessional Relations in the Western Regions of the Soviet Socialist Republic of Ukraine," *Religion in USSR,* No. 10 (October), 1990, pp. 28(1)–50(23).

34. *Moscow News,* No. 24, 1990, p. 12; *Keston News Service,* No. 359, September 27, 1990, p. 2.

35. *Moskovski Tserkovny Vestnik, Yezhenedelnik,* No. 22, October 1990, p. 3; *Pravoslavny Visnyk,* No. 7 (July), 1991, p. 8; Hugh Pope, "New Spirit Abounds for Enthronement of Church Leader," *Los Angeles Times,* November 2, 1991, p. F16; Hugh Pope, "Orthodox Patriarchs Decry Vatican 'Proselytism,'" *Los Angeles Times,* March 16, 1992, p. A4. The participants in the dialogue did not wholly support the restrictions the Orthodox placed on the ongoing talks.

36. William D. Montalbano, "Ukrainian Prelate in Emotional Return to His Homeland," *Los Angeles Times,* March 31, 1991, p. A4.

37. The Russian Orthodox Church Abroad calls itself the Russian Church Abroad and also the Russian Orthodox Church Outside of Russia.

38. Patriarchal spokesmen were referring to overt parishes, as distinguished from the True Orthodox, or catacomb church.

39. *Moscow News,* No. 7, February 18, 1990, p. 5; No. 20, May 27–June 3, 1990, p. 2; *Moskovski Tserkovny Vestnik, Yezhenedelnik,* No. 7, March 1990, pp. 1, 6; *Zhurnal Moskovski Patriarkhii,* No. 4 (April), 1991, p. 34; *Religion in USSR,* No. 9 (September), 1991, p. 9.

40. *Pravoslavnaya Rus* [Orthodox Russia], No. 13, July 1/14, 1992, p. 10; No. 21, November 1/14, 1992, pp. 7–8; No. 23, December 1/14, 1992, pp. 10–11, 13; No. 14, July 15/28, 1993, pp. 11–13; *Keston News Service,* No. 343, February 8, 1990, p. 4; No. 368, February 7, 1991, pp. 4–5.

41. In the spring of 1991, the Council for Religious Affairs estimated that "about forty" communities had registered themselves as under the jurisdiction of the Russian Orthodox Church Abroad. *Religion in USSR,* No. 5 (May), 1991, p. 12.

42. *Orthodox Life,* No. 1, January–February 1992, p. 23. Bishop Valentin (Rusantsov) claimed 52 functioning church societies, 30 church servers, and about 100 monks and lay brothers and sisters in December 1992. *Pravoslavnaya Rus,* No. 1, January 1/14, 1993, p. 11. From *Pravoslavnaya Rus* for 1992 and 1993, I identified 70 parishes adhering to the Russian Orthodox Church Abroad with 49 priests identified by name as having defected from the patriarchal church and having passed over to Metropolitan Vitali's authority.

43. *Pravoslavnaya Rus,* No. 4, February 15/28, 1992, interview with Archpriest Sergi Kostarev, p. 15; No. 9, May 1/14, 1992, letter from Monastic Priest Vladimir (Ovchinnikov),

p. 12. A priest who adheres to the Russian Orthodox Church Abroad may bring only a small number of his parishioners with him and may not retain control of his former church premises. The result is that such priests often have to celebrate the liturgy in a small private apartment with a very modest congregation.

44. *Moskovski Tserkovny Vestnik, Yezhenedelnik,* No. 7, March 1990, pp. 1, 6; No. 23, October 1990, p. 1; *Moscow News,* No. 7, February 18, 1990, p. 5; No. 20, June 3, 1990, p. 2; No. 38, October 7, 1990, p. 2; No. 51, December 30, 1990, p. 15. See also Vladimir Moss, "The True Orthodox Church of Russia," *Religion in Communist Lands,* Nos. 3–4, Winter 1991, p. 246. Archbishop Lazar (Zhurbenko), who lives in the village of Veliki Dalnik, five kilometers outside Odessa, signs himself as chargé d'affaires of the Russian Orthodox Free Church. *Pravoslavnaya Rus,* No. 1, January 1/14, 1993, p. 11.

45. Bishop Varnava (Prokofiev) of Cannes and Bishop Mark (Arndt) of Berlin have been active organizing parishes and administrative offices in the former USSR and—at least for a time—accepting the obedience of individual parishes, in Mark's case German-speaking Orthodox communities. Bishop Varnava sparked controversy by appearing to accept support from right-wing groups, Pamyat among them. *Pravoslavnaya Rus,* No. 10, May 15/28, 1992, p. 15; No. 20, October 15/28, 1992, p. 7; No. 8, April 15/28, 1993, p. 15; V. Molchanov, "Vstrecha s Rodinoi [Encounter with the Motherland]," *Pravoslavnaya Zhizn* [Orthodox Life], No. 5 (May), 1993, p. 10.

46. *Keston News Service,* No. 343, February 8, 1990, p. 4; S. Yurov, "Zatyanuvshayasya istoriya [A Murky Story]," *Moskovski Tserkovny Vestnik, Yezhenedelnik,* No. 3, February 1992, p. 7. Incidents have been reported from the dioceses of Alma Ata, Moscow, Novosibirsk, Simferopol, Smolensk (Kaliningrad oblast), Tambov, and Vladimir. Father Gleb Yakunin has taken up the cause of Free Church communities subjected to official abuse. *Keston News Service,* No. 376, May 30, 1991, p. 8; *Pravoslavnaya Rus,* No. 9, May 1/14, 1992, p. 13; No. 8, April 15/28, 1993, p. 15; No. 9, May 1/14, 1993, p. 12. For a failed attempt to seize a Free Church parish in Oboyan, Kursk oblast, see *Pravoslavnaya Rus,* No. 6, March 15/28, 1992, pp. 14–15. On the other hand, Father Vyacheslav Polosin, chairman of the Russian Supreme Soviet's Committee on Freedom of Conscience (a priest of the patriarchal church himself), has asserted that the leadership of the Russian Orthodox Church Abroad "made a mistake" in refusing to deal with the Russian governmental authorities. Adel Kalinichenko "Chernaya Messa [Black Mass]," interview of Father Vyacheslav Polosin, chairman of the Russian Supreme Soviet's Committee on Freedom of Conscience, *Posev,* No. 2, 1992, p. 52.

47. See B. Lyubimov, "Moi dom—moya tserkov [My Home—My Church]," *Moskovski Tserkovny Vestnik, Yezhenedelnik,* No. 22, October 1990, p. 8. The synod of bishops of the Russian Orthodox Church Abroad declined to meet with Aleksi II when he visited the United States in November 1991.

48. *Zhurnal Moskovskoi Patriarkhii,* No. 9 (September), 1990, p. 32. The articulation and enumeration of these conditions have varied somewhat over time. Patriarchate spokesmen allege for their part that Metropolitan Vitali's people cooperated with the World Council of Churches until Moscow entered the organization, after which they branded the Council as a promulgator of heresy. *Zhurnal Moskovskoi,* No. 2 (February), 1994, p. 16.

49. *Keston News Service,* No. 340, December 14, 1989, p. 11; No. 346, March 22, 1990, pp. 4–5.

50. *Moskovski Tserkovny Vestnik, Yezhenedelnik,* No. 22, October 1990, p. 2. The abolition of the requirement for clerical registration was made in response to a request of September 7, 1990, from Patriarch Aleksi II.

51. *Moskovski Tserkovny Vestnik, Yezhenedelnik,* No. 4, February 1990, p. 4; No. 5, March 1990, p. 1; No. 13, June 1990, p. 6; No. 17, August 1990, p. 5; N. Demina, "Shkola sester miloserdiya [School of Sisters of Charity]," *Moskovski Tserkovny Vestnik, Yezhenedelnik,* No. 22, October 1990, p. 7; *U Nas na Yugo-zapade* [With Us in the South-West (District of Moscow)], No. 5, April 1990, p. 3; *Vechernaya Moskva* [Evening Moscow], February 20, 1990, p. 2; *Moscow News,* No. 12, March 25, 1990, p. 11. *Russkaya Mysl,* No. 4022, March 25–31, 1994, p. 9.

52. *Zhurnal Moskovskoi Patriarkhii,* No. 12 (December), 1990, p. 8; No. 1 (January), 1991, p. 10; No. 5 (May), 1991, p. 10; *Moskovski Tserkovny Vestnik, Yezhenedelnik,* No. 6, April 1991, p. 2.

53. Archimandrite Sergi, "Poslednie dni zemnoi zhizni svyateishego Patriarkha Pimena [The Last Days of the Earthly Life of His Holiness, Patriarch Pimen]," *Zhurnal Moskovskoi Patriarkhii,* No. 8 (August), 1990, pp. 22–25.

54. Jane Ellis, "Obituary," *Religion in Communist Lands,* Vol. 18, No. 2, Summer 1990, p. 188; Jane Ellis, "End of an Era?" *Frontier,* July–August 1990, p. 15.

55. KGB, "Documents," *Glasnost,* No. 13, December 1987, p. 5; John-Thor Dahlburg, "Cleric's Death Paves Way for Change," *East Europe,* Moscow Edition (*Los Angeles Times*), May 4, 1990, p. 2; O. Gazizova, "Moskovski pustynnik [Moscow Hermit]," *Moskovski Tserkovny Vestnik, Yezhenedelnik,* No. 10, May 1990, p. 7.

56. Gazizova, p. 7. Metropolitan Nikodim (Rotov) was the source of many of the tendencies Gazizova deplored. See also the comments of the composer Georgi Sviridov in the same publication on page 3.

57. Sergei Belavenets, "Pamyati Patriarkha Pimena [Recollections of Patriarch Pimen]," *Zhurnal Moskovskoi Patriarkhii,* No. 9 (September), 1991, p. 31.

58. Nezhny, "Sudba Patriarkha," p. 32.

59. Apparently, Filaret won out over Metropolitan Aleksi of Leningrad by seven votes to five on the second ballot. *Argumenty i Fakty* [Arguments and Facts], No. 19, May 12–18, 1990, p. 7.

60. Gleb Yakunin asserted that church rules had not been strictly observed in selecting delegates from some dioceses. Aleksandr Nezhny said that 50 percent of the council delegates should have been laypersons, as in 1917, rather than about 25 percent. Gleb Yakunin, *Sobesednik* [Interlocutor], *Komsomolskaya Pravda* Supplement, May 22, 1990, p. 2; Aleksandr Nezhny, "Election of a New Russian Patriarch," *Moscow News,* No. 23, June 3–10, 1990, p. 4. According to Jane Ellis, church leaders explained the convening date for the council on the basis that it would afford an opportunity to have the forty-day requiem immediately following the council when bishops and faithful from the whole country could attend as a sign of respect. Ellis, "Hierarchs and Dissidents," p. 314.

61. *Sobesednik, Komsomolskaya Pravda* Supplement, May 22, 1990, p. 2; Yu. Golubev, "I tserkvi nuzhno yedinstvo [And Unity Is Needed Even for the Church]," interview of Met-

ropolitan Filaret (Denisenko), *Rabochaya Tribuna* [Labor Tribune], June 5, 1990, p. 3; *Moskovski Tserkovny Vestnik, Yezhenedelnik,* No. 13, June 1990, p. 2.

62. Aleksandr Nezhny, "Pered vyborom Patriarkha [Before the Election of the Patriarch]," *Moskovskie Novosti,* No. 21, May 27, 1990, p. 4.

63. Maksim Sokolov, "Kto zaimet patriarshi prestol? [Who Will Occupy the Patriarchal Throne?]" *Kommersant* [Businessman], No. 18, May 14, 1990, p. 11; Filipp Danilov, "Novy predstoyatel Russkoi Tserkvi [New Leader of the Russian Church]," *Kommersant,* No. 22, June 11–18, 1990, p. 10; Aleksandr Nezhny, "Teper mozhno verit v boga, ne riskuya popast v lager [Now It Is Possible to Believe in God Without the Risk of Landing in a Labor Camp]," *Ogonëk,* No. 45, November 3–10, 1990, inside front cover. Danilov, p. 10.

64. Following are descriptions of candidates less likely to be elected than the three front-runners:

• Metropolitan Filaret (Vakhromeev) of Minsk was admired for his courage. As rector of the Moscow academy and seminary he had admitted a medical doctor at the time when the Soviet government was preventing educated persons from pursuing priestly vocations and had been removed from the rector's job in consequence. In Byelorussia he had moved to open churches during the Brezhnev era. In the several years prior to 1990 his activism had been thought to diminish, however. Sources alleged that he engaged in a bitter rivalry with Filaret of Kiev and Metropolitan Pitirim (Nechaev) of Volokolamsk to position himself for possible elevation to the patriarchal throne, and the rivalry hurt all three men. Furthermore, the Byelorussian Orthodox Church had just been declared semiindependent (as the Ukrainian Orthodox Church had been).

• Archbishop Kirill (Gundyaev) of Smolensk was a second candidate of the reformers along with Vladimir of Rostov. Kirill was highly admired but regarded as still somewhat junior in seniority. Sokolov, p. 11.

• Metropolitan Pitirim (Nechaev) of Volokolamsk, as head of church publishing, was popular "in the world." This was due, in part, to his physical appearance, as he has a magnificent white beard and impressive bearing. I heard ordinary Soviet citizens— after his television appearance on February 23, 1990—remark that he was a "saintly looking man." He was also described, however, as a "courtier bishop" of doubtful theological views. Sokolov, p. 11. Pospielovsky called Pitirim "one of the most conformist . . . of the younger generation." Dimitry Pospielovsky, *The Russian Church Under the Soviet Regime, 1917–1982,* 2 Vols. [Crestwood, New York: St. Vladimir's Seminary Press, 1984], p. 430. Furov characterized him as being in the loyal, patriotic, and not overly zealous category. V. G. Furov, "Cadres of the Church and Legal Measures to Curtail Their Activities: A Secret Report by the Council for Religious Affairs," *Religion in Communist Dominated Areas,* Vol. XIX, Nos. 10–12, 1980, p. 150. Purported KGB documents from the late 1960s quoted Aleksi as saying Pitirim authorized the spending of considerable sums of patriarchate money without appropriate documentation. KGB, "Documents," p. 5.

• Metropolitan Yuvenali (Poyarkov) of Krutitsy formerly had a reputation for activism and courage, but this had faded in the years since Brezhnev's time. Allegations, true or otherwise, of homosexuality did not help his cause. A former associate of the metropolitan, Hegumen Lazar (Solnyshko), was also accused of homosexuality after Father Lazar's murder on December 26, 1990. *Keston News Service,* No. 366, January 10, 1991, pp. 9–10; No. 369, February 21, 1991, pp. 2–3; No. 370, March 7, 1991, pp. 16–18; *Zhurnal Moskovskoi Patriarkhii,* No. 5 (May), 1991, p. 39 (for Aleksi's condolences to Yuvenali over Father Lazar's death). In February of 1994 Father Gleb Yakunin sent an open letter to the patriarch referring to the "sin of sodomy" in the episcopate, but he named no names. *Russkaya Mysl,* No. 4017, February 17–23, 1994, p. 8.

• Archbishop Chrysostom (Martyshkin) of Vilnyus acquired a reputation for courage in defending church interests, ordaining priests, accepting dissident clerics, and opening churches. Furov numbered him among the least "cooperative" hierarchs (Furov, p. 150). He was generally regarded, however, as too junior in seniority to be considered.

• Metropolitan Gedeon (Dyukin) of Stavropol was regarded as courageous, activist, and accepting of dissident priests in his earlier days as bishop. Furov numbered him among the loyal but overly zealous (Furov, p. 150). Reportedly he was Pimen's choice to be the next patriarch. E. Strelchik, "V ozhidanii Patriarkha [Awaiting a Patriarch]," *Vechernaya Moskva,* June 6, 1990, p. 4. He was not known for extensive experience in central church administration, however, and stood a bit off the beaten track.

65. Jane Ellis, "Who Will Be Next Leader of the Russian Orthodox Church?" *Keston News Service,* No. 351, May 31, 1990, p. 17.

66. Sokolov, p. 11; Nezhny, "Election," p. 4; Mikhail Karelov, "Na krayu Raskola? [On the Edge of Schism?]" *Sobesednik, Komsomolskaya Pravda* Supplement, May 22, 1990, p. 2. Nezhny made an indirect reference to Filaret when he wrote of "rich and familied princes of the church," but Nezhny's article appeared after the council had selected Aleksi (Nezhny, "Sudba Patriarkha," p. 32). The accusations against Filaret were not that he was a philanderer but that he had quietly contracted a civil marriage and had raised children. Filaret's wife's name was reported to be Yevgeniya Petrovna Rodinova and their children were two daughters and a son. To the world Yevgeniya was said to be the metropolitan's "sister" and the children "adopted."

After the patriarchal election of 1990, numerous other accusations were leveled against Yevgeniya in the Russian press, including "legendary greed" that reportedly resulted in her receiving 2,000 rubles every month from St. Vladimir's Cathedral. Allegedly she called "on the Cathedral's icon-selling shop in person" in order to "confiscate the day's takings." She and Filaret were said to require clerics to genuflect before her. Some explained her power as "by witchcraft and black magic." The accusations continued: "When their son rebelled against his mother's power, she accused him of stealing, and he was put in prison." Vladimir Ruban, "Moscow Wants to Subdue Ukraine Through the Church," *Moscow News,* No. 29, July 19–26, 1992, p. 14. Reportedly Filaret's daughter Vera arrived in Kiev from Latvia in late 1992 and circulated a press release describing her father's family life. Vladimir Ruban, "Vozmozhno, Filareta vse zhe 'uidut' [Filaret Might Have to Go]," *Moskovskie Novosti,* No. 41, October 11, 1992, p. 20. As a note of caution, it should be added that Filaret's authoritarian ways left him with a number of clerics and church workers in Kiev prepared to circulate derogatory stories about him, and some of the accusations may have been exaggerations or distortions.

Sokolov asserted that the Council for Religious Affairs supported Filaret for *locum tenens,* perhaps because of the vulnerabilities described. Filaret's relations with the council had sometimes been tense over the years, and Furov had listed Filaret as loyal but over-zealous in defending church interests (Furov, p. 150).

67. Danilov, p. 10; Sokolov, p. 11; Ellis, "Who Will Be Next Leader," p. 19. Seniority among the bishops reflects rank and date of episcopal consecration.

68. Later, Archbishop Chrysostom (Martyshkin) commented: "With his peaceful and tolerant disposition Patriarch Aleksi will be able to unite us all." *Zhurnal Moskovskoi Patriarkhii,* No. 10 (October), 1990, p. 16; Sokolov, p. 11; Danilov, p. 10.

69. Aleksi himself said that the Ridigers "apparently" came from Sweden in Peter the Great's time and then lived for generations in St. Petersburg as Russian Orthodox military men and jurists. See Ilmira Stepanova, interview of Aleksi, *Russkaya Mysl* [Russian Thought], No. 3958, December 11, 1992, p. 9. Reportedly, the Ridigers emigrated from Petrograd to Estonia in 1917. *Muskovskie Novosty,* No. 16, April 17–24, 1994, p. 11A.

70. Pospielovsky, *The Russian Church,* p. 392; KGB, "Documents," pp. 3–5 (meetings with Aleksi in 1967 and 1968). Besides his comments about Pimen (see chapter 5, note 15), Aleksi told an unflattering story about the embattled Moscow archpriest, Vsevolod Shpiller. The contemporaneous KGB reports on Pimen's conversations have Pimen doing more backbiting than Aleksi did. The question must be asked whether the purported KGB reports were authentic. They have the look of authenticity, but that does not necessarily mean that the KGB officers who wrote them rendered an entirely fair version of what Aleksi and Pimen actually said. Referring to the foregoing documents, Father Georgi Edelshtein went so far as to call Aleksi a "hardened stoolpigeon." Georgi Edelshtein, "The Election of a Patriarch: Crossroads or Dead-End?" *Russkaya Mysl,* June 8, 1990, repro-duced in English translation in *Religion in Communist Lands,* Vol. 18, No. 3, Autumn 1990, p. 269. Valeri Nikitin also noted Aleksi's record of collaborative statements, although his judgments are more balanced than Edelshtein's. Nikitin, "New Patriarch, New Problems," *Russkaya Mysl,* June 29, 1990, reproduced in English translation in *Religion in Communist Lands,* Vol. 18, No. 3, Autumn 1990, p. 272; Furov, p. 150.

71. *Zhurnal Moskovskoi Patriarkhii,* No. 9 (September), 1990, p. 28.

72. *Zhurnal Moskovskoi Patriarkhii,* No. 9 (September), 1990, p. 29.

73. A fifth prelate, the deeply respected Metropolitan Antoni (Bloom) of Great Britain (the Surozh see), was proposed but disqualified, as he was not a Soviet citizen. The four nominated from the floor were Filaret of Minsk, Pitirim, Yuvenali, and Gedeon. Fifty percent of the 317 votes were necessary for a candidate to be included in the final balloting. *Zhurnal Moskovskoi Patriarkhii,* No. 9 (September), 1990, pp. 29–30; Aleksandr Nezhny, "Pyatnadtsaty patriarkh [The Fifteenth Patriarch]," *Moskovskie Novosty,* No. 24, June 17, 1990, p. 4; *Moskovski Tserkovny Vestnik, Yezhenedelnik,* No. 13, June 1990, p. 3.

74. *Zhurnal Moskovskoi Patriarkhii,* No. 9 (September), 1990, p. 30; *Pravda,* June 9, 1990, p. 5; Nezhny, "Pyatnadtsaty patriarkh," p. 4. In an interview reported in July 1992, Filaret explained that his poor showing was because he "was not satisfactory to certain influential circles in Russia's leadership, as well as in the Russian Orthodox Church and in Rome, because they know I am a staunch defender of Orthodoxy and its interests. They made it a secret ballot for appearance's sake. In real fact Aleksy [Aleksi] had already been

appointed by certain circles. . . . The pressure was high. Men were standing at each polling box who told every voter to cross out Filaret and leave Aleksy." Ruban, "Moscow Wants to Subdue Ukraine," p. 14.

75. G. Alimov and G. Charodeev, "Faith Without Deeds Is Dead: An Interview with Patriarch Aleksi II," *Izvestiya,* June 16, 1990, reproduced in English translation in *Religion in Communist Lands,* No. 3, Autumn 1990, p. 265.

76. Danilov, p. 10; Yakunin, p. 2.

77. The first reading of the freedom-of-conscience bill in the Supreme Soviet was on May 30, 1990; the second reading was on September 26, 1990. The law was proclaimed and put into effect on October 9, 1990.

78. According to Kharchev, the Politburo decided in early 1989 that the new law had to comply with the Vienna agreements on human rights, concluded in January of that year; therefore preliminary drafts had to be revised. Six offices were given responsibility for producing the draft: the Council for Religious Affairs (with administrative responsibilities), the Ministry of Foreign Affairs, the Ministry of Justice, the Ministry of Interior, the Committee for State Security (KGB), and the government Prosecutor's Office. Nezhny, "Treti razgovor s Kharchevem," p. 9.

79. Letter of April 19, 1989, to Nikolai Ryzhkov, chairman of the Soviet Council of Ministers. *Zhurnal Moskovskoi Patriarkhii,* No. 1 (January), 1990, p. 12; No. 2 (February), 1990, p. 11.

80. Nezhny, "Treti razgovor s Kharchevem," p. 9.

81. *Moskovski Tserkovny Vestnik, Yezhenedelnik,* No. 7, March 1990, p. 1; No. 9, April 1990, p. 3.

82. *Pravda,* April 12, 1990, p. 2; *Moskovskie Novosti,* No. 17, April 29, 1990, p. 1; *Religiya v SSSR,* No. 4 (April), 1990, p. 3.

83. *Pravda,* June 6, 1990, p. 5. *Izvestiya* published the text on June 5.

84. On June 8, 1990, the national council of the Russian Orthodox Church (besides electing Aleksi patriarch) published a declaration about the draft law, listing desired changes. *Religiya v SSSR,* No. 8 (August), 1990, pp. 1–6. See also *Keston News Service,* No. 358, September 13, 1990, p. 12; E. Lisavtsev, "Religiya v pravovom gosudarstve [Religion in a Lawful State]," *Pravda,* June 14, 1990, p. 2; Nezhny, "Pyatnadtsaty patriarkh," p. 4.

85. *Keston News Service,* No. 352, June 14, 1990, p. 6; No. 359, September 27, 1990, p. 15; No. 365, December 20, 1990, p. 17.

86. *Keston News Service,* No. 377, June 13, 1991, pp. 4–5. The Ukrainian law preserved an administrative role for the republic's Council for Religious Affairs, facilitated the appeal of delays and unfavorable governmental decisions to the courts, and gave added freedom to a congregation to change its allegiance from one central jurisdiction to another.

87. *The New York Times,* September 27, 1990, p. A3; *Los Angeles Times,* September 27, 1990, pp. A1, A15; *Moskovski Tserkovny Vestnik, Yezhenedelnik,* No. 22, October 1990, p. 3. The text of the new law and a clause-by-clause commentary are provided in Giovanni Codevilla, "Commentary on the New Soviet Law on Freedom of Conscience and Religious Organizations," *Religion in Communist Lands,* Nos. 1–2, Summer 1991, pp. 119–145.

88. Nezhny expressed regret that the legislation had "no clearly formulated norms separating the government from atheism." Nezhny, "Teper mozhno verit v boga," inside front cover. Educational authorities were given until the 1992–1993 academic year to carry

out necessary curriculum revisions eliminating atheist instructional programs. *Keston News Service,* No. 361, October 25, 1990, p. 16.

89. Religious communities did not get the right to organize denominational schools for general instruction.

90. Jane Ellis, "Soviet Legislation on Religion: A Complicated Picture," *Keston News Service,* No. 365, December 20, 1990, p. 20.

91. National Council of the Russian Orthodox Church, June 8, 1990, *Moskovski Tserkovny Vestnik, Yezhenedelnik,* No. 17, August 1990, pp. 2–3; Ellis, "Soviet Legislation," p. 18.

92. The national council had also asked that the central church authorities have the right to approve the establishment of new church societies and the dissolution of inactive ones. *Moskovski Tserkovny Vestnik, Yezhenedelnik,* No. 17, August 1990, pp. 2–3; No. 24, November 1990, p. 2.

93. Nezhny, "Teper mozhno verit v boga," inside front cover; *Moskovski Tserkovny Vestnik, Yezhenedelnik,* No. 17, August 1990, pp. 2–3; No. 24, November, 1990, p. 2.

94. Nezhny, "Teper mozhno verit v boga," inside front cover; *Keston News Service,* No. 361, October 25, 1990, p. 16; Ellis, "Soviet Legislation," p. 19. The Ukrainian Council for Religious Affairs and some other councils have continued to function.

95. *Keston News Service,* No. 363, November 22, 1990, pp. 15–17; *The Ukrainian Weekly,* April 26, 1992, p. 2.

96. For efforts by Pamyat to participate in Orthodox public activities, see Natalya Davydova, "Road to the Church," *Moscow News,* No. 39, October 7–14, 1990, p. 4. According to Victoria Pope, at least one right-wing, anti-Semitic publication was even then using the Orthodox cross as a logo on its masthead while ranting about "kikes" and "Jew-democrats" in its articles. Victoria Pope, "God and Man in Russia," *U.S. News and World Report,* March 2, 1992, p. 56.

97. Nezhny, "Pyatnadtsaty patriarkh," p. 4; Anatoli Tsirulnikov, "Iz zhizni dukhovnoi shkoly [From the Life of a Theological School]," *Ogonëk,* No. 5, January 28–February 4, 1989, p. 30; Victoria Pope, p. 57; *Moskovski Tserkovny Vestnik, Yezhenedelnik,* No. 18, December 1989, p. 3; *Moscow News,* No. 43, November 4–11, 1990, p. 1; Esther B. Fein, "Soviet Conservatives Try to Turn Back the Clock on Gorbachev's Policies," *The New York Times International,* February 27, 1989, p. A3; Dunlop, pp. 304–305.

98. *Keston News Service,* No. 358, September 13, 1990, p. 2.

99. The program was put on by an organization named Detektiv i Politika [Detective and Politics], which puts out a publication called *Sovershenno Sekretno* [Top Secret]. Tickets were sold in theater kiosks throughout Moscow.

100. Valeri Nikitin credited Aleksi with being the first permanent member of the Holy Synod to state unambiguously, in 1987, that Christian morality had nothing in common with primitive anti-Semitism. Nikitin, p. 274. See also Danilov, p. 10.

101. Aleksandr Minkin, "Ne rydaite obo mne [Don't Cry for Me]," *Ogonëk,* No. 39, 1990, pp. 32–33. In an interview, Men's widow quoted the examining doctor as saying that the death blow was "professionally" delivered. Yelena Svetlova, "On Whose Conscience a Cross?" *Sovershenno Sekretno,* No. 6, 1991, pp. 1, 4, reproduced by *U.S.S.R. Today,* No. 929, October 16, 1991, p. 20. *Keston News Service,* No. 359, September 27, 1990, p. 4; No. 368, February 7, 1991, pp. 2–3; No. 371, March 21, 1991, p. 5.

102. Billington stated that Men's murder "now appears to have been sanctioned at the

K.G.B.'s highest level." James H. Billington, "The True Heroes of the Soviet Union," *The New York Times,* August 30, 1991, p. A23; Victoria Pope, p. 59. According to *Argumenty i Fakty,* No. 39, October 1991, p. 1, Men had documents linking church, Communist Party, Soviet government, and KGB leaders in his briefcase when he was killed, and the documents disappeared. Men's widow told interviewer Yelena Svetlova that representatives of Pamyat had come to see Men during the summer before he died. Svetlova, p. 2.

103. Carey Goldberg, "Gorbachev Says He's Ready for Emergency Rule," *Los Angeles Times,* December 20, 1990, pp. A1, A10.

104. Deacon Andrei Kuraev, in "The Russian Orthodox Church and Patriarch Alexis II: Views and Stances," *Religion in USSR,* No. 4 (April), 1991, pp. 6–7, wrote that the declaration spoke of "Muslim, Orthodox and Buddhist churches," which is a phraseology a senior Orthodox prelate would never have used. (Aleksi would have said "religious communities," or some phrase that did not refer to Muslim and Buddhist "churches.")

105. *Keston News Service,* No. 369, February 21, 1991, p. 5.

106. Degtyarev reported 10,868 registered church societies on June 1, 1990. Yuri Degtyarev, "Religioznye obedineniya v S.S.S.R. i ikh registratsiya v 1990 godu [Religious Societies in the U.S.S.R. and Their Registration in 1990]," *Religiya v SSSR* [Religion in the USSR], No. 6 (June), 1990, p. 23.

107. Yuri Degtyarev, "Izmenenie chisla religioznykh obedinenii v S.S.S.R. v 1990 godu [The Change in the Number of Religious Societies in the U.S.S.R. in 1990]," *Religiya v SSSR* [Religion in the USSR], No. 6 (June), 1990, p. 23. Degtyarev reported 11,118 registered Orthodox societies on July 1, 1990, 11,262 on August 1, and 11,940 on September 30. Deregistrations had almost ceased with only one deregistration in June, one in July, and none in August and September. Of the 1,830 new parishes (net) registered in the first nine months of 1990, *Novosti* reported that 1,179 had received church buildings transferred to them, 542 were constructing new churches, and 110 were buying or adapting buildings to church use. Degtyarev, "Izmenenie chisla religioznykh obshchestv v S.S.S.R. v pervom polugodii 1990 goda [The Change in the Number of Religious Societies in the U.S.S.R. in the First Half of 1990]," *Religiya v SSSR,* No. 7 (July), 1990, p. 19; Degtyarev, "Religioznye obedineniya v S.S.S.R. i ikh registratsiya v yanvare-iyule 1990 goda [Religious Societies in the U.S.S.R. and Their Registration from January to July of 1990]," *Religiya v SSSR* [Religion in the USSR], No. 8 (August), 1990, pp. 1–2; *Religion in USSR,* No. 10 (October), 1990, p. 53. See also *Zhurnal Moskovskoi Patriarkhii,* No. 3 (March), 1991, p. 37; Degtyarev recorded only 71 Ukrainian Greek-Catholic registrations at the end of July 1990.

108. *Religion in USSR,* No. 6 (June), 1991, pp. 3, 4, 35. Degtyarev's exact figure was 10,087 registered Russian Orthodox Societies, but the diocesan breakdown gives the slightly higher figure of 10,118. Mikhail Ivolgin, first deputy of the Council for Religious Affairs, gave slightly different figures for January 1, 1991: 10,267 Russian Orthodox Church societies, 1,912 Greek-Catholic societies, and 811 Autocephalous societies. *Nauka i Religiya,* No. 1 (January), 1992, p. 7. These latter figures for Greek-Catholic and Autocephalous registrations are the same as those given me by archivists of the Council on Religious Affairs.

Radianska Ukraina reported on November 4, 1990, that the Ukrainian Autocephalists had 1,043 parishes at that time, all but 10 of them in Galicia (western Ukraine). Little, p.

90. According to Tataryn, many of the Autocephalists in western Ukraine are former Greek-Catholics converted under duress to Orthodoxy in and after 1946 who joined the Autocephalists out of Ukrainian patriotism and disappointment over uncompromising anti-Orthodox sentiment among some Greek-Catholic hierarchs, over Vatican opposition to patriarchal status for the Ukrainian Greek-Catholic Church, and over Vatican opposition to a Greek-Catholic married clergy in the West. Tataryn, pp. 312–313.

109. Most of Table 7.1 is based on reports of provincial commissioners of the Council for Religious Affairs. Archivists of the Central State Archive of the October Revolution (now of the Russian republic) kindly provided me with photocopies of these reports, which cover about 75 percent of the parishes in the former USSR. In this connection I am grateful to Marina Rebrova of MITEK Information Services in Moscow and Julia Petrakis of Facts OnLine in Camano Island, Washington, for their help in obtaining these materials. Statistics on the remaining 25 percent come from citations that appear at the end of this note, conversations with clerics in the former USSR, and my own parish listings compiled over the years. Although these last statistics may not all be accurate to the last digit, my cumulative total, reached by adding all the diocesan figures, came to 10,118, which lies between Degtyarev's and Ivolgin's published totals. *Zhurnal Moskovskoi Patriarkhii,* No. 6 (June), 1991, pp. 37, 39; No. 8 (August), 1991, p. 25; No. 10 (October), 1991, p. 21; *Moskovski Tserkovny Vestnik, Yezhenedelnik,* No. 16 (September), 1991, p. 11; No. 1 (January), 1992, pp. 8–9; No. 20–21, 1992, pp. 1, 2; *Pravoslavnaya Rus,* No. 20, October 15/28, 1992, p. 11; No. 2, January 15/28, 1993, p. 16; *Religion in USSR,* No. 1 (January), 1991, p. 14; No. 3 (March), 1991, p. 18; *Sibirski Blagovest* [Siberian Clarion] (published Novosibirsk), April 1992, First Issue; *Keston News Service,* No. 366, January 10, 1991, p. 17; No. 374, May 2, 1991, p. 4.

110. A cleric at the monastery of the Caves in Kiev told me in 1989 that there had been more than 200 churches in the diocese before the Chernobyl nuclear accident but not more than 180 after the disaster. Rar gave a figure of 220 in 1973. Sabant gave "over 200" in 1979. Gleb Rar, "Skolko v Rossii pravoslavnykh khramov? [How Many Orthodox Churches Are There in Russia?]," *Posev,* January 1974, p. 39; Philippe Sabant, "Religion in Russia Today, Part II," *The Tablet* (London), Vol. 234, No. 7280, January 19, 1980, p. 55.

111. Patriarch Aleksi II (Ridiger), "K sobytiyam v Pribaltike [Regarding Events in the Baltic States]," *Moskovski Tserkovny Vestnik, Yezhenedelnik,* No. 2, January 1991, p. 3. Aleksi said in addition that the Soviet authorities had mishandled the talks with the Lithuanians.

112. Father Serafim was priest-in-charge of the Church of the Birth of the Mother of God on Chekhov Street in Moscow. Reportedly, he had demonstrated proclivities favoring the Russian Orthodox Church Abroad when he was serving in the patriarchal church's mission in Jerusalem and had become involved with both Jewish and Palestinian Arab groups there before his premature recall. *Keston News Service,* No. 366, January 10, 1991, pp. 9–10; No. 368, February 7, 1991, pp. 2, 17; No. 369, February 21, 1991, pp. 2–3; No. 370, March 7, 1991 (erroneously printed as 1990), p. 3.

113. *Moskovski Tserkovny Vestnik, Yezhenedelnik,* No. 2, January 1991, p. 9; *Zhurnal Moskovskoi Patriarkhii,* No. 6 (June), 1991, pp. 6–7.

114. Schmemann, "Patriarch's Church Revives," p. 2.

115. *Zhurnal Moskovskoi Patriarkhii,* No. 10 (October), 1991, pp. 4–7. Official statistics of

the Council for Religious Affairs were 119 registered parish churches in Tallin diocese in January 1961, 90 in January 1966, and 82 in January 1986. This was a lesser toll of church closings than in the rest of the USSR, but not zero. Pyukhtitsa had 129 sisters (nuns and novices) in January 1960, 107 (48 nuns and 59 novices) in January 1966, 105 in 1970, 144 in 1985, and 148 at the beginning of 1988. Tsentralny Gosudarstvenny Arkhiv Oktyabrskoi Revolutsii [Central State Archive of the October Revolution], Vysshikh Organov Gosu-darstvennoi Vlasti i Organov Gosurdarstvennogo Upravleniya S.S.S.R. [of the Higher Organs of State Government and Organs of State Administration of the U.S.S.R.], Soviet po delam religii pri Sovete Ministrov [the Council for Religious Affairs attached to the Council of Ministers], Fond 6991s, Opis No. 2, Vol. I, delo No. 263; Fond 6991s, Opis No. 4, Vol. I, delo No. 574; Fond 6991, Opis No. 6, delo No. 3131; *Jane Ellis, The Russian Ortho-dox Church: A Contemporary History* [Bloomington, Indiana: Indiana University Press, 1986], p. 471; *Moscow News*, No. 8, 1985, p. 13; *Nauka i Religiya*, No. 3 (March), 1988, p. 46.

116. For the text of Aleksi's remarks, see *Zhurnal Moskovskoi Patriarkhii*, No. 10 (Octo-ber), 1991, pp. 9–10.

117. Vladimir Moss, p. 248, quoting Priest-Monk Tikhon Kazushin.

118. Paul D. Steeves in *Christianity and Crisis*, reprinted in *Rapprochement*, No. 91-3, October 1991, p. 2.

119. This was reported to me by two people who were present at the Kremlin service. Michael Bourdeaux asserted that the patriarch omitted the petition in the litany for the Red Army. Michael Bourdeaux, "Patriarch Aleksi II: Between the Hammer and the An-vil," *Religion, State and Society*, Vol. 20, No. 2, 1992, p. 231. John Arnold reported that the patriarch changed "two or three words in the intercession to make it clear that the faithful were praying for the people and not for the usurpers." John Arnold, "Patriarch Aleksi II: A Personal Impression," *Religion, State and Society*, Vol. 20, No. 2, 1992, p. 239.

120. Paul D. Steeves made this statement in a presentation at the convention of the American Association for the Advancement of Slavic Studies in Miami in November 1991.

121. Kalinichenko, p. 53.

122. Vladimir Moss, p. 248; Steeves, p. 2; Victoria Pope, p. 57.

123. Mikhail Frankov, "Mysteries of the Holy Synod," *Moscow News*, No. 6, February 9–16, 1992, p. 16. Frankov was clearly unsympathetic to the Holy Synod and suggested that Aleksi was perhaps in a "minority of one" in the body.

124. *Mirror* (U.S. National Council of Churches), Special Issue, Fall 1991, p. 1; *Frontier*, September–October 1991, pp. 14–15.

125. Francis X. Clines, "Resistance to Soviet Takeover Grows as Defiant Crowds Rally for Yeltsin," *The New York Times*, August 21, 1991, p. A1; Russell Chandler, "A Russian Force Is Reborn," *Los Angeles Times*, September 28, 1991, p. A1; Richard Lacaya, "The Silent Guns of August," *Time*, September 2, 1991, p. 38. The *Journal of the Moscow Patri-archate* printed Aleksi's first appeal of August 20 and his second appeal, made at 1:30 A.M. on August 21, condemning violence, bloodshed, and fratricide. *Zhurnal Moskovskoi Patri-arkhii*, No. 10 (October), 1991, p. 2.

126. Billington, p. A23. After the coup failed, Aleksi gave the blessing at the funeral of the two Christians among the three young men who had been killed defending the "White

House." Celestine Bohlen, "Moscow Mourns and Exalts Men Killed by Coup," *The New York Times,* August 25, 1991, p. A15.

127. Aleksi called on the Supreme Soviet to dissolve itself when that body's dissolution was sought by Gorbachev and Yeltsin. Steeves, p. 2; Chandler, p. A1; Carey Goldberg, "Supreme Soviet Session Ends in Spasms of Guilt," *Los Angeles Times,* September 1, 1991, p. A6; CNN, "Excerpts from Soviet Congress: Time for Drastic Changes," *The New York Times,* September 3, 1991, p. A7; Serge Schmemann, "Gorbachev Back as Coup Fails, but Yeltsin Gains New Power," *The New York Times,* August 22, 1991, pp. A1, A10.

128. Father Gleb Yakunin called for a general strike in support of Yeltsin on Monday while Aleksi was still hesitating. He and other Orthodox priests blessed the defenders and prayed with the crowds at the "White House" during the hours of peril. Father Aleksandr Borisov gave copies of Scripture to those in danger and to the troops; only one soldier refused to accept the gift. Clerics under the jurisdiction of the Russian Orthodox Church Abroad also joined in the defense of Yeltsin's forces at the "White House." It was asserted that Father Nikolai Artemov, a priest of the Russian Orthodox Church Abroad, celebrated the first supplicatory service to the new martyrs of Russia on the balcony. Celestine Bohlen, "Coup Sets Yeltsin at Center Stage," *The New York Times,* August 20, 1991, p. A11; Celestine Bohlen, "Bare-Fisted Russians Plot a Last Stand," *The New York Times,* August 21, 1991, pp. A1, A9; *Frontier,* September–October 1991, p. 15; Alan Geyer, "Three Days in August: Reflections on the Soviet Coup and Its Consequences" (distributed by the John T. Conner Center, 1991), p. 7; Lacaya, p. 43; Billington, p. A23; Vladimir Moss, p. 248; Anatoli Leshchinski, "Congress of Expatriate Russians in Moscow and Its Religious Program," *Religion in USSR,* No. 10 (October), 1991, p. 7.

129. Homes for old people were multiplying. *Keston News Service,* No. 369, February 21, 1991, p. 13. The Russian Christian Democratic Union was opening a Christian middle school. *Zhurnal Moskovskoi Patriarkhii,* No. 1 (January), 1992, pp. 36, 37; No. 2 (February), 1992, p. 16 (official section). *Moskovski Tserkovny Vestnik, Yezhenedelnik,* No. 1, 1993, pp. 7–10, 12.

130. The thirty-three-year-old widely admired bishop of Kostroma, Aleksandr (Mogilev), was elected chairman of the youth movement. *Moskovski Tserkovny Vestnik, Yezhenedelnik,* No. 2, January 1991, p. 3; No. 3, February 1991, p. 2; *Zhurnal Moskovski Patriarkhii,* No. 5 (May), 1990, p. 20; *Keston News Service,* No. 341, January 11, 1990, p. 16.

131. The recently organized Orthodox brotherhoods and sisters of charity spearheaded distribution, as did many parishes. Apparently importation was impeded by Polish demands for transit payments from German truckers. *Moskovski Tserkovny Vestnik, Yezhenedelnik,* No. 3, February 1991, p. 9; *Zhurnal Moskovskoi Patriarkhii,* No. 5 (May), 1991, p. 15.

132. On November 12, 1991, Mikhail Ivolgin observed that the evangelical Christians and Baptists were then running 120 hospitals, 145 children's homes and dormitories, 95 invalids' homes, and over 130 labor retraining institutes. *Nauka i Religiya,* No. 1 (January), 1992, p. 6. The international establishment of the Salvation Army also moved briskly in relief assistance, in part because the U.S. government and others turned to it.

133. *The Way,* December 29, 1991, p. 6.

134. The Russian Orthodox Church was opening new parishes throughout 1991, but there were continuing losses in western Ukraine, coupled with the fact that official statistics were increasingly reflecting the situation on the ground. For example, Lvov oblast alone recorded a loss of more than 400 parishes in 1991. Ternopol and other western Ukrainian oblasts also recorded losses. Church openings compensated for these losses and resulted in a modest net increase in functioning parishes in the country. At the November 1991 Inter-Confessional Forum in Kiev, the figure of "about 5.5 thousand" Orthodox parishes in Ukraine was given (up from 5,031 in January 1991), but the figure was probably rounded up by Metropolitan Filaret and his people, particularly as the figure of 5,500 was also given for mid-1992, and only 5,658 was given for 1993. *Zhurnal Moskovskoi Patriarchii*, No. 8 (August), 1991, p. 25; No. 3 (March), 1992, p. 12; No. 10 (October), 1992, p. 12; Metropolitan Filaret (Denisenko), quoted in *Moskovski Tserkovny Vestnik, Yezhenedelnik*, No. 6 (April), 1992, p. 8; No. 9–10, 1993, p. 14; *Pravoslavnaya Rus*, No. 11, June 1/14, 1992, p. 5; Khristina Lew, "Church Split Continues to Plague Orthodox Faithful in Ukraine," *The Ukrainian Weekly*, March 21, 1993, p. 3; *Frontier*, No. 1–3, 1993, p. 33; *L'Avvenire*, quoted by *Keston News Service*, No. 371, March 21, 1991, p. 16; Dimitri Pospielovsky, "The Eastern Rite Catholics and the Orthodox in Today's Ukraine," *Ecumenism*, September 1992, p. 20. Even in mid-1993, the patriarchal church in Ukraine was still being described as having "over 5,000 parishes." Viktor Elenski, "Kievski patriarkhat: Zadachi opredeleny, no nevypolnimy [The Kiev Patriarchate: Tasks Defined but Not Carried Out]," *Moskovskie Novosty*, No. 23, June 6, 1993, p. B8.

135. On December 3, 1991, Myroslav Ivan Cardinal Lubachivsky reported that the Ukrainian Greek-Catholics had 2,176 churches (*The Way*, December 29, 1991, p. 4). Serge Keleher reported that by late 1991 about 50 church buildings in Transcarpathia (the Mukachevo Orthodox diocese) had also passed over. Keleher, "Out of the Catacombs," p. 261. The *Journal of the Moscow Patriarchate* itself reported (quoting *Patriarkhat*, the U.S. Greek-Catholic magazine) that there were only 160 churches in Ternopol diocese still under the Orthodox in the spring of 1991. See *Zhurnal Moskovskoi Patriarkhii*, No. 8 (August), 1991, pp. 24, 25.

136. Soviet government sources estimated that there were "over 1,400" Autocephalist parishes in the spring of 1991. *Religion in USSR*, No. 5 (May), 1991, p. 15. At the November 1991 Inter-Confessional Forum in Kiev the figure of "about 1,600 parishes" was given. *Zhurnal Moskovskoi Patriarkhii*, No. 3 (March), 1992, p. 12.

137. *Orthodox Life*, No. 1, January–February 1992, p. 23. Other sources indicated that by late 1991 "several dozen" parish communities, most in the Russian republic, had gone over to the Russian Orthodox Church Abroad. Leshchinski, p. 5.

138. Gazizova, p. 7.

Chapter 8

1. The figure of 3,500–4,000 churches lost to the Ukrainian Greek-Catholics and Autocephalists between 1989 and 1994 does not represent the total number of churches in those two communities. As will be discussed later in the chapter, there were also newly estab-

lished Greek-Catholic and Autocephalist parishes that had never been under Moscow's authority.

2. Oleg Kalugin, quoted by John Dunlop, "Three Leading Moscow Hierarchs Unveiled as KGB Operatives," *Orthodox Life,* No. 3, May–June 1992, p. 25. The Kalugin interview, by *New Times,* No. 38, 1990, is reproduced in *Religion in Communist Dominated Areas,* Vol. XXIX, No. 3–4, Summer and Fall 1990, pp. 86–89.

3. The Russian Supreme Soviet gave its investigators, including Polosin and Yakunin, access to the records of the "Church Department" of the KGB and in Polosin's case records of the Communist Party Central Committee. Dunlop, p. 26. Father Gleb Yakunin became embroiled in a dispute with his ecclesiastical superiors (Metropolitan Yuvenali administers Moscow oblast, where Yakunin was serving) because the church had denied Yakunin permission to run for the Russian Supreme Soviet. Subsequently Yakunin retired from the active ministry, although he continued to appear dressed in clerical garb. Some alleged that he went over to the Russian Orthodox Church Abroad. In the autumn of 1993, when Yakunin entered the 1993 political campaign, the Holy Synod formally deprived Yakunin of his priestly office. See Interfax, November 3, 1993, and *Russkaya Mysl,* No. 4000, October 14–20, 1993, p. 7. Yakunin has continued to struggle against what he described as the church authorities' unjust, illegal, and uncanonical measures against him. *Russkaya Mysl,* No. 4016, February 10–16, 1994, p. 9; No. 4017, February 17–23, 1994; *Nezavisimaya Gazeta* (English Edition), Vol. IV, Issue 20–21, March-April, 1994, pp. 10–11.

4. P. Vasilev "'Abbat' vykhodit na svyaz ['Abbat' Emerges as Link]," interview of Father Gleb Yakunin, *Argumenty i Fakty* [Arguments and Facts], No. 1, January 1992, p. 5; "Trete Imya [Third Name]," *Ogonëk* [Little Fire], No. 4, January 1992, pp. 2–3. Allegations were made that Soviet churchmen following KGB orders were also instrumental in organizing the election of Emilio Castro as general secretary of the World Council of Churches. See *Izvestiya,* January 22, 1992, and *Megapolis-Express,* quoted in Dunlop, p. 26.

5. Dunlop, p. 26; Aleksandr Nezhny, *Ogonëk,* No. 18–19, 1992, p. 12; Aleksandr Nezhny, "Mitropolit Filaret kak zerkalo Moskovskoi Patriarkhii [Metropolitan Filaret as a Mirror of the Moscow Patriarchate]," *Russkaya Mysl* [Russian Thought], No. 3936, July 3, 1992, p. 9; *The Way,* April 19, 1992, p. 4. Mefodi (as well as Filaret) was accused of unchastity and producing offspring. Chrysostom (Khrizostom) of Vilnyus was quoted as calling Mefodi "an officer of the KGB, an atheist, and a vicious person." In 1994 Gleb Yakunin publicly accused Metropolitan Gedeon (Dyukin) of Stavropol (see also chapter 7, note 64), Metropolitan Serapion (Fadeev) of Tula, and Archbishop Melkhisedek (Lebedev) of Yekaterinburg of being notorious former stool pigeons. He also publicly denounced the church's and hierarchs' former practice of providing "black funds" to the KGB with no accounting to anybody, least of all the faithful widows whose mite they had originally been. *Russkaya Mysl,* No. 4016, February 10–16, 1994, p. 9; *Nezavisimaya Gazeta* (English Edition), Vol. IV, Issue 20–21, March-April, 1994, pp. 10–11.

6. Dunlop, p. 27, note 9, p. 29; Serhiy Plokhiy, "News Analysis: Ukrainian Orthodox Autocephaly and Metropolitan Filaret," *The Ukrainian Weekly,* August 2, 1992, p. 5; *Ukrainian Orthodox Word,* No. 5, September 1992, p. 9; Fen Montaigne, *The Philadelphia Inquirer,* in *The Way,* May 3, 1992, p. 4.

7. Mikhail Pozdnyaev, "Arkhiepiskop Vilenskii Litovski Khrizostom: 'Ya sotrudnichal s KGB . . . no ne byl stukachom' [Archbishop Chrysostom of Vilnyus and Lithuania: 'I worked together with the KGB . . . but I was not a stool pigeon']," *Russkaya Mysl,* No. 3926, April 24, 1992, p. 8.

8. For an example of church periodicals denouncing the press, see O. G., "Ne zavisimye ot faktov gazety [Newspapers Independent of Facts]," *Moskovski Tserkovny Vestnik, Yezhenedelnik,* No. 1, January 1992, p. 7. On page 6 of the same periodical (and in *Argumenty i Fakty,* No. 51, 1991) Archpriest Aleksandr Shargunov asserted that from his experience only about one priest in ten collaborated with the KGB. The patriarch and the Holy Synod addressed a declaration to the media in late 1991 appealing for an end to slander against the church and the inflaming of hatred in the land. *Zhurnal Moskovskoi Patriarkhii,* No. 1 (January), 1992, p. 9.

9. Adel Kalinichenko "Chernaya messa [Black Mass]," interview of Father Vyacheslav Polosin, *Posev,* No. 2, 1992, p. 53. Yevgeniya Albats, writing in *Moscow News,* suggested that the patriarch called on Ruslan Khasbulatov, chairman of the Russian Supreme Soviet, in order to dam the flow of additional revelations. Yevgeniya Albats, "The Parliament KGB Hearings," *Moscow News,* No. 6, February 9–16, 1992, p. 2. Yuri Afanasev, rector of the Russian State University for the Humanities, asserted that Yakunin and Ponomarev "categorically" should not have been given access to the KGB files of church hierarchs. Elliot Mossman, "The Case of the Russian Archives: An Interview with Iurii N. Afanas'ev," *Slavic Review,* Summer 1993, pp. 340–341.

10. Zoya Krakhmalnikova, editor of the samizdat publication *Nadezhda* [Hope], survivor of the Siberian GULAG, and noted Russian Orthodox author, was also a powerful voice.

11. *Moskovski Tserkovny Vestnik, Yezhenedelnik* [Moscow Church Herald, Weekly], No. 6, April 1992, p. 4.

12. *Keston News Service,* No. 341, January 11, 1990, p. 16.

13. Mikhail Karelov, "Na krayu raskola? [At the Edge of Schism?]," *Sobesednik* [Interlocutor], *Komsomolskaya Pravda* Supplement, May 22, 1990, p. 2; Victoria Pope, "God and Man in Russia," *U.S. News and World Report,* March 2, 1992, p. 59; Mikhail Frankov, "Mysteries of the Holy Synod," *Moscow News,* No. 6, February 9, 1992, p. 16.

14. Ukrainian Orthodox Church Council of November 1–3, 1991, *Moskovski Tserkovny Vestnik, Yezhenedelnik,* No. 2, February 1992, p. 6.

15. The transliteration of the name of the Ukrainian capital preferred by Ukrainians has become "Kyyiv" rather than "Kiev." As explained elsewhere in this book, I have not attempted a direct transliteration of all Ukrainian, Moldovan, or other non-Russian names.

16. Yevgeni Komarov, "Samostiinost, Nezalezhnost i Avtokefaliya [Autonomy, Independence in Action and Autocephaly]," *Moskovski Tserkovny Vestnik, Yezhenedelnik,* No. 2, February 1992, p. 6; *Zhurnal Moskovskoi Patriarkhii,* No. 2 (February), 1994, p. 14.

17. *Moskovski Tserkovny Vestnik, Yezhenedelnik,* No. 2, February 1992, p. 3; No. 4, March 1992, p. 13. Bishop Onufri (Berezovski) of Chernovtsy (a diocese with more than 350 parishes) was moved to Ivano-Frankovsk (a diocese where virtually all the parishes have been lost to the Ukrainian Greek-Catholics and the Autocephalists). A young bish-

op, Ilarion (Shukala), was moved from Ivano-Frankovsk to Chernovtsy. According to a commentary published in *Orthodox Russia,* Ilarion was fiercely in favor of Ukrainian autocephaly and quite friendly to the Greek-Catholics (*Pravoslavnaya Rus,* No. 11, June 1/14, 1992, pp. 3–5). Bishops Sergi (Gensitski) of Ternopol and Alipi (Pogrebnyak) of Donetsk were removed from their sees and made vicars of Filaret. The father superior of the monastery of the Caves in Kiev, Archimandrite Yelevferi (Didenko), who also opposed autocephaly, was also removed. *Moskovski Tserkovny Vestnik, Yezhenedelnik,* No. 3, February 1992, p. 2; No. 4, March 1992, p. 13.

18. *Moskovski Tserkovny Vestnik, Yezhenedelnik,* No. 3, February 1992, p. 12; No. 4, March 1992, p. 13; Aleksandr Nezhny, "Zapozdalye molnii [Delayed Lightning Bolts]," *Russkaya Mysl,* No. 3929, May 15, 1992, p. 9.

19. *Moskovski Tserkovny Vestnik, Yezhenedelnik,* No. 3, February 1992, p. 2.

20. Bishop Lazar (Shvets) of Odessa supported Filaret at the Moscow council. *Moskovski Tserkovny Vestnik, Yezhenedelnik,* No. 6, April 1992, pp. 4–9.

21. *Russkaya Mysl,* April 10, 1992, p. 1; *Moskovski Tserkovny Vestnik, Yezhenedelnik,* No. 7, May 1992, p. 3; Plokhiy, p. 12. On April 30, 1992, a convocation of some bishops, clergy, and laity of the Ukrainian Orthodox Church was held in Zhitomir. Resolutions were adopted of "no confidence" in Filaret; the assemblage called for his resignation, although Bishop Yakov (Iakov) (Panchuk) of the Dormition monastery in Pochaev did not support the other bishops in calling on Filaret to resign and was divested of his episcopal rank at a June 11 Russian Orthodox bishops' council meeting in Moscow.

22. Plokhiy, p. 12; Aleksandr Nezhny, "Mitropolit Filaret," p. 9; *Zhurnal Moskovskoi Patriarkhii* [Journal of the Moscow Patriarchate], No. 11 (November), 1984, p. 19. In an interview after his arrival in Kiev, Metropolitan Vladimir (Sabodan) asserted that the Moscow council (March 31–April 5, 1992) supported the idea of Ukrainian Orthodox Church independence "in the future." Vladimir also stated that Aleksi II was consulting the ecumenical patriarch, Bartholomeos I, and the heads of other national Orthodox communities about granting the Ukrainian church autocephaly. Aleksandr Ginzburg, "I lyudi napolovinu nashi [And People Half Ours]," *Russkaya Mysl,* No. 3941, August 7, 1992, p. 2.

23. According to Vladimir Ruban ("Moscow Wants to Subdue Ukraine Through the Church," *Moscow News,* No. 29, July 19–26, 1992, p. 14), Filaret deftly altered the Ukrainian bishops' council rule that the head of the Ukrainian church "must be elected by all the Ukrainian bishops" to read that he must be elected from among the Ukrainian bishops. Plokhiy, p. 12.

24. *Moscow News,* No. 25, June 21–28, 1992, p. 2. Marta Kolomayets, "New Leader of UOC Greeted by Faithful in Kiev," *Ukrainian Weekly,* June 28, 1992, p. 13; Plokhiy, p. 12. After Filaret came under widespread attack, additional charges against him began to surface. For example, Serge Keleher reported that "sources in Kiev claim that Filaret diverted church funds for the construction of the enormous metal statue of a Soviet warrior which disfigures the skyline near the Monastery of the Caves." Keleher also accused Filaret of having discharged clergy for preaching sermons in Ukrainian—despite his own Ukrainian nationality. Serge Keleher, "A Fading Star," *Frontier,* September–October 1992, p. 11.

25. *Ukrainian Orthodox Word,* No. 5, September 1992, p. 8.

26. Marta Kolomayets in *The Ukrainian Weekly,* June 28, 1992, pp. 1, 10; July 5, 1992, pp. 2, 14.

27. Plokhiy, p. 12. The proposed union of Filaret and the Autocephalists threatened to leave one Ukrainian hierarch adrift. Metropolitan Ioann (Bodnarchuk), then Bishop Ioann, had proclaimed the reestablishment of the Ukrainian Autocephalist Orthodox Church in October 1989. Because of Ioann's alleged KGB links, Mstyslav never fully accepted him. Ioann's position was further complicated by his involvement with the Canadian branch of the Ukrainian Orthodox Church during a year's stay in North America for health reasons. The Canadian Orthodox Church, according to commentator Frank Sysyn, "has accepted the jurisdiction of the patriarch of Constantinople, thereby implicitly questioning the status of the Ukrainian Autocephalous Orthodox Church in Ukraine and the church led by Patriarch Mstyslav in the U.S." Frank E. Sysyn, "The Russian Sobor and the Rejection of Ukrainian Orthodox Autocephaly," *The Ukrainian Weekly,* July 26, 1992, p. 8.

On Ioann's return from Canada, the Autocephalists demoted him to ruling bishop of Zhitomir. On March 20, 1992, Ioann broke with the Autocephalists and returned to Filaret's jurisdiction. This was before Filaret's final break with Moscow. Sysyn, p. 8; *The Ukrainian Weekly,* April 5, 1992, pp. 1, 2.

Later, anticipating Filaret's move to unite with the Autocephalists, Ioann applied to the Russian Orthodox Church for forgiveness and reinstatement. The June 11 bishops' council asked the Holy Synod to study the matter, and the synod passed Ioann's case to Metropolitan Vladimir (Sabodan) and the Ukrainian bishops at its December 22–23, 1992, meeting. *Ofitsialnaya Khronika, Zhurnal Moskovskoi Patriarkhii* [Official Chronicle, Journal of the Moscow Patriarchate], No. 1 (January), 1993, p. 58. *Moskovski Tserkovny Vestnik, Yezhenedelnik,* No. 1, 1993, pp. 2, 12. Considering the question still further on June 11, 1993, the Russian Holy Synod decided that the case could only be definitively resolved at the next meeting of the National Church Council (due in 1995). *Zhurnal Moskovskoi Patriarkhii,* No. 2 (February), 1994, pp. 38–39.

Subsequently, Ioann and the UOC-KP were reconciled and Ioann became a member of that church's permanent synod and head of the Drogobych see. *The Ukrainian Weekly,* October 31, 1993, p. 10.

28. Vladimir Ruban, "Vozmozhno, Filareta vse zhe 'uidut' [Filaret Might Have to Go]," *Moskovskie Novosti* [Moscow News], No. 41, October 11, 1992, p. 20.

29. Keleher, p. 13. The September 1992 issue of *Ukrainian Orthodox Word* (p. 9) continued to assert that Mstyslav had "not yielded" to the pressure to accept Filaret.

30. *The Ukrainian Weekly,* December 6, 1992, p. 2; December 20, 1992, pp. 1, 9. According to *Pravoslavnaya Rus,* Ioann (Bodnarchuk) attributed his demotion in the Autocephalous Orthodox Church in 1992 to his opposition to Antoni (Masendich), who he said had usurped the title of metropolitan while not having the appropriate education and having been a priest only a year and a half. *Pravoslavnaya Rus,* No. 16, August 15–28, 1992, p. 16.

31. *The Ukrainian Weekly,* June 20, 1993, p. 1.

32. *Ukrainske Pravoslavne Slovo* [Ukrainian Orthodox Word], No. 9, September 1993, p. 10; *Ukrainian Orthodox Word,* Nos. 7–8, July–August, 1993, p. 4; *The Ukrainian Weekly,* September 19, 1993, p. 3; No. 43, October 24, 1993, p. 2.

33. *Ukrainian Orthodox Word,* No. 10, October 1993, p. 12.

34. *The Ukrainian Weekly,* January 16, 1994, pp. 1, 8.

35. "Uproar in Ukraine," *Mirror* (U.S. Council of Churches), Special Issue, Fall 1992, p. 5.

36. Vladimir Ruban, "Moscow Wants to Subdue Ukraine," p. 14; Ruban, "Vozmozhno," p. 20; Ginzburg, p. 2.

37. Keleher, p. 13; Vladimir Ruban, "Izvergnut iz sana . . . [To Expel from Rank . . .]," *Moskovskie Novosti,* No. 28, July 12, 1992, p. 20.

38. *Frontier,* January–March 1993, p. 33. It appears that the Ukrainian authorities counted all the Autocephalists as part of the UOC-KP, which would be consistent with President Leonid Kravchuk's political position. No separate listing was made for the Autocephalists opposed to Filaret. In the autumn of 1993 the UOC-KP claimed more than 2,000 parishes and 1,600 priests. The anti-Filaret Autocephalists claimed 800 parishes and 300 priests. The Orthodox under Vladimir and the Moscow patriarchate were credited with 5,500 parishes, a figure close to the number (5,658) they were credited with in the spring. Jaroslaw Martyniuk, "News Analysis: The State of Ukraine's Orthodox Church," *The Ukrainian Weekly,* March 13, 1994, p. 2.

39. Khristina Lew stated that 27 of the 5,490 Moscow-affiliated Ukrainian Orthodox parishes in August 1992 had passed back over from the Autocephalists. Lew, "Church Split Continues to Plague Orthodox Faithful in Ukraine," *The Ukrainian Weekly,* March 21, 1993, p. 3.

40. Ginzburg, p. 3. Sources in Kiev reported in December 1992 that about 350 parishes were registered as members of the merged church and 1,300 had yet to do so. Marta Kolomayets and Borys Klymenko, "UOC of Kiev Rejects Patriarch's Demands," *The Ukrainian Weekly,* December 20, 1992, p. 9. Ukrainian Autocephalous Orthodox publications and headquarters in New Jersey include Filaret's parishes, sometimes explicitly noting the fact and sometimes not. For the number of autocephalous parishes prior to the merger, see Kolomayets, "New Leader of UOC," pp. 1, 13; Plokhiy, p. 12; Ginzburg, p. 2; *Nauka i Religiya* [Science and Religion], No. 1, January 1992, p. 6; Bohdan R. Bociurkiw, "The Reemergence of the Eastern Catholic Church in Ukraine," *Ecumenism,* No. 107, September 1992, p. 18. Reportedly Filaret claimed that a quarter of the twenty churches in the city of Kiev and more than two-thirds of the faithful in the 433 parishes in Kiev diocese supported him. Aleksi II estimated in July 1992 that Filaret took only a few more than 100 parishes with him, whereas Vladimir had the support of about 5,500 parishes. *Zhurnal Moskovskoi Patriarkhii,* No. 10 (October), 1992, p. 12.

41. *Moskovski Tserkovny Vestnik, Yezhenedelnik,* Nos. 18–19, 1992, p. 6; Ruban, "Vozmozhno," p. 20; Ginzburg, p. 3.

42. *Pravoslavnaya Rus,* No. 4, February 15/28, 1993, p. 16.

43. *The Ukrainian Weekly,* September 19, 1993, p. 3; December 26, 1993, p. 7; Marta Kolomayets, "UOC Enthrones Patriarch Volodymyr," *The Ukrainian Weekly,* October 31, 1993, pp. 1, 10.

44. The figures were approximately 2,200 at the end of 1991; about 2,700 in mid-1992; 2,800 in late 1992; 2,800 in early and mid-1993; almost 3,000 congregations (and 2,200 churches) at the end of 1993; "almost 3,000 parishes" in the spring of 1994. Myroslav Ivan Cardinal Lubachivsky, quoted in *The Way,* December 29, 1991, p. 4; *Pravoslavnaya Rus,*

No. 11, June 1/14, 1992, p. 5; *Frontier*, Nos. 1–3, 1993, p. 33; *Moskovski Tserkovny Vestnik, Yezhenedelnik*, Nos. 9–10, 1993, p. 14; *The Ukrainian Weekly*, December 26, 1993, p. 7; April 24, 1994, p. 3.

45. I. Arefeva, "V shkole kak v seme [In School as in the Family]," *Moskovski Tserkovny Vestnik, Yezhenedelnik*, No. 3, February 1992, p. 12; Nos. 18–19, 1992, p. 6; No. 1, 1993, p. 12.

46. The Latvian Orthodox Church had been under the ecumenical patriarch in the interwar period. Moscow was expected to establish an ecclesiastical mission church (*podvore*) in Riga. Mikhail Bombin, "Sudba Pravoslavnoi Tserkvi v Latvii [The Fate of the Orthodox Church in Latvia]," *Russkaya Mysl*, No. 3955, November 20, 1992, p. 9; *Pravoslavnaya Rus*, No. 11, June 1/14, 1992, p. 12.

47. *Moskovski Tserkovny Vestnik, Yezhenedelnik*, Nos. 14–15, 1992, p. 2.

48. Bombin, p. 9; *Ukrainian Orthodox Word*, No. 10, October 1993, p. 13; *Pravoslarnaya Rus*, No. 6, March 15–28, 1994, p. 9; *Zhurnal Moskovski Patriarkhii*, No. 2 (February), 1994, p. 14. The Phanar, a quarter of Constantinople, now Istanbul, is where the ecumenical patriarch has his palace, and it has come to be the identifying location of the seat of the patriarch.

49. Bombin, p. 9.

50. Nataliya Babasyan, "Spokoistvie narushaet Rumynski Patriarkhat . . . [The Romanian Patriarchate Disturbs the Peace . . .]," interview of Metropolitan Vladimir (Cantareanu), *Russkaya Mysl*, No. 3961, January 8, 1993, p. 9. See also *Moskovski Tserkovny Vestnik, Yezhenedelnik*, No. 1, 1993, pp. 2–3, 12; Nos. 2–3, 1993, p. 3; *Pravoslavnaya Rus*, No. 2, January 15/28, 1993, p. 16.

51. "Protest Moskovskogo Patriarchata [Protest of the Moscow Patriarchate]," *Russkaya Mysl*, No. 3961, January 8, 1993, p. 9.

52. Babasyan, p. 9.

53. Dan Ionescu, "Metropolis of Bessarabia Reactivated," *RFE/RL Daily Report*, No. 245, December 22, 1992; "Tserkovnoe polozhenie v Moldavii" (The Ecclesiastical situation in Moldavia), *Pravoslavnaya Rus*, No. 12, June 15–28, 1994, pp. 11, 15.

54. According to *Religion in USSR*, No. 11 (November), 1991, pp. 21–25, there is a registered pagan community in the region of Nizhni Novgorod, headed by Chief Magus Andrei Rybin. There are also pagan communities in Moscow, Vasenevo (near Shabalino), the Mari Republic, the Baltic states and Armenia. Carey Goldberg, "Russian Pagans Find Roots in the Forest," *Los Angeles Times*, November 28, 1992, p. A10, A11; the archive of the Ministry of Justice of the Russian federation. Even more disturbing to the Moscow Patriarchate is the rise of "satanism." The man who killed three members of the Optina hermitage community at Eastertime 1993 was found to be a satanist under the influence of demons, black magic, unclean carnal passions, and the "666" sign. Also in 1993, satanists were reported to have vandalized a Kiev cemetary. In the spring of 1994 police arrested two satanists in Liepaya, Latvia; they had killed two people and reportedly planned to kill 664 more, to a total of 666. *Moskovskoi Tserkovny Vestnik, Yezhenedelnik*, No. 9–10, 1993, pp. 1, 4–6; *Pravoslavnaya Rus*, No. 19, October 1–14, 1993, p. 16; No. 9, May 1–14, 1994, p. 16.

55. *Zhurnal Moskovskoi Patriarkhii*, No. 10 (October), 1990, p. 18.

56. It was reported that 46,000 people publicly witnessed for Christ. The team helped found the Leadership Development Center in Ukraine under a Baptist pastor with long-

term U.S. staff support. Myron B. Kuropas, "Religious Pluralism Growing in Ukraine," *The Ukrainian Weekly*, April 26, 1992, p. 7.

57. *Frontier*, January–March 1993, pp. 16–18.

58. *Mirror*, Special Issue, Fall 1991, p. 11. Billy Graham's crusade enlisted 3,000 church communities across the former USSR in a year-long preparatory effort.

59. I attended services at the Crystal Cathedral in Garden Grove, California, on May 9, 1993, immediately after Robert Schuller's return from Russia. Schuller asserted that his television sermons in Russia might have been decisive in Yeltsin's April 25, 1993, referendum success. (I doubt this.) In a *Russkaya Mysl* article, Irina Ilovaiskaya defended the freedom of Westerners to evangelize in Russia, noting practically that television time in Russia is available these days to the one "who pays the most." Irina Ilovaiskaya, "Otvet na pismo professora Krasikova [An Answer to Professor Krasikov's Letter]," *Russkaya Mysl*, No. 3981, May 28–June 3, 1993, p. 9. Among the motivations of the Russian government in allowing Western evangelical activity is the desire for tourist dollars and the humanitarian aid some of the missionaries bring with them.

60. *Pravoslavnaya Rus*, No. 24, December 15/28, 1992, p. 16.

61. Irina Ilovaiskaya and Aleksandr Ginzburg described the April meeting with Yeltsin and the patriarch's confidential letters in issue No. 3976 of *Russkaya Mysl* (April 23–29, 1993). See Irina Ilovaiskaya, "Tserkov i gosudarstvo [Church and State]," pp. 1, 7; Ginzburg, "Vsya presidentskaya rat [The Whole Presidential Array]," p. 3. Anatoli Krasikov, the head of Yeltsin's press service, answered Ilovaiskaya, correcting her description of the April 20 meeting—at which Krasikov had been present—but conspicuously failing to address her assertions about the patriarch's letters. See Krasikov, "Tserkov i gosudarstvo [Church and State]," *Russkaya Mysl*, No. 3981, May 28–June 3, 1993, p. 9.

62. Serge Schmemann, "Russia May Curb Foreign Religions," *The New York Times*, July 16, 1993, p. A9; "Lawmakers Add to Defiance of Yeltsin," *The New York Times*, July 24, 1993, p. A4; *The New York Times*, August 28, 1993, p. A5; *The Way*, August 8, 1993, p. 4; Mikhail Gokhman, "Religiozny 'Sevastopol' [A Religious Sevastopol]," *Russkaya Mysl*, No. 3989, July 22–28, 1993, p. 3; Margarita Petrosyan, "Sovest: ponyatie geopoliticheskoe [Conscience: A Geopolitical Understanding]," *Russkaya Mysl*, No. 3990, July 29–August 4, 1993, p. 9; No. 4017, February 17–23, 1994, p. 8; *Moskovskie Novosty*, No. 19, May 8–15, 1994, p. 5; *Zhurnal Moskovskoi Patriarkhii*, No. 2 (February), 1994, pp. 11, 32.

63. V. Spasski (a composer), "Pochemu? [Why?]" *Moskovski Tserkovny Vestnik, Yezhenedelnik*, Nos. 18–19, 1992, p. 12.

64. *Moskovski Tserkovny Vestnik, Yezhenedelnik*, No. 4, March 1991, pp. 3, 6; No. 12, July, 1991, p. 8; No. 2, February 1992, p. 3; No. 5, April 1992, p. 7; No. 6, April 1992, p. 5; Vladimir Semenko, "Tserkov i khristianskaya obshchestvennost [The Church and the Christian Community]," *Zhurnal Moskovskoi Patriarkhii*, No. 11 (November), 1990, p. 36; Georgi Shevkunov, "Ne uchastvuite v delakh tmy [Do Not Participate in the Works of Darkness]," *Zhurnal Moskovskoi Patriarkhii*, No. 12 (December), 1989, pp. 44–47; Deacon Andrei Lorgus, "'Krugly stol' po aktualnym problemam tserkovnoi zhizni: Vozrodit zhizn prikhoda ['Round Table' on Contemporary Problems of Church Life: To Resuscitate Parish Life]," *Zhurnal Moskovskoi Patriarkhii*, No. 6 (June), 1990, p. 22; No. 1 (January), 1992, pp. 14–15. Articles critical of Jesuit activities in the former Soviet Union are also appearing.

See *Moskovski Tserkovny Vestnik, Yezhenedelnik,* No. 3, February 1992, p. 13; Serge Schmemann, "Patriarch's Church Revives, but Will Spirituality?" *The New York Times,* November 9, 1991, p. 2; Christel Lane, *Christian Religion in the Soviet Union: A Sociological Study* (Albany, New York: State University of New York Press, 1978), p. 63; Donald J. Raleigh, "The Triumph of Glasnost in Scholarship: Raleigh Reaches Saratov," *Newsletter,* American Association for the Advancement of Slavic Studies, Vol. 30, No. 4, September 1990, p. 1.

65. *Moskovski Tserkovny Vestnik, Yezhenedelnik,* No. 3, February 1992, p. 6. See also *Kuranty* of December 6, 1991. Ignati Lapkin of the Russian Orthodox Free Church told an assemblage at the Holy Trinity monastery in Jordanville, N.Y., that "everywhere among us icons of Nicholas II can be seen." *Pravoslavnaya Rus,* No. 23, December 1/14, 1992, p. 5. For the White Gospel of the Third Testament, see Aleksandr Soldatov, "Heresy of the Last Times," *Pravoslavnaya Rus,* No. 9, May 1/14, 1993, p. 5.

66. It is said that both Ioann Bereslavski and Petr Bolshakov were ordained priests and tonsured by Metropolitan Gennadi (Sekach) of the True Orthodox catacomb church and were consecrated bishops by Metropolitan Ioann (Bodnarchuk). Apparently Metropolitan Feodosi confirmed that the ordination and tonsuring of Ioann and Petr had been done under Gennadi's authority in a circular message of May 21/June 3, 1992. See Aleksandr Soldatov, "Heresy of the Last Times," *Pravoslavnaya Rus,* No. 9, May 1/14, 1993, p. 5.

67. Soldatov, p. 5; *Pravoslavnaya Rus,* No. 9, May 1/14, 1993, p. 5; *Religiya v SSSR* [Religion in the USSR], No. 10 (October), 1990, pp. 12–27 (renumbered as pp. 1–16). The center is reported to be officially registered as a trade union. Svetlana Kolosovskaya, "Khotya den Strashnogo Suda otlozhena, [Even If the Date of the Judgment Day Is Postponed]," *Moskovskie Novosti,* No. 16, April 18, 1993, p. 9B. The position of the Moscow Patriarchate is that the center is not Christian. *Zhurnal Moskovskoi Patriarkhii,* No. 4 (April), 1993, p. 47.

68. V. Sergeev, "Profanatsiya very, ili 'Velikaya Liturgiya' v klube 'Krasny Oktyabr' [The Profanation of Belief, or the 'Great Liturgy' in the 'Red October' Club]," *Moskovski Tserkovny Vestnik, Yezhenedelnik,* No. 7, May 1992, p. 6. For alleged Russian Ministry of Defense ties with the Mother of God Center, see Kolosovskaya, p. 9B.

69. *Moskovskie Novosti,* No. 16, April 18, 1993, p. 9B; No. 25, June 20, 1993, p. 3A; No. 27, July 4, 1993, p. B8; *The New York Times,* November 7, 1993, p. 6; *Los Angeles Times,* November 9, 1993, p. A7; November 15, 1993, p. A4.

70. Aleksandr Kramov, "Poka Patriarkh molchit . . . [As the Patriarch Remains Silent . . .]," *Russkaya Mysl,* No. 3941, August 7, 1992, p. 8. Earlier, Bishop Lazar (Zhurbenko) of the Russian Orthodox Free Church had actually brought suit against Aleksi for making his conciliatory remarks to the rabbis. *Moscow News,* No. 13, March 29–April 5, 1992, p. 2. Sergei Bychkov, "Voskresenie mifa [Revival of a Myth]," *Moskovskie Novosti,* No. 10, March 7, 1993, p. 7B; No. 12, March 21, 1993, p. 5A; Aleksandr Nezhny, "Sumerki soznaniya [Twilight of Consciousness]," *Russkaya Mysl,* No. 3987, July 8–14, 1993, p. 9; (continuation) No. 3988, July 15–21, 1993, p. 9; No. 4025, April 14–20, 1994; Gokhman, p. 3; Celestine Bohlen, "Cradle of Russian Revolution a Hotbed of Disgust," *The New York Times,* June 22, 1993, p. A3.

71. *Moskovski Novosti,* No. 5, January 30–February 6, 1994, p. B10; No. 8, February 20–27, 1994, p. B11; No. 14, April 3–10, 1994, p. B5; No. 16, April 17–24, 1994, p. A11; *Russkaya*

Mysl, No. 4016, February 10–16, 1994, p. 8; No. 4017, February 17–23, 1994, p. 8; No. 4020, March 10–16, 1994, p. 7; No. 4032, June 2–8, 1994, p. 16. Other modernist ideas include the reciting of the so-called "secret" prayers aloud, individual confession separate from the liturgy, lay sermons, and having the gates of the Holy Door (*tsarskie vrata*) remain open during the liturgy. In the February 1994 issue of the *Journal of the Moscow Patriarchate* (pp. 62–67; see also pp. 68–90), A. A. Pletneva presents practical arguments on both sides of the language issue, noting that most of the church Slavonic texts cannot really be traced back to Sts. Cyril and Methodius but that literary Russian has many links to the old texts that might be lost in a vernacular revision; moreover, translation into Russian without careful supplementary explanation would not always clarify the meaning of the liturgy. Advocates of church renewal included a number of clerics working in the Patriarchate's Office of Foreign Church Relations.

72. *Moskovski Tserkovny Vestnik, Yezhenedelnik,* No. 5, April 1992, p. 12. Metropolitan Antoni (Bloom) of London (Surozh diocese) also wrote sympathetically of the canonization while explaining why the Russian Orthodox Church had declined to take the same action. For a defense of monarchism, see Vladimir Moss, "The Restoration of Romanity," *Orthodox Life,* No. 4, July–August 1992. *Zhurnal Moskovskoi Patriarkhii,* No. 2 (February), 1994, p. 39 Metropolitan Juvenali (Poyarkov) has been attacked by nationalists in the church for his perceived reluctance, as head of the responsible church commission, to move toward canonization of the czar. *Russkaya Mysl,* No. 4016, February 10–15, 1994, p. 8.

73. For the Vladimir funeral service, see *Moskovski Tserkovny Vestnik, Yezhenedelnik,* No. 7, May 1992, pp. 12, 13. For the Yu. Pubach letter, see p. 9. See *Moskovskie Novosti,* No. 11, March 13–20, 1994; *Ofitsialnaya Khronika, Zhurnal Moskovskoi Patriarkhii,* No. 4, 1993, pp. 16–19; *Moskovski Tserkovny Vestnik, Ezhenedelnik,* 7–8, 1993, pp. 3, 5.

74. Serge Schmemann, "Revolt in Moscow: How Yeltsin Turned the Tide, Hour by Hour," *The New York Times,* October 11, 1993, p. A4; Michael A. Hiltzik, "Yeltsin, Foes Reportedly Reach Accord on Siege," *Los Angeles Times,* October 1, 1993, pp. A1, A8; John-Thor Dahlburg, "Russians Stand Together at Rites for Fallen Countrymen," *Los Angeles Times,* October 11, 1993, pp. A6, A7; Aleksandr Nezhny, "Nedeistvitelnaya anafema [Inoperative Anathema]," *Russkaya Mysl,* No. 3999, October 7–13, 1993, p. 19 (also p. 15).

75. Most of Table 8.1 is based on reports of local authorities to the Ministry of Justice of the Russian republic and the authorities of other former constituent republics of the USSR. These reports cover about 80 percent of the parishes. In this connection I am grateful to Marina Rebrova of MITEK Information Services in Moscow and Julia Petrakis of Facts OnLine in Camano Island, Washington, for their help in obtaining these archival materials. Statistics on the remaining 20 percent come from conversations with clerics in the former USSR and from my own parish listings compiled over the years. For reasons of comparability of statistics, Table 8.1 continues to list the 67 dioceses within the USSR functioning during the quarter-century between the Khrushchev antireligious drive and the Millennium. Since then, about twenty new dioceses have been formed, most notably in Byelorussia (Belarus) and east of the Urals. Including dioceses abroad, the Russian Orthodox Church now has more than 100 dioceses.

76. See Metropolitan Kirill (Gundyaev), "Address" (in June 1992), *Zhurnal Moskovskoi Patriarkhii,* No. 10 (October), 1992, p. 20. The metropolitan was obviously not speaking in

very precise terms. He said that the number of parishes had "doubled" in four years. In June 1988, however, the number of parishes in the USSR was about 6,800, which is not half of 15,000. In the autumn of 1992 the patriarch gave a somewhat more modest figure of "over 14,000 parishes." *Zhurnal Moskovskoi Patriarkhii,* No. 20 (February), 1994, p. 9.

77. *Moskovski Tserkovny Vestnik, Yezhenedelnik,* No. 20–21, 1992, pp. 1, 2; *Zhurnal Moskovskoi Patriarkhii,* No. 1 (January), 1993, p. 112, No. 2 (February), 1993, p. 109; *Ofitsialnaya Khronika, Zhurnal Moskovskoi Patriarkhii,* No. 2 (February), 1993, p. 6.

78. *Ofitsialnaya Khronika, Zhurnal Moskovskoi Patriarkhii,* No. 2 (February), 1993, p. 47.

79. *Zhurnal Moskovskoi Patriarkhii,* No. 7 (July), 1992, p. 37.

80. Statistics are explained in this chapter and in Chapters 2–7. For 1961 the figures of 11,571 and 11,599 appear, but Georgian churches apparently were included in the 11,599 figure. The 1963 figure is for August 21, 1963, as transcribed by Sergi Gordun (Sergi Gordun, "Russkaya Pravoslavnaya Tserkov v period s 1943 po 1970 god [The Russian Orthodox Church in the Period from 1943 to 1970]," *Zhurnal Moskovskoi Patriarkhii,* No. 2 (February), 1993, p. 20). The 1964 figure is for October, when Khrushchev was deposed. Tsentralny Gosudarstvenny Arkhiv, Fond 6991s, Opis No. 2, Vol. I, delo No. 263. A table of virtually all of these data up to 1961 appears on page 56 in the folio, but the documents are not a continuous text and are sometimes out of order. Similar data with a few additions are presented in Fond 6991s, Opis No. 2, Vol. I, delo Nos. 156, 180, 181, 182, 183, 206, 209.

The *Journal of the Moscow Patriarchate* published the archive's figures for 1946, 1947, 1949, and 1955 in its February 1990 edition, although the author, Father Sergi Gordun, failed to subtract the Georgian churches. In his article published in 1993 he caught his error. *Zhurnal Moskovskoi Patriarkhii,* No. 2 (February), 1990, p. 76. Sergi Gordun, "Russkaya Pravoslavnaya Tserkov v period s 1943 po 1970 god [The Russian Orthodox Church in the Period from 1943 to 1970]," *Zhurnal Moskovskoi Patriarkhii,* No. 1 (January), 1993, pp. 39–49; Gordun, *Zhurnal,* No. 2 (February), pp. 11–24.

81. Nezhny, "Mitropolit Filaret," p. 9.

Chapter 9

1. Figures for the 1914–1917 period, in territories encompassing the post-1919 USSR, vary between 50,105 and 50,960 priests with approximately 15,000 deacons and 45,000 psalmists and readers in addition. Paul B. Anderson, *People, Church and State in Modern Russia* (New York: The Macmillan Co., 1944), p. 159; John Shelton Curtiss, *The Russian Church and the Soviet State, 1917–1950* (Boston: Little, Brown and Co., 1953), p. 10; Robert Tobias, *Communist-Christian Encounter in East Europe* (Indianapolis, Indiana: School of Religion Press, 1956), p. 225; Serge Bolshakoff, *The Christian Church and the Soviet State* (London: Society for Promoting Christian Knowledge, 1942), p. 56; Wassilij Alexeev and Theofanis G. Stavrou, *The Great Revival: The Russian Church Under German Occupation* (Minneapolis: Burgess Publishing Co., 1976), pp. 7, 29.

2. *Soviet War News,* August 22, 1941, as quoted by Stanley Evans, *Churches in the U.S.S.R.* (London: Corbett Publishing Co., 1943), p. 88. The figures include Renovationist (mostly Living Church) priests, but most of these men soon returned to Orthodox jurisdiction.

3. For example, in Leningrad oblast alone, Soviet records for July 1, 1944, showed that fifty-five clergy had fled with the Germans, and fifty-three had remained to serve forty-six churches. Tsentralny Gosudarstvenny Arkhiv Oktyabrskoi Revolutsii [Central State Archive of the October Revolution], Vysshikh Organov Gosudarstvennoi Vlasti i Organov Gosurdarstvennogo Upravleniya S.S.S.R. [of the Higher Organs of State Government and Organs of State Administration of the U.S.S.R.], Soviet po delam religii pri Sovete Ministrov [the Council for Religious Affairs attached to the Council of Ministers], Fond 6991s, Opis No. 2, Vol. I, delo Nos. 12, 15.

4. *Zhurnal Moskovskoi Patriarkhii* [Journal of the Moscow Patriarchate], No. 11 (November), 1945, p. 20. In 1946 the Council for Religious Affairs recorded 152 Orthodox Church societies in Transcarpathia and 407 Ukrainian Greek-Catholic ones. Tsentralny Gosudarstvenny Arkhiv, Fond 6991s, Opis No. 2, Vol. I, delo Nos. 4, 180, 206.

5. Tsentralny Gosudarstvenny Arkhiv, Fond 6991s, Opis No. 2, Vol. I, delo No. 4, Sidirov report, pp. 1, 5, 6.

6. *Pravoslavny Visnyk* [Orthodox Herald], No. 9 (September), 1989, p. 21; Albert Galter, *The Red Book of the Persecuted Church* (Westminster, Maryland: The Newman Press, 1957), p. 97. The council's figure for priests was 11,846 (including Georgian Orthodox). Tsentralny Gosudarstvenny Arkhiv, Fond 6991s, Opis No. 2, Vol. I, delo No. 206.

7. Tsentralny Gosudarstvenny Arkhiv, Fond 6991s, Opis No. 2, Vol. I, delo Nos. 206, 263; *Zhurnal Moskovskoi Patriarkhii*, No. 1 (January), 1980, p. 19. On December 1, 1949, the recorded number of priests and deacons was 13,483, and the ratio of priests to deacons has held quite steady at nine to one in the postwar period. Therefore, 90 percent of 13,483 is about 12,000.

8. Tsentralny Gosudarstvenny Arkhiv, Fond 6991s, Opis No. 2, Vol. I, delo Nos. 4, 12, 13, 15, 16, 60, 74, 180, 206, 263; *Pravoslavny Visnyk,* No. 9 (September), 1989, p. 21; *Zhurnal Moskovskoi Patriarkhii,* No. 1 (January), 1980, p. 19. Scattered dioceses east of Moscow and along the Volga River also had modestly greater numbers of priests than parishes.

9. Tsentralny Gosudarstvenny Arkhiv, Fond 6991s, Opis No. 2, Vol. I, delo Nos. 180, 206, 263. The figure for priests includes all priests, including bishops. Eastern and central Ukraine collectively lost 200 priests.

10. In western Ukraine 1,300–1,400 priests were serving 3,000 parishes at the end of 1953. The figures for January 1, 1954, were 11,912 bishops, priests, and deacons in the USSR, of whom approximately 10 percent were deacons. During the three years between the end of 1950 and the end of 1953, about 450 churches were closed, and the deficit of priests remained virtually constant at 2,700. In the traditionally Orthodox provinces of western Ukraine (Volyn, Rovno, and Chernovtsy), 750–800 priests served 1,100–1,150 parishes. Tsentralny Gosudarstvenny Arkhiv, Fond 6991s, Opis No. 2, Vol. I, delo Nos. 74, 206.

11. Bohdan R. Bociurkiw, *Ukrainian Churches Under Soviet Rule: Two Case Studies* (Cambridge, Mass.: Ukrainian Studies Fund, 1984), p. 109; Dimitry Pospielovsky, *The Russian Church Under the Soviet Regime, 1917–1982*, 2 Vols. (Crestwood, New York: St. Vladimir's Seminary Press, 1984), p. 354.

12. In 1956 Georgi Karpov, the chairman of the Council for Russian Orthodox Church Affairs, stated publicly that there were 8,000 churches and 6,000 clergy (bishops, priests, and deacons) in Ukraine. The council's official figures were 8,540 churches and 6,030

clergy, 4,735 in traditionally Orthodox Ukraine and 1,295 in formerly Greek-Catholic western Ukraine. Ivano-Frankovsk (formerly Stanislav) had 235 priests and 3 deacons for 646 registered parishes; Transcarpathia had 196 priests and 1 deacon for 512 parish churches and 133 auxiliary chapels; Lvov oblast had 301 priests and 5 deacons for 613 parish churches and about 300 auxiliary chapels. In Kiev oblast 289 priests and 19 deacons were serving 348 parishes, a ratio considerably more favorable than in western Ukraine. Tsentralny Gosudarstvenny Arkhiv, Fond 6991s, Opis No. 2, Vol. I, delo Nos. 180, 206, 208, 260.

13. The city figure included bishops, priests, and deacons. Tsentralny Gosudarstvenny Arkhiv, Fond 6991s, Opis No. 2, Vol. I, delo No. 206.

14. Pospielovsky, p. 332; Nikita Struve, *Christians in Contemporary Russia,* trans. Lancelot Sheppard and A. Manson (New York: Charles Scribner's Sons, 1967), p. 320. At least a few of these 200 priests who defected had been KGB infiltrators, so their abandonment of their vocation could have been counted as a gain for the church. This would not alter the fact, however, that the gap between the number of parishes and the number of priests to serve in them was widening.

15. Tsentralny Gosudarstvenny Arkhiv, Fond 6991s, Opis No. 2, Vol. I, delo No. 263.

16. Tsentralny Gosudarstvenny Arkhiv, Fond 6991s, Opis No. 4, Vol. I, delo Nos. 572–575. The figures were 6,800 priests and 625 deacons. The Russian republic had about 450 more priests than parishes, and Ukraine had almost 1,300 fewer priests than parishes. A figure of 1,000 fewer Orthodox priests than parishes was published by Yefim I. Shekhterman, *Vera ili znanie* [Faith or Knowledge] (Alma Ata: Kazakhstan, 1967), p. 249.

The figures of the vice chairman of the Council for Religious Affairs were 6,694 priests (including bishops) and 653 deacons on January 1, 1967. This means that about 100 priests were deregistered during 1966. V. G. Furov, "Cadres of the Church and Legal Measures to Curtail Their Activities: A Secret Report by the Council for Religious Affairs," *Religion in Communist Dominated Areas,* Vol. XX, Nos. 1–3, 1981, p. 4; Tsentralny Gosudarstvenny Arkhiv, Fond 6991s, Opis No. 2, Vol. I, delo No. 263.

17. The figures were 5,166 registered priests in Ukraine on January 1, 1960, and 3,261 priests on January 1, 1966. Tsentralny Gosudarstvenny Arkhiv, Fond 6991s, Opis No. 2, Vol. I, delo No. 263; Fond 6991s, Opis No. 4, Vol. I, delo No. 574.

18. Tsentralny Gosudarstvenny Arkhiv, Fond 6991s, Opis No. 4, Vol. I, delo No. 574.

19. In Ukraine as a whole, 3,261 priests were in active service in 4,540 parishes in January 1966. Tsentralny Gosudarstvenny Arkhiv, Fond 6991s, Opis No. 4, Vol. I, delo No. 574.

20. I calculated the retirement ratios by recording each year of retirement I could find for a priest (usually from his obituary) in the *Zhurnal Moskovskoi Patriarkhii.*

Furov reported 8,252 priests in 1961 but did not indicate whether the number was for the beginning or the end of the year. If it was for the end of the year, the figure would be quite consistent with the ratios I calculated. Moreover, it is probably not for January 1, 1961, because that would mean that about 2,150 of the 3,600 priests deregistered in the Khrushchev drive after January 1, 1960, were shorn of their registrations in the course of the single year of 1960. This is unlikely, as the program of systematic review and selective registration of priests was only initiated in 1961. The number of priests in the USSR dropped by about 600 in 1959. See Furov, p. 4.

21. Furov, p. 4. In January of 1972, there reportedly were 6,180 registered priests, for a

loss of 54 in the course of 1971. Pospielovsky, p. 401. See also Paul A. Lucey, "Religion," *U.S.S.R. Facts and Figures Annual,* ed. John L. Scherer, (Gulf Breeze, Florida: Academic International Press, 1973), p. 318. The loss of an average of 60 priests a year over the four years between January of 1971 and January of 1975 is consistent with the samizdat underground report cited by Jane Ellis, *The Russian Orthodox Church: A Contemporary History* (Bloomington, Indiana: Indiana University Press, 1986), p. 84. The samizdat report indicated that 297 new priests were ordained during this time and 537 priests died or retired; the difference matches Furov's net total of 240 fewer priests. The samizdat report also indicated that these were figures for 1972, 1973, and 1974, but the figure of 240 fits Furov's figure of a decline of exactly 240 priests between January of 1971 and January of 1975, and the Furov report is probably right.

22. The annual decline between January 1971 and the end of 1974 was about fifty churches per year and about sixty priests per year. Furov, p. 4; Konstantin M. Kharchev, "Garantii svobody [Guarantees of Freedom]," *Nauka i Religiya* [Science and Religion], No. 11 (November), 1987, p. 23, translated in *Religion in Communist Dominated Areas,* Vol. XXVI, No. 4, Fall 1987.

23. Furov, p. 4; George W. Cornell, "Worship Under the Red Star; Part II: The Careful Clergy," AP report, *The Gettysburg Times,* December 18, 1984, p. 19; Lucey, p. 318; Philip Walters, ed., with Keston College researchers, *World Christianity: Eastern Europe* (Monrovia, Calif.: Missions Advanced Research and Communications Center, 1988), p. 44; *Moskovski Tserkovny Vestnik* [Moscow Church Herald], No. 7 (July), 1988, p. 3.

24. Archbishop Aleksandr (Timofeev) was reporting as rector of the Moscow theological schools and chairman of the patriarchate's committee on instruction. *Zhurnal Moskovskoi Patriarkhii,* No. 9 (September), 1988, p. 18.

25. Not all seminary graduates become priests. A few decline to be ordained, although some of these men continue to serve the church as professors and in other vocations. Some seminary graduates, particularly the numerous correspondence-course students, were priests before entering seminary and therefore do not add to the number of new priests. Moreover, some seminarians are foreign students, Georgians, or Armenians, who also do not add to the number of new Russian Orthodox priests. Although some graduates go on to the academy courses, most of these men are ordained sooner or later—either as monastic or parish clergy—and do join the ranks of priests. Overall, it would appear reasonable to estimate that about half of seminary graduates swell the ranks of the Russian Orthodox priesthood.

Archpriest Nikolai (Gundyaev), then the rector of the Leningrad seminary and academy, told a group of Americans (including me) in June 1986 that the three seminaries graduated about 250 resident students a year. The Moscow seminary graduated 84 in 1987 and 73 in 1989. *Zhurnal Moskovskoi Patriarkhii,* No. 7 (July), 1987, p. 30; No. 10 (October), 1989, p. 26. Odessa graduated 50–60 students throughout the mid-1980s; roughly two-thirds became priests at the end of the course, as quite a few students were already ordained when they entered the seminary. *Zhurnal Moskovskoi Patriarkhii,* No. 7 (July), 1984, p. 68; No. 8 (August), 1985, p. 20; No. 2 (February), 1986, pp. 40–41; No. 8 (August), 1986, p. 31; No. 9 (September), 1987, p. 30; No. 10 (October), 1988, p. 30; *Pravoslavny Visnyk,* No. 9 (September), 1984, pp. 6–7; No. 8 (August), 1987, p. 7; No. 8 (August), 1988, p. 10. According to Oppenheim, 90 percent of resident seminarians at Moscow are ordained upon graduation. Raymond Oppenheim, "Russian Orthodox Theological Education in the Soviet Union," *Religion in Communist Lands,* Vol. 2, No. 3, 1974, p. 5.

26. The number of obituaries the *Journal of the Moscow Patriarchate* publishes each year is close to 100, but its obituaries are not a complete roster.

27. Paul Miliukov, "Religion and the Church," Part I, *Outlines of Russian Culture* (Philadelphia, Penn.: University of Pennsylvania Press, 1942), p. 204.

28. Tsentralny Gosudarstvenny Arkhiv, Fond 6991s, Opis No. 2, Vol. I, delo No. 206.

29. Furov, p. 4; *Zhurnal Moskovskoi Patriarkhii,* No. 9 (September), 1988, p. 25; *Religiya v SSSR* [Religion in the USSR], No. 12 (December), 1987, p. KKh4.

30. About 40 percent of those with academy training earned *candidat* (roughly, master of arts) or higher degrees. Furov, Vol. XX, Nos. 1–3, 1981, p. 4.

31. From biographies and obituaries in the *Journal of the Moscow Patriarchate,* I have recorded priests who were identified as graduates of theological schools and those who were ordained after informal instruction. The geographic distribution noted in the text comes from these files.

32. Furov, Vol. XX, Nos. 1–3, 1981, p. 5.

33. Furov, Vol. XX, Nos. 4–6, 1981, p. 53. Some observers say that the authorities tried to bar western Ukrainian candidates for seminary training altogether.

34. Furov, Vol. XIX, Nos. 10–12, 1980, p. 153; Vol. XX, Nos. 1–3, 1981, p. 5; Vol. XX, Nos. 4–6, 1981, p. 52; Pospielovsky, pp. 464–466.

35. E. Komarov, "Zapadnaya Sibir: Budet li svoya seminariya? [Western Siberia: Will It Have Its Own Seminary?]" *Moskovski Tserkovny Vestnik* [Moscow Church Herald], No. 7 (July), 1989, p. 2.

36. See also the bishops' council decision of October 1989. *Zhurnal Moskovskoi Patriarkhii,* No. 1 (January), 1990, p. 11; No. 3 (March), 1991, p. 38.

37. *Zhurnal Moskovskoi Patriarkhii,* No. 4 (April), 1965, p. 44; No. 5 (May), 1965, p. 17; No. 3 (March), 1990, p. 46.

38. Metropolitan Vladimir reported that the church had 74 bishops, 6,674 priests, 724 deacons, 1,190 cloistered monks and nuns, and 6,893 parishes in the USSR and abroad. That would translate into approximately 6,570 bishops and priests serving in 6,770 parishes in the USSR. *Zhurnal Moskovskoi Patriarkhii,* No. 9 (September), 1988, pp. 14–15.

39. *Keston News Service,* No. 325, May 11, 1989, p. 10; No. 335, October 5, 1989, pp. 4–5; No. 374, May 2, 1991, p. 4.

40. Metropolitan Vladimir (Sabodan) of Rostov, "O sovremennom sostoyanii Russkoi Pravoslavnoi Tserkvi posle prinyatiya novogo Ustava [About the Contemporary Situation of the Russian Orthodox Church After the Adoption of the New Statute]," *Zhurnal Moskovskoi Patriarkhii,* No. 2 (February), 1990, p. 9.

41. See *Keston News Service,* No. 341, January 11, 1990, pp. 21–22; No. 342, January 25, 1990, p. 17; No. 347, April 5, 1990, p. 8. In the spring of 1991 the Greek-Catholics were reported by Soviet government sources to have 720 priests (including both those who had served in Orthodox churches and those who had been in the catacomb Greek-Catholic church). *Religion in USSR,* No. 6 (June), 1991, p. 26.

42. In November 1990 the Novosti Press Agency reported 3,720 priests serving 6,505

parishes in Ukraine. This would indicate a continuing deficit of approximately 2,800 priests. *Religion in USSR*, No. 11 (November), 1990, p. 39 (p. 4 in the separately numbered article). The number of Ukrainian priests failed to reflect defections to the Ukrainian Greek-Catholics and Ukrainian Autocephalists.

43. *Zhurnal Moskovskoi Patriarkhii*, No. 9 (September), 1988, p. 15; No. 2 (February), 1990, p. 12. The church organized a pension committee in 1948 for priests, deacons, and a few others and expanded eligibility in 1970 to all employees of church offices, monasteries, theological schools, and shops making religious objects. In case of the death or the invalid condition of the breadwinner, widows, orphans, and incapacitated family members also became eligible to receive support. *Zhurnal Moskovskoi Patriarkhii*, No. 7 (July), 1971, p. 17; No. 1 (January), 1979, p. 13. See also Metropolitan Vladimir (Sabodan), "Sovremennoe sostoyanie Russkoi Pravoslavnoi Tserkvi" [The Present State of the Russian Orthodox Church], *Religiya v SSSR*, No. 10 (October), 1988, p. MV9.

44. Francis House, *The Russian Phoenix* (London: SPCK, 1988), p. 81.

45. A. Semenov, "Zhivoi ukor [A Living Reproach]," *Moskovski Tserkovny Vestnik, Yezhenedelnik* [Moscow Church Herald, Weekly], No. 23, October 1990, p. 4.

46. *U Nas na Yugo-zapade* [With Us in the South-West (District of Moscow)], No. 5, April 1990, p. 3. Archpriest Georgi Studenov was commuting from Zagorsk to St. Michael the Archangel Church in Moscow (Troparevo).

47. Konstantin M. Kharchev, "Religiya i perestroika [Religion and Perestroika]," speech to Higher Party School instructors, Moscow, March 1988 (transcribed by memory and abridged), *Russkaya Mysl* [Russian Thought], No. 3725, May 20, 1988, p. 4.

48. Kirill Golovin (pseudonym), "The Day Will Come . . . ," *The Samizdat Bulletin*, No. 174, October 1987, p. 11.

49. Deacon Andrei Lorgus, "Prikhodskaya zhizn: Tolko v ograde Khrama? [Parish Life: Only Within the Fence of the Church?]," interview of Archpriest Vladimir Rozhkov, *Zhurnal Moskovskoi Patriarkhii*, No. 6 (June), 1990, p. 20.

50. Kenneth L. Woodward and Rod Norland, "The Pope and the Pol," *Newsweek*, December 4, 1989, p. 90; Michael Bourdeaux, *Opium of the People* (Indianapolis, Indiana: The Bobbs-Merrill Co., 1966), pp. 73, 81; A. Makarov, "Put k vozrozhdeniyu [The Path to Revival]," *Moskovski Tserkovny Vestnik, Yezhenedelnik*, No. 1, January 1990, p. 3.

51. *Moscow News*, No. 41, October 21–28, 1990, p. 5.

52. Source data for the number of churches, or registered Orthodox parishes, are explained in Chapter 8, notes 75 and 80. Citations of sources for the number of priests are contained in this chapter, notes 3, 4, 6, 7, 8, 9, 10, 12, 15, 16, 20, 21, 22, 38, 40, and 42.

Chapter 10

1. Francis House, *The Russian Phoenix* (London: SPCK, 1988), pp. 91–92. House's figure of 48 million apparently was derived from a reported lecture in 1972–1973 by E. N. Klimov, an inspector of the Central Committee of the Communist Party of the Soviet Union. See Dimitry Pospielovsky, *The Russian Church Under the Soviet Regime, 1917–1982*, 2 Vols. (Crestwood, New York: St. Vladimir's Seminary Press, 1984), p. 374.

2. Nataliya Izyumova, "Russian Orthodox Church: Road to Rebirth," *Moscow News*,

No. 24, June 24–July 1, 1990, p. 15. Father Sergei Zheludkov, the indomitable Orthodox priest from Pskov who died in 1984, took Popov's position, characterizing an effective attempt to go underground as "unthinkable under a regime of this kind." See Trevor Beeson, *Discretion and Valor* (Philadelphia, Penn.: Fortress Press, 1974 and 1982), p. 78. Ludmilla Alexeyeva, in *Soviet Dissent: Contemporary Movements for National, Religious and Human Rights* (Middletown, Conn.: Wesleyan University Press, 1985), p. 11, expressed a similar view: "Members of contemporary secret organizations could be saved from the KGB only through complete inactivity. None of the known underground organizations managed to survive for more than two years [in conditions of extreme persecution]."

3. Wassilij Alexeev, *Russian Orthodox Bishops in the Soviet Union, 1941–1953*, text in Russian (New York: Research Program on the USSR, Mimeographed Series No. 61, 1954), p. 82.

4. *Zhurnal Moskovskoi Patriarkhii* [Journal of the Moscow Patriarchate], No. 12 (December), 1944, p. 7; No. 2 (February), 1945, p. 13; No. 4 (April), 1945, p. 3; No. 3 (March), 1947, p. 53; No. 2 (February), 1948, pp. 65–66; No. 5 (May), 1950, p. 12.

5. Jane Ellis, *The Russian Orthodox Church: A Contemporary History* (Bloomington, Indiana: Indiana University Press, 1986), p. 448.

6. Christel Lane, *Christian Religion in the Soviet Union: A Sociological Study* (Albany, New York: State University of New York Press, 1978), p. 42.

7. William C. Fletcher, *The Russian Orthodox Church Underground, 1917–1970* (London: Oxford University Press, 1971), p. 264.

8. Official Soviet statistics recorded that 130,067 of the 244,180 funerals conducted in Ukraine in 1985 were "by correspondence." In four provinces of Siberia and the Pacific maritime territories, 16,578 of 17,417 funerals in 1985 were by correspondence. In the northern Caucasus 28,452 of 30,883 funerals in 1985 were by correspondence. Tsentralny Gosudarstvenny Arkhiv Oktyabrskoi Revolutsii [Central State Archive of the October Revolution], Vysshikh Organov Gosudarstvennoi Vlasti i Organov Gosurdarstvennogo Upravleniya S.S.S.R. [of the Higher Organs of State Government and Organs of State Administration of the U.S.S.R.], Soviet po delam religii pri Sovete Ministrov [the Council for Religious Affairs attached to the Council of Ministers], Fond 6991, Opis No. 6, delo Nos. 3131, 3132.

9. M. K. Teplyakov, *Problemy ateisticheskogo vospitaniya v praktike partinoi raboty* [Problems of Atheist Education in Practice in Party Work] (Voronezh: Voronezh University Press, 1972), p. 152. Pospielovsky, p. 383, quoted a 1970 samizdat document of the catacomb church as including in the "catacombs" pastorally conscientious priests of the regular patriarchal church.

10. Nathaniel Davis, *Religious Collaboration and Resistance in the Communist World* (research paper submitted to Professor Philip E. Mosely, the Russian Institute, Columbia University, 1954), pp. 67, 68. See also Nathaniel Davis, *Religion and Communist Government in the Soviet Union and Eastern Europe,* dissertation, the Fletcher School of Law and Diplomacy, June 1, 1960, Appendix B.

11. Pospielovsky, pp. 375–376; House, p. 92; V. G. Furov, "Cadres of the Church and Legal Measures to Curtail Their Activities: A Secret Report by the Council for Religious Affairs," *Religion in Communist Dominated Areas*, Vol. XX, Nos. 4–6, 1981, p. 63.

12. Tsentralny Gosudarstvenny Arkhiv, Fond 6991s, Opis No. 2, Vol. I, delo Nos. 12, 15, 20, 70.

13. Drawing from official records of the USSR Council for Russian Orthodox Church Affairs, Father Sergi Gordun noted that local commissioners reported 783 unregistered Orthodox societies functioning illegally on January 1, 1962. Commissioners reported 672 such religious communities in the Russian republic, 89 in Ukraine, 17 in Kazakhstan, and 5 elsewhere. Internal documents indicate the council planned to have commissioners in each oblast approach local authorities and urge them to crack down, which implies that commissioners and local authorities were aware of the illegal activity but not doing much about it.

Sergi Gordun, "Russkaya Pravoslavnaya Tserkov v period s 1943 po 1970 god [The Russian Orthodox Church in the Period from 1943 to 1970]," *Zhurnal Moskovskoi Patriarkhii*, No. 2 (February), 1993, pp. 20–21. See also Igor Achildiev, "Zaboty upolnomochennogo Gubina [Anxieties of Commissioner Gubin]," interview of Mikhail V. Gubin, *Nauka i Religiya* [Science and Religion], No. 2 (February), 1988, pp. 23–25.

14. *Spravochnik propagandista i agitatora* [The Handbook of the Propagandist and Agitator] (Moscow: Izdatelstvo Politicheskoi Literatury [The Press for Political Literature], 1966), p. 150.

15. Konstantin M. Kharchev, "Religiya i perestroika [Religion and Perestroika]," speech to instructors of the Higher Party School, Moscow, end of March 1988 (transcribed by memory and abridged), *Russkaya Mysl* [Russian Thought], No. 3725, May 20, 1988, p. 4. For official knowledge of unauthorized religion in earlier times, see Merle Fainsod, *Smolensk Under Soviet Rule* (Cambridge, Mass.: Harvard University Press, 1958), p. 441; H. Petrus (pseudonym), *Religious Communes in the U.S.S.R.*, text in Russian (New York: Research Program on the U.S.S.R., Mimeograph Series No. 44, 1953), pp. 10–13, 22–24 and 38–42; Pierre Van Paasen, *Visions Rise and Change* (New York: The Dial Press, 1955), p. 198; E. Telyakovski, "Tserkov v nastoyashchee vremya [The Church in the Current Time]," *Antireligioznik* [The Antireligionist], February 1940, p. 24.

16. Father Petr Bolshakov, "The True Orthodox Church," *Religion in USSR*, No. 10 (October), 1990, p. 6.

17. *Zhurnal Moskovskoi Patriarkhii*, No. 6 (June), 1984, p. 33; No. 2 (February), 1985, pp. 34–35; No. 7 (July), 1990, p. 43.

18. See also Davis, *Religion and Communist Government*, pp. 269–270.

19. Ellis, p. 403.

20. Fletcher, pp. 133–143; John H. Noble, *I Found God in Soviet Russia* (New York: St. Martin's Press, 1959), pp. 107, 119–122, 129, 144–145, 190.

21. Olga Carlisle, "A Voice from the Third Russian Emigration," *The New York Times Book Review*, October 30, 1977, p. 50.

22. Dimitry V. Pospielovsky, *Soviet Studies on the Church and the Believer's Response to Atheism*, Vol. 3 of *A History of Soviet Atheism in Theory and Practice and the Believer* (New York: St. Martin's Press, 1988), pp. 231–232.

23. Fletcher, p. 141, quoting Dimitry Konstantinov.

24. Fletcher, p. 139.

25. Fletcher, p. 128.

26. Noble, p. 129; Fletcher, pp. 129, 138–139.

27. This was true not only in the contrast between the situation and activities of the religious communities in the old heartland of the USSR and the western lands but also in the contrast between religious life in the USSR and in the communist states of Eastern Europe after World War II. See Davis, *Religion and Communist Government,* pp. 152–175, 342–356.

28. A published Soviet sociological study of the Komi Autonomous Republic in 1967 found this to be true in notable degree. Fletcher, p. 226. See also Pospielovsky, *The Russian Church,* pp. 376–377.

29. The sensational trial of the True Orthodox Christian Wanderers in Alma Ata in 1963 revealed much about their coordination, leadership, and lateral communications. See Fletcher, pp. 180–229, 246–247.

30. Fletcher, pp. 197, 201, 275; Lane, pp. 82–90.

31. Fletcher, pp. 278–279, 284.

32. Fletcher, pp. 217–218; Lane, p. 87.

33. Fletcher, pp. 201–202.

34. Fletcher, pp. 184, 195, 214, 219, 225–226, 230–233, 235, 250, 278–280, 282–285; Lane, pp. 83–90; Pospielovsky, *The Russian Church,* p. 373. For discussion of True Orthodox women in the labor camps, see the December 1974 issue of *The Chronicle of Current Events,* quoted by John B. Dunlop, "The Contemporary Russian Orthodox Church," *Oberlin Alumni Magazine,* September–October 1976, p. 18.

The Khlysty (Flagellants in English) reject this appellation, calling themselves "Men of God." Khlysty is, nevertheless, what most people have long called them, as their secret, frenzied midnight dances, often in the deep woods, are accompanied by flagellation. Popular perception of them holds that these dances frequently evolve into sexual orgies and sacrificial rites, despite the sect members' vows of sexual abstinence. Gregory Rasputin was alleged to have been attracted to and influenced by the Khlysty. Their doctrine includes spiritual ecstasy, and their practice involves trances, fasts, and poetic songs. A member of the sect who succeeds in receiving the Spirit in full measure becomes a Christ, a God Zebaoth, or a Mother of God. Members of one offshoot of the sect, believing that modesty is a relic of the Fall, go naked at divine services and at home. See Karl K. Grass, "Men of God," *Encyclopaedia of Religion and Ethics,* ed. James Hastings (Edinburgh: T. and T. Clark, 1953), Vol. 8, pp. 544–546.

For a discussion of the role of women in the patriarchal church, see Lane, pp. 41–42; B. Lyubimov, "Moi dom—moya tserkov [My Home—My Church]," *Moskovski Tserkovny Vestnik, Yezhenedelnik* [Moscow Church Herald, Weekly], No. 22, October 1990, p. 8; L. Moshkina, "Prestolny prazdnik v sele [Church-altar Saint's Day in a Village]," *Moskovski Tserkovny Vestnik, Yezhenedelnik,* No. 2, January 1991, p. 7.

35. The description in the text is taken from Bolshakov, pp. 11 (1)–27 (16), and Vladimir Moss, "The True Orthodox Church of Russia," *Religion in Communist Lands,* Nos. 3–4, Winter 1991, p. 244. Apparently most priests in the branch of True Orthodoxy stemming from Metropolitan Gennadi's ministry are Melchizedekites, who hold that the canonical succession continues through the grace of God in the hearts of true believers even if the succession is disrupted.

36. Moss, p. 244.

37. The commissioner in Lipetsk reported in 1986 that there had been six True Orthodox Christian communities with two priests and a total of 120 members in 1975; he reported three communities with one priest and seventy-two members in 1980; and he reported three communities with no priest and fifty-five members in 1985. The commissioner in Krasnodar in the northern Caucasus reported in 1986 that there had been a small group of True Orthodox Christians in the province in 1980, but it had disintegrated in the course of the next several years. The commissioner in Cherkassy, Ukraine, reported one True Orthodox Church community and one True Orthodox Christian community in 1985 but he said both had disappeared. The commissioner in Odessa reported in 1986 that there had been three True Orthodox Church communities and one True Orthodox Christian community in the oblast in 1976 but none in the 1980s. Tsentralny Gosudarstvenny Arkhiv, Fond 6991, Opis No. 6, delo Nos. 3131, 3132.

In 1992 an Orthodox commentator asserted that by 1985 one could count the True Orthodox communities in the USSR "on one's fingers." This was clearly an underestimation, but the True Orthodox communities were surely quite reduced in number at that time. See S. Yurov, "Zatyanuvshayasya istoriya [A Murky Story]," *Moskovski Tserkovny Vestnik, Yezhenedelnik,* No. 3, February 1992, p. 7. The archive of the Ministry of Justice of the Russian federation listed four registered True Orthodox Church communities in Moscow oblast on January 1, 1994.

38. Moss, pp. 244–245. There have been additional reports of True Orthodox activity. A small True Orthodox community exists close to Rostov-on-Don consisting of followers of Father John, a spiritual elder (*starets*) who died about ten years ago. Bolshakov, p. 5. A community of the "Holy New Martyrs and Confessors of Russia," formerly a catacomb church, now registered, with ties to the Russian Orthodox Church Abroad, surfaced in the early 1990s in Yekaterinburg. It demanded that a church be built under its jurisdiction, rather than that of the patriarchate, on the site of the now-demolished house where Nicholas II and his family were killed. *Keston News Service,* No. 373, April 18, 1991, p. 7. A monarchist, Sergei Engelgardt-Yurkov, appeared on Soviet television in May 1990 claiming "ties with the catacomb True Orthodox Church throughout the Soviet Union" and with the Russian Orthodox Church Abroad.

The Russian Orthodox Church Abroad censured Guri in 1991 for having adhered to "an illegitimate and uncanonical group of Greeks." *Pravoslavnaya Rus,* No. 22, November 15–28, 1993, p. 2.

The former Soviet governmental publication *Religion in USSR* (No. 5, May, 1991, pp. 25–26) listed a dozen breakaway Orthodox communities and descriptive materials. The publication reported that the Ministry of Justice of the Russian republic officially registered the Inter-Regional Religious Administration of the True Orthodox Church in May 1991. See also Elena Laishuk, "The Life of New Martyr Archpriest Fr. Paul Levashov of Gomel," *Orthodox Life,* No. 1, January–February 1992, p. 26; John B. Dunlop, "The Russian Orthodox Church and Nationalism After 1988," *Religion in Communist Lands,* Vol. 18, No. 4, Winter 1990, pp. 303–304. *Pravda* reported on a little group of almost thirty True Orthodox "hermits" in the Altai in Siberia in 1990. *Pravda,* March 25, 1990, p. 3. See also Ellis, p. 485, note 54; Pospielovsky, *The Russian Church,* pp. 365, 367, 370, 373–375; *Mosk-*

ovski Tserkovny Vestnik, Yezhenedelnik, No. 23, October 1990, p. 7; No. 24, November 1990, p. 6; *Keston News Service,* No. 354, July 12, 1990, p. 2; No. 366, January 10, 1991, p. 14. Michael Bourdeaux described the discovery in 1976 of a network of True Orthodox monasteries and churches in Abkhazia. Michael Bourdeaux, *Risen Indeed: Lessons in Faith from the U.S.S.R.* (Crestwood, New York: St. Vladimir's Seminary Press, 1983), p. 77.

39. Moss, pp. 245–246. Father Konstantin Vasilev of the Dormition church in Kashira, Moscow oblast, who declared himself Bishop Lazar of the True Orthodox Church, is one such priest. Later Bishop Lazar called himself "Patriarch" Lazar of Kashira and All Russia. He attended at least one of the meetings at the Central Museum of the Armed Forces in Moscow described in Chapter 8. Bishop Vikenti (Viktor Vladimirovich Chekalin) of Tula, consecrated by Metropolitan Ioann (Bodnarchuk), is another. *Pravoslavny Visnyk* [Orthodox Herald], No. 4 (April), 1991, p. 49; *Keston News Service,* No. 369, February 21, 1991, p. 15; Serge Keleher, "Out of the Catacombs: The Greek-Catholic Church in Ukraine," *Religion in Communist Lands,* Vol. 19, Nos. 3–4, Winter 1991, p. 261. Archbishop Vladimir, in Ukrainian Volodymyr (Sternyuk), of the Ukrainian Greek-Catholics also accepted Bishop Vikenti, but his action was disavowed by the Holy See. Vikenti subsequently declared that he would unite the Orthodox east and the Catholic west under his leadership. Aleksandr Nezhny, "Metropolit Filaret kak zerkalo Moskovskoi Patriarkhii [Metropolitan Filaret as a Mirror of the Moscow Patriarchate]," *Russkaya Mysl,* No. 3936, July 3, 1992, p. 9. Several religious societies and brotherhoods have also declared their affiliation with the Russian Orthodox Free Church, among them the Society of the Tsar-Martyr Nicholas, the Society of St. Andrew (German Orthodox), and the Brotherhood of St. Iov of Pochaev in Moscow.

40. Moss, pp. 246–247, 249.

41. On ambivalence over policy in Rome, see Serge Keleher, "Church in the Middle: Greek-Catholics in Central and Eastern Europe," *Religion, State and Society,* Vol. 20, Nos. 3 and 4, 1992, pp. 293–299.

42. Vasyl Markus, *Religion and Nationalism in Soviet Ukraine After 1945* (Cambridge, Mass.: Ukrainian Studies Fund, Harvard University, 1985), pp. 71–72. For an account dating from the 1950s, see *Veritas Information Agency Bulletin,* 1953, quoted by Alexeev, *Russian Orthodox Bishops,* p. 58.

43. Tsentralny Gosudarstvenny Arkhiv, Fond 6991s, Opis No. 2, Vol. I, delo Nos. 12, 15, 18. See also A. Gaevski, "O roli sovetskoi obryadnosti i traditsii v kommunisticheskom vospitanii [About the Role of Soviet Ritualism and Tradition in Communist Upbringing]," *Kommunist Ukrainy* [Communist of Ukraine], No. 11 (November), 1963, pp. 36, 43.

44. Nevertheless, a Ukrainian priest was drafted into the army for six months in 1989 after publicly celebrating Holy Mass. See William D. Montalbano, "Half a Century Later, Ukrainian Priest Goes Home," *Los Angeles Times,* March 30, 1991, p. A10.

45. John Hands, "Uncertain Freedom," *Frontier,* January–February 1990, p. 14. Ukrainian Greek-Catholic bishop Pavlo Vasylyk said that Soviet authorities stopped giving fifteen-day jail sentences for participating in forbidden Catholic services in the summer of 1988.

46. Aleksandr Makarov, "Boi na stupenyakh very [Fight on the Steps of Faith]," *Moskovski Tserkovny Vestnik, Yezhenedelnik,* No. 17, December 1989, p. 7.

47. For repression of overt religion stimulating underground religious growth, see Fletcher, p. 278. For an apparent seesaw effect in the human rights movement in the early 1980s, see Alexeyeva, p. 384.

48. Kharchev, p. 4. See also Davis, *Religion and Communist Government*, p. 482; Nicholas S. Timasheff, *Religion in Soviet Russia, 1917–1942* (London: Sheed and Ward, 1944), p. 126.

49. Gerhard Simon, *Church, State and Opposition in the U.S.S.R.* (London: C. Hurst and Co., 1974), pp. 89, 102, 130. In 1937 Georgi Malenkov proposed to Stalin that the April 1929 decree be abrogated in favor of more direct suppression, as the decree had given an organizational underpinning to the continued activities of an essentially hostile religious organization in the country. P. A. Krasikov, head of the USSR Central Executive Committee Presidium's Standing Committee for Religious Questions successfully fought off Malenkov's proposal because it would make "legal" religious life impossible and encourage believers to go underground. Mikhail Odintsov, "The Soviet State and Laws on Religion," *Religion in USSR*, No. 12 (December), 1991, p. 51. See also Wassily (Wassilij) Alexeev, "L'Église Orthodoxe Russe sous l'occupation allemande, 1941–1944 [The Russian Orthodox Church Under the German Occupation, 1941–1944]," *Irénikon*, Vol. 29, 1956, p. 276; Robert Tobias, *Communist-Christian Encounter in East Europe* (Indianapolis, Indiana: School of Religion Press, 1956), p. 128; Wassilij Alexeev and Theofanis G. Stavrou, *The Great Revival: The Russian Church Under German Occupation,* (Minneapolis: Burgess Publishing Co., 1976), p. 28.

50. Fletcher, p. 279. For a defense of Metropolitan Sergi's 1927 loyalty declaration, see Lyubimov, p. 8.

51. Alexeev, "L'Église Orthodoxe Russe," p. 266; *Vsepoddanneishi otchet ober-prokurora svyateishago sinoda pravoslavnago ispovedaniya za 1911–1912* [Comprehensive Report of the Over-Procurator of the Holy Synod of the Orthodox Confession for 1911–1912] (Sankt-peterburg: Synodalnaya Tip., 1913), pp. 10–11; and Fainsod, pp. 430, 437. The figure of "about two hundred" operating churches in 1936 represents an adjusted estimate, based on data quoted in Fainsod, that takes into account changes in administrative boundaries in the region.

52. Friedrich Heyer, *Die Orthodoxe Kirche in der Ukraine von 1917 bis 1945* [The Orthodox Church in Ukraine from 1917 to 1945], Vol. III of *Osteuropa und der Deutsche Osten* [East Europe and the German East] (Köln-Braunsfeld: Rudolf Müller, 1953), p. 171; Alexeev, "L'Église Orthodoxe Russe," p. 266.

53. Fletcher, pp. 153, 182, 196, 198–201, 274. Some Soviet commentators expressed a note of caution about the spread of illegal, underground religious activity in the immediate postwar period. Shemetrov, for example, lamented that Orthodox Christians in the old territories of the heartland were "exhausted by World War II," even though "not all traces" of earlier outlawed activities of Christian brotherhoods were lost. N. Shemetrov, "Khristos posrede nas [Christ in our Midst]," *Moskovski Tserkovny Vestnik, Yezhenedelnik,* No. 11, May 1990, p. 3. Alexeyeva, p. 247, said "the majority" of True Orthodox returned to the patriarchal church after World War II and that True Orthodox influence became "practically unnoticed" by the mid-1980s.

54. See also Alexeev, *Russian Orthodox Bishops*, p. 83.

55. A book published in 1949 claimed that an extensive underground church existed after World War II in the Soviet Union. It was by "Father George" as told to Gretta Palmer, *God's Underground* (New York: Appleton-Century-Crofts, Inc., 1949). The book had factual errors, however, such as calling Metropolitan Sergi the head of the living church (pp. 48–49), and it had others (see pp. 168, 247, 250 and 253). Paul W. Facey, S.J., suggested in *America* of July 16, 1949 ("The Case of the Missing Underground"), that the circumstantial evidence was actually derived from Timasheff's account of the underground church before World War II; see particularly pp. 79–80. William C. Fletcher, on the other hand, was able—through a colleague—to identify "Father George" as a Croatian Catholic priest (which would explain at least some of his misunderstandings of the Soviet situation) who did have the experiences he described.

56. Fletcher, pp. 197, 201; Lane, pp. 82–83.

57. Aleksandr Soldatov, "Sibirskiya zarisovki [Siberian Sketches]," *Pravoslavnaya Rus*, No. 10, May 15/28, 1992, p. 14.

58. Fletcher, pp. 201, 276, 279; *Zhurnal Moskovskoi Patriarkhii*, No. 5 (May), 1946, p. 58; No. 1 (January), 1948, pp. 76–77; No. 2 (February), 1955, p. 61; No. 7 (July), 1955, pp. 8–9; No. 11 (November), 1956, pp. 10–11.

59. Fletcher, pp. 201, 246–253, 278–279. Fletcher, p. 279, also said that relaxed state policy results in underground churches turning away from aberrant practices; I agree. Alexeyeva, p. 247, noted the turn of True Orthodox Christians toward apocalyptic expectations in periods of suppression.

60. Fletcher, p. 260–262, 265; Ellis, p. 403. Pospielovsky reached conclusions similar to those presented in the text. In addition, he quoted a Russian Orthodox Church source as saying that "more than half" of the Orthodox priests in the country were operating unofficially in the late 1960s and early 1970s. The majority of them were loyal to the patriarchate, but "some" took the True Orthodox line of dissociating themselves from the collaborating patriarchal church. Dimitry Pospielovsky, "The Soviet State Versus the Russian Orthodox Church, 1959–1988," *Religion in Communist Dominated Areas*, Vol. XXVII, No. 4, Fall 1988, p. 107; Dimitry V. Pospielovsky, "Intelligentsia and Religion: Aspects of Religious Revival in the Contemporary Soviet Union, the Orthodox Church," *Religion and Communist Society*, ed. Dennis J. Dunn (Berkeley, Calif: Berkeley Slavic Specialties, 1983), p. 38, note 18.

61. E. Pazukhin, "Poiski puti [In Search of the Way]," *Moskovski Tserkovny Vestnik, Yezhenedelnik*, No. 9, April 1990, pp. 4–5. See also Vladimir Poresh, "Faith and Lack of Faith in Russia," *Religion in Communist Lands*, Vol. 19, Nos. 1–2, Summer 1991, p. 80.

62. Bohdan R. Bociurkiv and John W. Strong, eds., *Religion and Atheism in the U.S.S.R. and Eastern Europe* (London: The Macmillan Co., 1975), pp. 59–60. The criticism of the church for failure to protest was no doubt real and deeply felt, as was the criticism of Metropolitan Sergi after his 1927 loyalty declaration. Nevertheless, Aleksi and Nikolai did raise their voices in protest, with consequences disastrous for Nikolai.

63. Fletcher, p. 290.

64. For examples, see *Pravoslavnaya Rus*, No. 4, February 15/28, 1992, p. 11; No. 6, March 15/28, 1993, pp. 10–12; No. 6, March 15–28, 1994, p. 12; No. 8, April 15–28, 1994, p. 8; *Russkaya Mysl*, No. 4026, April 21–27, 1994, p. 12.

65. Fletcher, p. 262, 279. While the patriarch is obviously not a completely disinterested observer, he commented in mid-1993: "The Catacomb Church . . . existed in the 1920s and 1930s. It does not exist now." *Zhurnal Moskovskoi Patriarkhii*, No. 2 (February), 1994. p. 16.

66. I am indebted to William C. Fletcher for the rationale presented in this paragraph.

67. See also Fletcher, pp. 87, 252, 282–283.

68. For further discussion of this issue, see Davis, *Religion and Communist Government*, pp. 292–302, 441–446. It is true that the Old Believer communities not only survived but thrived in the years immediately prior to the Bolshevik revolution. It is also true, however, that the czarist government adopted a policy of toleration in 1905, and repression of the Old Believers essentially ceased. Many Old Believers were excellent businessmen, and some of them played important roles in the development of the Russian economy.

69. Timasheff, p. 89; Tobias, p. 140.

Chapter 11

1. For consistency, men's religious houses are called monasteries, women's are called nunneries, and either or both are called convents. Devout Christians could not, of course, visit openly functioning convents in the 1930s because Stalin had ordered them all closed. For an example of a *starets* and his influence, see the discussion of Archimandrite Tavrion (Batozski) of the Holy Trinity–St. Sergius nunnery in Riga later in this chapter.

2. Vladimir Vasilevich Pashkov, *Monastyri v S.S.S.R.: Ideologiya i deatelnost* [Monasteries in the U.S.S.R.: Ideology and Activity], dissertation for candidate's degree, full abstract (Moscow: Moscow State University named after Lomonosov, 1989), p. 16.

3. There are three degrees of monastic profession and characteristic habits. First is the *rasophorate*, taken from the *rason*, a black coat with long sleeves that is donned over the cassock. A male *rasophore* who is a priest (nuns may profess the same degrees) may be consecrated a bishop. Second is the little habit, which includes the *kamilavka*, a cylindrical hat, the *mandyas*, a wide black cope, and the *klobuk*, a black veil over the shoulders. Third is the *mega schema*, a cowled garment that falls below the knees in front and back and is decorated with many crosses. A bishop who takes the angelic habit must resign his episcopal dignity, and monks sometimes take the *mega schema* on their deathbeds. Victor J. Pospishil, "The Book of the Law," *The Way*, October 3, 1993, p. 3.

4. For "bondage," see Pashkov, p. 16. After being elevated to episcopal rank, Bishop Gavriil was removed from the see of Khabarovsk for abuse of power. *Moskovski Tserkovny Vestnik, Yezhenedelnik* [Moscow Church Herald, Weekly], No. 5, April 1991, p. 2. After serving the prescribed time of penance, he was reappointed to a territorially reduced Khabarovsk see in early 1994. *Moskovski Tserkovny Vestnik, Ezhenedelnik*, No. 1, 1994, p. 4.

5. Nina Chugunova, "Optina, zavyaz . . . [Optina, New Seed . . .]," *Ogonëk* [Little Fire], No. 34, August, 1989, p. 26.

6. *Nauka i Religiya* [Science and Religion], No. 3 (March), 1988, p. 46; *Zhurnal Moskovskoi Patriarkhii* [Journal of the Moscow Patriarchate], No. 8 (August), 1989, pp. 18–19; Savelii Tuberozov, "Monasteries and Theological Schools in the U.S.S.R.," *Eastern Churches Review*, Vol. I, 1966, p. 59.

7. *Zhurnal Moskovskoi Patriarkhii*, No. 10 (October), 1952, p. 37.

8. *Moskovski Tserkovny Vestnik* [Moscow Church Herald], No. 6 (June), 1988, pp. 6–7.

9. See *Komsomolskaya Pravda,* April 23, 1989, as reported in the *Keston News Service,* No. 327, June 8, 1989. Mother Nataliya, the mother superior, noted that educated women are sometimes not physically strong enough to stand up under the rigorous work schedule that the sisters carry out. O. Paukova, "Monastyr na ulitse Lenina [Convent on Lenin Street]," *Moskovski Tserkovny Vestnik, Yezhenedelnik,* No. 4, March 1991, p. 10.

10. *Nauka i Religiya,* No. 3 (March), 1988, p. 46.

11. The Moscow patriarchate noted in 1958 that the "majority" of convents are community living. Moscow Patriarchate, *The Russian Orthodox Church: Organization, Situation, Activity* (Moscow: Moscow Patriarchate, 1958), p. 98.

12. Jane Ellis, *The Russian Orthodox Church: A Contemporary History* (Bloomington, Indiana: Indiana University Press, 1986), p. 128; G. Gulichkina, "Pokrovski zhenski monastyr v Kieve [The Protection Nunnery in Kiev]," *Zhurnal Moskovskoi Patriarkhii,* No. 8 (August), 1989, p. 19; William J. Eaton, "Monks Keep Faith Alive in Old Russia," *Los Angeles Times,* January 24, 1986, Part I, pp. 1, 22–23. It should be borne in mind that services lasting two and a half to three hours are normal for the Russian Orthodox.

13. According to Father Sergi Gordun, USSR Council of Ministers Decree No. 1159 of October 16, 1958, had as a principal motivation a desire sharply to reduce convents' agricultural lands and to eliminate their work in the fields. Sergi Gordun, "Russkaya Pravoslavnaya Tserkov v period s 1943 po 1970 god [The Russian Orthodox Church in the Period from 1943 to 1970]," *Zhurnal Moskovskoi Patriarkhii,* No. 2 (February), 1993, pp. 11, 19.

14. *Moskovski Tserkovny Vestnik,* No. 6 (June), 1988, pp. 6–7; *Zhurnal Moskovskoi Patriarkhii,* No. 6 (June), 1990, p. 18. The arrangement is of long standing. Gerhard Simon, *Church, State and Opposition in the U.S.S.R.,* trans. Kathleen Matchett (Berkeley, Calif.: University of California Press, 1970), p. 117.

15. *Zhurnal Moskovskoi Patriarkhii,* No. 10 (October), 1988, p. 9.

16. Many diocesan bishops also maintain shops to make candles, vestments, and other religious objects. *Zhurnal Moskovskoi Patriarkhii,* No. 7 (July), 1971, p. 17; No. 2 (February), 1983, p. 48; No. 12 (December), 1985, p. 23.

17. *Moskovski Tserkovny Vestnik,* No. 6 (June), 1988, pp. 6–7.

18. Pierre Fontanieu, "Le problème religieux in U.R.S.S. [The Religious Problem in the U.S.S.R.]," *Christianisme Social* [Social Christianity], Vol. 63, Nos. 1–2 (January–February), 1955, p. 60; John Shelton Curtiss, *The Russian Church and the Soviet State, 1917–1950* (Boston: Little, Brown and Co., 1953), p. 84; Tsentralny Gosudarstvenny Arkhiv Oktyabrskoi Revolutsii [Central State Archive of the October Revolution], Vysshikh Organov Gosudarstvennoi Vlasti i Organov Gosurdarstvennogo Upravleniya S.S.S.R. [of the Higher Organs of State Government and Organs of State Administration of the U.S.S.R.], Soviet po delam religii pri Sovete Ministrov [the Council for Religious Affairs attached to the Council of Ministers], Fond 6991s, Opis No. 2, Vol. I, delo No. 206.

19. Tsentralny Gosudarstvenny Arkhiv, Fond 6991s, Opis No. 2, Vol. I, delo Nos. 206, 263. In August of 1941 the Soviet government gave a somewhat different figure of thirty-seven operating convents. See *Soviet War News,* August 22, 1941, London, quoted in Stanley Evans, *Churches in the U.S.S.R.* (London: Cobbett Publishing Co., 1943), p. 88. A "*skit,*" the dictionary definition of which is a "small and secluded monastery," is translated here

as a "hermitage" regardless of the sex of the religious persons living there. Usually, but not always, a "*skit*" is a filial establishment that is a dependency of a convent. The English translation of *skit* is skete, derived from the desert of Skete in lower Egypt, a region famous for the hermits found there from the third or fourth centuries.

20. Tsentralny Gosudarstvenny Arkhiv, Fond 6991s, Opis No. 2, Vol. I, delo Nos. 18, 206.

21. Tsentralny Gosudarstvenny Arkhiv, Fond 6991s, Opis No. 2, Vol. I, delo No. 61; Nikita Struve, "Tserkov v Sovetskoi Rossii [The Church in Soviet Russia]," *Vestnik Russkogo Studencheskogo Khristianskogo Dvizheniya* [Herald of the Russian Student Christian Movement], Nos. V–VI, 1954, p. 39; *Zhurnal Moskovskoi Patriarkhii,* No. 2 (February), 1949, p. 16.

22. Of the forty-one monasteries, twenty-four were in Ukraine; of the fifty-five nunneries, forty were in Ukraine. Eight convents were closed between October and early December and another three were closed during that month. Tsentralny Gosudarstvenny Arkhiv, Fond 6991s, Opis No. 2, Vol. I, delo Nos. 61, 206, 263.

23. Bohdan R. Bociurkiw, "The Orthodox Church and the Soviet Regime in the Ukraine, 1953–1971," *Canadian Slavonic Papers,* Vol. XIV, No. 2, Summer 1972, p. 197.

24. Of these sixty-four convents, twenty were monasteries, one was a hermitage for monks, thirty-seven were nunneries, and six were smaller establishments (*skits*) for nuns. Tsentralny Gosudarstvenny Arkhiv, Fond 6991s, Opis No. 2, Vol. I, delo No. 180.

25. The figures were sixty-three convents open (twenty monasteries, one hermitage for men, thirty-six nunneries, six women's hermitages) in January of 1959 and forty-four convents (fourteen monasteries, twenty-eight nunneries, and two hermitages for women) in January of 1960. Tsentralny Gosudarstvenny Arkhiv, Fond 6991s, Opis No. 2, Vol. I, delo Nos. 206, 263; Gordun, p. 11.

26. Francis House, *The Russian Phoenix* (London: SPCK, 1988), p. 90.

27. The struggle at Pochaev should not be seen as representative or typical of other convents' experiences. The authorities expected less resistance and earlier success than they were able to achieve, and the indomitable resistance set Pochaev apart. Moreover, the persecution of the monks became a cause célèbre in samizdat and tamizdat, which resulted in moral support from abroad that helped sustain the resistance and perhaps also contributed to the authorities' frustration and brutality.

28. *Zhurnal Moskovskoi Patriarkhii,* No. 10 (October), 1946, pp. 41–42.

29. Michael Bourdeaux, *Patriarch and Prophets: Persecution of the Russian Orthodox Church Today* (Oxford: A. R. Mowbray and Co., 1975), p. 170; also pp. 97–116. Arkadi Zhukovski, "Ukraïnska Pravoslavna Tserkva, dokumenti, materiyali Khristiyanski samvidav Ukraïni [The Ukrainian Orthodox Church, Documents and Materials of Christian Samizdat of Ukraine]," Vol. I of *Martirologiya Ukraïnskikh Tserkov* [Martyrdom of the Ukrainian Churches], eds. Osyp Zinkewych and Olexander Voronym, 4 Vols. planned (Toronto: V. Symonenko Smoloskyp Publishers, 1987), pp. 820–821, 832–839, 1059–1064; Dimitry Pospielovsky, *The Russian Church Under the Soviet Regime, 1917–1982,* 2 Vols. (Crestwood, New York: St. Vladimir's Seminary Press, 1984), p. 442. The confinement of religious and political resisters in psychiatric hospitals was widely practiced.

30. The monastery's population of monks and novices had already been reduced to

thirty-six in September 1962. Soviet official figures listed thirty-three monks and no novices in January 1966. Tsentralny Gosudarstvenny Arkhiv, Fond 6991s, Opis No. 4, Vol. I,
delo No. 574. See also Tuberozov, p. 59; *Posev,* January 15, 1965, p. 2; House, p. 90; Simon,
p. 78; Bourdeaux, p. 84.

31. William C. Fletcher quoted the Soviet newspaper *Trud* [Labor] as asserting that
underground True Orthodox activists had begun to appear at Pochaev by 1958 and from
there "began to spread throughout the country." The implication might be that the illegal,
underground activity based at Pochaev in some part caused the official crackdown.
Monks expelled from the monastery were also reported to have become wanderers. William C. Fletcher, *The Russian Orthodox Church Underground, 1917–1970* (London: Oxford
University Press, 1971), p. 265.

32. The listing of eighteen convents does not include convents abroad. The St. Pante-
leimon monastery on Mt. Athos (Afon) and the St. Andrew's hermitage are technically
under the jurisdiction of the Greek Orthodox Church. Between a dozen and two dozen
Russian Orthodox monks have lived there over the years. The Gorny nunnery in Jerusalem has had a dozen to two dozen Russian Orthodox nuns in residence. Two nuns were
murdered there in 1983. The Holy Ghost Russian Orthodox hermitage in Vanve, Paris,
also exists, but it does not appear to be a full-fledged resident community. Russian Orthodox prelates sometimes count one or more of these convents abroad when giving overall
figures. Inside the former USSR, the hermitage at Peredelkino (Lukino) is also sometimes
counted. It opened as a branch hermitage of the Trinity-Sergius monastery but was later
given over to the Greek Orthodox Church's jurisdiction.

33. Dimitry Pospielovsky, "The Soviet State Versus the Russian Orthodox Church,
1959–1988," *Religion in Communist Dominated Areas,* Vol. XXVII, No. 4, Fall 1988, p. 110.

34. The breakdown was 634 monks and 259 novices. Analogous figures for cloistered
women were 2,271 nuns and 1,497 novices, for a total of 3,768. Tsentralny Gosudarstvenny
Arkhiv, Fond 6991s, Opis No. 2, Vol. I, delo Nos. 180, 263.

35. Curtiss, p. 10.

36. I reached the estimate of 900–1,000 monastic priests by counting my records of
references to priests of every category in each diocese and calculating overall figures.

37. The word *lavra* comes from the Greek *laura,* originally a roadway or alley connecting hermitages under one superior jurisdiction. There were four *lavras* in the USSR: Trinity-Sergius; Dormition-Pochaev; Kiev-Caves (closed in 1961 and reopened in 1988); and
Alexander Nevsky in St. Petersburg (closed).

38. Of the eighty-three monks and novices at Zagorsk in 1956, about half were monks.
By 1960 the number was down to seventy-two. Of the sixty-two in 1966, three were novices. Tsentralny Gosudarstvenny Arkhiv, Fond 6991s, Opis No. 2, Vol. I, delo Nos. 180, 205,
263; Fond 6991s, Opis No. 4, Vol. I, delo No. 574. Western scholars and Russian Orthodox
Church sources give figures of about ninety in the post-Khrushchev years; they may include some seminary and academy students. See Tuberozov, p. 59; Simon, p. 115; *Eastern
Churches Review,* Vol. I, 1966, p. 60.

39. By 1980 the number was back to eighty, of whom fifteen to twenty were novices. See
a group picture of the monastery's monks published in the *Zhurnal Moskovskoi Patriarkhii,* No. 10 (October), 1980, before p. 57; Ellis, pp. 126, 131, 470–471; Marite Sapiets,

"Monasticism in the Soviet Union," *Religion in Communist Lands,* Vol. 4, No. 1, Spring 1976, p. 30; Philippe Sabant, "Religion in Russia Today, Part II," *The Tablet* (London), Vol. 234, No. 7280, January 19, 1980, p. 55; Trevor Beeson, *Discretion and Valor* (Philadelphia, Penn.: Fortress Press, 1974 and 1982), p. 56. James Moss, "The Russian Orthodox Church, 1986–1988," *Religion in Communist Dominated Areas,* Vol. XXVIII, No. 2, Spring 1989, p. 49. The official figure for January 1986 was seventy-one monks and novices, but that figure perhaps did not count monastic priests serving at the theological school and in other offices. Tsentralny Gosudarstvenny Arkhiv, Fond 6991, Opis No. 6, delo No. 3130. I was told in the summer of 1994 that there were eighty monks and novices in the cloister, not counting those at the theological schools.

40. Through the 1950s until 1957 Pskov-Pechory had forty to forty-five monks and a half dozen novices. Figures for 1958 from the archive records were sixty-five monks and novices and from the *Journal* sixty-eight. In 1966 there were fifty-eight monks and five novices. Tsentralny Gosudarstvenny Arkhiv, Fond 6991s, Opis No. 2, Vol. I, delo Nos. 180, 206, 231; Opis No. 4, Vol. 1, delo No. 574; *Zhurnal Moskovskoi Patriarkhii,* No. 2 (February), 1958, pp. 21, 24; No. 9 (September), 1969, p. 33.

41. Simon, p. 115; Ellis, pp. 127, 137, 471; Sapiets, p. 30; Sabant, p. 55; Beeson, p. 56; Eaton, p. 1; and data offered during my visit to Pskov-Pechory on July 5, 1986. The official figure for January 1986 was seventy-three. Tsentralny Gosudarstvenny Arkhiv, Fond 6996, Opis No. 6, delo No. 3130.

42. Of the monks, three had the *candidat* degree, four were theological academy students, five were seminary graduates, ten had at least some university education, and forty-one had at least some high school education. Data from documents of the Council for Religious Affairs, Russian State Archive, with the help of Marina Rebrova of MITEK Information Service, Moscow, and Julia Petrakis of Facts OnLine, Camano Island, Washington.

43. Ellis, p. 471. By 1978 there were about fifty monks, about twenty too aged or ill to work. *Khronika Tekushchikh Sobytii* [Chronicle of Current Events], No. 51, December 1, 1978, p. 125. In 1986 there were forty-six monks. Tsentralny Gosudarstvenny Arkhiv, Fond 6991, Opis No. 6, delo No. 3136.

44. Ellis, pp. 140–141; Pospielovsky, *The Russian Church,* p. 442; Zhukovski, p. 1063.

45. Archbishop Lavr of Syracuse (of the Russian Orthodox Church Abroad), "Palomnichestvo po svyatym mestam Kieva i Pochaeva [Pilgrimage to the Holy Places of Kiev and Pochaev]," *Pravoslavnaya Zhizn* [Orthodox Life], No. 12 (December), 1992, p. 20; MITEK (Rebrova).

46. The archive had an exact figure of sixty-five monks and three novices, a total of sixty-eight, in Odessa and Pochaev in January 1965. Pochaev alone had thirty-three monks and no novices in January 1966, and figures given by various observers for 1965 were about the same. By subtraction, this would put thirty-two monks, and three novices in Odessa. The Moscow Patriarchate, p. 98; Ellis, p. 133; Tsentralny Gosudarstvenny Arkhiv, Fond 6991s, Opis No. 2, Vol. I, delo No. 263; Opis No. 4, Vol. 1, delo Nos. 574, 575; *Zhurnal Moskovskoi Patriarkhii,* No. 6 (June), 1974, p. 31.

47. Ellis, pp. 133, 471 (forty-one monks of whom twenty-six were priests in 1968); Council for Religious Affairs figure in 1970 (thirty-nine monks); *Pravoslavny Visnyk* [Or-

thodox Herald], No. 8 (August), 1974, p. 2, picture (thirty-eight monks); Michael Binyon, *Life in Russia* (New York: Pantheon Books, 1983), p. 231 (forty-one monks); Council for Religious Affairs figure for January 1986, Tsentralny Gosudarstvenny Arkhiv, Fond 6991, Opis No. 6, delo No. 3136 (forty-three monks). For Council for Religious Affairs figure in 1991, see MITEK (Rebrova).

48. In 1956–1958 there were fourteen monks and sixteen novices at Zhirovitsy. For the 1981 figures, see Ellis, p. 128. In January 1986, the Council for Religious Affairs recorded five archimandrites, four hegumens, four monastic priests, four hierodeacons, one monk, and no novices. V. Menkov's report October 2, 1947, Tsentralny Gosudarstvenny Arkhiv, Fond 6991s, Opis No. 2, Vol. I, delo Nos. 61, 205, 206, 263; Fond 6991, Opis No. 6, delo No. 3137.

49. The monastery gained two men in 1956, as there were eleven monks and novices in January 1956 and thirteen in January 1957. By January 1958 there were ten monks and two novices, a total of twelve. By January 1959 the total had dropped to eight, but it increased to nine by January 1960. The 1966 figures were eight monks and seven novices at Vilnyus. In January 1986 the Council for Religious Affairs recorded nine monks at Vilnyus. Tsentralny Gosudarstvenny Arkhiv, Fond 6991s, Opis No. 2, Vol. I, delo Nos. 14, 180, 205, 206, 263; Opis No. 4, Vol. 1, delo No. 574; Fond 6991, Opis No. 6, delo No. 3130; *Religion in Communist Dominated Areas,* Vol. XXV, No. 1, Winter 1986, p. 40; *Zhurnal Moskovskoi Patriarkhii,* No. 4 (April), 1989, p. 12; my visit to the Holy Ghost monastery on July 2, 1986.

50. The figures were 129 nuns and novices in January 1960; forty-eight nuns and fifty-nine novices in January 1966, a total of 107; 105 nuns and novices in 1970; 144 nuns and novices in 1985; 148 nuns and novices in 1987. Until late 1991, the Pyukhtitsa nunnery also had a dependent cloister, the community of St. John, where St. John of Kronshtadt is venerated. The cloister was elevated in status and became independent of Pyukhtitsa. Tsentralny Gosudarstvenny Arkhiv, Fond 6991s, Opis No. 2, Vol. I, delo Nos. 74, 156, 180, 206, 231, 263; Opis No. 4, Vol. I, delo No. 574; Walter Kolarz, *Religion in the Soviet Union* (New York: St. Martin's Press, 1961), p. 122; Ellis, p. 471; *Zhurnal Moskovskoi Patriarkhii,* No. 11 (November), 1954, p. 12; *Moskovski Tserkovny Vestnik, Yezhenedelnik,* No. 4, March 1991, p. 2, and No. 2, February 1993, p. 3; *Moscow News,* No. 8, 1985, p. 13; Moss, p. 49; *Nauka i Religiya,* No. 3 (March), 1988, p. 46.

51. Friedrich Heyer, *Die Orthodoxe Kirche in der Ukraine von 1917 bis 1945* [The Orthodox Church in Ukraine from 1917 to 1945], Vol. III of *Osteuropa und der Deutsche Osten* [East Europe and the German East] (Köln-Braunsfeld: Rudolf Müller, 1953), p. 202 (130 nuns and novices); Wassilij Alexeev and Theofanis G. Stavrou, *The Great Revival: The Russian Church Under German Occupation* (Minneapolis: Burgess Publishing Co., 1976), p. 180 (130 nuns and novices); Tsentralny Gosudarstvenny Arkhiv, Fond 6991s, Opis No. 2, Vol. I, delo No. 74 (136 nuns and novices).

52. In 1958 there were seventy-nine nuns and ninety-three novices at the Trinity and Resurrection nunneries. Tsentralny Gosudarstvenny Arkhiv, Fond 6991s, Opis No. 2, Vol. I, delo No. 206.

53. Tsentralny Gosudarstvenny Arkhiv, Fond 6991s, Opis No. 2, Vol. I, delo No. 263.

54. The numbers were 164 nuns and 2 novices in January 1966; 144 nuns and novices in January 1970; 111 nuns and novices in January 1986; 110–120 nuns and novices in the mid-

dle to late 1980s; about 60–70 nuns and 40–50 novices in 1990, a total of 110. In 1984 the nunnery was put under the direct jurisdiction of the Moscow patriarchate making it "*stavropigiyalny*" (from *stavropegium,* planting of a cross received from the patriarch). Tsentralny Gosudarstvenny Arkhiv, Fond 6991s, Opis No. 4, Vol. I, delo No. 574; Fond 6991, Opis No. 6, delo No. 3136; Ellis, p. 471; *Literary Gazette International,* Vol. 1, No. 2, February 1990, p. 13. A picture taken in August 1990 showed 61 veiled nuns. *Zhurnal Moskovskoi Patriarkhii,* No. 12 (December), 1990, photographs appearing after p. 40; No. 6 (June), 1990, p. 18.

55. MITEK (Rebrova).

56. Isaac Glan, "An 'Unknown Land,'" *Literary Gazette International,* Vol. 1, No. 2, February 1990, p. 13.

57. Paukova, pp. 10–11. By 1958 the Protection nunnery had grown by about 10, to 254, of whom about 100 were novices. Tsentralny Gosudarstvenny Arkhiv, Fond 6991s, Opis No. 2, Vol. I, delo Nos. 18, 206. See also Heyer, p. 203; Alexeev and Stavrou, p. 181; *Zhurnal Moskovskoi Patriarkhii,* No. 6 (June), 1945, p. 13; Struve, p. 40; Ellis, p. 128.

58. Constantin de Grunwald, *The Churches and the Soviet Union* (New York: The Macmillan Co., 1962), p. 139.

59. The Protection nunnery had 140 nuns and 75 novices in January 1966. Tsentralny Gosudarstvenny Arkhiv, Fond 6991s, Opis No. 4, Vol. I, delo No. 574. *Posev* estimated 200 (January 14, 1966, p. 4), as did Gerhard Simon (Simon, p. 116).

60. Tsentralny Gosudarstvenny Arkhiv, Fond 6991s, Opis No. 4, Vol. I, delo No. 206. The Presentation nunnery had 142 sisters in 1958.

61. Ellis, p. 471. Sabant, p. 55, gave the figure of "over 100" for 1979. The mother superior of the nunnery said in February 1982 that the figure had been "about 100 for many years" (Ellis, p. 471).

62. See Ellis, pp. 128, 471, for the estimate of ninety-five in 1982. The figure of ninety-five was given by the *Journal of the Moscow Patriarchate* in 1989. *Zhurnal Moskovskoi Patriarkhii,* No. 8 (August), 1989, p. 19. On Tuesday, June 6, 1989, I counted eighty-five nuns and novices assembled at the nunnery, about half of them novices. The official figure was eighty-nine nuns and novices in January 1986. Tsentralny Gosudarstvenny Arkhiv, Fond 6991, Opis No. 6, delo No. 3130. For 1991, MITEK (Rebrova).

63. Of the 250 at St. Florus, only 8 were novices. Tsentralny Gosudarstvenny Arkhiv, Fond 6991s, Opis No. 2, Vol. I, delo No. 18; Heyer, p. 203; Alexeev and Stavrou, p. 181.

64. The numbers were 264 nuns and novices in December 1947; 167 nuns and 108 novices in 1957; 266 nuns and novices in 1958; 176 nuns and novices in 1966. Tsentralny Gosudarstvenny Arkhiv, Fond 6991s, Opis No. 2, Vol. I, delo Nos. 18, 61, 205, 206; Opis No. 4, Vol. I, delo No. 574; Fond 6991, Opis No. 6, delo No. 3130; *Zhurnal Moskovskoi Patriarkhii,* No. 10 (October), 1946, p. 22; Struve, p. 40; Ellis, pp. 128, 471; Sabant, p. 55; my visit to the nunnery on Tuesday, June 6, 1989; MITEK (Rebrova) for 1991.

65. In 1966 Krasnogorsk was reported to have seventy-two nuns and fourteen novices. In 1970 the Council for Religious Affairs reported eighty-five women at the nunnery. See Ellis, p. 471. For other figures see Tsentralny Gosudarstvenny Arkhiv, Fond 6991s, Opis No. 2, Vol. 1, delo No. 263; Opis No. 4, Vol. 1, delo No. 574; Fond 6991, Opis No. 6, delo No. 3136. For 1991, see MITEK (Rebrova).

66. Michael Bourdeaux, *Opium of the People* (Indianapolis, Indiana: The Bobbs-Merrill Co., 1966), p. 212.

67. The *Journal of the Moscow Patriarchate* published a picture of thirty-two nuns in full habit in 1968. *Zhurnal Moskovskoi Patriarkhii,* No. 11 (November), 1968, inside back cover. There had been seventy-five nuns and novices at St. Michael's nunnery alone in 1944 and 137 at the end of the 1950s. Tsentralny Gosudarstvenny Arkhiv, Fond 6991s, Opis No. 2, Vol. I, delo No. 74; Kolarz, p. 75. Simon, p. 116, estimated "over thirty" nuns at Aleksandrovka in 1969.

68. The Council for Religious Affairs recorded fifty nuns and novices in 1970. See Ellis, p. 471. In the mid-1970s, various sources recorded twenty-eight or twenty-nine nuns and sixteen novices, a total of about forty-five. *Pravoslavny Visnyk,* No. 2 (February), 1972, p. 72; No. 11 (November), 1972, p. 5; No. 2 (February), 1982, p. 32 (picture); *Zhurnal Moskovskoi Patriarkhii,* No. 4 (April), 1976, p. 27; No. 3 (March), 1982, p. 32; No. 2 (February), 1987, p. 22 (picture); No. 9 (September), 1987, p. 33 (picture); Sapiets, p. 32; Ellis, p. 129; Sabant, p. 55. The bishop consecrated ten novices as nuns in September of 1985. *Zhurnal Moskovskoi Patriarkhii,* No. 2 (February), 1986, p. 25. The Council for Religious Affairs figure for January 1986 was forty-six. Tsentralny Gosudarstvenny Arkhiv, Fond 6991, Opis No. 6, delo No. 3136. For 1991, see MITEK (Rebrova).

69. Soviet authorities reported 178 nuns and novices in 1947 and 258 in 1950. In 1957 they recorded 292 women, including 134 nuns, 96 novices in habit, and 62 novices not in habit. Tsentralny Gosudarstvenny Arkhiv, Fond 6991s, Opis No. 2, Vol. I, delo Nos. 72, 205, 208.

70. Sixty nuns were sent from the Lipcha nunnery to St. Nicholas; others came from as far away as Bulgaria. *Zhurnal Moskovskoi Patriarkhii,* No. 3 (March), 1986, p. 17; Tsentralny Gosudarstvenny Arkhiv, Fond 6991s, Opis No. 2, Vol. I, delo No. 208, 263.

71. Tuberozov, p. 59; Tsentralny Gosudarstvenny Arkhiv, Fond 6991s, Opis No. 4, Vol. I, delo No. 574.

72. In 1970 the Council for Religious Affairs reported 123 nuns and novices at Mukachevo; in 1976, 120 were reported by a Western observer. Ellis, p. 134; Sapiets, p. 32; Sabant, p. 55; *Pravoslavny Visnyk,* No. 10 (October), 1990, p. 15. Official figures for January 1986 were 97. Tsentralny Gosudarstvenny Arkhiv, Fond 6991, Opis No. 6, delo No. 3131.

73. *Zhurnal Moskovskoi Patriarkhii,* No. 6 (June), 1986, p. 34.

74. The Soviet authorities recorded forty-one nuns and novices at Chumalevo in 1970. Tsentralny Gosudarstvenny Arkhiv, Fond 6991s, Opis No. 4, Vol. I, delo No. 574; Fond 6991, Opis No. 6, delo No. 3130; Ellis, pp. 134, 471.

75. Ellis, pp. 147–148; Michael Bourdeaux, *Risen Indeed: Lessons in Faith from the U.S.S.R.* (Crestwood, New York: St. Vladimir's Seminary Press, 1983), pp. 80–83. According to Gordun, Patriarch Aleksi I proposed in 1962 that Archimandrite Tavrion be consecrated bishop of the large diocese of Kursk, but the Soviet authorities vetoed the proposed action, saying the archimandrite was reactionary and a fanatic. Gordun, p. 18.

76. Ivan Nikitich Shabatin of the Moscow theological academy. *Zhurnal Moskovskoi Patriarkhii,* No. 10 (October), 1952, p. 37.

77. There were fifty-one nuns and novices at the Riga nunnery and Yelgava hermitage in 1952; sixty in 1954; eighty-two in 1956; eighty-four in 1957; and eighty-eight in 1958

(thirty-three nuns and fifty-five novices). From ninety-one women in 1959, the number dropped back to eighty-eight in 1960. In 1966 there were sixty-nine nuns and one novice in residence. *Zhurnal Moskovskoi Patriarkhii,* No. 10 (October), 1952, p. 36; Struve, p. 40; Tsentralny Gosudarstvenny Arkhiv, Fond 6991s, Opis No. 2, Vol. I, delo Nos. 74, 180, 206, 263; Opis No. 4, Vol. I, delo No. 574.

78. N. Shemetrov, "Khristos posrede nas [Christ in our Midst]," *Moskovski Tserkovny Vestnik, Yezhenedelnik,* No. 11, May 1990, p. 3. The authorities recorded fifty-four nuns and one novice in 1970. Ellis, pp. 129, 131, 471. In 1989 the *Journal of the Moscow Patriarchate* showed a picture of twelve nuns in procession at the Transfiguration hermitage, perhaps all of the nuns residing at that ascetic branch of the nunnery. *Zhurnal Moskovskoi Patriarkhii,* No. 7 (July), 1989, before p. 41; No. 3 (March), 1992, p. 15 (official section). Tsentralny Gosudarstvenny Arkhiv, Fond 6991, Opis No. 6, delo No. 3130.

79. Almost half of the cloistered women at Vilnyus in 1955 were novices. In January 1956 there were thirty nuns and novices at Vilnyus, and in January 1957 there were thirty-two, but that year only one woman entered and six were lost, presumably aged nuns who died, and the numbers dropped to twenty-seven in January 1958. Tsentralny Gosudarstvenny Arkhiv, Fond 6991s, Opis No. 2, Vol. I, delo Nos. 74, 180, 205, 206, 263. The Council for Religious Affairs recorded "twenty-six" cloistered men and women at Vilnyus in 1970. This probably reflects a dozen monks and fourteen nuns (Ellis, p. 471). The Council for Religious Affairs listed thirteen nuns in 1983 (*Religion in Communist Dominated Areas,* Vol. XXV, No. 1, Winter 1986, p. 40). When I visited the monastery and nunnery on July 3, 1986, I was told that there were sixteen nuns and novices at the nunnery. In 1988–1989 the *Journal of the Moscow Patriarchate* showed a picture of eleven nuns and one novice at prayers. *Zhurnal Moskovskoi Patriarkhii,* No. 4 (April), 1989, after p. 40.

80. Tsentralny Gosudarstvenny Arkhiv, Fond 6991s, Opis No. 2, Vol. I, delo No. 74. In 1945 the council also recorded 467 monks, 162 male novices, and fifteen monasteries.

81. The numbers were 465 nuns and 621 novices. Equivalent figures for men were 309 monks and 167 novices, a drop of almost a quarter since 1945. Tsentralny Gosudarstvenny Arkhiv, Fond 6991s, Opis No. 2, Vol. I, delo No. 60.

82. Figures were: April 1949—497 nuns, 658 novices; January 1950—1,171 nuns and novices; 1955—1,079; 1956—1,059; 1957—549 nuns and 518 novices; 1958—1,049. Tsentralny Gosudarstvenny Arkhiv, Fond 6991s, Opis No. 2, Vol. I, delo Nos. 74, 180, 206, 231, 263.

83. Tsentralny Gosudarstvenny Arkhiv, Fond 6991s, Opis No. 2, Vol. I, delo No. 263. There were seven monasteries in January 1959; four of them were closed that year and the remaining three were closed before the Khrushchev drive was over.

84. Tsentralny Gosudarstvenny Arkhiv, Fond 6991s, Opis No. 4, Vol. I, delo No. 574.

85. The Council for Religious Affairs recorded seventy cloistered nuns and novices at Zhabka in 1970; in 1981, about sixty. Ellis, p. 471; *Zhurnal Moskovskoi Patriarkhii,* No. 7 (July), 1981, p. 20; Tsentralny Gosudarstvenny Arkhiv, Fond 6991, Opis No. 6, delo No. 3131.

86. Michael Bourdeaux, *Patriarch and Prophets,* p. 175; Pospielovsky, *The Russian Church,* p. 441; *Zhurnal Moskovskoi Patriarkhii,* No. 6 (June), 1979, p. 16.

87. In January 1957 the Grodno nunnery had fifty-two nuns and three novices; Polotsk

had forty-five nuns and six novices. Tsentralny Gosudarstvenny Arkhiv, Fond 6991s, Opis No. 2, Vol. I, delo Nos. 180, 205, 206.

88. The Council for Religious Affairs recorded fewer than fifty nuns and novices at Zhirovitsy in 1970. The figure of sixty-one given in 1970 must have included both the monastery and the nunnery. If there were fifteen monks, the number of nuns and novices was probably about forty-five. See Ellis, p. 471. By 1980 there were twenty-seven nuns and one novice who posed for a picture with Metropolitan Filaret (Vakhromeev). In 1981 Metropolitan Filaret stated that the nunnery had thirty-three nuns and novices. *Zhurnal Moskovskoi Patriarkhii,* No. 8 (August), 1980, before p. 9; Ellis, p. 128. In January 1986 the Council for Religious Affairs recorded one hegumen, one nun who had assumed the habit of the *mega schema,* twenty nuns, four senior novices, and ten junior novices. Tsentralny Gosudarstvenny Arkhiv, Fond 6991, Opis No. 6, delo No. 3137.

89. Metropolitan Filaret (Vakhromeev), letter to the Byelorussian authorities, *Moskovski Tserkovny Vestnik, Yezhenedelnik,* No. 6, April 1991, p. 15; No. 7, April 1991, p. 9; *Zhurnal Moskovskoi Patriarkhii,* No. 10 (October), 1989, p. 2.

90. *Zhurnal Moskovskoi Patriarkhii,* No. 9 (September), 1988, p. 15.

91. The Gorny nunnery had somewhere between a dozen and two dozen nuns and novices in the middle to late 1980s. Suzanne Massey in a television broadcast May 1, 1987, estimated twenty monks at the Danilov monastery. A picture in the *Journal of the Moscow Patriarchate* showed about the same number in a procession on September 12, 1987. *Zhurnal Moskovskoi Patriarkhii,* No. 1 (January), 1988, p. 40. I counted twenty-four monks and novices in a procession on January 28, 1990. Michael Warder was told in August 1988 that there were thirty-five monks and novices at Danilov. *Religion in Communist Dominated Areas,* Vol. XXVIII, No. 2, Spring 1989, p. 61. A fair estimate might be twenty-five to thirty-five. The *Moscow Church Herald* stated that there were nine nuns at the Tolga nunnery in June 1988. *Moskovski Tserkovny Vestnik,* No. 10 (October), 1988, p. 8. The *Moscow Church Herald* stated that there were four monks and four novices at the Optina hermitage in the summer of 1988. *Moskovski Tserkovny Vestnik,* No. 11 (November), 1988, p. 2. The low estimate for the total population of the four convents would be fifty-four and the high estimate seventy-six.

After June of 1988 both Tolga and Optina grew. By the end of 1988 there were fifteen to twenty nuns and novices at Tolga. *Moskovski Tserkovny Vestnik,* No. 12 (December), 1988, p. 2; *Zhurnal Moskovskoi Patriarkhii,* No. 12 (December), 1988, p. 25. I was told in the summer of 1994 that the number had grown to 100. This is also the number James R. Moss reported in 1992. *RCDA,* No. 4, 1992, p. 74. There were four monks and sixteen novices at Optina in the late months of 1988, a total of twenty; there were twenty-five at the end of the year; there were about forty in the summer of 1989; about fifty monks and novices, mostly novices, were claimed in May 1990; fifty-four monks and novices were reported in late 1990. *Zhurnal Moskovskoi Patriarkhii,* No. 2 (February), 1989, p. 21; No. 5 (May), 1989, p. 11; *Religiya v SSSR* [Religion in the USSR], No. 12 (December), 1988, p. 1AL; *Ogonëk,* No. 34, August 1989, p. 28; Dimitry V. Pospielovsky, "Religious Themes in the Soviet Press in 1989," *Religion in Communist Lands,* Vol. 18, No. 4, Winter 1990, p. 329.

92. Ellis, pp. 130–131, 471; Philip Walters, ed., with Keston College researchers, *World*

Christianity: Eastern Europe (Monrovia, Calif.: Missions Advanced Research and Communications Center, 1988), p. 44; Paul A. Lucey, "Religion," *U.S.S.R. Facts and Figures Annual,* ed. John L. Scherer (Gulf Breeze, Florida: Academic International Press, 1988), p. 318.

93. Early in 1990 church spokesmen claimed over forty functioning convents. *Zhurnal Moskovskoi Patriarkhii,* No. 10 (October), 1989, p. 16; No. 2 (February), 1990, p. 9; No. 5 (May), 1990, p. 26; *Nauka i Religiya,* No. 1, January 1990, p. 2.

94. The figure of fifty-six convents is from *Religion in USSR,* No. 10 (October), 1990, p. 53. *Keston News Service* reported sixty-one convents in January 1991 (No. 371, March 21, 1991, p. 4). For 121 convents in late 1991, see Serge Schmemann, "Patriarch's Church Revives, but Will Spirituality?" *The New York Times,* November 9, 1991, p. 2. Patriarch Aleksi had claimed 115 convents a few weeks earlier. See *Moskovski Tserkovny Vestnik, Yezhenedelnik,* No. 16, September 1991, p. 3. For the figures of 150 and 213, see *Zhurnal Moskovskoi Patriarkhii,* No. 10 (October), 1992, p. 20; No. 2 (February), 1994, p. 9.

95. Some newly established monasteries and nunneries have considerable populations of monks or nuns, of course, and many of the very small convents are growing. To illustrate the problem, however, the following are a few examples of small religious houses opened in the late 1980s and early 1990s:

- The Varnitsa hermitage of the Trinity-Sergius monastery, Yaroslavl oblast. A monastic priest and three monks dedicated themselves on September 12, 1989, to serve at the hermitage.
- Khust-Gorodilov, Makovitsya, Transcarpathia, the Trinity Monastery. In April 1990 the community was reported to number ten monks and novices and at the end of 1991, sixteen.
- Zadonsk, Voronezh oblast, Birth of the Mother of God monastery. Reportedly there were four monks in residence in mid-1990.
- Cossack Graves hermitage of the Pochaev monastery, Rovno oblast. Two monastic priests and a monastic deacon were reported to have been sent in 1991 to become the three men serving at the hermitage.
- Vyazma, Smolensk oblast. Eight monks and novices were reported in residence in January 1991.
- Vologda monastery. Four monks and novices were reported to be in residence in the summer of 1994.
- St. Petersburg, St. John Rylski–St. John of Kronshtadt mission community of Pyukhtitsa Dormition nunnery. In mid-1990 the community was reported to have nine sisters in residence.
- Kremenets, Ternopol oblast, Epiphany nunnery. In January 1991 a mother superior and six nuns and novices were reported to be in residence.
- Mogochin, Tomsk oblast, St. Nicholas nunnery. In 1992 a mother superior and five nuns and novices were reported in residence.

These are only a few selected examples. *Zhurnal Moskovskoi Patriarkhii,* No. 7 (July), 1990, p. 46; No. 10 (October), 1990, pp. 8–9, 24–26; No. 1 (January), 1991, p. 33; No. 8 (August), 1991, p. 23; No. 3 (March), 1992, p. 7; No. 4 (April), 1992, p. 8; *Pravoslavny Visnyk,* No. 4 (April), 1991, p. 5; No. 10 (October), 1991, p. 3; No. 4 (April), 1992, p. 6; *Moskovski*

Tserkovny Vestnik, Yezhenedelnik, No. 2, February 1992, p. 3; *Religion in the U.S.S.R.,* No. 6 (June), 1991, Supplement I, p. 34; MITEK (Rebrova), and reports to me in the summer of 1994.

96. *Izvestiya,* February 14, 1990, p. 6; *Zhurnal Moskovskoi Patriarkhii,* No. 11 (November), 1990, p. 32; *Moskovski Tserkovny Vestnik, Yezhenedelnik,* No. 2, January 1991, p. 11; *Zhurnal Moskovskoi Patriarkhii,* No. 10 (October), 1988, p. 9.

97. *Religiya v SSSR,* No. 11, 1990, p. 39(4).

98. Data for Figure 11.2 are from these sources: For 95,000 monks, nuns, and novices in imperial Russia, see Fontanieu, p. 61; Alexeev and Stavrou, p. 7. For 1939, see Ellis, p. 132. For 1945, see Fond 6991s, Opis No. 2, Vol. I, delo No. 263; for 1947, No. 61; for 1956 and 1957, No. 180; for 1958, No. 206; for 1959, 1960, and 1961, No. 263; for 1968 and 1970, Ellis, pp. 130, 131, 471, and Walters, p. 44; for 1976, Paul A. Lucey, "Religion," *The Soviet Union Today,* ed. James Cracraft (Chicago: Bulletin of the Atomic Scientists, 1983), p. 296; for mid-1980s and later, see *Zhurnal Moskovski Patriarkhii,* No. 9 (September), 1988, p. 15; No. 10 (October), 1992, p. 20; No. 2 (February), 1994, p. 9; *Pravoslavnaya Rus,* No. 20, October 15/28, 1992, p. 14.

99. I am indebted to William C. Fletcher for these thoughts.

Chapter 12

1. See Archpriest Andrei Sergeenko, "Sv. Ioann Zlatoust o pastyrskom sluzhenii [St. John Chrysostom on Pastoral Service]," *Zhurnal Moskovskoi Patriarkhii* [Journal of the Moscow Patriarchate], No. 5 (May), 1957, p. 40.

2. See Metropolitan Vladimir (Sabodan), "Zhizn i deyatelnost Russkoi Pravoslavnoi Tserkvi [Life and Activity of the Russian Orthodox Church]," report to the national council, June 7, 1988, *Zhurnal Moskovskoi Patriarkhii,* No. 9 (September), 1988, p. 15.

3. *Zhurnal Moskovskoi Patriarkhii,* No. 2 (February), 1990, p. 40; No. 9 (September), 1990, p. 7; No. 12 (December), 1990, p. 15; *Moskovski Tserkovny Vestnik, Yezhenedelnik* [The Moscow Church Herald, Weekly], No. 6, April 1992, p. 8. In 1989 the Russian Orthodox Church reduced the period of classroom instruction at the academies from four years to three and made the fourth year a time for the students to write their theses.

4. Jane Ellis, *The Russian Orthodox Church: A Contemporary History* (Bloomington, Indiana: Indiana University Press, 1986), p. 269; *Zhurnal Moskovskoi Patriarkhii,* No. 9 (September), 1944, inside front cover; No. 4 (April), 1945, inside front and back covers; No. 7 (July), 1947, pp. 26, 36; No. 1 (January), 1950, p. 28; No. 7 (July), 1963, p. 21; No. 5 (May), 1986, p. 15; No. 1 (January), 1990, p. 11; V. G. Furov, "Cadres of the Church and Legal Measures to Curtail Their Activities: A Secret Report by the Council on Religious Affairs," *Religion in Communist Dominated Areas,* Vol. XX, Nos. 4–6, 1981, p. 56. Originally, the *aspirantura* program offered courses to prepare a student for work abroad, including languages, other confessions, philosophy, and diplomatic practice. In later years the emphasis on foreign work faded, and under official pressure, the study of philosophy was curtailed.

5. M. Kozlov, "Prodolzhaya traditsiyu [Continuing in the Tradition]," *Moskovski Tserkovny Vestnik, Yezhenedelnik,* No. 23, October 1990, p. 6; *Zhurnal Moskovskoi Patriarkhii,*

No. 2 (February), 1990, p. 40. The requirements for admission published in 1993 (not republished in 1994) did not reflect the fifth year thesis. *Zhurnal Moskovskoi Patriarkhii,* No. 3 (March), 1993, p. 110.

6. Tsentralny Gosudarstvenny Arkhiv Oktyabrskoi Revolutsii [Central State Archive of the October Revolution], Vysshikh Organov Gosudarstvennoi Vlasti i Organov Gosurdarstvennogo Upravleniya S.S.S.R. [of the Higher Organs of State Government and Organs of State Administration of the U.S.S.R.], Soviet po delam religii pri Sovete Ministrov [the Council for Religious Affairs attached to the Council of Ministers], Fond 6991s, Opis No. 2, Vol. I, delo Nos. 204, 231, 232; Furov, Vol. XX, Nos. 4–6, 1981, p. 53.

7. *Zhurnal Moskovskoi Patriarkhii,* No. 3 (March), 1988, p. 32; No. 1 (January), 1990, p. 11; No. 2 (February), 1990, p. 41; No. 4 (April), 1990, p. 80; No. 5 (May), 1990, p. 28. Despite the decision of the bishops' council in 1989, the 1993 requirements for admission listed correspondence courses only in Moscow, St. Petersburg, Odessa, Kiev, and Zhirovitsy (Grodno oblast, Belarus). *Zhurnal Moskovskoi Patriarkhii,* No. 3 (March), 1993, p. 112.

8. *Zhurnal Moskovskoi Patriarkhii,* No. 11 (November), 1956, pp. 42–43; No. 3 (March), 1964, pp. 20–21; Moscow Patriarchate, *The Russian Orthodox Church: Organization, Situation, Activity* (Moscow: Moscow Patriarchate, 1958), p. 116.

9. Trevor Beeson, *Discretion and Valor* (Philadelphia, Penn.: Fortress Press, 1982), p. 56; *Moskovski Tserkovny Vestnik, Yezhenedelnik,* No. 15, November 1989, p. 7.

10. Dimitry Pospielovsky, *The Russian Church Under the Soviet Regime, 1917–1982,* 2 Vols. (Crestwood, New York: St. Vladimir's Seminary Press, 1984), p. 321.

11. *Zhurnal Moskovskoi Patriarkhii,* No. 3 (March), 1943, p. 24; No. 10 (October), 1946, p. 11. See also Raymond A. Davies, "The Patriarch on Church and State," *Soviet Russia Today,* November 1945, p. 13; Paul B. Anderson, *People, Church and State in Modern Russia* (New York: The Macmillan Co., 1944), p. 18.

12. Sergi Gordun, "Russkaya Pravoslavnaya Tserkov v period s 1943 po 1970 god [The Russian Orthodox Church in the Period from 1943 to 1970]," *Zhurnal Moskovskoi Patriarkhii,* No. 1 (January), 1993, p. 42; "50 let arkhiereiskogo sluzheniya Svyateishego Patriarkha Moskovskogo i vseya Rusi Aleksiya [Fifty Years of Episcopal Service of the Most Holy Patriarch of Moscow and All Russia Aleksi]," *Zhurnal Moskovskoi Patriarkhii,* No. 11 (November), 1945, p. 23; No. 7 (July), 1946, p. 6; Special Issue, December 1963, p. 76.

13. William B. Stroyen, *Communist Russia and the Russian Orthodox Church, 1943–1962* (Washington: The Catholic University of America Press, 1967), p. 71; *Zhurnal Moskovskoi Patriarkhii,* No. 9 (September), 1945, p. 38; No. 11 (November), 1945, pp. 22–23; No. 7 (July), 1946, p. 6; No. 6 (June), 1947, p. 6; No. 3 (March), 1986, p. 20; John Shelton Curtiss, *The Russian Church and the Soviet State, 1917–1950* (Boston: Little, Brown and Co., 1953), p. 294; Raymond Arthur Davies, *Inside Russia Today* (Winnipeg: Contemporary Publications, 1945), p. 48; "50 let arkhiereiskogo sluzheniya," p. 77. In the autumn of 1945, six of the seventy-four students at the Moscow theological institute were identified as taking an academy-level course of instruction.

14. Stroyen, p. 71; Moscow Patriarchate, pp. 116–117; *Zhurnal Moskovskoi Patriarkhii,* No. 11 (November), 1949, p. 10.

15. *American Churchmen Visit the Soviet Union* (New York: National Council of Churches), p. 11.

16. Pospielovsky, p. 322.

17. In 1948 only a third of the applicants were admitted; normal practice during the decade and a half after the war was to accept about half of those who applied. Nathaniel Davis, *Religion and Communist Government in the Soviet Union and Eastern Europe,* dissertation, The Fletcher School of Law and Diplomacy, June 1, 1960, pp. 374–378; Tsentralny Gosudarstvenny Arkhiv, Fond 6991s, Opis No. 2, Vol. I, delo Nos. 204, 231.

18. Close to 200 of the students in 1948 were in Moscow, roughly 150 were in Leningrad, and the remaining 200-plus were in the six other seminaries. Tsentralny Gosudarstvenny Arkhiv, Fond 6991s, Opis No. 2, Vol. I, delo No. 263.

19. Enrollment was 585 in the eight seminaries and 145 in the academies. Sergi Gordun, "Russkaya Pravoslavnaya Tserkov v period s 1943 po 1970 god [The Russian Orthodox Church in the Period from 1943 to 1970]," *Zhurnal Moskovskoi Patriarkhii,* No. 2 (February), 1993, p. 21.

20. Zhirovitsy had 164 students at the start of autumn classes in 1957 and Odessa had 159 as classes started in 1958. Davis, pp. 376–377; Tsentralny Gosudarstvenny Arkhiv, Fond 6991s, Opis No. 2, Vol. I, delo Nos. 177, 178, 204, 230–232; Walter Kolarz, *Religion in the Soviet Union* (New York: St. Martin's Press, 1961), p. 90; *Zhurnal Moskovskoi Patriarkhii,* No. 12 (December), 1947, p. 52.

21. Davis, pp. 376–377; Tsentralny Gosudarstvenny Arkhiv, Fond 6991s, Opis No. 2, Vol. I, delo Nos. 177, 178, 204; *American Churchmen Visit the Soviet Union,* p. 11.

22. Tsentralny Gosudarstvenny Arkhiv, Fond 6991s, Opis No. 2, Vol. I, delo No. 177. Leningrad offered seminary education by correspondence only for the latter two years of the four-year seminary course. The numbers in each class in September 1955, were third class seminary, 203; fourth class seminary, fifty-three; first class academy, eighty-nine; second class academy, thirty-four; third class academy, thirteen; fourth class academy, eleven. As is evident from the numbers, the school had been expanding for several years. There were 142 students at the two resident academies during the same academic year. By the next trimester, the two seminary classes had grown by twenty-three and ten students respectively. See also *Zhurnal Moskovskoi Patriarkhii,* No. 11 (November), 1949, pp. 10–11.

23. Enrollment increased from 403 in 1955, to 442 in 1956, to 488 in 1958. This gain probably reflected an increase from 400 to 500 in the officially imposed ceiling. Tsentralny Gosudarstvenny Arkhiv, Fond 6991s, Opis No. 2, Vol. I, delo Nos. 178, 204.

24. Attrition in the course of the academic year brought enrollment down to 117 (four failed, three left because of housing problems, fourteen left at the students' own choice, nine were inducted into the army, and two died). Tsentralny Gosudarstvenny Arkhiv, Fond 6991s, Opis No. 2, Vol. I, delo No. 178.

25. Tsentralny Gosudarstvenny Arkhiv, Fond 6991s, Opis No. 2, Vol. I, delo Nos. 177, 204, 231. Note that the statistics are for the number of students at the start of the academic year. All the schools experience some attrition in the course of the year, and some students fail their exams and drop out at the end of the year. A few new students are enrolled in the course of the autumn or in January. The authorities seem to have permitted small overages in initial enrollment, knowing that attrition would bring the numbers within bounds. *Zhurnal Moskovskoi Patriarkhii,* No. 1 (January), 1987, p. 19.

26. Tsentralny Gosudarstvenny Arkhiv, Fond 6991s, Opis No. 2, Vol. I, delo Nos. 204, 231, 232.

27. The military not only drafted those in seminary eligible for service but also tried to make sure applicants were drafted before matriculation. Gerhard Simon, *Church, State and Opposition in the U.S.S.R.,* trans. Kathleen Matchett (Berkeley, Calif.: University of California Press, 1970), p. 78.

28. Gordun, *Zhurnal,* No. 2 (February), p. 21; Pospielovsky, p. 322; *Russia Cristiana Ieri e Oggi* [Christian Russia Yesterday and Today], No. 18, June 1961, p. 18; No. 21, September 1961, p. 7.

29. Less than half of this loss could be accounted for by the closing of Kiev and Stavropol, and some of the students in those two schools had actually been transferred to seminaries like Odessa that were still functioning. Tsentralny Gosudarstvenny Arkhiv, Fond 6991s, Opis No. 2, Vol. I, delo No. 263.

30. Father Sergi Gordun quoted the instructions implementing Decree No. 263 of March 16, 1961, as explaining that the Soviet government had originally only authorized in-house (*statsionarny*) religious instruction. The text of the instructions forbade matriculation of new students, and it seems that some of the enrolled students were permitted to continue and perhaps to transfer to the Moscow correspondence schools when they opened. Gordun, *Zhurnal,* No. 2 (February), p. 19. Professor Nikolai D. Uspenski of the Leningrad academy reported that the Leningrad correspondence school operated until 1968. See Nikolai D. Uspenski, "K istorii bogoslovskogo obrazonvaniya v Leningrade [Commemorating the History of Theological Education in Leningrad]," *Zhurnal Moskovskoi Patriarkhii,* No. 4 (April), 1977, p. 11. It would be surprising if the correspondence schools at Leningrad managed to hang on quite so long, but a handful of students may have been allowed to finish theses, making Uspenski's statement technically accurate.

31. Simon, p. 78; Ellis, p. 106. The figures were 364 resident students in five seminaries and 197 resident students in two academies. In addition, Leningrad had an enrollment of 128 correspondence students in its seminary course and 65 correspondence students in its academy course. Gordun, *Zhurnal,* No. 2 (February), p. 21.

32. Gordun, *Zhurnal,* No. 2 (February), p. 21; Simon, p. 78; *Zhurnal Moskovskoi Patriarkhii,* No. 3 (March), 1964, pp. 22–24; No. 7 (July), 1964, p. 19; No. 5 (May), 1972, p. 21.

33. Gordun, *Zhurnal,* No. 2 (February), p. 21; Simon, p. 78; *Zhurnal Moskovskoi Patriarkhii,* No. 3 (March), 1990, p. 37.

34. At that time there were 177 correspondence seminarians and 157 correspondence academy students in the wasting Leningrad correspondence program and the newly opened Moscow correspondence schools. Gordun, *Zhurnal,* No. 2 (February), p. 21; *Zhurnal Moskovskoi Patriarkhii,* No. 4 (April), 1963, p. 30; No. 8 (August), 1982, p. 12.

35. Savelii Tuberozov, "Monasteries and Theological Schools in the U.S.S.R.," *Eastern Churches Review,* Vol. I, 1966, p. 60; Ellis, p. 120; Howard L. Parsons, *Christianity in the Soviet Union,* Occasional Paper No. 11 (New York: The American Institute for Marxist Studies, 1972).

36. Tsentralny Gosudarstvenny Arkhiv, Fond 6991s, Opis No. 2, Vol. I, delo No. 178; John S. Bonnell, "Will Atheism Triumph in Russia?" *The Fifth Avenue Voice,* September

1958, p. 4; Michael Bourdeaux, *Opium of the People* (Indianapolis, Indiana: The Bobbs-Merrill Co., 1966), p. 211. Foreign students are excluded from the figures.

37. Simon, p. 79; *Zhurnal Moskovskoi Patriarkhii,* No. 12 (December), 1967, p. 45 (group photo); No. 11 (November), 1970, p. 16 (group photo). Tuberozov, p. 60, estimated "nearly 500" resident students, which is very close to the figure of "about 475" given here. Simon, p. 79.

38. Raymond Oppenheim, "Russian Orthodox Theological Education in the Soviet Union," *Religion in Communist Lands,* Vol. 2, No. 3, 1974, p. 7. Oppenheim was the Episcopal chaplain at the U.S. embassy in Moscow during the 1970s.

39. Ellis, pp. 120–121; Oppenheim, p. 5; Philippe Sabant, "Religion in Russia Today, Part II," *The Tablet* (London), Vol. 234, No. 7280, January 19, 1980, p. 55; *Zhurnal Moskovskoi Patriarkhii,* No. 3 (March), 1989, p. 80; *Los Angeles Times,* February 19, 1989, p. 19; Francis House, *The Russian Phoenix* (London: SPCK, 1988), p. 102.

40. The figures of the Moscow seminary in the 1984–1985 academic year were 110 in class one, 110 in class two, 98 in class three, 94 in class four. Eleven of these students were aged eighteen to twenty; 369 were aged twenty-one to thirty; 32 were aged thirty-one to forty. Thirty-four students had a university degree; 3 had gone part way through university; 102 had a specialized middle-school education; 267 had a ten-year-school diploma; 6 had completed seven to nine classes of ten-year-school. Church servers numbered 182; 2 were priests; 103 were workers; 42 were service employees; 12 were collective farmers; 16 had been students; 45 had just been demobilized from the army; 10 were unemployed. Tsentralny Gosudarstvenny Arkhiv, Fond 6991, Opis No. 6, delo No. 3131.

41. *Zhurnal Moskovskoi Patriarkhii,* No. 1 (January), 1966, p. 25; No. 6 (June), 1988, pp. 6–7; Parsons, p. 31; Ellis, pp. 120–121; *Eastern Churches Review,* Vol. V, No. 1, Spring 1973, p. 79; House, p. 102; Sabant, p. 55; Pospielovsky, pp. 407, 458. Actually, double sections for entering students commenced in 1976.

42. *Zhurnal Moskovskoi Patriarkhii,* No. 7 (July), 1976, p. 4; No. 2 (February), 1971, p. 17 (group photo); *Pravoslavny Visnyk,* No. 12 (December), 1971, p. 11 (group photo); Ellis, pp. 120–121; Oppenheim, p. 8; Pospielovsky, p. 407; House, p. 102; Furov, Vol. XX, Nos. 4–6, 1981, p. 53. By 1973–1974 Odessa had almost 120 enrolled students.

43. In September 1977 the student body was at least 158 strong, although it dropped to 133 by the spring of 1978. Within a year or two the enrollment rose to 200. By 1979–1980 it had reached 245, and within a year after that, 260. *Pravoslavny Visnyk,* No. 11 (November), 1977, p. 14; No. 8 (August), 1978, p. 27; No. 11 (November), 1988, p. 10; Ellis, pp. 120–121; Michael Rowe, "Soviet Policy Towards Religion," *U.S.S.R. Facts and Figures Annual, 1981,* ed. John L. Scherer (Gulf Breeze, Florida: Academic International Press, 1982), p. 324; Sabant, p. 55; Pospielovsky, p. 407.

44. Furov, Vol. XX, Nos. 4–6, 1981, pp. 53, 56. Furov's figure for the seminary and academy enrollments at Moscow and Leningrad was 461 in June 1974. That was at the end of the academic year prior to the figure for 1974–1975 given in the text for Moscow, Leningrad, and Odessa.

45. In 1977 enrollment was 788. *Zhurnal Moskovskoi Patriarkhii,* No. 8 (August), 1978, p. 14. Metropolitan Vladimir (Sabodan), "Sovremennoe sostoyanie Russkoi Pravoslavnoi

Tserkvi [The Present State of the Russian Orthodox Church]," *Religiya v SSSR* [Religion in the USSR], No. 10 (October), 1988, p. MV2.

46. The enrollment figure for the Moscow correspondence schools for the 1973–1974 school year was 510. Furov, Vol. XX, Nos. 4–6, 1981, p. 56. The Leningrad correspondence schools had about 500 students in 1959, the year before those schools closed, and Moscow had over 800 in 1977. Rowe, p. 324. Late 1980s and early 1990s figures for the Moscow seminary and academy correspondence schools were January 1986—786; January 1988—810; early 1989—900; October 1990 to January 1991—921. *Nauka i Religiya* [Science and Religion], No. 1 (January), 1992, p. 7; Vladimir, "Sovremennoe sostoyanie," p. MV2; Anatoli Tsirulnikov, "Iz zhizni dukhovnoi shloly [From the Life of a Theological School]," *Ogonëk* [Little Fire], No. 5, January 28–February 4, 1989, p. 30; *Religion in USSR,* No. 10 (October), 1990, p. 53 (26); No. 12 (December), 1990, p. 37.

47. In 1947–1948 the Moscow theological schools had seven professors (four of them priests), six associate professors (docents—two of them priests), and five instructors (two of them priests). *Zhurnal Moskovskoi Patriarkhii,* No. 11 (November), 1948, p. 13; No. 1 (January), 1965, p. 4.

48. Thirty-seven members of the faculty were monastics and five were women. Oppenheim, p. 5; Ellis, p. 104.

49. In 1946 the Leningrad schools had three professors, five associate professors, and two instructors, for a faculty-student ratio of about one to seven. In 1956 there were seven professors, nine associate professors, and nine instructors. *Zhurnal Moskovskoi Patriarkhii,* No. 10 (October), 1946, p. 12; No. 7 (July), 1947, pp. 44, 46; No. 4 (April), 1977, p. 10. Tsentralny Gosudarstvenny Arkhiv, Fond 6991s, Opis No. 2, Vol. I, delo No. 178.

50. Pospielovsky, p. 458 (1982). Nine of the forty-three had secular degrees. In 1973–1974 there were five professors, six associate professors, and twenty instructors. Oppenheim, p. 7.

51. Between 1969 and 1974 the graduating students or sometimes all the students lined up most years and had their pictures taken, with the professors sitting in front. In 1969 there were six faculty members; in 1970, seven; in 1971, eight; in 1973, nine. Oppenheim, p. 8, reported for the 1973–1974 academic year that there were sixteen faculty members in all, nine of whom were ordained. *Zhurnal Moskovskoi Patriarkhii,* No. 9 (September), 1969, p. 19; No. 11 (November), 1970, p. 16; No. 2 (February), 1971, p. 17; No. 8 (August), 1973, p. 9. *Pravoslavny Visnyk,* No. 9 (September), 1973, p. 8.

52. In 1973–1974 there were sixteen faculty members at Odessa, and the number of ordained instructors had slowly increased from about six to nine, leveling off at about that number. Oppenheim, p. 8; Rowe, p. 326; Ellis, p. 104; *Zhurnal Moskovskoi Patriarkhii,* No. 3 (March), 1980, p. 36.

53. Father Sergi Gordun found a document in the archives of the Soviet government's Council for Russian Orthodox Church Affairs showing that the council in 1948 removed from the church's academies' teaching curriculum planned courses in Christian education, Christian psychology, the history of philosophy, and logic. The council also vetoed seminary courses in the foundations of psychology and a survey of philosophical pedagogy. Gordun, *Zhurnal,* No. 1 (January), p. 47.

54. Nikita Struve, "Tserkov v Sovetskoi Rossii [The Church in Soviet Russia]," *Vestnik Russkogo Studencheskogo Khristianskogo Dvizheniya* [Herald of the Russian Student Christian Movement], Nos. V–VI, 1954, p. 21.

55. William C. Fletcher, *The Russian Orthodox Church Underground, 1917–1970* (London: Oxford University Press, 1971), pp. 289–290. See also *Zhurnal Moskovskoi Patriarkhii,* No. 7 (July), 1947, p. 29.

56. Gordun, *Zhurnal,* No. 1 (January), p. 47.

57. *American Churchmen Visit the Soviet Union,* p. 12.

58. Nikolai Gavryushin, "Nasledie i nasledniki [The Heritage and the Heirs]," *Moskovski Tserkovny Vestnik, Yezhenedelnik,* No. 23, October 1990, p. 6.

59. In mentioning *Ogonëk,* the editor was referring to the numerous commentaries of Aleksandr Nezhny published in that magazine. In mentioning *Kommersant,* he was no doubt referring principally to its sensational exposé of Metropolitan Filaret (Denisenko) and his private life. Kozlov, p. 6.

60. In the autumn of 1990, the Odessa seminary appointed new instructors in philosophy, history, literature, and law. *Zhurnal Moskovskoi Patriarkhii,* No. 9 (September), 1988, p. 18; No. 2 (February), 1990, pp. 39–41; No. 2 (February), 1991, p. 32.

61. Matthew Spinka, *The Church in Soviet Russia* (New York: Oxford University Press, 1956), p. 96.

62. Furov, Vol. XX, Nos. 4–6, 1981, p. 56; *Zhurnal Moskovskoi Patriarkhii,* No. 9 (September), 1969, pp. 16–17.

63. Alan Geyer, "Three Days in August: Reflections on the Soviet Coup and Its Consequences," distributed by the John T. Conner Center, 1991, p. 7; Tsirulnikov, p. 30.

64. Ellis, p. 106, quoting Oppenheim and Theo van der Voort, a Dutch academy student at Leningrad between 1974 and 1977.

65. Furov, Vol. XX, Nos. 4–6, 1981, p. 55.

66. Ellis, p. 104.

67. Ellis, p. 107.

68. Tsentralny Gosudarstvenny Arkhiv, Fond 6991s, Opis No. 2, Vol. I, delo No. 178.

69. The collection hovered at about 200,000 for the next decade and a half. *Zhurnal Moskovskoi Patriarkhii,* No. 7 (July), 1947, p. 47; No. 9 (September), 1948, p. 28; No. 11 (November), 1971, p. 21; No. 4 (April), 1977, p. 12; Ellis, p. 107; Struve, p. 22; Tsentralny Gosudarstvenny Arkhiv, Fond 6991s, Opis No. 2, Vol. I, delo No. 178.

70. The St. Petersburg theological schools' reading room consists of several tables placed between the card catalogue on one wall and the counter where one requests materials. Most days I worked in the reading room alone without other scholars present.

71. Theo van der Voort, quoted in Ellis, p. 107.

72. Ellis, p. 107 (quoting Oppenheim and Alan Nichols, an Australian Anglican).

73. Oppenheim, p. 8; *Zhurnal Moskovskoi Patriarkhii,* No. 2 (February), 1990, p. 40.

74. Pospielovsky, p. 320. Pospielovsky was quoting Anatoli Levitin-Krasnov and other Russian Orthodox sources with approval.

75. Pospielovsky, p. 407. See also Bill Keller, "Russian Tells Shadowy Tale of Spying Inside the Church," *The New York Times,* June 21, 1987, pp. 1, 11; Bill Keller, "Ex-KGB Officer Asserts Spy Agency Is Unchanged," *The New York Times,* June 17, 1990, p. 12; [Oleg

Kalugin], "KGB: Former Soviet Spy Speaks Out," *Los Angeles Times,* July 23, 1990, p. A9. Dmitri Radyshevski, "Gonimye za veru [Persecuted for Their Faith]," *Moskovskie Novosti* [Moscow News], No. 18, May 6, 1990, p. 16.

76. "A. S.," *Posev,* Vol. XXIV, No. 5 (1132), May 1968, pp. 7–8.

77. *Posev,* Nos. 17–18 (1092–1093), April 30, 1967, p. 3.

78. In 1946 the ratio of applicants to acceptances at the Moscow seminary was about two to one. *Zhurnal Moskovskoi Patriarkhii,* No. 10 (October), 1946, pp. 3–4. In 1951 a Quaker delegation estimated that about half of seminary applicants were being accepted. Kathleen Lonsdale, ed., *Quakers Visit Russia* (London: East-West Relations Group of the Friends' Peace Committee, 1952), p. 29. In 1955 there were seventy candidates for the Moscow seminary, of whom thirty-six, or almost exactly half, were accepted. Paul B. Anderson, "Churchmen Visit Russia," *Christian Century,* April 18, 1956, p. 481. In 1957 Metropolitan Nikolai (Yarushevich) stated that the ratio of applicants to open places was three to one. *U.S.S.R. Illustrated Monthly,* No. 8, May 1957 (Washington, D.C.: Embassy of the U.S.S.R.), p. 54. In 1956 and 1957, for all ten theological schools, three quarters of those who applied presented themselves for entrance examinations, and about half of those who applied (47 percent) were accepted and matriculated. Tsentralny Gosudarstvenny Arkhiv, Fond 6991s, Opis No. 2, Vol. I, delo Nos. 204, 231. In 1965 Tuberozov estimated four candidates for each seminary opening in Leningrad. Tuberozov, p. 59. In 1973–1974 Oppenheim estimated about four candidates for each seminary opening in both Moscow and Leningrad. Oppenheim, pp. 6, 7. In 1983 there were 160 applicants to the Odessa seminary, and 60 were admitted. Helen Marmor, "The Church of the Russians," television broadcast on July 17, 1983, NBC Communications Commission, National Council of Churches, New York.

79. Oppenheim, p. 7. Oppenheim's figure was twenty-eight applicants for the twenty-five openings at the Leningrad academy for the 1973–1974 school year. The council's figures for 1956 and 1957 confirm that most applicants to the academies were accepted during that period. Tsentralny Gosudarstvenny Arkhiv, Fond 6991s, Opis No. 2, Vol. I, delo Nos. 204, 231. Since requirements for academy admission without special examination have reflected a slight relaxation of academic standards, as they have stipulated completion of seminary with grades of "4" or "5" (on a five-point scale), while earlier requirements stipulated only the top category of grades. *Zhurnal Moskovskoi Patriarkhii,* No. 4 (April), 1988, p. 79; No. 4 (April), 1987, p. 79.

80. Tsirulnikov, p. 30; Tsentralny Gosudarstvenny Arkhiv, Fond 6991s, Opis No. 2, Vol. I, delo Nos. 204, 231.

81. *Moskovski Tserkovny Vestnik, Yezhenedelnik,* No. 10, August 1989, p. 6.

82. Ellis, p. 103. Ellis said all three choir directors' schools were opened in 1969, but according to Leningrad academy professor Nikolai D. Uspenski, the school there opened in 1967. *Zhurnal Moskovskoi Patriarkhii,* No. 4 (April), 1977, p. 11.

83. Pospielovsky stated women were admitted to the Leningrad choir school in 1978. Pospielovsky, p. 403; *Zhurnal Moskovskoi Patriarkhii,* No. 8 (August), 1978, p. 14; No. 9 (September), 1979, p. 5; No. 5 (May), 1990, p. 29.

84. *Zhurnal Moskovskoi Patriarkhii,* No. 9 (September), 1988, p. 18; No. 12 (December), 1988, p. 27. The April 1992 issue of the *Journal of the Moscow Patriarchate* listed only the

choir directors' courses in Moscow (Sergiev Posad) and St. Petersburg when inviting applications from prospective students. *Zhurnal Moskovskoi Patriarkhii,* No. 4 (April), 1992, p. 16(x).

85. Moscow's splitting of classes reduced class size, enabled new learning disciplines to be introduced, and intensified the daily schedule of studies. *Zhurnal Moskovskoi Patriarkhii,* No. 10 (October), 1989, p. 25.

86. Russell Chandler, "A Russian Force Is Reborn," *Los Angeles Times,* September 28, 1991, p. A6. The increase in enrollments at the Moscow seminary and the accommodation of choir school students was facilitated by the decision of the Zagorsk city authorities in October 1986 to turn over additional buildings. The transfer was actually carried out in 1988, and the new facilities were consecrated on September 11, 1989. *Zhurnal Moskovskoi Patriarkhii,* No. 3 (March), 1990, p. 35.

87. Counting foreign students and commuters, there were about 450 students at St. Petersburg (then Leningrad) prior to the Millennium. The school authorities published a call for seminary and academy correspondence school applicants in April 1990, but Sorokin's figures probably do not include correspondence students. *Keston News Service,* No. 375, May 16, 1991, p. 7; *Zhurnal Moskovskoi Patriarkhii,* No. 4 (April), 1990, p. 80.

88. *Zhurnal Moskovskoi Patriarkhii,* No. 2 (February), 1991, p. 32; documents of the Council for Religious Affairs, Russian State Archive, with the help of Marina Rebrova of MITEK Information Service, Moscow, and Julia Petrakis of Facts OnLine, Camano Island, Washington.

89. In September, forty-two students selected from eighty applicants entered Minsk (Zhirovitsy). *Zhurnal Moskovskoi Patriarkhii,* No. 6 (June), 1989, p. 80; No. 7 (July), 1989, p. 12; No. 10 (October), 1989, p. 2; No. 6 (June), 1990, pp. 32, 54; *Moskovski Tserkovny Vestnik, Yezhenedelnik,* No. 2, May 1989, p. 6; *Keston News Service,* No. 337, November 2, 1989, p. 9; No. 353, June 28, 1990, p. 15. For Kiev, MITEK (Rebrova).

90. A fourth new seminary was reportedly being planned in late 1989 as a joint diocesan effort, shared by the dioceses of Kirov and Kostroma. Plans were modified in 1990, however, to provide initially for a theological training institution rather than a full-fledged seminary. *Nauka i Religiya,* No. 1 (January), 1990, p. 2; *Zhurnal Moskovskoi Patriarkhii,* No. 1 (January), 1990, p. 32; No. 11 (November), 1990, p. 23.

91. *Zhurnal Moskovskoi Patriarkhii,* No. 9 (September), 1988, p. 18; No. 12 (December), 1988, p. 27; No. 10 (October), 1989, p. 26; No. 11 (November), 1989, pp. 20, 21; No. 12 (December), 1989, pp. 25, 27; No. 2 (February), 1990, pp. 9, 39; No. 2 (February), 1991, p. 32; *Pravoslavny Visnyk,* No. 11 (November), 1988, p. 10; No. 12 (December), 1989, pp. 8, 10; *Religiya v SSSR,* No. 5 (May), 1988, p. 20.

92. The new seminary was at Stavropol, upgraded from a theological training institute. In May 1989 there had been seventeen students (twelve men and five women) at the institute; in September there had been forty-five students; in 1990 the institute became a seminary. New institutes (excluding the five opened in 1989) were Kolomna, Kostroma, Kursk, Lutsk, Omsk, Ryazan, Vologda, Kitskany, Kapriana, and Tashkent. *Moskovski Tserkovny Vestnik, Yezhenedelnik,* No. 2, May 1989, p. 6; No. 5, March 1990, p. 2; No. 22, October 1990, p. 2; No. 23, October 1990, p. 2; No. 27, December 1990, p. 5; *Religiya v SSSR,*

No. 3 (March), 1990, p. 5; *Religion in USSR*, No. 1 (January), 1991, p. 9; *Pravoslavny Vestnik Stavropolya* [Orthodox Herald of Stavropol], No. 5 (May), 1991, p. 3.

93. A figure of 200–250 students in the twelve institutes would seem low, but *Science and Religion* gave a figure of only 200 for late 1990. *Nauka i Religiya*, No. 1 (January), 1992, p. 7. In 1991, Chernigov had ninety-five students, Smolensk had fifty, and Lutsk had twenty-five. MITEK (Rebrova). Forty percent of the students at Smolensk were Ukrainians.

94. The Novosti Press Agency reported in October 1990 that there were 2,719 students in the theological schools exclusive of the theological institutes. *Religion in USSR*, No. 10 (October), 1990, p. 53 (26). In the December issue of the *Journal of the Moscow Patriarchate* figures were given for the Moscow schools. *Zhurnal Moskovskoi Patriarkhii*, No. 12 (December), 1990, p. 37. These combined data indicate estimated enrollments as follows: Moscow seminary resident students, 400–450; Leningrad seminary resident students, 350–400; Odessa seminary resident students, 250–300; five other seminaries, 225 students; total resident seminary students, 1,271; Moscow seminary correspondence students, 697. *Religion in USSR*, No. 10 (October), 1990, p. 53; *Nauka i Religiya*, No. 1 (January), 1992, p. 7. Reportedly, there were 206 resident academy students at Moscow and Leningrad and about 220 Moscow academy correspondence students. There were about 280 students at the Moscow and Leningrad choir schools with about 140 at each institution. When the 20 postgraduate students and 20 students at the Moscow icon-painting school, opened in the autumn of 1990, are included, the total is very close to the figure of 2,719 that the Novosti News Agency published in October 1990.

95. The latter was to be a four- to five-year course with four on-site sessions each year, two designed to further the students' academic preparation and two for examinations. *Zhurnal Moskovskoi Patriarkhii*, No. 6 (June), 1991, pp. 29–30; No. 4 (April), 1992, p. 16(x).

96. The 1991 enrollment was also a decline from the 870 or more students in the autumn of 1989. *Zhurnal Moskovskoi Patriarkhii*, No. 12 (December), 1990, p. 37; No. 1 (January), 1992, p. 35; *Religion in USSR*, No. 10 (October), 1990, p. 53(26). The figures for the autumn of 1990 were 697 students in the seminary correspondence school and variously 218 and 224 in the academy correspondence school.

97. *Zhurnal Moskovskoi Patriarkhii*, No. 12 (December), 1990, p. 37; No. 1 (January), 1992, p. 35; No. 2 (February), 1944, p. 9.

98. *Zhurnal Moskovskoi Patriarkhii*, No. 1 (January), 1994, p. 16; and information supplied by faculty members of the Institute. The patriarch's 1991 meeting with the rector of Moscow State University undoubtedly contributed importantly to the collaboration described.

99. *Moskovski Tserkovny Vestnik, Yezhenedelnik*, Nos. 2–3, 1993, p. 9; *Russkaya Mysl*, No. 4022, March 25–31, 1994, p. 9; No. 4027, April 28–May 4, 1944, p. 9.

100. Enrollments in short-term pastoral courses of a month or two are not included.

101. Both Saratov and Stavropol later upgraded the institutes to full seminary status. *Moskovski Tserkovny Vestnik*, No. 8 (August), 1989, p. 8; *Moskovski Tserkovny Vestnik, Yezhenedelnik*, No. 2, May 1989, p. 6. Stavropol also organized a school for church administrators and bookkeepers.

102. *Moskovski Tserkovny Vestnik, Yezhenedelnik,* No. 23, October 1990, p. 3.

103. Archpriest Aleksandr Pivovarov was a leader among these activist priests.

104. *Zhurnal Moskovskoi Patriarkhii,* No. 1 (January), 1990, p. 11; No. 9 (September), 1990, p. 7.

105. First Rule of the Sixth General Council, quoted in *Zhurnal Moskovskoi Patriarkhii, Spetsialny Nomer* [Special Number, Commemorating 500 Years of Autocephaly], 1948, p. 23. It is important to bear in mind that Russian Orthodoxy does not give the same value to seminal thinking and theological innovation as does Western Protestantism. Westerners must beware of projecting their values and priorities into the real situation and needs of the Russian Orthodox Church.

Chapter 13

1. *The National Council Outlook,* September 1956, p. 10; Paul B. Anderson, "Russian-American Visitations: A Prelude to Understanding," *Christianity and Crisis,* Vol. XVI, No. 12, July 9, 1956, p. 93; *Irénikon,* 4th Quarter, 1955, p. 424.

2. Deacon Vladimir Rusak, quoted in Jane Ellis, *The Russian Orthodox Church: A Contemporary History* (Bloomington, Indiana: Indiana University Press, 1986), p. 150.

3. Harrison E. Salisbury, "Russians Export New Bibles to U.S.," *The New York Times,* August 17, 1956, pp. 1, 11.

4. Ellis, p. 150; *Zhurnal Moskovskoi Patriarkhii* [Journal of the Moscow Patriarchate], No. 1 (January), 1977, p. 78.

5. *Zhurnal Moskovskoi Patriarkhii,* No. 1 (January), 1977, p. 78; No. 8 (August), 1978, p. 14; No. 3 (March), 1979, p. 7; No. 9 (September), 1983, p. 79; No. 4 (April), 1985, p. 11; *Religiya v SSSR* [Religion in the USSR], No. 7 (July), 1988, pp. 26–27; No. 11 (November), 1988, p. 13; Ellis, pp. 150–151. Jane Ellis (p. 151) expressed doubts that the 1983 edition actually appeared, but it may have been a reprinting of the 1979 edition.

6. *Keston News Service,* No. 357, August 30, 1990, pp. 6–7; *Ekspress-Khronika* [Express Chronicle], No. 7, February 13, 1990, p. 4.

7. *Los Angeles Times,* March 23, 1988, p. 2; Keston College staff, "Bibles in the Soviet Union," *Religion in Communist Lands,* Vol. 17, No. 3, Autumn 1989, p. 261, quoting *Izvestiya* of March 25, 1988; *Ekspress-Khronika,* No. 7, February 13, 1990, p. 4.

8. Keston College staff, pp. 261–262.

9. *Religiya v SSSR,* No. 7 (July), 1988, pp. 26–27.

10. *Zhurnal Moskovskoi Patriarkhii,* No. 2 (February), 1990, p. 24.

11. Nine-thousand New Testaments were reported to have been printed in Lvov. See *Foreign Broadcast Information Service,* February 10, 1989, pp. 67–68. For the 200,000 Bibles expected from the U.S.-based Ukrainian Family Bible Association, see Keston College staff, p. 258.

12. Keston College staff, p. 262.

13. *Zhurnal Moskovskoi Patriarkhii,* No. 2 (February), 1990, p. 24.

14. *Keston News Service,* No. 367, January 24, 1991, p. 7; No. 368, February 7, 1991, p. 9; No. 372, April 4, 1991, p. 5; No. 373, April 18, 1991, p. 9; No. 375, May 16, 1991, pp. 9–10; No. 378, June 27, 1991, p. 7; *Zhurnal Moskovskoi Patriarkhii,* No. 2 (February), 1990, p. 70; *Mir-*

ror (U.S. National Council of Churches), Special Issue, Fall 1991, p. 8. See also *Moskovski Tserkovny Vestnik, Yezhenedelnik* [Moscow Church Herald, Weekly], No. 7, May 1992, p. 10; *Ofitsialnaga Khronika, Zhurnal Moskovskoi Patriarkhii* (Official Chronicle, Journal of the Moscow Patriarchate), No. 3, 1993, p. 25.

15. N. S. Timasheff, "Religion in Russia, 1941–1950," *The Soviet Union, Background, Ideology, Reality,* ed. Waldemar Gurian (Notre Dame: University of Notre Dame Press, 1951), p. 167; *The New York Times,* March 21, 1947, and August 17, 1956. See also Robert Tobias, *Communist-Christian Encounter in East Europe* (Indianapolis, Indiana: School of Religion Press, 1956), p. 264.

16. Ellis, pp. 150–151; John Meyendorff, *The Orthodox Church,* 3d ed. (Crestwood, New York: St. Vladimir's Seminary Press, 1981), p. 157; *Zhurnal Moskovskoi Patriarkhii,* No. 9 (September), 1956, p. 79; No. 6 (June), 1979, p. 79.

17. *Religiya v SSSR,* No. 7 (July), 1988, p. 27; *Zhurnal Moskovskoi Patriarkhii,* No. 4 (April), 1988, p. 5; No. 2 (February), 1990, p. 24.

18. *Zhurnal Moskovskoi Patriarkhii,* No. 4 (April), 1989, p. 21; No. 2 (February), 1990, p. 24; *Keston News Service,* No. 328, June 22, 1989, pp. 8–9; Keston College staff, pp. 258, 262; John Dart, "Soviets Accept Offer of Scriptures from Two Bible-Smuggling Groups," *Los Angeles Times,* December 17, 1988, Part V, p. 16.

19. *Keston News Service,* No. 335, October 5, 1989, p. 6.

20. *Zhurnal Moskovskoi Patriarkhii,* No. 3 (March), 1991, p. 31.

21. The Ukrainian Orthodox monthly mentioned in the text is *Pravoslavny Visnyk* [Orthodox Herald]; Keston College staff, p. 262.

22. *Literaturnaya Gazeta* [Literary Gazette], Supplement, April 1990, pp. 1–32. *Keston News Service,* No. 371, March 21, 1991, p. 15.

23. The ability of well-supported, foreign evangelical missionaries to distribute large numbers of Bibles has assisted them in activities that many Russian Orthodox have come to regard as divisive and competitive.

24. Ellis, pp. 153–154, 168–171.

25. *Zhurnal Moskovskoi Patriarkhii,* No. 2 (February), 1990, p. 24; *Religiya v SSSR,* No. 7 (July), 1988, p. 27. Interestingly, 30,000 prayer books were printed in Smolensk diocese in September 1942 under the German occupation. Wassily Alexeev, "L'Église orthodoxe Russe sous l'occupation allemande, 1941–1944 [The Russian Orthodox Church Under the German Occupation, 1941–1944]," *Irénikon,* Vol. 29, 1956, p. 266.

26. *Zhurnal Moskovskoi Patriarkhii,* No. 2 (February), 1990, pp. 25, 26; No. 3 (March), 1990, p. 19; No. 12 (December), 1990, p. 21; No. 2 (February), 1994, p. 24.

27. Ellis, p. 155; *Zhurnal Moskovskoi Patriarkhii,* No. 7 (July), 1975, p. 79; No. 6 (June), 1983, p. 80; No. 8 (August), 1984, p. 80; No. 5 (May), 1986, pp. 79–80; No. 4 (April), 1987, p. 78; No. 3 (March), 1990, p. 19; No. 7 (July), 1990, p. 80; No. 12 (December), 1990, p. 21; Ellis, p. 155.

28. Tobias, p. 267; *Zhurnal Moskovskoi Patriarkhii,* No. 5 (May), 1956, p. 67; No. 3 (March), 1990, pp. 79–80; No. 12 (December), 1990, p. 80; Ellis, pp. 154–155. A concordance was published in 1989.

29. *Zhurnal Moskovskoi Patriarkhii,* No. 2 (February), 1946, p. 40.

30. K. M. Komarov, "40 let izdatelskomu otdelu Moskovskogo Patriarkhata [Forty

Years for the Publishing Department of the Moscow Patriarchate]," *Zhurnal Moskovskoi Patriarkhii* [Journal of the Moscow Patriarchate], No. 3 (March), 1985, p. 13. The *Journal* was a semimonthly in the 1930s.

31. An exception to the publishing rules also covered the publication of materials printed for dissemination abroad.

32. The patriarchate's *The Truth About Religion in Russia,* issued in 1942, conformed to the normal regulations. The *Journal of the Moscow Patriarchate* carried a permit number and the name of the printer through May 1947, omitted these data for the balance of that year, recommenced in 1948 for three months, stopped again, started again in 1950 for one issue, and then stopped completely. As for price and subscription, the patriarchate initially set a price of 5 rubles per issue, raised it to 100 rubles a year in 1944, and raised it to 120 rubles a year in 1945. This subscription price was printed in the *Journal* through May 1952 and was thereafter omitted. In 1943, the patriarchate invited private individuals to subscribe by sending money to its central offices at Chisty Pereulok in Moscow. In 1944, the church discontinued the practice and instructed would-be subscribers to approach their diocesan bishops or deans (*blagochinnye*). Copies were so grossly insufficient that subscription by laypersons was effectively abandoned. In the 1950s the *Journal* could be purchased occasionally at candle desks. In two years of attending Orthodox services virtually every Sunday between 1954 and 1956, I was able to purchase a May 1954 copy of the *Journal* for five rubles in Moscow and a May 1956 copy in Kharkov for twelve rubles.

When the *Journal* split out its *Official Chronicle* section at the end of 1992 to make a separate magazine of it, the regular *Journal* continued to omit the print run, but the *Official Chronicle* carried it (10,000 copies per issue). The *Official Chronicle* faltered, publishing irregularly in 1993 and sputtering out of print in 1994—although the publishing office of the patriarchate promised in June 1994 that there would be another issue "soon."

33. Pierre Van Paasen, *Visions Rise and Change* (New York: The Dial Press, 1955), p. 367; Dimitry Pospielovsky, *The Russian Church Under the Soviet Regime, 1917–1982,* 2 Vols. (Crestwood, New York: St. Vladimir's Seminary Press, 1984), pp. 330, 421; Walter Kolarz, *Religion in the Soviet Union* (New York: St. Martin's Press, 1961), p. 94; Ellis, pp. 156–157; V. G. Furov, "Cadres of the Church and Legal Measures to Curtail Their Activities: A Secret Report by the Council on Religious Affairs," *Religion in Communist Dominated Areas,* Vol. XX, Nos. 4–6, 1981, p. 59.

34. Rusak reported that 3,930 copies of the *Journal* were exported in the late 1970s. Ellis, p. 157.

35. In 1989 the print run was raised to 32,000. In addition, the width of the page was increased, which provided space for publication of about 15 percent more text. Ellis, p. 157; *Zhurnal Moskovskoi Patriarkhii,* No. 2 (February), 1990, p. 25; *Religion in USSR,* No. 5 (May), 1991, p. 7.

36. A. Vedernikov, "Russkaya Pravoslavnaya Tserkov v 1964 godu [The Russian Orthodox Church in 1964]," *Zhurnal Moskovskoi Patriarkhii,* No. 1 (January), 1965, pp. 10–16.

37. Pospielovsky, p. 430; *Keston News Service,* No. 339, November 30, 1989, p. 6; Jane Ellis, "Hierarchs and Dissidents: Conflict over the Future of the Russian Orthodox Church," *Religion in Communist Lands,* No. 4, Winter 1990, pp. 311–312.

38. *Zhurnal Moskovskoi Patriarkhii,* No. 10 (October), 1948, pp. 9–10; No. 11 (Novem-

ber), 1948, p. 28; No. 10 (October), 1953, pp. 55; No. 5 (May), 1955, pp. 22–23; *Pravoslavny Visnyk* [Orthodox Herald], No. 2 (February), 1948, p. 63; No. 2 (February), 1987, pp. 2–3.

39. Kolarz, p. 94. Copies of the *Pravoslavny Visnyk* have filtered abroad through unofficial channels. St. Andrew's Seminary in Winnipeg, Canada, has a virtually complete file.

40. According to James Moss, the *Pravoslavny Visnyk* continued publication until 1963. I have not been able, however, to locate any issues after May–June 1961. See also Furov, Vol. XX, Nos. 4–6, 1981, p. 66, note 3.

41. *Zhurnal Moskovskoi Patriarkhii*, No. 12 (December), 1978, p. 25.

42. N. Kolesnik, interview, *Foreign Broadcast Information Service*, February 10, 1989, pp. 67–68; Pospielovsky, p. 330.

43. *Pravoslavny Visnyk*, No. 12 (December), 1990, p. 46.

44. The *Keston News Service*, No. 339, November 30, 1989, p. 6, reported that the archbishop of Kuibyshev was publishing a weekly. The Krasnodar *Pravoslavny Golos Kubana* [The Orthodox Voice of the Kuban] is an eight-page, two-color journal with a print run of 15,000 copies. Metropolitan Aleksi of Leningrad sponsored a periodical entitled *Church Life of the North-West*, which petered out after he rose to the patriarchal throne. At least four other Orthodox periodicals are being published in St. Petersburg. *Religion in USSR*, No. 6 (June), 1991, Supplement III, pp. 40–41, listed eleven journals and twenty-seven "newspapers" (mostly diocesan bulletins) as then current periodicals of the Russian Orthodox Church.

45. Fifty thousand copies were being sold retail through Soyuzpechat in Moscow as of June, 1990. Paper supplies were insufficient to permit unrestricted subscription, and the state authorities, in consultation with the publications department of the patriarchate, decided that restricted subscriptions were undesirable. In subsequent months subscriptions were invited, but I have no confirmation that subscriptions from abroad were or are serviced. *Vechernaya Moskva* [Evening Moscow], June 16, 1990, p. 2; *Zhurnal Moskovskoi Patriarkhii*, No. 2 (February), 1990, p. 25.

46. *Moskovski Tserkovny Vestnik*, No. 11 (November), 1988, p. 3; *Zhurnal Moskovskoi Patriarkhii*, No. 2 (February), 1990, p. 25; *Moskovski Tserkovny Vestnik, Yezhenedelnik*, No. 2, January 1991, p. 7; No. 3, February 1992, p. 3.

47. In the summer of 1991 the Mossovet theater staged a production of Andrew Lloyd Weber's *Jesus Christ Superstar* with the libretto considerably influenced by Mikhail Bulgakov's long-suppressed novel, *The Master and Margarita*. Cindy Scharf, "A Resurrection in Moscow for *Jesus Christ Superstar*," *Los Angeles Times*, August 13, 1991, p. H6. I should add that the Russian Orthodox Church has bestowed no imprimatur on either *Jesus Christ Superstar* or *The Master and Margarita*. *Religion in USSR*, No. 12 (December), 1990, p. 3 (33); *Moskovski Tserkovny Vestnik, Yezhenedelnik*, No. 7, May 1992, p. 10.

48. *Zhurnal Moskovskoi Patriarkhii*, No. 2 (February), 1990, p. 26.

49. In the 1950s the exchange rate was four rubles to the dollar, although wages in the USSR were low, and four rubles could buy more goods and services (if one could find the goods) than a dollar could in the United States. Therefore, 700 million rubles was effectively worth more than $175 million.

The ten republics listed included virtually all the Russian Orthodox churches, as the two remaining Central Asian republics and the three Transcaucasian republics had only about a dozen Orthodox parishes among the five of them. Tsentralny Gosudarstvenny Arkhiv Oktyabrskoi Revolutsii [Central State Archive of the October Revolution], Vysshikh Organov Gosudarstvennoi Vlasti i Organov Gosurdarstvennogo Upravleniya S.S.S.R. [of the Higher Organs of State Government and Organs of State Administration of the U.S.S.R.], Soviet po delam religii pri Sovete Ministrov [the Council for Religious Affairs attached to the Council of Ministers], Fond 6991s, Opis No. 2, Vol. I, delo No. 263.

50. *Moskovski Tserkovny Vestnik, Yezhenedelnik,* No. 3, February 1991, p. 9. On the cited page, O. Gurbina discussed the plight of pensioners and invalids receiving up to 85 rubles a month, and a monastic priest named Roman described having had a salary of 60, 70, and 120 rubles at various times. These figures are not directly comparable to the church income figures of the 1950s, as Khrushchev carried out a currency reform exchanging one ruble for ten, effective January 1, 1961.

51. These "millions" would have been in the rubles of the 1950s. Jane Ellis reported an annual income of 1 million rubles for St. Nicholas Cathedral in Leningrad in 1977 (10 million before the 1961 currency reform) and 600,000 rubles for the great Trinity church at the Alexander Nevsky monastery site in Leningrad in 1979 (6 million before the currency reform). Ellis, *The Russian Orthodox Church,* p. 49.

52. Timasheff, "Religion in Russia, 1941–1950," p. 164. According to Timasheff, the patriarchal cathedral was taking in 32,000 rubles a day from the sale of candles alone. If the assumption is made that the sale of candles accounted for half to two-thirds of a church's official income, the patriarchal cathedral would have been taking in 15–20 million rubles a year, or about 4–5 percent of the total income of the church in the Russian republic in 1959. Timasheff said that one priest at the cathedral declared an income of 365,000 rubles in 1946—which would translate into 36,500 rubles after Stalin's 1947 ten-for-one currency reform or 3,650 rubles after Khrushchev's reform. Fifty times seventy rubles (the salary of the Ukrainian parish priest mentioned) is about 3,500 rubles.

53. Tsentralny Gosudarstvenny Arkhiv, Fond 6991s, Opis No. 2, Vol. I, delo No. 263.

54. Francis House, in Michael Bourdeaux, *Opium of the People* (Indianapolis, Indiana: The Bobbs-Merrill Co., 1966), pp. 89–90.

55. S. M. Gibbard, S.S.J.E., "Diary of a Visit to Russia," *Church Times,* July–August 1958.

56. Joseph H. Jackson, *The Eternal Flame* (Philadelphia, Penn.: The Christian Education Press, 1956), p. 16. Jackson wrote that he was given 1,000 rubles as spending money, the equivalent of several months salary for a Soviet worker.

57. Ellis, *The Russian Orthodox Church,* p. 49, p. 462, note 35.

58. The figures, quoted in Ellis, *The Russian Orthodox Church,* p. 134, were 2.5 million rubles of total convent income in 1970, of which Trinity-Sergius received over 1 million rubles and the two nunneries in Kiev received 415,000. The statistics came from a leaked report of the Council for Religious Affairs. They should be treated with some reserve, however, as Pochaev monastery reportedly also received over 1 million rubles a year in the 1970s (not necessarily the year 1970); that would have left less than 100,000 rubles income for all the fourteen other convents, which is difficult to credit. John B. Dunlop, "The Contemporary Russian Orthodox Church," *Oberlin Alumni Magazine,* September–Octo-

ber 1976, p. 18. Still, the general point is valid. The great convents receive the lion's share of the income and the smaller convents receive extremely little.

59. The income figures were as follows: 1982—Holy Ghost monastery complex, Vilnyus, 344,000 rubles, whole diocese, 779,100 rubles; 1983—complex 391,000 rubles, diocese 869,000 rubles. Leaked Council for Religious Affairs document, published in *Religion in Communist Dominated Areas,* Vol. XXV, No. 1, Winter 1986, p. 40.

A somewhat analogous situation could be seen in Byelorussia. Sources of income in 1985 for the Holy Dormition monastery and the Birth of the Mother of God nunnery at Zhirovitsy were as follows: loose plate offerings, 23,000 rubles; mailed contributions, 167,000; prayers for the dead, 182,000; sales of candles, 68,000; and other sales, 26,000. Expenditures were as follows: personnel, 87,000; sextons and charpeople, 36,000; land rent, utilities, and repairs, 82,000; center (diocesan and patriarchal offices), 240,000; Peace Fund, 16,000; Fund for the Preservation of Cultural Monuments, 1,000; Fund to Restore the Danilov Monastery, 30,000. Tsentralny Gosudarstvenny Arkhiv, Fond 6991, Opis No. 6, delo No. 3137.

60. Ellis, *The Russian Orthodox Church,* p. 134.

61. Paul Lucey estimated the patriarchate's annual income as 300 million rubles in 1982–1983; Jane Ellis gave a figure of 314 million rubles in 1985; and the atheist magazine *Science and Religion* reported the income of the church in early 1988 as 250 million rubles a year. Paul A. Lucey, "Religion," *The Soviet Union Today,* ed. James Cracraft (Chicago: Bulletin of the Atomic Scientists, 1983), p. 295; Ellis, *The Russian Orthodox Church,* p. 51; *Nauka i Religiya,* No. 6 (June), 1988, p. 16.

Ukrainian receipts were 32 million rubles in 1975 and 39 million rubles in 1980. Other income figures (in rubles) were maritime provinces (capital Vladivostok), 0.3 million in 1970, 0.4 million in 1985; Khabarovsk province, 0.3 million in 1985; Krasnoyarsk, 1 million in 1985; the Altai, 1.1 million in 1985; Krasnodar province, 3.8 million in 1980, 4.2 million in 1984, 4.2 million in 1985; Stavropol, 2.3 million in 1975, 2.9 million in 1980, 2.9 million in 1985; Belorussian convents, 0.5 million in 1985. Tsentralny Gosudarstvenny Arkhiv, Fond 6991, Opis No. 6, delo Nos. 3131, 3132.

62. Pospielovsky, p. 421; Tsentralny Gosudarstvenny Arkhiv, Fond 6991, Opis No. 6, delo Nos. 3131, 3132.

63. Over the years the arrangement between the Soviet government and the church was that the church pay the cost of renovating a working church; the state pay the cost of renovating and maintaining a church converted into a museum or secular facility; and the church and the state split the cost of restoring a historic monument that was also a working church. In 1988 about 2,000 of the almost 6,800 churches in the country were architectural monuments. For donations to the Soviet Peace Fund and other funds, see Aleksandr Nezhny, "Sovest svobodna [A Free Conscience]," *Ogonëk* [Little Fire], No. 21, May 1988, pp. 26–28; *Nauka i Religiya,* No. 6 (June), 1988, p. 16; and No. 11 (November), 1987; Georgi Edelshtein, "How to Plunder a Church," *Religion in Communist Dominated Areas,* No. 3, 1989, p. 68. The diocese of Poltava increased its "voluntary" contributions from 36,000 rubles in 1968 to 161,000 rubles in 1976. The contributions to the government actually grew to the point that they exceeded money expended in the diocese's own administra-

tion. Aleksi II, in an interview given after his enthronement, said: "In some regions up to 80 percent of the parish income was taken up by the [Soviet Peace] Fund." G. Alimov and G. Charodeev, "Faith Without Deeds Is Dead: An Interview with Patriarch Aleksi II," *Izvestiya*, June 16, 1990, reproduced in *Religion in Communist Lands*, No. 3, Autumn 1990, p. 266.

64. Tsentralny Gosudarstvenny Arkhiv, Fond 6991, Opis No. 6, delo Nos. 3131, 3132.

65. Russian Orthodox activities in the international peace movement have been described at length by many Western critics. For a 1989 commentary, see Kent R. Hill, *The Puzzle of the Soviet Church: An Inside Look at Christianity and Glasnost* (Portland, Oregon: Multnomah Press, 1989), Part IV. See also Ellis, *The Russian Orthodox Church*, pp. 271–276.

66. Thirteen percent of 250 million rubles would be 30 million rubles, so the figures check out quite closely. Ellis also reported contributions to the Peace Fund of 15 percent of income in the early 1980s. Ellis, *The Russian Orthodox Church*, p. 49.

67. The Russian republic set a stiff tax on candles and other religious objects sold in churches but reversed itself, after strenuous objections from church authorities, on October 21, 1991. *Moskovski Tserkovny Vestnik, Yezhenedelnik*, No. 2, February, 1992, p. 3.

68. "Miscellaneous expenses" are not listed, but they were small.

69. The successor organization to the Soviet Peace Fund, the Russian Peace Fund, began in 1992 to contribute to the restoration of semidestroyed churches, including the great and small churches of the Don monastery, and began to help meet the publishing costs of the *Moskovski Tserkovny Vestnik, Yezhenedelnik* (MTVE)—see No. 5, April 1992, p. 14.

70. *Zhurnal Moskovskoi Patriarkhii*, No. 4 (April), 1990, p. 7.

71. Ellis, "Hierarchs and Dissidents," p. 313.

72. *Zhurnal Moskovskoi Patriarkhii*, No. 12 (December), 1990, p. 13.

73. Metropolitan Mefodi (Nemtsov), "Khozyaistvennaya deyatelnost Russkoi Pravoslavnoi Tserkvi [Administrative Activity of the Russian Orthodox Church]," *Religiya v SSSR*, No. 10 (October), 1988, p. MM7; *Ofitsialnaga Khronika, Zhurnal Moskovskoi Patriarkhii*, No. 3, 1993, p. 24; No. 9–10, 1993, inside back cover; *Pravoslavnaya Rus*, No. 11, June 1–4, 1993, p. 16.

74. *Zhurnal Moskovskoi Patriarkhii*, No. 2 (February), 1990, pp. 13, 45; *Moskovski Tserkovny Vestnik, Yezhenedelnik*, No. 6, April 1992, p. 4.

75. In January 1991, the patriarchate announced the establishment of an entity to give interest-free loans to finance parishes restoring or building churches. Financing would come in part from "foreign citizens and organizations." *Moskovski Tserkovny Vestnik, Yezhenedelnik*, No. 2, January 1991, p. 7.

76. *Zhurnal Moskovskoi Patriarkhii*, No. 2 (February), 1990, pp. 12–14.

77. The publishing department also reported that it needed 15 million rubles to print badly needed texts for the theological schools but did not have the money. *Zhurnal Moskovskoi Patriarkhii*, No. 2 (February), 1990, pp. 42–46.

78. The Soviet government's share of receipts from Sofrino sales was high. Even before the dissolution of the USSR, the Russian Supreme Soviet was moving to impose its own high taxes on Sofrino's sales. See *Keston News Service*, No. 371, March 21, 1991, p. 4. For

further discussion of Sofrino, see *Ogonëk,* No. 4, January 1990, p. 22; *Moskovski Tserkovny Vestnik, Yezhenedelnik,* No. 6, March 1990, p. 3; *Moskovski Tserkovny Vestnik,* No. 7 (July), 1988, p. 8; *Zhurnal Moskovskoi Patriarkhii,* No. 7 (July), 1987, p. 26; No. 9 (September), 1987, p. 6; No. 9 (September), 1988, pp. 18–19; No. 2 (February), 1990, pp. 42–45; No. 2 (February), 1991, p. 28.

79. *Zhurnal Moskovskoi Patriarkhii,* No. 2 (February), 1990, pp. 42–45; No. 2 (February), 1991, p. 28.

80. *Zhurnal Moskovskoi Patriarkhii,* No. 2 (February), 1990, p. 12; No. 10 (October), 1990, p. 4.

81. In late 1990, the church had raised 390,000 rubles to restore the Valaam monastery on Lake Ladoga. Three quarters of the funds had come from the Leningrad diocese, although some funds had been donated by enterprises like the "Hammer and Sickle" factory in Moscow. Finns were helping restore the Smolensk hermitage at Valaam and had donated 154,000 rubles more. Compared to the need, all this was a drop in the bucket. *Zhurnal Moskovskoi Patriarkhii,* No. 12 (December), 1988, p. 25; No. 2 (February), 1991, p. 20. For the appeal of the rector of the Smolensk Theological Institute, see *Russkaya Mysl,* No. 4022, March 25–31, 1994, p. 18.

82. *Zhurnal Moskovskoi Patriarkhii,* No. 2 (February), 1990, p. 13.

Chapter 14

1. I was present at the July 2, 1986, meeting with a U.S. National Council of Churches delegation.

2. A by-product of the reduced crowding has been the installation of benches along the walls of many sanctuaries where the aged and infirm can sit. Heretofore this amenity almost never existed.

3. I estimated the size of the congregation and the adequacy of space in all my church visits. In ninety-two church visits I did head counts and amassed a sample of 9,523 churchgoers; I grouped them according to the split of men, women, young, and old. My overall sample was 26,000.

4. Fletcher described how in the 1960s more than twice as many collective farmers had icons in their homes (47 percent) as did families employed in state institutions (21 percent); workers' and business employees' families were somewhere in between (30 percent). A Soviet sociologist quoted in William C. Fletcher, "Introduction: The State of Soviet Sociology of Religion," Hans (J. J.) Mol, ed., *U.S.S.R., Western Religion: A Country by Country Sociological Inquiry* (The Hague, Paris: Mouton, 1972), pp. 578, 581.

5. A. I. Zalesski, "Ob otnoshenii Belorusskikh kolkhoznikov k religii i o roste ateizma [Concerning the Attitude of Byelorussian Collective Farmers Toward Religion and Concerning the Growth of Atheism]," *Sovetskaya Etnografia* [Soviet Ethnography], No. 2, 1957, p. 53. See also Wroe Alderson, G. Cary Stephen, William B. Edgerton, Hugh W. Moore, Clarence E. Pickett, and Eleanor Zelliot, *Meeting the Russians: American Quakers Visit the Soviet Union* (Philadelphia, Penn.: American Friends Service Committee, 1956), p. 56.

6. Father Nikolai Gainov, writing in *Religion in USSR,* No. 8 (August), 1991, p. 18.

7. The Reverend Michael A. Meerson, Orthodox Church in America, "The Decline in Religious Consciousness," *Religion in Communist Dominated Areas,* Vol. XXV, No. 2, Spring 1986, p. 52.

8. Kirill Golovin (a pseudonym), *The Samizdat Bulletin,* No. 173, September 1987, p. 12.

9. Monastic priest Innokenti, "O sovremennom sostoyanii Russkoi Pravoslavnoi Tserkvi [About the Present Situation of the Russian Orthodox Church]," *Religiya v SSSR* [Religion in the USSR], No. 8 (October), 1987, pp. VS1, 2, 4, 6.

10. John Shelton Curtiss, *The Russian Church and the Soviet State, 1917–1950* (Boston: Little, Brown and Co., 1953), p. 219.

11. Monastic priest Aleksi, quoted in "O dukhovnom sostoyanii Russkago naroda pod vlastyu bezbozhnikov [About the Spiritual Condition of the Russian Nation Under Atheist Rule]," *Doklad Soboru Pravoslavnoi Russkoi Zarubezhnoi Tserkvi s Uchastiem Klira i Miryan 7/20 Avgusta 1938 goda* [Report to the Council of the Russian Orthodox Church Outside Russia with the Participation of Clergy and Laity, of August 7/20, 1938], (napechatano po postanovleniyu plenarnago zasedaniya Sobora, 20-VIII-1938 [printed at the direction of the plenary session of the Council, 20-VIII-1938]), p. 2.

12. Dana L. Robert, "Grandmothers and the Millennium of Russian Christianity," *Christian Century,* December 24–31, 1986, p. 1175.

13. See Nicholas S. Timasheff, *Religion in Soviet Russia, 1917–1942* (London: Sheed and Ward, 1944), p. 143.

14. Metropolitan Nikolai (Yarushevich), quoted in *The New York Herald Tribune,* April 7, 1958.

15. Francis House referred to Orthodox leaders themselves as estimating 30 million churchgoers. House said that the 30 million represented "one-sixth of the population of European Russian," but there are only about 150 million people in the entire Russian republic, even in the mid-1990s. Francis House, *The Russian Phoenix* (London: SPCK, 1988), pp. 102–103.

16. Gerhard Simon, *Church, State and Opposition in the U.S.S.R.,* trans. Kathleen Matchett (Berkeley, Calif.: University of California Press, 1970), p. 106.

17. The patriarchal cathedral averages more than 2,000 on a normal Sunday, but its capacity appears to be 5,000–6,000, not the 10,000 and more sometimes claimed. A number of other churches in the top fifty average fewer than 2,000, and that figure appears to be ample as an average if all fifty are taken into account. It is true that my figures for attendance are for the number in the sanctuary at a given time in the service, and arrivals and departures swell the numbers of those present during the entire period of the celebration of the liturgy. This reality has also been taken into account in figuring overall attendance.

As a note of caution regarding casual estimates by foreign ecclesiastical visitors, it should be noted that distinguished visitors have been taken habitually by their hosts to selected churches where attendance is high.

18. For example, the Cathedral of St. Catherine in Krasnodar is one of the largest churches in the former USSR. *Zhurnal Moskovskoi Patriarkhii* [Journal of the Moscow Patriarchate], No. 4 (April), 1992, p. 61.

19. I visited forty city churches smaller than the fifty huge churches counted separately.

The congregations at a late Sunday morning service averaged 229; I rounded the figure up to 250.

20. Gauging average attendance in village churches has been more difficult than in urban ones, although I have attended services in a number of village churches. The *Journal of the Moscow Patriarchate* is also helpful, as it sometimes publishes photographs of the parishioners of a rural church lined up proudly when the bishop visits. Bishops, in describing their woes in church publications, also poignantly describe attendance in some of their troubled parishes. Priests estimate attendance in their parishes on occasion. Some village churches may have 100–150 worshipers attending on a Sunday morning; others that lack a priest may have very small attendance and services only a few times a year. See William C. Fletcher, *Soviet Believers: The Religious Sector of the Population* (Lawrence, Kansas: The Regents Press of Kansas, 1981), p. 180.

21. Poll results are notoriously imprecise, even in the West, particularly when they try to measure what people think or say. For example, some researchers have asserted that U.S. church attendance on an average Sunday is about half that reported consistently by Gallup polls. *Los Angeles Times,* September 18, 1993, p. B4; October 23, 1993, p. B5.

22. *Time,* December 21, 1987, p. 60; *Los Angeles Times,* September 20, 1986, Part II, p. 5; November 12, 1992, p. A12.

23. Fifty worshipers in each of the village churches on a normal Sunday morning would represent about half of the number of worshipers I calculated.

24. Christel Lane, *Christian Religion in the Soviet Union: A Sociological Study* (Albany, New York: State University of New York Press, 1978), p. 66; Fletcher, *Soviet Believers,* pp. 85–89, 181. Bociurkiw quoted a 1961 estimate of about 70 percent women. Bohdan R. Bociurkiw, "Religion and Atheism in Soviet Society," *Aspects of Religion in the Soviet Union, 1917–1967,* ed. Richard H. Marshall, Jr. (Chicago: University of Chicago Press, 1971), p. 56. In 1973, Simon estimated that "seventy to eighty per cent of regular church goers are women." Simon, p. 107.

25. All these church visits were after 1982, and a large proportion of them in 1990, when I spent from January to June in the USSR. The cumulative figures were 3,487 women and 621 men. I omitted visits to three very large churches (St. Nicholas and Trinity in Leningrad and St. Nicholas in Dushanbe on Trinity Sunday), fearing the very large numbers, arrived at by sampling, might skew the results. If these churches are added into the mix, the figures are 5,693 women and 902 men, or 86 percent women.

26. The weekday, Sunday evening, and early Sunday morning services were during twenty-three visits, with 2,423 women and 363 men counted. There is considerable variation in weekday attendance, depending on whether the service is on church holidays or saints' days, of which there are seventy during the year. For the preponderance of women in church, see also Vladimir Zelinsky, "Pastors and Their Flock," from the samizdat journal *Vybor* [Choice], No. 20, reproduced in *Religion in Communist Lands,* Vol. 17, No. 4, Winter 1989, pp. 345–348.

27. Nathaniel Davis, *Religion and Communist Government in the Soviet Union and Eastern Europe,* dissertation, The Fletcher School of Law and Diplomacy, June 1, 1960, p. 406 (where sources and methodology are explained).

28. Gosudarstvenny Komitet S.S.S.R. po Statistike, Informatsionno-izdatelski tsentr

[State Committee of the U.S.S.R. for Statistics, Information-Publishing Center], "Pol, vozrast i sostoyanie v brake naseleniya S.S.S.R., soyuznykh i autonomnykh respublik, kraev, i oblastei [Sex, Age and Marital Status of the Population of the U.S.S.R., Union and Autonomous Republics, Krais and Oblasts], Part I, Statisticheski sbornik [Statistical compilation]," Vol. II of *Itogi vsesoyuznoi perepisi naseleniya 1979 goda* [Results of the All-Union Census of Population of 1979] (Moscow, 1989), p. 32. The 1979 figures by population age group were age zero to forty-nine—varying between 51 and 48 percent; fifty to fifty-four—43 percent; fifty-five to fifty-nine—36 percent; sixty to sixty-four—34 percent; sixty-five to sixty-nine—33 percent; seventy to seventy-four—31 percent; seventy-five to seventy-nine—27 percent; eighty and over—25 percent. At the end of the 1980s each category would have been ten years older.

29. Eugene Carson Blake, *The New York Times Book Review,* November 2, 1958, p. 3.

30. Lane, p. 66; Fletcher, *Soviet Believers,* pp. 180–181. Fletcher reported scattered data, but 80 percent "old or middle aged" would, I believe, represent a reasonable approximation of his findings for Orthodox people.

31. Of the women whose faces I was able to see, 89 percent were older women (3,319 of 3,349). For the earlier years, see Davis, p. 406. Obviously, for me or anyone else to look at a person and tell how old he or she is, or whether the person is "old" or "older," must be a very rough judgment. A person over fifty would be someone I would call "older."

32. Of the men, 421 were old, and 616 appeared to be younger or young. Innokenti, p. VS2.

33. Protopresbyter Vitali M. Borovoi, quoted by Kent R. Hill, *The Puzzle of the Soviet Church: An Inside Look at Christianity and Glasnost* (Portland, Oregon: Multnomah Press, 1989), p. 146. See also George W. Cornell, "Belief Endures," AP report, *The Gettysburg Times,* December 17, 1984, quoting Father Vladimir Berzonsky.

34. Bill Keller, "The Kremlin Seeks a New Kind of Coexistence with Religion," *The New York Times,* August 23, 1987. For Patriarch Aleksi's observation of increased numbers of young people in church in Volgograd, see *Zhurnal Moskovskoi Patriarkhii,* No. 2 (February), 1994, p. 31.

35. Marcus Bach, in *The Chicago Daily News,* February 14, 1958.

36. *Presbyterian Life,* September 3, 1955, p. 2.

37. Alice S. Rossi, *Generational Differences in the Soviet Union,* Vol. 2, Project on the Soviet Social System—AF No. 33 (038)-12909, Russian Research Center, Harvard University, July 1954, a final report submitted to the director, Officer Education Research Laboratory AFP and TRC of ARDC, Maxwell Air Force Base, Montgomery, Alabama, p. A-34.

38. Marquis Childs, "The Puzzling Role of Soviet Religion," *The Washington Post and Times Herald,* July 8, 1958.

39. Timasheff, p. 145.

40. Fletcher, *Soviet Believers,* p. 92, was quoting M. K. Teplyakov, *Problemy ateisticheskogo vospitaniya v praktike partinoi raboty* [Problems of Atheist Education in Practice in Party Work] (Voronezh: Voronezh University Press, 1972), p. 128. Although Teplyakov's study was in 1972 and much has changed since 1988, such very basic data have changed less than other statistical measures. Fletcher devoted a chapter in *Soviet Believers*

to education and occupation (pp. 91–111). Christel Lane addressed the same subject and presented data that were similar to Fletcher's. Lane, p. 48. See also Zelinsky, p. 344–345.

41. Innokenti, pp. 3–5. See also Chris Pasles, "Bolshoi's Mikhail Lavrovsky Choreographs a Spiritual Quest," *Los Angeles Times,* May 6, 1988, Part VI, pp. 1, 12; Zelinsky, p. 345.

42. Anatoli Levitin-Krasnov quoted by Michael Bourdeaux, *Risen Indeed: Lessons in Faith from the U.S.S.R.* (Crestwood, New York: St. Vladimir's Seminary Press, 1983), p. 24.

43. Workers' attitudes were not always militantly atheistic or uniformly hostile to religion. For example, a study in Ukraine in the mid-1970s disclosed that only about half of a sample of 1,048 workers felt that religion exerted a bad moral influence. Considering the pressures for conformity in those days, the workers' attitudes could be regarded as quite benign. Christopher S. Wren, "Soviet Subdues Religion, but Zeal for Atheism Lags," *The New York Times,* March 1, 1976, p. 3.

44. Zelinsky, pp. 345–348.

45. Zelinsky, p. 345.

46. Anatoli V. Lunacharski, quoted by Lane, p. 224.

47. Emelyan Yaroslavski, quoted by Lane, p. 224.

48. Wassilij Alexeev and Theofanis G. Stavrou, *The Great Revival: The Russian Church Under German Occupation* (Minneapolis: Burgess Publishing Co., 1976), p. 26.

49. The figure of roughly 10 million Orthodox people annexed in the World War II period includes Ukrainian Greek-Catholics forcibly absorbed into the Russian Orthodox institution. These were believing people, and most of them worshiped in Orthodox churches until 1989.

For the 1950s, William Fletcher recorded a variety of figures for Orthodox believers or people attending church at least occasionally. Most of these estimates fell between 20 million and 60 million, although some were in the 100–140 million range. Fletcher, "Introduction," p. 579.

50. By "traditionally Orthodox" I mean the percentage of the population whose forebears were part of the Orthodox community and not Muslim, Buddhist, Jewish, Protestant, Catholic, and so on. This would be roughly 55–60 percent of the total population depending on territorial changes, higher Muslim birthrates over time, and the like. Official imperial Russian figures for the Orthodox population in 1914 are within this range. See John Meyendorff, *The Orthodox Church,* 3d ed. (Crestwood, New York: St. Vladimir's Seminary Press, 1981), p. 154, note 8.

51. Simon, p. 105; Bociurkiw, pp. 58, 60; Dimitry Pospielovsky, *The Russian Church Under the Soviet Regime, 1917–1982,* 2 Vols. (Crestwood, New York: St. Vladimir's Seminary Press, 1984), p. 454; Trevor Beeson, *Discretion and Valor* (Philadelphia, Penn.: Fortress Press, 1982), p. 57; Jane Ellis, *The Russian Orthodox Church: A Contemporary History* (Bloomington, Indiana: Indiana University Press, 1986), p. 175; Lane, pp. 66, 223–224.

52. Some Soviet sociologists reported 30 million believers and an additional 15 million "waverers," figures representing roughly 20 percent plus an additional 10 percent of the traditionally Orthodox population in the country. Pospielovsky, p. 454; Beeson, p. 57; Ellis, pp. 174–175; Lane, p. 223; William C. Fletcher, "Backwards from Reactionism: The

De-Modernization of the Russian Orthodox Church," *Religion and Modernization in the Soviet Union,* ed. Dennis J. Dunn (Boulder, Colo.: Westview Press, 1977), p. 228; Fletcher, *Soviet Believers,* pp. 208–211. Fletcher estimated 25–35 percent of the population in the traditionally Orthodox Russian-speaking areas to be religious believers. This would represent 35–55 million people. David K. Shipler quoted Western churchmen as estimating "at least thirty million members" in 1976–1977. He quoted a Moscow State University student as estimating that 3.5–5 percent of his university friends were religious. David K. Shipler, "Church in Soviet Finds Resilience as Millions Seek 'a Sense of Life,'" *The New York Times,* January 3, 1977, p. 1.

53. Dimitry Pospielovsky, "The Soviet State Versus the Russian Orthodox Church, 1959–1988," *Religion in Communist Dominated Areas,* Vol. XXVII, No. 4, Fall 1988, p. 110.

54. The Muslims were widely estimated to have higher levels of belief and practice than the Orthodox, but the levels of Orthodox belief in the western lands were also notably high. The figure of 40 million factored in a somewhat lower percentage level of Orthodox belief as compared to the Muslim population.

55. Seth Mydans, "In Soviet, Religion Ceases Outside Church Doors," *The New York Times,* July 15, 1984, p. 10. Another Russian Orthodox Church source estimated 30 million believers at the end of 1986. Public Radio Russian Orthodox Christmas broadcast on the program "All Things Considered," January 7, 1987. The chairman of the Council for Religious Affairs, Konstantin Kharchev, stated in 1987 that 10–20 percent of the population, depending on the region, were believers of all confessions. That would represent 30–60 million believers, with Orthodox believers totaling a little over half that number. Konstantin Kharchev, "Sovetskoe gosudarstvo i tserkov [The Soviet Government and the Church]," *Religiya v SSSR,* No. 10 (December), 1987, p. KKh5. *Nauka i Religiya* [Science and Religion], No. 6 (June), 1988, p. 16, reported that 10–20 percent of the population of the three Slavic republics were adherents of the Russian Orthodox Church. In 1987–1988 Francis House reported that there were over 50 million committed Orthodox Christians. House, p. 116. In 1989, Keston News Service reported an estimate that 25 percent of the population were believers, roughly 70 million people, of whom about 35 million would be Russian Orthodox. *Keston News Service,* No. 322, March 30, 1989, p. 17.

56. *Los Angeles Times,* September 27, 1990, p. A15.

57. Only 3 percent of the workers said religion played "a very great role." *Nauka i Religiya,* No. 7 (July), 1989, pp. 18–19.

58. The 1990 poll results were as follows: 8 percent of respondents affirmed that faith adds to self-respect; 5 percent said they were actively involved in religious matters; 66 percent had been baptized; 48 percent professed some belief (8 percent of the sample proudly called themselves believers, and 8 percent said religious values came first); 39 percent wanted to teach their children to believe, and 7 percent said they raised their children with the idea of retribution for their sins; 8 percent attributed the country's misfortunes to a loss of faith; 19 percent had some association with religious rites; 16 percent associated themselves with the omnipotence of God, 15 percent with prayer, and 15 percent with punishment for sins; 22 percent associated Christ with the supreme deity; 3 percent mentioned Christ among the outstanding historical persons of all times; for 20 percent religion meant church holidays, and for 10 percent it meant religious art. *Moscow*

News, No. 11, March 18, 1990, p. 11. For chaplains in 1994, see *Russkaya Mysl* No. 4025, April 14–20, 1994, p. 9.

59. Lane, pp. 67–69; Zalesski, p. 53.

60. *Keston News Service,* No. 347, April 5, 1990, p. 7; *Ogonëk,* No. 2–3, January, 1994, p. 23; *Moskovskie Novosti,* No. 1, January 2–9, 1994, p. A6.

61. A. Makarov, "Put k vozrozhdeniyu [The Road to Revival]," *Moskovski Tserkovny Vestnik, Yezhenedelnik* [Moscow Church Herald, Weekly], No. 1, January 1990, p. 1. Makarev was referring to actual parish church members, not members of the constituting "twenty" that legally had to form a registered church society.

62. Makarov, p. 1; *Keston News Service,* No. 353, June 28, 1990, p. 15. A poll conducted in November 1990 in six regions of the Russian republic indicated that 35 percent of the young adults aged eighteen to twenty-five said they believed in God, 40 percent said they did not, and 25 percent were agnostic. *Keston News Service,* No. 371, March 21, 1991, p. 16.

63. *Zhurnal Moskovskoi Patriarkhii,* No. 1 (January), 1993, p. 112. The poll question may have been phrased in such a way as to elicit an answer affirming Orthodox religious tradition more than actual religious commitment.

64. Marcus Bach, *God and the Soviets* (New York: Thomas Y. Crowell Co., 1958), p. 70.

65. Elena Kublitskaya, "Obshchestvo massogo ateizma [A Society of Mass Atheism]," *Nauka i Religiya,* No. 1 (January), 1990, p. 34. The poll was also conducted in north Ossetia and Tadzhikistan with results between the extremes reported in the text (21 percent believers in north Ossetia and 13 percent believers in Tadzhikistan). The population in both territories is mixed enough in religious tradition to make the results only marginally relevant to Orthodox belief.

66. Georgi Rozhnov, "Eto my, Gospodi [Here Are We, My Lord]," *Ogonëk* [Little Fire], No. 38, September 1989, p. 8; Elena Kublitskaya, Vyacheslav Lokosov, and Petr Olovyannikov, "Greko-katoliki v S.S.S.R. [Greek-Catholics in the U.S.S.R.]," *Religiya v SSSR,* No. 1 (January), 1990, p. 9. See also Lane, p. 223, and House, p. 266.

67. Lane, pp. 61, 224, 226–227; Fletcher, *Soviet Believers,* pp. 69, 86–87; Dimitry V. Pospielovsky, "Intelligentsia and Religion: Aspects of Religious Revival in the Contemporary Soviet Union, the Orthodox Church," *Religion and Communist Society,* ed. Dennis J. Dunn (Berkeley, Calif.: Berkeley Slavic Specialties, 1983), p. 14.

68. Pasles, pp. 1, 12; Pospielovsky, "The Soviet State," p. 11.

69. Bociurkiw, p. 59. Fletcher also cited research conducted in the 1960s, reflecting essentially the same motivations Bociurkiw described. Fletcher, "Introduction," p. 580; Lane, p. 225.

70. *Moskovski Tserkovny Vestnik, Yezhenedelnik,* No. 18, December 1989, p. 1.

71. The Communist Party lost over half the full confidence it enjoyed in early 1989, ending with about 40 percent of the respondents trusting it fully or in essence in mid-1990. *Ogonëk,* No. 7, February 1990, p. 3; *Moskovskie Novosti* [Moscow News], No. 21, May 27, 1990, p. 9 (*Moscow News,* June 3–10, 1990); *Moscow News,* No. 22, June 10–17, 1990, p. 7 (polling was carried out only in the Moscow region in this case).

72. *Izvestiya,* February 25, 1990, p. 2.

73. *Ogonëk,* No. 3, January 1990, pp. 32–33.

74. *Izvestiya,* March 21, 1990, p. 2.

75. *Keston News Service,* No. 358, September 13, 1990, p. 12.

76. *Sobesednitsa* [Interlocutor], *Komsomolskaya Pravda* Supplement, No. 10, March 1990, p. 3.

77. Lane, pp. 62–63; Bociurkiw, p. 59; Pospielovsky, *The Russian Church,* p. 457, note 130.

78. Curtiss, p. 222; Pospielovsky, *The Russian Church,* p. 171.

79. Zalesski, pp. 56–57; Protopresbyter Nikolai Kolchitski, administrator of the patriarchal offices, quoted by Pierre Fontanieu, "Le problème religieux en U.R.S.S. [The Religious Problem in the U.S.S.R.]," *Christianisme Social* [Social Christianity], Vol. 63, Nos. 1–2 (January–February), 1955, p. 60. For Sverdlovsk, Kolchitski's figure was "perhaps 30 percent" and Fontanieu's Soviet sources gave the figure of 20 percent.

80. The church officials are quoted in the preceding paragraph. Oblasts having high percentages were Pskov (62 percent), Yaroslavl (60 percent), Ivanovo (55 percent), Bryansk (53 percent), Kirov (49 percent), Kuibyshev (48 percent), Belgorod (48 percent), and Voronezh (48 percent); oblasts having low percentages were Khabarovsk (4.5 percent), Irkutsk (7 percent), Kurgan (9 percent), Tomsk (14 percent), Saratov (14 percent), Arkhangelsk (14 percent), the Mordovskaya Autonomous Republic (13 percent), and Sverdlovsk (14 percent). Tsentralny Gosudarstvenny Arkhiv Oktyabrskoi Revolutsii [Central State Archive of the October Revolution], Vysshikh Organov Gosudarstvennoi Vlasti i Organov Gosurdarstvennogo Upravleniya S.S.S.R. [of the Higher Organs of State Government and Organs of State Administration of the U.S.S.R.], Soviet po delam religii pri Sovete Ministrov [the Council for Religious Affairs attached to the Council of Ministers], Fond 6991s, Opis No. 2, Vol. I, delo No. 263.

81. Yu. G. Dobrynin and L. N. Mitrokhin, Chapter 7, *Stroitelstvo kommunizma i dukhovny mir cheloveka* [The Building of Communism and the Spiritual World of the Individual], ed. Ts. A. Stepanyan (Moscow: Nauka, Institute of Philosophy, Academy of Sciences, 1966), p. 221.

82. House, p. 90; Donald A. Lowrie and William C. Fletcher, "Khrushchev's Religious Policy, 1959–1964," *Aspects of Religion in the Soviet Union, 1917–1967,* ed. Richard H. Marshall, Jr. (Chicago: University of Chicago Press, 1971), p. 139; Michael Bourdeaux, *Patriarch and Prophets: Persecution of the Russian Orthodox Church Today* (Oxford: A. R. Mowbray and Co., 1975), pp. 197, 202. See also Konstantin M. Kharchev, "Religiya i perestroika [Religion and Perestroika]," speech to instructors of the Higher Party School, Moscow, end of March 1988 (transcribed by memory and abridged), *Russkaya Mysl* [Russian Thought], No. 3725, May 20, 1988, p. 4; Simon, pp. 81–82.

83. Selected specific data by oblast were Orel (52 percent), Lipetsk (40 percent), Moscow (39 percent), Novgorod (39 percent), Kaluga (26 percent), Leningrad (20 percent), Murmansk (18 percent), Krasnodar (18 percent, down from 25 percent in 1959), Orenburg (17 percent), Omsk (14 percent), Novosibirsk (11 percent), Krasnoyarsk (7 percent), Komi (2 percent), and Khabarovsk (2 percent, down from 4.5 percent in 1959). Tsentralny Gosudarstvenny Arkhiv, Fond 6991s, Opis No. 4, Vol. I, delo Nos. 572–573, 575. The figures were for January 1, 1966. See also Ellis, p. 177. Pospielovsky quoted a "secret study" by a Soviet scholar indicating that 19 percent of newly born children in the city of Leningrad were baptized in 1971, a figure very close to the council's figure of 20 percent in Leningrad

oblast in 1965. (The population of Leningrad oblast consisted, and still consists, mostly of the inhabitants of the city.) The "secret study" indicated that 26 percent of newborns in the city were baptized in 1976 and 1979. Pospielovsky, *The Russian Church,* p. 457.

84. Konstantin M. Kharchev, "Garantii svobody [Guarantees of Freedom]," *Nauka i Religiya,* No. 11 (November), 1987, p. 23 (translated in *Religion in Communist Dominated Areas,* Vol. XXVI, No. 4, Fall 1987); Gosudarstvenny Komitet S.S.S.R. po Statistike, p. 32. The figures were 1,017,228 baptisms of all Christian confessions in 1965 (data as of January 1966) and 965,188 in 1970. These figures included almost 30,000 school-age children baptized and more than 20,000 adults (many of whom were no doubt Baptists). Between 4 and 5 million children were born annually in those years, but close to 20 percent of those births were among the traditionally Muslim, Buddhist, Jewish, and other non-Christian peoples. See Lane, pp. 44, 60; Bociurkiw, p. 59.

85. Births were still running at 4–5 million a year, and Kharchev's figures for baptisms in 1975 (reported in 1976) were 808,478, of which 26,818 were adult baptisms, or a decline of 15–20 percent from the figures for 1965 and 1970. Ellis, p. 178; Kharchev, "Garantii svobody," p. 23; Gosudarstvenny Komitet S.S.S.R. po Statistike, p. 32. See also Simon, p. 105.

86. The figures were 259,484 baptisms in Ukraine in 1975, as compared to 808,478 in the whole country. Tsentralny Gosudarstvenny Arkhiv, Fond 6991, Opis No. 6, delo No. 3131.

87. Kharchev's figures were 830,596 people of all confessions baptized in 1980 (reported in 1981) and 774,747 people baptized in 1985 (reported in 1986). Kharchev, "Garantii svobody," p. 23. The 774,747 figure included the baptism of 52,000 adults (many of them Baptists) and 40,000 school-age children, leaving roughly 725,000 children of all denominations baptized annually and 685,000 infants baptized annually. Pospielovsky gave figures for Volgograd oblast indicating about 21 percent of the total number of newborn infants were baptized in 1970, 29 percent in 1977, and 34 percent in 1978. The baptismal figures apparently included adult baptisms, however, so the percentage figures for infants should be reduced in light of that factor. In fact, the sharp jump between 1970 and 1978 may considerably reflect adult baptisms. Pospielovsky, "Intelligentsia and Religion," p. 19; Gosudarstvenny Komitat S.S.S.R. po Statistike, p. 243.

88. The 1985 figure was 637,081, which was apparently for infant baptisms. This is somewhat less than the figure given by Kharchev (685,000) and may actually be the 1984 figure (reported in 1985), which would explain the difference. *Keston News Service,* No. 356, August 9, 1990, p. 16.

89. Tsentralny Gosudarstvenny Arkhiv, Fond 6991, Opis No. 6, delo No. 3131. Of the 154,578 baptisms in Ukraine in 1985, 1,230 were school-children and 2,109 were adults. This last figure strengthens the presumption that numerous baptisms were taking place in secret, as more than 2,109 Baptists were undoubtedly being baptized in Ukraine each year—without counting any Orthodox converts.

90. The figure was 700,000 baptisms in 1987. *Keston News Service,* No. 356, August 9, 1990, p. 16.

91. Metropolitan Vladimir (Sabodan) of Rostov, "Sovremennoe sostoyanie Russkoi Pravoslavnoi Tserkvi [The Present State of the Russian Orthodox Church]," *Religiya v SSSR,* No. 10, October 1988, p. MV2.

92. Michael Rowe gave the figure of 70 million baptized Orthodox Christians in the

USSR in 1981. This would appear to be a reasonable figure if the official statistics indicating close to 1 million infant baptisms a year in the 1970s and 1980s are accepted. Presumably a higher percentage of the older people had once been baptized. It would also tend to increase one's doubts that 30 million people, or almost half the total, could have been baptized in the period between 1971 and 1988. Michael Rowe, "Soviet Policy Towards Religion," *U.S.S.R. Facts and Figures Annual, 1981,* ed. John L. Scherer (Gulf Breeze, Florida: Academic International Press, 1982), p. 324.

93. *Zhurnal Moskovskoi Patriarkhii* [Journal of the Moscow Patriarchate], No. 6 (June), 1988, p. 6; No. 9 (September), 1988, p. 13; *The Samizdat Bulletin,* No. 180, Winter 1988, p. 14.

94. The statistics were that baptisms jumped from 700,000 in 1987 to 1.2 million in 1988 and to 1.6 million in 1989. *Keston News Service,* No. 356, August 9, 1990, p. 16.

95. Three times the 16–18 percent baptized in the late 1980s before the Millennium would bring the percentage up to 48–54 percent in 1990. *Zhurnal Moskovskoi Patriarkhii,* No. 10 (October), 1990, p. 10. Serge Schmemann in late 1991 gave the same figure of baptisms having "tripled" in late 1991. Serge Schmemann, "Patriarch's Church Revives, but Will Spirituality?" *The New York Times,* November 9, 1991, p. 2.

96. Zelinsky, p. 347; Col. Viktor Nechaev and Major Vladimir Mukhin, "Religiya: Mnenie voennikh [Religion: The Opinion of the Military]," *Religiya v SSSR,* No. 8, 1990, p. 2.

97. Alex de Jonge, *Stalin and the Shaping of the Soviet Union* (New York: William Morrow and Co., 1986), p. 70.

98. Curtiss, p. 222.

99. Tsentralny Gosudarstvenny Arkhiv, Fond 6991s, Opis No. 2, Vol. I, delo No. 263. The figures were 196,000 funerals out of 598,000 deaths. Ellis, p. 179.

100. The official figure for the USSR was 848,805 religious funerals of all religious communities in 1965 (reported in 1966). Kharchev, "Garantii svobody," p. 23. See also Lane, p. 60; Dobrynin and Mitrokhin, p. 223. Figures from scattered oblasts, mostly in Siberia, the Pacific maritime provinces, and the far north, were Omsk—5,700 religious burials and 12,000 deaths (48 percent); Novgorod—1,183 religious burials and 7,200 deaths (17 percent); Murmansk—77 religious burials and 1,698 deaths (5 percent); Orenburg—742 religious burials and 14,446 deaths (5 percent); Novosibirsk—685 religious burials and 17,067 deaths (4 percent); Komi—114 religious burials and 5,300 deaths (2 percent); Khabarovsk—111 religious burials and 7,100 deaths (1.6 percent). In the traditionally Russian Orthodox heartland there were some higher percentages. For example, there were 60 percent religious funerals in Orel oblast. Tsentralny Gosudarstvenny Arkhiv, Fond 6991s, Opis No. 4, Vol. I, delo Nos. 572–574.

101. The official figures were 990,618 religious funerals in 1970, or 14 percent more than in 1965. Kharchev, "Garantii svobody," p. 23. One Soviet sociologist stated that 32 percent of all funerals were religious in 1972, but this figure seems low in light of the official statistics. See Ellis, pp. 179–180. Lane gave a figure of 50 percent. Lane, p. 60. Some funerals in absentia may not be included in the official statistics, which Kharchev stated were from data submitted by the religious communities themselves. See also S. Petropavlovsky, "The Russian Orthodox Church," *Religion in Communist Lands,* Vol. I, Nos. 4–5, July–October 1973, p. 17.

102. The statistics reflected a true, gradual increase in religious funerals as a percentage of deaths, despite the demographic shifts in the elderly population, in both numbers and gender balance, created by World War II. During these years, approximately 2.5 million people were dying each year, and religious funerals rose to about 1.2 million in 1985, or 48 percent. Kharchev's figures were 1,096,190 religious funerals in 1975 (reported in 1976); 1,125,058 religious funerals in 1980 (reported in 1981); and 1,179,051 religious funerals in 1985 (reported in 1986). Kharchev, "Garantii svobody," p. 23. In the summer of 1990 *Argumenty i Fakty* published the figure of 249,033 religious funerals in 1985, or 9.6 percent of deaths. This figure differs radically from Kharchev's for the same time and is considerably less plausible. It could be true for Orthodox funerals in the Russian republic or some other such category. The *Argumenty i Fakty* article was carried by *Keston News Service,* No. 356, August 9, 1990, p. 16.

103. Kharchev also noted a high incidence of religious funerals in the north Caucasus, but many of these were no doubt Islamic rites. Kharchev, "Sovetskoe gosudarstvo i tserkov," p. 3.

104. *Argumenty i Fakty* reported in the summer of 1990 that religious funerals had increased from 249,033 to 324,291 between 1985 and 1989, a jump from 9.6 to 13 percent. Although the statistics appear garbled, the relative jump may be accurate, which would mean that religious funerals would have increased to about 65 percent in 1989. A jump in this range would be consistent with other available evidence. See *Keston News Service,* No. 356, August 9, 1990, p. 16.

105. *Information Service* (National Council of Churches of Christ in the U.S.A.), November 8, 1958, p. 4; Zalesski, p. 56.

106. Curtiss, p. 223; V. Mashchenko, "O rabote Uralskoi organizatsii [About the Work of the Ural Organization]," *Antireligioznik* [The Antireligionist], No. 11, 1929, p. 64.

107. Bach, p. 51; Tsentralny Gosudarstvenny Arkhiv, Fond 6991s, Opis No. 2, Vol. I, delo No. 263.

108. The actual statistics were as follows: Orenburg—399 church weddings out of a total of 13,000 (3 percent); Novgorod—44 of 5,500 (1 percent); Komi—19 of 8,000 (0.2 percent); Novosibirsk—32 of 20,730 (0.15 percent); Omsk—20 of 15,700 (0.1 percent); Murmansk—5 of 4,170 (0.1 percent); and Khabarovsk—7 of 13,000 (0.05 percent). Tsentralny Gosudarstvenny Arkhiv, Fond 6991s, Opis No. 4, Vol. I, delo Nos. 572–573.

109. Innokenti, p. VS4; Kharchev, "Garantii svobody," p. 23. Fletcher, in *Soviet Believers,* pp. 194–197, cited Soviet studies indicating that only 3 percent of marriages or less (outside of Roman Catholic areas) were religious.

110. Figures for religious marriages for all confessions were 1970—79,356; 1975—74,988; 1980—106,259; 1985—79,840. The official compilation date was January 1 of the year following. Kharchev, "Garantii svobody," p. 23. In 1990, *Argumenty i Fakty* gave the implausible figure of 30,085 religious marriages in 1985, or 1.4 percent of all weddings. This could have been a correct figure for religious weddings in the Russian republic or for Orthodox weddings in the country. *Argumenty i Fakty's* figure for 1989 was 83,767 as quoted by *Keston News Service,* No. 356, August 9, 1990, p. 16.

111. *Zhurnal Moskovskoi Patriarkhii,* No. 10 (October), 1990, p. 10. In late 1991 Schmemann reported a ninefold increase. Schmemann, p. 2.

112. Lane, p. 74.

113. Nikita Struve, *Christians in Contemporary Russia,* trans. Lancelot Sheppard and A. Manson (New York: Charles Scribner's Sons, 1967), p. 193.

114. Ellis, pp. 331–336, specifically p. 334. Meerson-Aksënov was then a layman.

115. V. Pokrovski, "Pastyri i Pastva [Pastors and Flock]," *Moskovski Tserkovny Vestnik, Yezhenedelnik,* No. 9, April 1990, pp. 4–5; Mikhail Meerson-Aksënov, "The People of God and the Pastors," quoted in Ellis, p. 334, and p. 493, note 8. See also Bishop Serafim (Chichagov), "Na puti iz krizisa [On the Way Out of Crisis]," *Moskovski Tserkovny Vestnik, Yezhenedelnik,* No. 3, February 1991, p. 7.

116. Mikhail Karelov, "Na krayu raskola? [At the Edge of Schism?]" *Sobesednik* [Interlocutor], *Komsomolskaya Pravda* Supplement, May 22, 1990, p. 2.

117. For discussion elsewhere of lay distrust of bishops and the danger of schism, see Chapters 7 and 15. See also Kenneth L. Woodward and Rod Nordland, "The Pope and the Pol," *Newsweek,* December 4, 1989, p. 90.

Chapter 15

1. Charles Williams, *The Descent of the Dove* (New York: Pellegrini and Cudahy, 1950), p. 44.

2. K. Marx, "K kritike Gegelevskoi Filosofii Prava [Critique of Hegel's Philosophy of Law]," *O Religii* [About Religion], K. Marx and F. Engels (Moscow: Gosudarstvennoe Izdatelstvo Politicheskoi Literatury, 1955), p. 30.

3. Friedrich Engels, "Die Lage Englands [The English Situation]," *Werke* [Works], Karl Marx and Friedrich Engels (Berlin: Dietz Verlag, 1956), p. 545.

4. V. I. Lenin, "Letter to Gorky," *Selected Works,* 12 Vols. (New York: International Publishers, 1935–1939), Vol. XI, pp. 675–676. Emphasis in the original.

5. John Shelton Curtiss, *The Russian Church and the Soviet State, 1917–1950* (Boston: Little, Brown and Co., 1953), pp. 200–201; Paul Miliukov, "Religion and the Church," Part I, *Outlines of Russian Culture* (Philadelphia, Penn.: University of Pennsylvania Press, 1942), p. 167.

6. Nathaniel Davis, *Religion and Communist Government in the Soviet Union and Eastern Europe,* dissertation, the Fletcher School of Law and Diplomacy, June 1, 1960, pp. 477, 482–484.

7. Michael Bourdeaux, *Risen Indeed: Lessons in Faith from the U.S.S.R.* (Crestwood, New York: St. Vladimir's Seminary Press, 1983), p. 47.

8. *The New York Times,* November 4, 1990, p. 1. For the same idea expressed in a slightly different way, see David K. Shipler, "Church in Soviet Finds Resilience as Millions Seek 'a Sense of Life,'" *The New York Times,* January 3, 1977, p. 8.

9. Serge Schmemann, "A Russian Holy Day Returns in Glory," *The New York Times,* April 8, 1991, p. A6.

10. Vsevolod Marinov, senior researcher, poll conducted for *Time,* published April 10, 1989, p. 63.

11. Victoria Pope, "God and Man in Russia," *U.S. News and World Report,* March 2, 1992, p. 56.

12. *The Way,* December 29, 1991, p. 6.

13. John Morrison, "The Bolshevik Who Came In from the Cold," *Los Angeles Times,* October 6, 1991, p. 16.

14. *Ogonëk* [Little Fire], No. 28, July, 1989, p. 17; *Religiya v SSSR* [Religion in the USSR], No. 4 (April), 1989, pp. 19–22.

15. For a presentation of these ideas, see Dimitry V. Pospielovsky, "Intelligentsia and Religion: Aspects of Religious Revival in the Contemporary Soviet Union, the Orthodox Church," *Religion and Communist Society,* ed. Dennis J. Dunn (Berkeley, Calif.: Berkeley Slavic Specialties, 1983), p. 32.

16. Dimitry V. Pospielovsky, *The Russian Church Under the Soviet Regime, 1917–1982,* 2 Vols. (Crestwood, N.Y.: St. Vladimir's Seminary Press, 1984), p. 421.

17. Francis House, *The Russian Phoenix* (London: SPCK, 1988), p. 92. It was also reported that Aleksi repeatedly expressed his readiness to retire in order not to be a witness and participant in the ravaging of the church. See Sergi Gordun, "Russkaya Pravoslavnaya Tserkov v period s 1943 no 1970 god [The Russian Orthodox Church in the Period from 1943 to 1970]," *Zhurnal Moskovskoi Patriarkhii,* No. 2 (February), 1993, p. 24.

18. Michael Bourdeaux, *Opium of the People* (Indianapolis: The Bobbs-Merrill Co., 1966), p. 210.

19. Forgiveness Sunday is the Sunday before Lent. Pospielovsky recounted this occurrence at a meeting of the American Association for the Advancement of Slavic Studies at Phoenix, Arizona, in November 1992.

20. Despite the freedom-of-conscience laws, the Russian Orthodox Free Church believes—correctly—that the authorities continue to support the patriarchal church against the adherents of the Russian Orthodox Church Abroad in many places.

21. Byelorussian (Belarusan) seminarians at Zhirovitsy are demanding and getting instruction in Byelorussian rather than Russian. John B. Dunlop, "The Russian Orthodox Church and Nationalism After 1988," *Religion in Communist Lands,* Vol. 18, No. 4, Winter 1990, p. 298. Metropolitan Filaret (Vakhromeev) welcomed the visiting head of the Byelorussian Autocephalous Church in Exile in February 1992, but did not conspicuously rush to the defense of Byelorussian (Belarusan) sovereignty when it seemed threatened in March. Jan Zaprudnik, *Belarus: At a Crossroads in History* (Boulder: Westview Press, 1993), pp. 214–215.

22. Well-informed observers reported that three-quarters of the vocations to the Russian Orthodox priesthood in the late 1980s came from Ukraine (see Dunlop, p. 295). If vocations from the Baltic states, Moldova, and other western lands are taken into account, the heartland church could claim about 20 percent of the vocations.

23. John Dunlop of the Hoover Institution noted that the "Russian imperial church would appear to be doomed" under conditions described in this paragraph. By "imperial" he clearly meant a multinational institution presiding over the Orthodox peoples of the former Soviet empire. Dunlop, p. 306. The Russian republic has non-Slavic Orthodox people within its borders, however, and the Russian Orthodox Church will be multinational regardless of the fate of the non-Russian republics.

24. Jonathan Peterson, "Many Soviets Wax Nostalgic for Stalin Rule," *Los Angeles Times,* September 29, 1991, p. A11.

25. *Pravoslavnoe Chtenie* [Orthodox Readings], No. 1 (January), 1990, pp. 2–3; *Zhurnal Moskovskoi Patriarkhii* [Journal of the Moscow Patriarchate], No. 10 (October), 1989, pp. 10–11.

26. *Moskovski Tserkovny Vestnik, Yezhenedelnik* [Moscow Church Herald, Weekly], No. 7, May 1992, p. 9.

27. Philip Walters discussed nationalism and religion in "Religion in the Soviet Union: Survival and Revival," Chapter 1, *Christianity and Russian Culture in Soviet Society,* ed. Nicolai N. Petro (Boulder, Colo.: Westview Press, 1990), pp. 11–12.

28. For additional commentary on this issue, see Davis, p. 484.

29. B. Sergeev, "Ya davno zhdal etoi vstrechi [I Have Been Waiting for the Meeting for a Long Time]," *Moskovski Tserkovny Vestnik, Yezhenedelnik,* No. 5, April 1991, p. 15.

30. Serge Schmemann, "Patriarch's Church Revives, but Will Spirituality?" *The New York Times,* November 9, 1991, p. 2. See also George Urban, "The Awakening," *The National Interest,* Spring 1992, pp. 40–42.

31. Sergei Belavenets, "S lyubovyu k Bogu i sostradaniem k cheloveku [With the Love of God and Compassion to the Person]," *Moskovski Tserkovny Vestnik, Yezhenedelnik,* No. 5, April 1991, p. 10.

32. Vladimir Semenko, "Tserkov i khristianskaya obshchestvennost [The Church and the Christian Community]," *Zhurnal Moskovskoi Patriarkhii,* No. 11 (November), 1990, p. 37.

33. Archbishop (now Metropolitan) Kirill (Gundyaev) of Smolensk, "Tserkov v otnoshenii k obshchestvu v usloviyakh perestroiki [The Church and Its Relationship to Society in the Circumstances of Perestroika]," *Zhurnal Moskovskoi Patriarkhii,* No. 2 (February), 1990, pp. 32–33.

34. Yevgeni Komarov, "Vzrastit rostki dobra [To Nurture the Sprouts of Goodness]," *Zhurnal Moskovskoi Patriarkhii,* No. 11 (November), 1990, p. 26.

35. *Moskovski Tserkovny Vestnik, Yezhenedelnik,* No. 13, June 1990, p. 4; Cindy Scharf, "A Resurrection in Moscow for *Jesus Christ Superstar,*" *Los Angeles Times,* August 13, 1991, p. H6; William E. Schmidt, "U.S. Evangelicals Winning Soviet Converts," *The New York Times,* October 7, 1991, p. A7.

36. Vladimir Poresh, "Faith and Lack of Faith in Russia," *Religion in Communist Lands,* Vol. 19, Nos. 1–2, Summer 1991, p. 77.

37. Poresh, p. 77, quoting an Open Christianity Society statement made in Leningrad at a May 18–20, 1990, conference in Leningrad.

38. B. Lyubimov, "Moi dom—moya tserkov [My Home—My Church]," *Moskovski Tserkovny Vestnik, Yezhenedelnik,* No. 22, October 1990, p. 8.

39. Some of the foregoing sentiments were expressed in a commentary in *Izvestiya* on June 5, 1990, p. 8.

40. For additional commentary, see Davis, pp. 484–485; Schmidt, p. A7.

41. V. N. Sachkov, letter, *Moskovski Tserkovny Vestnik, Yezhenedelnik,* No. 3, February 1991, pp. 8–9; personal comments made to me.

42. Marcus Bach, *God and the Soviets* (New York: Thomas Y. Crowell Co., 1958), pp. 156–157.

Selected Bibliography

Archives, Books, Pamphlets, and Dissertations

Alderson, Wroe, G. Cary Stephen, William B. Edgerton, Hugh W. Moore, Clarence E. Pickett, and Eleanor Zelliot. *Meeting the Russians: American Quakers Visit the Soviet Union*. Philadelphia, Penn.: American Friends Service Committee, 1956.

Alexeev, Wassilij. *Russian Orthodox Bishops in the Soviet Union, 1941–1953*. Text in Russian. New York: Research Program on the U.S.S.R., Mimeographed Series No. 61, 1954.

Alexeev, Wassilij, and Theofanis G. Stavrou. *The Great Revival: The Russian Church Under German Occupation*. Minneapolis: Burgess Publishing Co., 1976.

Alexeyeva, Ludmilla. *Soviet Dissent: Contemporary Movements for National, Religious and Human Rights*. Middletown, Conn.: Wesleyan University Press, 1985.

Anderson, Paul B. *People, Church and State in Modern Russia*. New York: The Macmillan Co., 1944.

Armstrong, John A. *Ukrainian Nationalism, 1939–1945*. New York: The Columbia University Press, 1955.

Bach, Marcus. *God and the Soviets*. New York: Thomas Y. Crowell Co., 1958.

Barron, J. B., and H. M. Waddams. *Communism and the Churches, a Documentation*. London: SCM Press, Ltd., 1950.

Beeson, Trevor. *Discretion and Valor*. Philadelphia, Penn.: Fortress Press, 1974 and 1982.

Bennett, John C. *Christianity and Communism*. New York: Hadden House Associated Press, 1948.

Berdyaev, Nicolas. *The Origin of Russian Communism*. London: Geoffrey Bles, 1948.

Bissonnette, Georges, A.A. *Moscow Was My Parish*. New York: McGraw-Hill Book Co., 1956.

Boas, Franz, ed. *General Anthropology*. New York: D.C. Heath and Co., 1938.

Bociurkiw, Bohdan R. *Ukrainian Churches Under Soviet Rule: Two Case Studies*. Cambridge, Mass.: Ukrainian Studies Fund, 1984.

Bociurkiw, Bohdan R., and John W. Strong, eds. *Religion and Atheism in the U.S.S.R. and Eastern Europe*. London: The Macmillan Co., 1975.

Bogolepov, Aleksandr A. *Tserkov pod vlastyu kommunizma* [The Church Under Communist Rule]. Munich: Instit. po izucheniya S.S.S.R., 1958.

Boiter, Albert. *Religion in the Soviet Union*. Beverly Hills, Calif.: Sage Publications, 1980.

Bolshakoff, Serge. *The Christian Church and the Soviet State*. London: Society for Promoting Christian Knowledge, 1942.

Bourdeaux, Michael. *Opium of the People*. Indianapolis, Indiana: The Bobbs-Merrill Co., 1966.

―――. *Patriarch and Prophets: Persecution of the Russian Orthodox Church Today*. Oxford: A. R. Mowbray and Co., 1975.

―――. *Religious Ferment in Russia*. London: The Macmillan Co., 1968.

―――. *Risen Indeed: Lessons in Faith from the U.S.S.R.* Crestwood, New York: St. Vladimir's Seminary Press, 1983.

Casey, Robert Pierce. *Religion in Russia*. New York: Harper and Bros., 1946.

Curtiss, John Shelton. *The Russian Church and the Soviet State, 1917–1950*. Boston: Little, Brown and Co., 1953.

Dallin, Alexander. *Odessa, 1941–1944: A Case Study of Soviet Territory Under Foreign Rule*. U.S. Air Force Project Rand, RM-1875, ASTIA Doc. No. AD 123552, The Rand Corp., February 14, 1957.

Davies, Raymond Arthur. *Inside Russia Today*. Winnipeg: Contemporary Publications, 1945.

Davis, Nathaniel. *Religion and Communist Government in the Soviet Union and Eastern Europe*. Dissertation. The Fletcher School of Law and Diplomacy, June 1, 1960.

―――. *Religious Collaboration and Resistance in the Communist World*. Research paper submitted to Professor Philip E. Mosely. The Russian Institute, Columbia University, 1954.

de Grunwald, Constantin. *The Churches and the Soviet Union*. New York: The Macmillan Co., 1962.

Dunn, Dennis J., ed. *Religion and Communist Society*. Berkeley, Calif.: Berkeley Slavic Specialties, 1983.

―――. *Religion and Modernization in the Soviet Union*. Boulder, Colo.: Westview Press, 1977.

Ellis, Jane. *The Russian Orthodox Church: A Contemporary History*. Bloomington, Indiana: Indiana University Press, 1986.

Evans, Stanley. *Churches in the U.S.S.R.* London: Corbett Publishing Co., 1943.

Fireside, Harvey. *Icon and Swastika: The Russian Orthodox Church Under Nazi and Soviet Control*. Cambridge, Mass.: Harvard University Press, 1971.

Fletcher, William C. *Nikolai: Portrait of a Dilemma*. New York: The Macmillan Co., 1968.

―――. *The Russian Orthodox Church Underground, 1917–1970*. London: Oxford University Press, 1971.

―――. *Soviet Believers: The Religious Sector of the Population*. Lawrence, Kansas: The Regents Press of Kansas, 1981.

―――. *A Study of Survival*. New York: The Macmillan Co., 1965.

Forest, Jim. *Religion in the New Russia*. New York: Crossroad, 1990.

Galter, Albert. *The Red Book of the Persecuted Church*. Westminster, Maryland: The Newman Press, 1957.

Gsovski, Vladimir, ed. *Church and State Behind the Iron Curtain*. New York: Frederick A. Praeger, 1955.

Gurian, Waldemar, ed. *The Soviet Union, Background, Ideology, Reality*. Notre Dame: University of Notre Dame Press, 1951.

Hayward, Max, and William C. Fletcher, eds. *Religion and the Soviet State: A Dilemma of Power*. London: Pall Mall Press, 1969.

Hebly, J. A. *The Russians and the World Council of Churches*. Belfast: Christian Journals Limited, 1978.

Heyer, Friedrich. *Die Orthodoxe Kirche in der Ukraine von 1917 bis 1945* [The Orthodox Church in Ukraine from 1917 to 1945]. Vol. III of *Osteuropa und der Deutsche Osten* [East Europe and the German East]. Köln-Braunsfeld: Rudolf Müller, 1953.

Hill, Kent R. *The Puzzle of the Soviet Church: An Inside Look at Christianity and Glasnost*. Portland, Oregon: Multnomah Press, 1989.

House, Francis. *The Russian Phoenix*. London: SPCK, 1988.

Hvat, Ivan. *The Catacomb Ukrainian Catholic Church and Pope John Paul II*. Cambridge, Mass.: Ukrainian Studies Fund, Harvard University, 1984.

Jackson, Joseph H. *The Eternal Flame*. Philadelphia, Penn.: The Christian Education Press, 1956.

Jenkins, Daniel. *The Strangeness of the Church*. Garden City, New Jersey: Doubleday, 1955.

Kolarz, Walter. *Religion in the Soviet Union*. New York: St. Martin's Press, 1961.

Konstantinov, Dimitry. *The Crown of Thorns*. London: Zarya, 1979.

———. *Stations of the Cross: The Russian Orthodox Church, 1970–1980*. London: Zarya, 1984.

Lane, Christel. *Christian Religion in the Soviet Union: A Sociological Study*. Albany, New York: State University of New York Press, 1978.

Little, *David. Ukraine: The Legacy of Intolerance*. Washington, D.C.: United States Institute of Peace Press, 1991.

Lonsdale, Kathleen, ed. *Quakers Visit Russia*. London: East-West Relations Group of the Friends' Peace Committee, 1952.

Markus, Vasyl. *Religion and Nationalism in Soviet Ukraine After 1945*. Cambridge, Mass.: Ukrainian Studies Fund, Harvard University, 1985.

Marshall, Richard H., Jr. and Thomas E. Bird, eds. *Aspects of Religion in the Soviet Union, 1917–1967*. Chicago: University of Chicago Press, 1971.

Meyendorff, John. *The Orthodox Church*. 3d ed. Crestwood, New York: St. Vladimir's Seminary Press, 1981.

Mol, Hans (J. J.), ed. *U.S.S.R., Western Religion: A Country by Country Sociological Inquiry*. The Hague, Paris: Mouton, 1972.

The Moscow Patriarchate. *The Russian Orthodox Church: Organization, Situation, Activity*. Moscow: The Moscow Patriarchate, 1958.

Noble, John H. *I Found God in Soviet Russia*. New York: St. Martin's Press, 1959.

Palmer, Gretta. *God's Underground*. New York: Appleton-Century-Crofts, Inc., 1949.

Parsons, Howard L. *Christianity in the Soviet Union*. Occasional Paper No. 11. New York: The American Institute for Marxist Studies, 1972.

Petro, Nicolai N., ed. *Christianity and Russian Culture in Soviet Society*. Boulder, Colo.: Westview Press, 1990.

Petrus (pseudonym), H. *Religious Communes in the U.S.S.R.* Text in Russian. New York: Research Program on the U.S.S.R., Mimeograph Series No. 44, 1953.

Pospielovsky, Dimitry V. *A History of Soviet Atheism in Theory and Practice, and the Believer*. 3 Vols. New York: St. Martin's Press, 1988.

————. *The Russian Church Under the Soviet Regime, 1917–1982.* 2 Vols. Crestwood, New York: St. Vladimir's Seminary Press, 1984.

Ramet, Sabrina Petra, ed. *Religious Policy in the Soviet Union.* New York: Cambridge University Press, 1993.

Shekhterman, Yefim I. *Vera ili znanie* [Faith or Knowledge]. Alma Ata: Kazakhstan, 1967.

Shirley, Eugene B., Jr., and Michael Rowe, eds. *Candle in the Wind: Religion in the Soviet Union.* Washington, D.C.: Ethics and Public Policy Center, 1989.

Simon, Gerhard. *Church, State and Opposition in the U.S.S.R.* Trans. Kathleen Matchett. Berkeley, Calif.: University of California Press, 1970; London: C. Hurst and Co., 1974.

Spinka, Matthew. *The Church in Soviet Russia.* New York: Oxford University Press, 1956.

Stepanyan, Ts. A., ed. *Stroitelstvo Kommunizma i dukhovny mir cheloveka* [The Building of Communism and the Spiritual World of the Individual]. Moscow: Nauka, Institute of Philosophy, Academy of Sciences, 1966.

Stroyen, William B. *Communist Russia and the Russian Orthodox Church, 1943–1962.* Washington: The Catholic University of America Press, 1967.

Struve, Nikita. *Christians in Contemporary Russia.* Trans. Lancelot Sheppard and A. Manson. New York: Charles Scribner's Sons, 1967.

Tancher, Volodymyr Karlovych. *Osnovi Ateizmu* [The Foundations of Atheism]. Kiev: Vydavnytsvo Kyivskogo Universytetu, 1961.

Teplyakov, M. K. *Problemy ateisticheskogo vospitaniya v praktike partinoi raboty* [Problems of Atheist Education in Practice in Party Work]. Voronezh: Voronezh University Press, 1972.

Timasheff, Nicholas S. *Religion in Soviet Russia, 1917–1942.* London: Sheed and Ward, 1944.

Tobias, Robert. *Communist-Christian Encounter in East Europe.* Indianapolis, Indiana: School of Religion Press, 1956.

Treadgold, Donald W. *Twentieth-Century Russia.* 6th ed. Boulder, Colo.: Westview Press, 1987.

Tsentralny Gosudarstvenny Arkhiv Oktyabrskoi Revolutsii [Central State Archive of the October Revolution], Vysshikh Organov Gosudarstvennogo Vlasti i Organov Gosurdarstvennogo Upravleniya S.S.S.R. [of the Higher Organs of State Government and Organs of State Administration of the U.S.S.R.] Soviet po delam religii pri Sovete Ministrov [the Council for Religious Affairs attached to the Council of Ministers].

Van Paasen, Pierre. *Visions Rise and Change.* New York: The Dial Press, 1955.

Vsepoddanneishi otchet ober-prokurora svyateishago sinoda pravoslavnago ispovedaniya za 1911–1912 [Comprehensive Report of the Over-Procurator of the Holy Synod of the Orthodox Confession for 1911–1912]. Sanktpeterburg: Synodalnaya Typ., 1913.

Walters, Philip, ed., with Keston College researchers. *World Christianity: Eastern Europe.* Monrovia, Calif.: Missions Advanced Research and Communications Center, 1988.

Williams, Charles. *The Descent of the Dove.* New York: Pellegrini and Cudahy, 1950.

Yaroslavski, E. M. *Na anti-religioznom fronte* [On the Antireligious Front]. Moscow: Krasnaya N., 1924.

Yudin, Nikolai I. *Pravda o Peterburgskikh "Svyatynyakh"* [The Truth about the Petersburg "Shrines"]. Leningrad: Lenizdat, 1962.

Zhukovski, Arkadi. "Ukraïnska Pravoslavna Tserkva, dokumenti, materiyali Khristiyanski samvidav Ukraïni [The Ukrainian Orthodox Church, Documents and Materials of Christian Samizdat of Ukraine]." Vol. I of *Martirologiya Ukraïnskikh Tserkov* [Martyrdom of the Ukrainian Churches]. Eds. Osyp Zinkewych and Olexander Voronym. 4 Vols. planned. Toronto: V. Symonenko Smoloskyp Publishers, 1987.

Zinkewych, Osyp, and Olexander Voronym, eds. *Martirologiya Ukraïnskikh Tserkov* [The Martyrdom of the Ukrainian Churches]. 4 Vols. planned. Toronto: V. Symonenko Smoloskyp Publishers, 1987.

Zinkewych, Osyp, and Taras R. Lonchyna. "Ukraïnska Kat. Tserkva [The Ukrainian Catholic Church]." Vol. II of *Martirologiya Ukraïnskikh Tserkov* [The Martyrdom of the Ukrainian Churches]. Eds. Osyp Zinkewych and Olexander Voronym. 4 Vols. planned. Toronto: V. Symonenko Smoloskyp Publishers, 1987.

Articles

Achildiev, Igor. "Zaboty upolnomochennogo Gubina [Anxieties of Commissioner Gubin]." Interview of Mikhail V. Gubin. *Nauka i Religiya* [Science and Religion]. No. 2 (February), 1988.

Albats, Yevgeniya. "The Parliament KGB Hearings." *Moscow News.* No. 6, February 9–16, 1992.

Aleksi II (Ridiger), Patriarch. "K sobytiyam v Pribaltike [Regarding Events in the Baltic States]." *Moskovski Tserkovny Vestnik, Yezhenedelnik* [Moscow Church Herald, Weekly]. No. 2, January 1991.

Alexeev, Wassily (Wassilij). "L'Église Orthodoxe Russe sous l'occupation allemande, 1941–1944 [The Russian Orthodox Church Under the German Occupation, 1941–1944]." *Irénikon.* Vol. 29, 1956.

———. "The Russian Orthodox Church 1927–1945: Repression and Revival." *Religion in Communist Lands.* Vol. 7, No. 1, Spring 1979.

Alimov, G., and G. Charodeev. "Faith Without Deeds Is Dead: An Interview with Patriarch Aleksi II." *Izvestiya.* June 16, 1990. Reproduced in English translation in *Religion in Communist Lands.* No. 3, Autumn 1990.

Anderson, John. "The Archives of the Council for Religious Affairs." *Religion, State and Society.* Vol. 20, Nos. 3 and 4, 1992.

Anderson, Paul B. "Churchmen Visit Russia." *Christian Century.* April 18, 1956.

———. "Russian-American Visitations: A Prelude to Understanding." *Christianity and Crisis.* Vol. XVI, No. 12, July 9, 1956.

Annin, Aleksandr. "Uzniki svobody [Prisoners of Freedom]." *Nedelya* [The Week]. No. 22, 1990.

Arefeva, I. "V shkole kak v seme [In School as in the Family]." *Moskovski Tserkovny Vestnik, Yezhenedelnik* [Moscow Church Herald, Weekly]. No. 3, February 1992.

Arnold, John. "Patriarch Aleksi II: A Personal Impression." *Religion, State and Society.* Vol. 20, No. 2, 1992.

Babasyan, Nataliya. "Spokoistvie narushaet Rumynski Patriarkhat . . . [The Romanian Patriarchate Disturbs the Peace . . .]." Interview of Metropolitan Vladimir (Cantareanu/Kantaryan). *Russkaya Mysl* [Russian Thought]. No. 3961, January 8, 1993.

Belavenets, Sergei. "Pamyati Patriarkha Pimena [Recollections of Patriarch Pimen]." *Zhurnal Moskovskoi Patriarkhii*. No. 9 (September), 1991.

————. "S lyubovyu k Bogu i sostradaniem k cheloveku [With the Love of God and Compassion to the Person]." *Moskovski Tserkovny Vestnik, Yezhenedelnik*. No. 5, April 1991.

Belyaev, Sergei. "Pamyati svateishego [Recollections of a Saintly Man]." *Literaturnaya Rossiya* [Literary Russia]. May 12, 1990.

Benedict, Ruth. "Religion." *General Anthropology*. Ed. Franz Boas. New York: D. C. Heath and Co., 1938.

Bisesti, A. "Attività religiosa clandestina nell' U.R.S.S. [Clandestine Religious Activity in the U.S.S.R.]." *Russia Cristiana Ieri e Oggi* [Christian Russia Yesterday and Today]. No. 18, June 1961.

Bociurkiw, Bohdan R. "Church-State Relations in the U.S.S.R." *Religion and the Soviet State: A Dilemma of Power*. Eds. Max Hayward and William C. Fletcher. London: Pall Mall Press, 1969.

————. "The Orthodox Church and the Soviet Regime in the Ukraine, 1953–1971." *Canadian Slavonic Papers*. Vol. XIV, No. 2, Summer 1972.

————. "The Re-Emergence of the Eastern Catholic Church in Ukraine." *Ecumenism*. No. 107, September 1992.

————. "Religion and Atheism in Soviet Society." *Aspects of Religion in the Soviet Union, 1917–1967*. Ed. Richard H. Marshall, Jr. Chicago: University of Chicago Press, 1971.

Bohlen, Celestine. "Bare-Fisted Russians Plot a Last Stand." *The New York Times*. August 21, 1991.

————. "Coup Sets Yeltsin at Center Stage." *The New York Times*. August 20, 1991.

————. "Cradle of Russian Revolution a Hotbed of Disgust." *The New York Times*. June 22, 1993.

————. "Moscow Mourns and Exalts Men Killed by Coup." *The New York Times*. August 25, 1991.

Bojcun, Marco. "Ukrainian Catholics Reject Orthodox 'Violence' Claims." *Keston News Service*. No. 341, January 11, 1990.

Bolshakov, Father Petr. "The True Orthodox Church." *Religion in USSR*. No. 10 (October), 1990.

Bombin, Mikhail. "Sudba Pravoslavnoi Tserkvi v Latvii [The Fate of the Orthodox Church in Latvia]." *Russkaya Mysl*. No. 3955, November 20, 1992.

Bonnell, John S. "Will Atheism Triumph in Russia?" *The Fifth Avenue Voice*. September 1958.

Bourdeaux, Michael. "Patriarch Aleksi II: Between the Hammer and the Anvil." *Religion, State and Society*. Vol. 20, No. 2, 1992.

Buldyk, Natalya. "Rushitsya barer neponimaniya [The Barrier of Incomprehension Crumbles]." *Religiya v SSSR* [Religion in the USSR]. No. 1 (January), 1989.

Bychkov, Sergei. "Voskresenie mifa [Revival of a Myth]." *Moskovskie Novosti* [Moscow News]. No. 10, March 7, 1993.

Chandler, Russell. "A Russian Force Is Reborn." *Los Angeles Times*. September 28, 1991.

Chaplin, Vs. "Khabarovskaya Yeparkhiya [The Khabarovsk Diocese]." *Moskovski Tserkovny Vestnik*. No. 5 (May), 1989.

Childs, Marquis. "The Puzzling Role of Soviet Religion." *The Washington Post and Times Herald.* July 8, 1958.

Chugunova, Nina. "Optina, zavyaz . . . [Optina, New Seed . . .]." *Ogonëk* [Little Fire]. No. 34, August 1989.

Clines, Francis X. "Bells Are Ringing as Soviets Return Churches to Faithful." *The New York Times.* April 16, 1989.

———. "Resistance to Soviet Takeover Grows as Defiant Crowds Rally for Yeltsin." *The New York Times.* August 21, 1991.

Codevilla, Giovanni. "Commentary on the New Soviet Law on Freedom of Conscience and Religious Organizations." *Religion in Communist Lands.* Nos. 1–2, Summer 1991.

Cornell, George W. "Analysts See Hopeful Stirrings of Improvements for Soviet Churches." *Los Angeles Times.* May 3, 1986.

———. "Belief Endures." AP (Associated Press) report. *The Gettysburg Times.* December 17, 1984.

———. "Worship Under the Red Star; Part II: The Careful Clergy." AP report. *The Gettysburg Times.* December 18, 1984.

Dahlburg, John-Thor. "Cleric's Death Paves Way for Change." *East Europe,* Moscow Edition. *Los Angeles Times.* May 4, 1990.

———. "Russians Stand Together at Rites for Fallen Countrymen." *Los Angeles Times.* October 11, 1993.

Danilov, Filipp. "Novy predstoyatel Russkoi Tserkvi [New Leader of the Russian Church]." *Kommersant* [Businessman]. No. 22, June 11–18, 1990.

Dart, John. "Soviets Accept Offer of Scriptures from Two Bible-Smuggling Groups." *Los Angeles Times.* December 17, 1988.

Davies, Raymond A. "The Patriarch on Church and State." *Soviet Russia Today.* November 1945.

Davydova, Natalya. "Road to the Church." *Moscow News.* No. 39, October 7–14, 1990.

Degtyarev, Yuri. "Greko-Katolicheskaya tserkov v S.S.S.R. i Perestroika [The Greek-Catholic Church in the U.S.S.R. and Perestroika]." *Religiya v SSSR.* No. 5 (May), 1990.

———. "Izmenenie chisla religioznykh obedinenii v SSSR v 1990 godu [The Change in the Number of Religious Societies in the U.S.S.R. in 1990]." *Religiya v SSSR.* No. 6 (June), 1990.

———. "Izmenenie chisla religioznykh obshchestv v SSSR v pervom polugodii 1990 goda [The Change in the Number of Religious Societies in the U.S.S.R. in the First Half of 1990]." *Religiya v SSSR.* No. 7 (July), 1990.

———. "More About Authorized Representatives." *Religion in USSR.* No. 7 (July), 1991.

———. "Neukosnitelno soblyudat zakon [To Observe the Law Strictly]." *Religiya v SSSR.* No. 6 (June), 1989.

———. "Religioznye obedineniya v SSSR [Religious Societies in the U.S.S.R.]." *Religiya v SSSR.* No. 5 (May), 1990.

———. "Religioznye obedineniya v SSSR i ikh registratsiya v 1990 godu [Religious Societies in the U.S.S.R. and Their Registration in 1990]." *Religiya v SSSR.* No. 6 (June), 1990.

———. "Religioznye obedineniya v SSSR i ikh registratsiya v yanvare-iyule 1990 goda

[Religious Societies in the U.S.S.R. and Their Registration from January to July of 1990]." *Religiya v SSSR.* No. 8 (August), 1990.

———. "Stalin and the Russian Orthodox Church." *Religion in USSR.* No. 12 (December), 1991.

Demina, N. "Shkola sester miloserdiya [School of Sisters of Charity]." *Moskovski Tserkovny Vestnik, Yezhenedelnik.* No. 22, October 1990.

Dunlop, John B. "The Contemporary Russian Orthodox Church." *Oberlin Alumni Magazine.* September–October 1976.

———. "The Russian Orthodox Church and Nationalism After 1988." *Religion in Communist Lands.* Vol. 18, No. 4, Winter 1990.

———. "Three Leading Moscow Hierarchs Unveiled as KGB Operatives." *Orthodox Life.* No. 3, May–June 1992.

Eaton, William J. "Monks Keep Faith Alive in Old Russia." *Los Angeles Times.* January 24, 1986.

Edelshtein, Georgi. "The Election of a Patriarch: Crossroads or Dead-End?" *Russkaya Mysl.* June 8, 1990. Reproduced in English translation in *Religion in Communist Lands.* Vol. 18, No. 3, Autumn 1990.

———. "How to Plunder a Church." *Religion in Communist Dominated Areas.* No. 3, 1989.

Ellis, Jane. "End of an Era?" *Frontier.* July–August 1990.

———. "Hierarchs and Dissidents: Conflict over the Future of the Russian Orthodox Church." *Religion in Communist Lands.* Vol. 18, No. 4, Winter 1990.

———. "Obituary." *Religion in Communist Lands.* Vol. 18, No. 2, Summer 1990.

———. "Some Reflections About Religious Policy Under Kharchev." *Religious Policy in the Soviet Union.* Ed. Sabrina Petra Ramet. New York: Cambridge University Press, 1993.

———. "Soviet Legislation on Religion: A Complicated Picture." *Keston News Service.* No. 365, December 20, 1990.

———. "Who Will Be Next Leader of the Russian Orthodox Church?" *Keston News Service.* No. 351, May 31, 1990.

Eshliman, Nikolai I., and Gleb P. Yakunin. "Declaration." *Religion in Communist Dominated Areas.* Vol. V, Nos. 9–10, May 15–31, 1966.

Facey, Paul W., S.J. "The Case of the Missing Underground." *America.* July 16, 1949.

Filaret (Denisenko), Metropolitan. "O podgotovke Pomestnogo Sobora Russkoi Pravoslavnoi Tserkvi i yubileinogo torzhestva v tselom [About the Preparation of the National Council (Pomestny Sobor) of the Russian Orthodox Church and the Celebration of the Jubilee in its Totality]." *Religiya v SSSR.* No. 4 (April), 1988.

———. "Tysyacheletie kreshcheniya Rusi [The Millennium of the Baptism of Rus]." *Religiya v SSSR.* No. 7 (July), 1988.

Filaret (Vakhromeev), Metropolitan. Letter to the Byelorussian authorities. *Moskovski Tserkovny Vestnik, Yezhenedelnik.* No. 6, April 1991.

Fletcher, William C. "Backwards from Reactionism: The De-Modernization of the Russian Orthodox Church." *Religion and Modernization in the Soviet Union.* Ed. Dennis J. Dunn. Boulder, Colo.: Westview Press, 1977.

———. "Introduction: The State of Soviet Sociology of Religion." *U.S.S.R., Western Reli-*

gion: A Country by Country Sociological Inquiry. Ed. Hans (J. J.) Mol. The Hague, Paris: Mouton, 1972.

Fontanieu, Pierre. "Le problème religieux en U.R.S.S. [The Religious Problem in the U.S.S.R.]." *Christianisme Social* [Social Christianity]. Vol. 63, Nos. 1–2 (January–February), 1955.

Fotiev, K. "Russkaya Pravoslavnaya Tserkov posle Yubileya [The Russian Orthodox Church After the Jubilee]." *Posev.* No. 4 (April), 1989.

Frankov, Mikhail. "Mysteries of the Holy Synod." *Moscow News.* No. 6, February 9–16, 1992.

Furov, V. G. "Cadres of the Church and Legal Measures to Curtail Their Activities: A Secret Report by the Council on Religious Affairs." *Religion in Communist Dominated Areas.* Vol. XIX, Nos. 10–12, 1980; Vol. XX, Nos. 1–6, 1981.

Gaevski, A. "O roli sovetskoi obryadnosti i traditsii v kommunisticheskom vospitanii [About the Role of Soviet Ritualism and Tradition in Communist Upbringing]." *Kommunist Ukrainy* [Communist of Ukraine]. No. 11 (November), 1963.

Garadzha, Viktor Ivanovich. "Pereosmyslenie [Rethinking]." *Nauka i Religiya.* No. 1 (January), 1989.

Gavryushin, Nikolai. "Nasledie i nasledniki [The Heritage and the Heirs]." *Moskovski Tserkovny Vestnik, Yezhenedelnik.* No. 23, October 1990.

Gazizova, O. "Moskovski pustynnik [Moscow Hermit]." *Moskovski Tserkovny Vestnik, Yezhenedelnik.* No. 10, May 1990.

Geertz, Clifford. "Religion as a Cultural System." *The Interpretation of Cultures.* New York: Basic Books, Inc., 1973.

Geruk, S. "Vremya yedineniya, a ne rozni [The Time for Unity, Not Dissension]." *Moskovski Tserkovny Vestnik, Yezhenedelnik.* No. 9 (27), 1990.

Geyer, Alan. "Three Days in August: Reflections on the Soviet Coup and Its Consequences." Distributed by the John T. Conner Center, 1991.

Gibbard, S. M., S.S.J.E. "Diary of a Visit to Russia." *Church Times.* July–August 1958.

Ginzburg, Aleksandr. "I lyudi napolovinu nashi [And People Half Ours]." *Russkaya Mysl.* No. 3941, August 7, 1992.

———. "Vsya presidentskaya rat [The Whole Presidential Array]." *Russkaya Mysl.* No. 3976, April 23–29, 1993.

Glan, Isaac. "An 'Unknown Land.'" *Literary Gazette International.* Vol. 1, No. 2, February 1990.

Gokhman, Mikhail. "Religiozny Sevastopol [A Religious Sevastopol]." Interview with Father Gleb Yakunin. *Russkaya Mysl.* No. 3989, July 22–28, 1993.

Goldberg, Carey. "Gorbachev Says He's Ready for Emergency Rule." *Los Angeles Times.* December 20, 1990.

———. "Supreme Soviet Session Ends in Spasms of Guilt." *Los Angeles Times.* September 1, 1991.

Golovensky, David I. "An American Rabbi in Russia." *Congress Weekly.* Vol. 23, No. 25, November 15, 1956.

Golovin, Kirill (a pseudonym). "The Day Will Come . . . ." *The Samizdat Bulletin.* No. 174, October 1987.

————. "Same Homeland, Different Future." *Sobornost*. No. 2, October (10), 1988 (Report dated July 17, 1988).

Golubev, Yu. "I tserkvi nuzhno yedinstvo [And Unity Is Needed Even for the Church]." Interview of Metropolitan Filaret (Denisenko). *Rabochaya Tribuna* [Labor Tribune]. June 5, 1990.

Gordun, Sergi. "Russkaya Pravoslavnaya Tserkov v period s 1943 po 1970 god [The Russian Orthodox Church in the Period from 1943 to 1970]." *Zhurnal Moskovskoi Patriarkhii*. No. 1 (January), 1993; No. 2 (February), 1993.

Gulichkina, G. "Pokrovski zhenski monastyr v Kieve [The Protection Nunnery in Kiev]." *Zhurnal Moskovskoi Patriarkhii*. No. 8 (August), 1989.

Hands, John. "Uncertain Freedom." *Frontier*. January–February 1990.

Henry, Catherine P. "Registration of Churches in the Soviet Union." *Religion in Communist Dominated Areas*. Vol. XXVI, No. 1, Winter 1987.

Hiltzik, Michael A. "Yeltsin, Foes Reportedly Reach Accord on Siege." *Los Angeles Times*. October 1, 1993.

Holmes, Larry E. "Fear No Evil: Schools and Religion in Soviet Russia, 1917–1941." *Religious Policy in the Soviet Union*. Ed. Sabrina Petra Ramet. New York: Cambridge University Press, 1993.

Ilarionov, Father Andrei. "Vesti iz Rossii [News From Russia]." *Pravoslavnaya Rus* [Orthodox Russia]. No. 23, December 1/14, 1992.

Ilovaiskaya, Irina. "Otvet na pismo professora Krasikova [An Answer to Professor Krasikov's Letter]." *Russkaya Mysl*. No. 3981, May 28–June 3, 1993.

————. "Tserkov i gosudarstvo [Church and State]." *Russkaya Mysl*. No. 3976, April 23–29, 1993.

Innokenti (probably Yazvikov, although Innokenti's surname is not given), Monastic Priest. "O sovremennom sostoyanii Russkoi Pravoslavnoi Tserkvi [About the Present Situation of the Russian Orthodox Church]." *Religiya v SSSR*. No. 8 (October), 1987.

Ionescu, Dan. "Metropolis of Bessarabia Reactivated." *RFE/RL Daily Report*. No. 245, December 22, 1992.

Irwin, Zachary T. "Moscow and the Vatican." *Religion in Communist Dominated Areas*. Vol. XXIX, No. 2, Spring 1990.

Izyumova, Nataliya. "Russian Orthodox Church: Road to Rebirth." *Moscow News*. No. 24, June 24–July 1, 1990.

Kalinichenko, Adel. "Chernaya Messa [Black Mass]." Interview of Father Vyacheslav Polosin, chairman of the Russian Supreme Soviet's Committee on Freedom of Conscience. *Posev*. No. 2, 1992.

Karelov, Mikhail. "Na krayu raskola? [At the Edge of Schism?]." *Sobesednik*, [Interlocutor], *Komsomolskaya Pravda* Supplement. May 22, 1990.

Keleher, Serge. "Church in the Middle: Greek-Catholics in Central and Eastern Europe." *Religion, State and Society*. Vol. 20, Nos. 3 and 4, 1992.

————. "A Fading Star." *Frontier*. September–October, 1992.

————. "Out of the Catacombs: The Greek-Catholic Church in Ukraine." *Religion in Communist Lands*. Nos. 3–4, Winter 1991.

Keller, Bill. "Atheist Preaches Glasnost, so a Priest Has Hope." *The New York Times*. June 8, 1987.

————. "Ex-KGB Officer Asserts Spy Agency Is Unchanged." *The New York Times.* June 17, 1990.

————. "The Kremlin Seeks a New Kind of Coexistence with Religion." *The New York Times.* August 23, 1987.

————. "Russian Tells Shadowy Tale of Spying Inside the Church." *The New York Times.* June 21, 1987.

Keston College staff. "Bibles in the Soviet Union." *Religion in Communist Lands.* Vol. 17, No. 3, Autumn 1989.

Kharazov, V. "Chudesa v Grusheve [Miracle in Grushev]." *Nauka i Religiya.* No. 5 (May), 1988.

Kharchev, Konstantin M. "Garantii svobody [Guarantees of Freedom]." *Nauka i Religiya.* No. 11 (November), 1987. Translated in *Religion in Communist Dominated Areas,* Vol. XXVI, No. 4, Fall 1987.

————. "Religiya i perestroika [Religion and Perestroika]." Speech to instructors of the Higher Party School, Moscow, end of March 1988 (transcribed by memory and abridged). *Russkaya Mysl.* No. 3725, May 20, 1988.

————. "Sovetskoe gosudarstvo i tserkov [The Soviet Government and the Church]." *Religiya v SSSR.* No. 10 (December), 1987.

Kirill (Gundyaev), Metropolitan. "Slovo" (Address). *Zhurnal Moskovskoi Patriarkhii.* No. 10 (October), 1992.

————. "Pravoslavnoe bogosluzhenie i problemy prikhodskoi zhizni [The Orthodox Service of Worship and Problems of Parish Life]." *Religiya v SSSR.* No. 3 (March), 1988.

————. "Tserkov v otnoshenii k obshchestvu v usloviyakh perestroiki [The Church and Its Relationship to Society in the Circumstances of Perestroika]." *Zhurnal Moskovskoi Patriarkhii.* No. 2 (February), 1990.

Kolesnik, N. Interview. *Foreign Broadcast Information Service.* February 10, 1989.

Kolomayets, Marta. "Believers and State at Odds Regarding Orthodox Churches." *The Ukrainian Weekly.* July 5, 1992.

————. "New Leader of UOC Greeted by Faithful in Kiev." *Ukrainian Weekly.* June 28, 1992.

————. "Orthodox Churches Announce Union." *The Ukrainian Weekly.* June 28, 1992.

————. "UOC Enthrones Patriarch Volodymyr." *The Ukrainian Weekly.* No. 44, October 31, 1993.

Kolomayets, Marta, and Borys Klymenko. "UOC of Kiev Rejects Patriarch's Demands." *The Ukrainian Weekly.* December 20, 1992.

Kolosovskaya, Svetlana. "Khotya den Strashnogo Suda otlozhena, [Even If the Date of the Judgment Day Is Postponed]." *Moskovskie Novosti.* No. 16, April 18, 1993.

Komarov, Yevgeni. "Iminy goroda [Saint's Name Day of a City]." *Moskovski Tserkovny Vestnik, Yezhenedelnik.* No. 1, January 1992.

————. Yevgeni. "Samostiinost, Nezalezhnost i Avtokefaliya [Autonomy, Independence in Action and Autocephaly]." *Moskovski Tserkovny Vestnik, Yezhenedelnik.* No. 2, February 1992.

————. "Vzrastit rostki dobra [To Nurture the Sprouts of Goodness]." *Zhurnal Moskovskoi Patriarkhii.* No. 11 (November), 1990.

————. "Zapadnaya Sibir: Budet li svoya seminariya? [Western Siberia: Will It Have Its Own Seminary?]" *Moskovski Tserkovny Vestnik.* No. 7 (July), 1989.

Komarov, K. M. "40 let izdatelskomu otdelu Moskovskogo Patriarkhata [Forty Years for the Publishing Department of the Moscow Patriarchate]." *Zhurnal Moskovskoi Patriarkhii.* No. 3 (March), 1985.

Kononenko, V. "Pamyat blokady [A Remembrance of the Blockade]." *Nauka i Religiya.* No. 5 (May), 1988.

Kozlov, M. "Prodolzhaya traditsiyu [Continuing in the Tradition]." *Moskovski Tserkovny Vestnik, Yezhenedelnik.* No. 23, October 1990.

Kramov, Aleksandr. "Poka Patriarkh molchit . . . [As the Patriarch Remains Silent . . .]." *Russkaya Mysl.* No. 3941, August 7, 1992.

Krasikov, Anatoli. "Tserkov i gosudarstvo [Church and State]." *Russkaya Mysl.* No. 3981, May 28–June 3, 1993.

Krasnov, A. "Zakat Obnovlenchestva [The Sunset of Renovationism]," *Grani* [Facets], No. 87–88, 1973.

Krikorian, Mesrob K. "The Armenian Church in the Soviet Union, 1917–1967." *Aspects of Religion in the Soviet Union, 1917–1967.* Ed. Richard H. Marshall, Jr. Chicago: University of Chicago Press, 1971.

Krivonos, F.P. "1000-letie khristianstva v Belorussii [A Thousand Years of Christianity in Belorussia]." *Zhurnal Moskovskoi Patriarkhii.* No. 2 (February), 1993.

Kublitskaya, Elena. "Obshchestvo massogo ateizma [A Society of Mass Atheism]." *Nauka i Religiya.* No. 1 (January), 1990.

Kublitskaya, Elena, Vyacheslav Lokosov, and Petr Olovyannikov. "Greko-katoliki v S.S.S.R. [Greek-Catholics in the U.S.S.R.]." *Religiya v SSSR.* No. 1 (January), 1990.

Kuraev, Deacon Andrei. "The Russian Orthodox Church and Patriarch Alexis II: Views and Stances." *Religion in USSR.* No. 4 (April), 1991.

Kuroedov, Vladimir. "Lenin's Principles of Freedom of Conscience in the U.S.S.R." *Nauka i Religiya.* No. 6 (June), 1968. Translated in *Religion in Communist Dominated Areas,* Vol. VIII, Nos. 7–8, Item 1436, April 1969.

Kuropas, Myron B. "Religious Pluralism Growing in Ukraine." *The Ukrainian Weekly.* April 26, 1992.

Lacaya, Richard. "The Silent Guns of August." *Time.* September 2, 1991.

Laishuk, Elena. "The Life of New Martyr Archpriest Fr. Paul Levashov of Gomel." *Orthodox Life.* No. 1, January–February 1992.

Lavr, Archbishop of Syracuse (of the Russian Orthodox Church Abroad). "Palomnichestvo po svyatym mestam Kieva i Pochaeva [Pilgrimage to the Holy Places of Kiev and Pochaev]." *Pravoslavnaya Zhizn* [Orthodox Life]. No. 12 (December), 1992.

Lebedev, V. "Da svetit svet vash [May Your Light So Shine]." *Moskovski Tserkovny Vestnik.* No. 6 (June), 1989.

Leshchinski, Anatoli. "Congress of Expatriate Russians in Moscow and Its Religious Program." *Religion in USSR.* No. 10 (October), 1991.

―――. "Tserkov v Tropareve: Posle osvyashcheniya [The Church in Troparev: After Its Consecration]." *Religiya v SSSR.* No. 4 (April), 1989.

Levitin-Krasnov, Anatoli. "Religion and Soviet Youth." *Religion in Communist Lands,* Vol. 7, No. 3, Autumn 1979.

Lew, Khristina. "Church Split Continues to Plague Orthodox faithful in Ukraine." *The Ukrainian Weekly.* No. 12, March 21, 1993.

Lewis, Flora. "Socialist Surrealism." *The New York Times.* June 29, 1987.

Lisavtsev, E. "Religiya v pravovom gosudarstve [Religion in a Lawful State]." *Pravda.* June 14, 1990.

Lorence, James J., and James G. Grinsel. "Amen: The Role of Religion in History Teaching." *Perspectives,* American Historical Association Newsletter. Vol. 30, No. 7, October 1992.

Lorgus, Deacon Andrei. "'Krugly stol' po aktualnym problemam tserkovnoi zhizni: Vozrodit zhizn prikhoda ['Round Table' on Contemporary Problems of Church Life: To Resuscitate Parish Life]." *Zhurnal Moskovskoi Patriarkhii.* No. 6 (June), 1990.

———. "Prikhodskaya zhizn: Tolko v ograde Khrama? [Parish Life: Only Within the Fence of the Church?]." Interview of Archpriest Vladimir Rozhkov. *Zhurnal Moskovskoi Patriarkhii.* No. 6 (June), 1990.

Lowrie, Donald A., and William C. Fletcher. "Khrushchev's Religious Policy, 1959–1964." *Aspects of Religion in the Soviet Union, 1917–1967.* Ed. Richard H. Marshall, Jr. Chicago: University of Chicago Press, 1971.

Lucey, Paul A. "Religion." *The Soviet Union Today.* Ed. James Cracraft. Chicago: Bulletin of the Atomic Scientists, 1983.

———. "Religion." *U.S.S.R. Facts and Figures Annual.* Ed. John L. Scherer. Gulf Breeze, Florida: Academic International Press, 1973, 1987, 1988.

Lyubimov, B. "Moi dom—moya tserkov [My Home—My Church]." *Moskovski Tserkovny Vestnik, Yezhenedelnik,* No. 22, October 1990.

Makari (Svistun), Metropolitan. "The Contemporary Status of Religion in the U.S.S.R.," Chapter 2. *Christianity and Russian Culture in Soviet Society.* Ed. Nicolai N. Petro. Boulder, Colo.: Westview Press, 1990.

Makarov, Aleksandr. "Boi na stupenyakh very [Fight on the Steps of Faith]." *Moskovski Tserkovny Vestnik, Yezhenedelnik.* No. 17, December 1989.

———. "Put k vozrozhdeniyu [The Path to Revival]." *Moskovski Tserkovny Vestnik, Yezhenedelnik.* No. 1, January, 1990.

Martyniuk, Jaroslaw. "News Analysis: The State of Ukraine's Orthodox Church." *The Ukrainian Weekly.* March 13, 1994.

Markus, Vasyl. "Religion and Nationality: The Uniates of the Ukraine." *Religion and Atheism in the U.S.S.R. and Eastern Europe.* Eds. Bohdan R. Bociurkiw and John W. Strong. London: The Macmillan Co., 1975.

Marx, K. "K kritike Gegelevskoi Filosofii Prava [Critique of Hegel's Philosophy of Law]." *O Religii* [About Religion]. K. Marx and F. Engels. Moscow: Gosudarstvennoe Izdatelstvo Politicheskoi Literatury, 1955.

Mashchenko, V. "O rabote Uralskoi organizatsii [About the Work of the Ural Organization]." *Antireligioznik* [The Antireligionist]. No. 11, 1929.

Meerson, Michael A. "The Decline in Religious Consciousness." *Religion in Communist Dominated Areas.* Vol. XXV, No. 2, Spring 1986.

Mefodi (Nemtsov), Metropolitan. "Khozyaistvennaya deyatelnost Russkoi Pravoslavnoi Tserkvi [Administrative Activity of the Russian Orthodox Church]." *Religiya v SSSR.* No. 10 (October), 1988.

Miliukov, Paul. "Religion and the Church." Part I. *Outlines of Russian Culture.* Philadelphia, Penn.: University of Pennsylvania Press, 1942.

Minkin, Aleksandr. "Ne rydaite obo mne [Don't Cry for Me]." *Ogonëk*. No. 39, 1990.

Molchanov, V. "Vstrecha s Rodinoi [Encounter with the Motherland]." *Pravoslavnaya Zhizn* [Orthodox Life]. No. 5 (May), 1993.

Montalbano, William D. "Half a Century Later, Ukrainian Priest Goes Home." *Los Angeles Times*. March 30, 1991.

———. "Ukrainian Prelate in Emotional Return to His Homeland." *Los Angeles Times*. March 31, 1991.

Morrison, John. "The Bolshevik Who Came In from the Cold." *Los Angeles Times*. October 6, 1991.

Moshkina, L. "Prestolny prazdnik v sele [Church-altar Saint's Day in a Village]." *Moskovski Tserkovny Vestnik, Yezhenedelnik*. No. 2, January 1991.

Moss, James. "The Russian Orthodox Church, 1986–1988." *Religion in Communist Dominated Areas*. Vol. XXVIII, No. 2, Spring 1989.

———. "The Russian Orthodox Church, 1988–1990." *Religion in Communist Dominated Areas*. Vol. XXIX, No. 1, Winter 1990.

Moss, Vladimir. "The Restoration of Romanity." *Orthodox Life*, No. 4, July–August 1992.

———. "The True Orthodox Church of Russia." *Religion in Communist Lands*. Nos. 3–4, Winter 1991.

Mossman, Elliot. "The Case of the Russian Archives: An Interview with Iurii N. Afanas'ev." *Slavic Review*. Summer 1993.

Mydans, Seth. "In Soviet, Religion Ceases Outside Church Doors." *The New York Times*. July 15, 1984.

Nechaev, Col. Viktor, and Major Vladimir Mukhin. "Religiya: Mnenie voennikh [Religion: The Opinion of the Military]." *Religiya v SSSR*. No. 8, 1990.

Nezhny, Aleksandr. "Election of a New Russian Patriarch." *Moscow News*. No. 23, June 3–10, 1990.

———. "Law and Conscience." *Moscow News*. No. 33, 1987. Translated in *Religion in Communist Dominated Areas*, Vol. XXVI, No. 2, Spring 1987.

———. "Mitropolit Filaret kak zerkalo Moskovskoi Patriarkhii [Metropolitan Filaret as a Mirror of the Moscow Patriarchate]." *Russkaya Mysl*. No. 3936, July 3, 1992.

———. "Nedeistvitelnaya anafema [Inoperative Anathema]." *Russkaya Mysl*. No. 3999, October 7–13, 1993.

———. "Pered vyborom Patriarkha [Before the Election of the Patriarch]." *Moskovskie Novosti*. No. 21, May 27, 1990.

———. "Pyatnadtsaty patriarkh [The Fifteenth Patriarch]." *Moskovskie Novosti*. No. 24, June 17, 1990. Translated in *Moscow News*, No. 24, June 24–July 1, 1990.

———. "Sovest svobodna [A Free Conscience]." *Ogonëk*. No. 21, May 1988.

———. "Sudba Patriarkha [The Fate of the Patriarch]." *Ogonëk*. No. 27, June 30–July 7, 1990.

———. "Sumerki soznaniya [Twilight of Consciousness]." *Russkaya Mysl*. No. 3987, July 8–14, 1993; No. 3988, July 15–21, 1993.

———. "Teper mozhno verit v boga, ne riskuya popast v lager [Now it is Possible to Believe in God Without the Risk of Landing in a Labor Camp]." *Ogonëk*. No. 45, 1990, inside front cover.

————. "Treti razgovor s Kharchevem [Third Conversation with Kharchev]." *Ogonëk.* No. 44, 1989.

————. "Zakon i sovest [Law and Conscience]." *Ogonëk.* No. 50, 1988.

————. "Zapozdalye molnii [Delayed Lightning Bolts]." *Russkaya Mysl.* No. 3929, May 15, 1992.

Nikitin, Valeri. "New Patriarch, New Problems." *Russkaya Mysl.* June 29, 1990. Reproduced in English translation in *Religion in Communist Lands.* Vol. 18, No. 3, Autumn 1990.

Nikolaeva, I. "Triumfi i tragediya [Triumph and Tragedy]." Interview of D. A. Volkogonov. *Nauka i Religiya.* No. 2 (February), 1989.

Nikolaeva, V. "Zakon Bozhi—malenkim Vyaticham [The Law of God—to Young Vyatkaites]." *Moskovski Tserkovny Vestnik, Yezhenedelnik.* No. 1, January 1992.

"O dukhovnom sostoyanii Russkago naroda pod vlastyu bezbozhnikov [About the Spiritual Condition of the Russian Nation Under Atheist Rule]." *Doklad Soboru Pravoslavnoi Russkoi Zarubezhnoi Tserkvi s Uchastiem Klira i Miryan 7/20 Avgusta 1938 goda* [Report to the Council of the Russian Orthodox Church Outside Russia with the Participation of Clergy and Laity, of August 7/20, 1938]. Napechatano po postanovleniyu plenarnago zasedaniya Sobora, 20-VIII-1938 [printed at the direction of the plenary session of the Council, 20-VIII-1938].

O. G. "Ne zavisimye ot faktov gazety [Newspapers Independent of Facts]." *Moskovski Tserkovny Vestnik, Yezhenedelnik.* No. 1, January 1992.

Odintsov, Mikhail. "Drogogo raza ne bylo . . . [There Never Was Another Time . . .]." *Nauka i Religiya.* No. 2 (February), 1989.

————. "The Soviet State and Laws on Religion." *Religion in USSR.* No. 12 (December), 1991.

Oppenheim, Raymond. "Russian Orthodox Theological Education in the Soviet Union." *Religion in Communist Lands.* Vol. 2, No. 3, 1974.

Parks, Michael. "Soviet Rights Group Urges Release of Jailed Believers." *Los Angeles Times.* August 10, 1988, Part I.

————. "Talks Set on Ukraine Church Status." *Los Angeles Times.* June 5, 1988, Part I.

Pasles, Chris. "Bolshoi's Mikhail Lavrovsky Choreographs a Spiritual Quest." *Los Angeles Times.* May 6, 1988.

Paukova, O. "Monastyr na ulitse Lenina [Convent on Lenin Street]." *Moskovski Tserkovny Vestnik, Yezhenedelnik.* No. 4, March 1991.

Pazukhin, E. "Poiski puti [In Search of the Way]." *Moskovski Tserkovny Vestnik, Yezhenedelnik.* No. 9, April 1990.

Peterson, Jonathan. "Many Soviets Wax Nostalgic for Stalin Rule." *Los Angeles Times.* September 29, 1991.

Petrochenkov, Valery. "Christian Patterns in Contemporary Soviet Prose." *Christianity and Russian Culture in Soviet Society.* Ed. Nicolai N. Petro. Boulder, Colo.: Westview Press, 1990.

Petropavlovsky, S. "The Russian Orthodox Church." *Religion in Communist Lands.* Vol. I, Nos. 4–5, July–October 1973.

Petrosyan, Margarita. "Sovest: Ponyatie geopoliticheskoe [Conscience: A Geopolitical Understanding]." *Russkaya Mysl.* No. 3990, July 29–August 4, 1993.

Pfaff, William. "Sweeping Soviet Retreat on Religion?" *Los Angeles Times.* May 5, 1988.

Pitirim (Nechaev), Metropolitan. "Ob izdatelskoi deyatelnosti Russkoi Pravoslavnoi Tserkvi [Concerning the Publishing Activity of the Russian Orthodox Church]." *Religiya v SSSR.* No. 11 (November), 1988.

Plokhiy, Serhiy. "News Analysis: Ukrainian Orthodox Autocephaly and Metropolitan Filaret." *The Ukrainian Weekly.* August 2, 1992.

Pokrovski, V. "Pastyri i Pastva [Pastors and Flock]." *Moskovski Tserkovny Vestnik, Yezhenedelnik.* No. 9, April 1990.

Pope, Hugh. "New Spirit Abounds for Enthronement of Church Leader." *Los Angeles Times.* November 2, 1991.

Pope, Victoria. "God and Man in Russia." *U.S. News and World Report.* March 2, 1992.

Poresh, Vladimir. "Faith and Lack of Faith in Russia." *Religion in Communist Lands.* Vol. 19, Nos. 1–2, Summer 1991.

Porubcansky, Mark J. "State Tolerance Increases as Russian Christianity Marks 1000th Year." *Los Angeles Times.* January 9, 1988.

Pospielovsky, Dimitry V. "The Eastern Rite Catholics and the Orthodox in Today's Ukraine." *Ecumenism.* No. 107, September 1992.

——— "Intelligentsia and Religion: Aspects of Religious Revival in the Contemporary Soviet Union, the Orthodox Church." *Religion and Communist Society.* Ed. Dennis J. Dunn. Berkeley, Calif.: Berkeley Slavic Specialties, 1983.

———. "Religious Themes in the Soviet Press in 1989." *Religion in Communist Lands.* Vol. 18, No. 4, Winter 1990.

———. "The Soviet State Versus the Russian Orthodox Church, 1959–1988." *Religion in Communist Dominated Areas.* Vol. XXVII, No. 4, Fall 1988.

Pospishil, Victor J. "The Book of the Law." *The Way.* October 3, 1993.

Potapov, Victor S. "The Celebration of the Millennium of the Baptism of Rus in the U.S.S.R." *Religion in Communist Dominated Areas.* Vol. XXVII, No. 4, Fall 1988.

Pozdnyaev, Mikhail. "Arkhiepiskop Vilenskii Litovski Khrizostom: 'Ya sotrudnichal s KGB . . . no ne byl stukachom' [Archbishop Chrysostom of Vilnyus and Lithuania: 'I Worked Together with the KGB . . . but I Was Not a Stool Pigeon']." *Russkaya Mysl.* No. 3926, April 24, 1992.

Pugach, Yu. Letter. *Moskovski Tserkovny Vestnik, Yezhenedelnik.* No. 7, May 1992.

Radyshevski, Dmitri. "Gonimye za veru [Persecuted for Their Faith]." *Moskovskie Novosti.* No. 18, May 6, 1990.

Raleigh, Donald J. "The Triumph of Glasnost in Scholarship: Raleigh Reaches Saratov." *Newsletter.* American Association for the Advancement of Slavic Studies. Vol. 30, No. 4, September 1990.

Rar (also Rahr), Gleb. "Skolko v Rossii pravoslavnykh khramov? [How Many Orthodox Churches Are There in Russia?]" *Posev.* January 1974.

Robert, Dana L. "Grandmothers and the Millennium of Russian Christianity." *Christian Century.* December 24–31, 1986.

Rothenberg, Joshua. "The Legal Status of Religion in the Soviet Union." *Aspects of Religion in the Soviet Union, 1917–1967.* Ed. Richard H. Marshall, Jr. Chicago: University of Chicago Press, 1971.

Rowe, Michael. "Soviet Policy Towards Religion." *U.S.S.R. Facts and Figures Annual, 1981.* Ed. John L. Scherer. Gulf Breeze, Florida: Academic International Press, 1982.

Rozhnov, Georgi. "Eto my, Gospodi [Here Are We, My Lord]." *Ogonëk.* No. 38, September 1989.

Ruban, Vladimir. "Izvergnut iz sana . . . [To Expel from Rank . . .]." *Moskovskie Novosti.* No. 28, July 12, 1992.

———. "Moscow Wants to Subdue Ukraine Through the Church." *Moscow News.* No. 29, July 19–26, 1992.

———. "Vozmozhno, Filareta vse zhe 'uidut' [Filaret Might Have to Go]." *Moskovskie Novosti.* No. 41, October 11, 1992.

Sabant, Philippe. "Religion in Russia Today, Parts I and II." *The Tablet* (London). Vol. 234, No. 7279, January 12, 1980, and No. 7280, January 19, 1980.

Sachkov, V. N. Letter. *Moskovski Tserkovny Vestnik, Yezhenedelnik.* No. 3, February 1991.

Safire, William. "Flirting with God." *The New York Times.* December 25, 1986.

Salisbury, Harrison E. "Russians Export New Bibles to U.S." *The New York Times.* August 17, 1956.

Sapiets, Marite. "Monasticism in the Soviet Union." *Religion in Communist Lands.* Vol. 4, No. 1, Spring 1976.

Sawatsky, Walter. "Secret Soviet Lawbook on Religion." *Religion in Communist Lands.* Vol. 4, No. 4, Winter 1976.

Scharf, Cindy. "A Resurrection in Moscow for *Jesus Christ Superstar.*" *Los Angeles Times.* August 13, 1991.

Schmemann, Serge. "Gorbachev Back as Coup Fails, but Yeltsin Gains New Power." *The New York Times.* August 22, 1991.

———. "Lawmakers Add to Defiance of Yeltsin." *The New York Times.* July 24, 1993.

———. "A Moment of Rapture as a Saint Is Marched Home." *The New York Times.* February 8, 1991.

———. "Patriarch's Church Revives, but Will Spirituality?" *The New York Times.* November 9, 1991.

———. "Revolt in Moscow: How Yeltsin Turned the Tide, Hour by Hour." *The New York Times.* October 11, 1993.

———. "Russia May Curb Foreign Religions." *The New York Times.* July 16, 1993.

———. "A Russian Holy Day Returns in Glory." *The New York Times.* April 8, 1991.

Schmidt, William E. "U.S. Evangelicals Winning Soviet Converts." *The New York Times.* October 7, 1991.

Semenko, Vladimir. "Tserkov i khristianskaya obshchestvennost [The Church and the Christian Community]." *Zhurnal Moskovskoi Patriarkhii.* No. 11 (November), 1990.

Semenov, A. "Zhivoi ukor [A Living Reproach]." *Moskovski Tserkovny Vestnik, Yezhenedelnik.* No. 23, October 1990.

Serafim (Chichagov), Bishop. "Na puti iz krizisa [On the Way Out of Crisis]." *Moskovski Tserkovny Vestnik, Yezhenedelnik.* No. 3, February 1991.

Sergeenko, Archpriest Andrei. "Sv. Ioann Zlatoust o pastyrskom sluzhenii [St. John Chrysostom on Pastoral Service]." *Zhurnal Moskovskoi Patriarkhii.* No. 5 (May), 1957.

Sergeev, B. "Ya davno zhdal etoi vstrechi [I Have Been Waiting for the Meeting for a Long Time]." *Moskovski Tserkovny Vestnik, Yezhenedelnik.* No. 5, April 1991.

Sergeev, V. "Profanatsiya very, ili 'Velikaya Liturgiya' v klube 'Krasny Oktyabr' [The Profanation of Belief, or the 'Great Liturgy' in the 'Red October' Club]." *Moskovski Tserkovny Vestnik, Yezhenedelnik.* No. 7, May 1992.

Sergi, Archimandrite. "Poslednie dni zemnoi zhizni svyateishego Patriarkha Pimena [The Last Days of the Earthly Life of His Holiness, Patriarch Pimen]." *Zhurnal Moskovskoi Patriarkhii.* No. 8 (August), 1990.

Serkora, O. V. Interview. *Foreign Broadcast Information Service.* December 16, 1988.

Shemetrov, N. "Khristos posrede nas [Christ in our Midst]." *Moskovski Tserkovny Vestnik, Yezhenedelnik.* No. 11, May 1990.

Shevkunov, Georgi. "Ne uchastvuite v delakh tmy [Do Not Participate in the Works of Darkness]." *Zhurnal Moskovskoi Patriarkhii.* No. 12 (December), 1989.

Shipler, David K. "Church in Soviet Finds Resilience as Millions Seek 'a Sense of Life.'" *The New York Times.* January 3, 1977.

Slovodchenko, V. "Vse shire sfera vliyaniya [Ever-Widening Sphere of Influence]." *Pravda Ukrainy* [Truth of Ukraine]. October 20, 1960.

Sokolov, Maksim. "Kto zaimet patriarshi prestol? [Who Will Occupy the Patriarchal Throne?]" *Kommersant.* No. 18, May 14, 1990.

Soldatov, Aleksandr. "Heresy of the Last Times." *Pravoslavnaya Rus.* No. 9, May 1/14, 1993.

———. "Sibirskiya zarisovki [Siberian Sketches]." *Pravoslavnaya Rus.* No. 10, May 15/28, 1992.

Sorokowski, Andrew. "Church and State, 1917–64." *Candle in the Wind: Religion in the Soviet Union.* Eds. Eugene B. Shirley, Jr., and Michael Rowe. Washington, D.C.: Ethics and Public Policy Center, 1989.

Spasski, V. "Pochemu?" (Why?) *Moskovski Tserkovny Vestnik, Yezhenedelnik.* Nos. 18–19, 1992.

Speranskaya, E. "Tserkovno-nauchnaya konferentsiya posvyashchennaya 400-letiyu ustanovleniya Patriarshestva v Russkoi Pravoslavnoi Tserkvi [The Church-Scholars' Conference Celebrating the 400th Anniversary of the Establishment of the Patriarchate in the Russian Orthodox Church]." *Zhurnal Moskovskoi Patriarkhii.* No. 2 (February), 1990.

Spuler, Berthold. "Die Orthodoxen Kirchen [The Orthodox Churches]." *Internationale Kirchliche Zeitschrift* [The International Church Journal]. Bern, No. 30, April–June 1940.

Steeves, Paul D. Writing in *Christianity and Crisis.* Reprinted in *Rapprochement.* The John T. Conner Center. No. 91–3, October 1991.

Stepanova, Ilmira. Interview of Aleksi. *Russkaya Mysl.* No. 3958, December 11, 1992.

Strelchik, E. "V ozhidanii Patriarkha [Awaiting a Patriarch]." *Vechernaya Moskva* [Evening Moscow]. June 6, 1990.

Struve, Nikita. "Tserkov v Sovetskoi Rossii [The Church in Soviet Russia]." *Vestnik Russkogo Studencheskogo Khristianskogo Dvizheniya* [Herald of the Russian Student Christian Movement]. Nos. V–VI, 1954; No. I, 1955.

Svetlova, Yelena. "On Whose Conscience a Cross?" *Sovershenno Sekretno.* No. 6, 1991. Reproduced by *U.S.S.R. Today.* No. 929, October 16, 1991.

Sysyn, Frank E. "The Russian Sobor and the Rejection of Ukrainian Orthodox Autocephaly." *The Ukrainian Weekly.* July 26, 1992.

Tataryn, Myroslav. "The Re-emergence of the Ukrainian (Greek) Catholic Church in the U.S.S.R." *Religious Policy in the Soviet Union*. Ed. Sabrina Petra Ramet. New York: Cambridge University Press, 1993.

Telyakovski, E. "Tserkov v nastoyashchee vremya [The Church into the Current Time]." *Antireligioznik* [The Antireligionist]. February 1940.

Timasheff, Nicholas S. "Religion in Russia, 1941–1950." *The Soviet Union, Background, Ideology, Reality*. Ed. Waldemar Gurian. Notre Dame: University of Notre Dame Press, 1951.

————. "Urbanization, Operation Antireligion and the Decline of Religion in the U.S.S.R." *The American Slavic and East European Review*. April 1955.

Tsirulnikov, Anatoli. "Iz zhizni dukhovnoi shkoly [From the Life of a Theological School]." *Ogonëk*. No. 5, January 28–February 4, 1989.

Tuberozov, Savelii. "Monasteries and Theological Schools in the U.S.S.R." *Eastern Churches Review*. Vol. I, 1966.

————. "News and Comment." *Eastern Churches Review*. Vol II, 1968–1970.

Urban, George. "The Awakening." *The National Interest*. Spring 1992.

Uspenski, Nikolai D. "K istorii bogoslovskogo obrazonvaniya v Leningrade [Commemorating the History of Theological Education in Leningrad]." *Zhurnal Moskovskoi Patriarkhii*. No. 4 (April), 1977.

Vadimov, R. "Eto agressiya [This Is Aggression]." *Moskovski Tserkovny Vestnik, Yezhenedelnik*. No. 1, January 1990.

————. "Khranit apostolskie zavety [Preserve Apostolic Precepts]." *Moskovski Tserkovny Vestnik, Yezhenedelnik*. No. 4 (22), 1990.

Vardys, V. Stanley. "Catholicism in Lithuania." *Aspects of Religion in the Soviet Union, 1917–1967*. Ed. Richard H. Marshall, Jr. Chicago: University of Chicago Press, 1971.

Vasilev, P. "'Abbat' vykhodit na svyaz ['Abbat' Emerges as a Link]." Interview of Father Gleb Yakunin. *Argumenty i Fakty* [Arguments and Facts]. No. 1, January, 1992.

————. "Uniaty [Uniates]." Interview of M. Odintsov. *Argumenty i Fakty* [Arguments and Facts]. No. 40 (469), October 7–13, 1989.

Vedernikov, A. "Russkaya Pravoslavnaya Tserkov v 1964 godu [The Russian Orthodox Church in 1964]." *Zhurnal Moskovskoi Patriarkhii*. No. 1 (January), 1965.

Veshchikov, Aleksandr Trofimovich. "Etapy bolshogo puti [Milestones of a Great Journey]." *Nauka i Religiya*. No. 11 (November), 1962. Translated in *Religion in Communist Dominated Areas*, Item No. 149, December 17, 1962.

Vladimir (Sabodan), Metropolitan. "O sovremennom sostoyanii Russkoi Pravoslavnoi Tserkvi posle prinyatiya novogo Ustava [About the Contemporary Situation of the Russian Orthodox Church After the Adoption of the New Statute]." *Zhurnal Moskovskoi Patriarkhii*. No. 2 (February), 1990.

————. "Sovremennoe sostoyanie Russkoi Pravoslavnoi Tserkvi [The Present State of the Russian Orthodox Church]." *Religiya v SSSR*. No. 10 (October), 1988.

————. "Soedinyaya veka [Uniting the Centuries]." *Moskovski Tserkovny Vestnik*. No. 9 (September), 1988.

————. "Zhizn i deyatelnost Russkoi Pravoslavnoi Tserkvi [Life and Activity of the Russian Orthodox Church]," report to the national council, June 7, 1988. *Zhurnal Moskovskoi Patriarkhii*. No. 9 (September), 1988.

Vvedenski, A. *Tserkov i gosudarstvo* [Church and State]. Moscow: Mospoligraf "Krasny Proletari," 1923.

Wallace, Charles P. "Orthodox Head Assails Soviet Religious Curbs." *Los Angeles Times.* April 9, 1988, Part I.

Walters, Philip. "Gorbachev: Is This the Breakthrough?" *Frontier,* March–April 1987.

———. "Religion in the Soviet Union: Survival and Revival," Chapter 1. *Christianity and Russian Culture in Soviet Society.* Ed. Nicolai N. Petro. Boulder, Colo.: Westview Press, 1990.

———. "A Survey of Soviet Religious Policy." *Religious Policy in the Soviet Union.* Ed. Sabrina Petra Ramet. New York: Cambridge University Press, 1993.

Warder, Michael. "Soviet Image-Building Through a Church Anniversary." *Religion in Communist Dominated Areas.* Vol. XXVIII, No. 2, Spring 1989.

Woodward, Kenneth L., and Rod Norland. "The Pope and the Pol." *Newsweek.* December 4, 1989.

Wren, Christopher S. "Soviet Subdues Religion, but Zeal for Atheism Lags." *The New York Times.* March 1, 1976.

Yakunin, Gleb. *Sobesednik* [Interlocutor], *Komsomolskaya Pravda* Supplement. May 22, 1990.

Yurov, S. "Zatyanuvshayasya istoriya [A Murky Story]." *Moskovski Tserkovny Vestnik, Yezhenedelnik.* No. 3, February 1992.

Zalesski, A. I. "Ob otnoshenii Belorusskikh kolkhoznikov k religii i o roste ateizma [Concerning the Attitude of Byelorussian Collective Farmers to Religion and Concerning the Growth of Atheism]." *Sovetskaya Etnografiya* [Soviet Ethnography]. No. 2, 1957.

Zelinsky, Vladimir. "Pastors and Their Flock." *Vybor* [Choice]. No. 20. Reproduced in *Religion in Communist Lands.* Vol. 17, No. 4, Winter 1989.

Newspapers and Periodicals

Argumenty i Fakty [Arguments and Facts].

Chas Pik [Rush Hour].

The Chicago Daily News.

Eastern Churches Review.

Ekspress-Khronika [Express Chronicle].

Filosofskie Nauki [Philosophical Sciences].

Foreign Broadcast Information Service.

Frontier.

Glasnost (Moscow).

Information Service (National Council of Churches of Christ in the U.S.A.).

Interfax.

Irénikon.

Izvestiya.

KC [Keston College], The Right to Believe.

Keston News Service.

Khronika Tekushchikh Sobytii [Chronicle of Current Events].

Komsomolskaya Pravda.

Kuranty.

Literary Gazette International.

Literaturnaya Gazeta [Literary Gazette], including Supplements.

Los Angeles Times.

Mirror (U.S. National Council of Churches).

Moskovski Tserkovny Vestnik [Moscow Church Herald].

Moskovski Tserkovny Vestnik, Yezhenedelnik [Moscow Church Herald, Weekly].

Moskovskie Novosti [Moscow News] (also published in English as *Moscow News* and in several other languages).

Nauka i Religiya [Science and Religion].

News from Behind the Iron Curtain.

Newsweek.

The National Council Outlook.

The New York Herald Tribune.

The New York Times.

Novoe Vremya [New Times In the English edition].

Ogonëk [Little Fire].

Orthodox Life.

Posev [Possev].

Pravda.

Pravoslavnaya Rus [Orthodox Russia] (an organ of the Russian Orthodox Church Abroad published in Jordanville, N.Y.).

Pravoslavnoe Chtenie [Orthodox Readings in the English edition].

Pravoslavny Vestnik Stavropolya [Orthodox Herald of Stavropol].

Pravoslavny Visnyk [Orthodox Herald].

Presbyterian Life.

Radianska Ukraina.

Religion in Communist Dominated Areas.

Religion in Communist Lands.

Religiya v SSSR [Religion in USSR in the English edition].

RFE/RL (Radio Free Europe/Radio Liberty) Daily Report

Russia Cristiana Ieri e Oggi [Christian Russia Yesterday and Today].

Russian Studies in History.

Russkaya Mysl [Russian Thought].

Russkoe Voskresenie [Russian Resurrection].

The Samizdat Bulletin.

Sibirski Blagovest [Siberian Clarion].

Sobesednik, Sobesednitsa [Interlocutor], *Komsomolskaya Pravda* Supplement.

Sovetskaya Rossiya [Soviet Russia].

Soviet Affairs Notes.

Soviet War News.

Sputnik Agitatora [Handbook of the Agitator].

Surviving Together.

Time.

U Nas na Yugo-zapade [With Us in the South-West (District of Moscow)].

The Ukrainian Weekly.

Ukrainian Orthodox Word.

U.S.S.R. Illustrated Monthly. (Washington, D.C.: Embassy of the U.S.S.R.).

Vechernaya Moskva [Evening Moscow].

Vestnik Russkogo Studencheskogo Khristianskogo Dvizheniya [Herald of the Russian Student Christian Movement].

Vozvrashchenie [Restoration]

The Way.

Zhurnal Moskovskoi Patriarkhii [Journal of the Moscow Patriarchate].

Other Media

Abuladze, Tengiz. *Pokayanie* [Repentance]. Tbilisi: Gruziafilm, 1987.

Bourdeaux, Michael. "Glasnost and the Churches: Developing a Perspective." Recording of Keston U.S.A. seminar, Dallas, Texas, May 6, 1989.

Marmor, Helen. "The Church of the Russians," television broadcast on July 17, 1983, NBC Communications Commission, National Council of Churches, New York.

About the Book and Author

Despite its problems, the Russian Orthodox Church manifests a luminous faith. It has achieved great political influence and is the former Soviet Union's most important vehicle for spiritual and ethical renewal. Nevertheless, it is still a long walk to church in that tormented land.

Making use of the formerly secret archives of the Soviet government, Nathaniel Davis offers the first complete account of the history of the Russian Orthodox Church in recent times. Twice in the past sixty years, the church hung on the brink of institutional extinction. In 1939, only four bishops and a few score widely scattered priests were still functioning openly in that vast land. In a single night, Stalin could have arrested them all. Ironically, Hitler's invasion and Stalin's reaction to it rescued the church—and parishes reopened, new clergy and bishops were consecrated, a patriarch was elected, and seminaries and convents were reinstituted.

In his paranoid last five years, Stalin reverted to his earlier policies of repression; after his death, Nikita Khrushchev resumed the onslaught against religion. Davis reveals the full scope of Stalin's last assault, the limited extent of the reprieve, and the relative continuity of policy in those brutal years of repression under Khrushchev. He shows that under Brezhnev, the erosion of church strength was greater than the world has been told, and that those decades witnessed the low point in the church's second great crisis of survival. It was none too soon when the Soviet government changed policy in anticipation of the millennium of Russia's conversion to Christianity in 988. One could travel a thousand kilometers on the Trans-Siberian Railroad without coming to a single functioning church.

The collapse of communism and the fragmentation of the Soviet empire have created a mixture of dizzying opportunity and daunting trouble for Russian Orthodoxy. Thousands of half-destroyed churches have been returned to believers, but the faithful do not have the money to restore them. Thousands of parishes are without priests. Ukraine, where most of the Orthodox churches were, has fallen into schism, with three feuding Orthodox factions struggling against each other and a resurgent Greek-Catholic community pushing all three eastward.

Across the former Soviet Union, the leaders of the Russian Orthodox Church bemoan a "spiritual vacuum," into which are rushing moneyed Protestant evangelists, Catholic proselytizers, Eastern mystics, and even Satanists and telesorcerers. Moreover, Orthodox Church leaders' past collaboration with the communist authorities has bedeviled the hierarchs as they struggle to assert moral leadership in a society where the communists worked for seventy-five years to lead the people astray.

Nathaniel Davis is the Alexander and Adelaide Hixon Professor of Humanities at Harvey Mudd College, Claremont, California. He served in the U.S. Foreign Service for thirty-six years, in Moscow, as assistant secretary of state, as ambassador in three posts, and as Lyndon B. Johnson's senior adviser on Soviet and Eastern European affairs.

Index